P9-DBP-691

Mastering Effective English

TRESSLER - LEWIS

Mastering Effective English

Third Edition

THE COPP CLARK PUBLISHING CO. LIMITED
Vancouver   Toronto   Montreal

Copyright 1937, 1950, 1961

by

The Copp Clark Publishing Co. Limited

All rights reserved. No part of the
material covered by this copyright may be
reproduced in any form without the
written permission of the publishers.

(1324)

PRINTED IN CANADA

Preface to the Third Edition

Important differences between the Third Edition and earlier editions of *Mastering Effective English* are the deletion of material specifically intended for Grade Ten, the expansion of several units to improve their usefulness, the addition of some new topics, and the division of the material into two parts instead of three. Part One is intended for Grade Eleven, and Part Two, for Grade Twelve. Schools that have used *Mastering Effective English* in Grade Thirteen will find that the Third Edition provides for more mature work than was provided for in the earlier editions.

Mention should be made of the extension of the list of Words Often Misused. The list has proved so useful that it has been more than doubled in length. The chapters dealing with the essay have been expanded, especially those on The Expository Essay and on Preparing the Research Essay. Similarly, the units on Literary Appreciation and Criticism and on Mass Media have been amplified. A chapter entitled Clear Thinking deals with logic, propaganda, and bias. Of particular importance are two chapters on The Précis, one for Grade Eleven and one for Grade Twelve. The Handbook has been retained and has been enlarged by the addition of units on Mechanics, and Spelling.

It is the hope of the authors that the new arrangement of the instructional material will make the text easier to use and will leave the teacher and the students more time for creative expression. The text is replete with models and stimulating examples of good writing, but effective writing requires a reflective and unhurried address to the topic in hand. It is hoped that the teacher will help to provide an atmosphere of creativity and will encourage the student to try his wings in figurative flight. One soaring sentence will do more to make a writer out of a pencil-chewer than hours of laborious attention to grammatical usage. Help the student to get his feet off the ground, and, in the glow that follows, it will be easy to teach him how to plant them firmly on the ground again.

The authors wish to acknowledge their indebtedness to many teachers whose reports have kept them informed of the needs of the classroom and the classroom teacher. The authors wish to thank the following teachers for specific and detailed help in organizing the materials for the Third Edition: Mr. D. Hager, East York Collegiate Institute; Mr. W. Sherwood, Agincourt Collegiate Institute; and Mr. K. P. Thompson, West Hill Collegiate Institute. Particularly, the authors are indebted to Mr. Art Hughes, W. A. Porter Collegiate Institute, who shouldered a great many specific tasks and supplied much useful material. Acknowledgement is made throughout the text to publishers and authors who have allowed us to use copyright material. Not least, we are indebted to many students who have allowed us to use their classroom exercises.

—J.C.T.
—C.E.L.

TABLE OF CONTENTS

PART ONE

PART TWO

HANDBOOK

Mastering Effective English

PART ONE

Chapter 1

The Words We Work With

THE ENGLISH LANGUAGE

We who speak the English language have reason to be proud of it. Fifteen hundred years ago, it was the language of a few thousand people; it had only a couple of thousand words. Today English is spoken by at least two hundred million people; it has more than three hundred thousand words. It is the language of world trade, and is one of the principal languages of international diplomacy. Of all languages it has proved to be the most adaptable and useful. It is still a living and changing language.

The development of the English language falls roughly into three periods:

(1) **Old English** (from the beginning to 1066)

(2) **Middle English** (1066 to 1485)

(3) **Modern English** (1485 to the present).

OLD ENGLISH

Old English began with the Jutes, Angles, and Saxons who invaded Britain about A.D. 450. They came from the Continent, in the region of north-west Germany; conquered the Britons and drove them into the west and north, into what is today called Wales and Scotland. The Angles settled north of the Humber (Northumbria); the Saxons, south of the Thames (Mercia and Kent); the Jutes occupied the territory between them (Essex, Wessex, and Sussex).

The oldest extant story in the language is the story of Beowulf.

This tale was carried down orally for many centuries and probably dates back to a time before the three tribes moved to Britain. The Angles were the first to record their language, which they called *Englisc* (English). Their land they called *Angle-land* (England). In the eighth century there rose among them two notable writers, Caedmon and the Venerable Bede. In the ninth century the West Saxon King, Alfred the Great, established his dialect as the literary language of the country, though it was still called English.

CHANGES IN THE LANGUAGE

Old English was a highly inflected language. Nouns had four or five cases and several declensions. *E.g.* The declension of *stan* (stone) is:

CASE	SING.	PLURAL
Nominative and Accusative	Stan	Stanas
Genitive	Stanes	Stana
Dative and Imperative	Stane	Stanum

It has, however, always been a characteristic of English to strive toward simplicity. Gradually many inflections were dropped and the position or order of the word indicated its use. By the fourteenth century, already, the genitive singular and plural were the same, *stanes, stanes*. Today the 'e' has been dropped and we indicate the possessive by the apostrophe only. "His lordes werre", of Chaucer has become "His lord's war".

In Old English many adjectives agreed with their nouns in number (*good*, sing.; *goode*, pl.)

His hors weren goode.—His horses were good.

In Old English, the verbs, too, had more inflections than we have today. These have been largely replaced by auxiliaries. Many past participles were preceded by *ge-* which gave way to *y-*, which was still common in Chaucer's time.

"At mete well *y-taught* was she withalle".
(She was, at the same time, well taught in table manners)

Plural verbs and infinitives sometimes ended in *en*.

And smale fowles *maken* melodye.
That *slepen* al the nyght with open eye.
(And small birds, that sleep all night with open eyes, make melody.)

A manly man to *been* an abbot able.
(A manly man, fit to be an abbot.)

FROM THE PROLOGUE TO THE CANTERBURY TALES

Chaucer's *Canterbury Tales* reveals a keenness of humour and a breadth of human sympathy to be found nowhere else in Middle-English literature. These qualities are most apparent in his description of the Prioress. In Chaucer's day the vowels were pronounced much as they are in modern French, German, or Italian. In general, pronounce as follows: accented **a** as in "father", **o** and **oo** like **o** in "lord", **ou** and **ow** like **oo** in "boot", **y** like **i** in "pin". The final **e** (marked with dot above) is pronounced like **ä** in "Emma". (The dots should facilitate your reading.)

> Ther was also a Nonne, a Prioressè,
> That of hir smylyng was ful symple and coy;
> Hire gretteste ooth was but by seintè Loy,
> And she was cleped madame Eglentynè.
> Ful weel she soong the servicè dyvynè,
> Entuned in hir nose ful semèly;
> And Frenssh she spak ful faire and fetisly,
> After the scole of Stratford attè Bowè,
> For Frenssh of Parys was to hire unknowè.
> At metè wel y-taught was she with-allè:
> She leet no morsel from hir lippès fallè,
> Ne wette hir fyngrès in hir saucè depè.
> Wel koude she carie a morsel and wel kepè
> Thát no drope ne fille upon hire brist;
> In curteisie was set ful muchel hir list.
> Hire over-lippè wypèd she so clenè
> That in hir coppe ther was no ferthyng senè
> Of grecè, whan she dronken hadde hir draughtè.
>
> —CHAUCER

It was natural that the language of the English conquerors should be influenced by that of their neighbours, particularly by borrowing new words used in daily converse, as in domestic life, trade and commerce. They borrowed from the Celts, whom they conquered, several words relating to the household and to the rearing of children: *gown, skein,* and *darn; cradle, brat,* and *babe; crock, pan,* and *griddle; mop* and *drudge.* Branches of the Celtic language have given us special words. From the Irish branch (Erse) we have taken *bog, brogue, galore, shamrock,* and *shillelagh;* from the Highland Scottish branch (Gaelic), *clan, crag, glen, loch, reel, slogan* (which originally meant "battle cry"), and *whisky* ("water of life"). Place names like *-aber,* river mouth (Aberdeen); *-avon,* river (Stratford-on-Avon); *-caer,* fortress (Cardiff, Carlyle); *-ben, -pen,* head or peak (Benlomond, Penzance); *-llyn, -lyn,* lake or pool (Liverpool, Roslyn); and *-loch,* lake (Lochlomond) are of Celtic origin.

Early contact between the Romans and the Germanic tribes on the Continent resulted in the adoption of such words as *street* (L. *strata*, a paved road), *wall* (L. *vallum*), and *mile* (L. *mille*); *pound* (L. *pondus*), *wine* (L. *vinum*), and *flask* (L. *flasca*); *kettle* (L. *catillus*), *cup* (L. *cuppa*), and *dish* (L. *discus*). These words deal with warfare, commerce, and domestic life.

From the Romans who occupied Britain from 45 B.C. to A.D. 400, they borrowed such words as *caster, chester, cester* (L. *castra, camp*); *port* (L. *portus*, a harbour); *mountain* (L. *mons, montem*, a hill); *tower* (L. *turris*, tower or rock); *village* (L. *vicus*, village). These words are evident in Lancaster, Manchester, Leicester, Portsmouth, Monteith, and Fenwick.

Modern English is the descendant of Anglo-Saxon (generally called Old English), which was brought to "Britain" by the Jutes, Angles, and Saxons in the fifth century. Most of the words that we use frequently, like *home, friend*, and *brother*, come from this parent language. Almost all our pronouns, prepositions, conjunctions, articles, and auxiliary verbs are native to our "Angle-ish", or English, tongue: *he, she, it, at, after, in, and, but, when, can, may, will.* Thus, though most of our words come from *French, Latin*, and *Greek*, a word count of a normal sentence would show a majority of Anglo-Saxon words.

The basic resemblances between English and modern German reflect the development of the English language.

GERMAN	ANGLO-SAXON	ENGLISH
Mutter	mōdor	mother
Bruder	brōther	brother
Schwester	sweoster	sister
See	sae	sea
Auge	ēage	eye
ich	ic	I
haben	habban	have
gegangen	gegan	gone

With the coming of the Roman missionaries to Britain (A.D. 597) came many new words connected with the church: *altar, priest, apostle, pope, school, candle.*

Similarly, the invasion of Britain by the Scandinavians (about A.D. 850) left imprints upon our language. Our pronouns *they, their, them,* and our verb *are* are the most notable of these. Such basic parts of speech are not often transferred from one language to another. From the Danes also came words like *billow, raft, anger, happy,* and *smile.* Words borrowed directly from the Scandinavians are generally pronounced with hard *sk, k,* or *g* sounds: *sky, skin, skill, scarpe, scrub, bask, kid, dike, give, get, egg* (which originally meant "instigate" as in our phrase "to egg on"). An interesting Danish word is *by*, meaning town. From this we get not only the place names such as Grimsby, Whitby, and Derby, but also our word *by-law*. Names ending in *son*, like Stevenson or Johnson, conform to a characteristic Scandinavian custom, the equivalent Old English patronymic being *-ing*, as in Browning. The Danish court influenced our language toward simplification. Since the stems of the English and Danish words were similar, inflections were dropped in order to make communication easier. English syntax— the way words are put together in phrases and clauses—was also influenced by Scandinavian. The placement of the preposition at the end of a sentence in the emphatic position is a Scandinavian influence: "He has someone to work for." That locutions like this are not good form in English is a misconception. "What is this cup made of?" is good idiomatic English and goes back to Scandinavian influence. To avoid such forms is unidiomatic and results in a stilted language.

MIDDLE ENGLISH

The Norman Conquest (1066) established French (Norman French) as the official language of England. For three hundred years French, with its Latin vocabulary, was the language of the English court, of English government, and of English art, society, and literature. But the conquered people and their language survived. True, the Anglo-Saxons had to learn French terms, words like *plaintiff, jury, state,* and *mutton;* but they stubbornly retained their own vocabulary too. This obstinacy proved a blessing. Because both conqueror and conquered had different words for similar things, English is unbelievably rich in synonyms providing fine shades of meaning. English can draw upon its Anglo-Saxon and Latin ancestry to choose between pairs like *home* and *mansion, work* and *labour, speed* and *velocity, stir* and *agitate.*

It was natural that the Norman invasion should bring with it the polite language of the French court. Sir Walter Scott's story *Ivanhoe* contains an illuminating passage—a conversation between Gurth, the swineherd, and Wamba, the jester—which explains the characteristic changes:

"Gurth," said Wamba, "I advise thee to call off Fangs, and leave the herd to their destiny, which, whether they meet with bands of travelling soldiers, or of outlaws, or of wandering pilgrims, can be little else than to be converted into Normans before morning, to thy no small ease and comfort."

"The swine turned Normans to my comfort," quoth Gurth, "expound that to me. Wamba, for my brain is too dull, and my mind too vexed to read riddles."

"Why, how call you those grunting brutes running about on their four legs?" demanded Wamba.

"Swine, fool, swine," said the herd, "every fool knows that."

"And swine is good Saxon," said the Jester; "but how call you the sow when she is flayed, and drawn and quartered, and hung by the heels, like a traitor?"

"Pork," answered the swineherd.

"I am glad every fool knows that too," said Wamba, "and pork, I think, is good Norman-French; and so when the brute lives, and is in charge of a Saxon slave, she goes by her Saxon name; but becomes a Norman, and is called pork when she is carried to the Castle-hall to feast among the nobles; what doest thou think of this, friend Gurth, ha?"

"It is but too true doctrine, friend Wamba, however it got into thy fool's pate."

"Nay, I can tell you more," said Wamba, in the same tone; "there is old Alderman Ox continues to hold his Saxon epithet, while he is under the charge of serfs and bondsmen such as thou, but becomes Beef, a fiery French gallant, when he arrives before the worshipful jaws that are destined to consume him. Mynheer Calf, too, becomes Monsieur de Veau in like manner; he is Saxon when he requires tendance, and takes a Norman name when he becomes matter of enjoyment."

It was natural that the new words which entered our language at that time should be words dealing with government, feudalism, the church, and the chase—words like *parliament, law, judge, armour, prisoner, homage, fealty, chivalry, tournament, pardoner, penance, forest, archery,* and *falconry.*

As the years passed, the languages fused to develop the Norman-English spoken in London and Oxford. The writings of Wycliffe and of Chaucer helped to establish this dialect as the permanent language of England. This was strongly influenced by the introduction of printing by Caxton (1476); spelling became more fixed, and grew less and less phonetic. It was never so easy afterwards for new dialects to get a wide acceptance.

MODERN ENGLISH

With the Revival of Learning and the coming of the great scholars to England, new words multiplied with great speed. Many Romance words and a large proportion of the Greek words in our language came during that time. Examples of the Greek words are *oxygen, hydrogen, chemist, narcissus, daffodil, crisis, athlete, fungus, skeleton,* and *elastic.*

World exploration and world trade added new words, as did the coming of machines and the industrial revolution. We have borrowed from all the world as we felt the need.

Yet it is significant that the majority of the words we use every day should be pure English. Words designating concrete objects, words of home and family and country, are largely English. Of the one hundred and seventeen words in the Twenty-third Psalm, one hundred and seven are of English origin.

OTHER EXAMPLES OF BORROWING

ITALIAN: opera, solo, piano, studio, stanza, fresco.
ARABIC: algebra, almanac, alkali, zero, sheik, salaam.
SPANISH: alligator, armada, cargo, cigar, negro, mosquito.
HEBREW: amen, hallelujah, cherub, seraphim, satan.
PORTUGUESE: molasses, veranda, caste, fetish.
DUTCH: sloop, yawl, skipper, yacht, skate, dollar.
RUSSIAN: steppe, knout, kopeck.
PERSIAN: bazaar, sofa, shah, caravan, dervish.
MALAYAN: amuck, gong, sago, bamboo.
INDIAN: squaw, papoose, wigwam, canoe, potato, tobacco.
CHINESE: silk, cash, tea, chop-suey.
INDIA: sugar, cheroot, cheetah, rupee.
AFRICA: kraal, gorilla, canary.
S. AMERICA: quinine, pampas, llama, condor.
POLYNESIA: taboo, tattoo.
AUSTRALIA: boomerang, cockatoo.
GERMAN: kindergarten, hamburger, hurrah.

HOW OUR LANGUAGE CHANGES

The addition of new words is only one of the processes at work in language. Others include (1) the loss of words; (2) changes in the meaning of words; (3) changes in grammatical structure—for example, the double negative, used by Shakespeare, is no longer considered acceptable; and (4) changes in pronunciation.

Loss of words. The dictionary labels "Obsolete" or "Archaic" words which have gone out of style. *Eftsoon* (*soon afterward*), *gleeman* (*minstrel*), and *shoon*, (old plural of *shoe*) are Anglo-Saxon words that have vanished from everyday speech and writing. Some words die because the objects they name are no longer used—for example *hauberk* (a suit of chain mail) and *greaves* (leg armour).

Changes in meaning. There are four principal ways in which words change their meanings:

ELEVATION OF MEANING   *marshal*—originally a servant in charge of horses, now an officer of high rank

DEGENERATION OF MEANING   *knave*—originally a boy or boy servant, now a tricky, deceitful person, a rogue

RESTRICTION OF MEANING *meat*—originally any solid food, now a particular kind of food

EXTENSION OF MEANING *box*—originally the box tree, then a receptacle made of boxwood, and now a receptacle in general

Changes in meaning tell us something about ourselves. Because people are likely to put things off, *soon*, *by and by*, *presently*, and *directly*, which once meant "instantly", now mean "in a little while". Because people generally look for short cuts, we now have *bus* (from *omnibus*), *taxi* (from *taximeter cabriolet*), *auto* (*automobile*), *zoo* (*zoological garden*), *phone* (*telephone*), and *gas* (*gasoline*).

PRACTICE 1. Studying Familiar Words with Less Familiar Meanings

Define the italicized word or words as they are used in each of the following sentences. Give one other meaning for each word.

1. That *horse* is too rickety to support the scaffold.
2. After falling into the water, Jack made a *sorry figure*.
3. The speaker asked all within the *compass* of his voice to come closer.
4. Persons who develop a heart *murmur* early in life often live to ripe old ages.
5. After the *signature* had been played, the regular broadcast began.
6. In the *morgue* the reporter found a complete file on the missing banker.

7. The flight should be pleasant, for weather conditions are ideal and the *ceiling* is unlimited.
8. *Play* the fish carefully, or you'll lose him.
9. The thieves *rifled* the house.
10. His attention was *arrested* by a cloud of smoke rising in the distance.

NEW WORDS FOR NEW PROCESSES

A living language never stops growing. As new processes and products are introduced, new words come along to enrich the language. Aviation has given us *fuselage, helicopter,* and *dead reckoning.* Radio and television have given us *telecast, commercial, transcription,* and *fringe area.* The automobile has given us *carburetor, motel,* and *drive-in.*

PRACTICE 2. Studying Words from Science and Industry

What science or industry was responsible for the addition to the language of each of the following words or expressions?

airstrip	chain reaction	FM	Oscar awards
animated cartoon	crash landing	isotope	simulcast
candid shot	disc jockey	octane	supermarket

NEW WORDS FOR CHANGING CONDITIONS

As political, economic, and social institutions change, words must be added to the language to describe new developments. New ways of life have given us *baby sitter, coffee break,* and *jukebox.* New fashions in dress and grooming have provided *crew cut, pony tail,* and *brunch coat.* The world around us is reflected in words like *automation, fringe benefit, supersonic, outer space,* and *roller derby.* New ideas in home building are preserved in words like *split-level, recreation room, carport, picture window,* and *ranch house.*

PRACTICE 3. Listing New Words

List and define five words added to the language in recent years. Do not include words already listed in this section.

HOW WORDS ARE COINED

Of the new words created almost daily a few, like *kodak* (coined by George Eastman), are pure inventions. Most have recognizable origins. Words like *cellophane, thermonuclear,* and *cyclotron* come from classical languages. *Walkie-talkie* is a humorous description of the apparatus it names. Humour and imitation often play a part in word formation. In hi-fi (high fidelity) language a *woofer* is a loudspeaker that "woofs", responds only to lower frequencies, while a *tweeter* responds only to high. Both terms are found in dignified engineering journals. Sometimes an expressive word is coined by an author and retained. Lewis Carroll joined *chuckle* and *snort* to produce *chortle*.

A common device is to form words from names of persons, places, literary characters. Often new inventions or discoveries are named after people responsible for them: *pasteurize, diesel, guillotine*.

PRACTICE 4. Studying Words from Names

In an unabridged dictionary find out how each of the following words came into the language and what it means.

Example

chauvinist—a person of exaggerated patriotism and military enthusiasm. Nicolas Chauvin was a Napoleonic veteran whose excessive devotion to Napoleon was ridiculed by his comrades.

ampere	galvanize	magnolia	protean
cravat	gerrymander	mesmerism	Pyrrhic victory
fez	hamburger	odyssey	rhinestone
forsythia	macadam	poinsettia	watt

CANADIAN AND BRITISH DIFFERENCES

"Cartwright stopped the lorry near a hoarding. Taking out his electric torch, he checked the petrol and the accumulator, wiped the windscreen, lifted the bonnet, and unsuccessfully tried to tighten the sparking plugs with a spanner."

Does this seem like another language? Now read it in our own language.

"Cartwright stopped the truck near a billboard. Taking out his flashlight, he checked the gas and the battery, wiped the windshield, lifted the hood, and unsuccessfully tried to tighten the spark plugs with a monkey wrench."

The development of the English language in North America has been somewhat different from its development in England. Though the differences are not of major importance, they include variations in spelling and pronunciation as well as in vocabulary.

PRACTICE 5. Canadian and British Differences

What do you think is the Canadian equivalent for each of these English words?

1. lift
2. pram
3. reel
4. flex
5. braces

6. treacle
7. underground
8. chemist's
9. dust bin
10. geyser

11. schedule
12. wood wool
13. ticket-of-leave
14. boots
15. drawing pin

16. saloon car
17. sock suspenders
18. potato crisp
19. vegetable marrow
20. tram

Give up? Answers are at the bottom of the next page.

WORDBUILDING

About 65 per cent of the words in the dictionary are of Latin or Greek origin. Learning common prefixes and roots that occur in dozens of words will give you a method of approaching many new words. Once you know, for instance, that *contra* means "against" and *dict* means "to speak," you can easily remember that *contradict* means "to speak against something, to disagree."

Because so many words in the dictionary are Latin derivatives, one needs to know at least the most common Latin prefixes and stems.

LATIN PREFIXES

PREFIX	MEANING	EXAMPLE	DEFINITION
a, ab	from	avert	turn from
ad	to, towards	attract	draw to
ante	before	antecedent	going before
bi	two	biped	a two-footed animal
circum	around	circumnavigate	sail around
contra	against	contradict	speak against
cum (com, con, cor, co)	together, with	convene	come together
de	from, down	depose	put down
dis (di, dif)	apart, from, not	dishonest	not honest
e, ex, (ec, ef)	out, out of, from	select	choose from
extra	beyond	extraordinary	beyond ordinary
in (il, im, ir)	in, into, not	insane	not sane
inter	between	interstate	between states
non	not	nondelivery	not delivery
ob (oc, of, op)	against, in front of	object	to throw against
per	through, thoroughly	perfect	thoroughly made
post	after	postscript	written after

prae	before	precede	go before
pro	for, forward	pronoun	for a noun
re	back, again	reconsider	consider again
se	apart	secede	go apart
semi	half	semicircle	a half circle
sub (suc, suf, sug, sum)	under	subscribe	write under
super	above	supernatural	above nature
trans	across, beyond	transgress	step beyond

Some of the prefixes are not readily detected because of consonant changes. *Ad* becomes *a(agree), ac(accede), af (affix), ag(aggrieve), al(ally), an(annex), ap(append), ar(arrive), as(assent).*

PRACTICE 6. Derivations of Words

1. Explain the meaning of the following words:

biweekly	indirect	prepaid	semicircle
coeducation	inhuman	prewar	sublet
disqualify	noninterference	reaction	subtitle
extra-hazardous	postgraduate	rearrange	transcontinental

2. *Irreligious* is the opposite of *religious*. What is the opposite of *polite, direct, legal, perishable, rational, fallible?*

3. Write lists of words in which the following prefixes are used: *sub, super, con (cor, col, com, co), trans.*

COMMON LATIN VERB ROOTS

VERB ROOT	MEANING	EXAMPLE	DEFINITION
ago, actum	do, act, drive	counteract	act against
audio, auditum	hear	auditor	one who hears
capio, capitum	take, seize, hold	captive	one taken
cedo, cessum	go, yield	precede	go before
credo, creditum	believe	credible	believable
curro, cursum	run	incur	run into

ANSWERS TO PRACTICE 5			
1. elevator	6. molasses	11. timetable	16. sedan
2. baby carriage	7. subway	12. excelsior	17. garters
3. spool of thread	8. druggist's	13. parole	18. potato chip
4. extension cord	9. ash can	14. shoes	19. squash
5. suspenders	10. water heater	15. thumbtack	20. streetcar

do, datum	give	data	facts given
dico, dictum	say	predict	say before
duco, ductum	lead, draw	induce	draw in
facio, factum	make, do	proficient	making progress
fero, latum	bear, carry, bring	differ	bear apart
flecto, flexum	bend	flexible	bending
fluo, fluxum	flow	fluent	flowing
frango, fractum	break	fracture	a break
gradior, gressus	go, walk, step	progress	go forward
jacio, jactum	throw, cast	eject	cast out
jungo, junctum	join	junction	a joining
lego, lectum	gather, read, choose	legible	readable
loquor, locutus	speak	elocution	a speaking out
mitto, missum	send, cast	remit	send back
pello, pulsum	drive, urge	expel	drive out
pendeo, pensum	hang, pay	suspend	hang under
pono, positum	place, put	postpone	place after
porto, portatum	carry, bear	import	carry into
rumpo, ruptum	break	rupture	a break
scribo, scriptum	write	scribe	a writer
seco, sectum	cut	section	a cutting
sedeo, sessum	sit, settle	session	a sitting
sequor, secutus	follow	execute	follow out
sto, statum	stand	distant	standing apart
tango, tactum	touch	contagion	touching together
traho, tractum	draw	attract	draw to
venio, ventum	come	convene	come together
verto, versum	turn	avert	turn aside
video, visum	see	vision	sight
voco, vocatum	call	vocation	calling

CAUTION Many words from Latin have been English citizens so long they have strayed far from the original literal meanings. *Mortify* doesn't now mean "make death", though one who is mortified might wish, for the moment, he were dead. A *volume*, originally a roll of writing, now has nothing to do with *roll*. Many expressions are now concealed metaphors. *Extravagant* spending *wanders beyond* normal limits. An *implication* is a hidden meaning *folded into* a statement. *Currency* is money that *runs continuously*. Knowing the derivation helps to fix the meaning once it is known.

SUFFIXES WORTH KNOWING

able, ible (capable of being): portable, credible
ance, ence, ity, tude (act, quality, or state of): reliance, independence, inequality, rectitude

ant, ent, er, or, ian (one who or pertaining to): servant, president, waiter, navigator, custodian, librarian

ion, tion, ation, ment (action, state of, or result): opinion, direction, conversation embarrassment

ish (like a): feverish, coltish, mulish, bookish

less (without): lifeless, hopeless, painless, worthless, stainless

ly (forming adverbs from adjectives, participles, or, rarely, nouns): slowly, badly, unexpectedly, timely

ous, y (full of): precipitous, miscellaneous, bounteous, bushy, husky

ship (skill, state, quality, office): championship, guardianship, partnership, horsemanship, craftsmanship, friendship

PRACTICE 7. Adding Prefixes and Suffixes

From the preceding lists choose one prefix (except *in, sub, super, cum,* and *trans*), one stem, and one suffix. Write five or more words containing each of the chosen forms. Be ready to explain the meaning of each word and to use it in a sentence.

PRACTICE 8. Meaning from Derivations

Show from its derivation how each of the following words has acquired its present meaning. When you don't find one part of a word, like *manuscript,* in the prefix and verb lists, look up the word in the dictionary.

Examples:

confer = *con + fero* = bring together
anticipate = *ante + capio* = take beforehand
capture = *captum* = seizing

1. Agent, actor, transact.
2. Accept, except, capable, deception, inception, precept.
3. Creditor, creditable, credential, creed.
4. Dictionary, dictator, edict, predict, benediction.
5. Aqueduct, educate, conduct, induce, deduct, reduce.
6. Factory, affect, facsimile, imperfect.
7. Conference, fertile, prefer, refer, reference, differ, offer.

LATIN NOUNS AND ADJECTIVES

annus, year	*finis,* end, limit
caput, capitis, head	*gratus,* pleasing, thankful
centum, hundred	*lex, legis,* law
civis, citizen	*lingua,* tongue
cor, cordis, heart	*littera,* letter
corpus, corporis, body	*magnus, major, maximus,*
dignus, worthy	great, greater, greatest

duo, two
mors, mortis, death
nomen, nominis, name
opus, operis, work
pars, partis, part

manus, hand
pes, pedis, foot
similis, like
terra, earth
via, way

COMMON GREEK PREFIXES AND ROOTS

anthrop, man, mankind
anti, against
astron, star
autos, oneself
chrom, colour
chronos, time
epi, upon
graphein, write
hyper, over, exceedingly
kratos, rule, government
logos, speech, reason, word, account

metron, measure
micro, small
monos, sole, alone
onoma, name
pan, all, whole
pathos, suffering
peri, around
philos, friend, lover
phon, sound
syn (becomes syl, sym, or sy), with

PRACTICE 9. Derivatives

Make a list of English words derived from the twenty-three Latin nouns and adjectives and from the Greek prefixes and roots. Know the meaning of the words listed.

PRACTICE 10. Sources of English Words

From what language are the words in each group derived? Add to as many of the lists as you can. Do the words in each group show anything about the people who use the language? If so, what?

a. bivouac, brunette, chapeau, chauffeur, chiffonier, cretonne, debutante, foyer, garage, matinee, rôle, trousseau

b. alto, andante, canto, gondola, lava, macaroni, opera, piano, regatta, sonata, sonnet, soprano, spaghetti, stanza

c. amen, cherub, jubilee, manna, Sabbath

d. alcohol, algebra, assassin, chemistry, cipher, coffee, cotton, mattress, zero

e. canoe, maize, moccasin, opossum, papoose, potato, squaw, tobacco, tomahawk, tomato, wigwam

f. armada, buffalo, canyon, cargo, cigar, corral, desperado, galleon, mosquito, mulatto, mustang, vanilla

g. ballast, boom, bowsprit, schooner, skates, skipper, sloop, yacht

TEST—WRITING VOCABULARY

By using the words in sentences which show clearly their meaning, prove that twenty of the following words are in your writing vocabulary. Underline in each sentence the word whose use you are illustrating. No credit will be given for any sentence whose context does not clearly set forth the meaning of the word.

Example

RIGHT The *genealogy* of Henry Adams reveals there were two presidents and several famous statesmen and writers among his ancestors.

WRONG His *genealogy* shows his family is a good one.

alliteration, annuity, aster, astrology, autobiography, biennial, centipede, conventional, eulogy, graphic, gratuitous, hexameter, hyperbole, ignominy, literal, logical, monotone, nominal, obliterate, panacea, panorama, psychology, subterranean, superannuated, symbolize.

PRACTICE 11. Adding to Your Word List

When you have used a word three times, it is yours. Hand to your teacher a list of new words that you have added to your word hoard by using them three times during the term. If your list now is short, get ready to hand in a longer list at the end of the term.

SYNONYMS

The person who is word poor uses the same word again and again—perhaps a dozen *gets*, *thens*, or *nices* on a page. One who has a synonym ready can avoid this unpleasant repetition.

Some synonyms, like *hard* and *difficult*, have almost the same meaning; others, like *fewer* and *less*, differ widely in either meaning or use. *Fewer* refers to number; and *less*, to quantity, as in the sentence, "I have fewer books and less money than my brother."

PRACTICE 12. Synonyms

Examine each group of synonyms. Do the words differ in meaning or in use? How?

1. Reputation, fame, notoriety.
2. Apparent, evident, doubtless.
5. Crowd, audience, spectators.
4. Approve, praise, flatter.
5. Job, vocation, profession.

PRACTICE 13. Choosing Synonyms

Write two or more synonyms of each of the following words. When necessary, consult the dictionary or a book of synonyms.

admit, awkward, big, brave, building, dress, fun, go hard, interesting, lazy, mistake, needful, odd, poor, promise, reply, sad, say, useful, walk, workman

ANTONYMS

Antonyms are opposites: *good, bad; happy, sad; friend, enemy.*

PRACTICE 14. Choosing Antonyms

What is the antonym of each of the following words?

accept, assemble, assets, cheerful, clumsy, conceal, courageous, deny, develop, doubt, feeble, gaily, healthy, lazy, prose, talkative.

peevish   petulant   meager   copious

SYNONYMS   ANTONYMS

PRACTICE 15. Finding Synonyms and Antonyms

In many placement tests young people are asked to pick words similar or opposite in meaning. For this test find a pair of synonyms and a pair of antonyms in each group of five words. Use your knowledge of Greek and Latin prefixes and roots whenever possible.

Example

>   boisterous, fantastic, grotesque, taciturn, ulterior
>   Synonyms—fantastic, grotesque Antonyms—boisterous, taciturn

1. amity, decorum, enmity, ignominy, infamy
2. congregate, disperse, end, saturate, terminate
3. amicable, avaricious, covetous, indispensable, inimical
4. adhesiveness, dejection, elation, privation, tenacity
5. authentic, genuine, pretentious, tractable, violent
6. aggravate, alleviate, remonstrate, repay, requite
7. despondency, deterioration, effrontery, improvement, impudence
8. ambiguous, astute, explicit, insurgent, shrewd
9. continuous, eminent, frivolous, perpetual, serious
10. adherent, brigand, partisan, predecessor, successor

HOMONYMS

Homonyms are pronounced alike but spelled differently: *right, write; scene, seen.*

PRACTICE 16. Using Homonyms

Use each of the following words in a good sentence of at least ten words:

1. aloud, allowed	11. principal, principle
2. by, buy	12. right, write
3. coarse, course	13. seen, scene
4. council, counsel	14. shone, shown
5. forth, fourth	15. site, cite
6. its, it's	16. stayed, staid
7. led, lead	17. their, there
8. new, knew	18. threw, through
9. piece, peace	19. to, too
10. plain, plane	20. ware, wear

PRACTICE 17. Distinguishing Meanings

Make clear the differences in meaning. Use each word in a sentence that shows its meaning.

1. Ability, capacity. 2. Adverse, averse. 3. Advise, advice, claim, say, state, maintain. 4. Allusion, illusion. 5. Angle, angel. 6. Apparent, evident. 7. Assent, ascent. 8. Choice, alternative. 9. Compare, contrast. 10. Deceased, diseased. 1. Deprecate, depreciate. 12. Disinterested, uninterested. 13. Distinct, distinctive. 14. Enunciation, pronunciation. 15. Famous, notorious. 16. Formally, formerly. 17. Habit, custom. 18. Last, latest, preceding. 19.

Later, latter. 20. Learning, intelligence, wisdom. 21. Loose, lose. 22. Personal, personnel. 23. Prevision, provision. 24. Purpose, propose. 25. Stature, statue, statute.

MALAPROPISM

A *malapropism* is a ludicrous misuse of words resulting from a confusion between two words that are similar in sound but different in spelling and meaning. The error occurs most frequently when the two words are formed from the same root: allusion, illusion; apathetic, pathetic; deciding, decisive; impetuous, impetus; momentary, momentous; perpetuate, perpetrate; populace, populous; precede, proceed.

The term is derived from a character, Mrs. Malaprop, in Richard Sheridan's play *The Rivals*. Mrs. Malaprop was constantly giving vent to such expressions as the following: "as headstrong as an allegory on the banks of the Nile" and "illiterate him, I say, quite from your memory".

PRACTICE 18. Eliminating Malapropisms

Replace the malapropisms in the following sentences with the words the writer should have used.

1. Although he is illegible for the team, he seems disinterested.
2. The affluence of the book on the students was not very great.
3. Winston Churchill is an imminent writer of our time.
4. In his speech the teacher inferred that he did not like the proposed schedule.
5. Her ingenious attitude convinced the jury of her sincerity.
6. The principal of the school is expressed in its motto.
7. I cannot except the statement without proof.
8. I refuse to ascent to such an unreasonable request.
9. After many months of privation the travellers looked weak and emancipated.
10. The cool wet spring produced luxurious growth.

WHAT IS GOOD USE?

"I got a bang out of the show."
"I liked the show."
"I enjoyed the performance."

Though all three sentences convey the same message, there is a difference in tone. You might use the first to a close friend, the

second to a classmate, the last to the adult coach of the play. You speak more informally to your closest friends than you do to your teachers, new acquaintances, or adults generally. Saying "Good evening, my friends," to your crowd at a wiener roast is as absurd as shouting "Hiya" at a dignified guest.

Words differ widely in appropriateness and acceptability. Some words, like *recondite*, *reticulate*, and *honorarium*, are as stiffly formal as a wedding invitation or a full-dress suit. Others are correct on all but the most stately occasions, while a few, like dirty fingernails at the dinner table, have no place in polite speech.

GOOD USE IS NOT DETERMINED BY LOGIC. For example, "Many a man have crossed this bridge" is logically correct, for *many a man* means more than one. Usage, however, has established the expression, "Many a man has crossed this bridge." In the same way, although "I don't think I shall go" is illogical because the negative is attached to the wrong verb, general usage has made the expression good idiomatic English. On the other hand, *in back of* is patterned after *in front of*, but is not in good use.

In speech and writing avoid any use of a word that is not sanctioned by the practice of a large body of educated and intelligent people. A dictionary is not a language law-maker or dictator of usage but a record, on the basis of wide observation and study, of the practice in speech and writing of intelligent people of the present. *A New English Dictionary* is the best authority on good use, because its editors investigated the use by many writers of every word in the language. This dictionary, which was completed in 1928 after seventy years of labour, contains 1,827,306 quotations showing how words are used.

CHOOSE THE BETTER

We use words to get results. If a speaker's language puts him on the defensive or needs explanation, he is not likely to accomplish his purpose. For example, *proven* is defensible in the sentence, "That statement was not proven." *Proven* is used by Tennyson, Bulwer-

Lytton, Lowell, Jowett, Thackeray, Spenser, Gladstone, Huxley, and Kipling, and is recognized by *A New English Dictionary* and by Webster. *Proved*, however, needs no defence and is the form used by most careful writers and speakers. Therefore it is better to avoid *proven*.

LEVEL OF USAGE

FORMAL ENGLISH is used in most magazine articles, in histories, and in formal letters, essays, and public speeches. It is also used in most biographies, novels, and short stories—except when informal conversation is recorded. Formal English shies away from contractions (*won't, should've, you'll*) and expressions like *movies, put on airs, do the town*. Formal English ranges, too, from the stiffly correct language of a legal document to the unpretentious correctness of a modern business letter or a well-written newspaper.

INFORMAL, OR COLLOQUIAL, ENGLISH is "spoken English", or "relaxed English". Informal English includes words and expressions like *a lot of fun, close* (meaning *stingy*), *funny* (*odd*), and *fixings* (for *decorations*), which would sound out of place in formal speaking or writing. It uses all kinds of short cuts (*TV, phone,* and *photo*) and contractions (*I'll, they're, you've*). Good informal English is not inferior to formal English; it is merely used on other occasions. For every occasion, the sensitive user of words selects those expressions which will suit both his meaning and his audience.

PROVINCIALISMS, OR LOCALISMS are words peculiar to certain parts of the country—for example, "allow" or "reckon" for *think;* "I want out"; "hisn"; "yourn"; and "right smart."

VULGARISMS are expressions used only by people without culture or education. There are no occasions appropriate for the use of expressions like these: *irregardless, shouldn't ought, this here book, them boys, disremember, should of, ain't, invite* (as a noun), *kinder* (kind of), *busted, critter.*

SLANG is "inelegant and unauthorized popular language."

WEAKNESSES OF SLANG

SLANG IS FILLED WITH OVERWORKED, SHOPWORN EXPRESSIONS THAT PRODUCE MONOTONY AND DEADLY REPETITION. To show approval or disapproval, some young people limit themselves to a few words like "great", "cool", or "terrible". Slang encourages language poverty.

SLANG TENDS TO ELIMINATE FINE DISTINCTIONS IN MEANING. "Swell" cannot have any exact meaning if it is applied to a party, a dog, an automobile, a swimmer, a view, a house, or a friend. Distinctions in words like *priceless, precious, exquisite, imposing, majestic, luxurious, brilliant, radiant* are lost in the slang word "super".

MOST SLANG GOES OUT OF DATE QUICKLY. Like a popular song played over and over to the point of exhaustion, slang usually has a brief popularity and dies. "Applesauce", "vamp", and "beat it" gave way to "corny", "scram", and "hit the road", to be followed by "you can say that again," "skip it", and "but definitely". If your vocabulary is chiefly slang, you'll need a new vocabulary every few months.

SLANG IS OFTEN LIMITED TO SMALL GROUPS OR SMALL AREAS OF THE COUNTRY. The slang of "hepcats" may not be understood by "shutterbugs".

SLANG IS OFFENSIVE TO SOME PEOPLE. Most adults, who have witnessed the death of thousands of slang expressions, wince when they hear "She's a doll" or "You're so right." To the majority of listeners an overuse of slang will stamp you as unintelligent, uneducated, or mentally lazy. Above all, don't use one slang expression like "gee" so frequently that even your friends groan when you begin to talk. A person with a large vocabulary is likely to use slang sparingly—never on formal occasions.

A GOOD WORD FOR SLANG

SLANG IS OFTEN CLEVER, PICTURESQUE, AND ECONOMICAL. The inventors of "stooge" (a partner who "feeds lines" to a comedian), a "washout" (complete failure), and "sob sister" (writer of sentimentalized news accounts) were using quicker, more effective language.

SLANG PROVIDES ENGLISH WITH NEW WORDS. Though most slang dies early, some few words stay on to enrich the language. Words like *highbrow, mob,* and *humbug* fill a need and become words in good standing. Colourful, apt slang is evidence of the imagination and exuberance of a people and of the vitality and vigour of the language they speak.

Occasional, discreet use of clever pictorial slang adds novelty, spice, and surprise to conversation.

PRACTICE 19. Studying Levels of Usage

At what language level (formal, informal, or slang) would you put each of the following?

1.

a. He's an old windbag.
b. He is extremely talkative.
c. He talks a lot.

2.

a. We're meeting our crowd at the usual spot.
b. We're meeting the gang at the old hangout.
c. We shall be meeting our friends at the usual place.

3.

a. When do we put on the feed bag?
b. At what time shall we dine?
c. When do we eat?

4.

a. Jones, I'm afraid, just doesn't like people.
b. Old Jonesey is certainly a sourpuss, isn't he?
c. I fear Mr. Jones has a disagreeable personality.

PRACTICE 20. Choosing the Right Expression

1. Bill Brown has been introduced to the parents of the girl he is taking to the formal dance. What should he say?
   a. Mighty glad to meetcha, folks.
   b. I'm very happy to meet you, Mr. and Mrs. Roberts.
   c. I am indeed proud and gratified to make your acquaintance this evening.
2. Ellen Owens has been formally invited to go to a meeting of the local Chamber of Commerce to act as representative of her school. In her letter of acceptance what should she write?
   a. I am honoured by your invitation and shall be delighted to appear as the representative of our school.
   b. I'll be there with bells on.
   c. Yes, I'll come; I wouldn't miss it for the world.

PRACTICE 21. Reputable English?

Indicate the standing (vulgarism, slang, localism, colloquialism, literary English) of each of the following expressions:

Back out; swell party; auto; a brainy man; brain trust; pep; a square deal; enthuse; exam; hire a hall; phone; raise a family; up against it; toe the mark; hit or miss; by hook or crook; put one over; gent; aboveboard; get away with it; namby-pamby; gabble; deliver the goods; bleachers; grouch; call-down; pell-mell; all in; giggle; bawl out; anyplace; a lot of people; kind of sorry.

PRACTICE 22. Translating into Good English

On what plane does each of the italcized expressions stand? Translate colloquial, slang, and vulgar expressions into literary English. Express the ideas accurately.

1. Open the door *quick*, for it is *awfully* cold out here.
2. Albert was *real mad* when he fell *off of* his horse.
3. It is *kind of funny* that Jerry didn't come.
4. I am *anxious* to verify the *above* statement and shall arrange to meet **you** *anyplace* you suggest.
5. My *folks claim* that I should enter Toronto when I *graduate* Revelstoke.
6. I am *mighty* glad he is *making* better wages ushering for the *movies*.
7. A *lot* of people *patronize* the new grocer.
8. She is *pretty* well *posted* on *receipts* for making bread.
9. He *sure* started *slow*.
10. We made their *star* pitcher look like *thirty cents*.

PRACTICE 23. Using Good English

Which expressions in the parentheses are colloquial? Write the sentences in literary English.

1. His self-assurance —— her. (aggravated, annoyed)
2. Do you still —— that you know nothing about the accident? (claim, maintain)
3. His impudence made me ——. (angry, mad)
4. Despite his parents' objection he is —— to study law. (bound, determined)
5. It is —— that the cackling of geese saved Rome. (funny, odd)
6. You must choose ——. (immediately, right away)
7. The speaker of the evening didn't ——. (arrive, show up)
8. How soon can you —— my shoes? (fix, repair)
9. I —— the attendance will be small today. (guess, think)
10. In Naples we —— at the Continental Hotel. (stayed, stopped)

SPECIFIC WORDS

Specific, the opposite of *general*, means *definite* or *particular*. *Animal* is a general term including whales and mice. *Quadruped*, a more specific word, excludes whales, robins, and snakes. *Bear* is more specific than *quadruped;* and *black bear* and *Japanese black bear* are in turn more specific than *bear*. *Go* is a general word; *walk* is more specific; *saunter, totter, paddle, stalk, trudge, plod, promenade, march, hobble, stride, toddle, waddle, mince, strut,* and *stroll* are more specific than *walk*. Specific words are more picturesque and accurate than general ones.

GENERAL: I remember how my uncle's house looked.

SPECIFIC: I can remember the bare wooden stairway in my uncle's house, and the turn to the left above the landing, and the rafters and the slanting roof over my bed, and the squares of moonlight on the floor, and the white cold world of snow outside, seen through the curtainless window.

—MARK TWAIN

GENERAL   SPECIFIC

fly —swoop, glide, float
food —chocolate ice cream, bacon and tomato sandwich toasted, lamb chops
reptile—snapping turtle, copperhead snake, horned toad
say —yell, whisper, mumble

PRACTICE 24. Choosing Specific Words

In the manner just shown, write three specific words after each of the following words or expressions:

building	flower	ship	to fasten
colour	insect	tree	to make
dessert	machine	vehicle	to make a sound
dog	music	to change	to take
fish	noise	to cook	to work

PRACTICE 25. Selecting Specific Words

Which words in the following sentences are specific?

1. And I was going to sea myself—to sea in a schooner, with a piping boat-swain, and pig-tailed singing seamen!—STEVENSON

2. Except on the crown, which was raggedly bald, he had stiff, black hair, standing jaggedly all over it, and growing down hill almost to his broad, blunt nose.—DICKENS

3. The big blue waves shouldered themselves up from the bosom of the sea, marched toward the beach, and tumbled to pieces in a roaring tumult of white and green.—JOSEPH C. LINCOLN

4. Troopers who have stood charge after charge while victory was possible will fly like sheep, and like sheep allow themselves to be butchered, when they have once turned the back.—WEYMAN

5. Strolling negroes patrolled the sidewalks, thrumming mandolins and guitars, and others came and went, singing, making the night Venetian.
—TARKINGTON

PRACTICE 26. Using Specific Words

In the following sentences substitute specific details for the italicized general expressions:

1. For our *meal* we had *soup, meat, vegetable, potatoes, salad,* and *dessert.*
2. In the *building* are two *dogs.*
3. "My *clothing* was torn in a *number of places,*" said the *boy.*
4. *One day some boys* and I *went* to a *lake.*
5. My *friend* read three *books* during *a vacation.*

6. The two *girls* and I *worked awhile* in the *room*.
7. My *friend* and I handed the *man some money* for the *flowers*.
8. The *animals made sounds* when the *man went* into the *building*.

ACCURATE WORDS

People who don't take pains to say precisely what they mean sometimes add to muddled stories or explanations, "Well, you know what I mean." How much better it is for us to say exactly what we mean than to assume that our hearers are mind readers! First, we should think out clearly what we wish to say and then search for accurate words to express our ideas.

The misuse of words is due sometimes to ignorance and sometimes to hurry or carelessness. If in the revision of our written work we ask ourselves often, "Does that word mean exactly what I want to say?" we shall correct many errors in word choice.

PRACTICE 27. Using Accurate Words

Improve each sentence by substituting an accurate word for the italicized one. Make no other change in the sentence.

1. When did you *loose* your ring?
2. I believe this article *answers* these topics.
3. Before the Constitution was *made*, there was but one house in Congress.
4. An essay may *compose* description, explanation, narration, and a little argument.
5. There is need for men and women who can discuss intelligently the great *factors* of the time.
6. Mr. Squeers was arrested for *robbing* the boys' money and clothing.
7. While Puck was *wandering* through the woods, he met a fairy.
8. People do not wish to live in a country in which they have no *say* in the government.
9. We must find out what steps are yet to be *done*.

EFFECTIVE WORDS

Effective words are words appropriate for the topic discussed and for the audience. As a rule, direct, simple, clear, brief wording is more effective than a lofty, far-fetched, roundabout style. Homely words like *stark, bleak, sheer, roar, prig, wheedle, boor, dolt, haggle, task, hobnob, job, glum,* and *hodgepodge* are more expressive than lengthy and pretentious ones.

PRACTICE 28. Effective Language

In each group do you consider *a* or *b* more effective? Why?

1

a. The play has not wit enough to keep it sweet.—JOHNSON
b. The play has not vitality enough to preserve it from putrefaction.
                                                                —JOHNSON

2

a. And sitting on the grass partook
   The fragrant beverage drawn from China's herb.—WORDSWORTH
b. And sitting on the grass had tea.—TENNYSON

3

a. He died poor.
b. He expired in indigent circumstances.

OVERWORKED WORDS

We need a Society for the Protection of Overworked Words. Some useful words have been worked so hard that they are worn threadbare and have little meaning left. Among them are: *awful, cute, fierce, fine, funny, gorgeous, get, grand, great, horrid, lovely, nice, pretty, quite, splendid, sure, sweet, swell, terrible, terrific, then, very, wonderful.* One book character, Alverna in Lewis's *Mantrap,* has only four adjectives, *cute, swell, dandy,* and *nice;* and some real people haven't a much longer list. To such people everything is a "thing" and all "things" are "grand", "swell", "awful", "nice", "terrible", "great", or "cute".

PRACTICE 29. Word Discrimination

Complete each sentence by selecting the better word or expression:

1. The cover of this magazine is ——. (very nice, artistic)
2. The examination was ——. (exceedingly difficult, just fierce)
3. Marion has —— new dress. (an attractive, a nice)
4. Our neighbours are —— people. (very nice, charming)
5. We had a —— sail up the Hudson and enjoyed the —— scenery while eating our —— lunch (nice, pleasant) (fine, unusual) (delicious, awfully good)
6. We had a —— party. (delightful, grand)
7. Elizabeth's new hat is ——. (nice, becoming)
8. I remained under the tree —— time. (a long, quite some)
9. *A Tale of Two Cities* is —— book. (a lovely, an exciting)
10. For rescuing the boy, John Binns —— a medal. (got, received)
11. By his —— explanations he helped the pupils to understand many difficult problems. (clear, splendid)
12. In the battle he —— in the foot. (was wounded, got a wound)

PRACTICE 30. Eliminating Overworked Words

In the following passage add or substitute specific, fresh, accurate words for the overworked general expressions. Instead of saying, for example, "it is a fine day," "he is at my feet," and "butterflies" tell what was fine about the day, use a more vivid verb, and add a descriptive adjective.

It is a fine day at last, after days and days of perfectly horrid weather! Our big pet named "Tummy" is at my feet on this lovely lawn. He is awfully upset by the doings of two butterflies which are very near his nose. Now everything is all right again. The trees are beautiful against the sky; the insects can be heard; a nice breeze faintly moves the trees' topmost leaves; and, changing all to gold, the sun shines. It's grand to be alive, and young, on such a marvellous day, and to be some part of it all, isn't it?

AVOID THE CLICHÉ

A *cliché* is a trite or hackneyed phrase that has lost vitality through over-use. The word is from the French verb *clicher* meaning "to stereotype". Stereotype ("to fix in lasting form; to make permanent") carries the connotation that the original was worth repetition or duplication. Indeed, many of our most continuous clichés had terrific power— when first used. Consider the following clichés of modern advertising:

Now you, too, can have . . .	The finest your money can buy . . .
At leading dealers everywhere . . .	Greatest in the history of . . .
The last word in . . .	Ready at last . . .

But cliché and stereotype also carry the connotations of something that has lost precise meaning, something lacking in originality, something commonplace and worn out. The following expressions have no place in writing that is sincere and natural.

all too soon	bright and early
favour us with a selection	sportsman's paradise
enjoyable occasion	safe and sound
bolt from a clear sky	teeth like pearls
dull, sickening thud	ruby lips, naked eye
was the recipient of	wee, small hours
long-felt want	fair maidens
had the privilege	chequered (checkered) career
tired but happy	the proud possessor
as luck would have it	sadder but wiser
method in his madness	beat a hasty retreat
sigh of relief	wended our way
working like Trojans	breakneck speed
it goes without saying	do justice to a meal
hungry as bears	abreast of the times

mother nature	doomed to disappointment
too funny for words	specimen of humanity
my better half	last but not least
make the supreme sacrifice	along these lines
filthy lucre	where ignorance is bliss
at the parting of the ways	conspicuous by his absence

PRACTICE 31. Eliminating Clichés

Re-write the following sentences, substituting fresh and original expressions for what is trite.

1. Tired but happy after our hike in God's great out-of-doors, we wended our way home.
2. A goodly number of newspapers reported the trials and tribulations of the survivors.
3. Conspicuous by his absence was the young hopeful who had embarked on the sea of life.
4. Hungry as bears, the boys did justice to the meal that the fair sex had prepared with breakneck speed.
5. Like a bolt from a clear sky, John became the proud possessor of a new automobile.
6. We had the privilege of listening to a mere slip of a girl who favoured us with a selection.
7. After working like Trojans to pack the suitcases, we were doomed to disappointment because Father did not arrive home until the wee, small hours of the morning.
8. The speaker beat a hasty retreat after gales of laughter greeted his proposal.
9. As my better half would say, "Don't act so high and mighty."
10. As luck would have it, mother nature provided us with a sportsman's paradise.

IDIOMS

An idiom, an expression peculiar to a language, either violates the laws of grammar or has a meaning as a whole entirely different from that obtained by putting together the meanings of its parts. The idiom "How do you do?" for example, doesn't mean exactly what the words say.

Idioms are important because they are the very life of the language. A free use of these homely, terse, vigorous expressions peculiar to the language makes one's English more natural, individual, forceful, sparkling, imaginative, effective. Examples of everyday idioms are *to make good, to fall in love, in the long run, to call in question, to laugh in one's sleeve, to run for office, a red-letter day, had better, side by side,* and *yours truly* (at the close of a letter).

PRACTICE 32. Using Idioms

Write sentences making clear the following idiomatic phrases:

1. Fall upon; fall back; fall short of; fall foul; fall on one's feet; fall through; fall to.

2. To turn; to turn a deaf ear; to turn round one's finger; to turn adrift; to turn one's hand to; to turn the scale; not turn a hair; to serve a turn; done to a turn.

3. To be a means of; by all means; by any means; by no means; in the meantime.

4. To take root; to take heart; to take pains; to take the place of; to take counsel; to take by storm.

5. To make much of; to make way; to make head against; to make sail; to make sure; to make up for; to make both ends meet; to make off with; to make a clean sweep of; to make one's mark; to make the most of.

Learn to use prepositions idiomatically. The following uses frequently cause trouble:

ability *to* do work	differ *from* or *with* an opinion
agree *to* a proposal	different *from*
agree *with* a person	fail *because of*
angry *at* or *about* a thing	in comparison *with*
angry *at* or *with* a person	in search *of*
bestow *upon*	to search *for*
charge a person *with*	independent *of*
compare *with* (for differences)	pleased *with*
compare *to* (for similarities)	possessed *by* or *with* an idea
correspond *to* or *with* a thing	possessed *of* goods
correspond *with* a person	prefer building *to* leasing
dependent *on*	superior *to*
devoted *to*	*with regard to*
differ *from* a person or thing	*as regards*

Do not violate idiom by the omission of needed words.

WRONG: He had no love or confidence in his employer.

RIGHT: He had no love for his employer and no confidence in him.

WRONG: I shall always remember the town because of the good times and the many friends I made there.

RIGHT: I shall always remember the town because of the good times I had and the many friends I made there.

WRONG: He acquired a knowledge and a keen interest in chess.

RIGHT: He acquired a knowledge of chess and a keen interest in the game.

Avoid faulty expressions used for idioms.

RIGHT	WRONG OR COLLOQUIAL
cannot help remembering	cannot help but remember
I have to	I have got to
I do not know whether I can	I do not know if I can
near enough for me to see	near enough that I could see
seldom or never	seldom or ever
there is no doubt that	there is no doubt but that
very much interested	very interested

PRACTICE 33. Using Idioms Correctly

Correct the following sentences.

1. Their love and devotion to their father is remarkable.
2. I am not only thoroughly familiar, but exceedingly fond of the game.
3. She is not only different but far more admirable than her brother.
4. She was in a constant state of discontent and rebellion against her lot.
5. He showed a distrust and opposition to his adviser.
6. He could not help but have a good time.
7. There is no doubt but that he came yesterday.
8. You have got to go down town at once.
9. I seldom or ever see him.
10. He was very delighted to have you come.

AVOID EUPHEMISMS

A euphemism is a mild, sometimes roundabout, expression substituted for one that may offend or suggest the unpleasant. A great many euphemisms are associated with death: *pass away, go West, to go to one's rest.* Some euphemisms attempt to disguise or dignify occupations—for example, *beauty consultant* for *hairdresser, tonsorial artist* for *barber,* and *lubritorium* for *garage.* Euphemisms used with kindly intent serve a valuable purpose, but usually the plain word is better.

AVOID GOBBLEDYGOOK

"The actual living through or participating in events is likely in the long run to provide incomparable instruction."

In this statement can you recognize the familiar proverb "Experience is the best teacher"? Such wordy, roundabout, indirect sentences are often called "gobbledygook". In discussing his plans for the future, one student wrote, "In the case of my choice of a career, it is felt by my mother and father that I ought to attend some hall of higher learning before starting on the road of life by myself." He might have written, "Mother and Dad think I should go to college."

To avoid gobbledygook (1) cut out padding; (2) use the simplest words that convey your meaning; (3) avoid vague, abstract nouns like *case, condition,* and *situation;* (4) use the passive voice sparingly; (5) avoid words like *swell, fine, grand,* and *interesting.*

PRACTICE 34. Recognizing Proverbs in Gobbledygook

What familiar proverb is concealed in each of the following sentences? Why is the original proverb preferable?

1. It is not at all feasible or even possible to judge accurately and justly the contents of a literary work merely by examining the outer cover.
2. In all the world, one's own residence is a place unique and incomparable.
3. It is extremely unwise under any circumstances to shed copious tears over lacteal fluid that has accidentally been let fall.
4. Aqueous fluids exhibiting nonagitated surfaces generally extend downward to a considerable depth.
5. An individual who vacillates when there is need of action will find himself beyond the hope of future success.

AVOID JARGON

With reference to departures from this vehicle it is requested that passengers proceed to the rear exit doors when they wish to leave the bus.

Is there a kernel of sense in all this "gobbledygook"? Yes; the sentence actually means "Please leave by the rear door." Sometimes because of conceit, ignorance, laziness, or a misguided desire to impress, writers avoid the simple, direct expression.

Writing should reveal thought, not conceal it. Length is no substitute for strength, unless additional words add specific details, as in the Mark Twain selection (page 26).

HINTS FOR AVOIDING JARGON

1. Avoid wordy expressions.

~~We wish to state that~~ ᵀ/his model place was designed ~~with the idea of~~ safety ᶠᵒʳ ~~in mind.~~

2. Use the shortest, simplest words necessary to express yourself exactly. Never use a longer, more learned word unless it expresses your idea more pointedly and satisfactorily. Ordinarily *go* is better

than *proceed; begin,* than *commence.* Simple, unpretentious words like *crisp, stark, bleak,* and *dour* are more effective than lengthy, pretentious ones.

DON'T SAY	SAY
domesticated feline	house cat
enjoyable sojourn	pleasant stay

Sometimes less common words are used for humorous effect, as when a sports writer calls a stolen base in baseball "pilfering" or "larceny". Use of long words is often unintentionally funny.

3. Avoid roundabout expressions (circumlocutions) and euphemisms (mild, vague, indirect expressions used instead of direct, blunt statements).

DON'T SAY	SAY
replied to the letter which I had put in the mails on the 15th of April	answered my letter of April 15
in two subjects received grades that reflected lower-than-acceptable accomplishment	failed two subjects
pass away	die

4. Avoid vague, woolly, abstract nouns, such as *asset, case, character, condition, degree, factor, instance, matter, nature, personality, persuasion, quality, subject, thing, in terms of, with reference to.*

Mr. Walker spoke to us ~~on the subject of~~ about the new cafeteria regulations.

5. Seldom use the passive voice.

Because of Skippy's sore arm ~~it is feared that our team may be defeated by Lincoln~~ we're afraid Lincoln may defeat us.

6. Avoid stilted "elegant variations". Repetition of a noun or the use of a pronoun is preferable to forced synonyms.

If you're planning to go ~~to the performance,~~ please buy your tickets for the play now to give ~~the production~~ it a boost.

7. Use figurative language with consistency and restraint. Don't mix metaphors.

DON'T SAY	SAY
He pulled up to a crossroads on the great sea of life. (Crossroads on a sea?)	He came to a crossroads in his life.
	or
	He faced a crisis in his life.

PRACTICE 35. Eliminating Jargon

Find the words or phrases which make jargon of the following sentences. Following the preceding rules, rewrite the sentences. Eliminate every unnecessary word.

1. It is requested that all pedestrians refrain from walking over those areas in the park which have been planted in grass.
2. Though he had sunk his roots deep in the life of the community, he pulled up anchor without hestiation or delay when the news was heard.
3. The reason that I made a selection of this particular book lies in the fact that some time before the problem of selection arose I was fortunate enough to have an opportunity to see the story of the book presented dramatically through the medium of the screen in a motion picture of real merit.
4. Macbeth informed Lady Macbeth that she would be most favourably impressed by a deed which he was contemplating though he did not wish her to achieve the status of actual complicity in the action.
5. Since Jo had never ridden a horse, Lester told her to ask for a gentle mount and pointed out a steed for her to use during her horseback riding experience.

Words Often Misused

Above. Sometimes used as an adjective: "the above statement", "the above paragraph". Most careful writers prefer *the preceding* or *the foregoing*.

Accept, except. *To accept* is *to receive*; *to except, to exclude*. *Accept* is a verb; *except* is commonly a preposition.
The meeting *accepted* the report of the committee.
All *except* me were called on.

Accept of. Better to omit the *of*. I *accept* your offer.

Ad. A colloquial abbreviation for *advertisement*. It has no relation to *add*, and should be written out in full.

Admittance, admission. *Admittance* means *allowing one to enter a building or location*; *admission, admitting to rights or privileges*.

Affect, effect. *Affect* is always a verb; *effect*, commonly a noun meaning *result*. To *affect* is *to influence*; *to effect, to bring about*.
Did the high-pressure ridge *affect* the course of the hurricane?
The hailstorm had little *effect* on the crop.
The students tried to *effect* a change in the constitution.

After. Redundant when used with the past participle. Say *after writing* instead of *after having written*.

Aggravate.   Means *make worse*.   Colloquial in the sense of *provoke, vex*, or *annoy*.

The constant whispering *annoyed* (not *aggravated*) the teacher.

The shock *aggravated* his misery.

All of.   *Of* is unnecessary.

I lost *all* my books (not *all of* my books).

All the farther, as far as.   *All the farther* is childish and low colloquial for *as far as*.   Avoid it.   *All the farther* correctly used means *by that amount, just so much*.

That was *as far as* we could go.

Our weariness made home seem *all the farther* away.

Allusion, illusion.   An *allusion* is an indirect reference; an *illusion* is a misleading appearance, a delusion.

Most literary *allusions* can be traced to the Bible, Shakespeare, or mythology.

We can see motion in motion pictures only because of an optical *illusion*.

Already, all ready.   *Already* means *previously*; *all ready* means *completely ready*.

By the time we were *all ready* to go, our taxi had *already* gone.

Alright.   The correct form is *all right*, two separate words.   In formal usage *very well* or *satisfactory* is preferred to *all right*. *Very well* (not *All right*), you may be excused.

His homework assignment was *satisfactory* (not *all right*).

Altogether, all together.   *All together* means *in one body*; *altogether, wholly, completely*.

At last the climbers were *all together* in their base camp.

The descent wasn't *altogether* free of accidents.

Among, between.   *Between* commonly applies to only two objects. *Among* is used for three or more.   *Between*, however, may be used with more than two objects to show the relationship of each object to the others; "a treaty between the three powers", "a railroad between the three cities".   Only dikes stand *between* much of low-lying Holland and the sea.

By the end of the fifth century the once powerful Roman Empire had been divided among the Goths, the Huns, and other barbarian tribes.

BUT   Mr. Endicott explained to us the differences between an element, a compound, and an alloy.

Amount, number. *Amount* refers to quantity; *number*, to things that can be counted.

A large *number* of townspeople contributed a substantial *amount* of money to the scholarship fund.

And etc. Never put *and* before *etc.* *Etc.* means *and the rest, and so on, and other things,* and *and* is redundant. *Etc.* is generally in bad form in any composition. Fowler says in *Modern English Usage,* "To resort to etc. in sentences of a literary character is amateurish, slovenly, and incongruous".

Anybody, anyone, everybody, everyone. These pronouns are singular and should be followed by singular pronouns (*he* or *she*) rather than by the plural (*they*).

Anxious. Colloquial for *eager* or *desirous.*

COLLOQUIAL   I am *anxious* to begin work at once.

LITERARY ENGLISH   I am *eager* to begin work at once.

Any place, every place, no place, some place. Incorrect. Use *anywhere, everywhere,* etc.

Anywheres, everywheres, etc. Incorrect for *anywhere, everywhere,* etc.

Appreciate means *estimate justly.* Hence we cannot say, "I appreciate your kindness highly."

Around, about, at about. *Around* refers to place, not time. Never say *around ten o'clock,* but *about ten o'clock.* Do not use *at about* when either *at* or *about* will do.

Father arrived home *about* (not *at about*) one in the morning.

As (1). Should not be used too frequently in the sense of *because.* Substitute *for, since,* or *because,* or omit the conjunction.

BAD: I want you to come home now, as it is time for dinner.

BETTER: I want you to come home now; it is time for dinner.

As (2). Not to be used in place of *that* or *whether.* "I don't know that (not *as*) we can go."

As (3). May be used as a relative pronoun after *same* and should be used after *such.* "Such as I have I give unto you." "These are the same books as (or that) you had."

As . . . as. Correct for affirmative expressions; for negative statements, *so . . . as* is preferable.

Your house is *as* large *as* mine.

Your house is not *so* large *as* mine.

As to whether.   Redundant for *whether.*

Athletics.   Commonly considered plural.

Audience, spectators.   The *audience* hear; the *spectators* see: "the audience at the lecture", "the spectators at the football game".

Avocation, vocation.   An *avocation* is a secondary occupation, such as music, fishing or boating.
A *vocation* is a regular occupation.   By derivation a *vocation* is a "calling"; an *avocation* is a "calling away" from a calling.
Many men who follow scientific *vocations* write science fiction as an *avocation.*

Awful, awfully.   Like *fine, great, grand, fierce,* and *cute,* the word *awful* has been misused so often that it has become meaningless. Do not use *awful* or *awfully* when you mean *very much, very great, disagreeable,* or *very bad.*   Say what you mean.   *Awful* means *full of awe* or *awe-inspiring,* as in "The awful majesty of the king."
Instead of "an awful mistake", say " a serious or disastrous mistake".
Instead of "an awful blunder", say "a ridiculous blunder".

Back of.   Colloquial or low colloquial for *behind.*
The garage stands *behind* (not *back of*) the house.

Badly.   Colloquially used for *a great deal* or *very much.*
I want *very much* (not *badly*) to see you.
The team was *badly* beaten yesterday.

Balance, remainder.   *Balance,* a bookkeeping term, means *the amount remaining after realizing assets and meeting obligations.* It should not be confused with *rest* or *remainder.*
John spent the *rest* (or *remainder*) of the day at home.

Be back.   Colloquial for *return* or *come back.*

Beat.   In everyday English correct for *defeat.*
Alberta was badly *beaten* on the football field.

Because.   See *Cause, reason.*

Being.   Always a participle—never a conjunction or part of a conjunction.
Because (not *Being that*)Alice had once acted the role of Yum-Yum, she was interested in seeing *The Mikado* done by a professional company.
Since (not *Being*) the motor wouldn't start, I was delayed.

Beside, besides. *Beside* is a preposition meaning *by the side of.* *Besides* is either an adverb meaning *in addition* or a preposition meaning *in addition to.*

The child sat close *beside* the mother.

Besides free tickets to the dance, the winner will receive ten dollars.

Aunt Martha not only gave the children cake and candies; she bought them ice-cream cones *besides.*

Between. See *Among.*

Blame . . . on. Crudely used instead of *blame.*

CRUDE   You needn't *blame* it *on* me.

RIGHT   You needn't *blame me* for it.

Borrow, lend, loan. A person *borrows from* a friend and *lends to* a friend. *Loan* is ordinarily a noun but may be used as a verb, particularly in banking.

Because I had been absent nearly a month, Ben *lent* me his history notes.

Boughten. Do not use instead of *bought.*

Bound. Colloquial for *determined.*

He was *bound* to succeed.

He was *determined* to succeed.

Bring, take, fetch. *To bring* requires one motion—toward the speaker: *to take,* one motion—away from the speaker; *to fetch,* two motions—from the speaker and to him again.

Take this message to Captain Morse; *bring* his reply to me; and then *fetch* my horse from the stable.

Bunch. Do not use *bunch* for a group of people or animals.

Mary took a *bunch* of flowers to her friend.

Bursted, bust, busted. Vulgarisms for *burst.* The principal parts of the verb *burst* are *burst, burst, burst.*

But what. Incorrect when used instead of *that* or *but that.*

I had no doubt *that* the dog would bite.

Bye-bye. Colloquial and playful for *good-bye.*

Can, may, might. Use *can* for ability and *may* for permission, probability, or possibility. Although in conversation *can* is allowable in asking permission, most careful speakers use *may.* *Might* is used after a verb in the past tense; *may* after a verb in the present tense.

Mother *says* that you *may* go to the dance.

Mother *said* that you *might* go to the dance.

Cannot help but. Avoid the double negative: *cannot help* and *cannot but*.

  I *cannot help* believing your story.

  I *cannot but* believe your story.

Can't hardly, can't scarcely. Avoid the double negatives.

Cause, reason. Complete such an expression as *the cause was* or *the reason was* with a predicate noun or a noun clause.

  POOR The cause of his failure in physics was on account of excessive absence.

  GOOD The cause of his failure in physics was excessive absence.

  GOOD The reason we did not use the throughway was that Dad prefers scenic back roads.

Character, reputation. *Reputation* is what people suppose a person's character to be. *Character* is what the person really is; it is his moral stature or worth.

Claim. Colloquial for *maintain*. The usage is popular, though objected to. I *maintain* that Cromwell was not a tyrant.

Compare to, compare with. To liken or to pronounce similar, use *compare to*; to make a detailed comparison, use *compare with*.

  She is not to be *compared to* Helen of Troy.

  He *compared me with* Julius Caesar and I was found wanting.

  BUT, C*ompared with* (or *to*) him, I am a bungler.

Complement, compliment. A *complement* is something that completes or makes perfect, A *compliment* is something said in praise of a person or his work.

  Is the predicate noun a *complement* of the verb?

  There is a difference between flattery and a sincere *compliment*.

  The newly assigned manager walked up to the receptionist of a large office and asked,
  "What is the usual complement of this office?"
  "Good morning, Beautiful!" replied the receptionist.

Conscience, consciousness. *Conscience* means sense of right and wrong; consciousness, awareness.

Consul, council, counsel, councillor, counsellor. A *consul* is a representative of a government; a *council* is a body of men; *counsel* as a noun is advice or a lawyer who gives advice; a *councillor* is a member of a council; a *counsellor* gives advice.

The Canadian *consul* in Istanbul gave the tourists excellent *counsel* about their visit to the site of Homer's Troy.

The post of secretary of our student *council* has always been filled by a girl.

COUNCIL

CONSUL

COUNSEL

Contemptible, contemptuous. *Contemptible* means *deserving contempt*; *contemptuous*, *showing contempt*.

The prisoners of war were *contemptuous* of Harlan's *contemptible* efforts to curry favour with the enemy guards.

Continual, continuous. *Continuous* means *uninterrupted*. *Continual* implies frequent repetition.

Since the rainfall was heavy and *continuous* throughout the night, Larry *continually* checked the roof of the tent for leaks.

Could and **might** have the same general distinctions as *can* and *may*.

Could of, might of, should of, would of. These illiteracies result from the contractions *could've, might've*, etc. The correct forms are *could have, might have*, etc.

You *should have* (not *should of*) returned sooner.

Credible (*believable*), **credulous** (*inclined to believe*—perhaps too quickly), **creditable** (*deserving praise*).

I'll admit I was *credulous* when Grant told what seemed like a very *credible* story about his encounter with a huge brown bear.

Canadian farmers have made a *creditable* showing in their efforts to grow superior grades of wheat.

Cute. Colloquial. Use *vivacious, entertaining, pretty,* or the appropriate designation.

Date. Colloquial for *engagement*.

Deadly, deathly. *Deadly* means *causing death; deathly, looking like death.*

Deal. Colloquial for *transaction, agreement,* or *arrangement*.

Deal of, many. *Deal of* refers to quantity; *many,* to number.

It cost me a great *deal of* trouble.

I have *many* entertaining books in my library.

Device, devise. *Device* is a noun; *devise,* a verb.

Differ from, differ with. Use *differ from* when *differ* means "be unlike"; use *differ from* or *differ with* when *differ* means "disagree".

German Christmas customs *differ from* ours.

I must *differ with* (or *from*) Bradley regarding his interpretation of Hamlet's melancholy.

Different than. A common colloquialism for *different from*.

WRONG   He plays it different than I.

RIGHT   His playing of it is different from mine. He plays it differently.

AWKWARD, BUT CORRECT   He plays it differently from what I do.

Discover, invent. *To discover* is to find out something that already exists; *to invent* is to produce something entirely new.

Disinterested, uninterested. *Disinterested* means *unselfish; uninterested, without interest.*

Mr. Jones was considered a *disinterested* judge.

John is an *uninterested* member of the class.

Dove. Use *dived*.

Due to. The two words *because of* are used as a preposition. *Due* is an adjective and should modify a noun.

Because of the drought the wheat crop was a failure.

The failure of the wheat crop *was due to the drought*.

Each other, one another. *Each other* should refer only to two. *One another* refers to more than two.

Either, neither. Should refer only to two: "I asked Tom and Bill, but *neither* was willing." If you wish to refer to more than two, say *any, any one, not one,* or *none*: "I asked Tom, Bill, and Dick, but *none* (*not one*) of them was willing." *Any one* of the three boys would make an excellent guide.

Elegant. Means *excelling in the power to discriminate properly and select properly,* or *giving evidence of such excellence*; as "an elegant gentleman", "elegant ornamentation". Should not be used loosely. Do not say "an elegant view", but "a beautiful view"; not "an elegant game of football", but an exciting (or thrilling) game"; not "an elegant march", but "a spirited (or rousing) march".

Else. To be followed by *but,* not by *than.* Often used redundantly, as "no one else but him" for "no one but him".

Emigrant, immigrant.
After *emigrating* from Russia, he became a Canadian *immigrant.*

Eminent, imminent. *Eminent* means *distinguished*; *imminent, threatening to occur immediately.*

The *imminent* storm forced the postponement of the address by an *eminent* scientist.

Enthuse. A colloquialism. Do not use for *be enthusiastic* or *show enthusiasm.*

Every so often. Childish. Use *at regular intervals* or *occasionally.*

Exceptional, exceptionable. *Exceptional,* which means *unusual,* is to be distinguished from *exceptionable,* which means *objectionable.*

It was an *exceptional* offer.

Your crude language is *exceptionable.*

Expect. Should not be used for *think* or *suppose.*

RIGHT I *suppose* the fish are biting this morning.

POOR I expect the fish are biting this morning.

Extra. Should not be used to mean *unusually,* as "an extra fine example".

Farther, further. *Farther* indicates "space"; *further,* "greater in degree, quantity, or time". *Further* also means *moreover, in addition to.*

He walked two miles *farther.*

Let us speak *further* on this topic.

Female. Do not use as a synonym for *girl* or *woman*.

Fewer, less. *Fewer* refers to number; *less*, to quantity.
The farmer had *fewer cows* and *less wheat* than usual.

Fine. Strictly the word means *refined, delicate, free from impurity, of excellent quality*: "fine flannels", "fine gold", "fine dust", "fine sense of honour". In colloquial use it is a general epithet of approval: "a fine fellow", "a fine ship", "a fine day".

Firstly. Not thoroughly established for *first*.

Fix. (1) Colloquial for *repair*: "He fixed the broken door."
(2) Colloquial for *plight, situation,* or *condition*.

Flaunt, flout, *Flaunt* means *display boldly; flout, treat with contempt.*
Only the ill-bred *flaunt* their wealth.
The newcomers *flouted* the posted regulations.

Folks. Colloquial for *people*.

Formally, formerly. *Formally* means *ceremoniously, according to established form or custom; formerly, previously.*
The mayor *formally* opened the conference with a brief address.
Our school is built on the site where the country club *formerly* stood.

Funny. Colloquial for *strange* or *odd*.

Gent. Do not use *gent* when you mean *man* or *gentleman*.

Gentleman, lady. Don't use these words for *man* and *woman*.
There were only four *women* and five *men* on the eleven o'clock trolley.

Get. Means *obtain, gain, win, earn, acquire, learn, receive, come to have, catch, contract, meet with, suffer*: "get cholera", "get sick", "get a fall", "get the worst of it", "get ten dollars a week", "get up", "get on", "get off", "get well", "get ready", "get ahead". Do not overwork this useful word. "Have you got a knife with you?" is colloquial.

Gotten. Affected, archaic in literary English, and should be avoided. Frequently used by American writers, but not by English or Canadian. It is correct in combinations, as in *misbegotten, ill-gotten*.

Graduated. Correct in active or passive voice.
He *graduated* from Manitoba.
Marion expects *to be graduated* from Queen's next June.

Grand. Means *on a large scale, imposing*; as, "a grand view". Should not be used loosely, as in "a grand day", when you mean "a beautiful (or brilliant) day".

Guess. Colloquial for *think*: "I *guess* I'll go." In some regions *reckon* is the colloquial equivalent of *think*.

Had have, had of. Incorrect for *had*.
If he *had* tried (not *had have* or *had of* tried), he would have succeeded.

Had ought. Incorrect for *ought* or *should*.
You *ought* (not *had ought*) to do your homework now.
Do you think I *should* (not *had ought to*) have accepted the invitation?

Hanged, hung. Use *hanged* with reference to capital punishment; otherwise, use *hung*. (What is a *hung* jury?)
The bandit was *hanged* for stealing horses.
Mother *hung* the clothes on the line.

Hardly, scarcely. Do not use a negative with these words. *Hardly* means *with difficulty*; scarcely, *barely*.
I *could hardly* (not *could not hardly*) hear the bell.

Hardly . . . when. See *Than, till, until*.

Healthy, healthful, wholesome. *Healthy* and *healthful* are often used interchangeably. Strictly, *healthy* means *having health* and *healthful* means *promoting health*: "healthy girl", "healthful climate", "wholesome food".

Home. Sometimes without a preposition expresses result of motion: "He is home from Europe."

Human. Not in good use as a noun. Say *Human being*.

If, whether. Use *if* in conditional clauses; use *whether* for alternatives.
If you are ready, we may leave.
I don't know *whether* it is one o'clock or two.
Although *if* may introduce a noun clause after *see, ask, learn, know, doubt; whether* is better.
ACCEPTABLE   He asked *if* the paper had been found.

Imply, infer. *To imply* means *to hint* or *insinuate*; *to infer, to draw a conclusion*. The speaker implies; the hearer infers.
From his faltering strokes, I *inferred* that the swimmer was tiring. My father *implied* that a good report card might mean an increase in my allowance.

In, at. *In* means *within.* When a place is thought of as a local point or a point along a course or on a map, *at* is more commonly used. We enjoyed ourselves *at* the Canadian National Exhibition *in* Toronto.

In, into. Use *into* ordinarily to express motion from one place to another. He fell *into* the pond. The fish swam *into* the trap we had set.

Notice the difference between "He jumped into the water" and "He jumped in the water."

In back of. Say *behind.*

Ingenious, ingenuous. An inventor is *ingenious*; a person of a frank trusting nature is *ingenuous.*

Inside of, outside of. Omit *of.* We went *inside* the building.

Inside of. A colloquial Americanism for *within*, in time expressions. It will disappear *within* (not *inside* of) a week.

Irregardless. Vulgarism (double negative) for *regardless.*

Is when, is where. Avoid these constructions. Do not begin a definition with *when* or *where.* The word after *is* should be a noun (the name of the class).

WRONG A tourniquet is when something is put on to stop bleeding.

RIGHT A tourniquet is a device to stop bleeding.

Its, it's. *Its* means *belonging to*; *it's* means *it is.*
That gull seems to have hurt *its* wing. *It's* time to start supper.

Kind, sort. These words are singular and therefore should be modified by singular adjectives.
I do not like *this kind* (not *these kind*) of apples.
OR I do not like *these kinds* of apples.

Kind of, sort of. Colloquial when used instead of *rather, somewhat,* or *in some degree.* Avoid these expressions in speeches and themes.
I am *rather* (not *kind of*) glad he was not elected.

Kind of a, sort of a. *Kind of* and *sort of* are preferably followed directly by a noun, not by an article.
He worked in a *kind of* (not *kind of a*) factory.

Later, latter. *Later* means *more recent*; *latter, the second of two.*
On the sundial was inscribed this motto: "It's *later* than you think."

Larry couldn't decide at first whether to take Spanish or French, but he finally chose the *latter.*

Lead, led. *Lead* (pronounced led) is a metal; *lead* (pronounced lēd) means *guide or conduct*; *led* is past tense of *lead*.
Dave *led* me to believe, incorrectly, that *lead* is heavier than gold.
Lead me to the water cooler!

Learn, teach. *To learn* is *to acquire knowledge or skill*. *To teach* is *to give instruction*.

Leave, let. *To leave* means *to allow to remain* or *to depart from*. *To let* means *to permit*.
Leave your *hat* in the hall.   *Let him have* the book.
We shall *leave you* for an hour.   *Let him be*.

Leave go, leave go of. Vulgarisms for *let go*. He *let go* the rope.

Lie, lay. *Lie* ("recline") is an intransitive verb. *Lay* ("put down or place") is a transitive verb. The principal parts of *lie* are *lie, lay, lain*; the principal parts of *lay* are *lay, laid, laid*.
Mr. Meredith *laid* the new linoleum in the kitchen and then *lay* down in the hammock to read the paper.

Like, as (as if). Do not confuse the preposition *like* with the conjunction *as* (*as if*). The preposition *like* should be followed by a noun or pronoun in the objective case.
It looks *as if* (not *like*) it will rain. (The subordinate clause requires a conjunction.)
It looks *like* rain. (The phrase requires a preposition)
He plays golf *like* a professional.

Likely, liable, apt. *Likely* indicates probability. *Liable* expresses obligation or the possibility of evil. *Apt* means *having a habitual tendency* or *quick to learn*.
You are liable to be hurt.
He is an *apt* pupil and is *likely* to succeed as a salesman.

Line. Vulgarism when used for *kind*: "What *kind* (not *line*) of work are you now doing?" Slang in such expressions as "He has a great line."

Loan. Only occasionally used as a verb. *Lend* is preferable.

Locate. Colloquialism for *settle* or *find*.
He settled in North Bay.
Find Saint John on the map.
Give the location of Kingston.

Loose, lose. *Loose* is usually an adjective meaning "not tight". *Lose* is a verb meaning "to misplace, not to have any longer".
Sew on that *loose* button, or you'll *lose* it.

Lose out, win out. Sporting slang for *lose* and *win*.

Lot, lots. Colloquial for *plenty of, many*. Say "many automobiles", not "lots of cars".

Lovely. A colloquialism when used loosely. Do not say "a lovely time", "a lovely dinner", "a lovely drive", but "a delightful time", "an excellent or delightful dinner", "an enjoyable drive". Choose the adjective that expresses definitely the meaning.

Mad. Colloquial or playful for *angry*. In standard English *mad* means *crazy*.

Majority, plurality. *Majority* means "more than half the votes" or "the excess of one candidate's votes over the votes for all other candidates combined." *Plurality* means "an excess of votes over those received by any other candidate."

Since Brad had 16 of the 27 votes cast, he had won a clear *majority*.

In the vote for class secretary Natalie had 12 votes; Jane, 9; and Clara 6. Natalie has a *plurality* of 3 votes over Jane, but she did not win a *majority*.

Make. Colloquial for *earn* or *gain*: "He makes ten dollars a week."

Manners, morals. *Manners* concern the minor forms of acting with others and toward others; *morals* include the important duties of life. Good manners make us good companions; good morals make us good members of society.

Mathematics. Singular noun.

May be, maybe. *May be* is a verb. *Maybe* is an adverb meaning *perhaps* or *possibly*.

Maybe it will be a pleasant day tomorrow.

It *may be* our last chance to go swimming.

Might. See *can, may, might*.

Mighty. Colloquial for *very*: "I'm *mighty* glad to see you." If in conversation you use *mighty* in this sense, do not overwork the word.

Most, almost. Use *almost* when you mean *nearly*.

Ted has finished *almost* all of the repair work on the car he bought.

Movies. Colloquial for *moving pictures*.

Mutual, common. *Mutual* means *reciprocal, interchanged.* Incorrect in the sense of *common to two or more.*

WRONG As we conversed, we found that we had several *mutual* friends.

RIGHT As we conversed, we found that we had several friends *in common.*

WRONG The two friends had a *mutual* interest in scultpure.

RIGHT The two friends had a *common* interest in sculpture.

Myself. A reflexive or emphatic pronoun. Do not substitute the compound personal pronoun for the simple personal pronoun. Tomorrow Joe and I (not *myself*) are going to the museum.

REFLEXIVE Did I cut *myself* with the can opener or the can?

EMPHATIC I *myself* was at fault.

Nice. In literary use *nice* means *minutely accurate, precise, discriminating, refined, finical, subtle*: "nice sense of touch", "nice distinction", "nice eye for distance". In colloquial use it is a general epithet of approval: "a nice fellow", "a nice long letter", "nice to me".

Do not say "a nice fellow", but "an agreeable, or admirable, or conscientious, or honourable fellow", not "a nice time", but "a pleasant time"; not "He is nice to us", but "He is kind or courteous to us". Choose the adjective that expresses your definite meaning.

No good. Colloquial when used adjectively. Say "It is worthless."

No sooner . . . than. See *Than, till, until.*

None. Either singular or plural.

None are to blame. None of the pupils was prepared.

Notorious, notable. *Notorious* means *infamous, of bad repute*: *notable* means *famous, celebrated, noteworthy.*

Nowhere near. Colloquial for *not nearly.*

I have *not nearly* finished my homework.

Off of. Vulgarism for *from* or *off.*

I got the knife *from* (not *off of* or *off*) Jack.

I took it *off* (not *off of*) the table.

Only. Incorrect for *but* or *except that.*

WRONG He would have been here, *only* he had to study.

RIGHT He wished to be here, *but* he had to study.

Or. Should not be correlated with *neither*; use *nor.*

WRONG *Neither* the long Arctic night *or* any other cause . . .

RIGHT *Neither* the long Arctic night *nor* any other cause . . .

Oral, verbal. *Verbal* means *in words*; *oral, in spoken words.*

Ought. Do not use with *had.*
> BAD   He *hadn't ought* to have done it.
> RIGHT   He *should not have* done it.

Out. "He *looked out* the window" is bad grammar. Say "He *looked out of* the window".

Out loud. Colloquial for *aloud.*

Outside of. Should not be used for *aside from.*
> WRONG   *Outside* of this mistake, it is very good.
> RIGHT   *Aside* from this mistake, it is very good.

Over with. *With* is superfluous.
> WRONG   The regatta is *over with.*
> RIGHT   The regatta is *over.*

Party, person. *Party*, except in legal language, means *body of people*: "dinner party", "Liberal party", "foraging party".

Passed, past. The verb is *passed.*
For the *past* three years I have *passed* that vacant lot every day.

Patronize. Colloquial for *trade with.* A *patron* helps, defends, protects, or supports.
We *trade with* the oldest *firm* in town.

Per. Use *per* with Latin words: *per annum, per capita, per cent, per diem.* Avoid its use with English words. Say, "Five dollars *a* week.".

Persecute, prosecute. *Persecute* means *to injure or harass, often because of religious belief; prosecute, to proceed against a person by legal process.*
At the Nürnberg trials the Allies tried to *prosecute* those war criminals who had *persecuted* innocent people.

Plan. Should not be combined with *on.*
> WRONG   We *planned on* taking a trip.
> RIGHT   We *planned* taking (to take) a trip.

Plenty. Colloquial if used as an adjective or adverb.
> BAD   She was *plenty* tired.
> RIGHT   She was *very* tired.
> BETTER   She was exhausted.

Politics. Commonly treated as plural.

Possessive before gerund. Nouns and pronouns preceding the infinitive ending in *ing* (gerund) should show the possession of the action named in the gerund.

You can depend upon *his* (not *him*) doing his best work.

My parents insisted on *my* (not *me*) returning early.

I never heard of a *person's* (not *person*) making excuses as readily as you do.

Posted. Colloquial in sense of *informed*: "Newspapers keep us posted on current events."

Practical, practicable. *Practical* is the opposite of *theoretical*. *Practicable* means *workable*.

He is a *practical mechanic*.

The *scheme* is delightful, but not *practicable*.

Precede, proceed. *Precede* means *to go before*; *proceed, to go or continue*.

Pretty as an adverb. Colloquial or familiar. "pretty cold", "pretty often", "pretty late".

Principal, principle. Use *a* in the adjective and in the name of the head of a school.

The *principal of our school* is a *man of principle*.

Proposition. Business jargon for *proposal*.

Proven. Has enemies. BETTER *proved*.

Providing. *Provided* is preferable.

I will lend you my pen, *provided* you agree to take good care of it.

Put in. Colloquial for *spend* or *occupy*.

COLLOQUIAL I *put in* three hours studying history.

RIGHT I *spent* three hours in studying history.

Quick. Correct as adverb.

Come quick. Come quickly.

Quite. Precisely used, quite means (1) *wholly* or (2) *really, truly, positively*: "quite correct", "quite alone", "quite a scandal", "quite a large party". Loosely or colloquially used, the word means *very* or *rather*: "quite sick", "quite tired".

Quite a few, quite a good deal, quite a little. Low colloquial and dialectal.

Quite some. A vulgarism.

Raise. Colloquial for the noun *increase* or the verb *rear*.
LITERARY ENGLISH   He deserved his *increase* in salary.
LITERARY ENGLISH   John was *reared* by his aunt.

Real. Dialectic or low colloquial for *very* or *really*. Say "a very good time", not "a real good time".

Reason is because. A noun clause is required.
The *reason* for his headache *was that* (not *was because*) he did not eat any breakfast.

Receipt. Correct for *recipe*: "the receipt for corn bread"; but *recipe* is in more common use.

Recollect, remember. *Recollect* usually suggests a conscious effort to recall a specific fact or a series of circumstances. *Remember* implies only that the impression remains.
I *remember* his main idea but can't *recollect* his exact words.
Beasts and babies *remember*; man alone *recollects.*—
SAMUEL TAYLOR COLERIDGE

Refer back, repeat again. *Back* and *again* are superfluous.

Respectfully, respectively. *Respectfully* means *with respect*; "Yours respectfully." *Respectively* means *each to each in order* or *in the order given.*
The letter *respectfully* requested the town council to consider replacing the old traffic lights.
Halifax, Toronto, and Winnipeg are the capitals *respectively* of Nova Scotia, Ontario, and Manitoba.

Right away. Colloquial for *at once, directly,* or *immediately.*

Rise, raise. *Rise* (ascend) is intransitive; *raise* (elevate) is transitive. The principal parts of *rise* are *rise, rose, risen*; the principal parts of *raise* are *raise, raised, raised.*
As the sun *rose* over the horizon, the troops *raised* the white flag.

Run. A colloquial Americanism in the sense of *manage* or *operate.*

Same. Crude and stilted when used instead of a personal pronoun.
WRONG Your letter came today, and I shall reply briefly to the same.

Scarcely . . . than. See *Than, till, until.*

Seldom ever. Illiterate. Say *very seldom* or *hardly ever.*
The captain of *H.M.S. Pinafore* declared that he had *hardly ever* been sick at sea.

Set, sit. Do not use *set* without an object to express mere rest; say "sit", "stand", "lie", "rest", or "*is set*".
WRONG The vase *sets* on the mantel.
RIGHT   The vase *stands* (or rests) on the mantel.
Four exceptions to the rule that *set* is transitive and *sit* intransitive are: "He *sits* his horse well", "This coat *sets* (or sits) well", "The sun *sets* in the west", and "He *set out* on a long journey".

Show. Colloquial for *play, opera, concert, entertainment.*

Show up. Colloquial in sense of *appear, attend, come,* or *expose.*

Size. Never use *size* as an adjective; say "sized", or "of size".
WRONG Any *size chain* will do.
RIGHT   A *chain of any size* will do.

Slow. Correct as adverb in some uses, especially when the emphasis is upon the slowness rather than upon the action. Cp. My watch runs *slow.* Go *slow.* They walked *slowly* homeward.

So. (1). Should not be used for *so that.*
WRONG They strapped it *so it* would hold.
RIGHT   They strapped it *so that it* would hold.

So. (2). Ordinarily vague and weak when used alone to modify an adjective.
WRONG Last week I was *so* lonely.
RIGHT Last week I was *very* lonely.

So. (3). So may be used as a conjunction only when it means *provided that, on condition that, in case that.* The sentence "We were down town, so we decided to have lunch at the Walker House" is wrong both grammatically and rhetorically, grammatically because *so* is here an adverb meaning *therefore,* and consequently the two clauses have no conjunction, and rhetorically because the second clause is the main idea and should be made the principal clause.
RIGHT As (or since) we were down town, we had lunch at the Walker House.
RIGHT He will sell anything, so (provided that) he gets a profit out of it.

Some. Colloquial for *somewhat.*
LITERARY ENGLISH He is *somewhat* better.
A provincialism when used as an adverb.
WRONG I worked *some* last winter.
RIGHT I did *some* work last winter.

State, say. *State* means *set down in detail*.

Stationary, stationery. *Stationary* (adjective) means *fixed, stable*; *stationery* (noun) means *writing paper*.

The ancients believe that the earth remained *stationary* while the sun and planets revolved around it.

For my birthday Mother gave me some *stationery* with my name printed on it.

Statue, stature, statute. *Statue* means *a sculptured or modelled figure*; *stature, height*; *statute, written law*.

Michelangelo's *statue* of David shows us a man tremendous in *stature*.

Many out-of-date *statutes* have been neglected rather than repealed.

Stop. Colloquial and dialectic for *stay*.

LITERARY ENGLISH In Winnipeg we *stayed* at the Fort Gray.

Such. When *such* is completed by a relative clause, the relative pronoun of the clause should be *as*.

I will act under *such* rules *as* (not *that*) may be fixed.

Sure. Low colloquialism or slang for *surely, certainly,* or *indeed*.

WRONG Will you come? Sure. RIGHT Will you come? Surely.

We were *certainly* (not *sure*) delighted with the gifts.

Take in. Slang.

SLANG We *took in* the show.

RIGHT We *went to* the show.

Terrible, terribly. See *awful, awfully*.

Than, then. *Than*, a conjunction, is used after the comparative degree of an adjective or adverb. *Then*, an adverb, means "at that time" or "next".

Than, till, until. Often improperly used for *when*. After *no sooner, than* is correct: "No sooner had we arrived than the play began."

WRONG *Scarcely* had he sat down *than* the horse started.

RIGHT *Scarcely* had he sat down *when* the horse started.

WRONG We had *hardly* got there and put things in order *till* John arrived.

RIGHT We had *hardly* got there and put things in order *when* John arrived.

That. Colloquial as an adverb: "I didn't intend to go that far."

That there, this here. Use *that* or *this*.

These kind, those kind. See *kind, sort*.

Thing. Choose a more specific word.

Through. Colloquial and childish when used as in the following sentence: "He is through writing." It should be: "He has finished writing."

Till, until. See *than, till, until.*

Toward, towards. Fowler says in *Modern English Usage*: "Of these two prepositions *towards* is the prevailing form, and the other tends to become literary on the one hand and provincial on the other."

Truth, veracity. *Truth* belongs to the thing; *veracity*, to the person.
  Because of the *veracity* of the narrator no one questioned the *truth* of the story.

Try and. Colloquial for *try to.*
  I shall follow your advice and *try to* do my best work.

Unless, without. Do not confuse the preposition *without* with the conjunction *unless* (*if not*).

Would have. Often incorrectly used instead of *had* in *if* clauses.
  WRONG If he would have stood by us, we might have won.
  RIGHT If he had stood by us, we might have won.

Unique. Means *the only one of its kind.* It may not be qualified, as "This is quite unique", or "fairly unique", or "the most unique".

United States. This form is correct only when used as an attributive noun, as in "United States laws and regulations". Used as a pure noun it should always be preceded by *the.*
  RIGHT: *The* United States is in North America.

Up. Should not be appended to the verbs *connect, cripple, divide, end, finish, open, polish, rest, scratch, settle.*
  WRONG He *opened up the box* and divided the *money up among* the men.
  RIGHT He *opened the box* and divided the *money among* the men.

Up to date. A colloquialism when used as an adjective; better used as an adverbial modifier.
  COLLOQUIAL His house is up to date.
  PREFERABLE His house is modern.
  RIGHT   He brought the house up to date.

Very. This word should be given a vacation. It is called upon for too much service by most young writers and speakers. When overworked *very*, instead of strengthening a statement, weakens it.

Wait on. Use *wait for*, unless you mean *serve*.
The waitress *waited on* the customer.
I will *wait for* you, if you hurry.

Want. "Want in", "want out", "want off", etc., are unauthorized localisms.
LOCALISMS Do you *want in*?
RIGHT   Do you want to *come in*?

Ways. The plural form should not be used when the singular is meant.
WRONG Go a little *ways* down stream.
RIGHT Go a little *way* down stream.
RIGHT He found *ways and means*.

Where. (1). Often misused for *that*.
WRONG I see in the morning paper *where* Cronin has been caught.
RIGHT I see in the morning paper *that* Cronin has been caught.

Where. (2). In an interrogative sentence do not add *to* or *at* to *where*.
WRONG *Where* are you going *to*?
RIGHT *Where* are you going?
WRONG *Where* is he *at*?
RIGHT *Where* is he?

PRACTICE 36. Using Troublesome Words Correctly

Select the correct or never-questioned expression in each of the following sentences. Justify your choice in each case.

1. A large (amount, number) of fallen trees blocked the trail after Dao, so that was (all the farther, as far as) he could go on horseback.
2. (Can, May) I have some ice cream to divide (among, between) the four boys who helped us with the decorations?
3. I don't doubt (but that, but what, that) (any one, either) of the three candidates will make a competent treasurer of the junior class.
4. (After, Following) a poor freshman year, Pat really buckled down and finally (graduated, graduated from) high school with high honours.
5. I don't know (as, whether) Clark will let you (borrow, have the lend of) his blanket roll for the hike.

6. Although (both, each) of them had a different reason for being optimistic neither Holmes nor Dr. Watson doubted (but that, but what, that) the other could be trusted.
7. Although a large (amount, number) of candidates tried out for the class play *Harvey*, we had (fewer, less) boys this year than last.
8. The reason we don't expect to go (anywhere, anywheres) this summer is (because, that) Dad is planning to paint the house.
9. Though Dunlap's (character, reputation) was injured by the slanderous statements, those who knew him best were rightly convinced of his upright (character, reputation).
10. If you (had, had of) (brought, taken) the message to Mrs. Owen as I asked you to, she would not have been concerned about Drew.
11. When during the Revolution the Tories had the choice of going back to England, fleeing to Canada, or remaining in the Colonies, a great (deal of, many) Loyalists, as they were called by the British, chose the (last, latter) course.
12. If the Rams (had, had of) thrown (fewer, less) forward passes, they might have won.

PRACTICE 37. Using Troublesome Words Correctly

Select the correct or never-questioned expression in each of the following sentences. Justify each choice.

1. Miss Baker (learned, taught) us how to dive gracefully (in, into) the water from the diving board.
2. By his confident manner, Lew (implied, inferred) that he had (passed, past) all his subjects.
3. Matt was (real, very) surprised to discover that he could do (almost, most) all of his homework in study hall when he tried.
4. Neither Lee (nor, or) Ed was born (at, in) Toronto.
5. Were you able to (learn, teach) your new puppy to stay (off, off of) the new sofa?
6. I was (real, very) happy to hear that he is (liable, likely) to win.
7. Harry was (real, very) badly bruised when he fell (off of, off) his horse.
8. (Almost, Most) all the players on the team said that the umpire had been unfair and (implied, inferred) by their statements that he had tried to give the game to Central High.
9. Earl received 22 votes for president; Roy, 14 votes; and Elwin, 6 votes. Earl had a (majority, plurality) of 2 and a (majority, plurality) over Roy of 8.
10. Just before the test Jennie borrowed the pen (from, off of) me as (per usual, usual).

PRACTICE 38. Using Troublesome Words Correctly

Select the correct or never-questioned expression in each of the following sentences. Justify each choice.

1. In describing suits of armour used in the Middle Ages, Mr. Greever commented that men were on the average much shorter (than, then) (than, then) now.

2. No sooner had we gone a little (way, ways) into the shadowy pine forest (than, when) Curtis remembered that he had left his compass back in the cabin.

3. Katie's Yorkshire terrier has a (most unique, unique) habit of sitting in its food dish and yelping until someone feeds (it, same).

4. I read in *Natural History* (that, where) wild animals that are unprovoked (hardly, seldom) ever attack man.

5. One can often (recollect, remember) without trying, but to (recollect, remember) may take some thought.

6. Jen was (certainly, sure) glad she did better on the second test (than, then) on the first.

7. I read in the paper today (that, where) a (most unique, unique) colonial silver pitcher was found in an abandoned barn.

8. I was so tired I was (certainly, sure) glad to hear the coach (say, state), "No practice today."

9. No sooner had I received a bright, newsy letter from Janet (than, when) I wanted to answer (it, same).

10. In August there are jellyfish a little (way, ways) out in the bay, but I have (hardly, seldom) ever been stung.

PRACTICE 39. Using Troublesome Words Correctly

Select the correct or never-questioned expression in each of the following sentences. Justify each choice.

1. Are you (quiet, quite) certain our (principal, principle) will approve a dance on a Wednesday night?

2. King George VI and Franklin D. Roosevelt were (eminent, imminent) men whose (avocation, vocation) was stamp collecting.

3. Our class wrote a letter to the (consul, counsel) at Lisbon (respectfully, respectively) requesting information about touring in Portugal.

4. (Beside, Besides) completing the heroic figure of Moses, Michelangelo worked on several others of the more than forty (statues, statures, statutes) he had originally planned for the tomb of Pope Julius.

5. Mr. Knox (complemented, complimented) us because we were (all ready, already) to leave for the picnic on time.

6. The storm had little (affect, effect) on our part of the shore (accept, except) to strew the beaches with driftwood and seaweed.

7. In a very (creditable, credulous) piece of research on Shakespeare's stage, Chris made many apt (allusions, illusions) to Sheldon Chesney's book on the theatre.

8. The Nazis were (contemptible, contemptuous) of the minority groups they (persecuted, prosecuted).

9. Anne, you should be more careful of your things; you're (continually, continuously) (loosing, losing) something.

10. Carl Schurz and Jacob Riis were (emigrants, immigrants) (respectfully, respectively) from Germany and Denmark.

11. (Beside, Besides) his regular job everyone should have a(n) (avocation, vocation).
12. I will (accept, except) all your suggestions (accept, except) one.
13. At the (consul, council, counsel) meeting, three officers (beside, besides) the president were present.
14. The (principal, principle) speaker at the town hall was an (eminent, imminent) scientist, who discussed atomic energy's peaceful uses.
15. With its full (complement, compliment) of officers and men, Mr. Roberts's ship, *The Reluctant,* was (all ready, already) to take another cargo from Tedium to Apathy.
16. The armed bands (flaunted, flouted) their revolutionary banners and (flaunted, flouted) the feeble authority of the collapsing government.
17. I didn't recognize the (allusion, illusion), but if Beth made it, it's no (complement, compliment).
18. Though he was (continually, continuously) interrupted, the sculptor finished the (statue, stature, statute) in time for the exhibition.
19. Though I am not usually (credible, credulous), I found Trim's strange explanation completely (credible, credulous).
20. Dunstan's (contemptible, contemptuous) act of stealing from an old man had great (affect, effect) upon the life of Silas Marner.

PRACTICE 40. Choosing the Correct Word

Select the correct or preferred word in each of the following sentences. Justify each choice.

1. —— my absence from school during the first two weeks all my subjects seem hard. (Because of, Due to)
2. Meriden was —— we went on Monday. (all the farther, as far as)
3. That our pupils are loyal to the school is shown by the large —— of them at the baseball games. (amount, number)
4. Oscar jumped —— the lake to rescue his little brother. (in into)
5. Harold —— me to write the ballad stanza. (learned, taught)
6. My father —— me go on the outing. (left, let)
7. His parents —— him do as he pleased. (left, let)
8. Mother, —— I go to the baseball game? (can, may)
9. My aunt didn't wish to be bothered with me and had me —— away to an orphan asylum. (brought, taken)
10. —— the mail from the village immediately. (Bring, Fetch)
11. I am —— this report to the office for Miss Lockwood. (bringing, taking)
12. Nausicaa promised to —— him to the village. (bring, take)
13. I shall endeavour to prove that in two periods a week a teacher could —— a girl how to make many of her own clothes. (learn, teach)
14. His mother thinks he is —— better. (some, somewhat)
15. I regret that I cannot —— your invitation for May 6. (accept, except)
16. The sign on the factory reads: Positively no ——. (admission, admittance).
17. I remained under the tree for —— time. (a long, quite some)
18. Henry and I went swimming —— every day. (almost, most)
19. If children were taught to be more careful, —— lives would be lost. (fewer, less)

20. The suit you received by mistake was made for another ——. (party, person)
21. He is —— to succeed. (liable, likely)
22. What will be the —— of the new tariff law? (affect, effect)
23. —— was one cause of the rapid growth of our population during the decade 1900-1910. (Emigration, Immigration)
24. The applicant has an excellent —— for honesty. (character, reputation)
25. Every year a certain —— of enlisted men are sent to the Royal Military College. (amount, number)
26. —— interruptions make —— work impossible. (continual, continuous)
27. His address was a highly —— performance, if the newspaper reports are ——. (credible, creditable)
28. The reports of the —— combat made him grow —— pale. (deadly, deathly)
29. ——, May 12 was the date for which the game was scheduled. (First, Firstly)
30. For your vacation select a —— spot; eat —— food; and become ——. (healthful, healthy, wholesome)
31. The —— machinist hit upon a —— device for reducing the friction. (practicable, practical)
32. He and his son are —— a lawyer and a journalist. (respectfully, respectively)
33. You —— always choose outdoor books. (almost, most, mostly)
34. The modifiers of the subject do not —— the number of the verb. (affect, effect)
35. Although he —— them well, he was embarrassed by his inability to —— their names. (recollected, remembered) (recollect, remember)
36. The —— applauded the pitcher. (audience, spectators)
37. Two of the party went to Oxford, but the —— spent the day in the Houses of Parliament. (balance, rest)
38. For president, John received 30 votes; Marion, 18; and Jaxon, 10. John had a —— of 2 and a —— of 12. (majority, plurality)
39. His many —— sap his energy and prevent his rapid advancement in his ——. (avocations, vocations) (avocation, vocation)
40. The town —— refused to admit to their meetings the —— for the railway. (council, counsel)

MASTERY TEST A—CORRECT WORD

Select the correct or preferred word or expression to fill each blank, and place it on your paper after the number of the sentence: (Right— Wrong = Score)

1. Paul —— me to write the composition heading correctly. (learned, taught)
2. He —— his sons drink and disgrace the family. (left, let)
3. —— the car to the nearest garage. (Bring, Take)
4. —— I go along on the fishing trip? (Can, May)
5. Harold jumped —— the water to save the child. (in, into)
6. Shylock would not —— the money. (accept, except)

7. I have —— books than you. (fewer, less)
8. What will be the —— of the new tariff law? (affect, effect)
9. A large —— of qualified voters remained away from the polls. (amount, number)
10. My mother divided the dozen apples equally —— us four boys. (among, between)
11. He tried to —— his dog a new trick. (learn, teach)
12. —— the dough rise in a warm place. (Leave, Let)
13. I gave him the note and told him to —— it to my father. (bring, take)
14. In my composition I made —— errors in punctuation. (a good deal of, many)
15. I cannot —— that statement without proof. (accept, except)
16. I see him —— every day. (almost, most)
17. He —— a history from his cousin. (borrowed, loaned)
18. They sailed away without —— their purpose. (affecting, effecting)
19. Will you please —— this note to the office. (bring, take)
20. Father —— me go with him to Boston. (left, let)

MASTERY TEST B—CORRECT WORDS

Select the correct or preferred word or expression to fill each blank, and place it on your paper after the number of the sentence: (Right— Wrong = Score.)

1. You —— put your books away now. (can, may)
2. Elwood fell from the dock —— the icy water. (in, into)
3. The farmer —— us sleep in his big red barn. (left, let)
4. There is a keen rivalry —— the six high schools in the city. (among, between)
5. I've decided to —— the hat back to the store. (bring, take)
6. —— boys and girls study music and art. (A great deal of, Many)
7. Fear —— a person in many ways. (affects, effects)
8. Peter —— Heidi many interesting things about the mountains and goats. (learns, teaches)
9. Edward —— the baker's offer. (accepted, excepted)
10. We have not —— him walk long distances. (left, let)
11. There were a large —— of booths at the fair. (amount, number)
12. Pete and John —— me horseback riding. (brought, took)
13. In our city there were —— drownings this year than there were last year. (fewer, less)
14. His presence had a quieting —— upon the crowd. (affect, effect)
15. From whom did you —— that book? (borrow, loan)
16. I cannot —— that for an answer. (accept, except)
17. —— everyone likes to write letters. (Almost, Most)
18. The farmer discovered that we were lost and offered to —— us back to our car. (bring, take)
19. Laura told me she would —— me how to swim. (learn, teach)
20. Why don't you —— the boy ride? (leave, let)

Chapter 2

Correct and Clear Sentences

To be correct and clear a sentence must have both unity and coherence. Unity means oneness. In a *unified sentence* every part must be related to ONE main idea. In a *coherent sentence* the parts must be worded and arranged so that they stick together.

Failure to observe these two basic principles produces major errors of sentence structure. The *lack of unity* may result in a fragment, a run-together sentence, a "cat-and-dog" sentence, a rambling or run-on sentence, an overlapping construction, or a choppy sentence. The *lack of coherence* may result in errors or subordination (misrelated words, phrases, and clauses), errors of co-ordination (faulty parallel structure), lack of consistency (careless shifts in tense, voice, mood, person, and number), or faulty ellipsis. You must avoid these errors if you wish to write sentences that are correct and clear.

A. Unity

Unity means oneness. A unified sentence expresses *one complete* thought. Logically this means that a sentence should make a statement about something; grammatically it means that a sentence should have a subject and a predicate. To write as sentences expressions that do not make complete sense when standing alone may confuse your reader or suggest to him that your thinking is not very clear. It is a common error to write subordinate clauses as if they were sentences or to use a participle or an infinitive in the place of a finite verb.

Do you know the difference between a sentence and a sentence fragment? Between one sentence and two sentences?

TEST A (Diagnostic) Sentence Unity

Indicate by *0, 1, 2,* or *3* the number of complete sentences in each of the following. On your paper place a period between the letter of the example and your answer.

Examples:

a. I left my baby brother and went to work on my homework soon I heard a thump and ran to see what had happened.

b. Hoping that you will visit us during either your Christmas or your spring vacation.

ANSWERS

a. 2
b. 0

The first example is two sentences. The 0 indicates that *b* is not a sentence.

THE TEST

a. Doctor Joachim an eye specialist from Montreal who had failed in an attempt to restore a man's eyesight and had moved to Labrador

b. I killed the snake and held the bird in my hands soon it flapped its wings and flew away

c. It is wise to use a small double boiler for this the upper part for cooking the syrup and the lower part filled with boiling water to keep the syrup hot

d. One September when my father mother sister and I arrived in Saint John on our way back to Fredericton after spending our vacation at Rye Beach New Hampshire

e. Jo set the table and Meg started the dinner they were going to have lobster salad bread strawberries and cream

f. A man on second base one down and Jimmy Foxx coming up to bat

g. Twelve members of the Cardinal Audubon Club went on a hike and picnic on Monday May 25 under the supervision of Miss Luciana Snyder the picnic was held at South Park before eating supper we saw about ten different kinds of birds in the fields and woods

h. What an awful feeling one gets when walking down a dark lonely road at night the trees swaying in the breeze the branches rubbing together making weird noises

i. Have you read *Robinson Crusoe* the story of an English sailor who was shipwrecked on a desert island it was written by Daniel Defoe

j. *The Animal Story Book* by Andrew Lang tells about the life of different animals where they are found how they live and what they eat

PHRASE, SUBORDINATE CLAUSE, AND SENTENCE

A phrase has neither subject nor predicate; a clause has a subject and a predicate. A sentence or a principal clause contains a subject and a predicate and needs no introductory word; a subordinate clause, except a direct quotation, needs an introductory word either expressed or understood. A sentence makes complete sense—really says or asks something—when standing alone; a subordinate clause, as a rule, does not make sense when standing alone.

Relative pronouns and subordinate conjunctions introduce subordinate clauses. The commonly used relative pronouns are *who*, *which*, *what*, and *that*. For a list of subordinate conjunctions see page 589.

PRACTICE 1. Phrases, Subordinate Clauses, Sentences

Which of the following are phrases? Subordinate clauses? Sentences? Can you tell why?

1. Every player on the team contributing his share to the victory against the seniors
2. Since every player on the team contributed his share to the victory against the seniors
3. Every player on the team contributed his share to the victory against the seniors

SENTENCE FRAGMENT

When a group of words that is not a sentence is written with a capital letter and a period, the expression is called a sentence fragment. In such a fragment usually the subject or predicate verb or both are missing from the principal clause.

SENTENCE AND SENTENCE FRAGMENT   Intercepting a long pass, Larry ran thirty yards. Before he was tackled. (The second group of words written as a sentence is a dependent clause.)

ONE SENTENCE   Intercepting a long pass, Larry ran thirty yards before he was tackled.

An exception is the elliptical sentence in which the subject and verb of the principal clause are sometimes omitted.

How old are you? Thirteen. (I am thirteen years old.)

What high school are you attending? La Grande. (I am attending **La Grande** High School.)

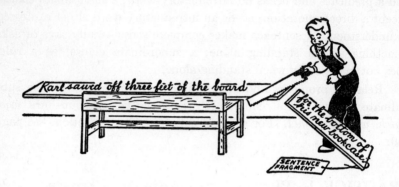

Karl sawed off three feet of the board

for the bottom of this new bookcase

SENTENCE FRAGMENT

To cure a sentence fragment (1) *complete* (make the fragment into a complete sentence, or (2) *attach* (attach the fragment to a sentence.)

Many good writers use sentence fragments for special effect. If you use a sentence fragment deliberately, place an asterisk (*) after it and write a footnote "*Sentence fragment" to show your teacher that you understand what you are doing. But first make sure that you always know a sentence fragment when you see it. Students' unintentional fragments are usually just bad writing.

THREE TYPES OF SENTENCE FRAGMENTS

1. A Group of Words Without a Predicate Verb

FRAGMENT   The many curious objects loose in the dead-letter and parcel department of the General Post Office, including alligators, baby chicks, boat hooks, and, once, a human eye.

SENTENCE   The dead-letter and dead-parcel department of the General Post Office has found loose in the mail many curious objects, including alligators, baby chicks, boat hooks, and, once, a human eye. (A predicate verb has been added to complete the sentence.)

SENTENCE AND FRAGMENT   The pony express riders braved snowstorms in the mountains and robbers in ambush to get the mail through on time. Also Indian attacks and other dangers which made carrying the mails a risky **venture.**

TWO SENTENCES The pony express riders braved snowstorms in the mountains and robbers in ambush to get the mail through on time. They also fought off Indian attacks and other dangers which made carrying the mails a risky venture. (Second sentence *completed*)

PRACTICE 2. Correcting Sentence Fragments

What is the sentence fragment in each of these? Correct.

1. We first sailed to Bermuda. Then to Cuba and Puerto Rico.
2. Following the band were soldiers carrying flags. Flags of all colours, flags of all nations, but mostly Union Jacks.
3. The well-dressed high school girl is always clean and tidy. Not only on one special day, but every day.
4. The flames were extinguished, but the ship, once an enormous sky bird, was transformed into a charred mass of wood and twisted steel. A sorrowful ending for such a giant.
5. The character of Aunt Polly in *Tom Sawyer* was modelled after Mark Twain's mother. A lovable, charitable, gentle woman.
6. My hobby now is collecting things. Stamps, coins, leaves, and curious stones.

2. PARTICIPIAL, GERUNDIAL, OR INFINITIVE PHRASES

A participle or an infinitive does not make a statement or ask a question and therefore never takes the place of the main verb of the sentence. No *ing* word by itself is a predicate verb.

FRAGMENT Bud hurrying down to breakfast, sniffing the tempting aroma of crisp bacon and fresh-out-of-the-oven biscuits.

SENTENCE Bud hurried down to breakfast, sniffing the tempting aroma of crisp bacon and fresh-out-of-the-oven biscuits. (Sentence *completed* with predicate verb.)

FRAGMENT The rays of the sun shining down on the water. (The participle *shining* does not make a statement or ask a question.)

SENTENCE The rays of the sun shone down on the water. (The verb *shone* makes a statement.)

SENTENCE AND SENTENCE FRAGMENT Good school spirit is what every school needs most. A loyal, hearty backing by the pupils of sports, dances, and other extracurricular activities. (In the sentence fragment the verbal noun *backing* does not make a statement or ask a question.)

TWO SENTENCES Good school spirit is what every school needs most. Pupils should loyally and heartily back sports, dances, and other extracurricular activities.

ONE SENTENCE Good school spirit is what every school needs most—a loyal, hearty backing by the pupils of sports, dances, and other extracurricular activities.

PRACTICE 3. Correcting Sentence Fragments

In each of the following get rid of the sentence fragment by writing one or two good sentences. Show that in each of your sentences there is a verb that makes a statement.

1. Lewis and Murray took part in "The Christmas Carol". Lewis taking the part of Scrooge, and Murray of Bob Cratchit.
2. To pilot a spaceship through the heavens and to be the first man on Mars. These are Davy's secret ambitions.
3. A sailing ship flying the British flag was becalmed on a placid expanse of water. The mariners lying on the deck with parched lips and throats.
4. Last summer we stayed at Briar Falls Inn. An old hotel famed for its comfort, its excellent food, and its facilities for summer sports.
5. That night we learned of an imminent enemy attack. By intercepting and decoding a message from their headquarters.
6. Canada has many lakes, rivers, and forests. The largest rivers being the St. Lawrence and the Mackenzie.

3. A SUBORDINATE CLAUSE STANDING BY ITSELF

Most sentence fragments have verbs that make statements. These verbs, however, are in subordinate clauses.

FRAGMENT Dr. J. W. Gray of Winnipeg, who is spending the summer in Nova Scotia. (The clause beginning with *who* is an adjective clause modifying *Dr. J. W. Gray*.)

SENTENCE Dr. J. W. Gray of Winnipeg is spending the summer in Nova Scotia.

SENTENCE AND SENTENCE FRAGMENT Later in our trip we lost our way repeatedly on the lonely Yorkshire moors. Where Charlotte and Emily Brontë had once wandered, planning strange and fantastic tales.

ONE SENTENCE Later in our trip we lost our way repeatedly on the lonely Yorkshire moors where Charlotte and Emily Brontë had once wandered, planning strange and fantastic tales. (Fragment *attached* to sentence.)

PRACTICE 4. Correcting Sentence Fragments

Correct the following. If necessary, supply a subject and a verb to make a principal clause. Draw one line under the simple subject and two lines under the predicate verb of the principal clause or clauses in each correct sentence you write.

1. I found a good friend in Tom Grogan. One whom I shall never forget.

2. Everyone should come out to see the game between the seniors and the juniors. The date of which will be announced later.

3. Rex proved to be a great pal to all of us, and we were very much attached to him. Till one sad day our happiness was turned to grief.

4. Igor Sikorski, who by years of experimentation conceived a new type of plane, a helicopter.

5. Bill Smith had will power, courage, and grit. All qualities which helped to make him a success in later years.

6. At the civilian defense meetings I learned what to do in case of bombings. That is, how to extinguish an incendiary bomb, how to aid the wounded, and, most important of all, how to conduct myself.

7. Then the pupils sang the school song. After which they went back to their classrooms for the next recitation.

8. In *Guadalcanal Diary*, Richard Tregaskis gives a clear picture of soldiers at the front. How they fought, how they thought, and how some died.

RUN-TOGETHER SENTENCE, OR COMMA FAULT

If a sentence ends with a comma and the next one begins with a small letter, the error is called a run-together sentence, a comma fault, or a comma splice.

There are four ways to correct this error. In a particular sentence one way is often more appropriate than another.

1. Insert a period or question mark after every principle clause with its modifiers.

Main Street expresses vividly Sinclair Lewis's resentment of the narrowness of life in a certain type of small town. It paints Gopher Prairie as crude, smug, and opinionated.

What do you think of our baseball team? It hasn't lost a game yet.

2. Connect the two principal clauses with *and, but* or *or* preceded by a comma.

The mountain streams froze, and snow covered the land.

The apples have been picked, but they have not been sorted.

3. Insert a semicolon between the principal clauses. (See the rules for the use of the semicolon.) When in doubt, use the period and the capital.

Instantly the tumult started; / the men yelled and beat upon tom-toms.

I have many friends; / among them are Esther, Estelle, and Gladys.

4. Rephrase the sentence, changing a principal clause to a subordinate clause or to a phrase to show the exact relationship between the ideas.

who
The cave was discovered by a hunter / ~~he~~ followed a wounded bear into it.

being
Canada has many lakes, rivers, and forests, the largest rivers ~~are~~ the St. Lawrence and the Mackenzie.

FUSED SENTENCE

If a sentence ends with *no punctuation mark* and the next one begins with a small letter, the error is called a fused sentence.

FUSED   Passengers of all sizes and ages crowded into the bus the young girls were in gay, summery dresses. (A period should be placed after *bus*, because that is the end of the first sentence. *Passengers* is the subject; *crowded*, the verb. The second expression is a complete sentence. *Girls* is the subject; *were*, the verb.)

CORRECT   Passengers of all sizes and ages crowded into the bus. The young girls were in gay, summery dresses.

The methods of correction are the same as those for the run-together sentence.

PRACTICE 5. Correcting Run-together Sentences

Punctuate and capitalize the following. Draw one line under the subject word and two lines under the verb of every simple sentence or principal clause.

1. When Dr. Jekyll changed his form he called himself Mr Hyde as Mr Hyde he was very dangerous
2. Jim hit a low ball over the first baseman's head it struck at least a foot inside the foul line
3. All evening as we drove along the fog had been growing thicker by ten o'clock we couldn't see five feet in front of us
4. I have sixty tropical fish in a tank last year I had only three pairs of them
5. Do not delay send your order today
6. It took me a half hour to mend the stocking neatly how I wished that I had taken a minute in the morning to fix that little run

7. Well just wait till we play you again we'll knock you right out of the championship race

8. The Indian called for water it was Deerslayer who got the water for him

9. Concentration has a great deal to do with studying if a person does not concentrate upon the subject he does not learn it

10. While the pirates were looking for the treasure a voice was heard in the trees above this frightened them

11. Robinson Crusoe was on a sailboat which was wrecked he was the sole survivor

12. Zane Grey's style of writing is free and easy he puts a humorous incident in to relieve the tension of a sad part

13. Hit the ball and run to first base if the pitcher catches the ball you are out

14. Agnes what kind of book are you reading is it a mystery story

15. On the top of a decayed branch of the tree I saw a woodpecker feebly struggling coming closer I saw that a bullsnake had wrapped itself around the bird and was slowly squeezing it to death

PRACTICE 6. Correcting Run-together Sentences

Correct each of the following in three ways. Star (*) the best of the three.

1. Odysseus' hall was filled with suitors every one of the suitors was determined to win Penelope in marriage.

2. In the winter some animals migrate others hibernate.

3. Some tabloids deal chiefly in sensational news they fail to give adequate space to stories of national and international significance.

4. *Giants in the Earth* makes one proud of the brave immigrants who came to this country and helped to settle the West it is an unromantic yet strangely poetic story of unbelievable hardships and undying fortitude.

5. Sourdough Sam, Paul Bunyan's lumber-camp cook, announced meals with an immense horn it was so large than ten acres of tall timber were blown down every time Sam sounded it.

To avoid the run-together sentence, use a period, a question mark, or an exclamation point after every independent clause with its modifiers unless it is clearly connected with another independent clause to form a compound sentence. When in doubt, use end punctuation. One way of finding where to put capitals and periods is by reading aloud what you write.

PRACTICE 7. Punctuating and Capitalizing

Punctuate and capitalize the following paragraph. Be sure to place a period at the end of a sentence and to begin a sentence with a capital. There are eight sentences.

ELECTRONICS—THE NEW SCIENCE

the discovery of electronics is one of the most important contributions science has made to the building of a new world through electronics every home will probably soon enjoy television programmes daily the electron microscope enables scientists to magnify 100,000 times the image of a mosquito larva the X-ray which is electronic in origin locates shell fragments detects tuberculosis and treats skin disorders electronic tubes turn on highway lights as the sky darkens and turn them off when morning comes electronic eyes inspect sheets of metal and spot tiny defects other electronic devices count traffic in tunnels inspect fruit aid ships to dock detect lurking submarines and fill tooth paste tubes only man's imagination limits the possibilities of electronics a new science for a new world—PUPIL.

PRACTICE 8. Punctuating and Capitalizing

Punctuate and capitalize this story. Be sure to place a period at the end of a sentence and to begin a sentence with a capital. Insert needed apostrophes and quotation marks.

A BEAR

While at camp last summer I spent a day that I shall never forget my friend Mildred and I were strolling through the woods on a sultry day in August suddenly I looked behind us and saw a strange black animal

Mildred whats that I asked excitedly

She turned around to see the cause of my disturbance and shouted I really dont know what it is but it looks like a bear

Impossible bears dont come around here I snapped striving to appear calm but not succeeding you must be wrong at least I hope so

Suddenly the creature growled my heart jumped without bothering to look again I started to run Mildred was at my heels what fate was to be ours suppose that queer beast overtook us I shuddered at the thought

After what seemed hours we reached camp with that animal peacefully trailing us Mildred and I ran into our tent and collapsed on the cot

The counsellor who had been reading a book glanced up

Whats the matter with you girls she asked you look as if you had seen a ghost

Wild animal we both shouted breathlessly

After looking us over carefully to see whether or not we were crazy she stepped out of the tent in a few minutes she returned giggling

You foolish girls she laughed its a dog with some burs in his hair after saying this she strolled out soon the whole camp knew of our mistake and we were the laughingstock for a few days

Since that day I have learned the difference between a dog and a bear

—PUPIL.

TEST B (Mastery).   Sentence Unity

Median—8.6

Indicate by *0, 1, 2,* or *3* the number of complete sentences in each of the following. On your paper place a period between the number of the example and your answer.

1. Penrod was a queer sort of child it seems as if the only pleasure he got out of life was in misbehaving
2. If air is removed from the siphon either by filling the tube with water or by sucking the air out
3. Have you ever wanted to read a book that was different from other books a book that does not have a beautiful girl for its heroine and that does not make the heroine the belle of the ball
4. For instance the scene in which Dr Grenfell is the only living object on an expanse of ice
5. The new members of the Press Club are purchasing pins the pins are silver with the word *Journalism* in blue enamel the pupils who were members of the club last year already have their pins
6. The next ball pitched was over the plate and Ott knocked a line drive between Vaughan and Reese both players ran after the ball as fast as they could but neither touched it
7. Thanking you again and hoping I haven't inconvenienced you in any way
8. The waves breaking over the rocks along the coast and the white foam that shot up out of the water from the terrific impact of the waves
9. Have you read *Rebecca of Sunnybrook Farm* the story of a carefree little girl who lived with two aunts it was written by Kate Douglas Wiggin
10. Three characters of *Tom Sawyer* are Tom a mischievous lad with a lively imagination Huckleberry Finn a homeless boy who is Tom's friend and Aunt Polly

CAT-AND-DOG-SENTENCE

Unity means oneness. Every part of a sentence must be related to *ONE* governing idea. If there are two main ideas in a sentence, they must be related parts of a larger idea. A "cat-and-dog" sentence is one that contains "unfriendly" ideas—statements that conspicuously lack connection with each other.

LACKING UNITY Sergeant Melville is a good leader of men and almost every day he receives mail from home. (The two ideas are not connected.)

HAVING UNITY Sergeant Melville is a good leader of men and will make, I believe, an outstanding lieutenant. (The two main ideas are parts of the large idea that Sergeant Melville has leadership ability.)

LACKING UNITY Bob is majoring in accounting in college and is making a name for himself on the university track team. (The two ideas are not connected.)

HAVING UNITY Bob is majoring in accounting in college and hopes eventually to become a CPA. (The two main ideas are on the subject of accounting.)

Correct a cat-and-dog error (1) by breaking the sentence into shorter sentences or (2) by subordinating one or more parts of the sentence to one main part. One main idea may have many modifiers.

LACKING UNITY We've enjoyed the water skiing at Cypress Gardens all this week, and we're looking forward to visiting Dad's brother in Miami.

TWO SENTENCES We've enjoyed the water skiing at Cypress Gardens all this week. Now we're looking forward to visiting Dad's brother in Miami.

LACKING UNITY My brother Fred is two years older than I am, and he's in first year at the University of Toronto.

ONE PART SUBORDINATED My brother Fred, who is two years older than I am, is in first year at the University of Toronto.

LACKING UNITY Punch never chases cats, and he is a Boston terrier.

ONE PART SUBORDINATED Punch, a Boston terrier, never chases cats.

PRACTICE 9. Correcting Cat-and-Dog Sentences

Improve the following sentences. In your revision show the correct relationship between the ideas expressed.

1. Robert Browning married Elizabeth Barrett, and his first poem was published in 1860.
2. My uncle was welcomed by a frail old man who had white hair and a large library.
3. Bob is an excellent swimmer, and last Christmas he visited his cousin in Vancouver.
4. Give my regards to your mother, and I hope you are enjoying your work on a farm this summer.
5. Mathematics is my hardest subject, and comes at eleven in the morning.

RAMBLING SENTENCE (THE "AND" HABIT)

Avoid rambling sentences consisting of three or more statements strung together with *and, but,* or *so.* Don't overwork *and.* The *and* habit is one of the worst English diseases.

RAMBLING Some people can't say good-bye gracefully, and they stand in the doorway talking on and on, and after a while their host and hostess wish they would hurry up and go home. (Three principal clauses.)

BETTER Because some people can't say good-bye gracefully, they stand in the doorway talking on and on, and after a while their host and hostess wish they would hurry up and go home. (One principal clause.)

RAMBLING The name of my book is *Adrift on an Ice Pan* and the name of the author is W. T. Grenfell and the call number is B41, so the book is a biography. (Four principal clauses.)

BETTER The call number of W. T. Grenfell's *Adrift on an Ice Pan*, a biography which I am reading, is B41. (One principal clause.)

PRACTICE 10. Correcting Rambling Sentences

Improve the following sentences.

1. Often Oliver Twist and some other boys would have to go away from the table hungry, so one day Oliver went up to the proprietor of the workhouse and asked for more food and when the proprietor heard this he turned him out into the street and poor Oliver was left penniless and homeless.
2. Mavericks were unbranded cattle and they belonged to whoever caught them, and they got their name from John Maverick, because he didn't brand his cattle.
3. Mark Twain took his pen name from the river pilot's call indicating that the mark on the sounding lead showed two fathoms of water, and he became fascinated with river boats during his childhood.
4. I was born in Brandon, Manitoba, and I was the son of a banker, and my parents died when I was young, so I went back to Ontario where they had come from, where later I entered the University of Toronto.
5. Herman Melville had been a sailor and had encountered unusual adventures at sea, and he returned home in 1842 and wrote novels about his experiences.
6. Mr. Decker lives next door to us, and he is a travelling representative for a publishing company, and so we rarely see him.
7. One of the scientists is Dr. Larson, and he is a very able man, and he believes that the photosynthesis experiments will yield new facts.
8. Just before his death Regan had been investigating labour disputes, and he worked long hours, and the overwork led to a run-down condition, and finally he became sick.

9. We can help with the chores Saturday morning, and then my father will take us in the car for a picnic at High Park, and don't forget to bring your portable radio.

10. My dog Pug first showed his intelligence when one Sunday he wanted to go out, and we had company, so he couldn't get our attention, so he went into the hall and got his leash out of the coat closet, and he brought it over to me.

11. *Main Street* expresses vividly Sinclair Lewis's resentment of the narrowness of life in a certain type of small town and it paints Gopher Prairie as crude, smug, and opinionated.

12. Mammoth Cave in Kentucky was discovered in 1809 by a hunter and he followed a bear into it.

OVERLAPPING CONSTRUCTION

Avoid using a series of overlapping adjective clauses or possessives. Tacking a *that, which,* or *who* clause onto another one results in a house-that-Jack-built sentence: "This is the dog that chased the cat that killed the rat that ate the malt that lay in the house that Jack built."

OVERLAPPING Among his minerals Ted displayed azurite, which is an ore from which copper is obtained.

CORRECT Among his minerals Ted displayed azurite, which is a copper ore.

———————

OVERLAPPING That's my brother's roomate's Thunderbird.

CORRECT That Thunderbird belongs to my brother's roommate.

PRACTICE 11. Avoiding Overlapping Construction

Improve the following sentences:

1. The sensation is carried to the brain, which in turn sends out a message to your muscles, which do the work.

2. The lecturer told us about the larch, which is a kind of pine tree which loses its needles in the fall.

3. The museum displayed an astrolabe which is an instrument which was used in early navigation.

4. *Ben-Hur* tells the story of the young prince who was one of those who tried to free his country from the oppression of Roman tyrants who held the throne.

5. The story tells about a ship which was caught on a reef near an island which was inhabited by cannibals.

6. The journalism students who meet in Room 311 the first period under the supervision of Mr. Donnelly, who is Head of the English Department, are comparing the Yearbooks of various schools.

7. Thousands of sightseers yearly climb the hundreds of steps which lead to the one-hundred-and-thirty foot statue of Christ which stands on the summit of Corcovado, which overlooks Rio de Janeiro.

8. John is a careful sailor who checks all the charts which show the landmarks and channel markings which are helpful to a pilot who navigates the Inland Waterway.

9. Another way we could improve our school yearbook is by securing more advertisements, which would help to pay for the halftones and cartoons which we desire.

10. *Oklahoma!* was a popular musical which had simple, bright settings which provided a cheerful background which set off the gay music and dancing which were in the show.

11. According to Mr. Kimmer, there should be more television programs that present authoritative information that helps listeners to think carefully and make wise decisions on important issues that confront them.

12. A. E. Housman wrote poetry which has a simple style which expresses thoughts and feelings which the reader understands and appreciates.

13. Alfred's sister's singing was the highlight of the concert.

14. The pike is a fresh-water fish which is known for its fighting qualities which terrify the smaller fishes which happen to go near it.

15. My cousin's friend's camera is a new Leica.

CHOPPY SENTENCE

In your effort to keep only *one* main thought in a sentence, do not chop up a single thought into several short sentences. Write it as a single unified sentence, subordinating the less important ideas.

CHOPPY Shakespeare is buried in the Stratford-on-Avon church. He is buried in the chancel. The church is a large, venerable structure. It is moldering with age.

ONE UNIFIED SENTENCE Shakespeare is buried in the chancel of the large, venerable Stratford-on-Avon church, which is moldering with age.

PRACTICE 12. Avoiding Choppy Sentences

Improve the following sentences:

1. Friction robs machines of efficiency. Much energy is lost in heat. Ball bearings are used to reduce friction. Lubrication serves the same purpose.
2. Mathematics stagnated for a long while. Then the zero was introduced. This eliminated the cumbersome system of the Romans. Great strides were made quickly.
3. With great reluctance Frederick opened the front door to leave the house. He found himself face to face with a stranger. The stranger was a powerfully built man and had ruddy cheeks. The stranger was ascending the steps.
4. The Greek patriots fought long and courageously. They had to face great odds. Their achievement will be remembered.
5. Two friends were to meet me in Montreal. We were to go to my home. They were to visit me. We were then going to camp together.

PRACTICE 13. Sentence Reconstruction

Include the substance of the following passage in four sentences, each containing only one principal clause. There are 156 words in the original. How many words are there in your revision?

On the north side of the road was a large white gate. A winding path led from the gate to a beautiful house. The house was about fifty yards from the road. Between the road and the house was a large lawn. About the lawn were scattered several flower beds. Many large trees were irregularly placed about the lawn. The house was a large white structure. Its architecture was of the colonial style. Along its entire front was a spacious veranda. The veranda was about three feet above the ground. The main entrance was at the middle of the front side of the house. One large door closed the entrance. On each side of the door was a large window. Each window was about half-way between the door and the nearest side of the house. The windows were four feet wide and ten feet high. Their lower edges were level with the floor of the veranda.

PRACTICE 14. Review of Unity

Correct the following sentences. How is unity violated in each?

A. 1. Molly has curly hair and blue eyes, and last week she beat me at tennis four sets out of five.

2. For my second supplementary report I read *Tarawa*. The author is Robert Sherrod. It is the stirring story of a Marine engagement.

3. There was a logical reason why General Nobile allowed himself to be taken first from the ice floe, but the outside world didn't know this, and on his return to civilization he was treated very coldly.

4. Edgar Allan Poe's life was short and tragic, and Poe is usually credited with the invention of the detective story.

B. 1. Petrovitch told the driver to wait. Then Petrovitch got out of the sleigh and entered the church. The church was feebly lit by two or three tapers.

2. Mr. Barclay began to read "Petit, the Poet", but just then the bell rang, so Mr. Barclay stopped reading, and he told the class to study the poem for Monday.

3. "The Spires of Oxford" is a poem honouring the Oxford men who were killed in World War I, in which many young men lost their lives.

4. *Wuthering Heights* is rather long, so I returned it to the library without finishing it, but I kept wondering how it ends, so finally I went back to the library and took the book out again.

B. Coherence

In a coherent sentence the parts are worded and arranged so that they stick together. Coherence includes (1) arrangement, (2) parallel structure, (3) connectives, (4) clear reference of pronouns, and (5) correct ellipsis.

1. ARRANGEMENT

DANGLING PARTICIPLES Put a participle close to the word it modifies. When a participle is used carelessly without a governing word (noun or pronoun) or when it is made to refer grammatically to a word that it does not actually modify, it is said to dangle. Past participles require special attention.

If a participle dangles, we may (1) get rid of the participle, (2) place it near the word it modifies, or (3) put into the sentence some word for it to modify

———————

DANGLING PRESENT PARTICIPLE Standing on the ferryboat, many cargo vessels can be seen. (*Standing* seems to modify *vessels*. The vessels are not standing on the ferryboat.)

PARTICIPLE REMOVED From the ferryboat many cargo vessels can be seen.

WORD SUPPLIED FOR PARTICIPLE TO MODIFY Standing on the ferryboat, a person can see many cargo vessels.

DANGLING PARTICIPLE   Coming into camp after a day's hike, a good hot supper was just what we needed. (*Coming* seems to modify *supper*.)

PARTICIPLE PUT NEAR THE WORD MODIFIED   Coming into camp after a day's hike, we needed a good hot supper.

DANGLING PAST PARTICIPLE   He was deaf, caused by an attack of scarlet fever.

PARTICIPLE REMOVED   He was deaf, as the result of an attack of scarlet fever.

PARTICIPLE CHANGED TO VERB   His deafness was caused by an attack of scarlet fever.

DANGLING PRESENT PARTICIPLE   The little ship was very light, causing it to ride the waves easily.

PARTICIPLE REMOVED   The little ship was very light; thus it rode the waves easily.

SITTING IN THE CAGE, I SAW THE MONKEY SCRATCH HIS HEAD.

PRACTICE 15.   Eliminating Dangling Participles

Correct the following. When you use a participle, tell what word it modifies.

Example:

GIVEN SENTENCE   Diving into the pool, the chill of the water shocked me.

CORRECTION   Diving into the pool, I was shocked by the chill of the water.

RELATIONSHIP OF PARTICIPLE   *Diving* is a participle modifying I.

1. Reaching into his pocket, his fountain pen came apart.
2. Not noticing who had entered the room, Mary's conversation continued unchecked.
3. Having eaten the canned cat food, Larry gave the kitten some milk.
4. Turning around, my eyes caught sight of a young stag emerging from the forest.
5. Having been planted in very poor soil, we moved the roses nearer the fence.
6. I felt very sick, caused by the motion of the boat.
7. He was well acquainted with the best literature, thus helping him to become an able critic.

DANGLING INFINITIVES AND GERUNDS Avoid dangling infinitives and gerunds. A gerund phrase (*in speaking, after pointing*) or an infinitive at the beginning of a phrase or clause should relate in thought to the subject.

DANGLING INFINITIVE　To get an unobstructed view of the valley, the car stopped at the look-out point. (Will the car stop to get an unobstructed view of the valley?)

CORRECT　To get an unobstructed view of the valley, the driver stopped the car at the look-out point.

DANGLING GERUND　After pointing out my errors, I was dismissed.

CORRECT　After pointing out my errors, the teacher dismissed me.
　　　　　When the teacher had pointed out my errors, he dismissed me.

PRACTICE 16. Eliminating Dangling Gerunds and Infinitives

Correct the following sentences.

1. Instead of gluing the top in place it was fastened with nails.
2. After prying the lock open the lid of the trunk was raised.
3. After riding for an hour or so a thunderstorm came up.
4. Upon arriving at the station our train had not yet been made up.
5. By letting a gun stand for several days without cleaning it will usually rust.
6. After getting out of Regina the road had very little traffic.
7. After rowing about a quarter of a mile the water became choppy.
8. To enjoy a walk thoroughly it should be taken early in the day.
9. To protect the children they were taken into the cellar.
10. After being late three times my teacher sent me to the principal.

DANGLING ELLIPTICAL CLAUSES Avoid dangling elliptical clauses. In an elliptical clause usually the subject and the verb are understood (*while watching* for *while I was watching; when only five* for *when I was only five*). To keep the elliptical clause from dangling (1) make the subject of the principal clause relate directly to the understood subject, or (2) supply the understood words.

DANGLING ELLIPTICAL CLAUSE While watching the helicopter circle the bay, a fine flounder slipped off Bob's hook.

CORRECT While watching the helicopter circle the bay, Bob let a fine flounder slip off his hook.

DANGLING ELLIPTICAL CLAUSE When only five, my father gave me a St. Bernard puppy. (Was your father only five?)
CORRECT When I was only five, my father gave me a St. Bernard puppy.

These rules about dangling expressions do not apply when the modifier designates a general action. The following are correct: "Generally speaking, the Studio One productions are spellbinding." "Allowing for possible mishaps, their sloop should reach port by tomorrow night."

PRACTICE 17. Correcting Dangling Modifiers

Correct the following. If you correct a sentence by placing a participle near the word it modifies, tell what word the participle modifies.

Example:

> Being a philatelist, most of my allowance is spent on stamps.
> Being a philatelist, I spend most of my allowance on stamps.
> *Being* is a participle modifying the pronoun *I*.

A. 1. Glancing through the magazine, the bright-coloured advertisements catch the eye.
2. Having carefully prepared my lessons, a friend came in.
3. At the age of fourteen his father died and left five sons.
4. While speaking to the class, the pupils in the back part of the room could not hear me.
5. While flying over the target, the antiaircraft fire became intense.
6. Being one of the earliest spring flowers, people greet the hepatica joyfully.
7. Entering the English office, a bust of Longfellow caught my eye.
8. When ill or in need, Florence was always ready to help people.

B. 1. Turning the page, my eye was attracted to a picture of an old open fireplace.

2. After a night of dreams the rising sun saw us again on the road.

3. One day while looking out the window, an organ-grinder stopped and played in the street below me.

4. Without rising from your chair, a book can transport you to foreign lands.

5. In applying for a position one's manners and English are important.

6. While wet, put the picture on a painting block and pin it down.

7. Being one of your pupils, you naturally wonder whether I enjoy writing and speaking.

8. Looking out my window, a runaway horse attracted my attention.

MISPLACED MODIFIERS Place modifiers near the words modified if clearness requires this arrangement.

MISPLACED WORDS

The recipe tells ↓ how to make a fudge cake ⌊clearly⌋ .

Because of injuries the coach has ⌈nearly⌉ lost↓ half his regulars.

John told his father that he ⌈only⌉ wanted ↓ five dollars.

MISPLACED PHRASES

One night I left ↑ the hundred-dollar violin my parents had given me.
⌊in a parked car⌋

Hamburgers ↓ were given to all the guests ⌊smothered in onions⌋

Dad says that ↑ drivers who hog the road or cut off other cars
⌊in four cases out of five⌋ are immature individuals with inflated egos.

(Do not place modifier where it may refer to either the preceding or the following word or words.)

MISPLACED CLAUSES

Tom ran to take the steak↓ off the grill ⌊which was burned to a cinder⌋

(A relative pronoun should follow its antecedent as closely as possible.)

A
↓Mr. Brown asked Tom ⌊As soon as the period was over⌋ to report to the office. (The circled clause may be placed at the *beginning* or at the *end* of the sentence. What is the difference in meaning?)

PRACTICE 18. Arranging Modifiers Correctly

Correct the following sentences. When you change the position of a modifier, tell what word or words it modifies.

Example:

> I missed the three first lessons.
> I missed the first three lessons. *First* modifies *three* lessons.

A. 1. I write a letter to my cousin who lives in Florida almost every week.

2. The blaze was extinguished before any damage was done by the local fire department.

3. The mortgage company urges owners to pay arrears of taxes and interest by letter, by telephone, and by personal visits.

4. One pupil was asked to write an account of the book he had read on the blackboard.

5. *Ivanhoe* and *Treasure Island* were the two first books I read in high school.

6. Repeat what you have read with your book closed.

7. A man was walking down the street with long gray hair.

8. Old Susan places a candle on the window sill, which flickers when the wind blows.

9. I only reviewed clausal analysis last night.

10. This news program is telecast over Channel 2 and is sponsored by a company that manufactures aluminum products at seven o'clock each evening.

B. 1. The steeds maintained a shambling gait through the sand that was neither a trot nor a lope.

2. I thought of going to bed several times but decided to complete my work.

3. Louis XVII, never actually the king of France, died when he was ten years old in prison.

4. In our club is a young group of boys and girls.

5. In Cairo bazaars tourists pointed at the things they wanted with a stick.

6. Tom Sawyer was a bloodthirsty pirate and dangerous cutthroat in his daydreams.

7. This is the story of a journey of one hundred and one days across the Pacific on a wooden raft named *Kon-Tiki* by Thor Heyerdahl.

8. Ralph edged closer as the deer sniffed suspiciously and snapped the picture.

9. In one day's sifting of beach sand the men nearly found one hundred dollars in small change.

10. I gave him a friendly slap as he left the room on his back.

PARALLEL STRUCTURE

Parallel structure is the use of the same form for words, phrases, or clauses which have equal value and similar function. By following the suggestions given below, you will develop skill in using parallel structure to represent parallel thoughts. As a result, your sentences will gain coherence.

a. AND, BUT   As a rule, use co-ordinate conjunctions (*and, but*) to connect like grammatical elements—for example, two nouns, two predicates, two adjectives, two prepositional phrases, two participial phrases, two adjective clauses.

Right   **Wrong**

WRONG   Hot weather makes people cross and say things that cause trouble. (*And* connects unlike grammatical elements—the adjective *cross* and the verb *say*.)

RIGHT   Hot weather makes people cross and quarrelsome. (*And* connects like grammatical elements—the adjectives *cross* and *quarrelsome*.)

RIGHT   Hot weather makes people cross and makes them say things that cause trouble. (*And* connects the verbs *makes* and *makes*.)

There are three ways to correct a sentence in which *and* connects a noun and a clause: (1) change the noun to a clause, (2) change the clause to a noun, (3) get rid of *and*.

WRONG   The Minister of Finance told the press conference his objections to current tax bills and what his plans were for meeting the problems of the new budget. (*And* connects the noun *objections* and the noun clause *what his plans were for meeting the problems of the new budget.*)

RIGHT   The Minister of Finance told the press conference his objections to current tax bills and his plans for meeting the problems of the new budget. (*And* connects two nouns, *objections* and *plans*.)

RIGHT   The minister of Finance told the news conference what objections he had to current tax bills and what his plans were for meeting the problems of the new budget. (*And* connects the two noun clauses.)

RIGHT   Having told the news conference his objections to current tax bills, the Minister of Finance outlined his plans for meeting the problems of the new budget. (No *and*.)

PRACTICE 19. Using Parallel Structure

Rewrite the following sentences, making parallel the elements that should be parallel. Separate the parallel elements from the rest of the sentence and number them. Under the sentence show that the numbered elements are parallel.

Examples:

a. Her sister was tall, black hair and eyes, and called by the Indians Wild Rose.
   Her sister
       (1) was tall,
       (2) had black hair and eyes,
   and (3) was called by the Indians Wild Rose.
   Members 1, 2, and 3 are parallel; they are predicates.

b. The treasure, filling two large chests, and which eight men could hardly carry, was seized by the police.
   The treasure,
       (1) which filled two large chests
   and (2) which eight men could hardly carry,
   was seized by the police.
   Members 1 and 2 are parallel; both are adjective clauses.

c. Then I formed the brilliant idea of climbing the sty fence and to hang from the top rail until the bull went away.
   Then I formed the brilliant idea of
       (1) climbing the sty fence
   and (2) hanging from the top rail
   until the bull went away.
   Members 1 and 2 are parallel; they are verbal nouns.

A. 1. Jeanne taught Eleanor to read and write, how to draw, and also French.
   2. The experience taught me two lessons: not to disobey Mother and I shall not again eat so much candy between meals.
   3. Hamlin would have enjoyed going to a library and read as many books as he wished.
   4. The book describes the struggles and hardships of Barnum and how he had to fight for fame and fortune.

5. I have learned this term in speaking always to keep to my subject, and do not discuss two topics in one paragraph.

6. Ichabod was a tall, thin man with a small head and having large eyes and an upturned nose.

7. This will teach the student self-control and to be economical.

8. Three qualities of sailors are quickness, coolness, and they have to be alert.

9. Miss Simmons teaches the piano, the violin, and vocal.

10. There is more to this hobby than finishing the scrapbook, putting it on a shelf, and forget it.

B. 1. You can improve your posture if you stand erect, correct breathing, and by sitting properly.

2. The highwayman wears doeskin breeches, a claret coat, a French cocked hat, and around his neck he has a ruffle of lace.

3. Since I didn't want to eat the food my brother prepared and having convinced my brother that I could cook, I got the job of cook.

4. Dickens' books are masterpieces because of his sly humour, his ability to weave characters into a mysterious plot, and because each of his characters portrays a certain type of person.

5. The chief traits of Bottom are overconfidence, and he uses words of which he doesn't know the meaning.

6. Many associates were unjust to Arrowsmith because they judged him by his outward and visible characteristics and not realizing his true character.

7. Have a reason for what you do and not because it is custom.

8. In assembly yesterday Jack Boswell said that just passing is not enough and to work for high marks in all subjects.

9. I enjoyed reading *To the Ladies* because of its humour and it holds the reader in suspense until the last scene.

10. I can't forgive a person for making an appointment and then leave a friend stranded on some street corner.

PRACTICE 20. Being Consistent

Improve the following sentences. Express each thought clearly and exactly.

1. That afternoon was Jud's first try at skin diving and needed some intensive coaching.

2. The girl who lands a job as Girl Friday to a public relations expert is in for an exciting time, for you get a chance to meet celebrities of stage, screen, TV, and radio, not to mention assorted literary people.

3. Two-year-olds like to say "no" just for the fun of it, and you mustn't take their negative attitudes too seriously.

4. By following a schedule is easier to get work done on time.

5. The coach rattled down the road, jolted over the cobblestones, shakes its passengers till their teeth rattle, and deposits them, bruised but still cheerful, at the hospitable door of the Juggler's Inn.

6. With one minute left in the game, Hamilton broke through for a touchdown and ties the score.

7. Mother had hysterics; Father phoned the police; then in walks Tommy and announces proudly, "I was losted."

8. All students in the class handed their notebook in on time.

9. I enjoy ice-skating because it gives you a chance to enjoy crisp winter weather.

10. The volunteer firemen left the firehouse within a few minutes of the alarm and discover that Jordan's wood lot was ablaze.

b. ADJECTIVE CLAUSE   Do not join an adjective (relative) clause to its principal clause or to a phrase by *and, but,* or *or.*

WRONG   The papers carried interviews with Dr. Jonas Salk, a daring and original leader in medical research, and who developed the polio vaccine.

RIGHT   The papers carried interviews with Dr. Jonas Salk, the daring and original leader in medical research who developed the polio vaccine.

c. SUBJECT, VOICE, MOOD, TENSE   Avoid unnecessary changing of the subject or of the voice, mood, or tense of the verb.

SHIFT IN MOOD   Arrive promptly for a job interview, and ~~you should be sure to~~ answer the interviewer's questions quickly and courteously.

SHIFT IN TENSE   Terry set her heart on a copy-writing job; then she ~~finds~~ *found* that what she really ~~wants is~~ *wanted was* to be a buyer.

SHIFT IN SUBJECT AND VOICE   The Masque members discussed the choice of a Christmas play, and ~~it was~~ finally decided to stage scenes from Dickens' *Christmas Carol.*

SHIFT IN NUMBER   In the outer office five crack stenographers were banging away on ~~a~~ typewriter*s* as if their ~~life~~ *lives* depended on finishing the manuscript before five o'clock.

SHIFT IN PERSON   A boy who earns part of his college expenses knows the value of a college education and ~~you~~ get*s* more out of it too.

d. UNFINISHED CONSTRUCTION   Don't begin a grammatical construction and leave it unfinished.

UNFINISHED CONSTRUCTION   When the tourist arrives in the Lake Country is a plesant surprise, because he finds there so many literary landmarks in so fine a state of preservation.

RIGHT When the tourist arrives in the Lake Country, he is pleasantly surprised to find there so many literary landmarks in so fine a state of preservation.

UNFINISHED CONSTRUCTION By making the most of every opportunity to speak in public will help a person to overcome his shyness.

IMPROVED Making the most of every opportunity to speak in public will help a person to overcome his shyness.

e. CORRELATIVE CONJUNCTIONS The most common correlative conjunctions are *either . . . or, neither . . . nor, both . . . and, not only . . . but also.*

Correlative conjunctions *join like grammatical elements*—for example, two nouns, two predicates, two adjectives, two prepositional phrases—and are placed *immediately* before the words or expressions they connect.

Patsy |both| enjoys ↓ watermelon and cantaloupe.
   (*Both* and *and* connect two nouns.)

| Either| ᶄou can ↓ take sandwiches or buy your lunch.
   (*Either* and *or* connect two predicates.)

We could |neither| reach the survivors ↓ by boat nor by plane.
   (*Neither* and *nor* connect two prepositional adverb phrases.)

                       d
|Not only| ~~did~~ I believe~~ ↓ that he was telling the truth but also that he had been treated unfairly.
   (*Not only* and *but also* connect two noun clauses.)

Correlatives may sometimes connect a word and a phrase of the same grammatical value.

A good dictionary |not only| will be helpful ↓ now but in later years also.
   (*Not only* and *but . . . also* connect the adverb *now* and the prepositional adverb phrase *in later years.*)

A correlative conjunction must be completed by its correct second part.

                  nor
Larry likes neither Latin ~~or~~ algebra.

PRACTICE 21. Using Correlatives Correctly

Improve the following sentences. Give a reason for each change.

1. The home-coming game is an event that not only appeals to the undergraduates but the alumni also.

2. Any afternoon you can find Sandy either tinkering with his jalopy or his tape recorder.

3. A jet pilot not only must be alert but also resourceful.

4. That pitcher is either big-league material, or I'm no judge of players.

5. Your notebook must either be on the hall table or on your desk.

6. Reading the newspaper daily not only will help a student in his current events class but also in his English assignments.

7. Bud not only wanted to break the wild colt but also to tame it and teach it tricks.

8. They would neither study nor would they read any books worth while.

9. In conversation one should neither whisper or shout.

10. The mosquitoes are not only bad but the black flies also.

PRACTICE 22. Parallel Structure

Improve the following sentences. Give a reason for each change.

A. 1. Ability to speak correctly and fluently is not only an asset in the business but also in the social world.

2. For the best results a very light rod should be purchased; then go out in your boat and catch the fish.

3. Instead of looking up the meaning of an unfamiliar word in my reading, I just skip it, and often the idea of the whole sentence is lost.

4. The long winter evenings were either spent in listening to the radio or reading aloud to the group before the open fireplace.

5. Mr. C. C. Woodruff, president of the Board of Trade and who is chairman of the Christmas Committee, was the next speaker.

B. 1. George Barry, editor of our school newspaper and who worked last summer in a newspaper office, expects to study journalism.

2. The president suggested that the club give a party, and each guest should bring an article of food or clothing for the Red Cross.

3. During the winter months I not only enjoy ice-skating but also skiing.

4. One's shoes should not only be stylish but also comfortable.

5. Either you must return the book or pay for it.

PRACTICE 23. Writing Coherent Sentences

Improve the following sentences. Give a reason for each change.

A. 1. No matter how bright the future may appear, we should not depend on it, but let us act in the present.

2. Surely the man in overalls was more of a gentleman than the man with gray gloves and who was swinging a cane.

3. Ralph neither likes to canoe nor to fish.

4. A pilot not only must be alert but also resourceful.

5. In building the paragraph I used four connectives, and all the ideas followed one another in order.

B. 1. Make the first sentence tell how far the paragraph will go, and the last sentence should tell how far the paragraph has gone.

2. During the term I not only read the required books but also eight supplementary books.

3. Helen Keller was taken to all the local doctors, and finally they took her to an eminent Boston physician.

4. Not only would the change help the fourth-year students but all other students as well.

5. Trini, considered one of the most beautiful women of Spain and who made a successful screen debut, will be at the Valencia on Saturday.

3. CONNECTIVES

ACCURATE CONJUNCTIONS

Use the conjunction that expresses accurately the relation of one clause to another. Think what each conjunction means. *And* equals plus; *but* equals minus. Don't use a plus or a minus word to express a subordinate relation. Use a subordinate conjunction—for example, *if, when, because, although*—to show condition (if it snows . . .), time, cause, or concession (although their team is good . . .).

THE AND—SO HABIT

Avoid the *and—so* habit. By substituting adverb or noun clauses for some of the independent clauses and by beginning new sentences, get rid of *and* and *so* joining clauses.

Since
ᴧI've always liked swimming, ~~so~~ I'm going to try out for the water-polo team.

Although it   ,
ᴧ~~It~~ snowed for two days ᴧ~~and~~ the mail came through as usual.

but
Fashion modeling sounds like an easy, glamorous job, ~~and~~ only patient, persevering girls can stand the strain of it.

who
No day was too dismal for Mr. Micawber, ~~and he~~ was an optimist of the unquenchable variety.

PRACTICE 24. Eliminating *And—So* Clauses

Improve the following sentences. Show that the conjunctions you use express accurately the relation between the ideas.

1. You have done superior work in physics this year, so you will not have to write the final examinations.

2. We were stuck in the traffic jam down town and we arrived home an hour late for dinner.

3. Well-forested areas hold precious water in reserve, so it is wise to maintain these areas as potential reservoirs.

4. Elizabeth's relatives at home wanted her to return, so she came back to Canada.

5. My uncle does not know where we live and is coming to visit us.

6. There was always a disagreement as to who would do the work, so they decided that Captain Jerry should marry to secure a housekeeper for them.

7. Tom failed to stop at the red light, so a patrol car followed him and ordered him to pull over.

8. A gold-plated Daimler is said to be the most expensive car in the world and it is valued at $100,000.

9. Small children can't read the labels on poison bottles and parents should be sure to store such things as weed killers, dye, and ammonia far out of reach of the younger members of the family.

10. The most desirable vocations are those requiring much preparation, so it is wise to plan a vocation early.

11. I had an umbrella and the rain came right through it.

12 So far I have seen but one hockey game, and I hope to see another soon.

WHEN, WHERE, BECAUSE

Use *when* for time and *where* for place. After *is* in a definition, use a noun or pronoun rather than *when, where,* or *because,* or rephrase the sentence. *Is* is an equal sign. Constructions like "The best part of the play was when . . ." and "An exciting scene is where . . ." are illogical. After verbs such as *read* or *learn,* use *that* rather than *where.*

NOT An exciting scene is when Pip discovers the identity of his secret benefactor. (The adverb clause "when . . . benefactor" is used as a noun-subjective completion of a copula verb.)

BUT An exciting scene is the one in which Pip discovers the identity of his secret benefactor.

OR An exciting scene occurs when Pip discovers the identity of his secret benefactor.

NOT The Hall of Mirrors is where the Treaty of Versailles was signed

BUT The Hall of Mirrors is the room in which the Treaty of Versailles was signed.

OR The Treaty of Versailles was signed in the Hall of Mirrors.

NOT The reason Ann is going to the fashion school is because she wants a career in merchandising.

BUT The reason Ann is going to the fashion school is that she wants a career in merchandising.

OR Ann is going to the fashion school because she wants a career in merchandising.

NOT I read in the newspaper where a man had been killed. (The clause "where . . . killed" functions as a noun—object of a transitive verb.)

BUT I read in the newspaper that a man had been killed.

NOT Because I am short is no reason for ridiculing me. (The adverb clause "Because . . . short" is used as a noun—subject of a verb.)

BUT That I am short (*or* My shortness) is no reason for ridiculing me.

PRACTICE 25. Correcting Misuse of Adverb Clauses

Improve the following sentences by correcting the misuse of the adverb clauses.

1. A democracy is where people rule themselves through their elected representatives.
2. We heard from our principal where television might be used in our school.
3. The reason why this sentence is objectionable is because it is not clear.
4. I read in the paper today where a company had declared bankruptcy.
5. A tourniquet is when something is put on to stop bleeding.
6. A first-class lever is where the fulcrum is between the weight and the effort.
7. The reason why I failed was because I did not study.
8. A compound sentence is when there are two principal clauses.
9. I saw in the paper where Marjorie Stanton has just entered the University of Manitoba.
10. A warrant officer is when an officer holds rank between that of commissioned officer and enlisted man.

CORRECT SUBORDINATION

Clear sentences require correct subordination. The main idea must be placed in the main clause; a secondary or subordinate idea, in a subordinate clause. Failure to think what each conjunction means sometimes results in incorrect subordination.

For example, a *when* clause fixes the time of an event told about in the principal clause.

After
ᴧI had driven only ten blocks ~~when~~ the tire blew.

After rowing
~~We rowed~~ on through the storm for an hour͵ᴧ~~when~~ we finally reached our dock.

As
ᴧI had become interested in English literature, ~~because~~ I decided to take the English Language and Literature Course at the university.

PRACTICE 26. Correct Subordination

Improve the following sentences by placing the main thought in the principal clause.

1. Ted was winding his watch when he heard the brakes squeal outside his door.
2. We fished for an hour when we were compelled by a storm to seek shelter.
3. We were down town, and so we decided to shop at Simpson's.
4. The China Clipper was far out over the Pacific when they saw a small fishing vessel.
5. We hiked about half the distance to the park when we decided to find a place to cook and eat our lunch.
6. Edison was almost in despair when unexpectedly the lamp stayed lit for many breathless hours.
7. I was very tired after the long trip, and so I went to bed early.

4. CLEAR REFERENCE OF PRONOUNS

Shirley's nose was sunburned, but it has now completely disappeared.
What is the boy's name who won the 220-yard dash?

If a sentence makes you blink and read again, it's probably not clear. Do your sentences say what you want them to say? If a reader complains "I don't know what this sentence means," the chances are that the writer was not thinking clearly. A sentence like "The difficulty can be practically eliminated by reading through the test paper upon answering the questions and then reread the test after completing it" is a product either of muddled thinking or of not enough thinking. The rules in the following pages will help you to avoid pronoun errors in **your own writing.**

AMBIGUOUS REFERENCE

Do not use a pronoun if, even for an instant, there can be doubt about its antecedent. Reword or rearrange the sentence. Supply a needed noun.

CONFUSING She wore a hat on her head which was made of brilliant crimson felt.

REARRANGED On her head she wore a hat which was made of brilliant crimson felt.

CONFUSING He had two mosquito bites on his arms, both of which have now disappeared.

REWORDED On his arms he had two mosquito bites, both of which have now disappeared.

CONFUSING May 11 would be a better day for our picnic than May 4 because it is the day after our history examination.

NOUN SUPPLIED May 11 would be a better day for our picnic than May 4 because May 11 is the day after our history examination.

The following appeared in a newspaper report. How would you correct the error?

Mr. Brown will start the $750,000 campaign with a dinner speech Tuesday evening. It will run one month.

CONFUSING Vickie told Cora that she had made a perfect score on the spelling test.

QUOTATION FOR CLARITY Vickie told Cora, "You have made a perfect score on the spelling test."

OR Vickie told Cora, "I have made a perfect score on the spelling test."

IMPLIED REFERENCE

Do not let a pronoun refer to a word that is not expressed. Supply a noun if it is needed.

CONFUSING The garage sign said, "Blow your horn, and we'll park it."

CLEAR The garage sign said, "Blow your horn, and we'll park your car."

This week Parliament will debate the question of Air Force expansion and
                            proposals
will weed out those˄which seem ill-timed or impractical.

My mother is a registered nurse and she hopes that at least one of her
                            nursing
daughters will choose i̶t̶ as a career.

BURIED REFERENCE

Avoid reference to a noun hidden in the possessive case or in a modifier. The antecedent should be prominent in the mind of the reader.

of the photographer

What's the ~~photographer's~~ name∧who took your cousin's wedding pictures?

ALLOWABLE   Have you seen Bob's new Jaguar? How can he afford it?

DOUBLE REFERENCE

Don't ordinarily use the same pronoun to refer to different antecedents.

CONFUSING   Mrs. Gage wrote Mother that she was going to put her cracker pie recipe in her new cookbook, *Treats for Special Occasions.*

CLEAR   Mrs. Gage wrote Mother, "I'm going to put your cracker pie recipe in my new cookbook, *Treats for Special Occasions.*"

PRACTICE 27. Using Pronouns Correctly

Correct the following sentences. Tell the antecedent of every pronoun you use except *I* and *you.*

Example:

Lila thinks court reporting is exciting and hopes to be one.
Lila thinks court reporting is exciting. In fact she hopes to be a court stenographer. (The antecedent of *she* is *Lila.*)

A. 1. Mr. Brink wants the salesman's name who made the best record last month.
   2. A student of Michelangelo's work soon realizes that he is a master of mass and line.
   3. Yesterday Ron told Dick that he had been accepted by McGill.
   4. This year insurance companies have raised the rates for young drivers and it's going to make life expensive for teen-agers who want to drive the family car.
   5. Every summer Jack's brother works as a lifeguard at Silver Beach and likes it very much.
   6. In the film's most exciting sequence a mongoose battled a cobra; after a long struggle it finally won.

B. 1. A person reading Wordsworth's poetry soon discovers that he is a nature poet.
   2. When Wordsworth discussed poetic expression with Coleridge he became certain of the need for a new kind of poetry.

3. Coleridge told Wordsworth that he did not share his view that the language of poetry should be the language of everyday life.

4. What was the poet's name who was a friend of Wordsworth and Coleridge and lived near them in the Lake District?

5. In *The Prelude* Wordsworth reminisces about his childhood and youth, describing vividly those which stirred his poetic imagination.

6. Because a knowledge of the Romantic poets is important to one's development as a reader and a thinker, every student should take at least a term of it.

INDEFINITE "IT", "YOU", "THEY".

In formal speech and writing avoid the indefinite use of *it, you,* and *they* except in expressions like "it is snowing," "it is hot," and "it appears".

~~It says here in~~ T̲his article͵ ᵃʸˢthat Donald Campbell broke the two-hundred-mile-an-hour "water barrier" in a jet-powered boat, the *Bluebird*.

Next September ~~they're establishing~~ a placement office͵ᵂⁱˡˡ ᵇᵉ ᵉˢᵗᵃᵇˡⁱˢʰᵉᵈ to help our students get part-time jobs.

Club members enjoy photography night, for then ~~you~~ ᵗʰᵉʸ have a chance to compare colour slides͵

WHICH, THAT, THIS

Do not use *which* in referring to a whole statement if that statement contains a noun to which the pronoun may erroneously refer. Be sure that the antecedent of the pronoun *this* or *that* is clear.

CONFUSING We read a number of articles on safe driving which gave us the information we needed for our debate.

CLEAR The safe-driving articles we read gave us the information we needed for our debate.

CLEAR We got information for our debate from a number of articles on safe driving.

PRACTICE 28. Clear Reference of Pronouns

Correct the following sentences:

A. 1. In this article it says that it took Richard Rodgers just six minutes to compose the music for "Oh, What a Beautiful Morning!"

2. Don't think about your speech for Tuesday if it makes you nervous.

3. You may rely on our staff to go over the contest mail carefully, setting aside those which are incompletely filled out.

4. Blanche likes the sea and her sister likes the mountains, which is why they always take separate vacations.

5. What's the pitcher's name who relieved Whitey Ford in the seventh?

6. At his news conference the Prime Minister announced that he would confer with leaders of the Western states on conservation problems and admitted that it had been long needed.

7. Byron told Shelley that he should learn to swim.

B. 1. The visibility is very poor and the fog is getting worse every minute which has grounded all planes along the Eastern seacoast.

2. In *Marty* by Paddy Chayefsky it tells about the struggle of a plain, ordinary fellow to find someone to love him.

3. The garage mechanic told Chuck that he couldn't get his old coupe to run again without putting in a whole new engine.

4. In the *Skeleton in the Clock* by John Dickson Carr it tells about a murder mystery that remained unsolved for about twenty years, only they didn't know it was a murder.

5. Julie and Ted have found they can't disagree without quarreling, which is why they have broken their engagement.

6. I used vanilla flavouring instead of chocolate which made the cakes too sweet.

7. The hunter finds his dog a great comfort to him on his hunting trips. He realizes that his sense of smell and his endurance far surpass his own.

5. ELLIPTICAL SENTENCES

We sometimes omit words which are important grammatically but which are not necessary to make our meaning clear. The sentence from which one or more such words have been omitted is elliptical.

Answers to Questions

Who is there? I [am here].
How long are you going to stay? [I am going to stay] About two weeks.
Whose book is this? [It is] Harry's [book].

Clause Introduced by **Than** *or* **As**

Our baseball team made a better record this year than [it made] last year.
Jenkins is not so good a pitcher as White [is good].

Conjunctions and Relative Pronouns

I wish [that] I knew the answer.
Had they started [If they had started] an hour earlier, they would have escaped the heavy traffic in the city.
You are the boy [whom] I mean.

Subject, Verb, or Subject and Verb

When [he was] only fifty years old, he retired.
[It is] Twenty-three, to be exact.
[That is] All right, I accept your offer.
[You] Hurry home.
Why [do you] not try harder to form the right kind of friendships?
While [I was] spending a week in Montreal, I enjoyed the tobogganing.

Avoiding Repetition

I shall complete Ernest Thompson Seton's *Lives of the Hunted* tonight **if** I can [complete it].
I shall not go to the play unless you wish to [go].

PRACTICE 29. Elliptical Sentences

Insert in brackets the grammatically important words which have been omitted because they are not necessary to make the meaning clear:

1. How old is Arthur? Fourteen.
2. What are you doing? Nothing.
3. Who is there? I.
4. Borup's *A Tenderfoot with Peary* is a more entertaining book than Schurz's *Abraham Lincoln*.
5. Thank you.
6. If necessary, I shall come earlier.
7. Murphy plays right end; Howe, left end.
8. If possible, meet me at nine o'clock tomorrow morning.
9. A tiger is physically stronger than a lion.
10. "Come back, then, and let me know what he says," yelled Harvey. "I certainly will," called Earl.

FAULTY ELLIPSIS

Faulty ellipsis is the ommission of subjects, verbs, objects, prepositions, or conjunctions which are necessary to make the meaning correct and clear. Faulty ellipses violate both unity and coherence.

Subject

FAULTY ELLIPSIS Hoping to receive the suit before December 1. (In this expression there is no subject. *Hoping* is a participle, not a verb form that makes a statement. To express the idea in a correct sentence we need to insert a subject and use a form of the verb that makes a statement.)

CORRECT I hope to receive the suit before December 1.

FAULTY ELLIPSIS When only four years old, George's father died. (This sentence seems to say that the father died at the age of four.)

CORRECT When George was only four years old, his father died.

Verb

FAULTY ELLIPSIS I never have, and never will, understand the mechanism of a radio. (*I never have understand* is ungrammatical.)

CORRECT I never have understood, and never will understand the mechanism of a radio.

Object

FAULTY ELLIPSIS The blind boy needs someone to educate and care for him. (In this sentence *him* is used as the object of the infinitive *to educate* and of the preposition *for*. A word may be the object of two verbs or of two prepositions, but not of one verb and one preposition.)

CORRECT The blind boy needs someone to educate him and care for him.

Preposition

FAULTY ELLIPSIS Carl graduated Riverside Collegiate before entering Toronto University. (*Graduate* in this sentence does not take an object; one does not "graduate a school".)

CORRECT Carl graduated from (or was graduated from) Riverside Collegiate before entering Toronto University.

Conjunction

FAULTY ELLIPSIS My English mark is always as high or higher than my French mark.

CORRECT My English mark is always as high as my French mark, or higher.

PRACTICE 30. Faulty Ellipsis

Supply the needed word or words. Give a reason for each change.

1. Jane says she has not and will not learn to play golf.
2. Each poem has a separate story to tell but are all linked together because of their relationship to King Arthur.
3. Elizabeth is as tall or taller than her mother.
4. Thanking you for the prompt shipment of the shoes.
5. I have never seen or spoken to him.
6. My brother graduated the University of Alberta last June.
7. When eight years old, my parents moved to Kamsack.
8. Did the boys and girls pity or make fun of the intoxicated man?

9. Is Chicago the chief railroad centre of United States?
10. This is a contest which everyone may compete.
11. The newsboy has a pair of broad shoulders and quite muscular.
12. I hope that your college career will be as successful as your high school.
13. The speed of the new car is almost equal to an airplane.
14. The record of our football team is as good as or better than last year's team.
15. There are two kinds of people who always have and always will exist.
16. He will have to serve a three-year term in jail or a thousand-dollar fine.
17. Geometry is interesting to me and therefore grasp it readily.
18. The town which Mary Antin lived in Russia was a dreary place.

6. SYNTACTICAL REDUNDANCE

Syntactical redundance—that is a hard name for a childish mistake. *Redundance* means *excess; syntactical* means *according to the rules of syntax.* Hence syntactical redundance is using two words to do the same grammatical job or using words that do no useful work in the sentence. Sometimes, for example, a pronoun and its antecedent are wrongly used as subject of the same verb.

RIGHT The kings at that time usually wore crowns.
WRONG The kings at that time they usually wore crowns.
RIGHT My father solved the problem for me.
WRONG My father he solved the problem for me.

They and *he* are omitted, because these words have no work to do in the sentences. *Kings* is the subject of *wore; father,* of *solved.*

A pronoun and its antecedent are not used as the subject of the same verb.

Occasionally a preposition is carelessly repeated, has no object, has no work to do in the sentence.

WRONG Antonio had no money with which to pay Shylock with.

This sentence should look about as queer to you as an automobile with a second engine behind the rear seat.

RIGHT Antonio had no money with which to pay Shylock.

Often a preposition is needlessly inserted.

RIGHT In the new building the principal will have an office about the size of our present library.

AWKWARD In the new building the principal will have an office of about the size of our present library.

The preposition is understood. Its omission avoids awkwardness.

RIGHT Clifford met a young man whose tastes and ambitions were like his own.

WRONG Clifford met with a young man whose tastes and ambitions were like his own.

Man is the object of the verb *met; with* is not needed.

RIGHT An example of a story having a lesson is Galsworthy's "Quality".

WRONG An example of a story having a lesson is in Galsworthy's "Quality".

"Quality" is the predicate nominative of the verb *is; in* is not needed.

Cross out every unnecessary preposition or conjunction.

PRACTICE 31. Sentence Correction

Correct the following sentences. Show that each word which you omit has no work to do in the sentence.

1. Jack one day he fractured his leg.
2. Where have you been at?
3. The trees they make the country gloomy on dark days.
4. Mr. Holmes told about some humorous anecdotes and jokes.
5. The number of classrooms in the new high school will be double over that in the old building.
6. The trustees, having worn themselves out in these quarrels, they had no energy left to make the necessary changes in the building.
7. In through the open window could be seen a boy of about eighteen years of age.
8. From whence did he come?
9. Susie she won't go.
10. He signed to the bond without reading it carefully.
11. We saw two rowboats approach towards us.
12. Leonard W. Wilson crashed to his death at Mitchell Field while he was trying out a gull-like plane on which he had laboured years to perfect.
13. My friend to whom I gave the book to did not return it.
14. The words to which I refer to are those ending in *ing*.
15. Would you like to know with what kind of boys I associated with?
16. A hero is a person to whom we look up to.
17. The great Canadian of whom I am going to write about is Bliss Carman.
18. Sonny selected the faith in which he wanted to be baptized in.
19. Vary your sentences in the ways in which you have studied in class.
20. It was agreed upon that Shylock should have a pound of Antonio's flesh.
21. Mrs. Floyd is a woman of about fifty years of age.

22. The pace set by the leader was killing, but nevertheless Bob stayed with his opponent.

23. They gave chase to the bandits, but, however, they soon gave up hope of catching them.

24. The instructor said that if anyone hadn't finished his composition that he should have it ready on Monday.

25. It is quite natural that when he found an opportunity to defeat his rival that he should take advantage of it.

26. I am trying to find the vocation to which I am best suited for.

27. Mabel was an attractive high school girl of about sixteen years of age.

28. They were looking in the direction from which the cart was to come from.

29. Pirate treasure is a subject about which everyone dreams about at one time or another.

30. The plot is surrounded by a hedge of about four feet high.

7. AWKWARDNESS

CLUMSY SENTENCE   Improve awkward, clumsy sentences. Your sentences should sound natural, smooth, idiomatic.

AWKWARD   The major reason for Stevenson's continuing popularity is due to his storytelling ability.

NATURAL   The major reason for Stevenson's continuing popularity is his story-telling ability.

WRONG ELEMENT   Don't use the wrong grammatical element.

CLAUSE FOR WORD   Another sport where a boy learns fair play is ~~if he plays~~ baseball.

PHRASE FOR WORD   The time the train actually started was ~~at~~ noon.

CLAUSE FOR PHRASE   Mrs. Elkins wanted ~~that~~ two boys ^{to} ~~should~~ go to the book-room for our new literature texts.

INFINITIVE PHRASE FOR GERUND PHRASE   I like to feel that I have the privilege of visiting ~~to visit~~ friends who have different beliefs.

PRACTICE 32. Avoiding Awkwardness in Writing

Correct the following sentences.

A. 1. Most of all, Sally enjoys to eat pistachio ice cream.

   2. I can visit my neighbour whenever I see it fit, without worrying about secret police.

   3. The reason Paul failed the last test was due to carelessness.

   4. I enjoy it very much to look up home-run records in the *Information Please Almanac.*

5. This book shows how Shirley because of her earnestness to be a good secretary helped her to become a secretary.

6. The first step in selecting a camp site is that it must be on high ground.

B. 1. The place where I can relax best is when I am in my own room.

2. If I succeed to get a job this summer, I hope to save my money for college.

3. We are looking forward to have you with us this coming week-end.

4. Good road signs prevent motorists to lose their way.

5. We had to get out a certain amount of work done in a day.

6. Another time where a girl is greatly aided if she knows how to type is if she belongs to a social club.

8. CLEAR THINKING

ACCURATE WORDS

Think what your words mean. Choose words which express your idea clearly, exactly, completely.

poor

My most serious composition problem is ~~good~~ handwriting.

"YOU GO FIRST, AND I SHALL PRECEDE YOU."

PRACTICE 33. Choosing Words That Say What You Mean

Decide what the writer or speaker was trying to say in each of the following sentences. Then express his thought exactly.

A. 1. The jet ace had had many narrow escapes ~~with~~ *from* death but had always come through safely.

2. Our crime bureau had ~~excess~~ *access* to files and criminal records of investigation departments in other countries.

3. Few novelists can compare with Dickens' characters. *the characters of Dickens*

4. Any defect in our appliances, if reported to the main office, will be greatly appreciated.

5. As he came to know her better, Darcy became in love with Elizabeth Bennet. *fell*

B. 1. Dad is going to analyze his golf game and try to improve his defects.

2. I've always excepted Muriel's annual invitation to spend Labour Day weekend at her cottage.

3. The thermometer has registered 90 degrees for over a week now, but the heat never effects me one way or the other.

4. Do you think that the reference to fifty dollars might defer small gifts?

5. The defense tried to show that the prisoner had been elsewhere at the time of the murder, but this was almost impossible to solve.

LOGICAL STATEMENT

Be logical. Make complete comparisons. Do not say a thing is what it isn't. Include every word necessary for clearness.

NOT The castle had big fireplaces that burned all day and night. (The fireplaces didn't burn.)

BUT Day and night fires blazed in the big fireplaces of the castle.

OR The castle had big fireplaces in which, day and night, fires blazed.

NOT Canadians feel that they are a leading country in world affairs. (Canadians aren't a country.)

BUT Canadians feel that their country plays a leading part in world affairs.

Two of my brother's classmates can't decide which profession to follow—engineering, dentistry, or law.
~~engineer, dentist, or lawyer.~~ (*Engineer, dentist, lawyer* are not professions.)

As his name suggests,
Rusty has red hair ~~like his name.~~ (Is the hair like his name?)

The setting of *Lost Horizon* is ~~in~~ a hidden valley in Tibet.　(The setting isn't *in* the valley; it *is* the valley.)

———

The action of

∧*The Talisman* takes place during the Third Crusade.　(Don't confuse the action in a book with its title.)

———

On a blistering hot day in August a baseball player's job is harder than an

　　　　　's·

office worker∧.　(Don't compare a job with a person.)

PRACTICE 34.　Building Clear Sentences

Change each of the following into a clear, sensible sentence.

A. 1. December 24 was a snowy, windy evening.

　2. In *A Tale of Two Cities* Dickens describes the plight of the French peasants who were dying ~~of lack~~ of hunger.

　3. Traffic Violators Cut in Half (notice in a newspaper)

　4. Our lettuce, onions, peas, and radishes are growing rapidly, but do not have the muskmelons and watermelons planted yet.

　5. Any discourtesy by our salesmen, if reported to the manger, will be appreciated.

　6. Three fine old English customs are the boar's head, the yule-log, and the Christmas service in the local church.

B. 1. Try Our Cakes—None like Them (sign in a bakery window)

　2. I'm trying to improve the criticisms the class made of my three-minute speech.

　3. Does a doctor's training take longer than a lawyer?

　4. If the furniture isn't delivered by Monday, May 5, I shall cancel all future orders.

　5. The plot of *The Caine Mutiny* takes place during World War II.

　6. A description in a recent magazine of Tibet and its people seems to be a very unusual country.

UTTER CONFUSION

Think first.　Some confused sentences defy classification.　If you write such a sentence, cross it out and begin all over.

WHAT THE CONFUSED WRITER SAID　By Stephen Crane's classic *The Red Badge of Courage* through which his descriptive words form lifelike pictures of what our men are going through in the War Between the States.

WHAT HE PROBABLY MEANT In the classic *The Red Badge of Courage* by Stephen Crane, the descriptions give the reader a lifelike picture of the sufferings of our soldiers during the War Between the States.

SAID *Hamlet* as compared with *Macbeth* for enjoyment I consider better.

PROBABLY MEANS I consider *Hamlet* more enjoyable than *Macbeth*.

PRACTICE 35. Bringing Order Out of Chaos

Decide what the writer of these hopelessly confused sentences probably meant. Then express the idea of each sentence clearly and concisely. You may have to use two sentences to express the thought of a single faulty sentence.

1. One reason that these classes are popular, everyone has some ability in that one subject.
2. Many times one enters his home and finds a marble, which is very common and is around nearly all homes with children near the door.
3. Insecurity as a child will lead to mistrust of people in later life when he is older.
4. Keats, in "Ode on a Grecian Urn," a simple object is presented to the reader in a pleasing manner which is therefore enjoyed and consider it one of the best poems.
5. Bad sports do not have to be only in athletics but also politicians who are disgruntled if they don't win an election and people who do not like to see other people have fun.
6. The result of a long period of procrastination is very serious indeed, and it should be done only once in a while, and then with caution.

PRACTICE 36. Rewriting a Letter

Rewrite the following letter for greater clarity and conciseness. Be ready to give a reason for each change you make.

Dear Larry,

In my opinion life here at Silver Lake is, I think, just about perfect. We start out each morning with a swim before breakfast and return back for a steaming bowl of oatmeal, country bacon, and fresh eggs. I've nearly gained five pounds already.

We're six miles away from the nearest post office, and the families in our area have agreed to take turns picking up and delivering mail. I'm writing this early in order that it may be mailed today. Mr. Brockway is coming at about 9:00 a.m. in the morning. Knowing him, he'll be early.

We'd enjoy to have you visit us the first week in August. Ask your parents and then you should let me know. I'll send full details, which you can expect to find in my next letter.

I read in our local paper where the first Monday in August is called Civic Holiday. In the article it tells how the city was founded in early times.

We'll enjoy hiking, swimming, and boating with a boy in the neighbouring cabin. The boy's name who has become our good friend is Fred Larson.

Oh, yes, we have a boat too. As a rule, we usually keep our boat moored to our dock, which has a bright red stripe around the white hull.

Hearing about all our fun, we hope you'll be able to come.

Your friend,
George

PRACTICE 37. Review of Clear, Correct Sentences

Correct or improve the faulty sentences. Give a reason for each change. One *A* sentence and one *B* sentence are clear and correct.

A. 1. Odysseus stopped in Sicily, where he was captured by Polyphemus, who ate some of his men who were not able to escape from the cave, which was the home of the giant.

2. Four weeks ago you sent us twenty dollars, leaving a balance of ten dollars, for which we thank you.

3. Children in ragged clothes and dirty faces were laying on the floor.

4. Uriah had no eyebrows and slight eyelashes, and his eyes were reddish brown, and he looked as if he wouldn't be able to go to sleep because of the scant covering of his eyes.

5. Martha has light hair, blue eyes, and good-natured.

6. Reading on in the story, there is another dog introduced.

7. The collie sat with his parched tongue hanging from his mouth feebly wagging his tail.

8. Jack Weel, famous as a football player at Yale and who was coach at Northwestern for years, talked at our last assembly.

9. I think, if you will follow my directions and by inquiring when you are in doubt, you will reach Somerset.

10. Poetry, according to Trevelyan, is in danger of becoming a dying art, appealing only to the cultured minority.

11. I nearly cried for joy when I read your letter, but as you do not know how to reach my house, I will give you the directions now.

12. Rip found his dog when he reached home, but he did not know him.

13. Use a coloured illustration, and also it is wise to have an attractive heading.

14. A classical high school educates the head only, but in a vocational high school attention is paid to the hands as well as the head.

15. *Ruggles of Red Gap* will keep you in fits of merriment, and please tell me when you are coming to visit us.

B. 1. A person who has to be told to do a thing two or three times will not advance rapidly in business.

2. In his will the dying monarch made Namgay king, because he had no children.

3. Standing on the bridge, a brown building is visible.

4. One can enjoy himself by going to the library and read good books.

5. Burrows neither succeeded as a clerk nor as a mechanic.

6. A teacher should not expect a pupil to know what he knows.

7. Going home, the wind blew a gale.

8. The reader is suddenly transported to the banks of the Congo, where ebony natives dance, rhythmically beat their drums, and perform fantastic rites.

9. After eating a hearty dinner, our carriages were brought to the door.

10. The carpenter is of medium height, ordinary looking, gray eyes, rather sallow cheeks, a long, thin, trailing mustache, and rather uncouth in his manner.

11. Eastern High School is overcrowded, and it has a commercial and a general course.

12. He said to his friend that since he ordered the fruit he ought to pay for it.

13. Poe invented the short story, and his home in New York has in it many relics.

14. We proved that air is a real substance because it occupies space and by showing that air has weight.

15. Flying at an altitude of ten thousand feet, the country for 132 miles in ﹐ all directions can be clearly seen.

IMITATING EFFECTIVE SENTENCE STRUCTURE

PRACTICE 38. Imitating Models

Using each of the following sentences as a model, write two sentences of your own, upon your own topic, in direct imitation of the model. Examine the model closely for its structure and do not neglect to imitate the punctuation.

Examples:

Model:

Her garments shone like the summer sea, and her jewels like the stars of heaven; and over her forehead was a veil, woven of the golden clouds of sunset.

Imitation:

1. The wheat waved like a billowy sea, and the grass like the rippling river; and on the field was a cloud-shadow, broken only by the drifting rack.

2. The castle stood like a mountain fixed, and the village like unmoving foothills; while over the scene broke the storm, driven by the desperate wind.

1. Here I observed, by the help of my perspective glass, that they were no less than thirty in number, that they had a fire kindled, and that they had meat dressed.

2. Here they used to sit on summer afternoons, talking listlessly over village gossip.

3. The spirit of my fathers grows strong in me, and I will no longer endure it.

4. From behind his stockade Jack watched them through his field glass as they landed from the launch and set off for the village.

5. She stopped a moment beneath the gently dripping trees and took off her knitted cap and shook it dry.

6. Martin Luther writes, "I was myself flogged fifteen times one afternoon over the conjugation of a verb."

7. A lingering winter and a tardy spring are what we always should like in this part of the world.

8. The fourth largest olive grove in the world is said to be on the outskirts of Beirut.

9. Do you know that the speaker will not disappoint you?

10. He never bluffs, and he dislikes bluffers.

11. At ten o'clock the crack of the starter's pistol announced that the annual six-mile free-style swim across Lake Henley had started.

12. Night after night, with only a flashlight, Ibram prowled about the Arab quarter, seeking adventure.

13. At dusk a slight flurry of snow heralded the coming storm, but by morning the outbuildings were buried under huge drifts.

14. The heavy fog and the still, damp air oppressed his mind and drained his body of strength and energy.

15. A century ago there had been a cart road across the peninsula, but it had been obliterated by jungle growth and floods.

16. At twilight a panther ventured within a stone's throw of our house, slaughtered a calf, and dragged it into the forest.

17. When Gladys had had a hot drink and had donned dry clothes, she felt better about her ducking.

18. That the rain was coming down in sheets, that the picnic lunch was the prey of ants, and that each of the boys had at least two wasp bites did not kill their enthusiasm for camping.

19. The Greeks and Romans thought that thunder and lightning were the punishment of the gods.

20. He corrected himself, blushing as he did so, though why he should blush was not known to Reuben.

Chapter 3

Effective Paragraphs

WHY PARAGRAPHS?

Have you ever, when selecting a novel for leisure reading, glanced through it to see how much conversation there was in it? If so, you know that the short paragraphs of conversation are easier reading than long paragraphs. How would you like to read a book that was just one long paragraph? If division into paragraphs helps you when you are reading, remember this fact when you write.

TEST—PARAGRAPHING

Recalling that in conversation each speech is in a separate paragraph, rewrite the following in correct form. Show that you have good eyes by spelling every word correctly and punctuating accurately.

A PATIENT FISHERMAN

About six o'clock on a fine morning in the summer I set out from Philadelphia on a visit to a friend, at the distance of fifteen miles; and passing a brook where a gentleman was angling, I inquired if he had caught anything. "No, sir," said he, "I have not been here long enough—only two hours." I wished him a good morning, and pursued my journey. On my return in the evening I found him fixed to the identical spot where I had left him, and again inquired if he had any sport. "Very good, sir," said he. "Caught a great many fish?" "None at all." "Had a great many bites though, I suppose?" "Not one, but I had a most glorious nibble."—BENJAMIN FRANKLIN

WHAT A PARAGRAPH IS

In dialogue each speech is a paragraph. Ordinarily, however, a paragraph is a group of sentences developing one topic. In the third paragraph of "A Patient Fisherman," for example, Franklin's topic is the happenings between the morning and the evening conversation with the fisherman.

Paragraphs vary widely in length from the short ones to an occasional long one of 250 or 300 words. A good length for ordinary writing is 100 to 150 words. In newspaper articles and business letters shorter paragraphs are used. The average length of paragraphs in business letters is about 60 words; in newspaper articles, about 75 words. Don't make the mistake of writing, in a composition or a test, a paragraph pages long or of starting a new paragraph for each sentence. We shall soon study when to stop one paragraph and begin a new.

TOPIC SENTENCE

When we travel by train, we first buy a ticket, on which our starting point and destination are shown. When we write or speak a paragraph, it is wise to start with a topic sentence making clear exactly what we are going to talk about. A topic sentence is a brief statement of the subject of a paragraph. At the beginning of the paragraph it furnishes a destination or goal for the writer or speaker and guides him in travelling towards his goal.

In a paragraph of narration the topic sentence is seldom expressed, in description it is often omitted, and in other writing sometimes omitted. Always, however, it is possible to sum up a good paragraph in a sentence. Commonly the first sentence in a paragraph of explanation or argument is a signpost telling in what direction and how far the speaker or writer expects to travel in the paragraph. The topic sentence may be placed in the middle of the paragraph or at the end. The beginner, however, progresses more rapidly if he forms the habit of expressing the main idea of a paragraph of explanation or argument in the first sentence and using the topic sentence as a foundation on which to build the paragraph. A master of the language writes paragraphs without much thought of topic sentences. In every field the artist has greater freedom than the mechanic.

Sometimes the first sentence of a paragraph links it with the preceding paragraph by taking a backward look, and the second announces the subject of the paragraph.

Example:

These faults perhaps we can overlook. (Transition and introductory sentence.) But his absolute disregard of the rights of others is a more serious matter. (Topic sentence.) During his youth he teased, tormented, bullied, and tortured his younger brother and other boys a size smaller than he, etc.

A good topic sentence, like a good guide, gives accurate and complete information. Some topic sentences are about as vague as the directions, "Go straight ahead for about a half mile, then turn right, then turn left, then turn left again."

One can develop a narrow topic sentence in a paragraph but usually needs two or more paragraphs to discuss a broad topic. "A true sportsman has many admirable qualities" and "A true sportsman is honest, courteous, self-controlled, courageous, loyal, and enthusiastic" are broad topic sentences. "A true sportsman must be a good loser" and "A true sportsman will never cheat to win" are narrower topic sentences.

PRACTICE 1. Topic Sentences

In each pair which topic sentence is the more useful guide to a person writing a paragraph?

1

a. Canoe tilting is a good sport.
b. Canoe tilting is a good sport, because it takes nerve, strength, and endurance to play the game.

2

a. Dogs often show great intelligence.
b. Dogs are good pets.

3

a. Last Saturday Jack and I fished all day.
b. Last Saturday Jack and I had great luck fishing for trout.

4

a. Camping is a form of recreation which is pleasingly blended with a form of learning.
b. For two reasons camping should appeal to boys and girls.

5

a. A stamp collector does more than gather coloured bits of paper.
b. Stamp-collecting is a good hobby.

PRACTICE 2. Choosing a Topic Sentence

Think of five topics you know something about. Then make a statement about each that you can "back up". For example, if you have read *Treasure Island*, you can "back up" the statement, "Jim was a quick thinker"; if you like to swim, can you prove the statement, "Swimming is a healthful sport"? Then write these five statements down as topic sentences that you can develop into paragraphs. A narrow topic sentence is ordinarily better than a broad one.

KEYS

If you examine the paragraphs which follow, you will notice that the topic sentence not only gives the name of the topic but suggests the thing which it is going to say about it. This key word or phrase is the most useful part of the topic sentence both to the reader and the writer. It is hard to write an incorrect paragraph if the key word is correct and clear.

1. THE POLICE DOG

The character of the police dog is complex. My best pal is one of these half-wild creatures, and from constant companionship I have discovered that he really has a dual personality. At night he slinks along with the stealthy tread of the world, nostrils quivering as he warily follows an imaginary scent and eyes gleaming like two phosphorus lights through the darkness. The ingrown fear of the unknown shows in the strained poise of his body or the suspicious turn of his head. But with the coming of daylight all the eerie illusions that are the companions of darkness vanish, and the police dog becomes a domesticated animal relying on man for the very substance of life. Gone is the cowardly and suspicious wolf, and in his place stands the dog, loyal-hearted and true.—PUPIL

2. THE LINNET CHORUS

One of the most delightful bird sounds or noises to be heard in England is the concert singing of a flock of several hundreds, and sometimes of a thousand or more linnets in September and October and even later in the year, before these great congregations have been broken up or have migrated. The effect produced by the small field finch of the pampas was quite different. The linnet has a little twittering song with breaks in it and small chirping sounds and when a great multitude of birds sing together, the sound at a distance of fifty or sixty yards is as of a high wind among trees, but on a nearer approach the mass sound resolves itself into a tangle of thousands of individual sounds resembling that of a great concourse of starlings at roosting time, but more musical in character. It is as if hundreds of fairy minstrels were all playing on stringed and winged instruments of various forms, each one intent on his own performance without regard to the others.

—W. H. HUDSON, *Far Away and Long Ago.*
By arrangement with J. M. Dent & Sons, London and Toronto.

Many things might be written about police dogs, but this paragraph deals with the complexity of its character. Similarly, "The Linnet Chorus" may be variously treated, but in these paragraphs we have respectively, variety of meanings, unusualness, and the delight of the music. Each of these is suggested in the topic sentence.

The topic sentence is not always first, but it should be as near the beginning as possible. Sometimes the clear-headed writer may write a clear and consistent paragraph by keeping the key in his mind only, but beginners are recommended to express it in the topic sentence.

PRACTICE 3. Selecting a Topic

What is the topic of each of the following paragraphs? What gives the key to each topic?

1

After Hautmont, the sun came forth again and the wind went down; and a little paddling took us beyond the iron works and through a delectable land. The river wound among low hills, so that sometimes the sun was at our backs and sometimes it stood right ahead, and the river before us was one sheet of intolerable glory. On either hand meadows and orchards bordered, with a margin or hedge and water flowers, upon the river. The hedges were of great height, woven about the trunks of hedgerow elms; and the fields, as they were often very small, looked like a series of bowers along the stream. There was never any prospect; sometimes a hill-top with its trees would look over the nearest hedgerow, just to make a middle distance for the sky; but that was all. The heaven was bare of clouds. The atmosphere, after the rain, was of enchanting purity. The river doubled among the hillocks, a shining strip of mirror glass; and the dip of the paddles set the flowers shaking along the brink.

—Robert Louis Stevenson, *An Inland Voyage*.
By permission of the publishers, Charles Scribner's Sons.

2

I remember having my juvenile imagination greatly excited by the appearance of a man on stilts. I would have given anything for a pair and the power to use them. What a thing it would be to go through the old town in such wise that the first-floor window-stool would be as familiar as the doorsteps. I thought I should never tire of them, never take them off. But reflection came later, and I bethought me that there were several highly desirable positions with which stilts were manifestly incompatible. How could I sit at meals; indeed, how sit conveniently at all? Above all, how could I go to bed o'nights? Stilts might be very desirable, but only for occasional use.

—Farrell, *Lectures*.

3

I found him seated on a bench before the door, smoking his pipe in the soft evening sunshine. His cat was purring soberly on the threshold, and his parrot describing some strange evolutions in an iron ring that swung in the centre of his cage. He had been angling all day, and gave me a history of his sport with as much minuteness as a general would talk over his campaign; being particularly animated in relating the manner in which he had taken a large trout, which had completely tasked all his skill and wariness, and which he had sent as a trophy to mine hostess of the inn.

—Washington Irving, *The Angler.*

4

There is nothing so horrible as languid study—when you sit looking at the clock, wishing the time was over, or that somebody would call on you and put you out of your misery. The only way to read with any efficacy is to read so heartily that dinner-time comes two hours before you expected it. To sit with your Livy before you, and hear the geese cackling that saved the Capitol; and to see with your own eyes the Carthaginian sutlers gathering up the rings of the Roman knights after the battle of Cannae, and heaping them into bushels; and to be so intimately present at the actions you are reading of, that when anybody knocks at the door, it will take you two or three seconds to determine whether you are in your own study, or in the plains of Lombardy, looking at Hannibal's weather-beaten face, and admiring the splendour of his single eye—this is the only kind of study which is not tiresome; and almost the only kind which is not useless; this is knowledge which gets into the system, and which a man carries about like his limbs, without perceiving that it is extraneous, weighty, and inconvenient.—Sidney Smith.

PRACTICE 4. Developing a Topic Sentence

Select two of the following topic sentences. Keeping in mind the key of each one, write an effective paragraph.

1. In the train opposite me sat the oddest-looking man I have ever seen.
2. My grandfather is an extraordinary man.
3. The Gordons' living-room (or any other room) is attractive.
4. The lake front by moonlight was a beautiful sight.
5. At a glance I knew I should like the cottage.
6. If you watch children at the age of three playing you can expect to have a good laugh.
7. My dinner last night came from many parts of the world.
8. A traveller must become accustomed to all sorts of inconveniences.
9. Shall I ever forget Victoria (or any other place)!
10. I have not always liked reading (skating, swimming, or any other thing in which you get keen pleasure now.)

CLINCHER SENTENCE

After driving home his idea in the paragraph, a writer may clinch it in the last sentence by restating tersely and vigorously the point of the paragraph.

Paragraphs illustrating topic sentences and clincher sentences:

1

Clearly, there is no need of bringing on wars in order to breed heroes. Civilized life affords plenty of opportunies for heroes and for a better kind than war or any other savagery has ever produced. Moreover, none but lunatics would set a city on fire in order to give opportunities for heroism to firemen, or introduce the cholera or yellow fever to give physicians and nurses opportunity for practising disinterested devotion, or condemn thousands of people to extreme poverty in order that some well-to-do persons might practise a beautiful charity. It is equally crazy to advocate war on the ground that it is a school for heroes.[1]

---

[1]*From Eliot's* Five American Contributions to Civilization *by permission of the publishers,* **D. Appleton-Century Company.**

2

A foolish consistency is the hobgoblin of little minds, adored by little statesmen and philosophers and divines. With consistency a great soul has simply nothing to do. He may as well concern himself with the shadow on the wall. Speak what you think now in hard words, and to-morrow speak what to-morrow thinks in hard words again, though it contradicts everything you said to-day.—"Ah, so you shall be sure to be misunderstood."—"It it so bad, then to be misunderstood?" Pythagoras was misunderstood, and Socrates, and Jesus, and Luther, and Copernicus, and Galileo, and Newton, and every pure and wise spirit that ever took flesh. To be great is to be misunderstood.

—EMERSON, *Self-Reliance.*

3

To most people the attic is just another place to store old furniture and unused household articles, but I have found it an unbelievably good place to study. For several years I have had a hard time doing homework conscientiously, because, you see, I have a brother and a sister, a dog (very lovable), a canary, two radios, a saxophone-playing neighbour, and company at very unexpected times. Imagine trying to study with all those around! Well. I stood it as long as I could and then rebelled and betook myself to the attic, and all my books and my typewriter went with me. There I actually studied in privacy. Now I wouldn't exchange that big old attic "study" for the most magnificent library there is, because no one wants to go up there but me. The whole family would congregate in our splendid library, if we had one, and they'd see that I got no work done. Although it's not much as far as appearance is concerned, the attic serves as a fine place to study—yes, and to dream also.—PUPIL

Principles of Paragraph Structure

The three principles of paragraph structure are unity, coherence, and emphasis. To be correct and clear, pleasing and forceful, a paragraph must adhere to these basic principles.

A. Unity

Unity means oneness. A paragraph has unity of thought if it sticks to one subject. While planning the paragraph, ask yourself frequently, "Is this on the subject?" If the answer is "No," cross out the detail or example. Likewise when you revise your paragraph, ask, "Have I held to my subject throughout?" If the completed paragraph is unified, you can sum it up in a sentence. If you do not forget your topic sentence and key word you are not likely to lose the unity of your paragraph.

PRACTICE 5. Paragraph Unity

Show that the following paragraphs lack unity of thought:

1

My favourite sport is baseball. Every fair day about a dozen of us go out to Forest Park after school and have a lively game. We knock the ball all over the lot, field it, run bases, and argue until the sun goes down. Then we race home to dinner. When I am reading or am in school, I wear glasses. I attend Jackson High School and am in the ninth grade.—Pupil

Methods of travel and transportation in Toronto have greatly improved. In the time of the early settlers the methods of travel and transportation in the city were very poor indeed. The only ways to travel in those days were by horseback, carriage, and foot. Travelling across the lake was done in sailing vessels, which depended upon the wind for motion. Therefore a trip from Kingston to Toronto was long and tedious. As time passed, the methods became better and better, until the steam engine was invented and put into practical use. A little later the steamship was also invented and used. But these motorized vehicles were yet to be greatly improved. And now we come to the present day with subways and expressways that greatly improve the method of travelling.—PUPIL

A good paragraph must have more than just unity of thought; it must have unity of impression. The impression may be love, hatred, peacefulness, turmoil, grandeur, beauty, solitude, vastness, heat, cold, and so on. A number of different effects may be introduced as long as they combine to form *one* dominant impression.

PRACTICE 6. Unity of Thought and Impression

For each of the following paragraphs, state the main thought and the dominant impression:

1

Nature was asleep. Not a breath rustled the drooping leaves or fanned the heated brow; not a chirp relieved the silence which was enhanced by the drowsy hum of the mysterious insect life. From my seat beneath a shady bush I gazed out over a wide, gently-rolling expanse of prairie backed in the distance by a dark line of trees, bluish in the heat haze which spread a delicate, gauzy film of transparent blue over distant objects. Far across the plain a flash of silver proclaimed the thread of a brook winding its glittering way between grassy banks to the river. The wavering heat-waves rising from the overheated prairie distorted and gave fantastic shapes to the solitary cattle that still persisted in grazing after their companions had sought refuge in the shade from the fiery sun. Their red and white hides gave an added note of colour to the scene which was bathed in the golden glory of the sunlight. The scene was devoid of other life save for a hawk which sailed majestically on "wings unweary" high up in the blue vault of heaven. Ever and anon its cry would come sifting faintly down to earth emphasizing the afternoon silence which had enveloped us in its all-embracing folds. And thus nature slept on that drowsy afternoon.—PUPIL

2

The aspect of this dreary town, half an hour before sunrise one fine morning, when I left it, was as picturesque as it seemed unreal and spectral. It was no matter that the people were not yet out of bed; for if they had all been up and busy, they would have made but little difference in that desert of a place. It was best to see it, without a single figure in the picture; a city of the dead, without one solitary survivor. Pestilence might have ravaged streets, squares, and marketplaces; and sack and seige have ruined the old houses, battered down their doors and windows, and made breaches in their roofs. In one part, a great tower rose into the air; the only landmark in the melancholy view. In another, a prodigious castle, with a moat about it, stood aloof: a sullen city in itself. In the black dungeons of this castle Parisina and her lover were beheaded in the dead of night. The red light, beginning to shine when I looked back upon it, stained its walls without, as they have many a time been stained within in the old days; but for any sign of life they gave, the castle and the city might have been avoided by all human creatures from the moment when the axe went down upon the last of the two lovers.—DICKENS, *Pictures in Italy*.

The use of a single physical point of view is an aid to paragraph unity. If, for example, you are standing directly in front of a building, you should not mention details that describe the windows at the side. Of course, should it be necessary to change the physical point of view so as to make a description complete, as is generally done in describing whole buildings, villages, towns, or cities, you must inform the reader of any change. (Point of view is discussed more fully in Chapter 8.)

Identify the physical point of view in the first paragraph in Practice 6.

PRACTICE 7. Point of View

Write a descriptive paragraph on one of the following topics. Make the physical point of view clear to the reader. Choose the most effective place, or person.

1. The village, the town, or the city in which you live, as it would appear from a high point of view.
2. A stretch of farmland, as seen from a neighbouring hill.
3. A harbour scene, as viewed from the deck of a steamer.
4. A scene on shore, as viewed from a canoe or rowboat.
5. The view from a window of your summer cottage.
6. The school campus on the day of an important rugby game.
7. A view from a bridge.
8. The second Saturday of September in the shoe department of a downtown store.
9. A service station about 4.30 on a Friday afternoon during summer.

B. Coherence

Coherence, literally "hanging together", includes two things: (1) the proper arrangement of the ideas and (2) bridging the gaps between sentences with connectives that show the exact relationship of part to part.

(1) ARRANGEMENT

In building a paragraph or a house, before beginning the actual construction, one needs, materials and also a plan in mind or on paper. When planning, arrange your ideas or points in a natural, sensible order. Sometimes—when you are writing about an experiment or happening, for example—the time order is best; when you are describing a scene or a picture, the space order is best. On other occasions you will find it wise to lead your reader from what he knows to facts you wish to make clear to him. Ideas and examples are often arranged in the order of importance—the best last.

The different sentences that compose a paragraph should follow one another in natural and logical order. If they do not, the attention of the reader is distracted, and he finds it difficult, if not impossible, to keep the thread of the discourse.

Examples of plans and paragraphs:

MY FIRST BIG GAME

Every ball player has his first big game.
> This first experience came to me when the regular pitcher was hurt and
>> I was allowed to replace him.
I was panicky and awkward.
I threw a fast ball in an attempt to fool the batter.
The batter hit the ball out of range of our outfielders.
I was dismissed from the game.

Every ball player has his first big game—I mean, one game among all games which he can look back upon and feel horrible sensations running up and down his spine. To me, this first experience came at the local field when the regular pitcher was struck by a line drive. There was no one else to put in. I was an outfielder, but, like many outfielders, I thought I was a better pitcher. I was sent in; immediately the demon panic seized me. I felt all arms and legs. I threw a few warm-up pitches, but instead of feeling better I felt worse. The ball seemed as big as a grapefruit. My hat was too tight, my pants too loose, and my arm as stiff and cold as an icicle. "Batter up!" I thought, "A fast ball; I'll fool him!" Well, I didn't fool him. The ball sailed over my head, over the head of the second baseman, and coyly out of range of the picturesque epithets of the outfielders—and out I came!—PUPIL

ON DOORS

There are many ways of opening a door.
> The waiter carrying a supper-tray
> The housewife before a book agent or pedlar
> The footman in a wealthy home
> The dentist's maid
> **The nurse after a baby is born**

There are many ways of opening doors. There is the cheery push of the elbow with which the waiter shoves open the kitchen door when he bears in your tray of supper. There is the suspicious and tentative withdrawal of a door before the unhappy book agent or pedlar. There is the genteel and carefully modulated recession with which footmen swing wide the oaken barriers of the great. There is the sympathetic and awful silence of the dentist's maid who opens the door into the operating room and, without speaking, implies that the doctor is ready for you. There is the brisk cataclysmic opening of a door when the nurse comes in, very early in the morning—"It's a boy!"

—CHRISTOPHER MORLEY, *On Doors.*

(2) CONNECTIVES

It is not enough that the sentences of a paragraph follow one another in proper order; the connection of each with the preceding context must be made clear and unmistakable.

A steel concrete, or wooden bridge joins the two banks of a river; a word bridge joins two sentences or paragraphs and keeps the reader's thought in the path the writer or speaker wishes him to take. Taine, speaking of connective words and phrases, says, "The art of writing is the art of using hooks and eyes."

Useful bridges, or, to change the figure, useful hooks and eyes are *this, that, these, those, such,* and *same,* personal pronouns, repeated nouns, synonyms, adverbs, conjunctions, and connective phrases. Some of these expressions carry the idea forward; most of them look backward.

The repeated word is called an "echo word."

FOR A GOOD PARAGRAPH USE CONNECTIVES TO RELATE THE SENTENCES TO EACH OTHER.

To add ideas use: *and, moreover, further, furthermore, also, likewise, similarly, too, in like manner, again, in the same way, besides.*   These words are plus signs.

To introduce statements opposing, negative, or limiting in some way the preceding statements use: *but, nevertheless, otherwise, on the other hand, conversely, on the contrary, however, yet, still.*   These words are minus signs.

To show time relation use: *then, now, somewhat later, presently thereupon, thereafter, eventually, at the same time, meanwhile.*

To indicate order use: *next, in the second place, to begin with, finally, secondly, in conclusion, first.*

To show space relation use: *to the right, in the distance, straight ahead, at the left.*

To introduce illustrations use: *for instance, for example.*

To indicate a consequence or conclusion use: *hence, consequently, thus, so, for this reason, accordingly, therefore, as a result, it follows that.*

To indicate a repetition of the idea use: *briefly, that is to say, in fact, indeed, in other words.*

To compare use: *similarly, likewise.*

When the thoughts are very closely related, no connective is required.

PRACTICE 8. Selecting Word Bridges

The following paragraph is a good example of effective arrangement in description. Select the connectives used to show space relation.

From the top of Notre Dame, Montreal, is certainly to be had a prospect upon which, but for his fluttered nerves and trembling muscles and troubled perspiration, the traveller might well look back with delight, and, as it is, must behold with wonder. So far as the eye reaches, it dwells only upon what is magnificent. All the features of that landscape are grand. Below you spreads the city, which has less that is really mean in it than any other city of our continent, and which is ennobled by stately civic edifices, adorned by tasteful churches, and skirted by full-foliaged avenues of mansions and villas. Beyond it rises a beautiful mountain, green with woods and gardens to its crest, and flanked on the east by an endless fertile plain, and on the west by another expanse, through which the Ottawa rushes, turbid and dark, to its confluence with the St. Lawrence. Then these two mighty streams, commingled, flow past the city, lighting up the vast champaign country to the south, where, upon the utmost southern verge, as on the northern, rise the cloudy summits of far-off mountains.—WILLIAM DEAN HOWELLS, *Their Silver Wedding Journey.*

By permission of the heirs of William Dean Howells.

PRACTICE 9. Supplying Word Bridges

Supply suitable bridge words to give the following paragraph coherence.

Every girl should learn how to make her own dresses because of the numerous advantages in knowing how to sew.   There is a great saving in money, which she can invest in more materials for new dresses.   A girl likes to have an extensive wardrobe.   Nobody likes to have a dress that is duplicated by almost everyone she meets.   In making one's own clothes, this danger is lessened. If a girl is clever, she can design her frocks herself, and so have exclusive models with an individual touch.   An advantage of sewing is that it teaches patience, an admirable virtue.   The girl who has learned to sew well has a substantial advantage over her helpless sister—PUPIL

PRACTICE 10. Using Word Bridges

On two of the following topic sentences plan and write paragraphs. Stick to your subjects.   Make your development full and complete. Use as many word bridges as are needed.   Underscore all conjunctions and connective phrases used to bridge the gaps between sentences.

1. Just then I heard a strange noise outside my window.
2. I fished a long time before I caught anything.
3. He showed great courage that time.
4. You can't get something for nothing.
5. Covering a book is a simple operation if it is done correctly.
6. One night while I was staying at Lake George (or another place) I had a strange experience.
7. There are books and plays that should have poison labels on them to warn us of their contents.
8. During a summer vacation at Lake Mahopac (or another place) one may enjoy many sports.
9. A place of interest I visited this summer was the Parliamentary Library (or another).
10. What you know after studying depends on the way you study.
11. My favourite movie actor is James Mason (or another).
12. Winter is a very enjoyable season.
13. Although some of us do not think so, Latin helps to prepare us for later years.
14. The Y.M.C.A. benefits every boy that joins.
15. He tramped in, where a surprise awaited him.
16. Eat at your table as you would eat at the table of a king.
17. Practice makes perfect.

18. Everyone ought to read *The Kon-Tiki Expedition* by Thor Heyerdahl (or another book).
19. Owning a dog has its disadvantages.
20. There are several reasons why I have chosen detective work (or another occupation) for my life work.

C. Emphasis

Emphasis requires that significant matters stand out and unimportant details keep in the background. The beginning and the ending of a paragraph, story, magazine article, or book are especially important. First impressions are lasting. and the ending is longest remembered.

If you have run a hundred-yard race, you know that it is important to be off with the crack of the pistol and to cross the finish line at top speed. To make a paragraph emphatic place the important ideas near the beginning and the end and give them the most space.

Some workmen when the quitting hour arrives just drop their tools and run. Others—bank clerks, for example—complete the work of the day before going home. There are likewise two ways of ending a paragraph—just stopping, and finishing it. A good way to end a paragraph is to close it with the most important sentence.

The chief devices of emphasis are (a) a forceful introduction, (b) an effective conclusion, (c) purposeful repetition, (d) examples and illustrations, (e) comparison and contrast, (f) climactic arrangement. and (g) good proportion. Some of these have been considered; others will be mentioned later.

PRACTICE 11. Studying Paragraphs

Examine each of the following paragraphs and answer these questions about it:

1. Has it a topic sentence? What?
2. Does it show evidence of planning? What?
3. Does the paragraph stick to its subject? Prove.
4. Are word bridges used? What?
5. Are the most important ideas placed near the beginning and the end and given most space?

1

With the crowding of people into the cities has come a greater appreciation of nature and increased interest in the *Nature Magazine*. Although we city dwellers are deprived of the joys of the fields and woods, we may turn the pages of the *Nature Magazine* and see the same sights, hear the same sounds, and smell the same fragrances as we could in the wide open spaces. Reading the *Nature Magazine* is like spending a holiday in the great outdoors; watching the wild ducks in their flight through the clear, blue sky; drinking in the pure air of the forests while sitting motionless on a rock; and watching and waiting, scarcely breathing, while the timid wild creatures carry on their daily life. What finer sentiment could be inspired in children than the love of living and growing things?—PUPIL

2

How much of our language do dogs understand? Perhaps a good deal more than we generally imagine. In learning a foreign language a person arrives at a stage where most of what the foreign people say is broadly intelligible to him, and yet he cannot express himself. Very young children understand a great deal before they are able to express themselves in words. Even horses—and horses are incomparably less intelligent than dogs—understand a complete vocabulary of orders. May not a dog of ability enter to some extent into the meaning of spoken language, even though he may never be able to use it?—PUPIL

PRACTICE 12. Studying Paragraphs

Find in a magazine article, a newspaper editorial, or a book two unusually good paragraphs and show that they are excellent. Has each paragraph a topic sentence? Unity? A plan? Word bridges? Emphasis?

METHODS OF PARAGRAPH DEVELOPMENT

Paragraph building is the development of the topic (usually the topic sentence) in some logical and natural manner.

After writing a topic sentence ask yourself the questions: "How?" "Why?" "What?" "What of it?" "What is it like or unlike?" "What example or illustration will make my point clear?" "How do I know?" If you know enough about the subject to write a paragraph, these questions will call forth particulars, details, examples, illustrations, instances, comparisons, contrasts, reasons, and results, which are, like the boards, stone, shingles, and beams of a house, the material out of which a paragraph is built.

The way to develop a paragraph depends, naturally, on what you have to say. You may picture the *details* of how your mile relay team won a close race, give *examples* of the spectators' behaviour at the meet, *compare* the differences in strategy between running the mile relay and the half-mile relay, *define* "sprint," or give your *reasons* for thinking your track team will win the county competitions.

SUPPLYING DETAILS

One way of developing a paragraph is by adding details. Paragraphs thrive on details.

Specific details which often answer the questions "What?" and "How?" may be used to develop or explain a general statement made in the topic sentence. Details make more vivid a word picture of a person, place, thing, or event. If you make a general statement that Helen is well dressed, you may make the picture clearer by describing her clothing, the colour scheme, the accessories, and the neatness and appropriateness of her outfit. It's the specific facts that put the paragraph across.

1

Many of the possessions in our family help me to know more about my ancestors. There is the old oak chest which stands in Mother's room. It was built by my grandfather, who took pride in his workmanship. In the den there are old muskets and rifles which revive the interests of my other grandfather, for not only are there several of them but they are remarkably well preserved. On our mantel there still ticks away a large clock that must be much older than my father. In the china closet there are many pieces of hand-painted china of which my mother is very proud, for they are the work of her mother's sister, and a fine example of the china-painter's art they are, too. I am myself proud of these family heirlooms, and of my ancestors, who must have been fine craftsmen.—PUPIL

1. What is the topic sentence?
2. What details are used to develop the topic?
3. What is the key word that gives unity to these details?
4. What makes the last sentence an effective clincher sentence?

2

The Frisby House, for that was the name of the hotel, was a place of fallen fortunes, like the town.   It was now given up to labourers and partly ruinous. At dinner there was the ordinary display of what is called in the West a two-bit house: the tablecloth checked red and white, the plague of flies, the wire hencoops over the dishes, the great variety and invariable vileness of the food, and the rough, coatless men devouring it in silence.   In our bedroom the stove would not burn, though it would smoke; and while one window would not open, the other would not shut.   There was a view on a bit of empty road, a few dark houses, a donkey wandering in its shadow on the slope, and a blink of sea, with a tall ship lying anchored in the moonlight.   All about that dreary inn frogs sang their ungainly chorus.—Stevenson

1. What is the topic sentence?
2. What details are used to develop the topic?

PRACTICE 13. Developing a Topic by Details

Choose two of the following topic sentences. Using details, prepare an oral paragraph based on one; develop the other into a written paragraph. Build clear, concise, varied sentences. Make certain that each paragraph has a strong clincher sentence.

A. 1. My dog (or other pet) shows in various ways that he recognizes me.
   2. Learning how to dance was (or was not) an ordeal for me.
   3. He's the sort of fellow that makes a worth-while friend.
   4. Our outing was spoiled at the start (or at the very end).
   5. The beaver is nature's construction engineer.
   6. Here's how to escape minding the baby (washing the dishes, mowing the lawn, or some other task).
   7. There are many advantages in being tall (or short).
   8. Bathing a pet can be a humorous experience.
   9. An impressive scene I observed during the summer holidays.
  10. My first-aid kit saved the day.
  11. Mr. Brown has an ideal back yard.

B. 1. When I was preparing for school this morning, everything went wrong.
   2. Yesterday I decided to dissect my alarm clock (the radio, the engine of our car, a lock, my harmonica, or something else).
   3. It is not difficult to make a marionette (hat, birdhouse, brass box, dress, model airplane, camp bed, shelter in the woods, apple pie, or something else).
   4. If I had fifty dollars, I know exactly how I would spend it.
   5. The most interesting room in the school is——.   (Supply the name of the room you like best).

6. In recent years many advances have been made in ——. (Supply the name of any industry, profession, or science in which you are interested: farming, advertising, raising chickens, protecting trees, irrigation, medicine, chemistry, physics, aviation.)
7. There are several ways in which I could improve my handwriting.
8. The storm did considerable damage in our neighbourhood.
9. The effects of the drought were visible everywhere on the farm.
10. Annabelle is a very superior cat. (You may substitute the name of any other animal.)
11. I had an ideal summer vacation.
12. The worst storm ever to hit our town struck on a quiet July afternoon.

SUPPLYING EXAMPLES

To make an explanation clear or to prove a point, give examples or illustrations. You may discuss fully one example or refer briefly to several. If you say, "The twentieth century has seen great progress in science," you may prove your point by discussing in detail one discovery such as the radio, or by briefly mentioning several—the radio, television, air conditioning, and others.

Paragraph developed by ONE example:

It is hard to be stern with a baby, yet it so often seems necessary. Let me give you an example from personal experience. Little George refuses to eat his soup. First I try cajolery, but when this fails, patience dies, and I sternly command that George partake of the delicious, life-giving substance or else—! He immediately assumes a wilted air and half-heartedly picks up the spoon. After stirring the soup awhile, he wails, "I can't eat—I—I fink I'm sick." Remembering that he usually likes this kind of soup, I think that he may be ill. After all, a baby is such a delicate bit of humanity. Soon enough my sympathies vanish when he asks if he can't have dessert now, please. I am angry because I have been fooled into feeling sorry for him, and attempt once more to force him to eat the soup. Alas, the end is always the same: he shrinks down into the seat and begins to sob, gradually working up to the most heartbreaking cries. As the tears stream down his face (and roll off into the soup), he looks so utterly woebegone that I haven't the heart to scold any more. Rather, I do everything in my power to placate him. How could anyone be stern after such a demonstration?—PUPIL

Paragraph developed by SEVERAL examples:

"Next" has a variety of meanings. To the small child sitting in the waiting room of a dentist's office that word means that his hour of torture has come. How different the customer in a crowded store feel when the "next" is meant for her. Generally she heaves a great sigh of relief. In the classroom that monosyllable always causes the pupil who is unprepared to have inward qualms. When the same pupil, however, is playing a game, "next" carries momentary joy with it.   To the boy who is seeking a position, "next" may have either of two meanings.   To the fellow who has already been interviewed, the word sounds cruel and unreasonable, for it means that he has failed to "land the job." But if he is the next to be interviewed, his hopes rise and his heart goes pitapat. What pictures are called up by the word "next!"—Pupil

PRACTICE 14.   Developing a Topic by Examples

Select two of the following topic sentences, or compose two of your own, making sure that they are narrow in scope, clear, and interesting. By giving examples develop one sentence into a good written paragraph.

A. 1. Canadian high school students are a mirror of the latest American fads.
   2. The subway (or bus) is as entertaining as a motion picture.
   3. Television has helped me to understand people in other countries (or some other subject).
   4. The radio (or television) has programs to satisfy every taste.
   5. The human hands are man's most remarkable tools.
   6. A practical joker soon gets a dose of his own medicine.
   7. Plastics administer to our everyday needs.
   8. Much information about a country can be gleaned from its postage stamps.
   9. Although friction is a cause of waste in all machines, it is put to good use in many.
  10. Truth is stranger than fiction.
  11. Fortunes have been made in peculiar ways.

B. 1. A chain is no stronger than its weakest link.   (Substitute any other proverb.)
   2. Chemistry (or another subject) has many practical applications (or is the most useful subject I have studied).
   3. Travel is becoming swifter each day.
   4. Successful work requires good equipment.
   5. Grown-up people really ought to be more careful.
   6. I have found from experience that the world can be seen and appreciated from my own doorstep.
   7. "Where there's a will there's a way" is illustrated by the lives of many poor boys who have become famous.
   8. We find the most colourful jewels in Woolworth's.
   9. There are many disturbers of the peace.
  10. There are mind poisons, just as there are body poisons.
  11. The endeavour of education to keep pace with the rapidly growing ignorance appears to be quite hopeless, since there are year by year so many new things of which to be ignorant.

USING COMPARISON AND CONTRAST

If you were describing a tiger to a small child who had never seen one, you would compare it with a cat. If you were describing how a child was educated in a dictatorship you would contrast his education with a child's schooling in a democracy. In describing to boys and girls the appearance of the human brain, one doctor compared it to a cauliflower. The doctor was trying to explain the appearance of something unfamiliar by showing that it is like something familiar to his audience. Comparisons (showing how two things are like or different) and contrasts (showing how two things differ) help to clarify our ideas. All the points on one side may be balanced against all the points on the other side, or the two objects may be compared a point at a time.

1

I prefer an apple to any other fruit. Unlike the orange, no bitter peel has to be stripped from the exterior. The orange conceals surprises for the unwary; one is liable to be sprayed with sticky juice. The pear, on being bitten into, contrives to make your chin a background for a flood. The disposal of the plum's slippery stone may cause embarrassment. The peach, unless one pays handsomely, is either too ripe or too hard, and only Merlin can detect whether it is fit for eating or not. But an apple takes to being bitten gracefully. The teeth sink into it smoothly, like a dagger into flesh. The juice behaves well, and gliding between the teeth, nectar-like, causes the saliva to flow freely. The greenish-white flesh resists pleasantly the pressure of the jaw. And the apple is no hypocrite. One glimpse at its hearty, flushed, honest surface tells the true story of its interior. One can eat it with confidence, knowing that one's face will not be smeared uncomfortably. Take the apple in the hand, a finger in each end, and when you have stripped the flesh from the core, the disposal problem is simple. The apple is the king of fruits, and the idea that it was the apple which caused Adam's and Eve's downfall is a vile slander circulated by crafty orange, peach, and plum growers.—PUPIL

1. What is the topic sentence?

2. With what fruits does the author of the paragraph contrast the apple? In what way does the apple differ from each of these fruits?

3. What comparisons can you find in the paragraph?

2

It is surprising how fighting fish differ in their manner of attacking the bait and in the times at which they bite. The bass will bite at any time he pleases. "As moody as a prima donna," says one expert, "as wary as a lynx, and fighting to the last gasp is the true black bass." He has a habit of mumbling the bait—that is running with the bait held in the front of his mouth, so that if you try to set the hook, you'll pull it right out of his mouth. Once this happens to a bass, he rarely bites again. But with the trout it's a different story.   The best time to fish for him is in the early morning or at night.   He rises lazily to the bait and sucks it down; then the fun begins.   When you have seventeen pounds of mad trout at the end of your line, there's no time to think of anything else.   One big fellow I hooked had his eye set on a distant mountain and seemed quite determined to reach it, when suddenly he turned about and came racing back for something he had forgotten.   You have to work fast with a full-grown muskellunge too.   He hits the bait as soon as it strikes the water, and his thirty to sixty pounds hit hard.   Once you hook a muskellunge it takes between forty minutes and an hour and forty minutes to end the argument.   All three of these fish, but particularly the bass, have a way of shooting out of the water and shaking themselves so that they often rip the hook out of their mouths.—PUPIL

1. What is the topic sentence?

2. What comparisons are made?

3. What contrasts are pointed out?

PRACTICE 15. Developing a Topic by Comparison and Contrast

Select two of the following topic sentences or compose two appropriate ones of your own.   By comparing or contrasting, develop one into a vivid oral paragraph and the other into a pointed written paragraph.

A. 1. It is safer to live in the country than in the city (or vice versa).
   2. There is a vast difference between a house and a home.
   3. Understanding is better than tolerance.
   4. The microscope has contributed more to man's progress than the telescope.
   5. A brunette should wear different colours from those worn by a blonde.
   6. Boys are better sports than girls (or vice versa).
   7. I would rather have a canoe than a rowboat. (Substitute any other possessions—a hampster than a white mouse, for example).
   8. It is more fun to be a guest than a host (or vice versa).
   9. I prefer a game of skill to a game of chance.
   10. My little brother (or sister) is more grown-up than I was at his age.

B. 1. My best friend looks different from the way he looked when I first met him.
   2. Human life has often been compared with the course of a stream. (Read Wordsworth's sonnet "It is not to be thought of . . .")
   3. I would rather join the Air Cadets than the Navy Cadets (or vice versa).
   4. Many games we play are like those our parents played as children.
   5. I like old clothes better than new ones (or vice versa).
   6. Hot water heat is preferable to steam heat.

7. A dog is a better pet than a cat (or vice versa).

8. I prefer to live in a private house rather than in an apartment (or vice versa).

9. The Diesel engine is similar to the gasoline engine.

10. The metric system is superior to the English system of weights and measures.

USING CAUSE AND EFFECT (GIVING REASONS)

A common way of building a paragraph is by starting with an assertion and then defending it by giving reasons or results—that is, causes or effects.

1

It has been estimated that more coal has been wasted than mined. This is due to several things. Mine owners take only the coal which can be mined easily, and in doing this they sometimes make it impracticable to return and get the rest because of caving in of shafts and tunnels. Much has been left for pillars and roof supports, and much more wasted as coal dust. Poor tools make it difficult to cut the coal economically. Mines have been opened for which there is little need. Factories waste valuable by-products because of inadequate machinery. Coke-making companies do not always obtain all the by-products. We waste coal through careless firing in our homes and in heating plants. Power is the very cornerstone of our industrial prosperity, and with the present wasteful methods of using fuel it will not last many generations[1].

—Maude Martin and Clyde Cooper, *The United States at Work.*

1. What is the topic sentence?

2. What reasons are given?

Novels certainly should not be illustrated. What is more disappointing than to see a picture of the heroine? The author may have made the lady gloriously beautiful, lithe, and gracefully slender; but you discover that her mouth is too big, that she looks queer and plump in the old-fashioned clothes and is much too stiff and ungainly to be lithe. If you glance too casually at another picture, you will mistake the hero for the villain. Certainly that odd little individual isn't the handsome, broad-shouldered hero! You've all had this experience, I'm sure; so you'll agree with me when I say we should have a new kind of prohibition—of illustrations in novels.—Pupil

1. What is the topic sentence? Clincher sentence?

2. What reason is given?

3. What comparisons make the paragraph more interesting?

---

[1]*Reprinted by permission of the publisher, D. C. Heath and Company.*

PRACTICE 16. Developing a Topic by Cause and Effect (Reasons)

Select one topic from each of the following groups. If you wish, you may choose a topic on why we should not do something, or why you dislike something. By giving reasons build one convincing oral paragraph and another good written paragraph. Speak and write in sentences.

Why we should

A.
1. have outdoor hobbies
2. cultivate more than one good friend.
3. be proud of our city (or state)
4. have a student court in high school
5. have homework
6. have coeducational high schools
7. study the customs of foreign peoples
8. learn to play musical instruments

Why I like

1. green (substitute your favourite colour)
2. to build model airplanes
3. a specific radio or television program
4. biology (or another subject)
5. a friend of mine
6. to entertain my friends in my home
7. bicycling (or some other sport)
8. to read travel books
9. to go shopping
10. sport clothes

B.
1. Novels should be illustrated.
2. The day was completely spoiled.
3. Advertising controls the very lives of people.
4. I soon discovered that it was wise to do my homework every day.
5. He did not receive his driving license.
6. Crash!
7. There was a sudden grinding of brakes, and then the car stopped dead.
8. The advantage of not being illiterate depends finally on the literature a people produces and reads.
9. The tabloid newspapers are a menace.
10. Liberty ends where law ends.
11. Every boy should learn how to do simple carpentry work.
12. Stamp-collecting (or another hobby) seems to me an ideal hobby.
13. Fear is the greatest enemy of man.
14. If the keynote of a successful life is service, homemaking (or another occupation or profession) is an occupation second to none.
15. Everyone should know how to cook. (You may substitute any other skill or activity.)
16. Why I decided to go to university.
17. Why I decided to ——.

18. Something should be done about the noise in study halls. (or about another school problem—homework, courtesy, assemblies, longer lunch periods, student court, or afterschool dances, for example.)

19. Our town's laws are unfair to dogs and dog owners. (Or take a stand on some other town regulation.)

20. I want to spend my summer vacation at the shore (in the north woods; in the mountains; right here at home; working).

USING DEFINITIONS

Often, to avoid misunderstanding, it is necessary to define. In explaining a term, one may supplement the dictionary by telling what the term includes and excludes or what it is and is not, by comparing or contrasting it with another term, or by giving an illustration.

1

First, then, of the distinction between the classes who work and the classes who play. Of course we must agree upon a definition of these terms—work and play—before going further. Now, roughly, not with vain subtlety of definition, but for plain use of the words, play is an exertion of body and mind, made to please ourselves, and with no determined end; and work is a thing done because it ought to be done, and with a determined end.

—JOHN RUSKIN, *The Crown of Wild Olive*.

2

The outstanding characteristic of American manufacturing development, distinguishing it from the industrial revolution which went on in other countries, was the utilization of the idea of standardized mass production with the help of automatic machinery. By standardized production is meant the production of innumerable articles or parts of articles exactly alike. Machines were built to do the work of making these articles. This process speeded up and cheapened production, while at the same time it gave a drab sameness to American life. The business genius of Henry Ford was the first to employ this principle on a wide scale in the production of his famous Model T automobile. In the organization of production Ford also adopted the principle of controlling all the various stages of production. He purchased coal and iron mines, railroads, steamships, in an attempt to control all the processes and do all the work involved in turning out an automobile from raw material to a finished product.—HAMM, BOURNE, AND BENTON, *A Unit History of the United States*[1].

[1]*By permission of the publisher, D. C. Heath and Company.*

1. What is the topic sentence?

2. What example is used in explaining standardized mass production?

PRACTICE 17. Developing a Topic by Definition

As if you were answering an examination question "What is —— ?" explain, in a paragraph for each, two of the following terms. Make your definitions clear, complete, and easy to understand. Include one or more illustrations. Use reference books to supplement your own knowledge.

1. Success (or Failure)
2. Ambition (or Laziness)
3. Optimism (or Pessimism)
4. Fear (or Courage)
5. Hero
6. Snob
7. "Square"
8. Beatnik
9. Tact
10. Charity
11. Integrity
12. Superstition
13. Culture
14. Libel
15. Propaganda
16. Patriotism
17. Government Subsidy
18. Leisure
19. Lobby
20. Atomic Fallout
21. Cyclotron
22. Daylight-saving Time
23. Tabloid Newspaper
24. Snorkel
25. Hybrid Corn
26. Radar
27. Radical, Conservative, or Liberal
28. Socialism, Democracy, Totalitarianism, or Communism
29. Sprint or Zone Defence (or a term from a sport in which you are interested)

TWO OR MORE METHODS

Commonly two or more methods are combined in the development of a paragraph. Details may be supported by examples; a definition may include details, illustrations, comparison, and contrast.

Each of the following paragraphs employs two methods of development. What are they?

1

A myth, in its simplest definition, is a story with a meaning attached to it other than it seems to have at first, and the fact that it has such a meaning is generally marked by some of its circumstances being extraordinary, or, in the common use of the word, unnatural. Thus, if I tell you that Hercules killed a water-serpent in the lake of Lerna, and if I mean, and you understand, nothing more than that fact, the story, whether true or false, is not a myth. But if, by telling you this, I mean that Hercules purified the stagnation of many streams from deadly miasmata, my story, however simple, is a true myth.

RUSKIN—*The Queen of the Air.*

2

An idiom is a group of words with a specialized meaning. When we say, "How do you do?" we don't mean what the words seem to say. We mean something like "Hello." When we look at the separate words that make up an idiom, we are puzzled, for the words don't seem to mean what they ordinarily mean. We can understand expressions like *by and large, all in all, right away,* and *just as soon* if we look at them as wholes, but if we take them apart, the words suddenly become meaningless. The idiom can only be studied as a unit. Because idioms are fairly common in all languages and because they are so puzzling in construction, they provide pitfalls for persons trying to learn a language.

PARAGRAPHS WITH HUMOUR

A short humorous paragraph is fun to write and fun to read. A funny experience, tongue-in-cheek advice, a light anecdote are perfect subjects for the humorous paragraph.

There is an art to eating watermelon. Though the watermelon tastes good by any method, it tastes twice as good when properly eaten. The setting is important: preferably the shade of a friendly tree on a hot and humid day. Eliminate all unnecessary encumbrances. Never use a fork or a spoon. Avoid a plate or a pan. Let there be just you, the tree, and the watermelon. Grasp the melon slice with both hands and place the face, with the mouth open to its maximum, into the delicious red heart. Sounds like "slurp" and "slosh" should blend with exclamations like "Mmmmmm!" Let the numerous seeds shoot off in all directions and fall where they will. Eat and drink your fill. Relaxation and simplicity are the secret of successful watermelon eating.—PUPIL

PRACTICE 18. Writing Humorous Paragraphs

Try your skill at writing a humorous paragraph using one of the following topics or another approved by your teacher.

1. The lost art of —— (You name it.) 2. Dogs are people. 3. Rain on a vacation. 4. Our puppy's first night. 5. Spectator types. 6. An unforgettable character. 7. What a good baby sitter must know.

PRACTICE 19. Studying Paragraph Development

Clip from the editorial page of a newspaper or from a magazine five well-developed paragraphs. If the topic sentence is expressed, underscore it; otherwise write it out. Explain how each paragraph is developed.

PRACTICE 20. Planning a Paragraph

What method or methods of paragraph development would you consider appropriate for each of the following topic sentences?

1. Sailboats are more fun than motorboats.
2. There is a fascinating view from the study-hall window.
3. I enjoy reading historical novels more than any other type.
4. The game fell to pieces in the ninth inning.
5. Holding a part-time job is good experience.
6. Of historical figures I have always greatly admired———.
7. Rainy days can be fun.
8. Childhood habits have a way of sticking.
9. I believe a house should have a great many windows.
10. Every high school student should learn to type.
11. The voting age should be lowered to eighteen.
12. Passengers as well as the driver have a responsibility.
13. There are three ways to study.
14. Take my advice and never attend a tea.
15. Television can perform a real public service.
16. The need for driver education is all too apparent.
17. The pedestrian isn't always right.
18. The farmer has all the comforts of the city and much more.
19. It is safer to live in the country than in the city (or vice versa).
20. There is a vast difference between a house and a home.

PRACTICE 21. Building a Paragraph

Using one of the following topics or topic sentences as a foundation, build a paragraph. First gather material, searching especially for examples, illustrations, comparisons, pictures, and other concrete support of the topic sentence. Ask, "How?" "Why?" "What?" "What of it?" "What is it like or unlike?" "What example or illustration will make my point clear?" and "How do I know?" Then write the paragraph, revise thoroughly and carefully, and copy it neatly before handing it in.

A. 1. There is one like him in every class.
   2. There are some people who think cats aren't intelligent, but I say they are.
   3. Everyone should learn how to swim.
   4. That was the busiest half hour of my life.
   5. Forgetfulness sometimes leads to much embarrassment.
   6. A hike through the woods is interesting.
   7. Clean-up week is essential for the safety of homes and lives.
   8. Many poor boys have become great men.
   9. During the month the moon presents different appearances to an observer.

10. All is not gold that glitters.

11. The grounds were liberally fringed with spectators, who had never before witnessed a scene so thrilling.

12. To be successful in any branch of business, one must be interested in one's work.

13. There are many things one can do in case of fire.

14. Prompt and intelligent first aid, deftly tendered, is a life-saving accomplishment when accidents occur on the road.

15. People often make fun of "stargazers," but they would be very badly off if it were not for the stargazers.

16. A hunter needs patience, endurance, and skill.

B. 1. Kitchen gadgets.
2. Hobbies and health.
3. A recent scientific discovery.
4. A recent advance in health.
5. College entrance requirements.
6. Teen-age drivers.
7. This year's automobiles.
8. Amateur weather forecasting.
9. Stargazing.
10. Exhibiting livestock.
11. Bargain hunting.
12. Buying a dress (or suit).
13. Commuting.
14. Learning to dance.
15. Children's programs on television.
16. A baseball immortal.
17. Football scholarships.
18. Cramming for examinations.
19. The value of discipline.

EFFECTIVE PARAGRAPHS

The following paragraphs should be studied carefully for construction, diction, and style, and then used as models for paragraphs of your own construction.

1. STORMING A WASPS' NEST

It is quite a sight to see a party of boys preparing to storm a wasps' nest. They go on an evening when all these fiery creatures are quiet in their holes, with their candle and lantern, their gunpowder made into a paste and fixed on the end of a stick, and with a spade to dig out the nest; and all armed with green boughs, ready if any of the wasps escape to beat them down. They light their gunpowder, and hold it to the hole. It burns hissing away in a stream of fiery sparks like a rocket, which, penetrating down to the nest, fill it with sulphurous fumes, and suffocate the wasps. A sod is clapped in the hole to keep in the fumes for a time; and when they think their purpose is effected, they dig out the nest. Then you may see every boy stand on his guard, with anxious looks and elevated bough, ready to defend himself, if it prove, as it often does, that they have not destroyed but merely irritated the wasps, and the wrathful insects rush out to take vengeance on the assailants. Hark! there is a hum!—the wasps rush out!—the cowards fly—some screaming amain, with a host of angry insects rushing after them, hissing in their ears, tangling in their hair, darting into their bosoms, and stinging them in a dozen places.

One brave boy stands at his post, waves his bough gallantly, defends himself stoutly, beats down the insects in clouds, and escapes without a single sting, bearing the nest, finally, away in triumph on the spade.—WILLIAM HOWITT, *The Boy's Country-Book.*

2. THE OLD ANGLER AT HOME

On parting with the old angler, I inquired after his place of abode, and happening to be in the neighbourhood of the village a few evenings afterward, I had the curiosity to seek him out. I found him living in a small cottage containing only one room, but a perfect curiosity in its method and arrangement. It was on the skirts of the village, on a green bank a little back from the road, with a small garden in front stocked with kitchen-herbs and adorned with a few flowers. The whole front of the cottage was overrun with a honeysuckle. On the top was a ship for a weather-cock. The interior was fitted up in a truly nautical style, his ideas of comfort and convenience having been acquired in the berthdeck of a man-of-war.

I found him seated on a bench before the door smoking his pipe in the soft evening sunshine. His cat was purring soberly on the threshold, and his parrot describing some strange evolutions in an iron ring that swung in the centre of his cage. He had been angling all day, and gave me a history of his sport with as much minuteness as a general would talk over a campaign, being particularly animated in relating the manner in which he had taken a large trout, which had completely tasked all his skill and wariness.

How comforting it is to see a cheerful and contented old age and to behold a poor fellow like this, after being tempest-tost through life, safely moored in a snug and quiet harbour in the evening of his days! His happiness, however, sprang from within himself, and was independent of external circumstances, for he had that inexhaustible good-nature which is the most precious gift of Heaven, spreading itself like oil over the troubled sea of thought and keeping the mind smooth and equable in the roughest weather.—WASHINGTON IRVING "The Angler" from *The Sketch Book.*

3. JACOB'S LADDER

If ever there was a vile, unnerving, and desperate place in the battle zone, it was the Mesnil end of Jacob's Ladder, among the heavy battery positions, and under perfect enemy observation.

Jacob's Ladder was a long trench, good in parts, stretching from Mesnil with many angles down to Hamel on the River Ancre, requiring flights of stairs at one or two steep places. Leafy bushes and great green and yellow weeds looked into it as it dipped sharply into the green valley by Hamel, and hereabouts the aspect of peace and innocence was yet prevailing. A cow with a crumbled horn, a harvest cart should have been visible here and there. The trenches ahead were curious, and not so pastoral. Ruined houses with rafters sticking out, with half-sloughed plaster and dangling window-frames, perched on a hill-side, bleak and piteous that cloudy morning; half-filled trenches crept along below them by upheaved gardens, telling the story of wild bombardment. Further on was a small chalk cliff, facing the river, with a rambling but remarkable dug-out in it called Kentish Caves. The front line was sculptured over this brow, and descended to the wooded marshes of the Ancre in winding and gluey irregularity. Running across it towards the

German line went the narrow Beaucourt road, and the railway to Miraumont and Bapaume; in the railway bank was a lookout post called the Crow's Nest, with a large periscope, but no one seemed very pleased to see the periscope. South of the Ancre was broad-backed high ground, and on that was a black vapour of smoke and naked tree-trunks or charcoal, an apparition which I found was called Thiepval Wood. The Somme indeed!—EDMUND BLUNDEN, *Undertones of War.*

By permission of the author and the publishers, R. Cobden-Sander, Ltd., London.

4. SINKING OF THE "LUSITANIA"

In the end my father owed his life to the fact that he chose the port side, for he would never have survived in the water. After looking about for a bit he realized that he had no life-belt and went downstairs to get one. Someone (a stewart, I think) gave him a Gieve. He tried to blow it up, but it would not blow, and so he went down to his cabin to get one off his bed, but they had all been taken. Finally he found three "Boddy" belts in his cupboard (the regulation ship's life-belt of that date and a most effective one). He came up on deck again just as the last boat—half empty—was being launched. The *Lusitania* "A" deck was by this time level with the water, and already the boat was about a foot away from the edge of the ship. A woman holding a small child hesitated whether to dare to step over to it. He gave her a shove and sprang after her himself. As the boat drew away, the *Lusitania* slowly sank, and one of her funnels came over to within a few feet of the boat. It seemed as if it must sink with it, but she was sinking by the bow as well as rolling over, and the funnel, passing within a few feet of their heads, sank just beyond them. My father had timed the explosion, and he looked at his watch when the ship disappeared. The whole thing had taken twelve and a half minutes.

VISCOUNTESS RHONDDA, *This Was My World.*

By permission of the publishers, The Macmillan Company of Canada, Limited.

5. THE MUSIC-MAKERS

A stout man with a pink face wears dingy white flannel trousers, a blue coat with a pink handkerchief showing, and a straw hat much too small for him, perched at the back of his head. He plays the guitar. A little chap in white canvas shoes, his face hidden under a felt hat like a broken wing, breathes into a flute and a tall thin fellow, with bursting over-ripe button boots, draws ribbons—long, twisted, streaming ribbons—of tune out of a fiddle. They stand, unsmiling, but not serious, in the broad sunlight opposite the fruit shop; the pink spider of a hand beats the guitar, the little squat hand, with a brass-and-turquoise ring, forces the reluctant flute, and the fiddler's arm tries to saw the fiddle in two.—KATHERINE MANSFIELD, "Bank Holiday" from *The Garden Party.*

By permission of the author's literary agents, Messrs. James B. Pinker & Son.

6.

A number of attempts have been made to provide for individual differences among pupils, two of the most important being classification on the basis of ability (called *homogeneous grouping* by school authorities) and individualized instruction. According to the plan of classifying pupils on the basis of ability, bright pupils are segregated into one class and slower pupils into another. This plan is thought to provide advantages for both groups, and it simplifies, to some extent, the procedure of the teacher. Pupils who learn at a slower rate are not discouraged by unfair contrast with brighter pupils, and the latter will be able to make greater progress. According to the second plan, the teacher tries to adjust assignments to the varying levels of ability. Pupils can read, write, speak, paint, draw, sing, play, construct, and in a variety of ways they give expression to their varying talents. Several methods such as the Dalton, Contract, Block, and Winnetka plans have been worked out in order to allow for these varying abilities. Many schools now use homogeneous grouping and individualized instruction.—WILLIAMSON AND WESLEY, *Principles of Social Science.*

Reprinted by permission of the publisher, D. C. Heath and Company.

For an example of evaluation of paragraph structure, see *The Cruel Sea,* p. 423.

Chapter 4

The Expository Essay

When you have a composition assignment, do you wonder what to write about (or which given subject to choose), how to get started, and how to find enough things to say? This chapter will give you suggestions about choosing a good subject, gathering material, and putting together a clear, readable composition.

A. CHOOSING A GOOD SUBJECT

A good subject for an expository essay is (a) one that interests you, and (b) one that you can make interesting to your readers. Your own experiences, your reading, your observation of people, places, and things, will give you ideas for essays. Are you interested in history, astronomy, atomic energy, baseball, fashions, square dancing, or pottery making? All these subjects contain the germs of possible essay themes. Your part-time job will provide you with half a dozen subjects. If you are a baby sitter, you may write on one of the following: Economic advantages of baby-sitting; How I became a baby sitter; How to "sit" efficiently; What I learned from my part-time job.

If you are limited to some special subject, like history, choose a period, a person, or a problem that appeals to you. You might as well enjoy what you are doing.

Narrow your subject to a size you can manage. Don't take "Astronomy"; take "Meteor Showers". Don't take "Music"; take "Calypso Music". Notice how the following broad subjects are gradually trimmed to manageable size.

Too Broad	A Little Better	Not Quite	Good!
Medicine	Methods of Fighting Disease	Fighting Polio	The Salk Vaccine
Conservation	Reforestation	The Importance of Forests	Forests and Our Water Supply
Music	Musical Instruments	Wind Instruments	The French Horn

Under the first heading we have a subject for a whole series of learned works; under the second, a subject for a book.

PRACTICE 1. Choosing Essay Subjects

Be sure your subject is narrow enough to be handled in the number of words alloted by your teacher. The following subjects are too broad, but they may suggest narrower ones to you.

1. A Canadian writer. 2. Magic as a hobby. 3. Animal care. 4. Modern explorers. 5. Changing fashions in home design. 6. Choosing a career. 7. Dolls of different countries. 8. The growth of magazines. 9. Health. 10. Leisure-time problems. 11. New strides in medicine. 12. New techniques in movie-making. 13. Pocket-book sales. 14. Television production problems. 15. Youth and community problems.

B. DECIDING YOUR PURPOSE AND STATING YOUR THESIS

An essay on "School Spirit" may have a number of purposes. It may be to congratulate the students on their display of school spirit; it may be to rouse a latent, or create a missing, school spirit; it may be to complain about the abuses which have grown up under the name of school spirit—or it might be others still. Be clear whether the object is instruction, admonition, reproof, or commendation, for this will materially affect the choice of material, and the arrangement of it. (See the essay on School Spirit at the end of this chapter.)

If your subject is Astronomy and your purpose is to interest fellow-students in your hobby, your thesis might be "Astronomy is a fascinating hobby". If, however, your purpose is to convey information to fellow-astronomers, your thesis might be "Making your own telescope".

PRACTICE 2. Stating Your Thesis

For three of the following subjects, indicate a purpose and state a thesis. Perhaps you would prefer to indicate three different purposes and three different theses for one subject.

1. Music. 2. Hockey. 3. Badminton. 4. Tennis. 5. Conservation. 6. Fishing. 7. Hunting. 8. Camping. 9. Hiking. 10. Baby-Sitting. 11. Working in a Supermarket. 12. Working at a Service Station. 13. Photography. 14. Dancing. 15. Nursing.

C. GETTING INFORMATION

Sometimes when we are faced with a subject not of our own choosing we are at a loss to know what to say about it. Under such circumstances—and under more favourable ones—remember Rudyard Kipling's serving men; they will serve you as they served him.

> I keep six honest serving men.
> They taught me all I know.
> Their names are *What*, and *Where*, and *When*,
> And *How*, and *Why*, and *Who*.

If your subject is personal, jot down notes of all you can remember about the experience. Ask yourself questions. Was the experience exciting? Why? Dull? Unexpected? Terrifying? Again, why? Try to pin down your reactions. Don't be satisfied with writing, "It was a good picture." Decide what made the movie good. Was it the acting? The sets? The plot? The direction? If your composition is going to explain "How I learned to dance," ask, Who taught me? Where? Why? How did I react to the lessons? Did I fall over my own feet? Trip my partner? Learn quickly?

You can write most clearly and effectively about the things you know firsthand. Often, however, you will have to supplement your knowledge by observing, conversing, reading, and thinking.

If your subject is one on which you need additional information, use the library. Sometimes an interview with a person who is an authority on the subject will be the best way of getting the necessary facts. Often you will use more than one source of information. For example, if you're writing about your local paper, you might examine the paper itself, read about it in the library, and interview someone on its staff.

You will probably find most of your material in books and magazines, but don't overlook other sources. Consider:

1. Your own experience and observation
2. The experiences of others—often obtained through interviews
3. Encyclopedias and other standard reference books
4. The card catalogue for books on your subject

5. The *Readers' Guide* for magazine articles
6. The library pamphlet and clipping file
7. Pamphlets and reports published by various agencies and available without charge

Various government agencies and private corporations publish many useful pamphlets for general distribution. Booklets like "Should Your Child Be a Doctor?" are written by competent authorities and provide useful information for researchers. Perhaps your librarian may be able to supply names of organizations to write to.

Find a number of books on your subject, either through the card catalogue or cross references in other books. Glance through the table of contents of each book to see whether the book is likely to be of help to you. If it seems to contain useful material, examine the index at the back to find specific references to your subject.

Read, talk to friends, think. These are the best ways of getting information.

PRACTICE 3. Discussing Essay Subjects

List and prepare to read to your class five subjects based on your own experience. You may find theme ideas in your social life, school life, and private life—your first date, your pet ambition, or why you hate your nickname. Be prepared to discuss which subjects would make good essay themes and why. The class may decide to list in their notebooks the subjects that sound most interesting as suggestions for future essays.

PRACTICE 4. Getting Information on the Subject

Discuss getting information on the following essay subjects. If the subject is personal, suggest questions that the writer might ask himself to unearth ideas about it. If the subject is impersonal, suggest sources of information that the writer might use.

1. High school fads. 2. Planning a career. 3. My hardest subject. 4. Student government in our school. 5. Collecting coins as a hobby. 6. The St. Lawrence Seaway.

Soon you will have such a bewildering array of material that you will lose yourself in scraps of paper and unrelated notes, unless you follow certain procedures.

D. PLANNING AND OUTLINING

No boy builds a model plane, a radio set, or a table without first planning. If the construction is very simple, he can, of course, carry the plans in his head. It is usually safer to have them on paper. Likewise you can plan in your head a simple explanation, but you will need pencil and paper for planning a longer or more complicated one.

The purpose of an essay is to give order, logical arrangement, and impressive form to its matter. It induces all possible brevity and assures proportion. It reduces the risk of confusion, repetition, or omission. Some students try to carry the outlines in mind and refuse to be finally bound by pre-conceived plans committed to writing. They feel that an outline cramps the ready flow of their discourse.

Such students usually labour under a misunderstanding of the use of the plan, which should never be a master but a patient and unobtrusive slave. *No plan should be so rigid as to preclude a desirable alteration*, but it should serve as a reminder, a guide, and a check. More good school essays are written with carefu planning than without it.

Three things you must determine in planning are (1) what facts to present, (2) the order in which to present them, and (3) the materials needed to make your explanation clear and entertaining. In deciding what to include, you will have to take into account the general intelligence of your reader or hearer and his knowledge of the subject. Explaining to one of the boys the fake kick that won the football game is quite different from making your grandmother understand.

A good general rule in arranging material is to give first the facts needed in understanding other facts. Plan to lead the reader or hearer, step by step, from what he knows to related facts or ideas you wish to make clear.

When you explain a process—making a cake, washing dishes, planting seeds, or building a kennel, for example—you will naturally want to arrange the details in *time order*—that is, the order in which you would do them. Try to carry out in imagination the process you are describing.

PRACTICE 5. Arranging Facts Sensibly

If you were explaining each of the following subjects, in what order would you arrange the topics?

How to apply artificial respiration. Applying pressure for two seconds. Placing hands on victim's ribs. Placing the victim in position. Straddling the victim. Continuing process as long as necessary.

How to make a dress. Pinning the pattern on the material. Hemming the skirt. Basting seams. Buying material and a pattern. Cutting out the dress. Sewing seams permanently by hand or on a machine.

An outline, which is a written plan of what you are going to say, should be definite and meaty. A vague or empty outline, so brief as to give little or no information about the subject, is neither interesting nor valuable. Put important facts into the outline and indicate clearly what you intend to say on every point.

Making an outline will help you (1) to find out whether you really understand your subject, (2) to arrange your ideas in a sensible order, and (3) to discover what additional material you need to secure.

Examine the following outline on choosing a college or university:

CHOOSING A UNIVERSITY

  I. Getting information about universities
    A. Asking friends and teachers
    B. Consulting guidance counsellor
    C. Writing for syllabi

 II. Reviewing my high school record
    A. My record in university preparatory subjects
    B. My extracurricular activities

III. Considering the cost
    A. University expenses
      1. Tuition
      2. Books
      3. Transportation
      4. Accommodation
    B. Possible financial resources
      1. Money supplied by parents
      2. Money in my bank account
      3. Scholarship possibilities
      4. Student aid programs (bursaries)

HOW TO OUTLINE

1. Write the title above the outline without a number or a letter.

2. Note in the example that the main topics are numbered I, II, III, and the subtopics under each main head, A, B, C. Print these capital letters. Subtopics under capital letters are numbers 1, 2, 3, 4; subtopics under arabic numerals, a, b, c, d.

3. Subtopics are begun farther to the right than main topics. The second line of a topic begins under the first word of the topic. Keep corresponding letters or numbers in vertical columns: I, II, III, IV; A, B, C, D; 1, 2, 3, 4.

4. Capitalize the first word of each topic and other words that would be capitalized in a sentence.

5. Place a period after each topic number or letter and at the end of each sentence.

6. Never write a single subtopic—that is, an A without a B following it, or a 1 without a 2 following it. Subtopics are subdivisions. When you divide, you have two or more parts. When you would like to write one subtopic, include the main point or fact in the main topic.

WRONG	RIGHT (*Subtopics Added*)
I. Sentimental songs	I. Sentimental songs
A. Old-time favourites	A. Old-time favourites
II. Music for dancing	B. Modern hit tunes
A. Music for the "lindy"	II. Music for dancing
III. Hits from musicals	A. Music for the "lindy"
A. Rodgers and Hammerstein highlights	B. Tunes for waltzing
	C. South American tempos
	III. Hits from musicals
	A. Cole Porter melodies
	B. Rodgers and Hammerstein highlights

7. Express all topics of the same rank in similar form. If I is a sentence, II and III should also be sentences; if A is a noun with or without modifiers, B and C should also be nouns with or without modifiers; if 1 is a phrase, 2 and 3 should also be phrases.

The topic outline is more concise and is used more often than the sentence outline. The sentence outline requires more effort to draw up but expresses ideas more thoroughly.

TOPICS IN A TOPIC OUTLINE

NOT PARALLEL	PARALLEL	
	All Participial Phrases	*All Nouns*
Looking for a job	Looking for a job	The job hunt
The letter of application	Writing letters of application	The letter of application
Preparing for a job interview	Preparing for a job interview	The job interview

TOPICS IN A SENTENCE OUTLINE

a. The job hunter must make use of all available sources of information.
b. A letter of application should try to meet the employer's needs.
c. The job interview requires careful preparation.

8. Avoid having a large number of main topics. A short theme cannot adequately cover more than four or five main points. Test your main topics by asking about each: Is this really one of the important divisions of the subject or only a subdivision?

LACK OF SUBORDINATION	PROPER SUBORDINATION
I. Organizing a club	I. Organizing a club
II. Electing a chairman	A. Electing a chairman
III. Electing officers	B. Electing officers
IV. Holding a meeting	C. Holding a meeting

9. Avoid overlapping of topics. Decide what basis of division you want to follow and then stick to it.

10. Cover the subject completely. Find subtopics that add up to the topic under which they fall. Cross out any topics not on the subject.

PRACTICE 6. Making Headings Parallel

Show that in the following examples the phrasing for co-ordinate headings in a set is not grammatically the same. Make the headings parallel in structure.

1
A. The people who attend the story conference
B. The animators sketch out a few principal scenes
C. The musical director suggests appropriate music
D. Breaking down finished scenario into scenes

2
A. Preparing criminals to earn an honest living
B. To deter others from committing crimes

3
A. Government inspection of food
B. Supervision of handling of milk
C. Purify water supply

4
A. Parking in downtown areas
B. Suburban centres have parking accommodations
C. Parking problems and car size
D. Enforcement of parking regulations

PRACTICE 7. Criticizing Main Headings

Show that the following sets of main headings overlap, do not cover the subject, or are not all on the subject.

EARLY AIRPLANES

I. Very early experiments
II. The *Giant* of Hiram Maxim
III. The successful plane of the Wright brothers
IV. Planes in World War I
V. Stratojets

TELEVISION COMMERCIALS

I. Cartoon commercials
II. Pay-as-you-go television
III. Live commercials
IV. Techniques of television commercials
V. Television spectaculars

THE SPIDER

I. Of what use each part of a spider's body is
II. How he builds his home
III. How he secures his food
IV. How he catches flies
V. How he cares for baby spiders
VI. Whether on the whole he is a friend or a foe
VII. What harm and what good he does

FOREST PROTECTION

I. Work of the forest rangers
II. Reforestation
III. Tree surgery
IV. Spraying young trees
V. Importance of forests

PRACTICE 8. Arranging an Outline

Below are the topics for a report on X-rays. Select the three main topics and write them on your paper. Then arrange the subtopics logically under the main topics. Capitalize, number, and indent the items correctly.

Invisibility
Heinrich Geissler
Professor Wilhelm Roentgen
Characteristics
Discovery of flaws in wood, iron, jewels
Diagnosing and curing disease

Powers of penetration
Discoverers
Similarity to light waves
Sir William Crookes
Detection of smuggled goods
Uses
Heinrich Hertz

PRACTICE 9. Preparing an Outline

Write an outline for an explanation of one of the following. If possible, select something you yourself have done. Arrange your material logically and include every necessary fact. Keep this outline; you will need it later.

A. 1. Making camp, or How to select a campsite. 2. Running a trap-line. 3. The pleasures of gardening. 4. Breeding pigeons. 5. Constructing bird-houses. 6. Sunday observance. 7. On behalf of the Y.M.C.A. (or Y.W.C.A.) 8. Life-saving. 9. Winter sports. 10. Amateur hockey. 11. Modern poetry. 12. Reading fiction. 13. The Red River settlement. 14. Pioneering. 15. The future of aviation. 16. The history of aviation. 17. Drought control. 18. Reforestation. 19. Apex (or Thatcher) Wheat. 20. Consumers' co-operatives. 21. A modern school of music. 22. Travelling libraries. 23. The library needs of our school. 24. Gandhi. 25. The schools of tomorrow. 26. Television comedies. 27. Space travel. 28. Blind dates. 29. Old-fashioned remedies. 30. Shopping manners. 31. Contour farming. 32. The St. Lawrence seaway. 33. The Columbia River project.

B. 1. Bargain hunters. 2. Hi-fi as a hobby. 3. New frontiers in science. 4. College scholarships. 5. Apartment living vs. home ownership. 6. What makes a happy marriage. 7. Places of interest in our community. 8. Getting out a school magazine. 9. How to give a good but inexpensive party. 10. Short cuts for the modern cook. 11. A new or unusual occupation. 12. The advantages (or disadvantages) of living in the suburbs. 13. A great engineering (or other) project. 14. A modern fire (or police) department. 15. How to shop wisely. 16. Experimental theatres. 17. Simple home experiments in chemistry. 18. Current movie favourites. 19. Recreation centres for teen-agers. 20. The Saskatchewan River Dam.

E. MAKING AN EXPLANATION

EXPLAIN COMPLETELY

If an explanation of raising head lettuce, pitching a tent, catching trout, or diving omits one necessary direction, it is worthless. In raising head lettuce, for example, both fertilizing and cultivating are necessary. If an amateur gardener follows directions that omit either of these essentials, his lettuce will be headless.

BE CLEAR AND INTERESTING

You may know how to swim, construct a radio set, play tennis, raise beans, or write verse, and yet fail to explain the subject clearly. Explanation is of value only if every important point is made clear to one who does not understand the subject, or perhaps knows nothing about it.

LOOK INTO YOUR READER'S MIND

Think of your reader or hearer as stopping you every ten seconds to ask, "Why?" "What for?" "How?" "What of it?" Answer every question in his mind. When you plan your explanation of how to dive or how to prune an apple tree, be an amateur mind-reader. Look into the minds of your classmates and find out what some will not understand or what mistakes others will make in carrying out your directions. Then take pains to make these points clear to everyone. Hang a red danger sign on each stumbling block. Spend more time or space on these difficult points and, if necessary, explain them in various ways.

USE EXAMPLES AND COMPARISONS

Often a comparison or an example helps a writer or a speaker to make his subject clear. In *Adventures with Living Things*, for instance, Kroeber and Wolff say, "Scientists have calculated that if all the red corpuscles of a normal person, microscopic as they are in size, were laid out next to one another, they would cover an area larger than that of a baseball diamond. This does not mean much to you unless you appreciate how extremely minute each corpuscle is: 5,000,000 of them would take up only about as much room as a coarse grain of sand." The comparison adds both clarity and force to the explanation.

USE DIAGRAMS, PICTURES, AND CHARTS

A diagram or a picture may show at a glance what many words would not make equally clear. A picture, says a Chinese proverb, is worth a thousand words. In explaining how to make or build something, you will almost always need a diagram. When your explanation deals with numbers, often a chart will help you to show the significance of a set of figures. Diagrams, pictures, and charts need not be artistic masterpieces but should be neat, clear, and accurate.

USE CLEAR, ACCURATE LANGUAGE

"When I use a word," says Humpty Dumpty in *Alice in Wonderland*, "it means just what I choose it to mean—neither more nor less." In real life, however, we cannot use words so casually. If your reader or hearer is to understand your explanation, you will need to express yourself in accurate, clear language. When you use a scientific or technical term, define it in simple words for those to whom it is unfamiliar.

BE CONCISE

Sometimes boys and girls have the idea that the more words they use the clearer will be their explanation. That, however, is not true. When you write or speak, aim to clear a path straight to your goal, not to wander in circles around it. In revision cross out repetitions and useless words. Whenever you can, substitute a simple sentence with a compound predicate for a compound sentence or two simple sentences.

By brevity an explanation gains not only clarity but also **vigour.** By compact wording, a writer or speaker can often in a single sentence explain adequately *how* or *why.*

Examples:

Because people found it inconvenient to carry around gold and silver for use in trading, governments printed paper certificates to represent the metal, which was kept as security in vaults.

Although the jellyfish is not a good swimmer, it can move through the water by waving its tentacles or contracting its body.

F. WRITING THE FIRST DRAFT

The first twenty words are the hardest. Even professionals sometimes find it difficult to get the first sentence on paper. If you catch yourself staring helplessly at a blank page, write something as simple as, "In this essay I am going to tell the reader about my favourite hobby, stamp collecting" and so on. Those first flat sentences can be thrown out when you revise your composition. Their sole purpose is to get you started, to break the block that is keeping you from writing.

In your first draft, follow your outline and write as freely and rapidly as the thoughts come to your mind. Change your outline if you see a good way to improve it. Express your thoughts simply and clearly. Use examples, illustrations, comparisons and details freely.

G. REVISING

Don't be afraid to revise. Get your first draft down on paper; then put the theme away for a while, overnight if possible. After the overnight wait, take the draft out and begin your revision. Ernest Hemingway rewrote one of his short stories eleven times; Dylan Thomas produced two hundred versions of "Fern Hill" before the poem satisfied him.

1. Check the arrangement of your material. What order have you followed in your essay? Four common patterns for the arrangement of material are (1) time order, (2) space order, (3) necessary-facts-first order, and (4) emphasis order, beginning with an important paragraph but keeping the best material for last. For example, if you are explaining a process—polishing a car, making a blouse, or painting a room—use the time order. Arrange the details in the order in which you would perform the actions.

2. Check the transitions. The relationship between paragraphs should be made clear. Any device used to connect ideas may be called a "transition." Here are some ways to lead the reader along easily and naturally.

a. Refer in the first sentence of a paragraph to the preceding paragraph. For example, after explaining that skin diving is your favourite hobby, you can write, "One of the first thrills that the skin diver experiences . . ."

b. Indicate in the last sentence of a paragraph the topic of the next paragraph.

c. Repeat at the beginning of a paragraph a word used at the end of the preceding one.

d. Use connective words and expressions—*for example, also, likewise, nevertheless, moreover, meanwhile, at the same time, consequently, for this reason, next, finally, first, secondly, to the right.*

e. Use a brief transitional paragraph.

3. Check for interest. Will your first sentence catch the attention of the reader? To get your reader interested in your subject, you might: (1) surprise him with an unusual statement or a novel phrase; (2) ask him a question which you will proceed to answer or explain; (3) tell an incident leading into the topic; (4) state an opposing theory and disprove it; (5) open with a bit of conversation; (6) state the purpose of your essay clearly and exactly.

REVISION OF A PARAGRAPH

~~It is a known fact that there are~~ ͚only 6000 stars are bright enough or near enough to be seen by unaided ~~in the skies that~~ the human eye ~~can see without the aid of a telescope. The other stars are not bright enough or near enough to be seen.~~ At the Palomar Observatory in California, however, the 48-inch Schmidt telescope can "see" millions of stars. ~~This is a 48-inch telescope.~~ ~~It can see~~ (hundreds of) ~~millions of stars.~~ Other telescopes at Palomar, the 100-inch and 200-inch, ones revealed have ~~seen~~ clusters of star galaxies, even those ~~stars that are running away from us~~ when galaxies were rushing through space at the rate of 38,000 miles a second.

As a further check on interest, ask yourself: Are the sentences varied (See pages 326—29). Are the figures of speech appropriate? (See pages 306–11.) Are the words and phrases specific and vivid? Hav you used examples, anecdotes, comparisons? Is your conclusion strong? Does it restate your most important ideas or emphasize your main point in a forceful way?

4. Cut where necessary. Get rid of deadwood. (*See* pages 315–19.)

5. Check spelling (*see* **pages** 658–71), **mechanics** (*see* **pages** 645–57), **and grammar.** When you revise, read your essay aloud. Reading a work aloud shows up weaknesses that a silent checking never reveals.

H. MAKING THE FINAL COPY ATTRACTIVE

Copy your revised essay carefully. Be sure to (1) leave a good margin on both sides, an inch at least; (2) indent each paragraph clearly and evenly; (3) centre the title of the essay and skip a line between the title and the first paragraph; (4) make any further corrections as neatly as possible.

PRACTICE 10. Writing an Expository Essay

Write an essay (from 200 to 500 words) based on the outline you prepared for Practice 9. Write rapidly; revise slowly and carefully.

or

Choose a subject from the following list or from the lists for Practice 9, gather material, and make an outline. Then write an essay (from 200 to 500 words) based on your outline.

1. Fashion fads. 2. Westerns, movie and television. 3. A local farm problem. 4. How to get a job. 5. Learning to understand people. 6. Foreign cars vs. Canadian cars. 7. A new discovery in medicine (or science). 8. Vacation on a budget. 9. Travel in outer space. 10. Freaks of the weather. 11. Top television announcers (or singers, or comedians). 12. What the neighbourhood (or school) library offers. 13. Misleading movie advertisements. 14. Using leisure time to advantage. 15. Opera in English. 16. Needed—superhighways. 17. Outdoor cooking. 18. The vote for eighteen-year-olds. 19. Book jackets.

I. EVALUATING STUDENT ESSAYS

PRACTICE 11. Evaluating Student Essays

SCHOOL SPIRIT

What is school spirit? This question has been discussed on many occasions both inside and outside school; definitions have been made and then torn to shreds to find the true meaning. True, it is vague and shadowy; even as an idea one has difficulty in grasping its full significance. It has been said, however, that students and teachers, in order to make a true success of school life, need to give their very best to the school which has undertaken the task of training us to think and act for ourselves.

School spirit is not restricted to club activities, but is exemplified toward the school as a whole. *I remember* hearing a young girl say, "I won't" under her breath to a teacher who had politely requested that she go and study. That answer was wearing down her school spirit; yet she did not realize it. No one does until the damage is irreparable. If every one of us continually broke rules, visitors to the school would consider us irresponsible. *I recall* one day that I tossed a piece of paper which fell short of the waste-paper basket. Now, I was tempted to leave it there, but a little voice asked me where my pride in keeping the school tidy was. So I picked it up. That, in some way was, I believe, school spirit.

Rugby games are a treat for the school spirit of both the player and the spectator. The player who, inflated with self-importance, "hogs" the ball is no asset to any team since he usually cancels the work of the rest, whereas the real hero co-operates with the team, effacing himself if necessary, to score the touch-down, and bring honour, not to himself but to the team. That is school spirit.

Some spectators think that it is heroic to drown the cheers of the opposing supporters; that is merely boorish! Quite noticeable at one game was the opposition that our own cheerleaders encountered. While they were trying to get the crowd to cheer en masse, several groups of our own gentlemen did their utmost to disorganize such attempts. There surely was an example of lack of school spirit.

Not only in clubs and games but in academic work, too, school spirit raises its ambitious head. The student who is always ready with the complete answer relieves the teacher of the necessity of extracting information piecemeal, thus saving valuable time—time which may be spent in acquiring further knowledge.

Our school life is only an apprenticeship for the future. The pride of keeping our school tidy, our students good sports, and our clubs well patronized would give each student an independence and self-reliance that would not be lost when he left school. Love of co-operation and pride in tradition would never leave us. School spirit embodies all these ideas.

—an editorial from a high school yearbook.

THE PLACE OF SPORT IN SCHOOL LIFE

A strong body! A strong mind! A strong character! What nobler ambitions could there be and where may they be more easily attained than in school sport?

From the standpoint of health, sport occupies an important scene in the drama of school life. The well-organized sports of today provide a diversion from the routine of academic studies and supply a form of recreation which exercises the mind and the body simultaneously as can no other subject on the course of study. Who would venture to say that the quarterback of a hard-fighting rugby team, planning the strategy for a "first-down" attack is not employing mental as well as physical ability? Besides developing muscles and the development of perfect co-ordination and timing. Also, reflex actions are strengthened and the mind of a good athlete becomes very alert. Furthermore, the student who witnesses a well-played game of any kind will gain a far greater incentive to be healthy than one who depends entirely on the health book. Thus, one sees that health is one of the prime factors in favour of school sport, and is not "health the key to happiness"?

Changing one's viewpoint and looking at school sport from a different angle, one finds that sport is also a fairly influential factor in the social development of a student. Intercollegiate sports promote a competitive spirit among different schools and provide wholesome entertainment as well as the opportunity for an exchange of ideas of social "get-togethers". One of the largest factors contributing to the overthrow of juvenile deliquency is properly supervised sport and this sport can take place in the school. In the field of sport, formalities are discarded like an unnecessary garment and a genuine air of friendship can be obtained. Racial differences are overcome and all students become equals in sport. It makes little difference to the cheering high-school crowd whether the speedy "half" running for a "touch-down" is black or white. It is clear that sports have a part to play in one's social life and in playing this part, enable one to think more democratically.

Do sports influence one's life in any other way? Definitely, for one finds that many of the highest ideals in the building of a fine character are attained in the world of sport. Among these, honesty, fair play, and team co-operation, stand foremost in the mind of a true athlete. Players can learn also, that it is as important to be a good loser as it is to win the laurels. Self-confidence and a feeling of importance may be gained in a game but possible conceit is checked by the spirit of team work necessary for a team to succeed. For example, the high-scoring forward of a hockey team soon realizes that the defense is indispensable and that although he forms an important link in the team, individually, in that sport at least, he is useless. In such ways, sport builds character, and is there a more solid stepping-stone to success?

Sport is as important in school life as any subject on the curriculum. Examinations in the other subjects are of temporary importance, but one is always being examined in, and judged on, the principles of good character achieved in sport. One may not always remember that Napoleon was born in 1769, nor may one be able to recall all the algebraic equations of book one but the principles of health, co-operation, fair play and good sportsmanship, maintained and practised in school sport are not easily forgotten. These become the building blocks of success!

—Grade X Student

SYMBOLS

Symbols mark the sufferings of the world; the joys and triumphs of the ponderous centuries that break over our struggling race.

Deep turbulent emotions immersed in human hearts burst forth and claim them.

Yet who can rise and say, "A symbol is—such and such"?

Every nation, generation, family, and individual has one, that for them takes on a different hue. Each heart resounds to different strains and has its individual thoughts concerning them.

Down through the ages symbols have heralded acts of chivalry, of devotion, love, duty, crime, and death. They have swayed the hearts and minds of men, have given them a goal, and bidden them to strive and win.

Symbols paint pictures, clear, concise, yet with impressions innumerable and vast in their scope.

Joan of Arc recalls to our minds the maid who became the symbol of fighting France. The maiden proclaimed a saint whose cross went into battle with the Free French Armies. Yet how profound and depth-sounding does it ring in the heart of a Frenchman? Our thoughts are but as the ripples caused by a sinking pebble compared to his.

Flags call forth the soldier unto battle. They stir the pride of the patriot and are admired by the onlooker. Is it just a gaudy piece of bunting that brings forth such a response? Could it be the symbol alone, or the power that lies behind it?

How simple, yet compound and complex it can be. How intense, how strong this word framed by but mortal lips, that stirs the smallest child or greatest genius. The word itself evokes a thought on the mysteries and complexities of man's mind and existence. Endowed with a brain capable of amazing discovery and wondrous construction, he is able to define in part alone a word; frustrated and eluded by something arising from his superiority over, and dominance of, the animal kingdom.

The time-washed halls of learning echo with our groping, faltering steps, ever bidden onward by such beacons, kindled by those who sought the higher things, as symbols.

—*Grade X Student*

Chapter 5

Explaining

All day long people use their powers of speech to instruct others. The teacher explains to his pupils; the coach, to his team; the foreman, to his men; the manager, to his department heads; the salesman, to his customers; the farmer, to his workmen; the physician, to his patients. You yourself explain something every time you answer a question beginning with "Why?" "How?" or "What?". "What is a quarterback sneak?" asks your brother. "What is osmosis?" asks your science teacher. "How do I get to the airport?" asks a motorist. "Why do leaves change colour?" asks your sister. To answer questions like these, you should know what you're talking about and make your explanations clear, brief, and easy to follow.

To succeed in a responsible position a person needs to be able to make good explanations. The engineer who can't explain the advantages of his plans may have a city council, board, or committee reject them for poorer plans the strong points of which are made clear. A salesman who knows his goods and has the best on the market may fail to sell because he can't make clear the superiority of his product. A teacher may know how to solve a problem yet be unable to make the solution clear to the class.

When your teacher calls on you to answer a question, he expects you to explain what you think or have learned, and gives no credit for the answer, "I understand that but can't explain it."

EXPLAINING BY DEFINING

Defining is an important part of explaining. To explain scoring in bowling, you'd need to define terms like *strike*, *spare*, and *frame*.

Make your definition accurate, clear, and concise. To define something, tell (1) what class of individual persons, places, things, or events it belongs to and (2) what characteristics distinguish it from other members of its class.

TERM TO BE DEFINED	= CLASS	+ PARTICULAR QUALITIES
A mackintosh is	a coat	made waterproof by cementing layers of cloth with rubber.
The ebony is	a tropical tree	having a hard, heavy, durable, black wood, prized for furniture and decorative work.
The polka is	a fast dance	having a hop followed by three short steps.

EXCEPTION   A synonym sometimes completes a definition satisfactorily: *Politeness* means *courtesy.*

TESTS FOR A LOGICAL DEFINITION

1. Does the class include all objects bearing the name but exclude objects not bearing the name?

TOO BROAD   A junior is a person who . . . (Use a broad class like *person, man,* or *object* only as a last resort.)

TOO NARROW   A junior is a boy who . . . (Girls are also juniors.)

BETTER   A junior is a third-year high school or college student.

2. Are the particular qualities complete and correct?

INCOMPLETE PARTICULARS   An avocado is a tropical fruit.

COMPLETE PARTICULARS   An avocado is a tropical fruit shaped like a pear and having a green to purplish black, thick skin, a single large seed, and yellow, buttery flesh.

3. Does the name of the class follow *is*?

NOT   A helicopter is when an aircraft is lifted and moved by a horizontal propeller. (Never use a *when* or *where* clause immediately after *is*.)

BUT   A helicopter is an aircraft lifted and moved by a horizontal propeller.

4. Is the key word in the definition after *is* or *means* the same part of speech as the word defined?

     noun   *participle*   *adjective*   *noun*
NOT   Valour is "being brave".   Dutiful means "obedience."

     noun   *noun*   *adjective*   *adjective*
BUT   Valour is "bravery."   Dutiful means "obedient."

5. Does the definition avoid including the word defined or a word derived from the same root?

NOT   A decoder is a device that automatically decodes scrambled messages.

BUT   A decoder is a device that automatically translates or deciphers scrambled messages.

If the dictionary defines *naturalization* as "the act of being naturalized," look up *naturalize*. There you will find the clue to the longer word.

6. Is the definition expressed in simpler terms than the word defined?

NOT   *Tycoon* was a title applied by foreigners to the former shogun of Japan. (What is a *shogun*?)

BUT   *Tycoon* was a title applied by foreigners to the former military governor of Japan.

7. Is the context you have in mind clear?

A *plane*, for example, means different things to a tree surgeon (*tree*), a carpenter (*tool*), and a geometry student (*flat surface*).

PRACTICE 1. Correcting Faulty Definitions

What is the mistake in each of the following definitions? Correct the definitions.

1. Wintergreen is a plant.
2. A parka is an article of clothing for protection from the cold.
3. An admiral is an officer of highest rank.
4. A canal is a waterway for navigation.
5. An adz is an ax-like tool.
6. A dictator is a king who does as he pleases.
7. A tractor is a farm machine.
8. An autobiography is an account of a person's life.
9. *Reliable* means "trust."
10. *Penury* means "to be very poor."
11. An insult is to hurt someone's feelings.
12. *Perseverance* means "to persist in a course of action."
13. A filibuster is when a minority group of a legislative body obstructs passage of a bill by making long and irrelevant speeches.
14. Smog is when smoke and fog mix.
15. A generator is a machine for generating electricity.
16. *Inflammable* means "flammable."
17. An editor is one who edits copy written by others.

18. Plumbing is the work or trade of a plumber.
19. A tyrant is a despot.
20. A democracy is a form of policy in which the people hold the supreme power.

PRACTICE 2. Writing Logical Definitions

Define ten of the following terms by giving the class and the particular qualities in the form shown on page 161. Check your definitions in a good dictionary.

alloy	harmonica
ammeter	harrow
ampere	hogshead
aquarium	kite
barnacle	lacrosse
cameo	mantilla
derrick	megaphone
escalator	octet
façade	pendulum
fez	satellite

EXPLAINING BY GIVING REASONS AND CAUSES

One of the commonest questions in school and out of school is "Why?" An answer to this question should be accurate and specific.

PRACTICE 3. Studying an Explanation

1. In the following explanation, does the pupil give specific reasons why the camel has a hump? If so, what are they?

2. Is her explanation clear, concise, and interesting?

WHY THE CAMEL HAS A HUMP

Although the camel is one of our most interesting animals, most of us who live in North America know but little about him, because we have had only a passing acquaintance with him through the menagerie of the circus, the zoo, the museum of natural history, or books. But in some other countries he is as familiar as the dog or cat is to us. Hence it is interesting to know why the camel has his hump.

The hump is the camel's "breadbasket". A camel can go several weeks with hardly any food, and all he is likely to get on a journey across the desert is a few mouthfuls of dry thorns.   Even at the end of the day he gets probably only a few dates, and he must live on this diet for several days while travelling forty or fifty miles a day.   During this time he secures his nourishment chiefly from his hump.   This consists almost entirely of fat and muscle; and as he marches along day after day, this fat passes back into his system and gives him renewed nourishment and energy.   By the time he reaches the end of his journey, his hump has almost disappeared, and little more is left than an empty bag of skin.   The camel is then unfit to work and is set out to graze for a few days until his hump fills out again.—Pupil

PRACTICE 4. Giving Reasons

Make up a title beginning with *Why I like, Why we should,* or *Why* followed by other words—for example, Why I wish to go to college ; Why science (or another subject) is my favourite; Why I'm glad I am a Canadian; Why I like to live in the suburbs (or the country); Why pupils fail in high school; Why I want to be a doctor (nurse, farmer, pilot, or something else); Why trees are valuable to the farmer; Why I wanted to join the orchestra (choir, band). Select pointed reasons and tell them clearly in a speech or written explanation.

EXPLAINING DIFFERENCES

When you are asked to explain the difference between two objects or persons commonly confused, first mention briefly the points of similarity.   Then explain exactly how the objects or persons differ. Explain clearly, completely, vividly. Give details. A topic sentence like "There are two important differences between an alligator and a crocodile" will serve as a guide and a reminder of the information you should include.

HOW DOES A STAR DIFFER FROM A PLANET?

Stars and planets are both heavenly bodies which may be seen through a telescope or perhaps even with the naked eye.   There are many scientific methods of differentiating stars from planets.   Two basic facts, however, will help the layman to distinguish between the two.   First, a star keeps the same position in relation to other stars.   It always appears in the same group or constellation.   A planet, however, is a wanderer, and may appear in different positions.   This is due to the fact that planets move about the sun.   Second, a planet has a steady, bright light, while a star twinkles on and off.   A further difference is that stars generate their own light and heat, but planets reflect the light of the sun. Even through a telescope, stars are small and appear as points of light. Planets, on the other hand, have considerable size and are seen as disks of light.—PUPIL

PRACTICE 5. Explaining Differences

Choose one of the following and be ready to explain clearly the difference between the two terms:

1. profession and job. 2. artery and vein. 3. volcano and mountain. 4. dew and rain. 5. telescope and microscope. 6. commissioned and non-commissioned officer. 7. hurricane and tornado. 8. reptile and fish. 9. spider and insect. 10. humour and wit. 11. disinfectant and antiseptic. 12. helicopter and ordinary airplane. 13. rotation and revolution. 14. planet and comet. 15. barometer and thermometer. 16. plain omelet and scrambled egg. 17. crosscut saw and ripsaw.

PLANNING AN EXPLANATION

To build a boat, you need a plan. To tell how to build a boat, you also need a plan. Unless an explanation is quite simple, put the plan on paper.

Of course, before you make your plan you will have to know your subject. You can't explain a subject that is hazy in your own mind. If you are in doubt about certain points, observe, experiment, ask someone who knows the subject, or look up the information in books or magazines.

Then arrange your facts and ideas in logical order. Start with the facts needed to understand other facts. Follow with the main points, and think of definitions, examples, details, comparisons, and contrasts you can use to make each step clear to your listener or reader.

PRACTICE 6. Studying an Outline

1. Why is it desirable to outline an explanation before writing it?

2. How are the topics in the outline arranged?

HOW TO BUILD A COLLECTION OF ROCKS AND MINERALS

I. *Aims*

    A. To learn about the earth's structure through study of rocks and minerals.

B. To build a colourful and representative collection.

II. *Preparation*

A. Reading two or three good books about rocks and minerals—for example, *Field Book of Common Rocks and Minerals,* by FREDERIC BREWSTER LOOMIS.

B. Acquiring equipment; small hammer, streak plate, pocket lens, spring scale, a set of scale-of-hardness minerals to help classify specimens.

III. *Procedure*

A. Prospecting for rocks and minerals in your vicinity.

1. Checking possible sites: new house foundations, quarries, new roadbeds, mines, caves, bare and exposed places.

2. Finding out from a science teacher or a librarian about books or pamphlets on local mineral resources.

B. Securing specimens approximately 2 x 3 x 4 inches if possible.

C. Classifying specimens.

1. If possible, comparing specimens with already labelled specimens in other collections.

2. Checking hardness, specific gravity, colour, lustre, crystalline structure, streak, and cleavage.

D. Labelling specimens uniformly: name, when found, where found.

E. Storing specimens in drawers or a display cabinet.

MAKING AN EXPLANATION

1. *Go straight to the point.* Avoid unnecessary words and round-about expressions.

NOT All you have to do to have a successful dance is to make some plans like asking your parents for the recreation room, inviting your friends to bring their favourite platters, and have some food.

BUT For a successful dance that will establish your reputation as a hostess, first clear the date with your family and arrange for the use of the recreation room. Then . . .

2. *Be a mind reader.* Think what may confuse or puzzle your listener or reader, and take pains to make difficult points clear to everyone. When giving an oral explanation, watch your listeners for blank or puzzled expressions. Arrange facts and ideas logically.

3. *Try to connect your explanation with something your hearer or reader already understands.* Use comparisons and examples freely.

Cite distances in terms of known distances—"as far as from here to the library"; compare rocket propulsion to the action of a released air-filled balloon.

4. *Use pictures, diagrams, charts or display materials.* In explaining a game, a machine, or a scientific process, provide a diagram.

5. *Use words your listeners or readers understand.* If a technical term or other unfamiliar word cannot be avoided, define it. You may speak about acetylsalicylic acid to a pharmacist, but you'd better say "aspirin" to the rest of us.

6. *Be concise.* Too many words spoil an explanation. Refer to Chapter 2 for help in building concise sentences. By compact wording you can often give a clearer explanation in one sentence.

7. *Explain thoroughly.* The more you know about a subject the more you must guard against leaving out important steps you take for granted. Will your friend have enough pudding for twelve guests if you forget to tell her your recipe makes four servings?

8. Use connective words to show the relation between the parts of the explanation. If the parts are not linked together, the explanation seems disjointed. For sentence connectives turn to pages 122—24.

SELF-CRITICISM OF AN EXPLANATION

1. *Do I understand my subject thoroughly?*
2. *Is my explanation accurate?*
3. *Is my explanation complete; that is, have I included all necessary facts and defined technical terms unfamiliar to my classmates?*
4. *Have I arranged my facts in logical order, giving first those that are necessary for an understanding of others?*

5. *Did I plan my explanation before attempting to speak or write it?*
6. *Have I tried to foresee points that will puzzle my classmates and taken pains to make such details crystal clear?*
7. *Have I used comparisons, diagrams, or pictures for greater clarity?*
8. *Is my explanation concise?*
9. *Are my pronouns and verbs correct?*

EXPLAINING PROCEDURES

1. HOW TO MAKE OR BUILD SOMETHING

An explanation of how to make or build something should include (1) the materials, and (2) the procedure, arranged step by step in time order. Reasons why the article is useful or enjoyable may be given at the beginning or the end.

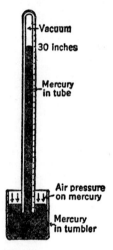

HOW TO MAKE A MERCURY BAROMETER

I. *Materials*
  A. Glass tumbler
  B. Glass tube thirty-four inches long, open at one end and marked off into inches
  C. Mercury

II. *Procedure*
  A. Filling tumbler and tube with mercury
  B. Inverting tube in tumbler of mercury

III. *Possible results*
  A. Dropping of mercury to thirty inches if at sea level
  B. Dropping below thirty inches at higher altitudes because of lower pressure

IV. *Reading barometer*
  A. Falling mercury probably accompanied by rain
  B. Rising mercury probably accompanied by fair weather

The necessary materials for making a mercury barometer are a glass tumbler, a glass tube about thirty-four inches long, open at one end and marked off into inches, and some mercury.

Fill the tumbler and the glass tube with mercury.   Holding the thumb over the open end of the tube, carefully invert the tube in the tumbler of mercury. Special care should be taken not to remove the thumb until the tube is under the surface of the mercury in the tumbler.

When the finger is removed, the pressure of the atmosphere on the mercury in the tumbler will force most of the fluid to remain in the tube.   If at sea level, the mercury will drop to thirty inches, because the weight of the air over a square inch at sea level is the same as the weight of a column of mercury thirty inches high over a square inch.   At higher altitudes, however, the mercury will drop lower, because the higher up one goes, the lighter the air becomes. With the graduated scale on the tube it is possible to measure the variations in the height of the mercury column resulting from increased or decreased air pressure.

If the instructions are properly carried out, the barometer will be accurate. When the mercury in the tube falls, the air pressure is decreasing and rain will probably follow.   If the mercury in the tube rises, however, the air pressure is increasing and the weather will usually be fair.—PUPIL

PRACTICE 7. Judging an Explanation

After reading the preceding explanation, could you make a mercury barometer? Is the explanation complete? Is it clear? Does the diagram help to clarify the directions? Judging the explanation by the standards on page 167, what rating would you give it? Why?

PRACTICE 8. Explaining How to Make or Build Something

Explain how to make or build one of the following: apple pie, apron, birdhouse, boat, bookcase, book ends, camp bed, canoe, chicken coop, Christmas cards, cookies, doghouse, grape jelly (or another kind), kite, lamp shade, leather pocketbook, model airplane, pair of socks, picture frame, pillow cover, round table, school dress, shelter in the woods, smock, Spanish omelet, willow whistle, workbench, Yorkshire pudding, any article you have made.

First write an outline. If you decide to explain how to build a birdhouse, assume that every member of the class is planning to build such a house but knows nothing about birdhouses and little about carpentry. Think what details in your explanation might confuse the class, and give these extra care. Your exposition will be successful if it is a clear and complete guide. A diagram saves words and makes clear. Judge your explanation by the self-criticism guide on page 167.

2. How To Do Something

When explaining how to do something, you can follow the same general plan you used in telling how to make or build something. Note the steps in the process and ask yourself frequently, "Will this point puzzle my reader? If so, how can I make it clear?"

PRACTICE 9. Studying an Explanation

1. Does Marilyn arrange logically the steps of the process she is explaining? Outline her explanation.

2. After reading her explanation do you think you could give yourself or someone else an attractive manicure?

HOW TO GIVE A MANICURE

Many women and girls think that to have a good manicure they must go to a beautician and pay for it. If you have the necessary equipment at home, however, you can easily take care of your own nails.

Before you start, collect everything you will need—a pan of lukewarm, soapy water, an orange stick, absorbent cotton, an emery board or nail file (preferably the former), polish remover, and nail polish or a buffer, which is a little gadget for polishing the nails. First, remove the old polish, if any, with the cotton saturated with polish remover. Then, preferably with the emery board, file the nails, following the natural shape of the fingertips. Next, soak each hand in the lukewarm water for five minutes, dry, and clean the fingernails. While the cuticle is soft, push it back with an orangewood stick covered with absorbent cotton.

If you use nail polish, apply it with a light stroke. You will get best results by outlining the moon first and then brushing the polish toward the end of the nails. If you don't like polish, you can use a buffer to make your nails smooth and shining.

After you have practised several times, your manicure will look like the work of a professional.—MARILYN B.

PRACTICE 10. Explaining How to Do Something

Give an accurate, clear, complete oral (or written) explanation of how to do one of the following. To avoid overlooking important points, prepare an outline. Draw a diagram on the blackboard, or exhibit materials that will make the explanation clear. Your classmates will listen to determine whether or not you follow the preceding suggestions for explaining. To test whether your explanation is clear, ask one of your classmates to repeat it.

1. How to oil a sewing machine. 2 How to care for a hot rod. 3. How to throw a curve, a knuckle ball, a slow ball, or a floater. 4. How to operate a fire in a fireplace. 5. How to dance the samba. 6. How to plan a motor trip. 7. How to take care of tropical fish or a parakeet. 8. How to train a bird dog. 9. How to put up a television antenna. 10. How to be an ideal baby sitter. 11. How to arrange flowers attractively. 12. How to raise chickens. 13. How to give a home permanent. 14. How to make a leaf (stamp, coin, or some other) collection. 15. How to judge cattle (or some other animals). 16. How to insert a new pane of glass.

3. How To Play a Game

Only a very simple game can be explained in a page or two. A complete explanation of football or basketball is a matter for a book, not for a short composition.

Here again you need to arrange steps carefully and to include every point your listener or reader needs to know.

PRACTICE 11. Explaining How to Play a Game

Select one of the following games, or any other game with simple rules, and explain it so that every member of the class will be able to play it.

1. Checkers. 2. Handball. 3. Bowling. 4. Shuffleboard. 5. Dominoes. 6. Charades. 7. Deck tennis. 8. Tug of war. 9. Hand wrestling. 10. Indian wrestling. 11. Potato race. 12. Three deep. 13. Pick-a-back relay. 14. Prisoner's base. 15. Horseshoes. 16. Volley ball. 17. Treasure hunt. 18. Anagrams. 19. Musical chairs.

As a check on the explanation and the listening, your teacher will ask a pupil to repeat the explanation, or a group to play the game if it is suitable for a classroom.

4. How Something Works

Make an outline and write a complete explanation of the construction and operation of one of the following. Draw a diagram if it will help to make your subject clear. Build clear, concise sentences.

The home—pressure cooker, washing machine, electric mixer, automatic dryer, electric eye, fluorescent lighting, hot-water heating system, vacuum cleaner, sewing machine, fire extinguisher, thermostat

Business—teletypewriter, photostat, dial phone, mimeograph, switchboard, dictaphone, adding machine, telephone transmitter or receiver

Farm—combine, cotton picker, grain drill, electric pump, food freezer, hay loader, corn picker, pulleys, tractor, baler, potato digger, milker

Amusement—polaroid camera, saxophone, television, television aerial, motion-picture projector, phonograph, motion-picture camera

Automobile—tubeless tire, automatic transmission, speedometer, shock absorber, brake, cooling system, carburetor

Aviation—parachute, guided missile, space satellite, helicopter, jet propulsion, propellers, wings, landing gears, radar

5. How to Give Directions

Before explaining how to reach a place, trace out in your mind the route called for. If there are several ways of reaching the place, choose the simplest and shortest way unless it presents some serious obstacle or other disadvantage. Use freely such terms as *right, left, three blocks north, at the junction of Peach Street and Harley Road.* Mention conspicuous landmarks or buildings—a grove of beech trees a white church with a steeple, the Bank of Commerce—which will enable the stranger to check his course. In directing someone on a route that has many curves and corners, diagram the route; appeal to both eye and ear.

Example of Directions:

To reach the high school, walk to the end of Newbold Place; turn left and walk to the end of Austin Street; then turn right on Lefferts Boulevard, cross the railway, pass the stores, and continue on Lefferts Boulevard for about three quarters of a mile to an elevated railroad. This is Jamaica Avenue. Turning right on Jamaica Avenue, follow the elevated for four blocks. Turn left on 114th Street and walk a block and a half. The large white brick building on the right is the high school.—PUPIL

PRACTICE 12. Giving Directions

In pairs dramatize the scene of a stranger asking his way to a railway station, the post office, a church, a bank, a baseball field, a swimming pool, a theatre, a race track, an airport, a library, a woods, a fish hatchery, a skating pond, a park, a store, a camp, a factory, a gymnasium, a city, or a town, and a courteous, clear-headed resident replying. Select a place that is not easy for the stranger to reach. The inquirer will ask a second question only if the directions aren't clear or complete. Watch your verbs (pages 603-19).

EXPLAINING FACTS AND IDEAS

In explaining why you think as you do, give the facts and ideas on which you base your opinions. Arrange your points in the order of their importance, emphasizing the most important point by placing it last. Touches of humour and bits of narration and description, if relevant to your subject, often make an explanation clearer and more entertaining.

PRACTICE 13. Studying an Explanation

1. Is the following explanation clear and concise?

2. What, according to the author, is wrong with student government at Staples? What details does he give to support his solution to the problem?

HOW TO IMPROVE YOUR STUDENT GOVERNMENT

I have heard many complaints about our government. Many students feel that they could do a better job than their elected officers, or they feel that they have a better solution to a specific problem. However, relatively few of these people take an active part in the congress.

One reason for the apparent apathy toward the government at Staples is that the bond between the officers and the student body is weak. It is' partly the fault of the home-room representatives that the students are not well informed about their government. There are few, if any, home rooms that have regular meetings to discuss current issues and to instruct their representatives as was planned when the senate started functioning.

Student government could be improved if home-room meetings were called during the activity period just preceeding the general congress meetings. Then the students would know what issues were to be discussed in congress meeting and would be more attentive and interested. Also, the representatives would know how their home rooms felt on subjects of importance to them and to the school and could vote accordingly, instead of merely doing their best and hoping that the students agree. If the leaders of the student government has the full and enthusiastic support of the student body, they would be more encouraged to do their jobs well.

Student government at Staples will never be more than we make it. It is the duty of every student to be informed about his government and to participate in it wholeheartedly.—STUDENT

PRACTICE 14. Explaining How You See It

Write a clear, interesting explanation of one of the following. Build clear, concise sentences (pages 63-110). Use correct verbs (pages 603-19). Which of the suggestions for explaining have you applied?

1. Who should go to college. 2. How to improve one's conversation. 3. What manners are important today. 4. Why I go to church. 5. ——is a book everyone should read. 6. —— is a television show for the whole family. 7. Controlled precipitation as a military weapon. 8. Air masses in weather forecasting. 9. The need for forests in watershed areas. 10. Responsibilities of an employee. 11. The father's role in bringing up children. 12. How to prepare gifted children for leadership. 13. Purposes of contour plowing. 14. Causes of juvenile delinquency. 15. The city manager plan. 16. The host's responsibilities at a party. 17. Advantages of a student court. 18. How to improve dairy stock. 19. The role of English in international affairs.

PRACTICE 15. Using Description for Exposition

Read the description of the Great Stone Face, and answer the following questions.

1. What was the Great Stone Face?

2. Does it look the same at different distances?

3. What details can you give of its appearance at different distances?

THE GREAT STONE FACE

The Great Stone Face, was a work of nature in her mood of majestic playfulness, formed on the perpendicular side of a mountain by some immense rocks, which had been thrown together in such a position as, when viewed at a proper distance, precisely to resemble the the the features of the human countenance. It seemed as if an enormous giant, or a Titan, had sculptured his own likeness on the precipice. There was the broad arch of the forehead, a hundred feet in height; the nose, with its long bridge; and the vast lips, which, if they could have spoken, would have rolled their thunder accents from one end of the valley to the other. True it is, that if the spectator approached too near, he lost the outline of the gigantic visage, and could discern only a heap of ponderous and gigantic rocks, piled in chaotic ruin one upon another. As he retraced his steps, however, the wonderous features would again be seen; and the farther he withdrew from them, the more like a human face, with all its original divinity intact, did they appear until, as it grew dim in the distance, with the clouds and glorified vapour of the mountains clustering about it, the Great Stone Face seemed positively to be alive.—NATHANIEL HAWTHORNE

Chapter 6

The Paraphrase

Paraphrasing is giving the meaning in other words, sometimes with greater fullness of detail or illustration. All thoughts of the original must appear and must appear exactly, and all compressed expression must be made explicit. No new or different thought should appear.

Example:

Swift to its close ebbs out life's little day.

Paraphrase:

Life is short. It passes away quickly, and its power weakens as it nears its close.

Three significant words give the key to this sentence. *Swift, ebbs,* and *little.* The last clause might have been overlooked had attention not centred on the significant verb *ebbs.*

Examples:

1. WORLDLY PLACE

Even in a palace life may be led well!
So spake the imperial sage, purest of men,
Marcus Aurelius. But the stifling den
Of common life, where, crowded up pell-mell,
Our freedom for a little bread we sell,
And drudge under some foolish master's ken
Who rates us if we peer outside our pen—
Match'd with a palace, is not this a hell?
Even in a palace! On his truth sincere.
Who spake these words, no shadow ever came;
And when my ill-school'd spirit is aflame
Some nobler, ampler stage of life to win,
I'll stop, and say: "There were no succour here!
The aids to noble life are all within."

—MATTHEW ARNOLD

175

Paraphrase:

"The compact language may be paraphrased as follows: 'What a strange thing to say, that even in a palace a man can be virtuous! Yet the man who said it was himself an emperor, a philosopher, and the purest of men in his own life. Yet, when we think of our own pain and trouble, how difficult it is for us to believe that the state of an emperor is not happier than the state of a common man. Think of the trouble that we have to earn a living—obligated to work every day in some uncomfortable position, watched by some man not wiser than ourselves, but often even more foolish, who is only watching our work in order to find fault with us. Surely the Emperor, who is the master of all men, and who is not obliged to obey anybody, or even obliged to do anything he does not wish to do, ought to be happier than we. But these are the words of the wisest and noblest of the Roman emperors—'Even in a palace!' Therefore we must understand that it is still harder for an emperor to be good and happy than it is for a common man. To believe this may be difficult, but Marcus Aurelius said it, and in his whole life he never told even the shadow of a lie. I believe him. When I feel myself dissatisfied, when I wish to leave the work that I now do, in order to obtain a higher or a better position, I remember the words of Marcus Aurelius. The secret of happiness and the power of virtue are in our hearts. That is the meaning of life as it was understood by that great teacher and great emperor'."—LAFCADIO HEARN, *Appreciation of Poetry.*

By arrangement with the publishers, Dodd, Mead & Company.

2. ON FIRST LOOKING INTO CHAPMAN'S HOMER

Much have I travell'd in the realms of gold
And many goodly states and kingdoms seen;
Round many western islands have I been
Which bards in fealty to Apollo hold.
Oft of one wide expanse had I been told
That deep-brow'd Homer ruled as his demesne:
Yet did I never breathe its pure serene
Till I heard Chapman speak out loud and bold:
—Then felt I like some watcher of the skies
When a new planet swims into his ken;
Or like stout Cortez, when with eagle eyes
He stared at the Pacific—and all his men
Look'd at each other with a wild surmise—
Silent, upon a peak in Darien.

—JOHN KEATS

Paraphrase:

I had always found great delight in works of the imagination, and, of course, was acquainted with much of the poetic literature of western Europe. But of one very important contribution to literature—the Homeric poems—I only knew by hearsay. It was not until I read the bold and striking translation of Chapman, that I really felt I had attained some insight into the calm and lofty spirit of these works. This translation seemed to reveal to me something altogether novel; my feelings may be best compared with those of an astronomer when he unexpectedly discovers a new planet, or with those of Cortez when in silent astonishment he gazed with keen and eager eye, for the first time, on the Pacific Ocean—a sight which offered a wide field for hopes and conjectures to him and his companions.

—STUDENT

PRACTICE 1. Paraphrasing Sentences

Find the meaning of the following sentences; then paraphrase them.

1. Time wasted is existence, used is life.
2. He is a skilled window-dresser of his own personality—H. H. MUNRO
3. It was a face filled with broken commandments.—JOHN MASEFIELD
4. The conversation fainted again, and again Mr. Lacey leapt forward with restoratives.—ANNE PARRISH
5. No man has a good enough memory to make a successful liar.—ABRAHAM LINCOLN
6. We live on one-third of what we eat and the doctors live on the rest.— ROYAL S. COPELAND
7. The Child is father of the Man.
8. Truth, crushed to earth, shall rise again.
9. One is never so near to another as when he is forced to be separated.
10. When faith is lost, when honour dies, the man is dead.
11. He who would search for pearls must dive below.
12. The applause of listening senates to command,
    The threats of pain and ruin to despise,
    To scatter plenty o'er a smiling land,
    And read their history in a nation's eyes,
    Their lot forbade; nor circumscribed alone
    Their growing virtues, but their crimes confined.—GRAY
13. The lunatic, the lover, and the poet
    Are of imagination all compact:
    One sees more devils than vast hell can hold,
    That is, the madman: the lover, all as frantic,
    Sees Helen's beauty in a brow of Egypt:
    The poet's eye, in a fine frenzy rolling,
    Doth glance from heaven to earth, from earth to heaven;
    And as imagination bodies forth
    The forms of things unknown, the poet's pen
    Turns them to shapes and gives to airy nothing
    A local habitation and a name.—SHAKESPEARE
14. Vice is a monster of so frightful mien
    As to be hated needs but to be seen;
    Yet seen too oft, familiar with her face,
    We first endure, then pity, then embrace.—POPE

PRACTICE 2. Paraphrasing

Paraphrase the following soliloquy spoken by Macbeth as he contemplates the advisability of murdering King Duncan.

If it were done when 'tis done, then 'twere well
It were done quickly: if the assassination
Could trammel up the consequence, and catch
With his surcease success; that but this blow
Might be the be-all and the end-all here,
But here, upon this bank and shoal of time,
We'ld jump the life to come.   But in these cases
We still have judgment here; that we but teach
Bloody instructions, which, being taught, return
To plague the inventor: this even-handed justice
Commends the ingredients of our poison'd chalice
To our own lips.   He's here in doubt trust;
First, as I am his kinsman and his subject,
Strong both against the deed; then, as his host,
Who should against his murderer shut the door,
Not bear the knife myself.   Besides, this Duncan
Hath borne his faculties so meek, hath been
So clear in his great office, that his virtues
Will plead like angels, trumpet-tongued against
The deep damnation of his taking off;
And pity, like a naked new-born babe,
Striding the blast, or heaven's cherubim, horsed
Upon the sightless couriers of the air,
Shall blow the horrid deed in every eye,
That tears shall drown the wind.   I have no spur
To prick the sides of my intent, but only
Vaulting ambition, which o'erleaps itself
And falls on the other—[side].

Chapter 7

The Précis

WHAT A PRÉCIS IS

A précis (pronounced *pray-see*) is a clear, concise, orderly summary of the contents of a passage and is ordinarily about one-third or one-fourth as long as the original. It is a passage boiled down so that only the essence, pith, or gist is left. Like frozen fruit-juice concentrate, a précis contains the heart of the original in smaller space.

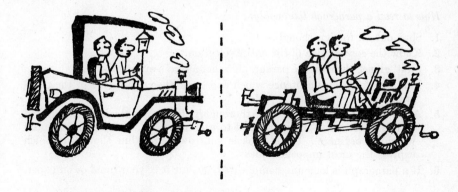

VALUE OF PRÉCIS-WRITING

One purpose of education is to help students to discover what they should not learn. The boy or girl who tries to learn everything in the books he reads and studies wastes his time and masters nothing. The student who is in the habit of searching for main points, understanding them, learning them, and reviewing them is educating himself.

Probably half the failures in school are due directly or indirectly to silent reading deficiency. Teachers of all subjects say that a high percentage of the pupils who fail in their classes fail because they can't read, can't understand the textbook, can't read the examination paper. Training in silent reading is training in the art of studying.

Moreover, the ability to get at the gist, pith, or essence of a matter is important professional, business, and social equipment. Précis-writing prepares for getting and explaining tersely the main points of legal papers, laws, rules and regulations, announcements and directions, business letters, speeches, conversations, interviews, books, and articles. The higher one goes in a profession, or the deeper one goes into any subject, the harder the reading one has to do. Practice in précis-writing also helps one to establish the habit of clear and concise expression, or putting a maximum of meaning into a minimum of words. Careful reading is one skill; concise writing is another. Précis-writing combines both.

PREPARING TO MAKE A PRÉCIS

The first and most important step in making a précis is *reading the passage thoroughly*. Thorough reading includes digging out the thought of every difficult sentence and discovering the relationship of the principal and subordinate ideas of each paragraph and of the whole passage.

How to read a paragragh thoroughly:

1. Shut out all foreign thoughts.
2. Know the central idea of the entire selection.
3. First, glance through the paragraph to get a bird's-eye view of it.
4. Find or construct a sentence which expresses the central idea of the paragraph.
5. As you read the other sentences thoroughly, think how the ideas are related to the topic of the paragraph and to each other, which are principal, and which subordinate. If the book is your own, underline the words which express the most important ideas.
6. If a paragraph is long and complicated, outline it in your mind or on paper.

HOW TO READ A DIFFICULT SENTENCE

1. Know the central idea of the entire selection and of the paragraph in which the sentence is imbedded. Each sentence is closely related in meaning to the rest of the paragraph. If a sentence may be interpreted in two or three ways, decide from the rest of the paragraph which interpretation is best.

2. Knowing what the preceding and the following sentences are about will help you to fathom the deepest sentence or unravel the most tangled one.

3. Look up in the dictionary the meaning of any word which is not perfectly clear to you.   Don't skip technical terms.

4. Look up allusions which are new to you.

5. In imagination see the pictures suggested by descriptive words and figures of speech.

6. Pick out the key words, think what their relation in thought is, and in this way find the central idea of the sentence.   Avoid giving great weight to an unimportant word.   Then read the sentence again, being careful to include all details.

HOW TO CONDENSE SENTENCES

RULE 1.   Since appositives are forms of repetition, you should choose the more significant idea.

> Vasco da Gama, *the famous Portuguese admiral,* was the first to round the Cape of Good Hope.
> Mr Jones, *our neighbour,* is a gardener.

RULE 2.   You may omit interjections, especially those enclosed by dashes or parentheses.

> That day—*a day he will always remember*—began uneventfully.
> Parts of the book (*I didn't read all of it*) were excellent.

RULE 3.   Omit words repeated merely for emphasis.

> Surely he hath borne our griefs, *and carried our sorrows.*
> —OLD TESTAMENT.
> Look out, *look out,* and see if we are pursued.—DICKENS

RULE 4.   Change similes and metaphors—imaginative comparisons used for their literary effect—into literal expressions or omit them entirely if they are unimportant.   The basic idea of the comparison can generally be expressed without the second part of the figure of speech.

Similes: Her thoughts in the morning are *as* tangled *as her hair.*
          He burst out of the door *like an explosion.*

Metaphors: He had a shrill, high *cock-crow of a* laugh.
          He had an expression of *enamelled* self-assurance.

Personification: At once the ghostly King of Terrors stood before him.

This may be reduced to, "Immediately Death appeared."

RULE 5.   Omit introductory subjects, since they are always used to emphasize the word or words that immediately follow.

> *It is* for these reasons *that* we still read with enthusiasm the diary of Samuel Pepys.

RULE 6.   Use a hyphenated expression, where possible.

writers of the seventeenth century	seventeenth-century writers
a box for carrying a hat	a hat-box
fame that is world wide	world-wide fame
a plank that is ten feet long	a ten-foot plank
a person who was once a judge	an ex-judge
a dog with only one eye	a one-eyed dog

(*See* the rules for the hyphen—pp. 659-60.)

PRACTICE 1. Condensing Sentences

Reduce the following sentences by employing the suggested rules. In each case, identify the rule that you are using.

1. I told him (and who would not?) just what I thought about the matter.
2. Pines and pines and the shadows of pines as far as the eye can see.
   —ROBERT SERVICE
3. The human mind should be like a good hotel—open the year round.
   —PHELPS
4. It was only with the approval of the staff advisor that the special dance was held.
5. And still Madame Defarge, pursuing her way along the streets, came nearer and nearer.—DICKENS
6. I had been all this time a very hedgehog, bristling all over with determination.
7. Pride goeth before destruction, and a haughty spirit before a fall.
   —*Old Testament*
8. All his arts were exhausted and proved fruitless, and then Tom knew that an evil spirit—a Wendigo—was on his trail.—ALAN SULLIVAN
9. The new edition has statistics which are up to date.
10. Old acquaintances—for such they soon grew to be, in this rapid current of affairs—continually departed.

RULE 7. Reduce a subordinate clause to a single word or phrase of the same grammatical value.

NOUN CLAUSE:	*What he said* is true	*His statement* is true.
	He loved to talk about *what he had done in his youth*.	He loved to talk about *his youth*.
ADJECTIVE CLAUSE:	A man *who is courageous* can conquer all fears.	A *courageous* man can conquer all fears.
	The task *that the officer had to perform* was very dangerous.	The *officer's* task was very dangerous.
	That was a day (that) *I never shall forget*.	That was a *memorable* day.
ADVERB CLAUSE:	He saved his money *so that he could buy a car*.	He saved his money *to buy a car*.

If an adverb clause of time or reason, or an adjective clause, contains a participle, it may be re-expressed by that participle.

When John had finished his homework, he turned on the radio.	*Having finished (On completing) his homework,* John turned on the radio. (*After his homework . . .*)
I watched the children *while they were swimming.*	I watched the children *swimming.*
They left *because they were displeased with the show.*	They left *displeased with the show.*

In using the participial phrase as a means of compression, you must make it modify the correct noun or pronoun. If you do not exercise caution here, you may produce such illogical constructions as the following:

Looking out my window, a runaway horse attracted my attention.
Having eaten our lunch, Father's car came to take us home.

RULE 8. Reduce a phrase to one or two words of the same meaning and part of speech.

occurring every night	nightly
with excitement	excitedly
without a sound	silently
of the south	southern
of glaciers	glacial

PRACTICE 2. Condensing Sentences by Reducing Clauses and Phrases

Reduce the length of the following sentences by substituting phrases or single words for clauses and phrases.

1. After she had used the new floor wax, Mrs. Jones was elated.
2. The suspect, who was apprehended by the police, pleaded innocence.
3. The cabin boy was well liked by the officers and crew of the ship.
4. We took nothing except what we absolutely needed.
5. Harry's dog, a Saint Bernard, was always so hungry that nothing could satisfy its ravenous appetite.
6. Canada's aid to the disaster victims came without hesitation or any prompting.
7. In Tom Moore, Alan Sullivan has created a character who sticks to his task, undaunted by disappointment or failure.
8. Some students expect teachers to explain that which cannot be explained or accounted for.
9. The coach was a man of unusual gifts or ability.
10. Mary pretended that she did not hear her mother's reply.

RULE 9.   Use a compendious or "suit-case" word—one that expresses a wealth of meaning.   Seek a store of concise and powerful words that do the job of long phrases: verbs like *acquiesce, insinuate,* and *elude;* nouns like *plagiarism, depredation,* and *travesty;* adjectives like *stoic, skeptical, subtle,* and *precocious.*   Properly used, these words provide punch with economy.

"A man who voluntarily endures great suffering for the sake of a principle" may be expressed more concisely and more effectively as "a martyr".

PRACTICE 3. Condensing Sentences by Compendious Words

Without changing the meaning, substitute one of the following words for all the italicized words in each sentence.   If some of the words are unfamiliar to you, turn to the dictionary for help.

deficit	improvise	incorrigible	perpetuate	tangible
depreciate	impunity	inscrutable	precarious	zenith

1. Some of Louis XVI's reforms only served to *give a lasting character or existence to* the evils that characterized eighteenth-century France. *perpetuate*
2. During periods of war and social upheaval money tends to *go down in real value.* *depreciate*
3. David's future position in the firm was *dependent on unknown circumstances or conditions.* *precarious*
4. Even in the tropics the sun is not usually at the *highest point overhead* at noon. *zenith*
5. After a full year's operation the *total loss shown in the books* was nearly ten thousand dollars. *deficit*
6. During the French Revolution the popular leaders thought they could continue the Reign of Terror with *no fear of punishment.* *impunity*
7. Eric had the rare gift of being able to *compose on the spur of the moment without previous preparation.* *improvise*
8. Though the rewards of honesty are not always *capable of being touched or felt,* they are none the less real. *tangible*
9. As Gerald sat there his expression was *incapable of being searched into or analyzed.* *inscrutable*
10. It was the judge's firm conviction that practically no criminal was *evil beyond hope of reform or correction.* *incorrigible*

PRACTICE 4. Finding Compendious Words

Reduce the length of the following sentences by using one compendious word for each italicized expression.

tradition

1. Many of our family's Christmas activities are *of a nature handed down from generation to generation.*

illiterate

2. The number of *people who can neither read nor write* is growing smaller every year.

tactics

3. In winning the game the quarterback displayed sound *skilful management in getting the better of an opponent.*

memoirs

4. Winston Churchill's *written recollections of his life* are literary masterpieces.

SERRATED

5. The back of the dinosaur, a stegosaurus, was *shaped like the edge of a saw.*

DISTORTED

6. Rumours, frequently are originally accurate accounts that have been *twisted out of shape in the retelling.*

PROCRASTINATING

7. Bill's main failing is his habit of *putting something off until the last possible moment.*

UNLIMITED

8. Tom has a supply of energy *that never comes to an end.*

INCONCLUSIVE

9. The judge said that the evidence was *not decisive or convincing.*

materialistic

10. George is *the type of person whose chief purpose in life is to make money.*

optimistic

11. Mary is always *looking at the bright side of everything.*

gullible

12. The Roman mob was *easily swayed by Antony's forceful persuasion.*

RULE 10. By finding a common factor, reduce a series of words **to a** class word which will include *all* the words in the original series.

apples, pears, peaches and plums   fruit
lemons, oranges, grapefruit and candy   (citrus) fruit and candy

Since the word "fruit" does not express the common factor in the second list, you must use the word "food" or the expression "fruit and candy". The latter is less generalized but more exact for précis-writing.

PRACTICE 5. Using Class Words

Using only the method of generalization (class words), reduce the following expressions to the number of words indicated in the parentheses.

1. English, French, German and Latin (1)
2. aunts, uncles, cousins, nephews, nieces and grandparents **(1)**
3. cooking, washing, ironing, dusting and vacuuming (1)
4. cats, dogs, horses and cows (1)
5. cats, dogs, horses, cows, chickens, ducks and snakes (4)
6. wagons, automobiles, trucks, trains and aeroplanes (1)
7. spring, summer, autumn and winter (1)
8. cement blocks, bricks, lumber and plaster (2)
9. people of England, Scotland and Wales (1 or 2)
10. Frenchmen, Germans, Italians, Spaniards and Belgians (2—*not* 1)

RULE 11. Omit rhetorical questions or change them to statements of fact. If the rhetorical question is simply a prelude to an answer, you should omit the question and concentrate on the answer. If the question is an expression of doubt, you should retain the idea. Thus "Will the people read the editorial? It seems unlikely." might be expressed as "The author doubted whether the people would read the editorial."

RULE 12. In précis-writing it is advisable to change direct narration into indirect or reported speech. If the direct narration is very short, or if the indirect speech seems unnatural or inappropriate, you should retain the original form. However, where you find it convenient for economy or for expression to avoid the first person or the present tense, avoid them.

Changing from direct to indirect speech involves changing *verbs* from the present to some form of the past tense.

tries	tried	may	might
is trying	was trying	can	could
has tried	had tried	must	had to

Pronouns usually change from first and second person to third person.

I, me (sing.)	he, she	ours, yours	theirs
me, you (pl.)	him, her	ourselves,	
		yourselves	themselves
mine, yours (s.)	his, hers	this, these	that, those
			(or such)

Pronominal adjectives change as follows:

my, your (sing.)	his, her	this, these	that, those
our, your (plural)	their		

Adverbs change also.

now	then, that time	yesterday	the day before
today	that day	here	there, that place

DIRECT STATEMENT: John said, "I am going to the cottage tomorrow."

INDIRECT STATEMENT: John said that he was going to the cottage the next day.

DIRECT QUESTION: He asked, "What are you going to do now?"
Lois asked, "Can you act as program chairman?"

INDIRECT QUESTION: He asked me what I was going to do then.
Lois asked (me) whether I could act as program chairman.

DIRECT COMMAND: "Be careful!" Mrs. Jones shouted.

INDIRECT COMMAND: Mrs. Jones shouted to them (ordered them) to be careful.

PRACTICE 6. Changing Direct to Indirect Narration

1. Jerry said, "I'll try out for the basketball team today."
2. Mrs. Allen yelled at the children, "Don't go too near the water!"
3. "Have you ever played badminton?" asked Jack.
4. The teacher suggested, "Use a direct quotation in this sentence."
5. "I have had many troubles in my life," said James Garfield, "but the worst of them never came."

RULE 13. Omit most examples and reduce long illustrations to bare facts.

1. (a) But often the routine seemed unbearable. Every minute of the day scheduled—even the exact spot in his clothespress where his collars were kept laid out for him. —T. BURTIS
   (b) But often he tired of the routine, the exact timing of every move.
2. (a) A party of girls, and one young man, on opposite sides of the car, found amusement in a game of ball. They tossed it to and fro, with peals of laughter that might be measured by mile-lengths; for, faster than the nimble ball could fly, the merry players fled unconsciously along, leaving the trail of their mirth afar behind, and ending their game under another sky than had witnessed its commencement.
   (b) A group of young girls and one young man *derived huge enjoyment* from a game of ball. (Notice how the adjective "huge" sums up the idea of the long illustration.)

PRACTICE 7. Omitting Examples

Reduce the following from 71 words to about 24 words.

Nearly all the changes in the English language, which now seem so clearly marked, took place very slowly and almost imperceptibly. We can easily trace the gorge cut by Niagara, though we cannot at any particular moment mark the wearing of the rock. As we review the history of the development of English speech, we can see, however, that these changes have come more rapidly at certain periods than at others.

RULE 14. Omit or condense descriptive or modifying expressions.

1. (a) A little later in the afternoon, when the rose of sunset lay on the snowy hills, a stranger knocked at the door of the cabin.
   (b) At sunset a stranger knocked at the cabin door.
2. (a) A poor and toil-worn peasant, bent with years, and groaning beneath the weight of a heavy faggot of firewood which he carried, sought, weary and sore-footed on a long and dusty road, to gain his distant cottage.—ÆSOP's *Fables*
   (b) A poor old man, carrying a heavy load of firewood, was toiling homeward.

RULE 15. Since economy of expression may depend to a considerable degree on sentence forms, combine a series of short, simple sentences into one or two well-constructed complex sentences.

> (a) The term "cowboy" was first used in England. It referred originally to a boy who took care of the cows. In the late nineteenth century the word took on a new meaning. It began to stand for the strong, silent hero of the American plains. This "cowboy" was the terror of rustlers. He was the defender of law and order in the cattle towns of the Wild West. (68 words)
>
> (b) The term "cowboy", originally used in England to refer to a boy who looked after cows, in the late nineteenth century came to stand for the strong, silent hero of the American plains, the terror of rustlers and the defender of law and order in the cattle towns of the Wild West. (52 words)

In (a) the wordiness results from the separate predication of each idea. In (b) the economy results from the subordination of less important ideas. This is *not* a précis; it is simply an example of economy through sentence structure.

PRACTICE 8. Condensing through Sentence Structure

By combining the short sentences and by using, where possible, compendious words, express each of the following series of sentences in a more concise form.

1. (a) John used to go to school with me. (b) I knew him quite well and we were great friends. (c) He is now a professional engineer. (Reduce to 12 words.)

2. (a) The man who kept me company on the camping trip was a French-Canadian. (b) He was about thirty years of age. (c) He was a person who never let anything ruffle him. (Reduce to 18 words.)

WRITING THE PRÉCIS

1. After thoroughly reading the passage, *write out clearly and tersely in your own words*—don't use sentences of the original—*the main points* of the selection. Subordinate or eliminate minor points.

2. Unless you receive specific instructions from your teacher, use about one-third or one-fourth as many words as there are in the original.

3. Look up in the dictionary words whose meanings are unfamiliar or not apparent from the context. The meaning of a key word may be crucial for your understanding of the passage.

4. Retain the paragraphing of the original unless the précis is extremely short.

5. Preserve the proportion of the original. Summarize the second half as thoroughly as the first.

6. Try to preserve the tone, attitude, and style of the original, but use the idiom of the present day.

7. Change direct narration to indirect, especially if the direct narration is long.

8. Omit figures of speech, repetitions, and most examples. Reduce lengthy illustrations.

9. Do not introduce any extraneous material by way of opinion, interpretation, or appreciation.

10. Make the précis a smooth, pointed composition. Show clearly by adequate transition and occasional connectives, such as *then, but, however, moreover,* the relation of ideas to each other.

11. Read the selection again and criticize and revise your work.

12. Finally, copy neatly and legibly your revised précis. If you write on every second line you will improve the general appearance of your work.

13. Record at the bottom of the passage the *exact* number of words that you have used.

SELF-CRITICISM CHART OF PRÉCIS

You should ask yourself these questions:

1. *Have I understood every statement?*
2. *Have I included all important ideas?*
3. *Have I excluded all minor details and crossed out all unecessary words? Are my sentences compact?*
4. *Is my language mainly my own?*
5. *Are my words, sentences and paragraphs correct?*
6. *Will my précis be clear to one who has not read the original selection?*
7. *Are my spelling, punctuation, grammar and sentence structure correct?*
8. *Does my finished work read smoothly? Does it have coherence?*

PRACTICE 9. Judging a Précis

Read carefully the following selection and evaluate the three précis. Apply the standards listed above. Which is best? Why?

A permanent reading habit based on a love of reading for all normal children is the most important purpose of the school's instructional effort. Achievement of this purpose would transform the whole program of inschool and afterschool education. It is widely recognized that children now read below the standards justifiably expected for their ages and intelligence. More disconcerting, great numbers of them fail to turn voluntarily to reading for information and recreation.[1]—GEORGE W. NORVELL (72 words)

Précis 1. Good reading would change the entire program of school life, but students show a lack of interest in better reading. (20 words)

Précis 2. Though establishing good reading habits is a major educational goal, children do not meet reasonable expectations. Many do not read freely for fun and profit. (25 words)

Précis 3. Normal children can be taught good reading. Good reading is very important. First, however, the students must turn voluntarily to reading for information and recreation. (25 words)

A PRÉCIS MODEL

In the following model the essential ideas of the original passage are underlined. Notice that minor details, repetitions and illustrations are omitted. The right-hand column contains the précis with each main idea boiled down to a sentence. Single words or phrases take the place of the clauses of the original. You should be able to justify all deletions. Refer to the rules for condensing sentences.

---

[1] *Reprinted from* The Reading Interests of Young People, *published by D. C. Heath and Company, by permission of George W. Norvell*

ORIGINAL (320 words)   PRÉCIS (104 words)

Within the car there was the usual interior life of the railroad, offering little to the observation of other passengers, but full of novelty for this pair of strangely enfranchised prisoners. It was novelty enough, indeed, that there were fifty human beings in close relation with them, under one long and narrow roof, and drawn onward by the same mighty influence that had taken their two selves into its grasp. It seemed marvellous how all these people could remain so quietly in their seats, while so much noisy strength was at work in their behalf. Some, with tickets in their hats (long travellers these, before whom lay a hundred miles of railroad), had plunged into the English scenery and adventures of pamphlet novels, and were keeping company with dukes and earls. Others, whose briefer span forbade their devoting themselves to studies so abstruse, beguiled the little tedium of the way with penny-papers. A party of girls, and one young man, on opposite sides of the car, found amusement in a game of ball. They tossed it to and fro, with peals of laughter that might be measured in mile-lengths; for, faster than the nimble ball could fly, the merry players fled unconsciously along, leaving the trail of their mirth afar behind, and ending their game under another sky than had witnessed its commencement. Boys, with apples, cakes, candy, and rolls of variously tinctured lozenges—merchandise that reminded Hepzibah of her deserted shop— appeared at each momentary stopping place, doing up their business in a hurry, or breaking it short off, lest the market should ravish them with it. New people continually entered. Old acquaintances—for such they soon grow to be, in this rapid current of affairs—continually departed. Here and there, amid the rumble and the tumult, sat one asleep. Sleep; sport; business; graver or lighter study; and the common and inevitable movement onward! It was life!—HAWTHORNE, *The House of Seven Gables*

Within the car the pair of emanicipated prisoners saw the usual train scene. To them, however, it was something strange and wonderful. They were held in close relationship with fifty other people by a common means of locomotion.

Some quietly read English novels; others, not travelling far, glanced over newspapers.

A group of young girls and one young man derived huge enjoyment from a game of ball.

At each station boys hurried aboard sold their tidbits, and dashed off again before the train started.

New passengers continually appeared, while others departed. All phases of life were represented here, from quiet sleep to joyous hilarity.

PRACTICE 10. Précis Exercises

Write précis of the following selections, reducing them to one-third as many words as there are in the originals. The total word count is given at the bottom of each passage.

1

The separate American ideals are all founded on the basic ideal of democracy. Political democracy means government founded on the consent of the governed; but socially, and we might say religiously, democracy means something much deeper. It means the recognition of the dignity of man, of the worthwhileness of every man, woman and child. Democracy also involves a recognition of the essential dignity of labour—that work is not the hallmark of the slave, but that the doing of a portion of the world's work, no matter how humble, is the rightful task and duty of every man and woman, justifying his claim to share in the bounty of the world. (111 words)—CHADSEY, WEINBERG, AND MILLER, *America in the Making*[1].

2

If vaccines and antitoxins are injected into a person, he is then immune to the particular disease for which the injection was made. This is acquired immunity. Vaccination results in a seven-year or longer immunity from smallpox. After vaccination, the cowpox, a mild form of smallpox, is the result, and the blood is filled with resisting bodies, called "antibodies," which remain there for years after there is no more trace of cowpox. If one has once had certain diseases, the body is then better able to resist these particular disease germs and will not get the disease again. Well-known examples are whooping cough and measles. This kind of freedom from disease is also called acquired immunity. (116 words)—PULVERMACHER AND VOSBURGH, *The World About Us*[2].

3

A panorama more deplorably desolate no human imagination can conceive. To the right and left, as far as the eye could reach, there lay outstretched, like ramparts of the world, lines of horridly black, beetling cliff, whose character of gloom was but the more forcibly illustrated by the surf which reared high up against it its white and ghastly crest, howling and shrieking forever. Just opposite the promontory upon whose apex we were placed, and at a distance of some five or six miles out at sea, there was visible a small, bleak-looking island; or more properly, its position was discernible through the wilderness of surge in which it was enveloped. About two miles nearer the land arose another of smaller size, hideously craggy and barren, and encompassed at various intervals by a cluster of dark rocks. (137 words)—POE, *Descent into the Maelstrom*.

4

On another of these desert journeys Lawrence was captured by a band of Kurd robbers. They took him to their secret refuge, high up on a mountaintop. They put him in a hut and left two of their men to guard him, while the rest of the band went off on another expedition. One afternoon the Kurd sentries were separated, one remaining inside with him and the other sitting outside in the sun. It was a very hot day. The Kurds had had their lunch, and the man on the outside had fallen asleep. The other sentry happened to turn his

[1], [2]*Reprinted by permission of the publisher, D. C. Heath and Company.*

back, and as he did so Lawrence jumped on his back and overpowered him. He did this without making enough noise to arouse the second man. Then he went out and disposed of the sleeper. The only approach to this rocky mountaintop was up a narrow, winding, precipitous path. Lawrence now had two rifles and plenty of ammunition. Hiding himself at a strategic point he picked off the rest of the band as they came up that evening. (179 words)—LOWELL THOMAS, *The Boys' Life of Colonel Lawrence.*

Reprinted by permission of the Century Company.

5

A circumstance which greatly tended to enhance the tyranny of the nobility and the sufferings of the inferior classes in England arose from the consequences of the Conquest of Duke William of Normandy. Four generations had not sufficed to blend the hostile blood of the Normans and Anglo-Saxons, or to unite, by common language and mutual interests, two hostile races, one of which still felt the elation of triumph, while the other groaned under all the consequences of defeat. The power had been completely placed in the hands of the Norman nobility by the event of the Battle of Hastings, and it had been used with no moderate hand. At court and in the castles of the great nobles, where the pomp and the state of a court was emulated, Norman-French was the only language employed; in courts of law, the pleadings and judgments were delivered in the same tongue. In short, French was the language of honour, of chivalry, and even of justice, while the far more manly and expressive Anglo-Saxon was abandoned to the use of rustics and hinds, who knew no other. (185 words)—SIR WALTER SCOTT, *Ivanhoe.*

6

Millions of people, presumably, are going to have in the near future, whether they want it or not, more time off than they ever dreamed of. An entire nation which has never learned to play has been presented with the great gift of leisure. Our playing is now, for the most part, done by proxy. We make paid entertainers rich by our inexperience in amusing ourselves. But vicarious amusements are not going to suffice to fill the spare hours which the future will bring. We must do better than that. We must acquire a new conception of play, one that demands active participation instead of passive acceptance. Radio, movies, athletic spectacles will all have a large place, but they will no longer suffice for a grown-up, healthy population. People must have something to make demands upon them physically and mentally, to develop and express them, and to give exercise to invention and imagination. If these diversions are of the kind that develops the complete man, mentally, socially, and physically, they will profoundly influence the course of human events. Indeed, the wise use of leisure may easily be an important, perhaps the most important, influence on the future course of our civilization. (201 words)—ERNEST ELMO CALKINS.

7

The great error in Rip's composition was an insuperable aversion to all kinds of profitable labour. It could not be from the want of assiduity or perseverance; for he would sit on a wet rock with a rod as long and heavy as a Tartar's lance, and fish all day without a murmur, even though he should not be encouraged by a single nibble. He would carry a fowling-piece on his shoulder for hours together, trudging through woods and swamps, and up hill and down dale, to shoot a few squirrels or wild pigeons. He would never refuse to assist a neighbour even in the roughest toil, and was a foremost man at all country frolics for husking Indian corn, or building stone fences; the women of the village, too, used to employ him to run their errands, and to do such little odd jobs as their less obliging husbands would not do for them. In a word, Rip was ready to attend to anybody's business but his own; but as to doing family duty, and keeping his farm in order, he found it impossible. (185 words)—WASHINGTON IRVING, *Rip Van Winkle*

8

There are those who hold, however, that the chief rivals of the novel are not non-literary media such as the radio and film, but the short story and the factual report.   To consider the case of the short story first, it is held that the speed of modern life militates against the sustained reading which the long novel demands and favours the shorter form.   In answer, one might simply point again to the fact that novels are still being read, and in great quantity; but it would be useful to seek a logical explanation of the novel's capacity to exist along with the short story.   The fact is that the two forms of fiction, for all their apparent similarity, are governed by different rules, perform different functions, and satisfy different tastes.   The short story is severely restricted in both space and time; it must seize upon some climactic event in the life of a character and can provide only a bare suggestion of what has gone before; the number of characters with which it can cope successfully is very small; there is space for only the briefest sort of treatment of the social and physical environment.   The novel, obviously, is far less hampered in these respects.   (206 words)—DESMOND PACEY, *The Future of the Novel.*   *By permission of the Author.*

9

A tree is an underground creature, with its tail in the air.   All its intelligence is in its roots.   All the senses it has are in its roots.   Think what sagacity it shows in its search after food and drink!   Somehow or other, the rootlets, which are its tentacles, find out that there is a brook at a moderate distance from the trunk of the tree, and they make for it with all their might.   They find every crack in the rock where there are a few grains of the nourishing substance they care for, and insinuate themselves into its deepest recesses.   When spring and summer come, they let their tails grow, and delight in whisking them about in the wind, or letting them be whisked about by it; for these tails are poor passive things, with very little will of their own, and bend in whatever direction the wind chooses to make them.   The next time you see a tree waving in the wind, recollect that it is the tail of a great underground, many-armed, polypus-like creature, which is as proud of its caudal appendage, especially in summer-time, as a peacock of its gorgeous expanse of plumage. (198 words)—OLIVER W. HOLMES, *Over the Teacups.*

10

Excellent results have been reported from high school classes in driving. It would be well if a driving course were made *compulsory* for American high school students, since *virtually* all of them will drive at one time or another. Book learning helps.   Once a boy knows that a head-on collision between two cars doing 30 miles an hour produces the same *impact* as a dive off a nine-story building he is apt to be a bit more careful.   Teen-agers are good mechanical drivers, of course, because of superior physical condition and fast reaction

time. Their judgment of speed and distance is often wonderfully good, but their judgment on questions of acceptable risk is often frightfully bad. But the most dangerous driver is not the teen-ager. Most dangerous is a man of 21 who has been driving for from six to eight years. Like the 5000-hour airplane pilot, he's just good enough to think that he's good. Women are safer drivers than men. Their mental attitude, as a group, is better (less *combative*) and their reaction times are faster. They go slower than men and thus get into fewer tricky situations. Once in a bad situation, though, women are more likely than men to have real trouble. (208 words—contractions counting as two words)—KEN W. PURDY, *The Kings of the Road.*
Reprinted by permission of Little, Brown and Company.

11

I've heard and read a great deal about the *necessity* of parents' understanding their sons and daughters, but there's very little said about the necessity of sons and daughters understanding their parents. Why not? We know that parents can get along much better with their sons if they understand the reasons why the boys act as they do—reasons the boys themselves do not understand. Parents who understand make allowances for the behaviour of their sons. Why shouldn't the boys know the reasons why their parents act as they do and make allowances for them? Did it ever occur to you, for example, that maybe your father was impatient or sharp with you because he was worried about something at the office, the mortgage, or the bills? Ever think that your parents disregarded your feelings? But did you ever think that perhaps you disregarded your parents' feelings? It is not my intention to make this a course for boys in understanding their parents, although it would be a good idea if someone did it. I do believe, however, if there was more understanding on both sides, of the desires, motives, and forces that cause people to act as they do, there would be greater happiness for both parents and sons and less friction. So, if your dad is griping, maybe he has had a bad day or something has gone wrong. (234 words)—DAVID W. ARMSTRONG, *Questions Boys Ask.*
Reprinted by permission of E. P. Dutton and Company, Inc. and the Author.

12

(Remember to use the idiom of the present day.)

Although we usually call reward and punishment the two hinges upon which all government turns, yet I could never observe this maxim to be put in practice by any nation except that of Lilliput. Whoever can there bring sufficient proof that he has strictly observed the laws of his country for seventy-three moons, has a claim to certain privileges, according to his quality or condition in life, with a proportionate sum of money out of a fund appropriated for that use; he likewise acquires the title of "snilpall" or legal, which is added to his name, but does not descend to his posterity. And those people thought it a prodigious defect of policy among us, when I told them that our laws were enforced only by penalties, without any mention of reward. It is upon this account that the image of Justice, in their law courts, is formed with six eyes, two before, as many behind, and on each side one, to signify circumspection; with a bag of gold open in her right hand, and a sword sheathed in her left, to show she is more disposed to reward than to punish. (192 words)—JONATHAN SWIFT, *Gulliver's Travels.*

13

The preparations for migration begin long before the coming of the fall.

They begin, in a real sense, with the moult, in latter summer when the care of the fledglings is over; for it is then that worn, frayed feathers are replaced by new ones and the bird's light-boned body acquires fresh buoyance. Like many another happening in fields and forests, the moulting of the bird is so casual and unspectacular an event that hardly one man in a thousand even remarks its occurrence; but it deserves rank among the minor miracles. Two feathers, and two feathers only, are shed at one time, and they are shed with perfect symmetry. The middle feather of each wing is the first to go. When the new replacement feathers for these gaps have achieved half their growth, another pair of quills loosens and is shed. With perfect precision the process continues until a whole new plumage has come into being. So gradual is the process, so nicely contrived, that at no time is more than a single pair of feathers missing; at no time is the bird's flight mechanism unbalanced or impaired. And in the case of certain of our species the miracle is of an even more arresting kind. There is the metmorphosis, for instance, which the male scarlet tanagers undergo. Before the moulting-time their flame-red plumage affords one of the gaudiest colours in our countryside. When the moult has ended, they are arrayed in dingy green. It will hide them, on their southward flight, from the sharp, preying eyes of hawks. (260 words)—ALAN DEVOE, "The Mystery of Migration" from *Down to Earth* by Alan Devoe, copyright 1939 by Alan Devoe.

Reprinted by permission of Coward-McCann, Inc.

14

The Moslem quarter of a city is lonely and desolate; you go up, and down, and on, over shelving and hillocky paths through the narrow lanes walled in by blank, windowless dwellings; you come out upon an open space strewed with the black ruins that some late fire has left; you pass by a mountain of cast-away things, the rubbish of centuries, and on it you see numbers of big, wolf-like dogs lying torpid under the sun, with limbs outstretched to the full, as if they were dead; storks or cranes, sitting fearless upon the low roofs, look gravely down upon you; the still air that you breathe is loaded with the scent of citron and pomegranate rinds scorched by the sun, or (as you approach the Bazaar), with the dry, dead perfume of strange spices. You long for some signs of life, and tread the ground more heavily, as though you would wake the sleepers with the heel of your boot; but the foot falls noiseless upon the crumbling soil of an eastern city, and Silence follows you still. Again and again you meet turbans, and faces of men, but they have nothing for you—no welcome—no wonder—no wrath—no scorn—they look upon you as we do upon a December fall of snow—as a 'seasonable', unaccountable, uncomfortable work of God that may have been sent for some good purpose, to be revealed hereafter. (238 words)—A. W. KINGLAKE.

PRACTICE 11. Writing a Précis

From the assignment for tomorrow in history, economics, chemistry, physics, biology, physiography, or any other science, pick one or more paragraphs which seem difficult to you. Make a précis of the passage, applying the rules for reading difficult sentences and paragraphs to help you understand the ideas.

Chapter 8

Description

SCIENTIFIC VERSUS LITERARY DESCRIPTION

In describing you transmit to others pictures of objects, persons, and places which have interested or pleased you. These pictures can be drawn, however, in two widely different ways. *Scientific description* presents a precise catalogue of details and excludes entirely the writer's personality and impressions; it resembles a diagram. In this type of description are included lost and found advertisements, descriptions in scientific textbooks, and police records. *Artistic description*, which is used in literature of all types, resembles a painting. With a few striking details the literary artist sets the reader's imagination to work at completing the picture and transmits to the reader the emotions and impressions the writer originally experienced.

Scientific Description of Air

Pure air is an invisible gas, colourless, odourless, and tasteless; very compressible and perfectly elastic. It is very mobile and, like all matter, has weight. Though under ordinary conditions gaseous, it may easily be made to assume the liquid state.—AREY, BRYANT, CLENDENIN, AND MORREY, *New Physiography*

Literary Description of a Person

Once more the door banged, and a slight, slim-built boy perhaps fifteen years old, a half-smoked cigarette hanging from one corner of his mouth, leaned over the high footway.—KIPLING

PRACTICE 1. Studying Descriptions

1. How many facts about air are given in the brief scientific description?

2. What facts are given in the literary description of **Harvey Cheyne**?

3. "A half-smoked cigarette hanging from one corner of his mouth" arouses the reader's imagination to finish the portait of Harvey Cheyne and also to tell what kind of boy he was. What is your picture of Harvey?

OBSERVING

To paint word pictures one needs to observe the object, scene, or person, and then to picture what one sees. To observe means to see and note, to examine and note, to watch closely, to look at attentively, not just to look at. When an artist paints a person's picture, he doesn't just glance at his subject or take one look at him and then paint; instead, with the subject "sitting" for his picture, he observes and paints, observes and paints, and continues to observe and paint.

All five senses bring us information about an object. Often, however, our senses, like a knife, become dull and need whetting. This can best be done by using them actively in gathering impressions of our surroundings. Describing is telling what our senses find out for us about the world in which we live—our eyes by seeing, our ears by hearing, our noses by smelling, our tongues by tasting, and our fingers by feeling.

PRACTICE 2. Words that Describe

Pick out the words that describe sounds, tastes, smells, feelings, and sights.

Example:

The next wave crashed and roared over me and filled my mouth with bitter salt water.
Crashed and *roared* describe sounds.   *Bitter* and *salt* describe tastes.

1. Even as I looked, there came a red flash and another report that sent the echoes clattering, and once more a round shot whistled through the air.
    —STEVENSON
2. The unceasing vibration of the engines throbbed through their bodies and numbed their brains.
3. Still tingling from the cold water, we tramped toward camp, hungrily sniffing the sharp, pungent odour of frying bacon.
4. Down his throat trickled a thick, tart liquid that made him cough, choke, and gasp for breath.

5. The drummer walloped his drums, a saxophone squawked, and fiddles squeaked.—TARKINGTON

6. Wavelets of creamy-crested green water lapped gently on the mossy rocks.

7. A large oak door creaked dismally as it swung back and forth on its one rusty hinge.

8. Sand gritted between their teeth, seared their eyeballs, and lashed their faces with stinging blows.

9. The monarch is a little, keen, fresh-coloured old man, with protruding eyes, attired in plain, old-fashioned, snuff-coloured clothes and brown stockings.

10. André stood before her, a shadowy figure in the obscurity, pale, unshaven, muddy, smiling a strange, dim, tired, infinitely tender smile.—FISHER

PRACTICE 3. Picture-making Words

In a sentence for each, describe a sound, a sight, a taste, a smell, and a feeling suggested by the following. Choose accurate picture-bringing words.

1. A storm. 2. The tea kettle. 3. Olives. 4. Pop-corn. 5. Coffee boiling. 6. A plunge in the lake. 7. Birch trees. 8. A wood fire. 9. A hinge that needs oiling. 10. Wild strawberries. 11. Polished wood. 12. Rain on a tin roof. 13. A sunset. 14. Newly ploughed earth. 15. Toasted marshmallows. 16. Satin. 17. Icicles. 18. Salt water. 19. Fog. 20. My kitten's fur. 21. A baby's hand. 22. A service station.

PRACTICE 4. Picture-making Words

Write vivid words appealing to each of these senses: sight, hearing, touch, smell.

Example:

taste—nibble, devour, gulp, gorge, guzzle, crunch, salty, bitter, tangy, spicy, creamy, delicious, sour, sharp, tender, tough, toothsome, flat, nauseating, savoury, tart, sharp, mellow, mild, tasty, gritty, slippery, sugary, peppery

PRACTICE 5. Picture-making Verbs

For each of the following verbs or word-groups find four or more specific, picture-making equivalents: *be active, speak, sleep, work, hasten, eject, depart, make a noise, smell an odour, feel a fabric, taste a food.*

Example:

Be inactive—lounge, loaf, loiter, loll, lag, dawdle, vegetate, let the grass grow under one's feet, kill time, burn daylight, sleep at one's post, swim with the stream.

WORD PICTURES

"There were clouds in the sky" states a simple fact, but "Feathery clouds scudded across the sky" paints a word picture. The difference lies in two words used: *feathery* and *scudded*. Just as a painting in fresh, vivid colours is more arresting than a drawing in black and white, so the use of vigorous, picture-making adjectives, adverbs, and verbs will produce in your speaking and writing a more telling effect than the colourless verbs and bald nouns so frequently employed. After observing sharply we need to search out vivid, exact words to picture what we see.

PRACTICE 6. Picture-making Words

Select the picture-making words in each of the following sentences:

Example:

Big Junko sported a wide, ferocious, straggling moustache and low eyebrows, under which gleamed little fierce eyes.—STEWART EDWARD WHITE

The picture words are *wide, ferocious, straggling, moustache, low, eyebrows, gleamed, little, fierce, eyes*.

1. Lou Gehrig has a jolly face with a smile that has won him many friends, broad shoulders, immense hands, powerful forearms, and a pair of sturdy legs, commonly called "bottle" legs because of their appearance.
2. Claude Bowers is a short, slim, dark, studious, scholarly, quiet man in his middle years.—*Time*
3. Donald's apple-like cheeks, ham-like hands, and big, puffy body are accentuated by his tiny round cap, tight-fitting clothes, and choking collar.
4. A silvery moonlight flooded the white beach, and in the inky black lake the stars and moon beheld their reflections.
5. Except on the crown, which was raggedly bald, he had stiff, black hair, standing jaggedly all over it, and growing down hill almost to his broad, blunt nose.—DICKENS
6. I remember him as if it were yesterday, as he came plodding to the inn door, his sea chest following behind him in a handbarrow; a tall, strong, heavy, nut-brown man; his tarry pigtail falling over the shoulders of his soiled blue coat; his hands ragged and scarred, with black, broken nails; and the sabre cut across one cheek, a dirty, livid white.—STEVENSON
7. There was Ben Gunn's boat—homemade if ever anything was homemade: a rude, lopsided framework of tough wood, and stretched upon that a covering of goatskin, with the hair inside.—STEVENSON
8. A last tremendous crash, a deep-throated grunt, and a mighty moose, a colossal bull, broke out of the woods and stalked stiff-legged toward them through the berry bushes, staring suspiciously from side to side.—MACMILLAN

PRACTICE 7. Creating a Word Picture

In a good sentence or two for each, describe ten of the following. Observe. Use picture-making words.

1. An old house. 2. A new house. 3. A storm at sea. 4. A sea gull in flight. 5. A canoe. 6. A sailboat. 7. A baseball player sliding to second base. 8. An elm tree in a storm. 9. A tramp. 10. A bald head. 11. A thick head of hair. 12. A skinny boy. 13. A fat girl. 14. A rug. 15. A motion picture actor. 16. A motion picture actress. 17. The Prime Minister of Canada. 18. A face in the crowd. 19. A tennis player returning a hard high ball. 20. Grandfather. 21. A lively street corner. 22. A cat watching a bird. 23. Father landing a fish. 24. A boy scoring a touchdown.

DESCRIBING SOUNDS

How many radio voices can you describe? Have you ever listened to your own voice carefully enough to know how it sounds? To describe sounds listen attentively and thoughtfully and then find words which will cause another to hear what you heard.

PRACTICE 8. Describing Sounds

In a sentence for each, describe six voices or sounds. Listen sharply and then choose words which accurately describe what you hear.

Examples:

1. The booms were *tearing* in the blocks, the rudder was *banging* to and fro, and the whole ship was *creaking, groaning,* and jumping like machinery. —STEVENSON
2. In the park today I heard the *barking* of a squirrel, the *chattering* of a blue-jay, the *chirping* of a cricket, and the *shrill piping* call of a tree-toad.

1. My voice. 2. Father's voice. 3. Mother's voice. 4. A radio voice. 5. Outside the radio store. 6. At a country fair. 7. The school cafeteria. 8. A touchdown. 9. A mouse in the wall. 10. A robin. 11. An airplane propeller. 12. A dilapidated automobile. 13. A streetcar. 14. A home run. 15. A thunder storm. 16. The riveter. 17. Main Street on election night. 18. Victoria Day. 19. The huckster. 20. In the barn. 21. The baby. 22. Our neighbour's dog. 23. In the kitchen. 24. A cat fight. 25. Any other sound or voice you have heard recently.

COMPARING

Often the quickest and most effective way to picture an object or a scene is by the use of an apt, striking comparison or figure of speech. Three common kinds of figures are simile, metaphor, and personification.

202 MASTERING EFFECTIVE ENGLISH

A **simile** is a definitely stated comparison of two unlike objects that have one point in common. Regularly *as* or *like* is used to make the comparison.

> The grass rustled like silk.
> He talks like a dictionary on its best behaviour.—Concordia Merrel

A **metaphor** is an implied comparison between unlike objects that have one point in common. *As* or *like* is not used.

> The road was a narrow ribbon unwinding before us.
> Everest, cold and imperious monarch of mountains, has repulsed with death man's latest attempt to conquer her.

Personification, a kind of metaphor, assigns personal attributes to inanimate objects or abstract ideas.

> The wind shrieked with fury and rained blows on the house.
> The waves danced.

For vividness use figures of speech and comparisons. Avoid, however, hackneyed comparisons: "pearly teeth," "old as the hills," "wise as an owl," "good as gold." If you wish to describe an animal your hearers or readers have never seen, compare it with an animal they have seen. Stevenson calls sea lions "huge slimy monsters—soft snails, as it were, of incredible bigness—two or three score of them together, making the rocks to echo with their barkings."

PRACTICE 9. Comparisons and Figures of Speech

Pick out the effective descriptive words, comparisons, and figures of speech in the following sentences.

1. He was a scraggly bearded individual in a ragged shirt, which offered glimpses of a hairy chest in need of soap.—Henry Sydnor Harrison
2. His voice was like a buzz saw striking a rusty nail.—Folwell
3. Captain Cunningham was a great, florid, burly, drunken brute, not less than sixty years old.—S. Weir Mitchell
4. He had a strongly cut face and a soft, purring voice.
5. The moaning and howling of the wind outside served to emphasize the coziness and security of our kitchen.
6. The film moves along with the sweeping speed of an overfed caterpillar.
   —*New York Evening Post*
7. Love is a breath of fresh air from the highest Heaven brought somehow into the stuffy cellar of our existence.—De Morgan
8. They were led up a corkscrew staircase to a squat-ceilinged closet lit by the arched top of a high window, the lower panes of which served for the floor below.—Edith Wharton

9. On her mouth is a smug, self-satisfied, conceited smile.
10. His face looked as if it were one freckle, and his pug nose loomed up handsomely between a pair of roguishly blue eyes.

PRACTICE 10. Adding Vivid Details

Add details to make each of the following pictures more vivid:

Examples:

1. We walked along in the rain.
   With the cold raindrops merrily trickling down our backs, we paddled along, entertained by the steady squish-squosh of our rubbers.
2. He was fat and poorly dressed.
   He was a fat, amiable, seedy, down-at-heels looking man.

1. On the table was a dish containing fruit.
2. There are many flowers in the garden.
3. We had a good dinner.
4. Ted has three dogs.
5. Mr. Norton has two cars.
6. Mr. Jeff's home is very attractive.
7. There are several trees in front of our school.
8. The room was disorderly.
9. In the kitchen the cook was preparing dinner.
10. Two birds were sitting on the fence.
11. The trees last fall were beautifully coloured.
12. Last week we had a bad storm.
13. In the woods I heard a number of interesting sounds.
14. In the tree was a nest full of young birds.
15. A giraffe is a queer-looking animal.

OBSERVATION AND SENSE IMPRESSIONS

Without accurate observation there can be no description. Look carefully at details and fix them well in mind. Learn to employ actively the sense of taste, touch, smell, and hearing as well as that of sight, for these five senses furnish all descriptive material. Be an artist gathering material, not an ordinary unobservant person who can't describe accurately from memory his breakfast table, his home, his living room, the face of his watch, or the faces of the members of his family.

Recording a sense impression is painting for your reader the picture of some memorable sense experience. If your mental picture is clear and your word picture vivid, your reader will himself experience that same sense impression. Take for example, this record of a sense impression: "Weather-beaten walls sagged despondently under the weight of overhanging eaves, and a single remaining shutter swung disconsolately on a rusty hinge, creaking dismally." In a sentence the writer has conjured up a picture of an ancient, dilapidated house.

PRACTICE 11. Sense Impressions

In a sentence or two for each, record five sense impressions, one for each sense, suggested by the following. Have a clear picture in mind and choose vivid descriptive words.

Example:

Each wild strawberry as it touched my lips was a drop of nectar and a crumb of ambrosia, a concentrated essence of all the pungent sweetness of the wildwood, sapid, penetrating, and delicious.—VAN DYKE

1. A clover field. 2. The hoot of an owl. 3. A blanket. 4. A street light through a mist. 5. Mint leaves. 6. A waterfall. 7. A wild rose bush. 8. A train whistle. 9. A bakery. 10. The bark of a tree. 11. The ocean. 12. A fog horn. 13. A moss-covered stone. 14. Sand. 15. A sea shell. 16. A ripe tomato. 17. A sty full of small pigs. 18. A fire siren. 19. A lump of sugar. 20. A wheat field. 21. A bass drum. 22. A pebble. 23. Ginger ale. 24. Newly mown hay. 25. Coffee.

BREVITY AND ACCURACY

The best description is short and accurate. No one, Flaubert tells us, can write an effective description more than half a printed page in length. Faguet says, "However considerable M. Valois's nose was, a whole page devoted to its description is, I confess, too much for me."

HOW TO PICTURE

1. Observe. Flaubert says, "Study an object till its essential difference from every other is perceived and can be rendered in words." The "seeing eye" and the "hearing ear" are the foundation of good description.

2. Decide whether your description is to be a scientific or a literary one. Do you wish to take a snapshot or, like most artists, emphasize a central idea or feeling, called an impression? The description of an office, for example, may produce the impression of neatness, untidiness, prosperity, system, or confusion.

3. Describe from a favourable point of view. No one sets up his camera and snaps pictures at random. A word painter commonly makes clear at the outset from what point he is viewing the room, building, or landscape. He may, for example, say, "When we had clambered over the last steep rocks to the summit of Whiteface, we sat down to rest and looked first towards the St. Lawrence River," and then picture what we saw from that point. A snapshot of a home taken at noonday from the middle of the street or road in front of it is quite different from a picture of it at dusk or by moonlight from a point a distance away.

When, as in the description of a town or the exterior of a house or school, the point of view is changed, notify the readers of the shift. In "Westminster Abbey," Irving shows a change of point of view in the following sentence: "From Poet's Corner I continued my stroll towards that part of the abbey which contains the sepulchres of the kings."

4. As a rule, present first such a picture or impression as one would get from a glance at the object. The passenger on an express train, for example, notices the size, shape, and colour of the buildings he passes.

5. Decide how many and what details will make your picture most vivid. Select the most striking, interesting, or significant features. If you present every detail observed, you may weary the reader or hearer and also puzzle him, because he will be unable to hold the parts of the picture in mind long enough to put them together. The picture in his mind will resemble a cut-up picture of which some pieces have been lost. In an impressionistic description select the details that give the idea or feeling desired. If you are describing an untidy school-room in which the books on one desk are neatly arranged, either picture this desk as a contrast with the rest of the room, or omit it because it does not change the impression of untidiness produced by the room.

6. Arrange details in the order of observation. The first detail observed is the most striking or unusual one. After especially striking details have been presented, the order of observation is commonly the space order: foreground to background, top to bottom, centre to circumference, or right to left.

7. For vividness use picture-making nouns, verbs, adjectives, and adverbs, figures of speech, and comparisons. Avoid overworked general words such as *nice, fine, lovely, wonderful, grand,* and *interesting.*

Use *very* and superlatives sparingly. "He is honest" is stronger than "He is very honest" or "He is most honest."

8. Use "signposts." Such phrases as *on the right, on the extreme right, just beyond, farther along, somewhat lower, in the distance, farther to the left,* and *just in front of* help the mind to put the parts of the picture together.

9. End the description with a salient detail or with an effective statement of the central feeling or impression.

ORDER AND ARRANGEMENT

No fixed rule can be laid down, but as already suggested, the commonest arrangement is

> General impression on first view.
> Details in any number.
> General effect after closer scrutiny.

DOMINANT IMPRESSION

We have already learned that a good paragraph requires a key sentence to lead the mind to anticipate what is to come. This topic sentence is then developed to a more complete understanding. So, too, in description, success depends upon a judicious selection of details to maintain a dominant impression favourable or unfavourable. This must be determined before the first sentence is written, and borne in mind throughout the whole of the writing.

Models:

1. MAY IN IRELAND

That was a pleasant drive. May in Ireland! What does it mean? It means coming out of a dark tunnel into blinding sunshine; it means casting off the slough of winter, and gliding with crest erect and fresh habiliments under leafy trees and by the borders of shining seas, the crab-apple blossoms, pink and white, scenting the air over your head, and primroses and violets dappling the turf under your feet; it means lambs frisking around their tranquil mothers in the meadows, and children returning at evening with hands and pinafores full of the scented cowslips and the voluptuous woodbine; it means the pouring of wineblood into empty veins, and the awakening of torpid faculties, and the deeper, stronger pulsations of the heart, and the fresh buoyancy of drooping and submerged spirits, and the white clouds full of bird-music, as the larks call to their young and shake out the raptures of their full hearts, and the cheery salutations of ploughmen, as the coulter turns over the rich, brown soil, and the rooks follow each furrow for food.—SHEEHAN, *My New Curate.*

By permission of the publishers, The Talbot Press Ltd., Dublin.

2. TINK, TINK, TINK

From the workshop of the Golden Key there issued forth a tinkling sound, so merry and good-humoured that it suggested the idea of some one working blithely, and made a pleasant music. *Tink, tink, tink,*—clear as a silver bell, and audible at every pause of the street's harsher noises, as though it said, "I don't care; nothing puts me out; I am resolved to be happy."

Women scolded, children squalled, heavy carts went rumbling by, horrible cries proceeded from the lungs of hawkers. Still it struck in again, no higher, no lower, no louder, no softer; not thrusting itself on people's notice a bit the more for having been outdone by louder sounds—*tink, tink, tink, tink, tink.*

It was a perfect embodiment of the still small voice, free from all cold, harshness, huskiness, or unhealthiness of any kind. Foot-passengers slackened their pace, and were disposed to linger near it. Neighbours who had got up splenetic that morning felt good-humour stealing on them as they heard it, and by degrees became quite sprightly. Mothers danced their babies to its ringing—still the same magical *tink, tink, tink,* came gayly from the workshop of the Golden Key.—DICKENS.

PRACTICE 12. Dominant Impression

Write a descriptive composition in which one chief impression is dominant. Determine beforehand what that impression is to be. It may be confusion, peace, silence, tranquillity, grandeur, beauty, mystery, fright, comfort, cosiness, joyousness, oddity, ugliness, dullness.

1. A sunset. 2. A sunrise. 3. A mountain valley. 4. A limestone cave. 5. Mirror Lake. 6. Lake Louise. 7. Midnight Lake. 8. Hot summer afternoon. 9. Noon in a hay field. 10. Under the elms. 11. Three o'clock in the morning. 12. A tropical scene. 13. Sunset Bay. 14. Harvest field. 15. A tramp. 16. A pedlar. 17. Your own choice.

A FIXED POINT OF VIEW

A single point of view may be fixed in place (doorway, hilltop, the road, the boat, the garden gate); or it may be a mental point of view (owner, borrower, traveller, stranger, artist, businessman, woman, hermit). We do not see the same things from different places, nor do people of different interests or temperaments see the same thing from the same local point.

Models:
1. PRAIRIE HUSH

Nature was asleep. Not a breath rustled the drooping leaves or fanned the heated brow; not a chirp relieved the silence which was enhanced by the drowsy hum of the mysterious insect life. From my seat beneath a shady bush I gazed out over a wide, gently-rolling expanse of prairie backed in the distance by a dark line of trees, bluish in the heat haze which spread a delicate, gauzy film of transparent blue over distant objects. Far across the plain a flash of silver proclaimed the thread of a brook winding its glittering way between grassy banks to the river. The wavering heat-waves rising from the over-heated prairie distorted and gave fantastic shapes to the solitary cattle that still persisted in grazing after their companions had sought refuge in the shade from the fiery sun. Their red and white hides gave an added note of colour to the scene which was bathed in the golden glory of the sunlight. The scene was devoid of other life save for a hawk which sailed majestically on "wings unweary" high up in the blue vault of heaven. Ever and anon its cry would come sifting faintly down to earth emphasizing the afternoon silence which had enveloped us in its all-embracing folds. And thus nature slept on that drowsy afternoon.—STUDENT.

2. THE PASS OF FUENCEBADON

It is impossible to describe this pass or the circumjacent region, which contains some of the most extraordinary scenery in all Spain; a feeble and imperfect outline is all that I can hope to effect. The traveller who ascends it follows for nearly a league the course of the torrent, whose banks are in some places precipitous, and in others slope down to the waters, and are covered with lofty trees, oaks, poplars, and chestnuts. Small villages are at first continually seen, with low walls, and roofs formed of immense slates, the eaves nearly touching the ground; these hamlets, however, gradually become less frequent as the path grows more steep and narrow, until they finally cease at a short distance before the spot is attained where the rivulet is abandoned, and is no more seen, though its tributaries may yet be heard in many a gully, or descried in tiny rills dashing down the steeps. Everything here is wild, strange, and beautiful; the hill up which winds the path towers above on the right, whilst on the farther side of a profound ravine rises an immense mountain, to whose extreme altitudes the eye is scarely able to attain, but the most singular features of this pass are the hanging fields or meadows which cover its sides. In these, as I passed, the grass was growing luxuriantly, and in many the mowers were plying their scythes, though it seemed scarcely possible that their feet could find support on ground so precipitous: above and below were driftways, so small as to seem threads along the mountain side. A car, drawn by oxen, is creeping round yon airy eminence; the nearer wheel is actually hanging over the horrid descent; giddiness seizes the brain, and the eye is rapidly withdrawn. A cloud intervenes, and when again you turn to watch their progress, the objects of your anxiety have disappeared. Still more narrow comes the path along which you yourself are toiling, and it turns more frequent. You have already come a distance of two leagues, and still one-third of the ascent remains unsurmounted.—GEORGE BORROW, *The Bible in Spain*.

3. NIGHT SOUND

As I thus lay, between content and longing, a faint noise stole towards me through the pines. I thought, at first, it was the crowing of cocks or the barking of dogs at some very distant farm; but steadily and gradually it took articulate shape in my ears, until I became aware that a passenger was going by upon the high-road in the valley, and singing loudly as he went. There was more of good-will than grace in his performance; but he trolled with ample lungs; and the sound of his voice took hold upon the hillside and set the air shaking in the leafy glens. I have heard people passing by night in sleeping

cities; some of them sang; one, I remember, played loudly on the bagpipes. I have heard the rattle of a cart or carriage spring up suddenly after hours of stillness, and pass, for some minutes, within the range of my hearing as I lay abed. There is a romance abo it all who are abroad in the black hours, and with something of a thrill we try to guess their business. But here the romance was double; first, this glad passenger, lit internally with wine, who sent up his voice in music through the night; and then I, on the other hand, buckled into my sack, and smoking alone in the pine-woods between four and five thousand feet toward the stars.—ROBERT LOUIS STEVENSON, *Travels with a Donkey.*
By permission of Charles Scribner's Sons, New York.

PRACTICE 13. Point of View

In writing on the following topics, keep in mind the value of picture words, vital observation, and dominant impression. Write three descriptions based on three of the following themes, making the local point of view clear to the reader. Choose the most effective place, or person.

1. Our summer camp. 2. A city park. 3. The old swimming hole. 4. The old mill. 5. Woodland scene. 6. Prairie landscape. 7. January morning. 8. The bridge. 9. The orchard. 10. The sentinel tree. 11. The caravan.

PRACTICE 14. Points of View

Write three paragraphs of description, each one of the same object, seen by three different persons:

1. The valley (hunter, lumberman, artist). 2. The hotel (beggar, architect, guest). 3. The lake (fisherman, discoverer, poet). 4. The school (freshman, teacher, alumnus). 5. The monument (tourist, next of kin, sculptor).

A CHANGING POINT OF VIEW

Description is seldom used in literary writing except as part of the narrative structure. In consequence it is frequently narrative in form, a series of brief pictures at various times, and often in different places. The secret of success in this running description is to keep the reader clear where the scene has shifted in time or place, and to make keen, crisp observations, not so much detailed as etched with deft strokes, a succession of bright miniatures.

Models:

1. THE VALLEY OF THE TARN

The valley below La Vernède pleased me more and more as I went along. Now the hills approached from either hand, naked and crumbling, and walled in the river between cliffs; and now the valley widened and became green. The road led me past the old castle of Miral on a steep; past a battlemented monastery, long since broken up and turned into a church and parsonage; and past a cluster of black roofs, the village of Cocurès, sitting among vine-lands, and meadows, and orchards thick with red apples, and where, along the highway, they were knocking down walnuts from the roadside trees, and gathering them in sacks and baskets. The hills, however much the vale might open, were still tall and bare, with cliffy battlements and here and there a pointed summit; and the Tarn still rattled through the stones with a mountain noise. I had been led, by bagmen of a picturesque turn of mind, to expect a horrific country after the heart of Byron; but to my Scottish eyes it seemed smiling and plentiful, as the weather still gave an impression of high summer to my Scottish body; although the chestnuts were already picked out by the autumn, and the poplars, that here began to mingle with them, had turned into pale gold against the approach of winter.—ROBERT LOUIS STEVENSON, *Travels with a Donkey.*

By permission of Charles Scribner's Sons, New York.

2. UNDERN HALL

Undern Hall, with its many small-paned windows, faced the north sullenly. It was a place of which the influence and magic were not good. Even in May when the lilacs frothed into purple, paved the lawn with shadows, steeped the air with scent; when soft leaves lipped each other consolingly; when blackbirds sang, fell in their effortless way from the green height to the green depth, and sang again—still, something that haunted the place set the heart fluttering. No place is its own, and that which is most stained with old tumults has the strongest fascination.

So at Undern, whatever had happened there went on still; someone who had been there was there still. The lawns under the trees were mournful with old pain, or with vanished joys more pathetic than pain in their fleeting mimicry of immortality.

It was only at midsummer that the windows were coloured by dawn and sunset; then they had a sanguinary aspect, staring into the delicate skyey dramas like blind, bloodshot eyes. Secretly, under the heavy rhododendron leaves and in the future sunlight beneath the yew-trees, gnats danced. Their faint motions made the garden stiller; their smallness made it oppressive; their momentary life made it infinitely old. Then Undern Pool was full of leaf shadows like multitudinous lolling tongues, and the smell of the mud tainted the air—half sickly, half sweet. The clipped bushes and the twisted chimneys made inky shadows like steeples on the grass, and great trees of roses beautiful in desolation, dripped with red and white and elbowed the guelder roses and the elders set with white patens. Cherries fell in the orchard with the same rich monotony, the same fatality, as drops of blood. They lay under the fungus-riven trees till the hens ate them, pecking gingerly and enjoyably at their lustrous beauty as the world does at a poet's heart. In the kitchen-garden also the hens took their ease. banqueting sparely beneath the straggling black boughs of a red-currant grove. In the sandstone walls of this garden hornets built undisturbed, and the thyme and lavender borders had grown into forests and obliterated the path. The cattle drowsed in the meadows, birds in the heavy trees; the golden day-lilies drooped like the daughters of pleasure; the very principle of life seemed to slumber. It was then, when the scent of elder blossom, decaying fruit, mud and hot yew brooded there, that the place attained one of its most individual moods—narcotic, aphrodisiac.

In winter the yews and firs were like waving funeral plumes and mantled, headless goddesses; then the giant beeches would lash themselves to frenzy, and, stooping, would scourge the ice on Undern Pool and the cracked walls of the house, like beings drunken with the passion of cruelty. This was the second mood of Undern—brutality. Then those within were, it seemed, already in the grave, heavily covered with the prison frost and snow, or shouted into silence by the wind. On a January night the house seemed to lie outside time and space; slow, ominous movement began beyond the blind windows, and the inflexible softness of snow, blurred on the vast background of night, buried summer ever deeper with invincible, caressing threats.
—MARY WEBB, *Gone to Earth.*

By arrangement with the publishers, Jonathan Cape, Limited, Toronto.

3. THE SONG MY PADDLE SINGS

August is laughing across the sky,
Laughing while paddle, canoe, and I,
Drift, drift,
Where the hills uplift
On either side of the current swift.

The river rolls in its rocky bed;
My paddle is plying its way ahead;
Dip, dip,
While the waters flip
In foam as over their breast we slip.

And oh, the river runs swifter now,
The eddies circle about my bow!
Swirl, swirl!
How the ripples curl
In many a dangerous pool awhirl!

And forward far the rapids roar,
Fretting their margin for evermore.
Dash, dash,
With a mighty crash,
They seeth, and boil, and bound, and splash.

Be strong, O paddle! be brave, canoe!
The reckless waves you must plunge into.
Reel, reel,
On your trembling keel,—
But never a fear my craft will feel.

We've raced the rapid, we're far ahead!
The river slips through its silent bed.
Sway, sway,
As the bubbles spray
And fall in tinkling tunes away.

—E. PAULINE JOHNSON.

From Flint and Feather, *published and copyrighted by The Musson Book Company Ltd., Toronto*

PRACTICE 15. Changing Point of View

Describe a scene from two or more points of view, keeping the reader clearly aware of each change.

1. The river drive. 2. The castle (inside and out). 3. The stadium (near and far). 4. A tour of the city (waterfront, lake side, beach). 5. The park. 6. The steamer, 7. The streamlined train. 8. The river-bank (spring, summer, autumn, winter). 9. A masquerader (before and after the unmasking). 10. The church (you saw it building and completed). 11. The nursery garden (spring, summer, autumn). 12. A bird's nest (from the ground, at closer view). 13. A swarm of bees (swarming, gathered on a branch). 14. A street as you see it while driving along in a car.

ACTION

When possible, describe an action. For pure description the action should be limited to a moment. Commonly, however, the short story and the novel, like the motion picture, combine story and picture so closely and effectively that it is both difficult and useless to separate the description from the narration.

PRACTICE 16. Studying Action Picture

1. What impression does the following selection from Anthony Gibb's *Peter Vacuum* produce?

2. What words vividly describe sights?

3. What words describe sounds?

4. What action is pictured?

The saxophone reared it brazen head in the air, swayed like some sort of gleaming python intoxicated by the charmer's pipe, sent an excruciating whinny reeling across the room, and squirted a little sport of sucking chuckles to gibber in its wake. A very fat man, with his plump cheeks creased by the thin end of this infernal machine, sent an inspired blast of carbon dioxide roaring through its sweating innards, which, being wrought on by his pudgy fingers, issued forth in the form of weird moans, choking coughs, dyspeptic signs, and the bleating of lambs.

"It hadda be yew," tittered the violinist through the megaphone.

And the banjos thrummed eternally, and a lean man with india rubber fingers hurled himself at the piano until it squeaked at the violence of his onslaught, or rippled over it placid surface in a rush of twitterings, as if all the sparrows in London had gone suddenly mad, and the saxophone hoicked, and the drum throbbed its insinuating rhythm, and the violin shrieked like a soul in pain, and all the demons in hell swayed to this diabolical syncopation of demented monsters lumbering through fetid swamps; and the pulsing agony became more and more insistent with the last verse, and the music mounted up and up, modulating through penetrating quarter tones that have no place in a printed score, and the time became more and more fantastically distorted, and the cornet lifted up his voice to heaven and let forth a cry of vengeance, until, with a crash of cymbals, and a last howling discord, the band laid down their instruments with every appearance of haste, and disappeared through a small door in the back. *Reprinted by permission of the Dial Press.*

Models:

BANK HOLIDAY

A crowd collects, eating oranges and bananas, tearing off the skins, dividing, sharing. One young girl has even a basket of strawberries, but she does not eat them. "Aren't they *dear!*" She stares at the tiny pointed fruits as if she were afraid of them. The Australian soldier laughs. "Here, go on, there's not more than a mouthful." But he doesn't want her to eat them, either. He likes to watch her little frightened face, and her puzzled eyes lifted to his: "Aren't they a *price!*" He pushes out his chest and grins. Old fat women in velvet bodices—old dusty pin-cushions—lean old hags like worn umbrellas with a quivering bonnet on top; young women, in muslins, with hats that might have grown on hedges and, high pointed shoes; men in khaki, sailors, shabby clerks, young Jews in fine cloth suits with padded shoulders and wide trousers, "hospital boys" in blue—the sun discovers them—the loud, bold music holds them together in one big knot for a moment. The young ones are larking, pushing each other on and off the pavement, dodging, nudging; the old ones are talking: "So I said to 'im, if you wants the doctor to yourself, fetch 'im, says I."

"An' by the time they was cooked there wasn't so much as you could put in the palm of me 'and!"

The only ones who are quiet are the ragged children. They stand, as close up to the musicians as they can get, their hands behind their backs, their eyes big. Occasionally a leg hops, an arm wags. A tiny staggerer, overcome, turns round twice, sits down solemn, and then gets up again.

"Ain't it lovely?" whispers a small girl behind her hand.

And the music breaks into bright pieces, and joins together again, and again breaks, and is dissolved, and the crowd scatters, moving slowly up the hill.

At the corner of the road the stalls begin.

"Ticklers! Tuppence a tickler! 'Ool 'ave a tickler? Tickle 'em up, boys." Little soft brooms on wire handles. They are eagerly bought by the soldiers.

"Buy a golliwog! Tuppence a golliwog!"

"Buy a jumping donkey! All alive-oh!"

"*Su*-perior chewing gum. Buy something to do, boys."

"Buy a rose. Give 'er a rose, boy. Roses, lady!"

"Fevvers! Fevvers!" They are hard to resist. Lovely, streaming feathers, emerald green, scarlet, bright blue, canary yellow. Even the babies wear feathers threaded through their bonnets.

And an old woman in a three-cornered paper hat cries as if it were her final parting advice, the only way of saving yourself or of bringing him to his senses: "Buy a three-cornered 'at, my dear, an' put it on!"

It is a flying day, half sun, half wind.   When the sun goes in, a shadow flies over; when it comes out again it is fiery.   The men and women feel it burning their backs, their breasts and their arms; they feel their bodies expanding, coming alive . . . so that they make large embracing gestures, lift up their arms, for nothing, swoop down on a girl, blurt into laughter.

Lemonade!   A whole tank of it stands on a table covered with a cloth; and lemons like blunted fishes blob in the yellow water.   It looks solid, like a jelly, in the thick glasses.   Why can't they drink it without spilling it?   Everybody spills it, and before the glass is handed back the last drops are thrown in a ring.

Round the ice-cream cart, with its striped awning and bright brass cover, the children cluster.   Little tongues lick, lick round the cream trumpets, round the squares.   The cover is lifted, the wooden spoon plunges in; one shuts one's eyes to feel it, silently scrunching.—KATHERINE MANSFIELD, "Bank Holiday" from *The Garden Party and Other Stories.*

By permission of the author's literary agents, Messrs. James B. Pinker & Son.

THE PIED PIPER'S MUSIC

Once more he stept into the street
    And to his lips again
    Laid his long pipe of smooth straight cane;
And ere he blew three notes (such sweet
Soft notes as yet musician's cunning
    Never gave the enraptured air)
There was a rustling that seemed like a bustling
Of merry crowds justling at pitching and hustling,
Small feet were pattering, wooden shoes clattering,
Little hands clapping and little tongues chattering,
And, like fowls in a farm-yard when barley is scattering
Out came the children running.
All the little boys and girls,
With rosy cheeks and flaxen curls,
And sparkling eyes and teeth like pearls,
Tripping and skipping, ran merrily after
The wonderful music with shouting and laughter.
      —ROBERT BROWNING, *The Pied Piper of Hamelin.*

PRACTICE 17. Action Shorts

Describe one or more still scenes or scenes with action in them. Limit the action to a moment. Your purpose is to paint a picture in colours, not to tell a story. If you select a topic like number 1, describe both sights and sounds.

1. An election night scene.   2. At the beach.   3. An exciting moment in a play, a motion picture, or real life.   4. The subway or a streetcar at rush hour.

5. The bargain counter. 6. The bleachers after the home run or winning touchdown. 7. A busy office or street corner. 8. Harvesting wheat. 9. The crowd coming from a factory. 10. A wedding. 11. A market scene. 12. The toy department just before Christmas. 13. A fire scene. 14. A storm on the lake, river, or ocean. 15. A street parade. 16. A humorous scene. 17. A country fair. 18. My favourite view. 19. A farmyard. 20. A back yard. 21. The garden. 22. Main Street on Saturday night. 23. Ten minutes before the bell rang. 24. Three minutes after the game ended. 25. The crowd waiting for a parade. 26. When the five o'clock whistle blows. 27. A study in colour. 28. A banquet. 29. A political meeting. 30. A stage spectacle. 31. A fight.

LANDSCAPE—STILL SCENES

In description of scenery you have a fine opportunity to choose dominant effects and to describe sound and colour. Study the models for arrangement, tones, diction. Notice the guide words with which positions are marked.

Models:

1. DEDLOW MARSH

The vocal expression of the Dedlow Marsh was also melancholy and depressing. The sepulchral boom of the bittern, the shriek of the curlew, the scream of passing brant, the wrangling of quarrelsome teal, the sharp, querulous protest of the startled crane, the syllabled complaint of the "killdeer" plover were beyond the power of written expression. Nor was the aspect of these mournful fowls at all cheerful and inspiring. Certainly not the blue heron standing midleg deep in the water, obviously catching cold in a reckless disregard of wet feet and consequences; nor the mournful curlew, the dejected plover, or the low-spirited snipe, who saw fit to join him in his suicidal contemplation; nor the impassive kingfisher, reviewing the desolate expanse; nor the black raven that went to and fro over the face of the marsh continually, but evidently couldn't make up his mind whether the waters had subsided and felt low-spirit in the reflection that, after all this trouble, he wouldn't be able to give a definite answer. On the contrary it was evident at a glance that the dreary expanse of Dedlow Marsh told unpleasantly on the birds, and that the season of migration was looked forward to with a feeling of relief and satisfaction by the full-grown, and of extravagant anticipation by the callow brood.

But if Dedlow Marsh was cheerless at the slack of the low tide, you should have seen it when the tide was strong and full. When the damp air blew chilly over the cold, glittering expanse, and came to the faces of those who looked seaward like another tide; when a steel-like glint marked the low hollows and the sinuous line of slough; when the great shell-encrusted trunks of fallen trees arose again, and went forth on their dreary, purposeless wanderings, drifting hither and thither; when the glossy ducks swung silently, making neither ripple nor furrow on the shimmering surface; when the fog came in with the tide and shut out the blue above, even as the green below had been obliterated; when boatmen, lost in that fog, paddling about in a hopeless way, started at what seemed the brushing of mermen's fingers on the boat's keel, or shrank from the tufts of grass spreading around, and knew by these signs that they were lost upon Dedlow Marsh, and must make a night of it, and a gloomy one at that,—then you might know something of Dedlow Marsh at high water.—BRET HARTE, *High-Water Mark*

By arrangement with the publishers, Houghton Mifflin Company, Boston.

The following questions are based on the *second* paragraph:

1. What word in the first sentence suggests the dominant impression of this scene?
2. Show that the details selected are significant in creating this impression.
3. What is the effect of the repetition of the word "when"?
4. Show that the details have been arranged to work up to a climax.

2. EVENING ON THE HUDSON

The sun gradually wheeled his broad disk down into the west. The wide bosom of the Tappan Zee lay motionless and glassy, excepting that here and there a gentle undulation waved and prolonged the blue shadow of the distant mountain A few amber clouds floated in the sky, without a breath of air to move them. The horizon was of a fine golden tint, changing gradually into a pure apple green, and from that into the deep blue of the mid-heaven. A slanting ray lingered on the woody crests of the precipices that overhung some parts of the river, giving greater depth to the dark gray and purple of their rocky sides. A sloop was loitering in the distance, dropping slowly down with the tide, her sail hanging uselessly against the mast; and as the reflection of the sky gleamed along the still water, it seemed as if the vessel was suspended in the air.—IRVING, *Legend of Sleepy Hollow.*

3. A CALM ON A SCOTCH LOCH

The lake lies stilled in sleep, reflecting every isle and every tree along the shore, its bright plain dimmed here and there by faint breezes, that remain each in its place with singular constancy, as if invisible angels hovered over the waters and breathed upon them here and there. And under the dark mountain what a dark unfathomable calm! What utter repose and peace! It is incredible that ever wind blew there, and though but yesterday this shining liquid plain was covered with ten thousand crested waves, and countless squalls struck it all over like swooping eagles flying from every quarter of the heavens, it lies so calmly to-day in its deep bed, that one cannot help believing, in spite of all evidence, that thus it has been from the foundation of the world, and thus it shall be forever and forever!

The hills are clothed with purple, slashed with green. The sky is not cloudless, but the clouds move so languidly that their slowness of movement is more expressive of indolence than the uttermost stony stillness. Like great ships on a rippling sea, with all their white sails spread, they float imperceptibly westwards, as though they had eternity to voyage in. And just under them, in blinding light, beyond the shining crests of snow.—HAMERTON, *A Painter's Camp.*

4. EVENING

From upland slopes I see the cows file by,
Lowing, great-chested, down the homeward trail,
By dusking fields and meadows shining pale
With moon-tipped dandelions.   Flickering high,
A peevish night-hawk in the western sky
Beats up into the lucent solitudes,
Or drops with griding wing.   The stilly woods
Grow dark and deep, and gloom mysteriously.
Cool night winds creep, and whisper in mine ear;
The homely cricket gossips at my feet.
From far-off pools and wastes of reeds I hear,
Clear and soft-piped, the chanting frogs break sweet
In full Pandean chorus.   One by one
Shine out the stars, and the great night comes on.

—Archibald Lampman, *Lyrics of Earth.*

Published and copyrighted by The Musson Book Company, Ltd., Toronto.

PRACTICE 18.

1. Choose another topic from Practice 12 of this chapter and write upon it.

2. Write upon one of the following. Use clear guide and "echo" words; make sure of the dominant impression.

1. The park after a wet clinging snow.   2. The same on a crisp, biting day in mid-winter.   3. A scene along the river.   4. My favourite view.   5. A landscape you have seen on a holiday excursion.   6. Castle Mountain (or another). 7. Scene from a mountain side.   8. Level prairie.   9. Our favourite hunting marsh.   10. Among the pines.   11. On the silver beach.   12. From the lake. 13. From my bedroom window.   14. The bad lands.

NATURE IN MOVEMENT

With the introduction of movement there is also the introduction of time usually, so that in this kind of description there will probably be—and it is quite proper that there should be—an introduction of narrative. All that is desirable is that we should know whether it has been done, whether we wish to do it.

Models:

1. CANADIAN NIAGARA

But there they change. As they turn to the sheer descent, the white and blue and slate-colour, in the heart of the Canadian Falls at least, blend and deepen to a rich, wonderful, luminous green. On the edge of disaster the river seems to gather herself, to pause, to lift a head noble in ruin, and then, with a slow grandeur, to plunge into the eternal thunder and white chaos below. Where the stream runs shallower it is a kind of violet colour, but both violet and green fray and frill to white as they fall The mass of water, striking some ever-hidden base of rock, leaps up the whole two hundred feet again in pinnacles and domes of spray. The spray falls back into the lower river once more; all but a little that fines to foam and white mist, which drifts in layers along the air, graining it, and wanders out on the wind over the trees and gardens and houses, and so vanishes.—RUPERT BROOKE, *Niagara Falls*, from *Letter from America.*

By permission of the author's representatives and of the publishers, Sidgwick & Jackson Ltd., London.

1. Select the expressions which suggest that the author is following the course of the river with his eyes.

2. What would be the effect on the description if these expressions were removed?

3. What evidence is there that the writer has a clear picture in his own mind?

4. Show that the first and the last sentence make an effective introduction and conclusion to this paragraph.

2- THUNDER AND LIGHTNING

A light flapped over the scene, as if reflected from phosphorescent wings crossing the sky, and a rumble filled the air. It was the first arrow from the approaching storm, and it fell wide.

The second peal was noisy, with comparatively little visible lightning. Gabriel saw a candle shining in Bathsheba's bedroom, and soon a shadow moved to and fro upon the blind.

Then there came a third flash. Manoeuvres of a most extraordinary kind were going on in the vast firmamental hollows overhead. The lightning now was the colour of silver, and gleamed in the heavens like a mailed army. Rumbles became rattles. Gabriel from his elevated position could see over the landscape for at least half a dozen miles in front. Every hedge, bush, and tree was distinct as in a line engraving. In a paddock in the same direction was a herd of heifers, and the forms of these were visible at this moment in the act of galloping about in the wildest and maddest confusion, flinging their heels and tails high into the air, their head to earth. A poplar in the immediate foreground was like an ink-stroke on burnished tin. Then the picture vanished, leaving a darkness so intense that Gabriel worked entirely by feeling with his hands.

He had struck his ricking-rod, or poniard, as it was indifferently called— a long iron lance, sharp at the extremity and polished by handling—into the stack to support the sheaves. A blue light appeared in the zenith, and in some indescribable manner flickered down near the top of the rod. It was the fourth of the larger flashes. A moment later and there was a smack—smart, clear, and short. Gabriel felt his position to be anything but a safe one, and he resolved to descend.

Not a drop of rain had fallen as yet. He wiped his weary brow, and looked again at the black forms of the unprotected stacks. Was his life so valuable to him, after all? What were his prospects that he should be so chary of running risk, when important and urgent labour could not be carried on without such risk? He resolved to stick to the stack. However, he took a precaution. Under the staddles was a long tethering chain, used to prevent the escape of errant horses. This he carried up the ladder, and sticking his rod through the clog at one end, allowed the other end of the chain to trail upon the ground. The spike attached to it he drove in. Under the shadow of this extemporized lightning conductor he felt himself comparatively safe.

Before Oak had laid his hands upon his tools again, out leaped the fifth flash, with the spring of a serpent and the shout of a fiend. It was as green as an emerald, and the reverberation was stunning What was this the light revealed to him? In the open ground before him, as he looked over the ridge of the rick, was a dark and apparently female form. Could it be that of the only venturesome woman in the parish—Bathsheba? The form moved on a step; then he could see no more.

"Is that you, ma'am?" said Gabriel, to the darkness.

"Who is there?" said the voice of Bathsheba.

"Gabriel. I am on the rick, thatching."

"Oh, Gabriel!—and are you? . . . Can I do anything to help? Liddy is afraid to come out. Fancy finding you here at such an hour! Surely I can do something?"

"You can bring up some reed-sheaves to me, one by one, ma'am, if you are not afraid to come up the ladder in the dark," said Gabriel. "Every moment is precious now, and that would save a good deal of time. It is not very dark when the lightning has been gone a bit."

"I'll do anything," she said resolutely. She instantly took a sheaf upon her shoulder, clambered up close to his heels, placed it behind the rod, and descended for another. At her third ascent the rick suddenly brightened with the brazen glare of shining majolica—every knot in every straw was visible. On the slope in front of him appeared two human shapes, black as jet. The rick lost its sheen—the shapes vanished. Gabriel turned his head. It had been the sixth flash which had come from the east behind him, and the two dark forms on the slope had been the shadows of himself and Bathsheba.

Then came the peal. It hardly was credible that such a heavenly light could be the parent of such a diabolical sound. "How terrible!" she exclaimed and clutched him by the sleeve. Gabriel turned, and steadied her on her aerial perch by holding her arm. At the same moment, while he was still reversed in his attitude, there was more light, and he saw as it were a copy of the tall poplar tree on the hill drawn in black on the wall of the barn. It was the shadow of that tree thrown across by a secondary flash in the west.

The next flare came. Bathsheba was on the ground now, shouldering another sheaf, and she bore its dazzle without flinching—thunder and all—and again ascended with the load. There was then a silence everywhere for four or five minutes, and the crunch of the spars as Gabriel hastily drove them in, could be distinctly heard again. He thought the crisis of the storm had passed. But there came a burst of light. "Hold on!" said Gabriel, taking the sheaf from her shoulder and grasping her arm again.

Heaven opened then, indeed. The flash was almost too novel for its inexpressibly dangerous nature to be at once realized, and Gabriel could only comprehend the magnificence of its beauty. It sprang from east, west, north, south. It was a perfect dance of death. The forms of skeletons appeared in the air, shaped with blue fire for bones—dancing, leaping, striding, racing around and mingling altogether in unparalleled confusion. With these were intertwined undulating snakes of green. Behind these was a broad mass of lesser light. Simultaneously came from every part of the tumbling sky what may be called a shout; since, though no shout ever came near it, it was more of the nature of a shout than of anything else earthly. In the meantime one of the grisly forms had alighted upon the point of Gabriel's rod, to run invisibly down it, down the chain, and into the earth. Gabriel was almost blinded, and he could feel Bathsheba's warm arm tremble in his hand—a sensation novel and thrilling enough: but love, life, everything human seemed small and trifling in such juxtaposition with an infuriated universe.—THOMAS HARDY, *Far From the Madding Crowd.*

By arrangement with the publishers, The Macmillan Company of Canada, Ltd.

PRACTICE 19. Nature in Movement

Describe vividly one of the following scenes. Strive to achieve the distinction of style of Hardy's writing. Etch every picture with clear, accurate strokes.

1. A thunderstorm on the prairies.   2. A thunderstorm in the mountains 3. A cyclone.   4. A dust storm.   5. A hail storm.   6. The blizzard.   7. A wind at the lake.   8. A squall on the lake (on the sea).   9. Remarkable cloud effects. 10. An unusual whirlwind.   11. A field of waving wheat.   12. Cloud galleons. 13. Birches (elms, maples, poplars, oaks) in the gale.   14. A gentle fall of snow. 15. Landscape in the rain.   16. A Scotch mist.   17. A drizzly day.

PRACTICE 20.

Using the model "A Calm on a Scotch Loch" page 216, write a description of one of the themes in Practice 18 or 19, giving by contrast the same scene in a moment of quiet and again in motion or commotion. Work the contrast in your account as skilfully as Hamerton has done.

OBJECTS OF NATURE, AND OTHERS

Picture-making words, and phrases that live are the main concern in the description of most objects. Apart from scientific description, these have little value unless informed with beauty, grace, sentiment, human association, or reflected human emotions. We should be led to admire, to resent, to condemn, to love, to desire these objects. They must rouse our feelings.

1. THE BULL-FINCH'S NEST

Once I found a bull-finch's nest in a rosebush.   It looked like a pink shell holding four blue pearls.   Nodding over it hung a rose heavy with dew-drops. The male bull-finch, motionless, stood guard on a neighbouring shrub, like a flower of azure and purple.   These objects were mirrored in a glassy pool, with the reflection of a walnut tree for background, behind which was to be seen the light of dawn.   God gave me in that little picture an idea of the loveliness with which he has clothed nature.—CHATEAUBRIAND.

2. BIRCHES IN THE BREEZE

See the silver birch in a breeze; here it swells, there it scatters, and it is puffed to a round and it streams like a pennon; and now gives the glimpse and shine of the white stem's line within, now hurries over it denying that it was visible, with a chatter along the sweeping folds, while still the white peeps through.—GEORGE MEREDITH, *The Egoist.*

By permission of the publishers, Constable & Company Limited, London.

3. THE HERON

Pale, shimmering green, and soaked in sun, the miles of sedge-flats lay outspread from the edges of the slow bright water to the foot of the far, dark-wooded, purple hills.   Winding through the quiet green levels came a tranquil little stream.   Where its sleepy current joined the great parent river, a narrow tongue of bare sand jutted out into the golden-glowing water.   At the extreme tip of the sand-pit towered, sentry-like, a long-legged gray-blue bird, as motion-less as if he had been transplanted thither from the panel of a Japanese screen.

The flat narrow head of the great heron, with its long, javelin-like yellow beak and two slender black crest-feathers, was drawn far back by a curious undulation of the immensely long neck, till it rested between the humped blue wing-shoulders.   From the lower part of the neck hung a fine fringe of vaporous rusty-gray plumes, which lightly veiled the chestnut-coloured breast. The bird might have seemed asleep, like the drowsy expanses of green sedge, silver-blue water, and opalescent turquoise sky, but for its eyes.   Those eyes, round, unwinking, of a hard, glassy gold, with intense black pupils, were un-mistakable and savagely wide awake.—CHARLES G. D. ROBERTS, *Neighbours Unknown.*

By permission of the publishers, The Macmillan Company of Canada Limited.

4. PORTRAIT OF RAB

I wish you could have seen him.   There are no such dogs now.   He belonged to a lost tribe.   As I have said, he was brindled and gray like Rubislaw granite; his hair short, hard, and close, like a lion's; his body thick-set, like a bull —a sort of compressed Hercules of a dog.   He must have been ninety pounds' weight, at the least; he had a large, blunt head; his muzzle black as night, his mouth blacker than any night, a tooth or two—being all he had—gleaming out of his jaws of darkness.   His head was scarred with the record of old wounds, a sort of series of fields of battle all over it; one eye out, one ear cropped off as close as was Archbishop Leighton's father's; the remaining eye had the power of two; and above it, and in constant communication with it, was the tattered rag of an ear, which was forever unfurling itself like an old flag; and then that bud of a tail, about one inch long, if it could in any sense be said to be long, being as broad as long—the mobility, the instantaneousness of that bud was very funny and surprising, and its expressive twinklings and winkings, the intercommunication between the eye, the ear and it, were the oddest and swiftest.

Rab had the dignity and simplicity of great size, and having fought his way all along the road to absolute supremacy, he was as mighty in his own line as Julius Caesar or the Duke of Wellington, and had the gravity of all great fighters.

You must have often observed the likeness of certain men to certain animals, and of certain dogs to men.   Now I never looked at Rab without thinking of the great Baptist preacher, Andrew Fuller.   The same large, heavy, menacing, combative, sombre, honest countenance; the same deep, inevitable eye, the same look—as of thunder asleep, but ready; neither a dog nor a man to be trifled with.—JOHN BROWN, *Rab and His Friends.*

5. GUNPOWDER

The animal he bestrode was a broken-down plough-horse, that had outlived almost everything but his viciousness.   He was gaunt and shagged, with a ewe neck and a head like a hammer; his rusty mane and tail were tangled and knotted with burrs; one eye had lost its pupil, and was glaring and spectral, but the other had the gleam of a genuine devil in it.   Still he must have had fire and mettle in his day, if we may judge from the name he bore, of Gunpowder.   He had, in fact, been a favourite steed of his master's, the choleric Van Ripper, who was a furious rider, and had infused, very probably, some of his own spirit into the animal; for, old and broken-down as he looked, there was more of the lurking devil in him than in any young filly in the country.
—WASHINGTON IRVING, *Sketch-Book.*

6. THE COLLAR OF PRESTER JOHN

The priest raised the necklace till it shone above his head like a halo of blood.   I have never seen such a jewel, and I think there has never been another such on earth.   Later I was to have the handling of it, and could examine it closely, though now I had only a glimpse.   There were fifty-five rubies in it, the largest as big as a pigeon's egg, and the least not smaller than my thumb-nail.   In shape they were oval, cut on both sides *en cabochon,* and on each certain characters were engraved.   No doubt this detracted from their value as gems, yet the characters might have been removed and the stones cut in facets, and these rubies would still have been the noblest in the world.   I was no jewel merchant to guess their value, but I knew enough to see that there was wealth beyond human computation.   At each end of the string was a great pearl and a golden clasp.   The sight absorbed me to the exclusion of all fear.   I, David Crawfurd, nineteen years of age, and assistant-storekeeper in a back-veld dorp, was privileged to see a sight to which no Portuguese adventurer had ever attained.   There, floating on the smoke-wreaths, was the jewel which may once have burned in Sheba's hair.

As the priest held the collar aloft, the assembly rocked with a strange passion.   Foreheads were rubbed in the dust, and then adoring eyes would be raised, while a kind of sobbing shook the worshippers.—JOHN BUCHAN, *Prester John.*

By permission of the copyright holders, Jonathan Cape, Limited, Toronto.

7. THE EAGLE

He clasps the crag with crooked hands;
Close to the sun in lonely lands,
Ringed with the azure world he stands.

The wrinkled sea beneath him crawls;
He watches from his mountain walls,
And like a thunderbolt he falls.

—TENNYSON

8. NIGHTINGALE'S SONG

Thou wast not born for death, immortal Bird!
No hungry generations tread thee down;
The voice I hear this passing night was heard
In ancient days by emperor and clown:
Perhaps the self-same song that found a path
Through the sad heart of Ruth, when, sick for home,
She stood in tears amid the alien corn;
The same that oft-times hath
Charm'd magic casements, opening on the foam
Of perilous seas, in faery lands forlorn.

—JOHN KEATS, *Ode to a Nightingale.*

PRACTICE 21. Describing Objects

Describe three of the following. Use a good topic sentence, observe closely, choose an interesting point of view as the writer has in the description of Prester John's collar in your model.

1. A bird's nest (robin, oriole, gull, partridge, woodpecker). 2. Silver birches in the moonlight. 3. Weeping birches in a storm (day or night). 4. A bird (bittern, red-winged blackbird, pelican, gull, sparrow, peacock). 5. The Canada goose in flight. 6. A modern luxury liner. 7. A yacht. 8. A young fox. 9. Kittens four months old. 10. A young calf. 11. A mastiff. 12. A Great Dane. 13. My pet. 14. A curio. 15. A rare coin. 16. An interesting stamp. 17. A well-printed book. 18. A statue (bust, group, memorial). 19. A beaver. 20. A beautiful piece of china.

SEASONS

Perhaps no natural phenomenon has waked such enthusiastic praise and portrayal as the pageant of seasons. As with sunrise and sunset, the seasons are best described by their accompanying changes and effects upon nature. The subject seems to invite poetry and poetic prose.

Models:

1. THE FALL OF LEAVES

At this season a sky which is of so delicate and faint a blue as to contain something of gentle mockery, and certainly more of tenderness, presides at the fall of leaves. There is no air, no breath at all. The leaves are so light that they sidle on their going downward, hesitating in that which is not void to them, and touching at last so imperceptibly the earth with which they are to mingle, that the gesture is much gentler than a salutation, and even more discreet than a discreet caress.

They make a little sound, less than the least of sounds. No bird at night in the marshes rustles so slightly; no men, though men are the subtlest of living things, put so evanescent a stress upon their sacred whispers or their prayers. The leaves are hardly heard, but they are heard just so much that men also, who are destined at the end to grow glorious and to die, look up and hear them falling.—HILAIRE BELLOC, *Hills and the Sea.*

By permission of the publishers, Methuen & Co. Ltd., London.

1. What evidence is there that the writer's aim was not to present a photographic view of the fall of leaves?

2. What was his aim?

3. Show how the selection of details, the choice of words, and the structure of the sentences help him to achieve that aim.

4. Select three words which indicate that the author had in mind readers who are more mature than children in elementary schools.

2. LAKE SEDGES

Taller than the grass and lower than the trees, there is another growth that feels the implicit spring. It had been more abandoned in winter than even the short grass shuddering under a wave of east wind, more than the dumb trees. For the multitude of sedges, rushes, canes, and reed were the appropriate lyre of the cold. On them the keen winds played their dry music. They were parts of the winter. It looked through them and spoke through them. They were spears and javelins in array to the sound of the drums of the north.—ALICE MEYNELL, *Rushes and Reeds.*

By permission of Mr. Wilfred Meynell and the publishers, Burns, Oates and Washbourne Limited, London.

3. GARDEN SNOW SCENE

It has snowed all night. I have been to look at our primroses; each of them had its small load of snow, and was bowing its head under its burden. These pretty flowers, with their rich yellow colour, had a charming effect under their white hoods. I saw whole tufts of them roofed over with a single block of snow; all these laughing flowers thus shrouded and leaning one upon another made one think of a group of young girls surprised by a shower and sheltering under a white apron.—MAURICE DE GUERIN, trans. by Matthew Arnold, *Essays in Criticism.*

4. AUTUMN IN THE SOUTH

The colour of the leaves deepened, and there came a season of beauty, singular and sad, like a smile left upon the face of the dead summer. Over all things, near and far, the forest where it met the sky, the nearer woods, the great river, and the streams that empty into it, there hung a blue haze, soft and dream-like. The forest became a painted forest, with an ever-thinning canopy and an ever-thickening carpet of crimson and gold; everywhere there was a low rustling underfoot and a slow rain of colour. It was neither cold nor hot, but very quiet, and the birds went by like shadows—a listless and forgetful weather, in which we began to look, every hour of every day, for the sail which we knew we should not see for weeks to come—MARY JOHNSTON. *To Have and to Hold.*

By permission of the publishers, Houghton Mifflin Company.

5. RICH DAYS

Welcome to you, rich Autumn days,
   Ere comes the cold, leaf-picking wind;
When golden stooks are seen in fields,
   All standing arm-in-arm entwined;
And gallons of sweet cider seen
On trees in apples red and green.

With mellow pears that cheat our teeth,
   Which melt that tongues may suck them in
With cherries red, and blue-black plums,
   Now sweet and soft from stone to skin;
And woodnuts rich, to make us go
Into the loveliest lanes we know.

—W. H. DAVIES.

By permission of the publishers, Jonathan Cape Limited, Toronto.

PRACTICE 22. Describing the Seasons

An eye to see, an imagination to interpret, and words adequate to your need, are the requisites to good seasonal description. When Davies says that the young leaves of spring have not "outgrown their curly childhood yet," he has combined all these. Use all your skill in writing upon the following topics.

1. Autumn on the prairie. 2. Autumn among the hills (mountains). 3. A forest scene in autumn. 4. A poplar (maple, oak, elm, plane) tree in colour. 5. Orchards in bloom. 6. Spring comes to the valley (mountain, prairie). 7. Along the waterfront (at any season). 8. In the old muskeg (any season). 9. The garden after the first soft snow. 10. Winter landscape. 11. A sleet-crusted landscape. 12. Pine trees in the snow. 13. Wrapped in hoar-frost. 14. "Season of mists and mellow fruitfulness." 15. "When the frost is on the pumpkin." 16. "What is so rare as a day in June." 17. "When icicles hang by the wall." 18. "Spring, the sweet spring."

EXTERIOR OF BUILDINGS

In describing the exterior of buildings the general dominant impression is the chief thing. Look at the picture and remember to make an attractive snapshot of it.

Models:

1

At length we stopped before a very old house bulging out over the road; a house with long low lattice-windows bulging out still farther, and beams with carved heads on the ends bulging out too, so that I fancied the whole house was leaning forward, trying to see what was passing on the narrow pavement below. It was quite spotless in its cleanliness. The old-fashioned brass knocker on the low arched door, ornamented with carved garlands of fruit and flowers, twinkled like a star; the two stone steps descending to the door were as white as if they had been covered with fair linen; and all the angles and corners, and carvings and mouldings, and quaint little panes of glass, and quainter little windows, though as old as the hills, were as pure as any snow that ever fell upon the hills.—CHARLES DICKENS.

2. MRS. STUBBS'S

Mrs. Stubbs's shop was perched on a little hillock just off the road. It had two big windows for eyes, a broad veranda for a hat, and the sign on the roof, scrawled MRS. STUBBS'S, was like a little card stuck rakishly in the hat crown.

On the veranda there hung a long string of bathing-dresses, clinging together as though they'd just been rescued from the sea rather than waiting to go in, and beside them there hung a cluster of sand-shoes so extraordinarily mixed that to get at one pair you had to tear apart and forcibly separate at least fifty. Even then it was the rarest thing to find the left that belonged to the right. So many people had lost patience and gone off with one shoe that fitted and one that was a little too big . . . Mrs. Stubbs prided herself on keeping something of everything. The two windows arranged in the form of precarious pyramids, were crammed so tight, piled so high, that it seemed only a conjuror could prevent them from toppling over. In the left-hand corner of one window, glued to the pane by four gelatine lozenges, there was—and there had been from time immemorial—a notice.

> LOST! HANDSOME GOLD BROOCH
> SOLID GOLD
> ON OR NEAR BEACH
> REWARD OFFERED

> —KATHERINE MANSFIELD, "At the Bay" from
> *The Garden Party and Other Stories.*
> By permission of the author's literary agents, Messrs. James B. Pinker & Son.

3

As I approached the house, I noticed that the windows were broken out, or shut up with rough boards to exclude the rain and snow; that the doors were supported by wooden props instead of hinges, which hung loosely on the panels; and that long luxuriant clover grew in the eaves, which had been originally designed to conduct the water from the roof, but becoming choked up with dust and decayed leaves, had afforded sufficient food for the nourishment of coarse grasses. The portico, like the house, had been formed of wood, and the flat surface of its top imbibing and retaining moisture, presented a mass of vegetable matter, from which had sprung up a young and vigorous birch tree, whose strength and freshness seemed to mock the helpless weakness that nourished it. I had no desire to enter the apartments; and indeed the aged ranger, whose occupation was to watch over its decay, and to prevent its premature destruction by the plunder of its fixtures and more durable materials, informed me that the floors were unsafe. Altogether the scene was one of a most depressing kind.—HALIBURTON, *The Clockmaker.*

4. MELROSE ABBEY

If thou woulds't view fair Melrose aright,
Go visit it by the pale moonlight;
For the gay beams of lightsome day
Guild but to flout the ruins grey.
When the broken arches are black in night,
And each shafted oriel glimmers white;
When the cold light's uncertain shower
Streams on the ruin'd central tower;
When buttress and buttress, alternately,
Seem framed of ebon and ivory;
When silver edges the imagery,
And the scrolls that teach thee to live and die;
When distant Tweed is heard to rave,
And the owlet to hoot o'er the dead man's grave,
Then go—but go alone the while—
Then view St. David's ruin'd pile;
And home returning, soothly swear,
Was never scene so sad and fair!
—SIR WALTER SCOTT, *The Lay of the Last Minstrel.*

PRACTICE 23. Exteriors of Buildings

Write a description of the exterior view of some building which has struck you as distinctive for its beauty, architectural design, commodiousness, ruin, picturesqueness, oddity—or other distinctions.

If you are describing a railway station, decide first the effect produced upon you, whether it is imposing, ugly, smoky and dirty, noisy, a scene of activity or of rapid changes. State the effect you feel and follow with details that bear upon your point of view.

Suggestions:

1. A hovel. 2. A beautiful residence. 3. A grand hotel. 4. A skyscraper. 5. The Art Gallery. 6. Empire State Building. 7. Toronto City Hall.

8. Parliament Buildings. 9. A cosy cottage. 10. A cabin—"of clay and wattles made." 11. Log cabin. 12. A sod hut. 13. The lodge. 14. The pavilion. 15. Banff Springs Hotel. 16. Chateau at Lake Louise. 17. Jasper Park Lodge. 18. The bridge. 19. The observatory. 20. Our school.

INTERIOR OF BUILDINGS—ROOMS

A soon as we step inside a building we realize, even more than outside, the reflection of a personality. This must always be made evident—this atmosphere of habitation. Stress the dominant impression.

Models:

1.

The room in which I found myself was very large and lofty. The windows were long, narrow, and pointed, and at so vast a distance from the black, oaken floor as to be altogether inaccessible from within. Feeble gleams of encrimsoned light made their way through the trellised panes, and served to render sufficiently distinct the more prominent objects around. The eye, however, struggled in vain to reach the remoter angles of the chamber, or the recesses of the vaulted and fretted ceiling. Dark draperies hung upon the walls. The general furniture was profuse, comfortless, antique, and tattered. Many books and musical instruments lay scattered about, but failed to give any vitality to the scene. I felt that I breathed an atmosphere of sorrow. An air of stern, deep, and irredeemable gloom hung over and pervaded all.—POE, *The Fall of the House of Usher.*

1. What is the outstanding characteristic of the room?

2. List some of the details that help to convey this impression.

3. Select three or four expressions which indicate that the author's choice of words was governed by his desire to create this impression.

4. Why does the author not mention pictures on the wall?

5. Writers frequently begin a description by indicating the mood or impression they wish to create. What does Poe gain by delaying his statement of the dominant mood until the last sentence?

2. FAGIN'S ROOM

Oliver, groping his way with one hand, and having the other firmly grasped by his companion, ascended with much difficulty the dark and broken stairs that his conductor mounted with an ease and expedition that showed that he was well acquainted with them. He threw open the door of a back room, and drew Oliver in after him.

The walls and ceiling of the room were perfectly black with age and dirt. There was a deal table before the fire, upon which were a candle stuck in the neck of a ginger-beer bottle, two or three pewter pots, a loaf and butter, and a plate. In a frying-pan, which was on the fire, and which was secured to the mantel-shelf by a string, some sausages were cooking; standing over them with a toasting-fork in his hand, was a very old, shrivelled Jew, whose villainous-looking and repulsive face was obscured by a quantity of matted red hair. He was dressed in a greasy flannel gown, with his throat bare, and seemed to be dividing his attention between the frying-pan and a clothes horse, over which a great number of silk handkerchiefs were hanging. Several rough beds made of old sacks were huddled side by side on the floor. Seated round the table were four or five boys, none older than the Dodger, smoking long clay pipes and drinking spirits, with the air of middle-aged men. These all crowded about their associate as he whispered a few words to the Jew; then they turned and grinned at Oliver. So did the Jew himself, toasting-fork in hand.—CHARLES DICKENS, *Oliver Twist*.

3. MR. BADGER'S KITCHEN

The floor was well-worn red brick, and on the wide hearth burnt a fire of logs, between two attractive chimney-corners tucked away in the wall, well out of any suspicion of draught. A couple of high-backed settles, facing each other on either side of the fire, gave further sitting accommodations for the sociably disposed. In the middle of the room stood a long table of plain boards placed on trestles, with benches down each side. At one end of it, where an arm-chair stood pushed back, were spread the remains of the Badger's plain but ample supper. Rows of spotless plates winked from the shelves of the dresser at the far end of the room, and from the rafters overhead hung hams, bundles of dried herbs, nets of onions, and baskets of eggs. It seemed a place where heroes could fitly feast after victory, where weary harvesters could line up in scores along the table and keep their Harvest Home with mirth and song, or where two or three friends of simple tastes could sit about as they pleased and eat and smoke and talk in comfort and contentment. The ruddy brick floor smiled up at the smoky ceiling; the oaken settles, shiny with long wear, exchanged cheerful glances with each other; plates on the dresser grinned at pots on the shelf, and the merry firelight flickered and played over everything without distinction.—KENNETH GRAHAME, *The Wind in the Willows*.

By permission of Charles Scribner's Sons, New York.

4. DAVID'S BEDROOM

Peggotty opened a little door and showed me my bedroom. It was the completest and most desirable bedroom ever seen—in the stern of the vessel; with a little window which the rudder used to go through; a little looking-glass just the right height for me, nailed against the wall, and framed with oyster shells; a little bed which there was room enough to get into; and a nosegay of seaweed in a blue mug on the table. The walls were whitewashed as white as milk, and the patchwork counterpane made my eyes quite ache with its brightness.—DICKENS, *David Copperfield*.

PRACTICE 24. Describing Interiors

Describe the interior of a building, or a room, making some one characteristic predominate. If you choose to describe your class-room, make a list of every detail you observe. Then decide the dominant impression you would like to create in describing this room to a friend. Go through the list of details striking out those that would not help convey this impression. Determine the order of description you intend to use and number the details accordingly. Write the paragraph.

1. A living room (comfort). 2. A living room (luxury). 3. A library (quiet, studiousness). 4. A drawing room (comfort, cheerfulness). 5. A kitchen (bright, cheery, savoury). 6. A den (homely). 7. An attic (disorder, neglect). 8. Theatre (attractiveness). 9. Audience chamber (formal). 10. Dining room (old-fashioned spaciousness). 11. A church (solemn, loftly, stately). 12. A church (reverence). 13. A cathedral (beauty, dignity). 14. A restful room. 15. Foyer of a hotel (stir, convenience, comfort). 16. A tea-room. 17. An untidy room. 18. An unkept room. 19. Bedroom after a hurried exit. 20. The living room 'dressed' for vacation. 21. Moving in. 22. After a fire. 23. Marjorie is unpacking. 24. A gymnasium dressing room. 25. The pool at the "Y". 26. An art gallery. 27. A museum. 28. Your class-room. 29. Any other.

TOWNS AND CITIES

In describing towns and cities it is of the utmost importance to form a dominant impression, and not to overload the description with too many details. Watch arrangement of details; but particularly watch selection of details towards a unified impression.

Models:

1. FERRARA

The aspect of this dreary town, half an hour before sunrise one fine morning, when I left it, was as picturesque as it seemed unreal and spectral. It was no matter that the people were not yet out of bed; for if they had all been up and busy, they would have made but little difference in that desert of a place. It was best to see it, without a single figure in the picture; a city of the dead, without one solitary survivor. Pestilence might have ravaged streets, squares and marketplaces; and sack and siege have ruined the old houses, battered down their doors and windows, and made breaches in their roofs. In one part, a great tower rose into the air; the only landmark in the melancholy view. In another, a prodigious castle, with a moat about it, stood aloof: a sullen city in itself. In the black dungeons of this castle Parisina and her lover were beheaded in the dead of night. The red light, beginning to shine when I looked back upon it, stained its walls without, as they have many a time been stained within in the old days; but for any sign of life they gave, the castle and the city might have been avoided by all human creatures from the moment when the axe went down upon the last of the two lovers.—DICKENS, *Pictures in Italy.*

2. THE ROYAL EXCHANGE

There is a place in front of the Royal Exchange where the wide pavement reaches out like a promontory. It is the shape of a triangle with a rounded apex. A stream of traffic runs on either side, and other streets send their currents down into the open space before it. Like the spokes of a wheel, converging streams of human life flow into this agitated pool. Horses and carriages, carts, vans, omnibuses, cabs, every kind of conveyance cross each other's course in every possible direction. Twisting in and out by the wheels and under the horses' heads, working a devious way, men and women of all conditions wind a path over. They fill the interstices between the carriage and blacken the surface, till the vans almost float on human beings. Now the streams slacken, and now they rush amain, but never cease; dark waves are always rolling down the incline opposite, waves swell out from the side rivers, all London converges into this focus. There is an indistinguishable noise— it is not clatter, hum, or roar, it is not resolvable; made up of a thousand thousand footsteps, from a thousands hoofs, a thousand wheels—of haste, and shuffle, and quick movement, and ponderous loads, no attention can resolve it into a fixed sound.

Blue carts and yellow omnibuses, varnished carriages and brown vans, green omnibuses and red cabs, pale loads of yellow straw, rusty-red iron clanking on paintless carts, high white wool-packs, grey horses, bay horses, black teams; sunlight sparkling on brass harness, gleaming from carriage panels; jingle, jingle, jingle! An intermixed and intertangled, ceaselessly changing jingle, too, of colour; flecks of colour champed, as it were, like bits in the horses' teeth, frothed and strewen about, and a surface always of dark-dressed people winding like the curves on fast-flowing water.—RICHARD JEFFERIES, *The Story of My Heart.*

3. COMPOSED UPON WESTMINSTER BRIDGE

Earth has not anything to show more fair:
Dull would he be of soul who could pass by
A sight so touching in its majesty:
This City now doth, like a garment, wear
The beauty of the morning; silent, bare,
Ships, towers, domes, theatres, and temples lie
Open unto the fields and to the sky;
All bright and glittering in the smokeless air.
Never did sun more beautifully steep
In his first splendour, valley, rock, or hill;
Ne'er saw I, never felt, a calm so deep!
The river glideth at his own sweet will:
Dear God! the very houses seem asleep;
And all that mighty heart is lying still!

                     —WILLIAM WORDSWORTH

PRACTICE 25. Describing Towns and Cities

Suggested topics for description of towns and cities:

1. A mountain village seen from a height above. 2. A prairie village. 3. Prairie town in a snow storm. 4. Vancouver (Victoria, Quebec, Saint John, New York) seen from the water. 5. The city by night (choose advantageous

point of view). 6. The city square. 7. Across Burrard Bridge. 8. A bird's-eye view of Calgary (Regina, Saskatoon, Vancouver, Winnipeg, Toronto, Halifax, Quebec or another). 9. At the Corner of Portage and Main (Scarth and Eleventh). 10. Beacon Hill Park. 11. Volunteer Park. 12. Victoria Park. 13. View of the city from —— (name of vantage point, Fort Garry Hotel, Chateau Frontenac, Plains of Abraham, Bessborough Hotel, Capitol Building). 14. Sunset over the city. 15. The city at sunrise.

PEN-PORTRAITS

The pen-portrait is often the beginning of a character portrayal, and differs from it largely by refraining from much comment upon the interpretation of the actual picture. The pen-portrait should bring before the mind's eye an image of the person described. It will need, then, to be vivid, not too detailed, but clear and definite. These portraits are frequently merely impressions, but the better ones give actual pictures. Examine the following models for order and arrangement, for material included and excluded. This kind of description is very important for it is the commonest of all forms in literary writing. Frequently these are very brief.

Models:

1. THE UNCOMMISSIONED MASTER OF HORSE

The door opened, and the uncommissioned master of horse made his appearance. His appearance was at once strikingly majestic and prepossessing, and the natural ease and dignity with which he entered the room might almost have become a peer of the realm coming to solicit the interest of the family for an electioneering candidate. A broad and sunny forehead, light and wavy hair, a blue cheerful eye, a nose that in Persia might have won him a throne, healthful cheeks, a mouth that was full of character, and a well-knit and almost gigantic person, constituted his external claims to attention, of which his lofty and confident, although most unassuming carriage, showed him to be in some degree conscious. He wore a complete suit of brown frieze, with a gay-coloured cotton handkerchief around his neck, blue worsted stockings, and brogues carefully greased, while he held in his right hand an immaculate felt hat, the purchase of the preceding day's fair. In the left he held a straight-handled whip and a wooden rattle, which he used for the purpose of collecting his ponies when they happened to straggle. An involuntary murmur of admiration ran amongst the guests at his entrance.—GRIFFIN, *The Collegians.*

By permission of the publishers, The Talbot Press Ltd., Dublin.

2. ICHABOD CRANE

The cognomen of Crane was not inapplicable to this person. He was tall but exceedingly lank, with narrow shoulders, long arms and legs, hands that dangled a mile out of his sleeves, feet that might have served for shovels, and his whole frame hung most loosely together. His head was small and flat at the top, with huge ears, large green glassy eyes, and a long snipe nose, so that it looked like a weather-cock perched upon his spindle neck, to tell which way the wind blew. To see him striding along the profile of a hill on a windy day, with his clothes bagging and fluttering about him, one might have mistaken him for the genius of famine, descending upon the earth, or some scarecrow eloped from a cornfield.—WASHINGTON IRVING, *The Legend of Sleepy Hollow.*

3. MARY

She was not more than fifteen. Her form, voice, and manner belonged to the period of transition from girlhood. Her face was perfectly oval, her complexion more pale than fair. The nose was faultless; the lips, slightly parted, were full and ripe, giving to the lines of the mouth, warmth, tenderness, and trust; the eyes were blue and large, and shaded by drooping lids and long lashes; and, in harmony with all, a flood of golden hair, in the style permitted to Jewish brides, fell unconfined down her back to the pillion on which she sat. The throat and neck had the downy softness sometimes seen which leaves the artist in doubt whether it is an effect of contour or colour. To these charms of feature and person were added others more indefinable—an air of purity which only the soul can impart, and of abstraction natural to such as think much of things impalpable. Often, with trembling lips, she raised her eyes to heaven, itself not more deeply blue; often she crossed her hands upon her breast, as in adoration and prayer; often she raised her head like one listening eagerly for a calling voice. Now and then, amidst his slow utterances, Joseph turned to look at her, and, catching the expression kindling her face as with light, forgot his theme, and with bowed head, wondering, plodded on.—LEW WALLACE, *Ben-Hur.*

4. SELINA STONE

Apart from the rest, in deepest black, stood a tall, rather harsh-featured woman, who seemed to have about her something of the atmosphere of the pariah. She leaned against the churchyard wall in the purple shadow of the yew tree, which spread its flat, dark masses over the daisied lawn from the dank enclosure of the churchyard, and she had the look of a creature at bay —sullen, and inexpressive. She was of the age that corresponds to the apple-tree's time of hard, green fruit, half way between maturity and middle age. She had the spare angularity and weathered complexion of all field-workers. Yet, although she had no beauty, she was, in a curious, subtle way, arresting. She had the air of remoteness that some people always take with them, so that their lives seem to move in a different rhythm from the lives around them, and one surprises in their eyes an impassioned secrecy, and feels in their presence the magnetism of great things for ever unrevealed.—MARY WEBB, "The Prize" from *Armour Wherein He Trusted.*

By permission of the publishers, Jonathan Cape Limited, Toronto.

5. OLD SUSAN

When Susan's work was done, she would sit,
With one fat guttering candle lit,
And window opened wide to win
The sweet night air to enter in.
There, with a thumb to keep her place,
She would read, with stern and wrinkled face,

Her mild eyes gliding very slow
Across the letters to and fro,
While wagged the guttering candle flame
In the wind that through the window came.
And sometimes in the silence she
Would mumble a sentence audibly,
Or shake her head as if to say,
"You silly souls, to act this way!"
And never a sound from night I would hear,
Unless some far-off cock crowed clear;
Or her old shuffling thumb should turn
Another page; and rapt and stern,
Through her great glasses bent on me,
She would glance into reality;
And shake her round old silvery head,
With—"You!—I thought you was in bed!"—
Only to tilt her book again,
And rooted in Romance remain.

—WALTER DE LA MARE

By kind permission of the author and Messrs. James B. Pinker & Son.

6. SATAN

He, above the rest
In shape and gesture proudly eminent,
Stood like a tower. His form had yet not lost
All his original brightness, nor appeared
Less than Archangel ruined, and the excess
Of glory obscured: as when the sun new-risen
Looks through the horizontal misty air
Shorn of his beams, or, from behind the moon,
In dim eclipse, disastrous twilight sheds
On half the nations, and with fear of change
Perplexes monarchs. Darkened so, yet shone
Above them all the Archangel: but his face
Deep scars of thunder had intrenched, and care
Sat on his faded cheek, but under brows
Of dauntless courage, and considerable pride
Waiting revenge.

—JOHN MILTON, *Paradise Lost.*

PRACTICE 26. Writing a Pen-Portrait

Withholding the name, write a pen-portrait of some well-known historical figure, movie actor or actress, or comic figure from the cartoons and comic strips. The test of your skill will be the ability of the class to recognize the portrait. You may entitle the portrait when the class has had an opportunity to test it.

PRACTICE 27. Another Pen-Portrait

Write a pen-portrait of some person whom you have known: a member of the class, some striking or unusual person you have met, a prominent member of the community. Remember that unkindness and discourtesy have no place in class work. Avoid caricature in writing of real persons.

GROUPS AND ASSEMBLIES

Composite groups are, of necessity, well selected impressions, first of the whole group, and secondly a few of the outstanding individuals within the group—a general impression followed by a series of miniatures vividly drawn.

Models:

1. PRESTER'S MEN

The next thing I remember was a movement among the first ranks. The chiefs were swearing fealty. Laputa took off the collar and called God to witness that it should never again encircle his neck till he had led his people to victory. Then one by one the great chiefs and indunas advanced, and swore allegiance with their foreheads on the ivory box. Such a collection of races has never been seen. There were tall Zulus and Swazis with *ringkops* and feather head-dresses. There were men from the north with heavy brass collars and anklets; men with quills in their ears, and ear-rings and nose-rings; shaven heads, and heads with wonderfully twisted hair; bodies naked or all but naked, and bodies adorned with skins and necklets. Some were light in colour, and some were black as coal; some had squat negro features, and some thin, high-boned Arab faces. But in all there was the air of mad enthusiasm. For a day they had forsworn from blood, but their wild eyes and twitching hands told their future purpose.—John Buchan, *Prester John.*

By permission of the publishers, Jonathan Cape, Limited, Toronto.

2. THE MARKET-PLACE

In the market-place at Goderville was a great crowd, a mingled multitude of men and beasts. The horns of cattle, the high and long napped hats of wealthy peasants, the head-dresses of the women, came to the surface of that sea. And voices clamorous, sharp, shrill, made a continuous and savage din. Above it a huge burst of laughter from the sturdy lungs of a merry yokel would sometimes sound, and sometimes a long bellow from a cow tied fast to the wall of a house.

It all smelled of the stable, of milk, of hay, and of perspiration, giving off that half-human, half-animal odour which is peculiar to men of the fields.
—Guy de Maupassant, *The Odd Number.*

By permission of the publishers, Harper & Brothers, New York.

3. ELEVEN O'CLOCK, NOVEMBER 11

They stood on the curb while the crowd, noisy, cheerful, exaggerated, swirled back and forwards around them. Suddenly eleven o'clock boomed from Big Ben. Before the strokes were completed there was utter silence; as though a sign had flashed from the sky, the waters of the world were frozen into ice. The omnibuses in Trafalgar Square stayed where they were; every man stood, his hat in his hand. The women held their children with a warning clasp. The pigeons around the Arch rose fluttering and crying into the air, the only sound in all the world; the two minutes seemed eternal . . .

The moment was over; the world went on again, but there were many there who would remember.—From *The Young Enchanted* by HUGH WALPOLE.

Copyright 1921, by Doubleday, Doran and Company, Inc.

PRACTICE 28. Describing a Crowd

Describe one or more of the following groups of people, and try to avoid mere cataloguing. Pick out the picturesque, the colourful.

1. The Midway at the Fair. 2. A crowd at a football game. 3. A college crowd rooting for a team. 4. The assembly hall or auditorium on a gala occasion. 5. A street scene, such as a parade. 6. A school (or church, or C.G.I.T. or Boy Scout) bazaar. 7. A department store at Christmas shopping time. 8. The concert. 9. A solemn occasion such as the Trooping of Colours, Memorial Day exercises, Armistice Day ceremonies at the Cenotaph. 10. A welcome to the Governor-General. 11. A political rally. 12. A crowd at Market Square. 13. A mob scene. 14. A police court scene.

MOODS AND MENTAL STATES

Success in novel and short story writing often depends upon ability to re-create moods and mental states. This may be only to outward appearance, or it may go very deep, or into the very heart of the characters. It is not so difficult as it first appears, requiring only accurate observation and patient selection of most effective phenomena —with persons, facial and bodily reactions in each mood; with crowds, the more obvious demonstrations. Watch verbs and adverbs closely. The introduction of conversation helps in the portrayal.

Models:

1. VILLION

Suddenly his heart stopped beating; a feeling of cold scales passed up the back of his legs, and a cold blow seemed to fall upon his scalp. He stood petrified for a moment; then he felt again with one feverish movement; and then his

loss burst upon him, and he was covered at once with perspiration.—ROBERT
LOUIS STEVENSON, *A Lodging for the Night.*

By permission of Charles Scribner's Sons, New York.

2. AFRAID?

I do not know if I was what you call afraid; but my heart beat like a bird's
both quick and little; and there was a dimness came before my eyes which I
continually rubbed away, and which continually returned. As for hope, I
had none; but only a darkness of despair and a sort of anger against all the
world that made me long to sell my life as dear as I was able. I tried to pray,
I remember, but that same hurry of my mind, like a man running, would not
suffer me to think upon the words; and my chief wish was to have the thing
begin and be done with it.—ROBERT LOUIS STEVENSON, *Kidnapped.*

By permission of Charles Scribner's Sons, New York.

3. THE SINKING OF THE "LUSITANIA"

The next thing I can remember was being deep down under the water.
It was very dark, nearly black. I fought to come up. I was terrified of being
caught on some part of the ship and kept down. That was the worst moment
of terror, the only moment of acute terror, that I knew. My wrist did catch
on a rope. I was scarcely aware of it at the time, but I have the mark on me
to this day. At first I swallowed a lot of water; then I remembered that I
had read that one should not swallow water, so I shut my mouth. Something
bothered me in my right hand, and prevented me striking out with it: I discovered that it was the life-belt I had been holding for my father. As I reached
the surface I grasped a little bit of board quite thin, a few inches wide and
perhaps two or three feet long. I thought this was keeping me afloat. I was
wrong. My most excellent life-belt was doing that. But everything that
happened after I had been submerged was a little misty and vague; I was
slightly stupefied from then on.—VISCOUNTESS RHONDDA, *This Was My
World.*

By permission of the publishers, The Macmillan Company of Canada Limited.

4. THE SPELL OF THE ROAD

Next moment, hardly knowing how it came about, he found he had hold
of the handle and was turning it. As the familiar sound broke forth, the old
passion seized on Toad and completely mastered him, body and soul. As if
in a dream, he found himself, somehow, seated in the driver's seat; as if in a
dream, he pulled the lever and swung the car round the yard and out through
the archway; and, as if in a dream, all sense of right and wrong, all fear of
obvious consequences, seemed temporarily suspended. He increased his pace,
and as the car devoured the street and leapt forth on the high road through
the open country, he was only conscious that he was Toad once more, Toad
at his best and highest, Toad the terror, the traffic-queller, the Lord of the lone
trail, before whom all must give way or be smitten into nothingness and everlasting night. He chanted as he flew, and the car responded with sonorous
drone; the miles were eaten up under him as he sped he knew not whither,
fulfilling his instincts, living his hour, reckless of what might come to him.
—KENNETH GRAHAME, *The Wind in the Willows.*

By arrangement with Charles Scribner's Sons, New York.

6. A GREAT TIME

Sweet Chance, that led my steps abroad,
    Beyond the town, where wild flowers grow—
A rainbow and a cuckoo, Lord,
    How rich and great the times are now!
Know, all ye sheep
And cows, that keep
On staring that I stand so long
    In grass that's wet from heavy rain—
A rainbow and a cuckoo's song
    May never come together again;
        May never come
        This side the tomb.

                                    —W. H. DAVIES.

By permission of the publishers, Jonathan Cape Limited, Toronto.

PRACTICE 29. Presenting a Mood

Write a descriptive composition representing an individual who, in some appropriate circumstance, is in a mood pronounced enough to be easily observable. Represent one of the following:

1. Terror. 2. Awe. 3. Nervousness. 4. Joy. 5. Ecstasy. 6. Cheerfulness. 7. Sadness. 8. Sullenness. 9. Melancholy. 10. Suspicion. 11. Doubt. 12. Enthusiasm. 13. Rapture. 14. Despondency. 15. Bitterness. 16. Cynicism. 17. Contentment. 18. Any other.

PRACTICE 30. Emotional Reaction of a Crowd

Describe an assembly in which conflicting emotional reactions will be represented.

Suggestions:

1. Crowd waiting at the palace hear of death of their monarch. 2. Rain at last! 3. A court room hears the jury deliver its verdict. 4. A school hears announcement of unexpected holiday. 5. The first snow of winter (children, parents, old folk). 6. A room full of people hear a boy on the street shout "Extra!" 7. At the dance. 8. The train is pulling out (newly-weds on honeymoon, business men on business trips, prisoners being escorted to prison, holidayers leaving for holidays, etc., etc.)

WORKS OF ART

With works of art the chief concern is to create an emotional response, which is usually subjective. The writing itself must rise to the level of art—not ornate but sincere and true. The words, for this reason, must be carefully chosen. The models give descriptions of musical compositions, speeches, and painting.

Models:

1. THE MOONLIGHT SONATA

He suffered himself to be led back to the instrument. The moon shone brightly in through the window and lit up his glorious, rugged head and massive figure. "I shall improvise a sonata to the moonlight!" looking up thoughtfully to the sky and stars. Then his hands dropped on the keys, and he began playing a sad and infinitely lovely movement, which crept gently over the instrument like the calm flow of moonlight over the dark earth. This was followed by a wild, elfin passage in triple time—a sort of grotesque interlude, like the dance of sprites upon the sward. Then came a swift, breathless, trembling movement, descriptive of flight and uncertainty, and vague, impulsive terror, which carried us away on its rustling wings, and left us all in emotion and wonder.—ANONYMOUS.

2. PRESTER JOHN'S SPEECH

I had heard him on board the liner, and had thought his voice the most wonderful I had ever met with. But now in that great resonant hall the magic of it was doubled. He played upon the souls of his hearers as on a musical instrument. At will he struck the chords of pride, fury, hate, and mad joy. Now they would be hushed in breathless quiet, and now the place would echo with savage assent. I remember noticing that the face of my neighbour 'Mwanga, was running with tears.

He spoke of the great days of Prester John, and a hundred names I had never heard of. He pictured the heroic age of his nation, when every man was a warrior and hunter, and rich kraals stood in the spots now desecrated by the white man, and cattle wandered on a thousand hills. Then he told tales of white infamy, lands snatched from their rightful possessors, unjust laws which forced the Ethiopian to the bondage of a despised caste, the finger of scorn everywhere, and the mocking word. If it be the part of an orator to rouse the passion of his hearers, Laputa was the greatest on earth. "What have ye gained from the white man?" he cried. "A bastard civilization which has sapped your manhood; a false religion which would rivet on you the chains of the slave. Ye, the old masters of the land, are now the servants of the aggressor. And yet the oppressors are few, and the fear of you is in their hearts. They feast in their great cities, but they see the writing on the wall, and their eyes are anxiously turning lest the enemy be at their gates?" I cannot hope in my prosaic words to reproduce that amazing discourse. Phrases which the hearers had heard at mission schools now suddenly appeared, not as the white man's learning, but as God's message to His own. Laputa fitted the key to the cipher, and the meaning was clear. He concluded, I remember, with a picture of the overthrow of the alien, and the golden age which would dawn for the oppressed. Another Ethiopian empire would arise, so majestic that the white man everywhere would dread its name, so righteous that all men under it would live in ease and peace.

By rights, I suppose, my blood should have been boiling at this treason. I am ashamed to confess that it did nothing of the sort. My mind was mesmerized by this amazing man. I could not refrain from shouting with the rest. Indeed I was a convert, if there can be conversion when the emotions are dominant and there is no assent from the brain. I had a mad desire to be of Laputa's party.—JOHN BUCHAN, *Prester John.*

By permission of the publishers, Jonathan Cape Limited, Toronto.

3. THE ANGELUS

"A PAINTED PRAYER"

Millet was one of the famous group of French painters who founded what is now known as the "Barbizon" School. He was the son of a peasant farmer, and his outlook was coloured by the incidents of peasant life which find such eloquent expression in his pictures. His work is distinguished by an absolute truthfulness to Nature which was the guiding principle of his life. He saw the peasant bent at his work in the fields, and he pictured him in all his gaunt poverty and weariness, while he invested him, by his inspired vision, with the symbolical dignity of labour. Thus, in painting life, Millet reveals the sublime in the commonplace, the promise hidden in the pain, and the mercy that hovers over sorrow.

"The Angelus" completes a series of three pictures by Millet which are considered his masterpieces. "The Sowers" typifies the labourer going forth bearing good seed with him. "The Gleaners" shows the end of the harvest which has supplied the people's wants and left something over for the needy. "The Angelus" depicts the labourers' thanks for the gift of plenty.

The last picture is the most popular of all the works of this artist, and it expresses in full measure the simplicity and devoutness of his nature. His wish was to make the spectator realize the vesper hour, when the soft chimes call the toiler to thankful rest. The man and the woman have worked well,

as their full sacks bear witness, and they are bending their heads in gratitude
to their Creator for His gifts. On a small canvas, twenty-five inches long and
twenty-one inches high, the painter has created a scene that is at once a prayer
and an inspiration, which will hold its strong appeal as long as the colours
last.—From *Famous Paintings*, Vol. I.

By permission of the publishers, Cassell & Company, Ltd., London.

4. THE MAN WITH THE HOE

Bowed by the weight of centuries he leans
Upon his hoe and gazes on the ground,
The emptiness of ages in his face,
And on his back the burden of the world.
Who made him dead to rapture and despair,
A thing that grieves not and that never hopes,
Solid and stunned, a brother to the ox?
Who loosened and let down this brutal jaw?
Whose was the hand that slanted back this brow?
Whose breath blew out the light within this brain?

What gulf between him and the seraphim!
Slave of the wheel of labour, what to him
Are Plato and the swing of Pleiades?
What the long reaches of the peaks of song,
The rift of dawn, the reddening of the rose?
Through this dread shape the suffering ages look;
Time's tragedy is in that aching stoop;
Through this dread shape humanity betrayed,
Plundered, profaned, and disinherited,
Cries protest to the Judges of the World,
A protest that is also prophecy.
                                   —EDWIN MARKHAM

Copyright by the author and used with his permission.

PRACTICE 31. Describing a Work of Art

Describe some picture, poem, or piece of music which you admire.
Try to justify your admiration by presenting, in words, what is admirable. Do not depend upon apostrophe and emotional ejaculation.
State **explicitly and clearly** what is beautiful about the object **you
describe**.

Chapter 9

Writing a Social Letter

As an ambassador represents his country at the court to which he is attached, so your letters represent you to the friends, relatives, or acquaintances to whom they are addressed. Newsy, entertaining letters will win for you a favourable report. Timely, considerate letters will win for you a reputation for thoughtfulness and courtesy. Most of us do not sufficiently cultivate the opportunities that present themselves for friendly and interesting communication. Moreover, it can be fun to write letters as well as to receive them.

HOW TO WRITE A GOOD LETTER

Good Beginning. Arouse interest with a lively beginning. **Avoid** useless, unnecessary words.

GOOD What an exciting time you and Aubrey had on your holidays!

DULL I got your letter Tuesday telling us about your holidays.

Conversational Style. Write much as you would talk. Use contractions. Keep your language clear, simple, and direct. **Avoid** wordiness and artificiality.

GOOD We've had a good time ourselves.

WORDY If I bestir myself, maybe I can recall some of our own experiences.

Friendly Tone. The warmth of tone should vary with the purpose

242

of your letter, the age of your reader, and the intimacy of your friendship. Be enthusiastic and cheerful. Say what you mean and mean what you say. Avoid complaints and malicious gossip. Don't send an important letter while you are angry, depressed, or tired. Wait until you have read it the next day.

Well-chosen Details. Do not try to tell everything. Stick to a few topics and give definite, well-chosen details.

Good Ending. When you have said what you want to say, stop. Don't make excuses or add pointless remarks. If possible, talk about your reader, not about yourself, in your last sentence.

GOOD   Do you like living in Montreal?

WEAK   I must close now as I have a lot of work to do.

Attractive Appearance. The appearance of your letter tells as much about you as does your dress.

Correct Form. Be sure to use correct form. Mistakes in the heading, salutation, closing, or envelope address create a bad impression.

HOW TO MAKE YOUR LETTER ATTRACTIVE

Margin on Four Sides. A margin on all four sides is a pleasing frame for a letter page. At least leave a half-inch margin on the left. Indent each paragraph a half-inch or more.

Stationery. White stationery is always good. Girls may use pale grey, tan, or blue paper, paper with a gay border, or envelopes with a frilly lining. Avoid green, violet, and vivid pink. Gilt-edged, ruled, or highly-scented paper is taboo.

Blue or Black Ink. Use blue, black, or blue-black ink. Type a friendly letter, if you wish, but write by hand an invitation, a reply, a thank-you, or other social note. If you cannot erase a mistake neatly, take a fresh sheet of paper.

Pages in Order. If you use double sheets of paper, write on the pages in 1, 2, 3, 4 order as if they were pages in a book. If you haven't much to say, use pages 1 and 3.

REVIEWING THE FIVE PARTS OF A LETTER

Study the following letter outline and the reminders below it.

INDENTED STYLE

180 Strathallan Boulevard,
                        Toronto 12, Ontario.
                        March 5, 19—

SALUTATION   Dear Betty,

BODY   _____

         _____

CLOSING   Affectionately,
SIGNATURE   Joan

REMINDERS

1. Form: if you prefer block form, write the second and third lines of the heading directly beneath the first; begin the signature beneath the first letter of the closing.

2. Heading: give your address unless you are sure that your reader knows it; always include the day or date; avoid abbreviations.

3. Salutation: Dear Jed, Dear Mrs. Fowler, Dear Aunt Laura, My dear Mrs. Martin, (more formal), Ginny dear, (more intimate)

4. Closing: Cordially yours, With love, Gratefully yours, Affectionately, Your loving nephew, Yours as ever,

5. Capitals: heading—street, town or city, state, month; salutation—the first word and all nouns; closing—the first word.

6. Punctuation: four commas—(1) after city, town, or zone number; (2) between day and year; (3) after salutation; (4) after closing.

Joan Smithers,
   180 Strathallan Boulevard,
      Toronto 12, Ont.

            Miss Betty Ferguson,
               1632 Côte des Neiges,
                  Quebec 10, P.Q.

PRACTICE 1. Evaluating a Friendly Letter

Does Marion's letter (below) have (a) conversational style; (b) friendly tone; (c) contents to fit the reader? Give examples to illustrate your answers.

2. Are the beginning and ending effective? What improvements would you suggest?

3. List the main topics and the definite details she gives about them.

Dear Claire,

Your post card from Halifax looked so exciting that I almost forgot I had had a fine trip myself. In fact we got home two days ago.

I thought of you and your fear of snakes when we stopped near Washington at a snake farm. Yes, a snake farm—where they milk snakes for venom. Raising snakes is actually an important job. Serum used to treat snake bite is made from the venom of poisonous snakes. At the farm we saw the king cobra, the coral snake, and lots of others, both poisonous and nonpoisonous. I actually held some of the harmless snakes. Snakes aren't really horrible at all, I've decided.

Thanks for suggesting that I read "Please Don't Eat the Daisies" by Jean Kerr. Have you read "Story of the Gypsies" by Konrad Bercovici? It's the best book I've read in months. I had always imagined that gypsies were fierce and frightening, but Bercovici pictures them as happy, fun-loving, and music-loving. The author's anecdotes show the gypsies' great loyalty to one another and their scorn of anyone who is not a gypsy.

I've been helping Dad with the garden and have learned a good deal, mostly through sad experience. We had planted three dozen gladioli bulbs, and the plants were coming up green and healthy. One Sunday the *Times* printed a terrifying article about thrips and advocated spraying glads with DDT to protect them. The next day Dad, who is never one to dillydally, gave our plants a dousing. Within a few hours the glads collapsed in a horrible yellow-brown mass.

A gardener friend explained that there are two kinds of DDT—one for plant insects and one for other insects. Dad had used the latter.

Dad and Mother hope you all are well and are not baking, broiling, or scorching this summer.

Yours affectionately,

Marion

PRACTICE 2. Studying Social Letters

After reading each of the following letters answer these questions about it:

1. Would you like to receive such a letter? Why?
2. Is it entertaining? Why?
3. What information does it contain?
4. Does it sound like conversation? If so, how does the English differ from that of an ordinary composition?
5. How would you write the heading?
6. What is the salutation? The complimentary close?
7. What does the letter show about the writer?
8. What deliberate devices to maintain the unusual has each writer used?

1.

Lewis Carroll writes to a child friend[1]

Christ Church, Oxford, March 8, 1880.

My dear Ada,—(Isn't that your short name? "Adelaide" is all very well, but you see when one is *dreadfully* busy one hasn't time to write such long words—particularly when it takes one half an hour to remember how to spell it—and even then one has to go and get a dictionary to see if one has spelt it right, and, of course, the dictionary is in another room, at the top of a high bookcase—where it has been for months and months, and has got all covered with dust—so one has to get a duster first of all, and nearly choke oneself in dusting it—and when one *has* made out at last which is dictionary and which is dust, even *then* there's the job of remembering which end of the alphabet "A" comes—for one feels pretty certain it isn't in the *middle*—then one has to go and wash one's hands before turning over the leaves—for they've got so thick with dust one hardly knows them by sight—and, as likely as not, the soap is lost and the jug is empty, and there's no towel, and one has to spend hours and hours in finding things—and perhaps after all one has to go off to the shop to buy a new cake of soap—so, with all this bother, I hope you won't mind my writing it short and saying, "My dear Ada"). You said in your last letter you would like a likeness of me—I won't forget to call the next time but one I'm in Wallington.

Your very affectionate friend,
Lewis Carroll

2.

Robert Louis Stevenson to Miss Adelaide Boodle. (Stevenson heard that his friend was teaching a class of children at Kilburn in London, so he wrote this letter to be read to them.)

Vailima [Samoa],
January 4th, 1892.

My dear Adelaide,

We were much pleased with your letter and the news of your employment. Admirable, your method. But will you not run dry of fairy stories? Please salute your pupils, and tell them that a long, lean, elderly man who lives right

---

[1]*Taken by permission from* The Life and Letters of Lewis Caroll, *published by the Century Company.*

through on the other side of the world, so that down in your cellar you are nearer him than the people in the street, desires his compliments.

This man lives in an island which is not very long, and extremely narrow. The sea beats round it very hard, so that it is difficult to get to shore. There is only one harbour where ships come, even that is very wild and dangerous; four ships of war were broken there a little while ago, and one of them is still lying on its side on a rock clean above water, where the sea threw it, as you might throw your fiddle-bow on the table.

All round the harbour the town is strung out; it is nothing but wooden houses, only there are some churches built of stone, and not very large, but the people have never seen fine buildings. Almost all the houses are of one storey.

Away at one end lives the king of the whole country. His palace has a thatched roof which stands upon posts; it has no walls, but when it blows and rains, they have Venetian blinds which they let down between the posts and make it very snug. There is no furniture, and the king and the queen and the courtiers sit and eat on the floor, which is of gravel; the lamp stands there too, and every now and then it is upset.

These good folk wear nothing but a kilt about their waists, unless to go to church or for a dance, or the New Year, or some great occasion. The children play marbles all along the streets; and though they are generally very jolly, yet they get awfully cross over their marbles, and cry and fight like boys and girls at home.

Another amusement in the country places is to shoot fish with a bow and arrow. All round the beach there is bright, shallow water where fishes can be seen darting or lying in shoals. The child trots round the shore, and whenever he sees a fish, lets fly an arrow and misses, and then wades in after his arrow. It is great fun (I have tried it) for the child, and I have never heard of it doing any harm to the fishes: so what could be more jolly?

The road up to this lean man's house is uphill all the way and through forests; the forests are of great trees, not so much unlike the trees at home, only here and there are some queer ones mixed with them, cocoanut palms, and great forest trees that are covered with blossom like red hawthorn, but not nearly so bright; and from all the trees thick creepers hang down like ropes, and nasty-looking weeds, that they call orchids, grow in the forks of the branches; and on the ground many prickly things are dotted, which they call pine-apples: I suppose everyone has eaten pine-apple drops . . .

On the way up to the lean man's house you pass a little village, all of houses like the king's house, so that, as you ride through, you can see everybody sitting at dinner; or if it be night, lying in their beds by lamplight; for all these people are terribly afraid of ghosts, and would not lie in the dark for any favour. After the village there is only one more house and that is the lean man's; for the people are not very many, and live all by the sea, and the whole inside of the island is desert woods and mountains . . .

Here is a tale the lean man heard last year. One of the islanders was sitting in his house, and he had cooked fish. There came along the road two beautiful young women, who came into his house and asked for his fish.

It is the fashion in the islands always to give what is asked, and never to ask folk's names. So the man gave them fish and talked to them in the island jesting way.

Presently he asked one of the women for her red necklace, which is good manners and their way; he had given the fish, and he had a right to ask for something back.

"I will give it you by and by," said the woman, and she and her companion went away; but he thought they were gone very suddenly, and the truth is they had vanished.

The night was nearly come, when the man heard the voice of the woman crying that he should come to her, and she would give the necklace. He looked out, and behold she was standing calling him from the top of the sea. At that, fear came on the man; he fell on his knees and prayed, and the woman disappeared.

It was known afterwards that this was once a woman indeed, but should have died a thousand years ago, and has lived all that while as a devil in the woods beside the spring of the river. Sau-mai-afe (Sow-my-affy) is her name, in case you want to write to her.

Ever your friend Tusitala (tale-writer),

alias Robert Louis Stevenson.

Reprinted from "The Letters of Robert Louis Stevenson, 1868-1894." *Edited by Sir Sidney Colvin. By kind permission of Sir Sidney Colvin and Messrs. Methuen & Co., Ltd.*

SOME BEGINNINGS

As with other kinds of writing, the beginning sentences of a letter may prove its making or its unmaking. It should set writer and reader in a common frame of mind, so that communion and communication is ready and pleasing.

PRACTICE 3. Opening Sentences

Consider these openings, and say what kind of relationship of acquaintance or intimacy, what mood or attitude exists between writers and receivers of the letters.

1. Thomas Bailey Aldrich writes to William Dean Howells:

Dear Howells,

We had so charming a visit at your house that I have about made up my mind to reside with you permanently.

2. Robert Louis Stevenson, to his parents, after receiving an offer for *Treasure Island:*

My dearest People,

I have had a great piece of news. There has been offered for *Treasure Island*—how much do you suppose? I believe it would be an excellent jest to keep the answer till my next letter. For two cents I would do so. Shall I? Anyway, I'll turn the page first.

—By arrangement with Charles Scribner's Sons

3. Leigh Hunt, English essayist and poet, to Shelley and his wife who were resident at Leghorn, Italy:

My dear Friends,—

Whenever I write to you, I seem to be transported to your presence. I dart out of the window like a bird, dash into a southwest current of air, skim over the cool waters, hurry over the basking lands, rise like a lark over the mountains, fling like a swallow into the valleys, skim again, pant for breath, there's Leghorn—how d'ye do?

4. George Bernard Shaw, holidaying in Suffolk, writes to Ellen Terry, the famous actress:

The Rectory, Stratford St. Andrews,
Saxmundham

There are no clocks and no calendars here, but surely it must be September by this time. If not, keep this letter till it *is*, and then read it.

5. Ellen Terry, to George Bernard Shaw, after a long and weary rehearsal of *Cymbeline:*

11 September, 1896, Savoy Hotel,
Victoria Embankment, London.

" 'Tis now the witching hour of night." Churchyards yawn and so do I. Oh, the long speeches!

PRACTICE 4. Writing Social Letters

1. Write to a boy or girl of your age in New Zealand, Japan, Denmark, or Brazil about life in a Canadian high school or in your city or town.
   (If you would like to correspond with a student from overseas, write for information to Mrs. R. T. Tanner, Overseas Correspondence Department, United Nations Association in Canada, Box 178, Markham, Ont., Canada.)
2. All boys will write their names on slips of paper and drop them into a hat. Each boy will draw a slip from the hat. From another containing the names of the girls each girl will draw a name. Then write an entertaining letter to the pupil whose name you draw.
3. Reply to the letter received from your classmate.
4. Write a cheery, sympathetic letter to a sick friend or classmate.
5. Write to a cousin in Florida about northern winter sports or to a cousin in Australia about Canadian winter sports.
6. Arrange to meet a friend. Make clear the time and the place.
7. To a friend who has asked, "What is a good book to read?" write entertainingly about a book you have read recently.
8. To a friend who has asked, "What is a good magazine to read?" write entertainingly about your favourite magazine.
9. In a letter to your parents, who are away, tell entertainingly the family news.

10. To a friend write a true travel letter based on a trip you have taken or an imaginative letter based on a travel book you have read. Share the new scenes and acquaintances with your friend.

11. The pupils in rotation have arranged to write a daily letter to an injured classmate and to include the English homework assignment. Write your letter.

12. Write to a friend who has moved to another city. Include school news.

13. As a character in a book you are studying, write a letter about your experiences. For example, if you are studying *Ivanhoe*, as Cedric write about the rudeness of the Normans at the banquet, or as Rowena tell of your being chosen Queen of Love and Beauty and your discovering that the Disinherited Knight is Ivanhoe.

INFORMAL DISCUSSION

Friendly letters are not limited to personal matters, experiences, descriptions, and reading, but often include discussions on a great variety of subjects. In the following letter Paul tries to persuade Jack to join a club or an athletic team at his high school.

49 Eighth Street
Govan, Saskatchewan
October 14, 1949

Dear Jack,

You old bookworm! If you were here, I'd take that chem book away from you, drag you out into the open air, and let the wind drive those chemical cobwebs out of your brain.

So you don't think every student should take part in at least one extra-curricular activity! Did you ever stop to think that when you've graduated you'll have to mingle with other people in your business or profession? If you cloister yourself in a chem lab, you'll never learn how to meet people, talk to them, or enjoy the comradeship of those who share your interests. School clubs will help you to make many lasting friendships and prepare you for life outside your high school walls.

Besides, think of the mental stimulation. Do you rise to the bait, my learned friend? It's perfectly all right to formulate your own theories and test them alone, but other people have theories, too. Defending your ideas in club meetings will clear up many hazy points and help you to see the flaws in your own reasoning. You'll learn a lot from the other fellows.

As for athletics—can't you see me beam—a good workout every afternoon would do you good. You can't think clearly or study at your best if you insist on hurrying home to your books immediately after classes every day. You'll never live to a ripe old age if you spend all the best years of your life over a test tube or a dusty tome.

Have I convinced you? Write soon and let me know whether this letter flabbergasted you completely.

Your friend,
Paul

PRACTICE 5. Informal Argument

Choose, by drawing names from a hat or in some other way, an opponent who will reply by letter to an informal argument you write him. Suppose for example, that he, at the end of his third year in high school, has been offered a position with a fair salary and excellent opportunity for advancement. Try to convince him that he should complete his high school course, and then wait for his reply. Instead, you and your opponent may argue about college, poetry, the value of Latin, a candidate for school or public office, the best method of crime prevention, the youth of to-day, the value of athletics, the effects of football, the influence of the movies or the radio, abolishing home work, student government, the use of slang, or any other subject mentioned —or not mentioned—in the unit on discussion, argument, and debate.

LETTER OF INTRODUCTION

Because the purpose of a letter of introduction is to establish a friendship between two people, the letter should make clear what the two people have in common—for example, a love of travel, literature, music, or adventure. It should also explain why the bearer of the letter happens to be in the city of address.

Near the centre of the envelope write the name of the person addressed; and in the lower left corner, *Introducing Alfred Jordan*. Hand Alfred the letter, unsealed and unstamped.

630 Clarence Avenue
Sudbury, Ontario

Dear Edward,

Do you remember Alfred Jordan about whose exploits I told you? Well, here he is. He is going to spend his summer at Rocky Hill Camp, right next to your place.

Al played fullback on Excel's team at the same time that you were quarterback at Fulton. And his ideas about life are very similar to yours. He believes that the best life is under the blue sky out in the open spaces. You'll find him a likeable chap, very sociable, and exceedingly clever. You two scouts will, I'm sure, have some good times together.

Write to me soon, and tell me about your various feats.

Cordially yours,
Nathaniel Boyle

PRACTICE 6. Letter of Introduction

When you lived in Halifax (or another city or town), you had one real friend. Now one of your pals is moving to Halifax. Write the letter of introduction.

LETTERS OF COURTESY

Thoughtful, sympathetic people write many letters of courtesy; young, selfish, ignorant, and lazy ones frequently neglect these opportunities to make others happy and to increase their circle of friends. Letters of courtesy, which include letters of thanks, congratulation, and condolence, must be written promptly. If a month after a visit you thank your hostess, or months after a death you write a note of sympathy, the letter is of little value.

Letters of courtesy are not lengthy, literary efforts but sincere, direct, genuine expressions of feeling. To express simply what is in one's heart is much better than to search for lofty, meaningless phrases.

LETTER OF APOLOGY AND EXPLANATION

A letter of apology in which the writer spends most of his time defending himself is useless—and amusing. Why write at all if you are not ready frankly to admit you're wrong? Of course, one must differentiate between an apology for wrongdoing and an explanation of an unavoidable failure to keep an appointment or a promise.

> 289 Twelfth Street
> Saint John, New Brunswick
> December 11, 1960

Dear Paul,

I'm deeply sorry I failed to keep my appointment with you Saturday morning. It was due to my carelessness entirely. When I awoke I had forgotten all about our plans for the day. About ten o'clock I remembered and hurried to the station. Of course, you were no longer upon the platform, but I went to the museum as planned. As you know, I didn't meet you there, and the day was spoiled for both of us.

Please forgive me. I assure you that I'll be less forgetful next time.

> Your friend,
> Walter Arnoldi

LETTER OF THANKS

Every young person understands one must thank a friend for a gift or hospitality, but many people, young and old, neglect to write notes like the following to thank those who help them in a variety of ways.

> 301 West Twentieth Street
> Wetaskiwin, Alberta
> October 9, 1959

Dear Mr. Gleason,

The material that you sent will, I am sure, prove helpful in the coming debate. It was kind of you to give me so much of your time in writing such a full explanation.

I am very grateful for your assistance.

Sincerely yours,
Lucille Comstock

217 Judge Street
Prince Albert, Saskatchewan
January 9, 1959

Dear Alice,

The impassive face of your Buddha smiles at me through the clouds of incense that create an oriental atmosphere in our most prosaic living-room. I wonder what fairy told you that I am a slave to the mystic East and that the slightest reminder of that far away land will always be dear to me.

Because your attractive gift is so full of this subtle charm, I appreciate it and the kind thought that prompted you.

I hope that the past holiday was a merry one and that this new year will be filled with happiness.

Your loving friend,
Harriet Munro

LETTER OF CONGRATULATIONS

In congratulating a friend write him an entertaining note showing your joy in his success. When you receive a letter of congratulation, remember that it should be answered.

1643 North Second Street
Brandon, Manitoba
May 17, 1960

Dear Richard,

You cannot imagine how glad I was when I heard of your winning the French medal. It was a wonderful achievement, and we're all proud of you.

I can picture you standing upon the platform on commencement night in front of several thousand people, with your chest thrown out and your head high, receiving the award. I can see you striding across the stage and down the steps like Napoleon himself, while the whole vast auditorium rings with applause. I can see, too, the entire French class gazing with envy at the medal. It must be a fine one, and you must bring it with you the next time you visit us.

Remember me to your parents and write soon.

Your old friend,
Harvey

LETTER OF CONDOLENCE

In a letter of condolence show simply and directly that you sympathize with your sorrowing friend.

230 College Street
Toronto, Ontario
June 6, 1948

Dear Margaret,

Your father's death must have been a great shock; I guess it is only human to suppose that sorrow may come near us, but that it will not touch us. Maybe it is better so.

At such a time words seem idle. I wish there were something that I could do instead of just sending my deepest sympathy.

I hope that you will be a great help to your mother in her grief and find comfort in her love for you.

Affectionately yours,
Isabel Landon

PRACTICE 7. Courtesy Letters

1. Your friend in a distant city wrote a letter of introduction for you to a chum in the town to which you have just moved. Thank your friend for his kindness and write an entertaining account of your first meeting with his chum.

2. Thank a friend or relative for a gift on your birthday, at Christmas or graduation, or on another occasion.

3. Congratulate a friend on an honour or an achievement: winning a medal, a pin, or a prize in an essay, short-story, scholarship, pig-raising, good-citizenship, or athletic contest; election to the captaincy of a team or to a school or other office; a successful piano recital, debate, speech, or radio talk; winning a scholarship; passing his university matriculation examinations; gaining admittance to a first-class college.

4. You have asked for material for an essay or debate, a letter of recommendation or introduction, or advice about the choice of a college or vocation. In a letter thank the person who helped you.

5. Thank a hostess for a delightful week-end visit.

6. Imagine that sorrow has come to one of your friends. Write him (or her) a letter of condolence.

7. You have been mean, cranky, unreasonable, rude, untruthful, or disagreeable. Apologize to a friend who has been a victim.

8. In a letter explain why you were unable to keep an appointment **or a** promise.

9. Send birthday or anniversary greetings to a friend or relative.

10. To a friend who is recovering from a serious illness write a cheery, entertaining letter.

11. Congratulate a man who is soon to be married, or send best wishes to a girl who has just announced her engagement.

12. Seize the next opportunity to write an actual letter of courtesy. Show it to your English teacher before mailing it.

FORMAL NOTES

Formal notes are sent as invitations to weddings, receptions, and dinner parties. The answer, written on letter paper or a correspondence card, should be similar in wording to the original note.

INVITATION

Mr. and Mrs. James Hamilton
request the pleasure of
Mr. and Mrs. Timothy Gamble's
company at dinner
on Wednesday, the twelfth of December,
at eight o'clock.

ACCEPTANCE

Mr. and Mrs. Timothy Gamble
accept with pleasure
Mr. and Mrs. Hamilton's
kind invitation for dinner
on Wednesday, the twelfth of December,
at eight o'clock.

REGRET

Mr. and Mrs. Timothy Gamble
regret extremely that a previous engagement
prevents their accepting
Mr. and Mrs. Hamilton's
kind invitation for dinner
on Wednesday, the twelfth of December.

Notice that—

1. The note and the replies are in the third person.

2. Formal notes lack heading, salutation, complimentary close, and signature.

3. The present tense is used in the answer.

4. No abbreviations except *Mr., Mrs., Jr.,* and *o'clock* are used.

5. Numbers are written words.

6. The acceptance mentions the day and the hour of the dinner.

7. In a regret the hour may be omitted.

A formal invitation need not be engraved but may be written by hand on the first page of a sheet of good note paper. Follow the arrangement and the spacing of the model on page 255. Also arrange your pen-written reply like the acceptance or the regret shown. Above everything else, answer an invitation promptly.

VISITING-CARD INVITATIONS

The hostess' card with the time and kind of entertainment on it is commonly used in inviting to an informal dance, musicale, picnic, or a tea to meet a guest, or for bridge.

The answer to an invitation on a calling card is exactly the same as the reply to a formal penned or engraved invitation. To a close friend a calling card with "With pleasure! Friday at 4" written on it is also correct.

To meet
Miss Mildred Drew

Mrs. Arnold S. Proudfoot

Thursday, May 4
Dancing at 10 o'clock
275 Park Lane

PRACTICE 8. Formal Notes

1. Write both an acceptance of Mrs. Proudfoot's invitation and a regret.

2. Write a correct formal note to Dr. and Mrs. Stokes requesting the pleasure of their company at dinner on Friday, October 22, at eight o'clock. Write an acceptance and a regret from Dr. and Mrs. Stokes.

3. Mr. and Mrs. James Howland Wilson have invited you to be present at the marriage of their daughter Hester to Mr. James Ferguson at four o'clock on June 6 at their home, 4 West 187th Street. Write both an acceptance and a regret.

Chapter 10

Writing Business Letters

Why Learn to Write Business Letters?

THE business letter is the backbone of business. Because time, distance, and expense often prevent men's doing business with each other face to face, a business man needs to know how to write a letter which will have a personal touch and will somehow appeal to the particular man written to. To know what he wants to say is not enough. "The vehicle of expression," says a publisher, "even from the purely business standpoint, is quite as important as the thing said."

PROMPTNESS

A business letter calls for a prompt reply. Delay often means loss of business or of an opportunity. Most successful executives try to clear their desks each day before leaving their offices.

PRECISENESS

A business letter demands the highest degree of clarity. It must be free of any ambiguities. The business letter must be explicit about orders, rejections, quantities, and shipping or delivery instructions.

258

PARTS OF A BUSINESS LETTER

The six parts of a business letter are heading, address, salutation, body, complimentary close, and signature.

OPEN PUNCTUATION—SLANT FORM

```
                                    Moose Jaw, Saskatchewan
                                       December 2, 1960

The Radio Electric Company
   Ninth Street and Broadway
      New Westminster, British Columbia

Gentlemen:
        _____

_____

                              Yours truly,
                              (Miss) Grace Glidden
```

OPEN PUNCTUATION—BLOCKFORM

(The block form is commonly used in typed letters; the slant, in pen-written letters.)

```
                                    1013 Ballantyne Avenue
                                    Lethbridge, Alberta
                                    December 12, 1960

Mr. James Stern, Manager
Canadian Bank of Commerce
62 West Fourteenth Street
Edmonton, Alberta

Dear Sir:
        _____

_____

                              Very truly yours,
                              Jay Electric Company
                              by  M. J. Williams
```

CLOSE PUNCTUATION—SLANT FORM

536 Marsden Place,
Fort William, Ontario,
December 4, 1960

Mrs. Samuel Warner,
1024 Wabash Avenue,
Chicago, Illinois.

Dear Madam:

_____

_____

Yours very truly,

J. G. Phillips

ADDRESS

1. The name and address of the firm written to are placed **regularly at** the left margin just below the heading and rarely at the end of the letter. When writing to a firm, write the name exactly as it appears on the company's letterhead: *The J. H. Fidler Co., Dominion Messenger & Signal Co., Ltd., G. & C. Merriam Company, Henry Holt and Company.*

2. The arrangement and punctuation must follow the system of the heading. If the heading has no punctuation after lines and has **a** sloping margin, don't change the style in the address.

SALUTATION

1. Common business salutations are—

Dear Sir: *Gentlemen:*
My dear Sir: *Ladies: or Mesdames:*
Dear Mr. Hawkins: *Dear Madam:*
My dear Mr. Page: *My dear Madam:*

In a letter to a person you know use *Dear Dr. Scott* or *Dear Mrs. Leonard,* not *Dear Sir* or *Dear Madam.*

2. Begin the salutation at the margin two spaces below its **address in a** typed letter and one space below in a script letter.

3. Use a colon after the salutation.

4. Capitalize the first word **and** all nouns.

LETTER FORM MODEL

The following letter is dictated and has one enclosure. The writer addresses it to a particular member of the firm.

Attention of Mr. C. H. Duell is centred two spaces below the salutation or on the same line with it. Usage varies.

Letterhead	**THE CANADIAN PRINTERS** PRINTING AND ENGRAVING ◈ 316 THIRD AVE., SASKATOON, SASK.
Date	January 2, 1960
Address	John Underwood & Co., 90 Richmond Street, Toronto, Ontario.
Salutation	Gentlemen:
Particular Address	Attention of Mr. C. H. Duell.
Body	
Complimentary Close	Very truly yours, THE CANADIAN PRINTERS
Signature	*J. E. Dewitt* Manager
Dictator and typist *Enclosure*	JED/SM Enc.

BODY

Our letters are written representatives of ourselves.

1. Indent all paragraphs alike. Don't make the first paragraph an exception.

2. Good English is good business English. Vary the sentence length. The short simple sentence is emphatic but usually not so precise as the longer complex sentence.

3. A good business letter is correct, clear, complete, accurate, courteous, and concise. Have clearly in mind what you wish to say and express your ideas exactly and fully in simple, direct language. As a rule, confine a letter to one subject. Clearness requires also a separate paragraph for each idea. Because short paragraphs are easier to read than long ones, paragraphs in business correspondence are shorter than in a book chapter or a magazine article. They should not average more than sixty words and should seldom exceed one hundred.

4. The first sentence is especially important. It should arouse interest and create a favourable impression by telling the reader something he wishes to know, and may refer in a definite and original way to the letter to which it is in reply. Notice these beginnings:

We have asked our representative, Mr. S. J. Tucker, to see that your cash register is put in proper working order at once. Thank you very much for reporting this matter on your card of November 10.

A duplicate shipment of the bedroom set, which you won in the Spring Contest, has been ordered.

5. Because the last sentence also occupies an important position, it should be clean-cut and complete. Avoid the participial conclusion beginning with *hoping, trusting, believing, thanking* or *regretting*. And *oblige* is obsolete. Don't insert *We beg to remain, We remain,* or *I am* before the complimentary close.

Aim to clinch your point and bring the reader "over to your side." Add a few friendly words if you can—for example:

We thank you for placing the order with us and hope the shipment will arrive promptly.

As it is necessary for us to have this information, won't you please telephone to us the first thing tomorrow morning.

6. Conciseness requires that the writer courteously make his point in the fewest possible words. "It has always been the habit of greatness to say much in little." Don't, however, omit such necessary words as the subject, the verb, articles, or prepositions. A business letter is not a telegram. Instead of *Received your letter,* say *I received your letter.* Business men now avoid the hackneyed expressions which were correct in the days of our grandfathers.

Old-fashioned:

a. Your esteemed favour of the 30th ult. is at hand; are sorry that the twenty pounds of Royal Oak coffee have not arrived.

b. Yours of recent date received and contents carefully noted and in reply to same would say that your order was shipped on December 10th.

c. Enclosed herewith please find—

d. Regretting our inability to serve you along these lines, we beg to remain—

Better:

a. We regret to learn from your letter of November 30 that you have not received the twenty pounds of Royal Oak Coffee.

b. We are glad to find that the order about which you inquired in your letter of December 14 was shipped on December 10.

c. I enclose—

d. We regret that our stock of Humphrey Radiantfires is exhausted.

7. The secret of success in letter writing and salesmanship is putting yourself in the other fellow's place. Remember that courtesy is politeness plus kindness. The *Correspondence Manual* of the Stanley Works, New Britain, Connecticut, says, "Then before you sign your name to a letter ask yourself, 'Would this letter suitably answer me if I were in the customer's place?' "

8. It is better to use no abbreviations except *Mr., Mrs., Messrs., Dr., St.* (*Saint*), f.o.b., A.M., *Y.M.C.A., C.O.D.*, B.C., A.D. Do not use *etc.* if you can avoid it.

When preparing to write a reply read thoroughly the letter you are answering, think what kind of man the writer is, decide what you wish to accomplish with the reply, then plan your letter.

10. Write *January 19*, not *January 19th* or *January nineteenth* Use figures also for house numbers and page numbers.

11. Use freely such courteous expressions as *thank you, please, we are glad, it is a pleasure,* and such positive words as *confidence, success, enjoy, achieve, approve, energetic, substantial, attractive, genuine, happy, trustworthy,* and *straight-forward.* Use sparingly such negative words as *complaint, misunderstanding, grievance, trouble delay, mistake,* and *inconvenience.*

PRACTICE 1. Good Business English

For the following stereotyped or old-fashioned expressions substitute fresh, terse, conversational ones. If necessary, supply information to complete the sentence.

1. *Kindly* deliver the *same at an early date.*

2. *Enclosed please find as per your request* an itemized bill.

3. *Thanking you in advance* for suggestions *along this line* and *awaiting your further favours, we remain.*

4. Your *kind* order has *come to hand,* and *same shall receive attention at the earliest possible moment.*

5. Your *valued favour* is *at hand* and *in reply would say* that *our* Mr. Johnson will call on you next Thursday.

6. *Kindly* send the cheque *by return mail, and oblige.*

7. *Your complaint of recent date rec'd* and *contents carefully noted* and *in reply would state for your information* that the shoes were shipped on January 14.

8. *Trusting this will prove satisfactory, we beg to remain.*

COMPLIMENTARY CLOSE

1. The complimentary close may be—

Yours truly,   *Very truly yours,*
Truly yours,   *Yours very truly,*

Respectfully yours and *Yours respectfully* are sometimes used in letters to superiors—for example, a student to his principal, the Department of Education, or the Mayor. A business letter to an acquaintance may close with *Cordially yours, Sincerely yours, Yours cordially,* or *Yours sincerely.*

2. Place a comma after the complimentary close.

3. Capitalize the first word only of the complimentary close.

4. Begin the complimentary close about halfway across the page.

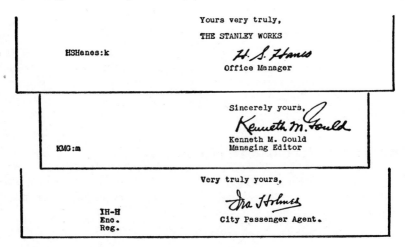

SIGNATURE

1. The signature is placed below the complimentary close and begins farther to the right in slant style and directly underneath the first word of the complimentary close in block style.

2. A period is not necessary after the signature but may be used if the period is used after the address and the heading.

3. Write the signature legibly. Typewritten letters frequently have the signature both typed and pen-written.

4. A woman addressing a stranger should make clear what title he should use in the reply.

UNMARRIED WOMAN: *(Miss) Catherine Thompson*
MARRIED WOMAN: *Catherine Thompson*
(Mrs. James Thompson)

5. In a letter from a firm, if the letterhead does not show the writer's position, the signature should make this clear.

PRACTICE 2. Letter Form

Write the heading, address, salutation, complimentary close, and signature of each letter:

1. Juliet Reiss (wife of John Reiss), 100 Newbury Street, North Battleford, Saskatchewan, writes to Dr. Samuel Pearse, Bethesda Hospital, Oak Street, Weyburn, Saskatchewan.
2. Andrew King, president of Thomson and Company, 297 Washington Street, Dauphin, Manitoba, writes to Hare & Smith, Pittsburgh, Pennsylvania.
3. H. J. Moss, manager of Olney and Warren, 297 Laval Street, Montreal, P.Q., writes to James R. Ross, The Senate, Ottawa, Canada.
4. From your home address write to Miss Jean Royce, Registrar, Queen's University, Kingston, Ontario.

LETTER PICTURE

Most typewritten letters are single spaced, except for double spacing between the parts and the paragraphs. In a letter so typed, if the heading and address are in the block form, paragraphs may begin flush with the margin. Most business men, however, think that indention makes the paragraph division clearer and prefer to have all paragraphs indented. Short letters are sometimes double spaced.

A letter makes a more pleasing picture if it is centred on the page.

Like the mat of a picture, the margin should extend around the letter and be approximately the same width on the four sides. For a short letter the left and right margins should be two inches wide; for a longer letter, an inch and a half or slightly less. The margin at the bottom of a full-page letter should never be less than the side margins.

PAPER AND FOLDING

Paper, ink, and envelopes of good quality add distinction to correspondence. Use regularly white, heavy paper 8½ by 11 inches in size. For a short letter, paper about 6 by 9½ inches in size may be used. The envelope should match the paper, be strong enough to stand rough handling, and be heavy enough to prevent the writing showing through.

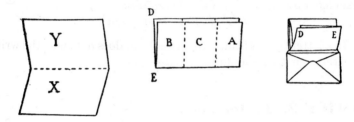

To fold a sheet 8½ by 11 inches, first place the lower half X over the upper half Y with the lower edge a quarter or a half inch from the upper edge. Then over the centre C fold in turn from the right and the left A and B, each slightly less than one-third of the folded sheet. Place the letter in the envelope with the loose edges DE up and next to the flap. Fold the enclosures with the letter.

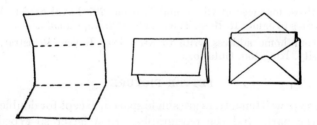

When for a short letter paper 6 by 9½ inches is used, fold the lower third up and the top quarter down. Place the letter in the envelope "with the two flaps next to the back, not the face, of the envelope and with the top edge of the letter at the bottom of the envelope."

REFERENCE DATA AND ENCLOSURES

A business letter should show who dictated it and who typed it. In the model on page 261, *JED* are the initials of the dictator, and *SM*, of the typist. This might be *JED:SM*, *JED-SM*, *jed–sm*, or *J. E. Dewitt-SM*.

A notation at the left margin below these initials refers to enclosures, if there are any. The common forms are:

2 Enclosures
Enc.

THE SECOND PAGE

The second page of a long letter is on paper of the same size and quality as the first page but has no letterhead. The name of the recipient is commonly placed in the upper left corner, the page number in the centre, and the date in the upper right corner:

On the last page there should be at least three lines of the body of the letter.

ENVELOPE ADDRESS AND RETURN CARD

1. The margin, straight or slant, and the punctuation, open or close, should correspond with that of the letter. If close punctuation is used, a period is placed after the last line and a comma after each preceding line.

CLOSE PUNCTUATION, SLANT STYLE

```
    J. H. HOLMES,
      BROADWAY,
NUTANA, SASKATCHEWAN.


            Mr. T. H. Reading,
              724 Business Avenue,
                Fort Hamilton,
                  Ontario.
```

OPEN PUNCTUATION, SLANT STYLE

JOHN T. WELSH
25 WILMOT AVENUE
LONDON, ONTARIO

                    The Scott Enamel Company
                      300 Ferry Street
                          Winnipeg
                          Manitoba

OPEN PUNCTUATION, BLOCK STYLE

STEPHEN P. CARR
29 KIRBY AVENUE
ALSASK, SASKATCHEWAN

                    Dr. P. T. Thomas
                    608 East Fortieth Street
                    Prince George
                    British Columbia

ASKING FOR INFORMATION

1. In your opening sentence explain in general the type of information you desire. If your letter goes to a large business house, the correspondent will be able, without reading the entire contents, immediately to turn it over to the person best fitted to answer your inquiry.

2. Then ask the specific questions you would like to have answered.

3. Make your questions clear, correct, and courteous.

1436 Arbor Boulevard,
Winnipeg, Manitoba,
November 10, 1948.

Brigden's of Winnipeg Limited,
Notre Dame at Langside Street,
Winnipeg, Manitoba.

Gentlemen:

The English 3 B Class of Commercial High School would like to have you estimate the cost of binding in durable dark blue cloth a collection of the best work of the members of the class. On the cover we should like to have stamped in gold the title, "Writer's Cramp".

The classbook consists of two hundred pages of 8½ × 11 inch heavy typewriting paper with an inch and a half margin at the left for binding.

Very truly yours,

Doris McDermott,
Secretary.

4. Include any information which may be of assistance to your reader in answering your questions fully and accurately. (See the model above).

5. Explain why you want the information.

6. Enclose a stamped and self-addressed envelope unless you are likely to repay your informant in another way—with an order, for instance.

7. Don't write for information that you can secure in the library or ask questions calling for long answers. If a man's opinion is worth much, he is usually extremely busy.

PRACTICE 3. Asking for Information

1. Your class is planning to spend Easter week in Hamilton, Ontario. Write to the New Raleigh Hotel for rates. Be specific about the number in the party, the length of time you are to stay, and the accommodations desired.

2. You are preparing to debate the question of moving picture censorship. Write to the National Board of Review of Motion Pictures, 70 Fifth Avenue, New York City, for pamphlets and information. Ask several pointed questions which can be answered briefly.

3. In a letter to the president or the registrar of a college ask what scholarships are open to freshmen, whether an examination is required, when the examination is held. Ask also for any available printed information on the subject.

4. Write to Mr. John Noel, Public Relations Department, Canadian National Railways, Toronto, Ontario, and ask whether his department will lend pictures or lanterns slides to your club.

5. You are planning a trip down the St. Lawrence from Clayton to Quebec. Write for information to the Canada Steamship Lines Limited, Montreal, Canada.

LETTER OF APPLICATION

PURPOSE AND IMPORTANCE:

The letter of application is the one type of letter that practically everyone who earns a living is called upon to write at one time or another. It has been called the "personal sales letter" because it sells the writer—his training, skill, knowledge, service, and ability. It is usually the application letter which launches the student into the business world. Since a person's whole future may depend upon the success of this letter, it is worth every effort to do it well. As there are generally several people competing for a position, the applicant's chief hope of selection is to make his letter stand out among others. He must influence the reader to think favourably of him and of his abilities and to grant an interview in which the applicant tries to complete the sale of his services.

APPEARANCE:

A good-looking letter suggests a good applicant. Attractive appearance and correct form cannot be over-emphasized. The information should be well-organized, the letter correctly margined and spaced, faultless in grammar, spelling, and punctuation. It should be revised and rewritten until satisfactory in every respect. The following points should be noted:

STATIONERY: Use white bond paper of fairly good quality, standard size, with envelope to match. Do not use the letterhead of an employer, hotel, or any organization.

TYPEWRITTEN   Unless asked for a penwritten letter, type the letter to
or   ensure ease in reading. Submit only a neatly typed,
PENWRITTEN: properly set-up letter, free of strikeovers and erasures. It is sometimes advisable to submit both a typewritten and a penwritten copy.

ARRANGEMENT: Restrict the letter to one page if possible although it is permissible to use two pages. Set up the letter in one of the more common approved styles. The general practice is to submit a *penwritten letter in the indented style*.

CONTENTS:

Write a letter which is clear, correct, complete, concise, and courteous. Do not follow model letters too closely. The letter should contain the following:

1. One or two opening sentences to establish contact or attract attention and arouse the reader's interest.
2. A statement explaining how your qualifications, experience, and training enable you to measure up to the required standards, or enclose a data sheet giving this information.
3. The characteristics which qualify you for the position (for example, ability to accept responsibility and work without supervision).
4. Definite statements about what you can do, have done, and want to do.
5. Proof of qualifications in the form of letter of recommendation or the submission of references.
6. Request for an interview.
7. *All* the desired information requested in the advertisement.

PERSONAL QUALITIES:

Often the prospective employer is more interested in certain basic personal qualities, such as reliability, initiative, good judgment and accuracy, than in specialized knowledge. These assets can best be indicated by listing successful experience in work which required such qualities.

PROOF OF QUALIFICATIONS:

Unless specified in the advertisement, letters of recommendation should *not* be enclosed. However, if specific letters are requested, do not send the originals. Make carbon copies, mark each letter COPY at the top of the sheet and type SIGNED before the typed signature. In giving references, three names are usually enough. If you are an experienced worker, give the names of your most recent employers. If you are inexperienced, give the name of your school principal or guidance counsellor. It is correct and desirable to include the name of some person of standing in the community who can vouch for your personal qualities. Obtain permission before using a person's name as reference.

QUESTION OF SALARY:

This is best discussed at the interview, but if the advertisement asks you to state it, do not evade the question. Be clear in your mind about the salary you expect to get and be sure that it is reasonable and in line with current wage rates. Following are a few examples of how this subject may be referred to:

"My present salary is $150.00 per month. I am willing to start at this amount if the possibilities of promotion justify it." "I understand that beginners are being paid $35.00 to $40.00 per week for positions of this type. I should be glad to discuss the details at an interview."

The closing of the letter should suggest action—interview or appointment to the position. Make action easy by providing all the information necessary for the convenience of the reader. "May I have an interview at your convenience? My telephone number is CR. 8-4407" "I am keenly interested in the position which you offer and hope I may have an interview in which I can give you more details of my qualifications. Kindly telephone MAyfair 5-6908."

RELIGION AND NATIONALITY:

It is not lawful for the employer to ask about your religion, although it is often done. However, do not volunteer the information.

Sometimes names give away our nationality. However, there is no need to stress this point. Some employers are prejudiced against a certain race and an applicant stating that nationality will not be given an interview. However, quite often after the applicant has been seen, the employer realizes that nationality does not really enter into the question.

THE DATA SHEET:

The use of the data sheet permits the applicant to turn the application letter into a sales letter where the reader is referred to the second

---

> STENOGRAPHER—Experienced, with some knowledge of bookkeeping and general office work: salary $40. B.W., Box 357, The Globe and Mail.

```
                                   171 Bell Avenue,
                                   Toronto, Ontario
                                   June 26, 1960.

B. W., Box 357 The Globe and Mail,
   Toronto, Ontario.

Dear Sir:

     This letter is in reply to your
advertisement which appeared in yesterday's Globe
and Mail.

My qualifications are as follows:

     Age: Seventeen.

     Education: Graduate of four-year Commercial
Course of Northern Vocational School, Toronto,
Ontario. I have had three years of bookkeeping
and French, two years of stenography and
typewriting, one year of commercial arithmetic,
commercial geography, commercial law, Canadian
history, and business English and correspondence,
and four years of English. I have a knowledge of
single and double entry and corporation
bookkeeping, can operate the standard makes of
typewriters at about sixty words a minute, can
take dictation at the rate of one hundred words
per minute, can use the dictaphone and mimeo-
graph, and understand the filing systems.
```

---

sheet for detailed information. "I am enclosing a personal data sheet that will give you the necessary information concerning my training and experience." (Remember to write the word "Enclosure" at the

        Experience: During my last summer vacation
I was employed as stenographer and typist by
J. I. Black, 110 Yonge Street.

        Reference: For further information about my
experience, ability, character, and habits you
may communicate with——

Mr. J. I. Black,
   110 Yonge Street,
      Toronto, Ontario.

Mr. James McQueen, M.A., B.Paed.,
   Principal, Northern Vocational School;
      Toronto, Ontario.

Mr. Wm. J. Brown, B.A., B.Com.,
   Head of the Commercial Department,
      Northern Vocational School,
         Toronto, Ontario.

        Salary: The salary mentioned in the
advertisement is satisfactory.

        I hope you will give me a chance to
demonstrate my ability.

                              Yours truly,

                              Fred Joerger

left-hand margin, two lines below the line of the signature.) The data sheet creates an impression of business-like efficiency. Many employers welcome such a display of organization and it provides them with a concise record of the application which may be filed for further reference.

DATA SHEET

NAME:	James J. Grant
ADDRESS:	158 Pinecrest Avenue, Scarborough
TELEPHONE:	ROger 7-4575
AGE:	Fifteen years last February
EDUCATION:	R. H. King Collegiate, Scarborough: First and Second year, Academic Course; W. A. Porter Collegiate, Scarborough: Third year, Academic Course
STUDENT ACTIVITIES:	Member of School Orchestra Member of Championship Rugby Team Member of Cadet Corps
BUSINESS TRAINING:	Part-time position as cashier at Loblaws Summer position as sales clerk at Jack Fraser Men's and Boys' Wear
FUTURE PLANS:	To obtain Honour Graduation Diploma and enter the English Language and Literature Course, University of Toronto
REFERENCES:	Mr. J. Smith, Manager, Jack Fraser Men's and Boys' Wear 1886 Eglinton Ave. East, Scarborough RIverdale 3-6363
	Mr. A. Johnson, Manager, Loblaws Groceteria, 1450 Kingston Rd., Toronto 13, OXford 9-8395
	Mr. E. Dobie, Guidance Counsellor, W. A. Porter Collegiate, 40 Fairfax Crescent, Scarborough, PLymouth 7-3658

DATA SHEET

NAME: Joyce Smith

ADDRESS: 158 Pinecrest Avenue, Scarborough

TELEPHONE: ROger 6-4575

AGE: Fifteen years last February

EDUCATION: R. H. King Collegiate, Scarborough: First and Second
                   years, Commercial Course;
                   W. A. Porter Collegiate, Scarborough: Third year,
                   Commercial course

STUDENT ACTIVITIES: Member of School Orchestra
                   Member of School Glee Club

BUSINESS TRAINING: Typewriting: three years, about 55 words per minute
                   Shorthand: two years, about 80 words per minute
                   Bookkeeping, Business Correspondence, and other
                   Commercial Subjects
                   Part-time position as cashier at Loblaws
                   Summer position as typist for the legal firm of Canfield
                   and Carter

FUTURE PLANS: To obtain Senior High School Graduation and enter the
                   Commerce and Finance Course, University of Toronto

REFERENCES: Mr. E. Dobie, Guidance Counsellor,
                   W. A. Porter Collegiate,
                   40 Fairfax Crescent, Scarborough,
                   PLymouth 7-3658

                   Mr. A. Johnson, Manager,
                   Loblaws Groceteria,
                   1500 Kingston Rd., Toronto 13,
                   OXford 9-8395

                   Mr. J. A. Canfield, Barrister,
                   2026 Classon Ave., Scarborough
                   ROger 7-2345

PRACTICE 4. Letter of Application

Answer one of the following advertisements or another clipped from the Help Wanted column of the morning paper:

GIRL—Intelligent, neat high school student with interest in home nursing to care for baby, 20 months, on Saturdays. $5 per day and meals. P.O. Box 49.

BOY—High school graduate who has studied chemistry to do general work in laboratory Opportunity for experience and advancement. Give age, experience, education, and references. Post Office Box 93.

BOY

An opportunity is offered to a boy who is willing to learn the import and export business; offering many opportunities for advancement; initial salary $35 per week, with bonus twice per annum; high school graduate preferred; applicant must be alert and give full details in first letter. V 773 *The Sun.*

CLERK—Bright young woman in large departmental store; splendid opportunity; short hours; hot lunch at cost and other benefits; state age, education, experience, if any, and salary expected. V 691 *The Free Press.*

BANK wants boys and girls just out of school. Only high school graduates considered. Handwriting must be good. Openings in bookkeeping and stenographic departments. State age, references, etc. *Leader-Post* D 2897.

LETTER TO A LEGISLATOR OR CITY EXECUTIVE

A democracy needs citizens who not only are honest and think straight but also let their legislators and executives know what they are thinking.

PRACTICE 5. Writing to Officials

1. Write to your member of parliament, senator, or member of the legislative assembly to convince or persuade him to support or oppose a bill before parliament or the provincial legislature.

2. Write to the mayor or another city or town official, urging that he exert his influence in favour of better schools, school buildings, police protection, street cleaning, parks, or another improvement.

REPORTING AN ACCIDENT

In case of an automobile accident a person who carries liability and property-damage insurance should promptly write to his insurance company a letter giving as much as possible of the following information:

1. Time and place of accident, speed of both cars at time of accident, and a description of how the accident happened (draw a diagram).

2. Operator of your car at the time of the accident and his license number.

3. License number, owner, driver, and make of other car, and owner's address.

4. Damage to each car.

5. Names and addresses of the occupants of the two cars.

6. Nature of injuries sustained and care of the injured—name of doctor and hospital.

7. Names and addresses of other witnesses.

8. Your policy number.

(For example of letter, see pages 279-80)

PRACTICE 6. Reporting an Accident

In a letter to the General Accident Assurance of Canada, Toronto, Ontario, in which your car is insured, report an automobile accident. Make your report clear and complete.   Include a diagram.

CHANGE OF ADDRESS

In requesting that a magazine be sent to a different address, give the name of the magazine and your old and your new address, and tell how long the magazine is to be sent to the new address if the change is a temporary one. Instead of writing in the body of the letter your new address, you may refer to the address in the heading. Give accurate and complete information. Write legibly.

REPORTING AN ACCIDENT

908 Park Lane South,
Brantford, Ontario,
January 15, 1959.

General Accident Assurance of Canada,
357 Bay Street,
Toronto Ont.

Gentlemen:

I wish to report an automobile accident that took place in Rockville Centre, Ontario, yesterday, January 14, 1959.

About one o'clock my brother and I were proceeding westward along Sunrise Highway through Rockville Centre in his 1958 Studebaker at a speed of about thirty-five miles an hour. From our right a car dashed out along Waverly Place into Sunrise Highway. My brother applied his brakes and swerved to the left as quickly as possible but could not avoid a collision. The other car had swerved slightly to the right. Our bumper and right front fender smashed into the left rear wheel of the other car, a 1958 seven-passenger Buick.

The Buick's left rear wheel was badly damaged. Our right front tire was blown out, the steering gear was broken, and the speedometer cable snapped.

My brother, William Arnoldi, whose driver's license number is 6487, owns the Studebaker and was driving at the time of the accident. The owner and driver of the Buick was Albert Hendrickson of 157 Washington Boulevard, Long Beach, New York. He had no passengers. His driver's license number is 8694N.

My brother was thrown against the steering wheel by the impact and knocked unconscious, but I was not hurt, as I was in the back seat. He was taken into the office of Dr. Weber of 23 Waverly Place. His right arm is fractured and his cheek cut. Later the doctor drove him to our home. Mr. Hendrickson was uninjured.

The only witness was Mr. George Hamilton of 37 Elton Place, Rockville Centre, who was standing on the street corner when the accident occurred.

Because my brother is unable to write, I am reporting the accident for him. His policy number is M68947.

Yours truly,

Walter Arnoldi.

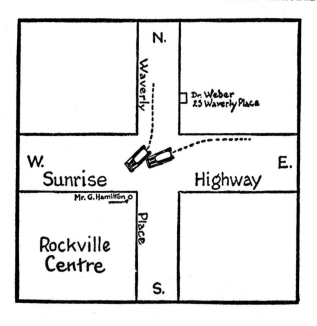

PRACTICE 7. Business Letter

1. *The Reader's Digest* is published by The Reader's Digest Association (Canada) Ltd., 276 St. James St. W., Montreal, P.Q. Assuming that you are a subscriber for this magazine, ask the company to change your address for the summer vacation. Be definite.

2. You have moved to another street, city, or town. Write to *Maclean's*, Maclean-Hunter Publishing Company Limited, 481 University Avenue, Toronto 2, Ont., to change the address of your magazine.

3. You are spending the Christmas vacation with your aunt. Write to the postmaster of your town or city, asking that your mail be forwarded.

4. Write to a farmer to arrange for his supplying your family with eggs, butter, apples, peaches, or potatoes.

5. Your father wishes to have some work done: trees trimmed, lawn improved, car repaired, floors refinished, rooms redecorated, furnace repaired, coal bin enlarged, bookcase or table built, or house repainted. Write for him a letter explaining to a workman exactly what is to be done.

6. Request a catalogue of sporting goods from A. G. Spalding and Brothers, 1410 Stanley Street, Montreal, Quebec, or a seed catalogue from Patmore Nurseries, Brandon, Manitoba.

7. Write a business letter for your father or mother; and, before mailing it, show it to your English teacher.

8. While motoring, you stayed over night at the Fort Garry Hotel, Winnipeg, Manitoba. In your room you left a fountain pen. Ask the manager to mail it to you. Enclose postage.

9. Write to the owner of a vacant plot, asking for permission to use his property as a baseball diamond. Promise to clear the ground and to do no damage.

TELEGRAM

The telegram is written in an abbreviated style. Most conjunctions, prepositions, and articles are omitted, and adjectives and adverbs are used sparingly. Yet clearness is the first essential of a telegram; and brevity, the second. Because punctuation marks are ordinarily omitted in transmission, the telegram should be clear without them. If there is a possibility of misinterpretation, however, the word *stop* should be inserted to show the break in thought.

Notice that the telegram has no salutation or complimentary close, that the numbers are written in words, and that the writer inserts *stop*, when he thinks it is needed to make the message absolutely clear.

COUNTING WORDS:

The minimum charge is for ten words. Each additional word increases the cost. *Four thousand* is counted as two words; *fifty thousand*, as two; *4000, as four; 50000*, as five. A figure counts as a word. Dictionary words, names of countries, cities, towns, and provinces, and some abbreviations are each counted as one word: *per cent, cannot, New York City, North Vancouver, C.O.D.,* A.M., O.K. The following are counted as two words each: *Canadian Airways, James Corson.* The name and address of the sender and receiver are not charged for, but a title like *football manager* after the signature is counted.

NIGHT LETTER

The night letter is a telegram sent at night to be delivered the next morning. The rate for a fifty-word night letter is the same as for a ten-word day telegram.

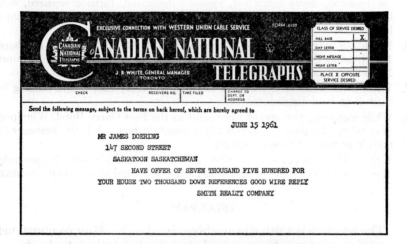

EXCLUSIVE CONNECTION WITH WESTERN UNION CABLE SERVICE   FORM 6102

CANADIAN NATIONAL TELEGRAPHS

J. R. WHITE, GENERAL MANAGER
TORONTO

CLASS OF SERVICE DESIRED

FULL RATE   X
DAY LETTER
NIGHT MESSAGE
NIGHT LETTER

PLACE X OPPOSITE
SERVICE DESIRED

CHECK   RECEIVERS NO.   TIME FILED   CHARGE TO DEPT. OR ADDRESS

Send the following message, subject to the terms on back hereof, which are hereby agreed to

JUNE 15 1961

MR JAMES DOERING
147 SECOND STREET
SASKATOON SASKATCHEWAN
HAVE OFFER OF SEVEN THOUSAND FIVE HUNDRED FOR
YOUR HOUSE TWO THOUSAND DOWN REFERENCES GOOD WIRE REPLY
SMITH REALTY COMPANY

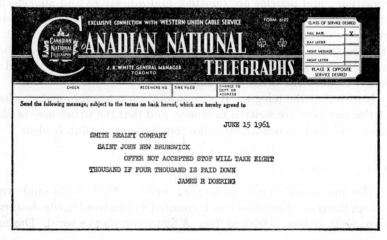

EXCLUSIVE CONNECTION WITH WESTERN UNION CABLE SERVICE   FORM 6102

CANADIAN NATIONAL TELEGRAPHS

J. R. WHITE, GENERAL MANAGER
TORONTO

CLASS OF SERVICE DESIRED

FULL RATE   X
DAY LETTER
NIGHT MESSAGE
NIGHT LETTER

PLACE X OPPOSITE
SERVICE DESIRED

CHECK   RECEIVERS NO.   TIME FILED   CHARGE TO DEPT. OR ADDRESS

Send the following message, subject to the terms on back hereof, which are hereby agreed to

JUNE 15 1961

SMITH REALTY COMPANY
SAINT JOHN NEW BRUNSWICK
OFFER NOT ACCEPTED STOP WILL TAKE EIGHT
THOUSAND IF FOUR THOUSAND IS PAID DOWN
JAMES R DOERING

PRACTICE 8. Telegrams

1. On your way home you missed connections. Telegraph your father, who has planned to meet you at the station.
2. As manager of a baseball team cancel a game by telegraph. It is raining, and even if the rain stops, the field will be muddy and soggy.
3. On an automobile trip your expenses are substantially higher than you anticipated. Telegraph home for money.
4. As manager of the school football team telegraph to arrange a game with a neighbouring school. Give full information about dates, officials, field, expenses, and division of the gate receipts.
5. Telegraph your mother on her birthday.

OTHER TYPES OF BUSINESS LETTER

PRACTICE 9. Business Letters

Jot down points to keep in mind in writing each type of letter. Outline your letter by paragraphs before writing it.

1. As manager of a school team write to another school to arrange a game. Be specific about the place, available dates, expenses, officials, and division of gate receipts.
2. Invite another school or a society of another school to hold a joint contest —debate, algebra contest, art contest, or pronunciation contest.
3. Ask a college to send you a catalogue or a bulletin giving information about expenses, entrance requirements, and courses.
4. Your school needs a new building, an addition, a swimming pool, a gymnasium, an athletic field, or additional equipment. Write to the Chairman, Board of Trustees.
5. Resign from a club or office, giving good reasons.
6. Request a room reservation in a dormitory or a hotel.
7. As secretary of a club write a postcard notice of the next meeting, a letter requesting someone to address the club, and a letter thanking some person for a service to the club.
8. Write to the president of the Alumni Association, urging the establishment of a fund to help needy pupils. Explain why the fund is needed. Suggest a plan for raising the money and administering the fund.
9. Write to a transportation company or express company about discourteous treatment, personal injury, damage to property, or loss of baggage. Write the reply of the company.
10. To the proper city or town official write about a choked drain in your neighbourhood, dangerous holes in the streets or street obstructions, a local nuisance, or another matter which needs his attention.
11. Write to Henry Birks & Sons, Ltd., 1240 Phillips Square, Montreal, P.Q., about class pins. Ask for designs and prices.
12. Write a letter to someone who has been of service to the school. Only the best letter will be mailed.

13. You have more points than are required for admission to a college. In a letter to the Committee on Admission state the facts clearly and fully and ask whether by taking examinations or in some other way you can secure college credit for the courses.

14. Before mailing a business letter you have written at home on your own account, or for your father or mother, show it to your teacher.

FORM OF ADDRESS

PERSON	ADDRESS	SALUTATION	COMPLIMENTARY CLOSE
Prime Minister of Canada	To the Right Honourable John George Diefenbaker, Q.C. Prime Minister of Canada Ottawa, Canada	Honourable and dear Sir: *or* To the Honourable the Prime Minister of Canada:	Yours respectfully, Yours very truly,
Members of the Dominion Cabinet	(May not always be addressed by name, address the office) The Honourable, The Minister of—	To the Honourable the Minister of—	Yours respectfully, Yours very truly,
The Lieutenant-Governor	The Honourable Frank L. Bastedo Government House Regina, Saskatchewan (Also correct: His Honour the Honourable..........)	To His Honour the Lieutenant-Governor of Saskatchewan	Yours respectfully, Yours very truly,
The Premier of the Province	Honourable Dufferin Roblin Parliament Buildings Winnipeg, Manitoba	To the Honourable the Premier of Manitoba: *or* Honourable and dear Sir:	Yours respectfully, Yours very truly,
The Mayor of a City	Mayor Sidney Buckwold City Hall Saskatoon	To His Worship the Mayor of Saskatoon: *or* Your Honour:	Yours respectfully, Very truly yours, Yours very truly,
A Senator	Honourable John Smith Parliament Buildings Ottawa, Canada	Sir: *or* Dear Sir:	Yours respectfully, Very truly yours, Yours very truly,
Member of Parliament, or Member of Legislative Assembly	C. W. Morrow, M.L.A. Parliament Buildings Victoria, British Columbia	Sir: *or* Dear Sir:	Yours respectfully, Very truly yours, Yours very truly,
Protestant Clergyman	Reverend Nelson Chappel	Dear Sir: *or* Reverend Sir; *or* My dear Mr. Chappel	Yours respectfully, Yours sincerely,
Bishop	To the Right Reverend, the Lord Bishop of—	My Lord: *or* My Lord Bishop:	I remain, my Lord Bishop, Your Lordship's most obedient servant.
Priest	Reverend Francis X. Dolan, D.D.	Reverend and dear Father Dolan:	Yours faithfully, Yours sincerely,
Sisters of Various Orders	Sister M. Jeanette	Reverend and dear Sister Jeanette	Yours respectfully, Yours sincerely,
Canon	The Reverend Canon Armitage	Reverend Sir:	Yours respectfully, Yours sincerely,
Rabbi	Rabbi Jacob W. Stern	Reverend Sir: *or* Dear Sir: *or* My dear Rabbi Stern:	Yours respectfully, Yours cordially, Yours sincerely,

Chapter 11

Interviewing and Talking Business

WHAT are you going to do after you complete your education? To secure a position you will have to be interviewed. An interview is a rather formal type of conversation. The impression you make on an employer or personnel manager will largely determine whether you'll join the ranks of wage earners. If you wish to secure a summer or part-time job while you are still in school, this unit will give you some practical hints for your interview.

ASKING FOR INFORMATION OR ADVICE

One of the best ways to gain information is to interview a person who is an authority on the subject, for his knowledge will be thorough and his point of view fresh and practical. First, make an appointment for the interview, by letter, in person, or by telephone. In this request give your name and your reason for asking for an interview, but let the person to be interviewed name the day and the hour.

Prepare for the interview by learning enough about the subject to ask questions and listen intelligently, and enough about the person to phrase your questions tactfully. Think out in advance several specific questions covering the subject.

Be punctual. Politely introduce yourself. When the person to be interviewed has asked you to be seated, state briefly your purpose in coming and introduce your subject with a good question. It is always courteous to address a person by name—for example, "What qualities must a boy have to become a successful physician, Dr. Saunders?"

If you are well prepared, you will be able to keep the discussion **on** the topic in which you are interested and secure the information you wish. If you are courteous, earnest, and enthusiastic, the person interviewed will respond with interest, friendliness, and helpfulness. Be as punctual to leave as you were to arrive, and express your appreciation for the interview.

PRACTICE 1. Enacting an Interview

Choose a partner and prepare to present before the class an interview, one pupil acting as interviewer, the other as an authority on some subject: raising chickens, camping, catching trout, teaching a dog tricks, gardening, baking cakes, taking care of an automobile, table manners, kites, radio programs, motion pictures, stamp collecting, making model airplanes, maintaining a home aquarium, football, photography, or the like. Speak distinctly and pronounce every word correctly.

PRACTICE 2. Reporting an Interview

Interview a person and write a report including (1) the person's name and position, (2) why you interviewed him, (3) where you interviewed him, (4) his personal appearance and (5) your questions and his answers. Do not record every word spoken, but include the main points of the discussion and any especially important remarks. Build clear, concise, varied sentences (pages 326-39). Capitalize and punctuate direct quotations correctly (pages 638-39). Some interesting people to interview are:

1. A teacher of your favourite subject. 2. The football, baseball, track, **or** swimming coach. 3. The librarian. 4. The oldest resident of your town or neighbourhood. 5. The teller in charge of pupil bank accounts. 6. A public official in your community. 7. The manager of a department store. 8. The editor of a newspaper. 9. The police captain in the school precinct. 10. Any person who does interesting work—farmer, gardener, actor, musician, architect, carpenter, traffic officer, social worker, soldier, sailor, or merchant seaman. 11. A scout troop leader. 12. Director of an employment office. 13. A member of the student council. 14. The faculty adviser of a school club, a publication, dramatics, or another activity. 15. A V.O.N. nurse.

ASKING PERMISSION OR MAKING A SUGGESTION

As a preparation for asking permission or making a suggestion, marshal as many sound reasons as you can. Don't take up a person's time unless you have convincing reasons to support your request or idea. Find out what you can about the person to be interviewed, put yourself in his place, and try to foresee his objections. Your courtesy, sincerity, and correct English will help you to win your case.

After introducing yourself, come to the point immediately and state your purpose clearly and briefly. With his possible objections in mind, state your soundest and most convincing arguments first; then follow up with other reasons. Stress those points which will appeal to him most. If you have carefully studied your subject, you will be able to answer his questions intelligently.

At the end of the interview, even if your request is refused, thank the person courteously for granting you the interview.

PRACTICE 3. Asking Permission

Is Anne's method of making a request good? Why?

ANNE BLAKE. Mr. Nichols, my name is Anne Blake. I should like to make a change on my option card for next term.

MR. NICHOLS. Miss Young, will you please find Miss Blake's option card in the files. What is the trouble, Anne?

ANNE. A month ago I decided to register for a course in typing next term. When I made out my program, however, I neglected to include typing in my list of subjects desired. If it isn't too late to make a change on my option card, I should like to register for the course now.

MR. NICHOLS. You are an academic student, aren't you, Anne? Why do you want to take typing?

ANNE. I think typing is a skill that is valuable to everyone, Mr. Nichols. At present I plan to go to college after graduating from high school. Ability to type will enable me to prepare assignments more quickly and to hand in neater reports. Then, too, when I graduate I may find that I can't go to college. In that case I shall probably have a much better chance of finding a job if I know how to type.

MR. NICHOLS. Those are sound reasons, Anne. Let me see—you have four majors for next term. Typing would make your second minor. Yes, we can include typing on your program.

ANNE. Thank you very much, Mr. Nichols. I won't be so forgetful next term. Good afternoon.

PRACTICE 4. Asking Permission

Choose a partner and act out an interview in which you ask the proper authority for permission to take some action—for example:

1. To visit a printing establishment, a cannery, a creamery, or a factory.
2. To make a change in your program for next term. 3. To visit a biological experiment station. 4. To use the auditorium for a club entertainment. 5. To use a science laboratory for a meeting of the Science Club. 6. To organize a club or a team. 7. To use the gymnasium for a basketball game. 8. To hold

a party or a contest. 9. To use the visual education room one period. 10. To go home for lunch every day. 11. To run a cake sale for the benefit of the Senior Girls' Club. 12. To use your minister's (or another's) name as a reference for a part-time job. 13. To make up the work in English you missed when you were absent.

APPLYING FOR A PART-TIME OR VACATION JOB

PREPARING FOR AN INTERVIEW

How you prepare before you see your prospective employer may determine the success or failure of your interview. Get ready for your interview by following these suggestions:

1. Get a full night's sleep before the interview.

2. Bathe and put on fresh, clean, pressed clothes. Polish your shoes. Your outfit need not be expensive but it should be harmonious. Avoid the extremes of sportswear and party clothes. Girls, shun jingling jewelry and bright make-up. Boys, select quiet socks and neckties.

3. Brush your teeth, clean your nails, and comb your hair.

4. Know exactly what job you are applying for. Don't make yourself ridiculous by saying, "I can do anything."

5. Think about your qualifications as a worker. What qualities and skills can you offer an employer? Are you healthy, punctual, trustworthy, industrious, intelligent? Do you get on well with others? Can you type, sell, sew, clean, take care of children, deliver packages, take care of a lawn and garden? What special qualifications have you for the job you want? If the job is to deliver packages, do you know the delivery area thoroughly? If the job is to take care of children, can you say that you haven't had a cold in two years or that you like children and that children like you?

6. Anticipate questions you might be asked, and prepare to answer them clearly and honestly. Some questions for which you should have clear-cut answers are:

What hours can you devote to the part-time job? When do you plan to do your homework for school?
What salary do you expect?
How many days have you been absent from school in the past year?
How many times have you been late?
How good a record have you made in high school?
What extracurricular activities have you engaged in?
Does your family need your financial help?
How do you spend your spare time?

What vocation are you planning to enter?
Why do you want to work here? Who referred you to us?

7. Make a clear, accurate list of the names and addresses of two, three, or four responsible persons who know you well and will answer questions about your character, training, and experience. Avoid, if possible, giving the names of relatives; they are likely to be prejudiced.

8. If you have had experience in the work for which you are applying, take with you the name and address of your former employer and the exact dates of your employment.

9. If you have never had a job, think of the unpaid experience you have had which fits you for the job—for example, a hobby, or service as assistant in the school office, as secretary to a teacher, as junior leader of a church club, or as messenger for the local Red Cross chapter. Prepare to tell the exact dates of service and the name of the person in charge.

10. Be ready to tell what training your school courses have given you for the job, how long you studied each subject, and what your marks were. If the courses were stenography and typewriting, know your speed in taking dictation, typing from straight copy, and transcribing your notes.

11. Your interviewer may ask you whether you have any questions. Think out in advance what you want to know about the work. You may be judged as much by the intelligence of your questions as by the persuasiveness of your answers.

12. Fill your fountain pen. You may need it to make out an application blank.

INTERVIEW

The qualities your interviewer will look for are courtesy, modest self-confidence, energetic health, alertness, earnestness, straightforwardness, neatness, and clear, natural, correct speech. If you follow these suggestions, you will be more likely to secure the job.

1. Walk in briskly, and introduce yourself with a smile. Say, "Good morning, Mr. Burton. I am Sylvia Wells," not "I am Miss Wells." If you have an appointment for four o'clock, be there when the clock strikes four.

2. State at once your purpose in coming. "Mrs. Norton suggested that I apply for the job of taking care of your son Bobby on Saturday

evenings," or "I wish to apply for the job of junior camp counsellor which you advertised in this morning's *Times*."

3. Don't sit down until invited. Unless Mr. Burton extends his hand, don't offer to shake hands. Don't park your hat on his desk.

4. Sit easily erect. Don't edge up to your hearer while you talk.

5. Park your nervousness and mannerisms outside. Relax. Girls, don't open and close your bag, fuss with your hair or clothes, or fidget. Boys, don't smooth your hair, look at the floor or out the window, play with a pencil, or wriggle.

6. Look your interviewer straight in the eye. Listen sharply. Never interrupt.

7. Answer questions frankly, honestly, fully, but don't talk too much.

8. Never chew gum during an interview.

9. Speak clearly, distinctly, earnestly, and keep your voice pitched low.

10. Use grammatical language. Avoid slang.

11. If you are asked to fill out a written application, fill accurately, neatly, and legibly every blank that applies to you. Be brief. Spell and punctuate correctly. Your application will be considered an example of how you work.

12. Avoid, if possible, making negative statements about yourself. Don't volunteer, "I haven't had any experience in office work," even if you intend to follow this immediately with a "but I have had high marks in stenography, typing, and accounting." To the direct question, "Have you ever held a paid selling job, Miss Gardner?" however, answer, "No, Mr. Lewis, but I have sold war stamps, school papers, and baseball tickets in my home room. I like to sell." Tell what your strong points are and express your eagerness to work and learn. Be self-confident but modest—never cocky.

13. At the end of the interview stand up, thank the interviewer, and leave promptly. Walk with firm, rather quick steps.

PRACTICE 5. Applying for a Job

With a partner acting as interviewer, apply for one of the following jobs or another one. Put your best foot forward. The class will decide whether you followed the preceding suggestions and whether you will secure the position in preference to other applicants. Use natural, pleasing tones.

care of children	garage helper	receptionist
cashier	gardener	salesperson
delivery boy	junior camp counsellor	shipping or stock
dentist's assistant	office boy or page	clerk
farm hand	packer in department	tutor
file clerk	store	typist

HINTS ON MAKING A PURCHASE

1. *If people are ahead of you at the counter, wait your turn patiently.*
2. *Describe clearly the article you wish to see: quality, colour, size, material, manufacturer, or anything else which will help the salesperson to find it quickly. Use vivid, accurate words.*
3. *Be courteous. Say ,"Will you please show me" or "I should like to see," not "Show me" or "I want."*
4. *If an article does not meet your requirements, explain why; perhaps the salesman can show you a more satisfactory one. Don't, of course, leave while the salesman is looking for an article you asked about.*
5. *Don't compare unfavourably the article shown you with a competitor's goods. Such criticism is, as a rule, both ill-mannered and useless, for ordinarily the salesman has no control over the price or the type of articles given him to sell.*
6. *Never lose your temper and argue loudly with a salesperson; if you have a legitimate grievance, take it to the proper authority.*
7. *Avoid needless handling and disarrangement of merchandise on a counter.*
8. *Above all, never make a salesperson display his entire stock when you have no intention of buying.*

PRACTICE 6. Studying Sales Conversations

Read examples 1 and 2 below. Then, by referring to the preceding hints, explain which customer was the more efficient in making her purchase. What necessary information did one customer omit at the start?

Example 1:

MISS GRAHAM. I'd like to see some gloves.
CLERK. Certainly. What size do you wear?
MISS GRAHAM. Size 6¼.
CLERK. Have you any particular colour in mind?
MISS GRAHAM. Yes, brown.
CLERK. This pair is made of exceptionally soft kid.
MISS GRAHAM. I prefer suède to kidskin.

CLERK. Here's a pair of handsewn, washable, brown suède gloves in your size for $6.50.

MISS GRAHAM. Oh, that's more than I care to spend! Have you a pair for about three dollars in a darker shade of brown?

CLERK. Yes, here's a good value in your size for $3.35.

MISS GRAHAM. They're good-looking, aren't they?

Example 2:

CLERK. May I help you, madam?

MRS. KINGSLEY. Yes, please. I should like to see an all-wool, sleeveless pull-over sweater in olive drab, suitable for a soldier, in size 40, for about four dollars.

CLERK. Surely. Here are two of the most popular soldier's pull-overs. This one, priced at $3.60, is 85% new wool and 15% reprocessed wool. This sweater, priced at $4.50, is 95% new wool and 5% new brushed rabbit's hair.

MRS. KINGSLEY (*after examining the sweaters*). Are these sweaters washable?

CLERK. We can guarantee our sweaters only if they are dry-cleaned, madam.

MRS. KINGSLEY. I'll take the $4.50 sweater.

PRACTICE 7. Dramatizing Purchases

Dramatize purchases suggested by the following list. In each, one pupil will act as the salesperson and another as the customer. Speak distinctly. Use pleasing tones.

baseball or baseball glove

birthday present for a member of your family

butter and eggs, or vegetables

dress, suit, coat, or hat

fountain pen

handbag or wallet

loose-leaf notebook

necktie or scarf

pair of shoes

pair of skates

shoeshine kit for a serviceman

stationery

sweaters for a basketball team

swimming suit

tennis racket

wrist watch

another article

BUSINESS TELEPHONING

When you transact business by telephone, be brief, clear, and definite. Before you pick up the receiver, know exactly what you wish to accomplish. Have clearly in mind names, dates, sizes, and other detailed information. Have handy a pencil and pad, also a catalogue or price list if you will need it.

Most telephone directories have a classified section, in which business and professional subscribers are listed according to the product or service they offer. A few classifications are beauty shops, carpenters, carpet cleaners, florists, laundries, painters' supplies, physicians and surgeons, storage. The classes are arranged alphabetically, and under each classification subscribers are listed alphabetically.

When the person or company called answers, say at once who you are and what you want—for example, "This is Frank Evans calling. I should like to make an appointment with Dr. Howard for Tuesday evening." Using your natural tones, speak directly into the mouthpiece with your lips about half an inch from it. Don't mumble, shout, or talk fast. When your call is concluded, replace the receiver gently.

PRACTICE 8. Using the Telephone Directory

1. On your paper arrange alphabetically the following as they would appear in a telephone directory. For help study the arrangement of names in the telephone directory.

Paul Luber	Edwin Lucien
Ludlow Valve Manufacturing Company	The Lucy Ann Hat Company
	John C. Lozier
Luber Pharmacy, Inc.	Claire Ludwin
The Loyal Dairy	Ludewig and Deutch, Inc.
Lucht Dress Company	R. J. Ludlow, Jr.
Loyal Dress House	The Lucy-Bern Hat Corporation
Mrs. Lucy Lozier	Dr. Frances Lucton
Joseph Luckow	Ludlow and Minor
Lucille Beauty Shop	Ludlow Studios Inc.

2. Using the classified section (the yellow pages) of the directory, write on your paper the name, address, and telephone number of a subscriber who offers for sale each of the following products:

brick	flags	shoes	lumber
automobile supplies	pets	storm windows	meat
adding machines	coal	automobile parts	paint

3. In the classified section of the directory find the name, address, and telephone number of each of the following:

a veterinarian	a piano tuner	a church	a hospital
a business school	a nurse	a mover	a hotel
an accountant	an architect	an auctioneer	a doctor

HINTS ON SHOPPING BY TELEPHONE

1. *Think out in advance questions to secure the information you want. Know on what basis you will make your decision—for example, price, quality, brand, style, colour, date of delivery, or a combination of two or more of these.*

2. *Without wasting time tell exactly what type of product you want to purchase. Mention size, colour, style, price, and other details that will help the store to fill your order accurately.*

3. *Before concluding the call, repeat for verification prices, sizes, dates, and other details quoted by the store.*

4. *Don't forget to give your name and address. Spell your name, unless it is Jones, Brown, or the like. Find out when the purchase will be delivered.*

PRACTICE 9. Studying a Telephone Order

Does Mrs. Leeds waste any words in placing her order? How does she know that the clerk has understood her order?

DEPARTMENT STORE. The Rogers Company.

MRS. LEEDS. I wish to place an order.

[*The telephone operator of the Rogers Company connects Mrs. Leeds with the Order Department.*]

ORDER DEPARTMENT. Order Department.

MRS. LEEDS. I should like to order the number three gift package for overseas which you advertised for four dollars in yesterday's *Post*. That is the box containing two pounds of icebox cookies, one pound of fruit-filled hard candies, one pound of mixed dried fruits, one pound of pure strawberry jam, and one pound of grade A peanut butter.

ORDER DEPARTMENT. Yes, madam, that is our number three package. To whom shall we send it?

MRS. LEEDS. To Mr. Raymond J. Dean (D-e-a-n), 341 Lansing Place, Oxford, England. Charge this purchase to my account. I am Mrs. Philip Leeds (L-e-e-d-s), 207 West End Avenue. My account number is 325,784. On the card write, please, "From Marie and Philip Leeds."

ORDER DEPARTMENT. Yes, Mrs. Leeds. We shall enclose a card reading, "From Marie and Philip Leeds" (L-e-e-d-s), in the number three package, to be sent to Mr. Raymond J. Dean (D-e-a-n), 341 Lansing Place, Oxford, England. The gift is to be charged to Mrs. Philip Leeds, account number 325,784. Is that correct?

MRS. LEEDS. Yes, thank you. Good-bye.

PRACTICE 10. Dramatizing a Telephone Order

With a partner dramatize a scene in which you order by telephone one of the following articles or another article. Speak distinctly. Use pleasing tones.

book	vegetables or fruit	flowers
box of candy	gloves	stationery
house dress	chicken, leg of lamb, pork	bread and cookies
stockings	chops, or other meat	canned goods

MAKING AN APPOINTMENT

When making an appointment by telephone, mention:

1. Your name.

2. The time for which you desire the appointment.

3. The purpose of the appointment unless it is obvious.

If it is necessary to change an appointment:

1. Give your name.

2. Tell the time of the appointment to be broken.

3. Briefly give your reason for breaking the appointment.

4. Ask courteously for another appointment, suggesting a day and time.

PRACTICE 11. Making an Appointment by Telephone

With a partner dramatize a scene in which you make an appointment with one of the persons listed below, and later change the appointment. Enunciate distinctly. Use your best voice.

doctor or dentist	principal of your school
club or scout leader	hairdresser
minister, priest, or rabbi	worker in a field that interests
music teacher	you

EMERGENCY CALLS

When an emergency occurs, the first and most important rule to remember is, Keep calm. Go quickly to the telephone, dial or call the operator, and say, "I want a policeman," "I want to report a fire", "I want an ambulance," or something similar. Be sure to tell the operator accurately where help is needed.

Mastering Effective English

PART TWO

Chapter 12

Effective Diction

When a writer sits down to write, what does he try to do? Joseph Conrad has given us his answer: "My task," he says, "which I am trying to achieve is, by the power of the written word to make you hear, to make you feel—it is, before all, to make you *see*. That—and no more, and it is everything."—'By the power of the written word . . .'—

To learn to write, then, is to discover the power of words—how to make written words communicate forthright, definite pictures, sounds, feelings.

Put in this way, the task may seem immense; but put in the words of H. G. Wells, it may not seem so formidable. Wells says, "I write as I walk because I want to get somewhere, and I write as straight as I can, just as I walk as straight as I can, because that is the best way to get there."

The Power of Words

PICTURES

Because words are the chief tools of expression, we must learn to use words with discrimination. There are words that chuckle, as there are words that sigh. There are thundering words as there are gentle words. Our task is to learn to use the words that give the effect we want to achieve. An editorial writer has said, "You can put tears into words, as though they were so many little buckets; and you can hang smiles along them, like Monday's clothes on the line; or you can starch them with facts and stand them up like a picket fence; but you won't get the tears out unless you first put them in."

299

Command of words enables one to convey thought accurately and swiftly. Select concrete, picture-bringing words that exactly fit the meaning. Many words are unemployed, while others are worn to the bone from overwork.

GENERAL   The sound came loudly from a distance.
CONCRETE   The shot echoed like thunder from the hills.
GENERAL   The bird sat lightly on my hand.
CONCRETE   The sparrow perched gingerly on my index finger.
GENERAL   The wind blew hard against the house.
CONCRETE   The blast beat fiercely against the window.
GENERAL   The boat went quickly to the shore.
CONCRETE   The canoe shot like an arrow to the wooded shore.

PRACTICE 1. Choosing Words

Using your imagination and the dictionary or Roget's *Thesaurus of English Words and Phrases*, write as many colourful words as you can for each of the following:

Example:

eat—chew, crunch, devour, gnaw, gobble, gulp, munch, peck

ask	do	good	nice	take
answer	fall	help	old	tell
begin	frightful	injury	pleasant	want
big	get	interesting	pretty	walk
break	give	leave	see	work
change	go	like	show	young

SUITING THE SOUND TO THE SENSE

Words have a definite music of their own, and often suggest their meaning by their sound. Consider the variations of sound in these words, and listen attentively, first to the vowel sounds, and then to the consonant modifications of them: *purl, murmur, babble, chatter, rilling, swish, splash, gush, whirl, eddy.*

Notice the lightness of short vowels: *twinkle, twitter, shimmer, glimmer;* and the emphasis secured by long vowels and monosyllables; *deep, hole, pool, fine.*

From some of these—*babble, chatter, twitter, shimmer, glimmer*—we notice the effect of double consonants. Consider the prolonging effect of *l*, as in *howl, hill, yell*, and contrast with the short crisp *k* sounds in *bark, crag, crack.*

Many words are imitative of the sounds of nature whence they are derived: *buzz, whisper, cuckoo, whip-poor-will.*

Some sounds seem suited to dolorous expressions, as the long *o:* *woe, moan, alone;* as others are bright, as the long *i; "Arise, shine,* for the *light* of the Lord is upon you."

Poetry has been quicker than prose to make use of this imitative harmony.

1. The lights begin to twinkle from the rocks.—TENNYSON
2. The long day wanes, the slow moon climbs, the deep
   Moans round with many voices.—TENNYSON
3. And ere three shrill notes the piper uttered,
   You heard as if an army muttered;
   And the muttering grew to a grumbling;
   And the grumbling grew to a mighty rumbling;
   And out of the houses the rats came tumbling.—BROWNING

Yet every effective author must write with the sound of the words in his ear.

PRACTICE 2. Suiting the Sound to the Sense

1. Use in effective sentences:

2. List five or more other words the sound of which suggests the sense.

clamour	clatter	hissed	roar	slam
clang	hammer	moan	shriek	squeak

3. List five or more soft, smooth, musical words like *moon, lily, cool, lowly, mole, rill.*

4. Copy into your note book at least a dozen effective passages where the sound resembles the sense. See that not fewer than three of them are from prose.

PRACTICE 3. Choice of Words

Read the following passage carefully and answer the questions that follow it.

Soon the stars are hidden. A light breeze seems rather to tremble and hang poised than to blow. The rolling clouds, the dark wilderness, and the watery waste shine out every moment in the wide gleam of lightnings still hidden by the wood, and are wrapped again in ever-thickening darkness over which thunders roll and jar and answer one another across the sky. Then, like the charge of ten thousand lancers, come the wind and the rain, their onset covered by all the artillery of heaven. The lightnings leap, hiss, and blaze; the thunders crack and roar; the rain lashes; the waters writhe; the wind smites and howls. For five, for ten, for twenty minutes—for an hour, for two hours—the sky and the flood are never for an instant wholly dark, or the thunder for one moment silent; but while the universal roar sinks and swells, and the wide, vibrant illumination shows all things in ghostly half-concealment, fresh floods of lightning every moment rend the dim curtain and leap forth; the glare of day falls upon the swaying wood, the reeling bowing, tossing willows, the seething waters, the whirling rain, and in the midst the small form of the distressed steamer, her revolving paddle-wheels toiling behind to lighten the strain upon her anchor chains; then all are dim ghosts again, while a peal, as if the heavens were rent, rolls off around the sky, comes back in shocks and throbs, and sinks in a long roar that before it can die is swallowed up in the next flash and peal.—GEORGE W. CABLE, *Bonaventure*.

By permission of Charles Scribner's Sons, New York.

1. Point out the verbs, adjectives, and nouns that help to produce the vivid impression created by this paragraph.
2. Show that the comparison used in the fourth sentence is suitable to describe the coming of the wind and the rain.
3. Select four words that suggest their meaning by their sound. What is the value of using such words?
4. What does the author gain by using the word "toiling" instead of "turning" to describe the motion of the paddle-wheels?

To make your description powerful, use words that are definite, concrete, and pictorial. Specific nouns, vivid verbs, adjectives, and adverbs appeal to the various senses and give your reader a clear strong image of the picture you are presenting. Good comparisons help to make the picture meaningful. In choosing words and figures of speech, however, be careful that you do not draw attention from what is being said to the way it is being said: use only those words that are necessary to give the impression you wish to create.

THE ROMANCE OF WORDS

Besides the exact connotation, the derivation, and the sound, every word carries with it an air of association. Some words have persistently kept bad company and others good; some have a halo of holiness, others an atmosphere of romance, adventure, ecstasy. We must learn to choose our words as we choose our friends for their character and tastes.

WORDS

How I love the mere words, the picturesque and dear words,
  Romany and Patteran and Caravan and Chal—
How they lilt and sing to me; flame-lit, how they bring to me
  Heathered moors and bending skies and gypsy carnival.

The sun-swept and the wild words I dreamed of as a child, words
  Like Lariat and Chaparral, Coyote, Pinto, Sage;

How they flung a dare to me of life without a care to me;
  How the flying hoofbeats rang across the printed page!

The lanthorn-lit, the old words, the scarlet and the gold words,
  Palfrey, Jerkin, Yeoman, Falcon, Glebe, and Glade;
Minstrel, Lance, and Tourney—what an age-long journey
  Through the posterns of the Past, alone and half afraid.

The wind blown and the sea words, the lawless and the free words,
  Spindrift, Doubloon, Cutlass, Jib, Corsair, Yardarm Crew;
Whispering wild tales to me—ah, how each unveils to me
  Palm-fringed islands rising green against the ocean blue!

The balsam-scented North, words that call untamed hearts forth, words
  Like Wanigan, and Mackinaw, Duffel, Tumpline, Trail;
While the languid South to me turns a lover-mouth to me
  Jasmine-scented, passion-flowered, by the Bayou pale.

Some may live their fair dreams, costly, jewelled, rare dreams;
  Some may rove the luring world as free as homing birds;
But still I'll find my all for me, close-waiting at my call for me,
  In my printed palaces, bright-tapestried with words.
                                        —Martha Haskell Clarke.
By arrangement with the publishers, The Youth's Companion.

THE EXACT WORD

Discrimination, the ability to make fine distinctions, is essential in conveying exact impressions. Flaubert says, "Whatever may be the thing one wishes to say, there is but one word for expressing it, only one verb to animate it, only one adjective to qualify it. It is essential to search for this word, for this verb, for this adjective, until they are discovered, and to be satisfied with nothing else." In a garden a person who uses his eyes sees asters, roses, larkspurs, zinnias, marigolds, and petunias, not just flowers, and one who is moderately intelligent about flowers also knows the names.

PRACTICE 4. Choosing the Exact Word

1. List fifteen or more colours—for example, lilac-blue, scarlet, crimson, indigo
2. Prepare a list of as many kinds of each of the following as you know: dogs, animals, birds, trees, bushes, flowers, grasses, vegetables, farm crops, chickens, houses, apples, chairs, carpets or rugs, tools, jewels, cloth.
3. In a sentence for each describe (1) a loud noise, (2) the taste of lemon, (3) the colour of the sunset, (4) the feel of kid gloves, (5) the odour of roses.

COMBINING WORDS

Although "adjectivitis"—that is, piling one adjective on top of another—is one of the commonest diseases among young writers, it is possible sometimes to combine two simple words into a vivid expression which causes the reader to hear a sound or see, feel, smell, or taste an object. A boat may be "a wave-tossed canoe", "a flat-bottomed row-boat", "a full-rigged yacht", or "a 30,000-ton battleship".

PRACTICE 5. Two-Word Modifiers

Describe each of the following with a two-word modifier:

Examples:

dog-eared book, thumb-marked page, confetti-strewn streets, carelessly-scrawled message, owl-eyed shoe buttons.

| automobile | book | factory | lips | schoolboy |
| beach | coat | hair | park | street |

SUITING THE MOVEMENT TO THE MOOD

As words have an onomatopoetical sound, suiting the sound to the sense, so sentences and paragraphs may have a movement suitable to the mood. If the mood is dreamy or sentimental, then smooth rhythmic sentences are appropriate; if the mood is vigorous, or hurried, or argumentative, a short, quick or staccato movement is suitable. Sometimes the sentiment requires dignity or grandeur.

Rhythmic style:

1. DEATH OF LITTLE PAUL

Paul had never risen from his little bed. He lay there, listening to the noises in the street, quite tranquilly; not caring much how the time went, but watching it and watching everything about him with observing eyes.

When the sunbeams struck into his room through the rustling blinds, and quivered on the opposite wall like golden water, he knew that evening was coming on, and that the sky was red and beautiful. As the reflection died away, and a gloom went creeping up the wall, he watched it deepen, deepen, deepen into night. Then he thought how the long streets were dotted with lamps, and how the peaceful stars were shining overhead. His fancy had a strange tendency to wander up the river, which he knew was flowing through the great city: and now he thought how black it was, and how deep it would look, reflecting the hosts of stars—and more than all, how steadily it rolled away to meet the sea.—DICKENS, *Dombey and Son.*

2. THE SONG OF THE SIRENS

And all things stayed around and listened; the gulls sat in white lines along the rocks; on the beach great seals lay basking, and kept time with lazy heads; while silver shoals of fish came up to hearken, and whispered as they broke the shining calm. The wind overhead hushed his whistling, as he shepherded his clouds toward the west; and the clouds stood in mid blue, and listened dreaming, like a flock of golden sheep.—KINGSLEY, *The Heroes.*

Quick-moving style:

THE BARRAGE

The British barrage struck. The air gushed in hot surges along the river valley, and uproar never imagined by me swung from ridge to ridge. The east was scarlet with dawn and the flickering gunflashes; I thanked God I was not in the assault, and joined the subdued carriers nervously lighting cigarettes in one of the cellars, sitting there on the steps, studying my watch. The ruins of Hamel were soon crashing chaotically with German shells, and jags of iron and broken wood and brick whizzed past the cellar mouth. When I gave the word to move, it was obeyed with no pretence of enthusiasm. I was forced to shout and swear, and the carrying party, some with shoulders hunched, as if in a snowstorm, dully picked up their bomb buckets and went ahead. The wreckage around seemed leaping with flame. Never had we smelt high explosive so thick and foul, and there was no distinguishing one shell-burst from another, save by the black or tawny smoke that suddenly shaped in the general miasma. We walked along the river road, passed the sandbag dressing-station that had been rigged up only a night or two earlier where the front line ("Shankill Terrace") crossed the road and had already been battered in; we entered No Man's Land, past the trifling British wire on its knife-rests, but we could make very little sense of ourselves or the battle.—EDMUND BLUNDEN, *Undertones of War.*

By permission of the author and publishers, R. Cobden-Sanderson, Ltd., London.

Dignified style:

SAMUEL JOHNSON TO LORD CHESTERFIELD

Is not a patron, my lord, one who looks with unconcern on a man struggling for life in the water, and, when he has reached ground, encumbers him with help? The notice you have been pleased to take of my labours, had it been early had been kind; but it has been delayed till I am indifferent, and cannot enjoy it; till I am solitary and cannot impart it; till I am known, and do not want it. I hope it is no very cynical asperity not to confess obligations where no benefit has been received, or to be unwilling that the public should consider me as owing that to a patron, which Providence has enabled me to do for myself.—SAMUEL JOHNSON.

PRACTICE 6. Writing Rhythmic Prose

Using the *Death of Little Paul* or *The Story of the Sirens* as a model, write a piece of rhythmic prose. Analyze your model, notice the parallel clauses, the repetitions, and the variations. Use the same devices in your own paragraph. These topics may be suggestive:

1. Dr. Manette in prison watches the sunlight on the walls of his cell and recalls his home. 2. An old negro sits beside the river and in reverie recalls his southern home. 3. An old Highlander sits dreaming of his highland home. 4. A young man, stirred by an incident he has witnessed or read about, builds dreams of the future. 5. A description of a field of waving wheat lying between rolling hills.

PRACTICE 7. Writing About Action

With *The Barrage* as model, write a paragraph of prose imitative in its movement of action, commotion, haste. Are these suggestions helpful?

1. A frightened child races through the woods. 2. A kingbird chases a hawk. 3. Terror stricken people scramble from a circus tent. 4. A runaway car careens down a street. 5. Hornets chase a boy who has molested the nest.

FIGURES OF SPEECH

WHAT IS A FIGURE OF SPEECH?

Notice the two ways of expressing each of the following ideas:

1. When we are in trouble, we find who our real friends are.
2. The light of friendship is like the light of phosphorus—seen plainest when all around is dark.
3. Everybody has some envy in his make-up.
4. Envy lurks at the bottom of the human heart, like a viper in its hole.
5. He was nervous and excited.
6. He was about as calm and collected as a man with St. Vitus dance walking a tight rope over Niagara Falls in a hurricane.—WITWER.

Numbers 1, 3, and 5 are straightforward, matter of fact expressions of the ideas. In 2, 4, and 6 figures of speech are used to make the ideas concrete, vivid, beautiful, forceful, or amusing. A striking comparison may incalculably enhance the effectiveness of a sentence.

Moreover, comparisons enable a speaker or writer to say much in little. When a writer says, "He was the Machiavelli of the twentieth century," he has conveyed as much as could be said in a biography.

SIMILES AND METAPHORS

There are two common figures of speech in use, metaphors and similes.

SIMILE

A simile is a definitely stated comparison of two unlike objects that have one point in common. Regularly *as* or *like* is used to make the comparison.

Her thoughts in the morning are as tangled as her hair.
He burst out of the door like an explosion.
Red as a rose is she.
You have about as much chance as a woodpecker trying to make a nest in a concrete telephone pole.

Likening one man to another, one house to another, or one river to another is not a figure of speech: "He looks like his father."

METAPHOR

The metaphor is a more completely integrated comparison. The resemblance is so complete that the writer, instead of saying one thing is *like* another, implies that, in features compared, the one thing is identical with the other.

> She is a rose of Sharon.
> Ted waltzed into the room wearing a rainbow tie.
> The Prime Minister moved to eliminate bottlenecks in production.

As and *like* are not used in the metaphor.

> Exactitude in small matters is the soul of discipline.
> Some books are to be tasted, others to be swallowed, and some few to be chewed and digested.—BACON
> The Giants uncorked a devastating six-run rally in the fifth inning.
> As runs began to pour over the plate in a torrent, the crowd roared itself purple.

A mixed metaphor results from using in a sentence two or more contradictory metaphors. Occasionally metaphors are effectively mixed for humorous effects. Avoid, however, in serious speech or writing such ridiculous mixtures as the following:

> The politicians will keep cutting the wool off the sheep that lays the golden eggs, until they pump it dry.
> I smell a rat, I see it floating in the air, but I shall nip it in the bud.

A mixture of a metaphor and a literal expression is often absurd.

> Boyle was the father of chemistry and the brother of the Earl of York.

As two of the preceding sentences indicate, metaphors are frequently used in sports stories. Many slang expressions are metaphors: *bats in his belfry, crash the gate, dry up, spill the beans, step on the gas, get his goat, high-hat, hit the hay, peachy, the big cheese, hold your horses, a good egg, also-ran.*

PRACTICE 8. Metaphors in Slang

To the list just given add five slang expressions that are metaphors.

Metaphors are commonly used in advertising—for example, "a fleet of superb trains"; "a whale of a success"; "weigh the evidence"; "breeze-swept apartments"; "an oasis in the blistering desert of torridity"; "you'll be convinced in the wink of a humming bird's eyelash."

PRACTICE 9. Metaphors in Advertisements

Find five metaphors in advertisements.

PRACTICE 10. Simile or Metaphor?

Name the figure in each of the following. What are compared? What is the point of likeness? Which figures seem to you particularly striking or effective? Why?

Example:

> Life's but a walking shadow, a poor player,
> That struts and frets his hour upon the stage
> And then is heard no more.—SHAKESPEARE

Metaphor. Life is compared with a shadow and with a poor actor. Life, like a walking shadow or the performance of a poor actor, doesn't last long. This is an effective figure because in a striking, unusual, and rememberable way Shakespeare reminds us that life is short.

1. He felt like the symptoms on a medicine bottle.
2. Contentment is a pearl of great price.
3. To listen to the advice of a treacherous friend is like drinking poison from a golden cup.
4. Your face, my thane, is as a book where men
   May read strange matters.—SHAKESPEARE
5. Good nature, like a bee, collects honey from everywhere. Ill nature, like a spider, sucks poison from the sweetest flower.
6. Life is an isthmus between two eternities.
7. The woman was a tigress in the defense of her children.
8. Writing is like pulling the trigger of a gun; if you are not loaded, nothing happens.—CANBY
9. The human mind should be like a good hotel—open the year round.— PHELPS
10. Spare moments are the gold dust of time.
11. There are many minds that are like a sheet of thin ice. You have to skate on them pretty rapidly or you'll go through.—MORLEY
12. For joy is the best wine, and Silas's guineas were golden wine of that sort.— GEORGE ELIOT
13. I had been all this time a very hedgehog, bristling all over with determination.—DICKENS
14. Liddy, like a little brook, though shallow, was always rippling.—HARDY
15. He has the sense of humour of a crocodile.
16. She sings as if mere speech had taken fire.—YEATS

NOTEBOOK

Watch for striking similes and metaphors and copy them on the page of your notebook reserved for figures of speech.

PRACTICE 11. Changing Figures of Speech

Complete the similes and then change the first ten of them to metaphors:

1. Marie was as quiet as a *mouse*.
2. They were as swift as *eagles* and as strong as *oxen*.
3. Her locks were yellow as *gold*.
4. Gloom hung like a *veil* over the land.
5. Fred's shoes look like *new*.
6. Father is as wise as *owl*.
7. He is as sly as *fox*.
8. Tom is as noisy as *tin can*.
9. Jack was blinking like *mad*.
10. He was as restless as *door mouse*.
11. He is as angry as *bull*.
12. The answer came clear as *a bell*.
13. When Juliet's father heard of her refusal to marry the prince, he roared like a *bull*.
14. Some clever folk are as changeable as *the weather*.
15. She is as sad as *anything*.
16. Her heart beat quickly like *clock*.
17. His reasoning was as clear as *the sky*.
18. It was as hard to catch as *a shadow*.
19. He was as agile as *fox*.
20. He is as faithful as *Christ*.

PRACTICE 12. Using Figures of Speech

Express these thoughts in metaphorical language. Then change the first ten metaphors to similes. Do you prefer the similes or metaphors? Why?

1. He is a hard worker. *works like an ox*
2. He is stubborn. *stubborn like a mule*
3. You are foolish. *foolish as a chimp*
4. When he knows what he wants, he tries until he gets it.
5. Everyone in the schoolroom was busy. *busy as a bee*
6. He is innocent. *innocent as a new born child*

7. He was brave in the fight.
8. He swims well.
9. He thought quickly.
10. She had black hair.
11. There were a great many faces in front of me.
12. He was thoroughly indignant.
13. He kept his eyes on the floor.
14. She walks softly.
15. In love he was fickle.
16. She arose quickly.
17. The children ran to **him.**
18. She spoke quickly.
19. He was eager to go.
20. She had soft skin.

OTHER FIGURES

PERSONIFICATION, a kind of metaphor, consists in giving personal attributes to inanimate objects or abstract ideas. Sometimes the names of the things personified are capitalized.

> The wind whistled, wailed, sobbed, and whispered.
> But I am faint; my gashes cry for help.—SHAKESPEARE
> Joy and Temperance and Repose
> Slam the door on the doctor's nose.
> The gloom slinks up the tenement stairs.

APOSTROPHE is an address to the absent as if present, or the inanimate as if human.

> Shine! Shine! Shine!
> Pour down your warmth, great sun—WHITMAN
> Byron! how sweetly sad thy melody!
> Attuning still the soul to tenderness.—KEATS

METONYMY is a figure of speech in which one word is put for another which it suggests. Four common relations that give rise to metonymy are—

1. Container and thing contained

Please address the chair (chairman).

2. Sign and thing signified

The pen (books, newspapers, and magazines) is mightier than the sword (armies and navies).

Have you no respect for gray hairs (age)?

3. An author and his books

We are reading George Eliot (her novels).

4. The part for the whole

She has seen sixteen summers (years).
All hands (men) to the deck!

ANTITHESIS is a contrast of words or ideas. As white seems whiter when placed beside black, and a sound seems loudest on a quiet night or in a quiet place, so words or ideas which are contrasted are emphatic. Antithesis is most effective if the phrasing of the contrasted ideas is parallel.

His body is active, but his mind is sluggish.
Easy writing makes hard reading; hard writing, easy reading.
Whoso loveth instruction loveth knowledge, but he that hateth reproof is brutish.—BIBLE
To use too many circumstances ere one come to the matter is wearisome; to use none at all is blunt.
A bird in the hand is worth two in the bush.

HYPERBOLE is exaggeration not intended to deceive. Some humorists—Mark Twain, for example—use hyperbole freely as a device for making people laugh.

His hands dangled a mile out of his sleeves.—IRVING
Waves mountain-high broke over the reef.
When he told me the joke, I almost died laughing.
The movie bored me to death.
So frowned the mighty combatants that hell grew darker at their frown.—MILTON
His voice could be heard a mile away.

IRONY is saying the opposite of what is meant in a tone or manner that shows what the speaker thinks.

After Norman had wasted his evening in nonsense, his father remarked, "Don't you think you have studied too hard this evening?"
It was very kind of you to remind me of my humiliation.
To cry like a baby—that's a fine way for a man to act.

PRACTICE 13. Effective Figures of Speech

Name the figures of speech in the following sentences. If the figure is a comparison, name the objects compared. Which figures do you consider most effective? Why?

1. The greatest art is always as obvious as the sea, and as immense.
2. Thy word is a lamp unto my feet.—BIBLE
3. Our birth is but a sleep and a forgetting.—WORDSWORTH
4. O wild West Wind, thou breath of Autumn's being.—SHELLEY
5. His trousers are a mile too short.
6. Now Rumour the messenger went about the street, telling the tale of the dire death and fate of the wooers.—HOMER
7. All the world's a stage.—SHAKESPEARE
8. Pleasures are like poppies spread.—BURNS
9. The train flew at lightning speed.
10. The Puritan hated bear-baiting, not because it gave pain to the bear but because it gave pleasure to the spectators.—MACAULAY
11. Sport that wrinkled Care derides,
    And Laughter holding both his sides.—MILTON
12. I have no spur to prick the sides of my intent.—SHAKESPEARE
13. Roll on, thou deep and dark blue Ocean, roll.—BYRON
14. At one stride comes the dark.—COLERIDGE
15. Walter the Doubter was exactly five feet six inches in height and six feet five inches in circumference.—IRVING
16. His bump of humour is a dent.—JOSEPH LINCOLN
17. The express train ran so fast that the mile posts looked like fence rails.
18. He bought a hundred head of cattle.
19. There is a tide in the affairs of men,
    Which, taken at the flood, leads on to fortune.—SHAKESPEARE
20. One occasion trod upon the other's heels.—DICKENS
21. You look about as fat as a stall-fed knitting needle.—WHITE
22. Life is a leaf of paper white,
    Whereon each one of us may write
    His word or two.—LOWELL
23. They work to pass, not to know; and outraged Science takes her revenge. They do pass, and they don't know.—HUXLEY
24. Every man would live long, but no man would be old.
25. The tale of his ungentle past was scarred upon his face.—LOCKE
26. When people have wooden heads, you know, it can't be helped.—GEORGE ELIOT
27. To err is human; to forgive, divine.—POPE
28. Character is what we are; reputation is what men think we are.
29. The harbour was crowded with masts.
30. What has the gray-haired prisoner done?
    Has murder stained his hand with gore?
    Not so; his crime is a fouler one—
    God made the old man poor.—WHITTIER

PRACTICE 14. Effective Expressions

Of the two expressions of each idea, which is more effective? Tell why you prefer it. Name the figure of speech if there is one.

1. He wore canoes on his feet.
   He wore very big shoes.
2. There are five hundred houses in the village.
   It is a village of five hundred chimneys.
3. Night's candles are burnt out.
   The stars, which are like candles, are gone since it is morning.
4. His clothes did not fit him.
   His garments fitted him like a shirt on a handspike.
5. He bent with dour determination to pluck a coy snail from its reverie beneath a head of lettuce.
   He leaned over to pick up the snail that was under a head of lettuce.
6. Rain scampers over the shingles.
   The rain falls lightly and quickly on the roof.
7. He had a big snow-white beard which hid his whole face.
   He was lost behind his beard, as behind a snowdrift.
8. The birches stood like frozen feathers.
   The tall thin birches were frozen and looked like feathers.
9. She doesn't like anything that is not what it seems to be.
   She prefers genuine cotton to imitation silk.
10. His vest pocket was crowded with pencils and cigars.
    His vest pocket was so filled with cigars and pencils, he looked like a miniature pipe organ.
11. She had a sudden thought, but it vanished as quickly as it came.
    A little mouse of a thought went scampering across her mind and popped into its hole again.
12. It is disappointing to meet a well-dressed but unintelligent woman.
    A well-dressed but mindless woman is like a silly book in a beautiful binding.
13. Life has for everyone happy experiences and unpleasant ones.
    Life is made up of marble and mud.
14. The short evening flew away on gossamer wings.
    The evening passed quickly.
15. You have put the cart before the horse.
    You have put first what should be last.

TOWARDS A MORE PICTURESQUE SPEECH

The use of metaphor is habitual with some people, and gives to their conversation a vitality which is lacking in most of us. It is not the prerogative of university graduates. Peasants, farmers, and artisans often shame the more literate both by the penetration of their observation and the picturesqueness of their language. The *Reader's*

Digest quotes, month by month, some of the most striking of the phrases and sentences which it has gleaned. Let us try to keep our language alive by vigilance and effort, speaking and writing as vividly as we can.

PRACTICE 15. Choosing Picturesque Expressions

Cull from your reading picturesque phrases and sentences and make a note-book collection of them. For a taste:

1. She's learned to say things with her eyes that others waste time putting into words.—CAREY FORD
2. A sleight-of-tongue performance.—MARGARET AYRES BARNES
3. She felt in italics and thought in capitals.—HENRY JAMES
4. The wrinkled half of my life.—THOMAS HARDY
5. The sky had been washed with rain and scrubbed with wind until it shone. —ANNE PARISH
6. The bells and clocks of the town were discussing midnight.—KATE O'BRIEN
7. He lights one question on the stub of the last.—MARGUERITE HENRY
8. Fireflies were lighting matches on black shadows.—CAPTAIN FREDERICK MOORE
9. A smile as contagious as a yawn.—R. H. MACDONALD
10. Sleet wrapped the land in cellophane.—WALTER B. PITKIN

Chapter 13

Pleasing, Forceful Sentences

STYLE means *finish* and *polish*. It is the result of carefully choosing the most distinctive way of saying what you mean, of expressing yourself with individuality. It means rejecting the commonplace sentence and insisting on the best. Conciseness, clarity, force, and variety are difficult to achieve, but they are worth striving for. Generalizing is much easier than giving examples, but illustrations clarify and reinforce ideas. The following suggestions will help you to write sentences that are pleasing and forceful.

A. Concise Sentences

Coleridge says, "Whatever is translatable in other and simpler words of the same language, without loss of sense or dignity, is bad." The historic radio message, "Sighted sub; sank same," illustrates both calm heroism and terse English. Not a word is wasted. Conciseness and compression lend life and vigour to writing. Learn to cross out in your editing and revision.

1. OMIT UNNECESSARY WORDS

Say what you have to say simply and directly. Cross out dead-wood—words that add nothing to your thought. Padding a twenty-word idea out to one hundred words does not make a one-hundred-word idea

PADDED Anyone who confines his interests to himself and his own affairs is bound, in the end, to amount to very little in life, because the narrowness of his selfish outlook has stunted his chances of self-development.(36 words).

CONCISE A man wrapped up in himself makes a very small bundle. (11 words) —BENJAMIN FRANKLIN

PADDED In a discussion an individual should be careful to keep his temper, because if he gets angry he will lose his case because he will say things that don't really support his side of the question. (37 words)

CONCISE Keep cool; anger is not argument. (6 words)—DANIEL WEBSTER

When possible, cut a phrase to a single word and cut a clause to a phrase or a single word. Strike out every useless *which* and *that*.

The shipment of tile ~~which we had~~ ordered May 3 arrived only yesterday.

What stores in my vicinity carry the new type of oven ~~that was~~ recommended in the February *Good Housekeeping?*

MAX ALLEN IS A ~~MAN WHO IS A VERY~~ SKILLFUL MECHANIC. ~~IN HIS FIELD~~

W
~~That is most~~ ̸Wonderful!

an entertaining
David Copperfield is ~~the kind of~~ book. ~~that one enjoys reading.~~

AVOID	SAY AND WRITE
at all times	always
at the present time	now
due to the fact that, for the reas̶ that, in view of the fact that	as, because, since

inasmuch as	since
in order to, with a view to	to
in the amount of	for
in the case of, in the event that, in the event of	if
in the meantime	meanwhile
in the near future	soon
in the neighborhood of	nearly, about, around
in this place	here
previous to, prior to	before
there can be no doubt that	doubtless
with reference to, with regard to	about

2. AVOID NEEDLESS REPETITION Avoid tautology—the needless repetition of an idea in different words: "the reason why", "co-operate together", "write down".

~~at~~ about one o'clock	over ~~with~~
cheap ~~in price~~	rarely ~~ever~~
combined ~~together~~	refer ~~back~~
connect ~~up~~, finish ~~up~~, end ~~up~~, join ~~up~~, divide ~~up~~, hurry ~~up~~	requirements ~~needed~~ for
	remember ~~of~~
~~every~~ once in a while	round ~~in shape~~, small ~~in size~~
fell off ~~of~~ the porch	such as . . . ~~and others~~
gray ~~in colour~~	the fingers ~~on her hand~~
~~in my opinion~~, I think	the sun rose ~~in the east~~
inside ~~of~~	the ~~two~~ twins
long ~~length of~~ time	throughout the ~~whole~~ night
meet ~~up with~~	win ~~out~~, lose ~~out~~
modern schools ~~of today~~	

~~In my opinion~~ I think *The Haunted Bookshop* should be added to our reading list.

3. OMIT UNNECESSARY PRELIMINARIES

~~We are writing to tell you that~~ We are sorry that your order for slip covers has been delayed.

~~I wish to state that~~ I have not ~~yet~~ received the shoes ~~which~~ I ordered on October 16.

4. AVOID FLOWERY LANGUAGE Don't pile adjective upon adjective, adverb upon adverb. Don't overload your sentences with hackneyed metaphors or extravagant, high-sounding phrases.

The ~~magnificent,~~ golden, ~~glorious~~ rays of the setting sun contrasted with the gloomy, ~~deathlike, murky, dismal~~ shadows in the valley.

FLOWERY Every intelligent boy and girl, whose interest in the things of the mind is keen and very much alive, should be granted the happy opportunity of pursuing further the pleasant paths of learning.

PLAIN Every qualified student should have a chance to go to college.

FLOWERY   The powerfully swung bat met the whizzing ball with a sharp, cracking sound, and the huge crowd in the vast stadium, expecting to see a home run, loudly and excitedly yelled their heartfelt joy.

PLAIN   Bat met ball with a sharp crack, and the crowd, expecting a home run, yelled joyfully.

5. AVOID WORDY, IMPERSONAL CONSTRUCTIONS   There were, it is.

~~It was~~ Tommy Henderson ~~who~~ drove in the winning run.

F
~~There were~~ five juniors and six seniors ~~who~~ won prizes in the essay contest.

PRACTICE 1. Eliminating Useless Words

Strike out the unnecessary words.   Express each idea more briefly.

A. 1. I have had no business experience at all.

2. At about half past nine my aunt phoned.

3. Gordon told the both of us what he wanted to be done.

4. How can I repay you back for your kindness?

5. Enclosed you will please find a recommendation from my shop teacher.

6. In reply to your advertisement in the *Globe and Mail* for artificial flower makers, I beg leave to apply for the position.

7. In my opinion I consider Lowell Thomas one of the best and finest news reporters and commentators on the air.

8. Another interesting feature of the *American Girl* is the section where they have jokes.

9. Announcements could be made telling of future games that are going to be played.

10. In my estimation, I believe the play has already proved itself a success.

B. 1. The population of Venezuela is 3,492,747 people.

2. Dickens will always be read for the many human and real characters he has created, such as Mr. Micawber, Oliver Twist, Tiny Tim, Little Nell, David Copperfield, and many others.

3. Some of the interesting features of the *Toronto Daily Star* are: it has very good book reviews; it runs a very interesting sports section; and its editorial page and letters to the editor are very informative.

4. The poets deal with such topics as spring, Indian summer, a brook, the clouds, and similar subjects.

5. In my opinion, I believe that Judge Pyncheon brought about Cliffords' imprisonment.

6. There is a brief biography of E. J. Pratt's life on page 19.

7. On reaching home I found the door to be locked.

8. Another reason why *Hamlet* is worth studying is due to the fact that there is much comedy in this tragedy.

9. There is no doubt that Raymond deserved the reprimand.

10. The authors feel and believe that a high school education is almost indispensable in order to succeed in the business world.

B. Forceful Sentences

1. PICTURE-MAKING WORDS

Use simple specific, vigorous, picture-making words.

COLOURLESS The turtle walked over the grass by the roadside.

COLOURFUL The turtle's hard legs and yellow-nailed feet threshed slowly through the grass, not really walking, but boosting and dragging his high-domed shell along.—JOHN STEINBECK

COLOURLESS Uriah tried to give the impression of great humility.

COLOURFUL Uriah's nostrils quivered, he wriggled his body obsequiously, and kept squeezing his palms together.—CHARLES DICKENS

COLOURLESS Mr. Bumble was never moved by appeals to emotion.

COLOURFUL Tears didn't affect Mr. Bumble. His heart was waterproof.
—CHARLES DICKENS

PRACTICE 2. Writing Colourful Sentences

Make eight of the following sentences more forceful by using specific, suggestive, vigorous, picture-bringing words. Make the sentences graphic by using your imagination and giving sharp details.

Example:

Sunday dinner at Aunt Nan's was very good.

For Sunday dinner Aunt Nan served pineapple mint cup, crisp, brown, savoury roast turkey with chestnut dressing, creamy mashed potatoes, smooth, rich gravy, fresh green peas, little white onions, mixed green salad, and hot apple pie.

1. The crowd cheered the touchdown.
2. The storm came suddenly.
3. Japanese beetles attacked our garden in force.
4. The tree outside my window is beautiful.
5. The tuba player was very comical.
6. At the park there was an unusually large crowd of people of all kinds.
7. Jerry is a fine boy.
8. Phil's soda fountain is always busy after school hours.
9. Marie was attractively dressed.
10. We have various kinds of flowers in our garden.
11. In his beautiful summer home he had most of the conveniences of the city.
12. His speech was poor.
13. When Dad cooks, he messes up the kitchen.
14. The beach was crowded with people.
15. Sue was nervously waiting for the telephone to ring.
16. Mrs. Pringle's voice is unpleasant.
17. The bride looked lovely.
18. The planes moved across the sky.
19. The little boy was frightened.
20. He is the funniest person I ever saw.

2. BEGINNING THE SENTENCE

Begin a sentence with important words. Placing key words at the beginning of a sentence connects it with the preceding sentence and challenges the reader's interest.

Liberty is to the collective body what health is to every individual body. *Without health* no pleasure can be tasted by man; without liberty no happiness can be enjoyed by society.—HENRY ST. JOHN BOLINGBROKE

3. ENDING THE SENTENCE

End the sentence with an important word or phrase. Like a bee a good sentence should carry the sting in its tail.

WEAK   To national downfall national injustice is the surest road.

FORCEFUL   National injustice is the surest way to *national downfall.*—WILLIAM E. GLADSTONE

WEAK   The day that you first have a laugh at your own expense is the day that you really grow up.

FORCEFUL   You grow up the day you have your first real laugh—at yourself.
—ETHEL BARRYMORE

WEAK   Although Alfred Lunt likes to plan things on a grand scale, he doesn't forget to be practical, too.

FORCEFUL   Alfred Lunt has his head in the clouds and his feet in the box office—NOEL COWARD

4. SANDWICHING NONESSENTIALS

Acquire the habit of sandwiching parenthetic expressions between the key words of your sentences.   By placing parenthetic expressions in the middle of your sentences you will reserve the emphatic beginning and end positions for key words.   Avoid ordinarily beginning with *however, therefore, I think, it seems to me,* or a similar expression.

WEAK   *Dr. Jekyll and Mr. Hyde* is a masterpiece in my opinion.

FORCEFUL   *Dr. Jekyll and Mr. Hyde* is, *in my opinion,* a masterpiece.

5. CLIMACTIC ORDER

Arrange a series as a climax (from the least important to the most important) unless you wish to make an anticlimax for the sake of humour.

CLIMAX   Quality, will power, geographical advantages, natural and financial resources, the command of the sea, and, above all, a cause which rouses the spontaneous surging of human spirit in millions of hearts—these have proved to be the decisive factors in the human story.—WINSTON CHURCHILL

CLIMAX   I am in earnest.   I will not equivocate; I will not excuse; I will not retreat a single inch; and I will be heard!—W. L. GARRISON

ANTICLIMAX   Men will confess to treason, murder, arson, false teeth, or a wig. How many of them will own up to a lack of humour?—FRANK M. COLBY

6. DIRECT QUOTATION

Report conversation directly.

WEAK   Bernard Shaw commented speculatively that youth is too precious a thing to waste on children.

FORCEFUL   "Youth," commented Bernard Shaw speculatively, "is too precious a thing to waste on children."

WEAK   Jonathan Swift said that a lady of his acquaintance wore her clothes as though they had been thrown on her with a pitchfork.

FORCEFUL   "She wears her clothes," said Swift, "as though they were thrown on her with a pitchfork."

PRACTICE 3. Building Forceful Sentences

Improve the following sentences. Give a reason for each change.

Example:

Al commanded the dog to come to him at once.
"Come here, Peter," snapped Al. (Al's command is reported directly.)

A. 1. Kipling's "Gunga Din" is the best poem I've ever read, I think.
   2. It is time that the world took steps to prevent future wars, wholesale slaughter, and unfair trade discrimination.
   3. In time of crisis men will fight for their country, their rights, and their freedom, invariably.
   4. Alice's father asked whether Alice had put away his briefcase.
   5. Collecting minerals is an educating and fascinating pursuit. However, you must spend a little time studying the properties of minerals, their classification, and ways of distinguishing them.

B. 1. The outstanding characteristic of the Canadian variety of European civilization is our faith in education, according to the best observers.
   2. Cynthia's mother said that whenever Cynthia felt blue it was a good idea to find someone who was bluer than she was.
   3. The invading army murdered, robbed, and annoyed defenseless civilians.
   4. Humanity has had a "sweet tooth" for ages, according to a recent history of sugar.
   5. Shakespeare ranks first among writers as a philosopher, a poet, and a creator of human beings, as I have pointed out.

7. CORRECT SUBORDINATION

Place the principal thought of a complex sentence in the principal clause. A *when* clause fixes the time of an event told about in the principal clause.

After
ʌ I had driven only ten blocks ~~when~~ the tire blew.

After rowing
~~We rowed~~ on through the storm for an hour ~~when~~ we finally reached our dock.

When t
ʌThe Englishmen and their Sherpa guides were halfway up the glacier,ʌ ~~when~~ they spotted the tracks of the "abominable snowman." (The main thought is that the climbers spotted the tracks, not that they were halfway up the glacier.)

's
Jimmyʌ~~has a~~ pet snake ~~that~~ is black and ugly and completely harmless.

8. Active Voice

The active voice is usually more direct and forceful than the passive.

Passive   Twenty feet in a single leap can be covered by the great gray kangaroo.

Active   The great gray kangaroo can cover twenty feet in a single leap.

Use the passive when the doer is unknown or unimportant or when you want to put particular emphasis on the receiver.

The Eskimo hunter was marooned for nine days on the floating ice.
Except under certain specific conditions, wire tapping is banned by law.

PRACTICE 4. Substituting the Active for the Passive

Make each sentence clearer and more forceful by changing the passive voice to the active voice.

1. A pleasant atmosphere was created in the store by the recorded music.
2. The earth was circled by the first man-made satellite about once every ninety-five minutes.
3. The leading parts of our class production of *The Admirable Crichton* will be played by Evelyn Foster and Ted Bowers.
4. No one would have thought that the tennis tournament would be won by the inexperienced Williams team.

5. More than a hundred million road maps will probably be given out this year by service stations.

PRACTICE 5. Building Forceful Sentences

Improve each of the following sentences in one of these three ways: correct subordination, direct quotation, active voice.

A. 1. Will Rogers said that everything is funny as long as it is happening to somebody else.
2. Joe has a new car that is low-slung, fast, and fire-engine red.
3. Mother and Aunt Mary were hanging out the wash when they smelled the biscuits burning.
4. The part of Peter was played by Mary Martin in the television production of Sir James Barrie's *Peter Pan*.
5. Sis warned us that we had better not forget that we had promised to bring potato chips, hot dogs, and marshmallows to the picnic.

B. 1. James Jr. had always been called "J. J." by the family.

    2. The Police Department Glee Club had barely finished "Take Me Out to the Ball Game" when the audience broke into excited cheering and clapping.

    3. The fire chief yelled to us to get back from the fire lines and to keep clear of the hose.

    4. "Winter Wonderland" was sung by our glee club as the opening number of the Valentine show.

    5. Judy called to Pete that he shouldn't let Buddy dive off the high board.

9. Comparisons

Comparisons enable a speaker or writer to say much in little. This important method of gaining vividness and force is used constantly by newspaper columnists and radio commentators, as well as by poets. Many of our common expressions, like "stole second base", "blossomed forth in a new dress", and "swamped with calls", are metaphorical in origin. "A face like a cross pansy" paints a fresher picture than the tarnished comparison "cross as a bear".

PRACTICE 6. Studying Comparisons

Note the condensation and colour in the following. Numbers 1 to 3 are metaphors and 4 to 6 are similes. What are compared in each?

1. Ted waltzed in wearing a rainbow tie.
2. Armed only with a hunting knife, pint-sized, hickory-tough Captain James Kehoe set out on foot through one of the world's densest jungles.
3. The Prime Minister moved to eliminate bottlenecks in production.
4. She barged in with her six children, like a bomber escorted by fighters.
—Harold Mynning
5. Restless as the tip of a cat's tail.—Jack Morris
6. Grandfather sat quiet as a stone under the fan-shaped elm.

PRACTICE 7. Writing Similes and Metaphors

Construct similes or metaphors for eight of the following. Avoid worn-out comparisons; make them vivid, not far-fetched.

Example:

anger. When angry, he is hasty as fire.

an airplane	an old house	a battered hat
an old dog	a book	an apple orchard
the wind	a voice	Vancouver's skyline

a tried friend   silence   hot rolls
a hypocrite   envy   clouds

10. WRITING OBJECTIVELY

For the most part write objectively, picturing actions rather than describing emotions. Subjective writing depends principally upon the analysis of feeling or the description of emotion. Objective writing does not eliminate feeling but lets the reader draw his own conclusions from a graphic description of what is happening. Because objective writing describes what you could *see* and *hear* if you were present, it can be transferred directly to stage or screen.

SUBJECTIVE When his turn to recite came, Little Tom felt so nervous that he thought he would never be able to say the poem.

OBJECTIVE Little Tom walked to the front of the room, tremblingly blurted out the title of his poem, and burst into tears. (The sentence shows how Tom felt by picturing him in action.)

NOTE. There is room for occasional good subjective writing which does not merely tell the emotion a person feels, but pictures it from his point of view. Thus the preceding subjective sentence may be improved:

When his turn to recite came, little Tom felt himself go cold, as though someone had poured ice water into his veins.

PRACTICE 8. Writing Objectively

Change the following subjective analyses into objective descriptions. Show what the people do. Make your classmates see the actions and, as a result, know what emotion is felt.

Example:

Cold, bitter anger welled into Joan.

With narrowed eyes, tightly closed lips, and clenched fists, Joan rose and advanced toward her tormentor.

A. 1. Dad welcomed Uncle Jack heartily.

   2. Toby felt deep unrest and uneasiness as the time for his father's arrival passed.

   3. Little Dora felt overwhelming pity for the poor homeless dog.

   4. Ted was badly frightened when he heard an owl for the first time.

   5. The sight of the little black box stirred Marie's curiosity.

B. 1. George had a great affection for his ragged chum.
2. Harold is a very shy boy.
3. Mother was enthusiastic about my new hat.
4. Susie was greatly pleased with her new doll.
5. The two boys were dead tired when they returned from the hike.

C. Varied Sentences

Vary the length and type of sentence you use. There is no one best kind of sentence. Each kind helps the writer to achieve a particular effect.

1. VARIED IN LENGTH

a. A *short* sentence is easier to understand than a long one. Use a short sentence to (1) express strong feeling or create a dramatic effect; (2) follow several long sentences; (3) begin and end a paragraph.

Tyranny is always weakness.—JAMES RUSSELL LOWELL
Responsibility educates.—WENDELL PHILLIPS
Thinking makes the man.—AMOS BRONSON ALCOTT

If, however, many short, choppy sentences are used together, the composition sounds like a primer.

b. In a *long* sentence you can (1) express a complicated idea more fully and accurately; (2) develop suspense; (3) show similarity or contrast; (4) give examples or proof.

The English-speaking people are quite ready to follow a leader for a time as long as he is serviceable to them; but the idea of handing themselves over lock, stock, and barrel, body and soul, to one man and worshipping him as if he were an idol—that has always been odious to the whole theme and nature of our civilization.—WINSTON CHURCHILL

PRACTICE 9. Using Both Short and Long Sentences

Improve the following selection by using a few short sentences and changing the rest into longer unified sentences.

THE STRATOSPHERE

The atmosphere is a blanket of air. This blanket surrounds the earth. The upper atmosphere is the stratosphere. The air in the stratosphere is thin. Its depth is unknown. The stratosphere begins about nine miles above the earth at the equator. It begins about six miles above the earth in the polar regions. The temperatures of the stratosphere rarely change. Above the polar regions the stratosphere is around —60° F. It is —90°F. above the equator. Scientists have sent balloons into the stratosphere. These contained instruments for collecting information. Some balloons reached a height of 100,000 feet.

2. VARIED IN ARRANGEMENT

a. A *loose sentence* makes complete sense if brought to a close at one or more points before the end.

The beautiful constellation Scorpius towers high || in the southern sky || in the early summer evenings. ||

b. A *periodic sentence* makes complete sense only at the end.

High in the southern sky in the early summer evenings towers Scorpius.

The loose sentence is simpler, clearer, and more natural than the periodic; but the periodic sentence keeps the hearer in suspense until the last word is reached. Because it holds the attention, impresses the point, and varies the usual subject-verb order, it should be used frequently for effect.

PRACTICE 10. Writing Periodic Sentences

Change each loose sentence into a periodic sentence.

Example:

We reached home toward dark, after a long ride and some unusual experiences.

Toward dark, after a long ride and some unusual experiences, we reached home.

1. Father Hubbard, the Glacier Priest, enjoyed climbing California's mountains at an early age even though he was not robust.
2. He became interested in geology and paleontology while other boys of his age thought only of sports and frolic.
3. He didn't neglect sports despite his keen interest in natural science.
4. He has made many contributions to science as a result of his years spent in Alaska and the Bering Sea region.
5. His language is colourful, whether he is addressing a large group, writing a book about his explorations, or speaking conversationally to a few people.
6. The Army and the Navy have used his scientific data in the compilation of information on Alaska and the Aleutian Islands.

c. *Parallel structure* is the use of the same form for words, phrases, or clauses which have equal value and similar function. (See page 85.)

I have nothing to offer you but blood, sweat, toil, and tears.—WINSTON CHURCHILL

. . . that government of the people, by the people, and for the people shall not perish from the earth.—ABRAHAM LINCOLN

. . . Undulating hills were changed to valleys, undulating valleys (with a solitary stormbird sometimes skimming through them) were lifted up to hills; masses of water shivered and shook the beach with a booming sound; every shape tumultuously rolled on, as soon as made, to change its shape and place, and beat another shape and place away; the ideal shore on the horizon, with its towers and buildings, rose and fell; the clouds fell fast and thick; I seemed to see a rending and upheaving of all nature.—CHARLES DICKENS

Identify the grammatical elements that have been made parallel.

Parallel structure is an excellent device for achieving pleasing, forceful sentences. The similarity of structure may convey equality (if the paired ideas are equal in importance), emphasize a contrast (if the paired ideas are opposite), provide a climax or anticlimax (if the ideas are arranged in an ascending or descending scale of interest or importance), or suggest a rhythmic effect.

PRACTICE 11. Using Parallel Structure

Using parallel structure, complete the following sentences:

1. Every week end Bud washes the car, fills the gas tank and——.
2. Terry took the ball, faded back for a pass, and ——.
3. College freshmen have to get used to new books, new study habits, and ——.
4. A successful musical comedy needs gay tunes, ——, and ——.
5. By the time we got home Dad had peeled the potatoes, set the table, and ——.
6. Vince grabbed his lunch box, leaped down the front steps, and ——.
7. Three duties of a secretary are receiving callers, ——, and ——.
8. Buck, our star quarterback, was able to pass, run, and —— better than any other player in the high school league.
9. When I interviewed Miss Seton, I asked her what high school and college she had attended, why she had entered the teaching profession, and ——.
10. I think that most high school seniors have a sense of responsibility, ——, and ——.

    d. A *balanced sentence* has two parts that are similar in form.

Silence is as deep as eternity; speech is as shallow as time.—THOMAS CARLYLE

Not that I loved Caesar less, but that I loved Rome more.—WILLIAM SHAKESPEARE

A wise son maketh a glad father, but a foolish son is the heaviness of his mother.—Bible

In each of these sentences the structural repetition emphasizes a contrast.

e. Long sentences, especially compound and compound-complex sentences, may sometimes combine two or more of the types mentioned above. Such sentences are called *mixed.*

PRACTICE 12. Writing Balanced Sentences

Construct balanced sentences containing statements about five of the following:

Example:

Youth and age.   The young man who has not wept is a savage, and the old man who will not laugh is a fool.—George Santayana

1. the country and the city
2. winter and summer
3. sleeping and daydreaming
4. wit and wisdom
5. student and teacher
6. hope and despair
7. war and peace
8. Champlain and Sir Wilfrid Laurier
9. poverty and riches
10. subjects of your own choice

3. Varied in Grammatical Purpose

An occasional interrogation, exclamation, or command adds variety and life to your writing. "Who is equal to him?" is livelier than "He has no equal." "How beautiful!" is stronger than "This is beautiful."

Who will tell us why only in winter do we see that strange chill apple green in the sunset sky?—Donald Peattie

Dost thou love life?   Then do not squander time, for that is the stuff life is made of.—Benjamin Franklin

How are the mighty fallen!—Bible

Have you ever been caught in a squall?   How suddenly the waves seem to turn into angry breakers, all intent on pounding your small boat!   How dim the shore line seems, and how distant!   When a squall strikes, put about and make for a quiet harbor, or prepare to drop anchor and ride out the gale.

PRACTICE 13. Improving Sentence Interest

Add spirit and interest to the following sentences by turning an indirect quotation into a direct quotation, or by changing a statement to a question, an exclamation, or a command.

A. 1. Harold E. Palmer said that language is primarily the thing we think with; it is more than mere communication.

2. Emily Dickinson's poems are short and compressed.

3. I should like you to give me your opinion of this editorial after you have read it.

4. Whenever you write a composition, you should keep a dictionary and a book of synonyms near at hand.

5. Bing Crosby replied to the London newspaper that as a crooner he had stretched his talent over a thirty-year period.

B. 1. The early fur traders were fearless adventurers.

2. Father called to us to hurry back, as it was going to rain.

3. Perhaps you cannot react quickly and intelligently in an emergency.

4. Stevenson said that when he speaks of writing it is rewriting that he has chiefly in mind.

5. I should like you to try the accordion for a week to see whether or not you like it.

PRACTICE 14. Different Sentence Forms

Express the meaning of each of the following questions in the form of an assertion, a command, or a wish.

Example:

"Shall I never hear the end of this?" means "I am weary of having this brought up to me."

1. When shall we be rid of him?

2. Will you please be quiet?

3. When can we have silence?

4. Can you imagine anything more lovely?

5. Am I never to be rid of this pest?

6. Am I my brother's keeper?

7. Will no one rid me of this turbulent priest?

8. What do you expect to gain by this lying?

9. Canst thou not minister to a mind diseased?

10. Of whom then shall I be afraid?

4. VARIED IN GRAMMATICAL STRUCTURE

a. A *simple* sentence has *one* subject and *one* predicate, either or both of which may be compound. Its singleness enables a writer to present concisely and emphatically *one* main idea.

The *quality* and *quantity* of a harvested crop *depend* to a large extent upon the proper timing of the harvest. (Compound subject)

A searching *beam dipped* from the sky and *swept* across the bay. (Compound predicate)

Big three-place torpedo *planes* and tiny, stubby *fighters* **roared** away from the field in groups and **headed** for the carrier.

By building sentences with compound predicates, avoid the overuse of compound sentences with *and I, and we, and he, and she,* and *and they.*

The pirates killed the crew in a bloody fight and then ~~they~~ transferred the cargo to their own ship.

PRACTICE 15. Using Compound Predicates

Improve these sentences by making of each compound sentence a simple sentence with a compound predicate.

A. 1. At an early age Stephen Vincent Benét began writing, and he won prizes offered by *St. Nicholas* magazine.

2. He prepared for college at Summerville Academy, and in 1915 he was admitted to Yale University.

3. As a writer he brought American folklore into the limelight, and he made Americans proud of their heritage.

4. "The Devil and Daniel Webster", his famous short story, was successful as a play and an opera, and it was even more impressive on the screen as *All That Money Can Buy.*

5. He was not satisfied to go on writing short stories, and on a Guggenheim fellowship he spent two years in France writing an epic poem.

6. This long poem, *John Brown's Body,* presents a fresh view of a familiar event, and it won the Pulitzer prize for poetry in 1928.

7. His work is not bulky but it is of high quality.

B. 1. Alice read the advertisement, she hesitated a moment, and then she went to the telephone.

2. Dwarf trees three feet high may be over five hundred years old, and they can cost as much as four thousand dollars.

3. Flying fishes use their pectoral fins as wings, and they often fly six feet above the water for about one hundred feet.

4. During the forest fire season, some forest rangers stay constantly in high lookout towers, and they watch for signs of smoke.

5. Per Hansa threw himself out of the sleigh, and he fumbled his way along the traces to the oxen.

b. *A compound* sentence is made up of two or more independent statements, questions, or commands. Its arrangement enables a writer to show the relationship (equality or contrast) of two main ideas.

Suddenly a window opened, and a young boy looked out.

c. A *complex* sentence has one main clause and one or more subordinate clauses. Its arrangement enables a writer to emphasize *one* main idea and to indicate the close relationship of secondary ideas to it.

> The high wind rattled the windows of the deserted house until it creaked like a ship in a heavy sea.

d. A *compound-complex* sentence has two or more principal clauses and one or more subordinate clauses. Its arrangement permits both subordination and co-ordination of ideas.

> Now and then a blue cart filled with peasants drew aside *as the tourists approached,* or a shepherd in a vividly embroidered cloak guided his flock into a huddle at the roadside and stood watching, pipe in mouth, *as they passed.* (The two subordinate clauses are in italics.)

e. A *complex-complex* sentence is a complex sentence in which a subordinate clause is itself complex.

> I remembered what Silver had said about the current that drifts northward along the whole west coast of Treasure Island. (*What Silver had said about the current* is a noun clause used as direct object of the verb *remembered; that drifts northward along the whole west coast of Treasure Island* is an adjective clause modifying *current.*)

To avoid overworking *and, but,* and *so,* write complex sentences.

WEAK, CHILDISH   Vegetation grows rapdily in the hot, rainy regions of the Amazon basin and they might be the most productive parts of the world but men don't know how to cultivate them.

FORCEFUL, GROWN-UP   Vegetation grows so rapidly in the hot, rainy regions of the Amazon basin that they might be the most productive parts of the world if men knew how to cultivate them.

PRACTICE 16. Writing Complex Sentences

By subordinating one of the ideas change a compound sentence or a group of two sentences into a complex sentence. Whenever possible, place an adverb clause before the principal clause it modifies. Select conjunctions that show exactly how the clauses are related in thought.

Example:

Dr. Samuel Johnson became the most celebrated literary figure of his time. He had a youth of hard work, bitter poverty, and repeated failure.

Dr. Samuel Johnson, who became the most celebrated literary figure of his time, had a youth of hard work, bitter poverty, and repeated failure.

1. Samuel Johnson was the son of a poor bookseller. He managed to attend college with the help of financial assistance from friends.

2. After three years his money ran out. Despite his brilliant record, he had to leave Oxford without a degree.

3. Years later, Johnson became famous. The University of Oxford bestowed on him the honorary degree of Doctor of Laws.

4. In 1737, Johnson, practically penniless, hiked to London with David Garrick. Garrick was destined to become the greatest actor of his time.

5. In after years Johnson often recalled their early struggles. They reached London with five pence halfpenny between them.

6. Two poems, "London" and "The Vanity of Human Wishes," and two periodicals, the *Idler* and the *Rambler*, gained Johnson some measure of success. This consoled him for the failure of his play *Irene*.

7. In 1755, Johnson published his *Dictionary of the English Language* and this work made his reputation and won for him the title of "the great lexicographer."

8. His novel *Rasselas* was written to pay for his mother's funeral. He finished it in a single week.

9. Eventually, a government pension made Johnson financially independent. His generosity to those in want kept him always relatively poor.

10. In his later years Johnson dominated the conversations of the Club. Its members included such men as the stateman Burke and the painter Reynolds.

11. Johnson's *Lives of the Poets* is a landmark of literary criticism. It firmly established his reputation as the last great representative of the classical school.

12. Boswell's *Life of Johnson* is considered the best biography in the English language, and it gives us a matchless picture of Johnson's tenderness, his courage, his unflinching honesty, and his magnificent common sense.

PRACTICE 17. Sentence Reconstruction

A. By introducing correct subordination, reconstruct the following passage into an effective paragraph of four or five sentences.

La Vérendrye and his successors had penetrated to the western prairies. They had begun to cut off at its source the Hudson's Bay Company's supply of furs. The Company sent out Henday. They told him to re-establish trading relations with the Indians. He travelled into the southern part of the modern province of Alberta. He encountered a fort. The French had established it. Henday exchanged civilities with the officer in charge of the French post. Beneath the surface there was an undercurrent of rivalry. The meeting presaged a struggle lasting over half a century. It ended in 1821. At that time the Hudson's Bay Company united with the North West Company.

B. By introducing correct subordination, reconstruct the following passage into an effective paragraph of two or three sentences.

Lord Durham arrived in Canada. He landed at Quebec. It was at the end of May, 1838. He issued a proclamation. Its style was like that of a dictator. It was not in any way unworthy of the occasion. The occasion called for the intervention of a brave and enlightened man acting as a dictator. He declared that he would unsparingly punish any persons if they violated the laws. He frankly invited the colonists to co-operate with him. He wished to form a new system of government. This was to be really suited to their needs. It was to be suited to the altering conditions of civilization.

C. By introducing correct subordination, reconstruct the following passage into an effective paragraph of *five or six sentences*. Most of the ideas may be arranged in the order suggested.

To recover Milan, Francis raised a great army and advanced into Italy. Here he met a Swiss army. This army was composed of mercenaries of the Duke of Milan. Francis won a brilliant victory. The fame of this victory spread far and wide. He returned to France. He was received as a hero. This reception inflamed his ambition. Nothing seemed impossible. He presented himself as a candidate for the imperial throne. He wanted glory for himself. He wanted to prevent the king of Spain from increasing his power. The king of Spain ruled the Netherlands and Naples. Francis put his hopes in his personal popularity and his extravagant spending of money. Francis was defeated. Charles became Emperor.

D. (a) Using correct subordination, co-ordination, parallel construction, etc., reconstruct the following sentences into *two* effective paragraphs totalling nine or ten sentences.

(b) In sentence form, explain the reason for your choice of paragraph division.

Grenville's financial policy culminated in 1765. It ended with the Stamp Act. A year before its enactment Grenville announced his intention. It was to frame such legislation. The colonial agents in London discussed the project with him. Grenville said he would accept American suggestions for raising the money. Some of the colonial agents notified their colonial governments. They said that the colonies might tax themselves. The colonial assemblies took no other action but protestation. The agents presented the colonial objections to taxation by the British Parliament. They urged that revenue should be obtained from the colonial assemblies. Grenville asked, "Can you agree on the proportions each colony should raise?" They admitted the impossibility of agreement. Grenville proceeded with his legislation. In America the act raised a storm. Royal officials were attacked by mobs. Agreements not to import British goods were formed among the merchants. Delegates from the majority of the colonies came together in the Stamp Act Congress. The delegates met to protest Grenville's measure. The resolution of the Congress was expressed in moderate terms. It raised a fundamental issue. This issue was taxation without representation.—LUNT: *History of England*

By permission of Harper & Brothers Publishers.

5. VARIED IN POSITION OF SUBJECT

Vary your sentences according to the meaning you wish to convey. To emphasize a word, phrase, or clause, place it at the beginning or at the end of the sentences. Do not, however, sacrifice naturalness or clarity.

Frequently place a word or words before the complete subject. Most pupils overuse the simple sentence beginning with the subject.

Use both subject-first and subject-not-first sentences.

ADVERB   *Grimly* the garrison held out, waiting for the relief that never came.

EXPLETIVE AND VERB   *There is* a special gaiety in Calgary at Stampede time.

(*There* and *it* are often used to invert sentences.)

PREPOSITIONAL PHRASE   *With its six-foot wingspread and its soaring flight,* the eagle is one of the most spectacular birds of prey.

ADVERB CLAUSE   *Although billions of snowflakes fall to the ground,* no two of them are exactly alike.

PARTICIPIAL PHRASE   *Buzzing angrily,* the jets shot across the sky.

INFINITIVE PHRASE   *To secure for themselves certain basic rights,* the English barons forced King John to sign the *Magna Carta.*

NOUN CLAUSE AS OBJECT OF VERB   *What we learn by experience* we remember longest.

ADVERB AND PREDICATE ADJECTIVES   *How daring and self-sufficient* were the free trappers of the old frontier.

PRACTICE 18. Building Subject-not-first Sentences

Revise each sentence by placing a word or words before the complete subject. Then tell what grammatical event or elements you placed before the subject.

A. 1. Walt Disney is well loved for his contribution to the happiness of the world.
   2. Children and adults everywhere shout their unqualfied approval of his work in every conceivable tongue and dialect.
   3. Dale Carnegie says of him. "He made a fortune out of a mouse and three pigs."
   4. Mickey Mouse, the first of Disney's many successes, has become an international figure, achieving a fame equalled by few living persons.
   5. The idea for Mickey Mouse was born when Disney befriended a playful mouse on the floor of an old wooden garage.
   6. He recalled the mouse years later when his cartoon, "Oswald and the Rabbit", failed to arouse interest.

B. 1. Disney, capitalizing on the success of Mickey Mouse, introduced new characters.
   2. He added Minnie Mouse to provide romantic interest for Mickey.
   3. Donald Duck, Pluto Pup, and many other beloved characters soon came from Mr. Disney's studio.
   4. *Three Little Pigs* was the greatest success in the history of animated cartoons up to its time.
   5. His longer pictures, beginning with *Snow White*, stamped cartoons as a striking, original, and beautiful movie art form.
   6. Disney puts whatever profits he makes back into his great love, his pictures.

6. VARIED IN POSITION OF MODIFIERS

ADJECTIVE AFTER NOUN   Occasionally place adjectives after the nouns they modify.

In these regions, hot, arid, and barren, most of the rainfall evaporates.
The Camembert, velvety-crusted and creamy-centred, was Dr. Adams' favourite cheese.

SOMETHING BETWEEN SUBJECT AND VERB

Occasionally place adjectives, an adverb, an infinitive, or a parenthetic or adverb clause or phrase between the subject and the verb. Use this arrangement only if the sentence sounds natural.

The royal barge, like an ancient Roman galley, glided along under the rhythmic dip of many oars.
The winters in England, though cold enough to be stimulating, are not so cold as to interfere seriously with most occupations.

7. PARTICIPLES FOR STYLE

Use participial phrases in place of some clauses, sentences, or compound predicates. Participles add meaning and compactness to a sentence.

WEAK   The tall sailing ship towered above me as I stood on the dock. It seemed like a pale ghost in the moonlight.

FORCEFUL   The tall sailing ship, towering above me as I stood on the dock, seemed like a pale ghost in the moonlight.

PRACTICE 19. Using Participles

Improve these sentences by substituting participles for some of the verbs in principal or subordinate clauses.

1. Robert E. Peary, who was brought up on the coast of Maine, acquired at an early age a deep love for outdoor life.
2. Peary completed a course in civil engineering at Bowdoin College, and he first worked as a surveyor for a private company and then entered the service of the United States government.
3. In a Washington bookstore one day he found a paper which described the interior of Greenland.
4. In 1886 Peary, who was fired with enthusiasm for the North, applied for a leave of absence and sailed for Greenland.
5. Five years later the Academy of Natural Sciences supplied him with the money which was needed to lead a second expedition.
6. He explored the frozen country by sledge, and he proved on his second trip that Greenland is an island.

7. On his eighth voyage, which was made in 1909, Peary reached the North Pole and planted there the flag of the United States.

8. Especially happy at his success was his daughter Marie, who was born in the far North and was called by the Eskimos "the snow baby."

8. Appositives for Variety

Use appositives to save words and improve sentence structure. Unless you write better than the oridinary pupil in high school, you should use about twice as many appositives as you are in the habit of using.

WEAK Samuel Johnson was a man to dominate the conversation in any company.   He was a scholar, an essayist, a lexicographer, and a moralist.

FORCEFUL Samuel Johnson—scholar, essayist, lexicographer, and moralist —was a man to dominate the conversation in any company.

PRACTICE 20. Using Appositives

In each of the following, combine the sentences by substituting an appositive for one of them.

1. On his first day in a fashionable school at Ascot, Winston Churchill was whipped twice.   He was a small, red-headed, big-eared boy of seven.
2. At twelve Winston entered Harrow.   It is one of the most famous private schools in England.
3. His mother was an American.   She was a famous beauty of London society.
4. At Harrow, Winston ranked high in two fields.   He was the school champion in fencing and gained a mastery of English.
5. In later life Churchill once said that if he were a teacher he would whip a boy for only one reason.   Any boy deserved a birching, he believed, for not knowing English.

6. At Harrow he prepared to take the examinations for entrance to Sandhurst. This military school is England's West Point.
7. When he graduated from Sandhurst at the age of twenty, he was commissioned as a sublieutenant in a famous cavalry regiment. His regiment was
   Her Majesty's Fourth Hussars.
8. As an officer of hussars Churchill wore on his head a busby. This is a tall
   fur hat with a beautiful plume and a bag hanging from the top over the
   right side.

D.   Pleasing the Ear

Read the first draft of your story, essay, or report aloud and listen
to it carefully. Good writing has a pleasing sound and cadence.

1. SOUND AND SENSE

Make your style fit your content. Use short, staccato sentences to
describe rapid action.

It was all a trap. Suddenly those close forests would bristle with rifle
barrels. Ironlike brigades would appear in the rear. They were all going
to be sacrificed.—STEPHEN CRANE

Use longer, slower-paced sentences to convey a quiet mood.

The tide of darkness flowed on swiftly; and with tropical suddenness
a swarm of stars came out above the shadowy earth, while I lingered yet, my
hand resting lightly on my ship's rail as if on the shoulders of a trusted friend.
—JOSEPH CONRAD

The round open vowels and the consonants *l*, *m*, *n*, and *r* give
ease and a liquid quality to the sound: *momentum, lowly, mole, moonlight, nevermore, rolling.*

When lilacs last in the dooryard bloom'd,
And the great star early droop'd in the western sky in the night,
I mourn'd, and yet shall mourn with ever-returning spring.
—WALT WHITMAN

2. PURPOSELESS REPETITION

Don't repeat a sound or a word at too close an interval without a
good reason. Purposeless repetition is a mark of the writer who is too
lazy to reword his sentence or hunt for a synonym.

PURPOSELESS REPETITION OF A SOUND   Tom took the train to Toledo.
REWORDED   Tom caught the train for Toledo

AWKWARD REPETITION OF SYLLABLES   The sound of a shot resounded through
    the cave.
REWORDED   The sound of a shot echoed through the cave.

LAZY REPETITION OF WORDS The music at the Thanksgiving dance was very nice and the decorations were nice and, all in all, there was a nice turnout at the dance.

REWORDED The music and decorations at the Thanksgiving dance were topnotch, and there was a good turnout for the affair.

3. PURPOSEFUL REPETITION

Purposeful repetition of a sound may create the proper atmosphere; purposeful repetition of a word may drive home a point.

When *befriended,* remember it; when you *befriend,* forget it.—BENJAMIN FRANKLIN

My idea of *an agreeable person* is *a person who agrees* with me.—BENJAMIN DISRAELI

A wise man is never less *alone* than when he is *alone.*—JONATHAN SWIFT

Even a *waiter* finally comes to him who *waits.*

At a *glance* I didn't like Judy, and during the nine weeks at camp I had more than a *glance* at her.

And the silken sad uncertain rustling of each purple curtain

Thrilled me—filled me with fantastic terrors never felt before.

—EDGAR ALLAN POE

PRACTICE 21. Improving the Sound of Sentences

Improve the following sentences by eliminating unnecessary repetitions of sounds or words.

Example:

If the furniture cannot be repaired, we shall furnish you with new furniture.
If the furniture cannot be repaired, we shall replace it.

1. Every pupil in our school takes examinations at the termination of each term and is marked according to the marks on these examinations.
2. When you asked me to come, you didn't tell me what time you wanted me to come.
3. In a friendly fashion Frank tried to make friends by speaking gently to the unfortunate foundling.
4. If that time is not convenient for you, write and tell us when it will be convenient for you to have our repairman call to repair you oil burner.
5. The magazine is a monthly magazine coming out on the 25th of every month.
6. That is a country that offers to the oppressed all that they desire.
7. It is not profitable for a company to employ a careless employee whose carelessness results in costly accidents.
8. I fear you were not near enough to hear the weary speaker.
9. Tom tried to tidy up the tent before the two tenderfeet returned.

4. Too Many Modifiers

Don't overload your writing with useless modifiers.

CLUMSY The gray-coated, undersized, furtive-looking man hurried down the shadowy, winding, cobblestoned alley.

BETTER The furtive-looking man hurried down the cobblestoned alley.

5. Jerky Rhythm

Don't break the flow of a sentence by chopping it up into small units set off by commas.

JERKY The Trident Cup, we felt sure, would go to Don, who had, in the junior races, brought his sloop in first.

SMOOTH We felt sure that the Trident Cup would go to Don, who had brought his sloop in first in the junior races.

6. Rhyme

In prose avoid rhyme and a regular rhythm (metre).

RHYME AND METRE If Dad and Marty have their way we'll have that outdoor grill by May.

BETTER If Dad and Marty can manage it, our outdoor grill will be finished by May.

RHYME AND METRE They tried to win at any cost. They knew not that the game was lost.

BETTER Fighting on with a never-say-die spirit, they failed to realize the game had already been lost.

PRACTICE 22. Improving the Sound of Sentences

Improve the sound of the following sentences. Two of the sentences are good.

A. 1. Down the foggy, muddy, murky street slowly crept the thin, sinister, silent figure of the mysterious whistler.

   2. If you make a good impression in a job interview, you have a good chance of getting the job for which you had the interview.

   3. If the furniture cannot be repaired, we shall furnish you with new furniture.

   4. The big, bouncy, cheerful, always-smiling quarterback jumped eagerly to his feet as the keen-eyed, quick-tempered coach brusquely threw him a short, sharp word of command.

   5. There were papers on the desk, papers under the desk, papers in the wastebasket, and papers on the floor—mute evidence of Jerry's struggles to write a five-hundred word theme.

B. 1. Give me Jack's letter to mail, and I'll mail it without fail in the box on Taylor Street.

2. Come on in and shut the door and don't track mud on Mom's clean floor.

3. The parrot, Aunt Marion discovered, to her everlasting embarrassment, could be counted on to startle company with phrases which, long ago, it had picked up from its former owner, a sea captain.

4. This action has been taken with the consent of the community and for the good of the community.

5. The leaders that our country chooses should be chosen intelligently from all parts of the country.

PRACTICE 23. Different Ways of Saying the Same Thing

Here are seven ways of saying "Isn't he thin!"

How thin he is!
He is thin as a rail.
What a thin man!
Did you ever see so thin a man!
There are few men as thin as he.
Isn't he a roly-poly?   (Said ironically)
Here comes another Ichabod Crane.

With these suggestions find at least four ways of saying each of the following:

1. He is exceedingly wise.
2. What a pigmy he is!
3. The building is unusually tall.
4. The sunset was lovely.
5. How quiet the lake is!

PRACTICE 24. Changing the Subject

Following each of these sentences there is one word or more in parentheses. Give the meaning of the sentence in another sentence, the subject of which is the word or words in parentheses.

Example:

Why do you look at me so reproachfully, as if I were the guilty party? (Your reproachful looks)
Your reproachful looks would imply that I am the guilty party.

1. I have a veneration for the hard hand, although it may be crooked and coarse.   (The hard hand)

2. I thank God that my faculties are not much impaired.   (My faculties)
3. I have loved Jacob, but I have hated Esau.   (Jacob .. Esau)
4. Actions are better than words for the basis of judgment.   (I)
5. Two men and no third are honourable to me.   (I)
6. The enthusiastic recognition of certain qualities in others turns most of us into hero-worshippers.   (Hero-worship)
7. Is there a person who thinks of turning into ridicule our great and ardent hope of a world to come?   (Who)
8. It is said that Solomon's axe spared certain cedars when he was busy with his temple.   (There are cedars)
9. A sickening suspicion was inspired within the fortress by the death-like stillness which reigned there.   (A death-like stillness)

PRACTICE 25.   Review of Building Pleasing, Forceful Sentences

In one or more of the ways suggested in this section improve each sentence or change its grammatical structure.

A. 1. Nothing is more welcome than an unexpected holiday, in my opinion.
  2. The French National Library, which was founded in 1367, is the oldest library in Europe.
  3. Her narrow, green, impenetrable eyes smouldered with sullen savagery.
  4. The retina of the eye is sensitive to light, like the film of a camera.
  5. My rubber boots have had many adventures.
  6. Perhaps you have wondered how men are able to foretell the weather.
  7. Captain Larsen said that if I ever happened to be in want of employment, I should remember that as long as he had a ship I had a ship too.
  8. The society again repeated the concert a second time for the benefit of the building fund.
  9. Now these treasures, which are bound in purple and gold, are preserved in the National Library.
 10. It was about eight o'clock on a July evening, and Fred and I were hiking toward camp.

B. 1. The farmer carved the turkey with a sharp knife that didn't require whetting.
  2. The enemy is preparing to slaughter our people, devastate our fields, burn out houses, and devour our poultry.
  3. The new beginner quickly snatched his hat as soon as the bell rang.
  4. It was dastardly of Chilton to dynamite a building in which women and children were hard at work.
  5. That tall building is built beautifully with its massive dome, and it has mighty columns to beautify it.
  6. John Singer Sargent's father was a well-known physician and surgeon, and he taught the boy the value of keen observation and hard work.

7. Michael Faraday invented the dynamo after years of experimentation, and thus he paved the way for the work of Morse, Field, and Bell.

8. After escaping from a South American jungle, Lieutenant Harmon said that he certainly was thankful for his years of football.

9. However, temperatures remained normal yesterday, and little of the snow and ice melted.

10. In my opinion, Oslo is a comfortable city to live in.

E.   Imitating Model Sentences

PRACTICE 26. Imitating Models

Following the rhythm and construction of these models, make sentences of your own as effective as you can devise.

Example:

Model: The more irksome any habit is in its formation, the more pleasantly and satisfactorily it sticks to you when formed.—TOM HUGHES

Imitation: The more pleasant any incident is in our experience, the more lasting and valuable will it be in our memory.

1. Except a living man, there is nothing more wonderful than a book!—CHARLES KINGSLEY

2. One of the best rules in Conversation is, never to say a thing which any of the Company can reasonably wish we had rather left unsaid.—JONATHAN SWIFT
(You may omit the old fashioned capitals.)

3. Savoury was the smell of fried pilchard and hake; more savoury still that of roast porpoise; most savoury of all that of fifty huge squab pies.—CHARLES KINGSLEY

4. "Drown me, will you?" said I; "I should like to see you!"—GEORGE BORROW, *Lavengro.*

5. The old gods, worshipped by youth and beauty, are dead; and no immortal power can place a living heart in this stony bosom or lend to these matchless limbs the warm flexibility and rosiness of life.—LAFCADIO HEARN, *Fantastics and Other Fancies.*

6. The stars in their silent courses looked down through the crannies of the tomb and passed on; the birds sang above him and flew to other lands; the lizards ran noiselessly above his bed of stone and as noiselessly departed; the spider at last ceased to renew her web of magical silk; the years came and went as before, but for the dead there was no rest.—LAFCADIO HEARN, *A Dead Love.*

7. Imagine a man in the Sahara regretting that he had no sand for his hourglass.—GILBERT KEITH CHESTERTON, *A Piece of Chalk.*

8. He crossed, snake-like, toward the fire. There that bullying fellow had stood with his back to it—confound his impudence!—as if the place belonged to him.—JOHN GALSWORTHY, *The Stoic.*

9. The night had come, black, inevitable, long. And to those who have no house the night is a wild beast. In every chimney a hollow wind spoke its uncontent.—MARY WEBB, *Over the Hills and Far Away.*

F. Evaluating Sentence Structure

A FIGHT WITH A CANNON

A gun that breaks its mooring becomes suddenly some indescribable supernatural beast. It is a machine which transforms itself into a monster. This mass turns upon its wheels, has the rapid movements of a billiard ball; rolls with the rolling, pitches with the pitch, goes, comes, pauses, seems to meditate; resumes its course, rushes along the ship from end to end like an arrow, circles about, springs aside, evades, rears, breaks, kills, exterminates. It seems as if the power of evil hidden in what we call inanimate objects finds a vent and bursts suddenly out. The mad mass has the bounds of a panther, the weight of the elephant, the agility of the mouse, the obstinacy of the axe, the unexpectedness of the surge, the rapidity of lightning, the deafness of the tomb. It weighs ten thousand pounds, and it rebounds like a child's ball. What is to be done? How to end this? How to control this enormous brute of bronze? In what way can one attack it?—VICTOR HUGO, *'Ninety-three.*

SAMPLE COMMENT ON SENTENCE STRUCTURE

The sentence structure used by the author in developing this passage greatly enhances its effectiveness. The variety in types of sentences, alone, protects it from any charge of monotony.

Moreover, the structure of each sentence suits its purpose. The author's effective use of parallel structure is perhaps most noticeable. The third sentence contains several series of parallel expressions, each series different and yet appropriate. The series of single verbs "goes, comes, pauses" emphasizes how numerous the cannon's movements are, and how swift and varied. The sudden effect of the series imitates the suddenness of the movements. In the same sentence, the series of parallel phrases "rolls with the rolling, pitches with the pitch" suggests the slower movements of the cannon, the pauses between the swift movements. And the parallelism of the whole sentence draws attention to the ideas expressed in the sentence, just because of the repetitive structure.

Similarly, the parallel structure of "The mad mass . . . the tomb" is effective. The monotony of the constant repetition emphasizes the myriad features of "the mass", and the very similarity of their description emphasizes their differences.

Closely allied with the above sentence is the one beginning "It weighs ten thousand pounds." The partial balance emphasizes the paradoxical contrast in the cannon's qualities—heavy and agile.

Equally effective in emphasizing the danger the cannon offers, and the helplessness of the people, is the series of short questions at the end of the paragraph. The fact that these sentences are short, draws our attention to them. They stand out in contrast to the long loose sentences preceding them. Their effectiveness lies particularly, however, in the fact that they are all rhetorical questions; the assertive tone in which the cannon's nature was described is gone. Emphasized now is the uncertainty, the hopelessness of the situation. "What is to be done?"

PRACTICE 27. Evaluating Sentence Structure

For the following paragraph write a critical evaluation in which you consider the merits of the sentence structure.

Into the teeth of the gale pushed this pigmy caravan—a gale that was born on the flat shores of Hudson Bay, that breasted the slopes of the Height of Land, that raged across the blank white expanse of Lac Seul, and was now shrieking down, dire and desolate, to the ice-bound and battlemented borders of Lake Superior. It was a wind that had weight. Tom Moore felt its vast and impalpable force, as he leaned against it when he stopped for breath. It assaulted him—it tore steadily, relentlessly, at him, as if seeking to devour—it lashed the stinging grains into his face, and into the open mouths of his panting dogs— it smoothed out the crumpled trail as the wake of a ship is obliterated by closing waters—till, a moment after his passing, the snow ridges lay trackless and unruffled. Still, however insignificant in these formless wastes, that silent progress held steadily on; and so it had held from early morn. These black specks on a measureless counterpane, guided by some unfailing instinct that lurked far back in the big half-breed's brain, were making an unswerving line for a wooded point that thrust out a faint and purple finger, far ahead in the gathering dusk. As they drew slowly in, the wind began to abate its force, and Tom, peering out from the mass of ice that was cemented to his mouth and eyes, looked for some sheltering haven. The dogs smelled the land, and more eagerly flung themselves into the taut traces, while over them gathered the shadows of the welcome woods.—ALAN SULLIVAN, *The Essence of a Man*.

Reprinted by permission of the publishers, J. M. Dent (Canada) Limited.

Chapter 14

Mastering Connected Paragraphs

MAINTAINING UNITY

Most of the writing you will have to do will require more than single paragraphs. It is well, then, to learn how to write themes consisting of more than one paragraph. You have learned already that sentences must have unity—that is, they must deal with one central theme. You have learned, too, that paragraphs must possess unity and coherence. The same is true of themes of more than one paragraph.

The most important way to maintain unity of theme is to see that every sentence, every paragraph deals with the principal topic. If the writer does not deviate from the topic, then the exercise will possess unity. Sometimes this is made easier by directional signals which indicate to the reader just what the writer is going to write about. For example, he may say, "There are three points I want to make . . ." If he does this, he is not likely to wander from the point until he has told the reader what the three points are.

Examine the following theme, which discusses the fundamental causes of war.

THE FUNDAMENAL CAUSES OF WAR

Although there are many conditions which contribute to war, *imperialism, militarism, and nationalism* are *its three fundamental causes. Imperialism* is the acquisition of backward areas by an industrially developed country for the purpose of obtaining materials, markets for surplus products, and places for investment of capital. It is true that the conquest of backward areas is more or less essential to the prosperity of the different countries. The nations realize it and are willing to go to any ends to acquire such territory. The nations which have succeeded in increasing their territory are considered the greatest nations. Italy, Germany, and Japan were good examples of imperialistic countries.

To increase its land or to continue to hold land, a country must follow a course of *militarism*. Militarism is spending large sums of money to build up a powerful army and navy. As long as there is rivalry for land, there will be suspicion and fear. As long as there is fear, there will be militarism. The nation that owns certain desired land says that it must maintain a large fighting force to defend its property. The underdog nation must equal a more powerful rival for fear that the enemy may attempt to add to its possessions. Thus the two nations build. When other countries see what is happening, they become fearful for their own well-being and join the race. Thus the arms-building contest goes on until each nation feels that she is unbeatable and is willing to display her strength at the slightest provocation.

Nationalism now plays its part in starting the war. By definition, it is the feeling which binds together people of the same land, history, race, and customs. It is this feeling which diplomats toy with to urge the people to conflict. First, people are shown the battleships, airplane forces, and the army. They are told that their country has the greatest fighting force in the world. Then the government, if it desires war, points out the rank injustices that their nation is being submitted to by some foreign country. Usually this injustice is imagined or, at the least, exaggerated. Feeling throughout the country becomes strong. Nationalism becomes greater and greater. In the other country the same state of affairs exists. Only a match is needed to touch off the explosion. It usually comes in the form of a comparatively minor quarrel, perhaps over some rights in Africa or elsewhere. Each country reasons that it is the stronger. Being anxious to come to blows, they soon do and the war is on. The war could not, of course, have occurred without land greed, or imperialism, or without fighting forces which justify great national pride, or nationalism.—PUPIL

1. What is the topic of each paragraph?
2. By what method or methods is each paragraph developed?

In order to point the way for the reader, the author has stated in the first sentence the three fundamental causes of war. In Para. 1 the writer defines and writes about the first of the three causes, imperialism. In Para. 2 he writes about militarism, the second fundamental cause. In Para. 3 he writes about nationalism, the third cause. Notice that the writer manages to include in the last sentence a brief summary of all three of the causes he had set out to consider.

BRIDGES FOR COHERENCE

You will have noticed that the three paragraphs are further held together by connecting words and phrases. The most obvious of these have been printed in italics. Go through the theme and underline the other connectives that help bind the essay into a closely knit and clearly defined whole.

PRACTICE 1. Unity and Coherence in a Multi-paragraphed Essay

Point out how the author of the following exposition has maintained unity and coherence in his theme.

PUNISHMENT AND CONSCIENCE

Punishment is a blessed thing. I pity the young who have grown up without it. I pity the old, the masters and the mistresses of households, whom nobody dares to contradict, who are never, never put into the corner or whipped as they deserve. I pity the kings and emperors who have gone murderous-mad because no one stood up to them or made them behave themselves. But punishment is of no positive value; only negative.

For any positive help towards living a nobler life, apart from the influence of friendship and of education, I can only fall back on that real and widespread possession of the human race of which we have already spoken: that instinct which shows itself in the existence of the Internal Censor. It is an instinct both moral and aesthetic, which rejects things both because they are bad and because they are ugly, and pursues things both because they are good and because they are beautiful.

Philosophers insist on drawing a distinction between these two, but I confess that I never can feel it very real. As far as I can analyze my own feelings, I should say that the motive which keeps me from a bad action is a feeling that, as I contemplate it, I do not like the look of it or the smell of it. I feel it to be ugly or foul or not decent—not the sort of thing with which I want to be associated. And, similarly, the thing that nerves me towards a good but difficult action is a feeling that it seems beautiful or fine, the sort of thing that I love as I look at it and would like to have for my own.

Though not infallible, this moral of aesthetic instinct is a true fact. I believe it to be generally very strong in young people, at any rate in those who have real life in them, and, though often misdirected while they make their usual experiments, it has a way of correcting its own errors and ultimately finding its right course. It, and perhaps it alone, answers the most troublesome of all questions which the cynic can put to the moralist: "Granted that it is useful to society that I should be honest, why should I mind about society if I can find my own profit in stealing?"—GILBERT MURRAY

PRACTICE 2. Unity of Theme

Make an outline showing the orderly arrangement of details that go to developing the theme "Punishment and Conscience".

PRACTICE 3. Bridges for Coherence

Underline the connective words and phrases that bind the paragraphs together in "Punishment and Conscience".

DEVELOPING A THEME

In Chapter 3 (p. 111) you learned how sentences are joined together to develop paragraphs. In a similar manner, and by the same methods, paragraphs are joined together to develop complete themes.

These methods may be listed as:

Supplying Details
Supplying Examples
Using Comparisons and Contrasts
Using Cause and Effect
Using Definitions
Using Two or More Methods Together
Using Humour or Humorous Juxtaposition

PRACTICE 4. Developing a Theme

By analyzing the paragraph arrangement, show how each of the following themes is developed.

CEDRIC'S DINING-HALL

In a hall, the height of which was greatly disproportioned to its extreme length and width, a long oaken table, formed of planks rough-hewn from the forest, and which had scarcely received any polish, stood ready prepared for the evening meal of Cedric the Saxon. The roof, composed of beams and rafters, had nothing to divide the apartment from the sky except the planking and thatch; there was a huge fireplace at either end of the hall, but as the chimneys were constructed in a very clumsy manner, at least as much of the smoke found its way into the apartment as escaped by the proper vent. The constant vapour which this occasioned had polished the rafters and beams of the low-browed hall, by encrusting them with a black varnish of soot. On the sides of the apartment hung implements of war and of the chase, and there were at each corner folding-doors, which gave access to other parts of the extensive building.

The other appointments of the mansion partook of the rude simplicity of the Saxon period, which Cedric piqued himself upon maintaining. The floor was composed of earth mixed with lime, trodden into a hard substance, such as is often employed in flooring our modern barns. For about one quarter of the length of the apartment, the floor was raised by a step, and this space, which was called the dais, was occupied only by the principal members of the family, and visitors of distinction. For this purpose, a table richly covered with scarlet cloth was placed transversely across the platform, from the middle of which ran the longer and lower board, at which the domestics and inferior persons fed, down towards the bottom of the hall. The whole resembled the form of the figure T, or some of those ancient dinner tables, which, arranged on the same principle, may be still seen in the antique colleges of Oxford or Cambridge. Massive chairs and settles of carved oak were placed upon the dais, and over these seats and the more elevated table was placed a canopy of cloth, which served in some degree to protect the dignitaries who occupied that distinguished station from the weather, and especially from the rain, which in some places found its way through the ill-constructed roof.

The walls of this upper end of the hall, as far as the dais extended, were covered with hangings or curtains, and upon the floor was a carpet, both of which were adorned with some attempts at tapestry, or embroidery, executed with brilliant or rather gaudy colouring. Over the lower range of table, the roof, as we have noticed, had no covering; the rough plastered walls were left bare, and the rude earthen floor was uncarpeted; the board was uncovered by a cloth, and rude massive benches supplied the place of chairs.

In the centre of the upper table were placed two chairs more elevated than the rest, for the master and mistress of the family, who presided over the scene of hospitality, and from doing so derived their Saxon title of honour, which signifies "the Dividers of Bread".

To each of these chairs was added a footstool, curiously carved and inlaid with ivory, which mark of distinction was peculiar to them. One of these seats was at present occupied by Cedric the Saxon, who, though but in rank a thane, or, as the Normans called him, a franklin, felt, at the delay of his evening meal, an irritable impatience, which might have become an alderman, whether of ancient or of modern times.—SIR WALTER SCOTT, *Ivanhoe*.

CHEERFULNESS

I have always preferred cheerfulness to mirth. The latter I consider as an act, the former as a habit of the mind. Mirth is short and transient, cheerfulness fixed and permanent. Those are often raised into the greatest transports of mirth who are subject to the greatest depressions of melancholy: on the contrary, cheerfulness, though it does not give the mind such an exquisite gladness, prevents us from falling into any depths of sorrow. Mirth is like a flash of lightning, that breaks through a gloom of clouds, and glitters for a moment; cheerfulness keeps up a kind of day-light in the mind, and fills it with a steady and perpetual serenity.

Men of austere principles look upon mirth as too wanton and dissolute for a state of probation, and as filled with a certain triumph and insolence of heart, that is inconsistent with a life which is every moment obnoxious to the greatest dangers. Writers of this complexion have observed, that the sacred Person who was the great pattern of perfection was never seen to laugh.

Cheerfulness of mind is not liable to any of these exceptions: it is of a serious and composed nature; it does not throw the mind into a condition improper for the present state of humanity, and is very conspicuous in the characters of those who are looked upon as the greatest philosophers among the heathens, as well as among those who have been deservedly esteemed as saints and holy men among Christians.

If we consider cheerfulness in three lights, with regard to ourselves, to those we converse with, and to the great Author of our being, it will not a little recommend itself on each of these accounts. The man who is possessed of this excellent frame of mind is not only easy in his thoughts, but a perfect master of all the powers and faculties of his soul: his imagination is always clear, and his judgment undisturbed: his temper is even and unruffled, whether in action or in solitude. He comes with a relish to all those goods which nature has provided for him, tastes all the pleasures of the creation which are poured about him, and does not feel the full weight of those accidental evils which may befall him.

If we consider him in relation to the persons whom he converses with, it naturally produces love and good-will towards him. A cheerful mind is not only disposed to be affable and obliging, but raises the same good humour in those who come within its influence. A man finds himself pleased, he does not know why, with the cheerfulness of his companion: it is like a sudden sun-shine that awakens a secret delight in the mind, without her attending to it: the heart rejoices of its own accord, and naturally flows out into friendship and benevolence towards the person who has so kindly an effect upon it.

When I consider this cheerful state of mind in its third relation, I cannot but look upon it as a constant habitual gratitude to the great Author of nature. An inward cheerfulness is an implicit praise and thanksgiving to Providence under all its dispensations: it is a kind of acquiescence in the state wherein we are placed, and a secret approbation of the divine will in his conduct towards men.

There are but two things, which, in my opinion, can reasonably deprive us of this cheerfulness of heart. The first of these is the sense of guilt. A man who lives in a state of vice and impenitence can have no title to that evenness and tranquility of mind which is the health of the soul, and the natural effect of virtue and innocence. Cheerfulness in an ill man deserves a harder name than language can furnish us with, and is many degrees beyond what we commonly call folly or madness.

Atheism, by which I mean a disbelief of a Supreme Being, and consequently of a future state, under whatsoever titles it shelters itself, may likewise very reasonably deprive a man of this cheerfulness of temper. There is something so particularly gloomy and offensive to human nature in the prospect of non-existence, that I cannot but wonder, with many excellent writers, how it is possible for a man to outlive the expectation of it. For my own part, I think the being of a God is so little to be doubted, that it is almost the only truth we are sure of, and such a truth as we meet with in every object, in every occurrence, and in every thought. If we look into the characters of this tribe of infidels, we generally find they are made up of pride, spleen, and cavil: it is indeed no wonder that men who are uneasy to themselves should be so to the rest of the world: and how is it possible for a man to be otherwise than uneasy in himself, who is in danger every moment of losing his entire existence, and dropping into nothing?

The vicious man and atheist have therefore no pretence to cheerfulness, and would act very unreasonably should they endeavour after it. It is impossible for any one to live in good-humour, and enjoy his present existence, who is apprehensive either of torment or of annihilation; of being miserable, or of not being at all.

After having mentioned these two great principles, which are destructive of cheerfulness in their own nature, as well as in right reason, I cannot think of any other that ought to banish this happy temper from a virtuous mind. Pain and sickness, shame and reproach, poverty and old age, nay, death itself, considering the shortness of their duration, and the advantage we may reap from them, do not deserve the name of evils: a good mind may bear up under them with fortitude, with indolence, and with cheerfulness of heart. The tossing of a tempest does not discompose him, which he is sure will bring him to a joyful harbour.

A man who uses his best endeavours to live according to the dictates of virtue and right reason, has two perpetual sources of cheerfulness, in the consideration of his own nature, and of that Being on whom he has a dependence. If he looks into himself, he cannot but rejoice in that existence which is so lately bestowed upon him, and which, after millions of ages, will be still new, and still in its beginning. How many self-congratulations naturally arise in the mind, when it reflects on this its entrance into eternity, when it takes a view of those improveable faculties, which in a few years, and even at his first setting out, have made so considerable a progress, and which will be still receiving an increase of perfection, and consequently an increase of happiness? The consciousness of such a being spreads a perpetual diffusion of joy through the soul of a virtuous man, and makes him look upon himself every moment as more happy than he knows how to conceive.

The second source of cheerfulness to a good mind, is its consideration of that Being on whom we have our dependence, and in whom, though we behold him as yet but in the first faint discoveries of his perfections, we see everything that we can imagine as great, glorious, or amiable. We find ourselves everywhere upheld by his goodness, and surrounded with an immensity of love and mercy. In short, we depend upon a Being, whose power qualifies him to make us happy by an infinity of means, whose goodness and truth engage him to make those happy who desire it of him, and whose unchangeableness will secure us in this happiness to all eternity.

Such considerations, which every one should perpetually cherish in his thoughts, will banish from us all that secret heaviness of heart which unthinking men are subject to when they lie under no real affliction, all that anguish which we may feel from any evil that actually oppresses us, to which I may likewise add those little cracklings of mirth and folly, that are apter to betray virtue than support it; and establish in us such an even and cheerful temper, as makes us pleasing to ourselves, to those with whom we converse, and to him whom we were made to please.—JOSEPH ADDISON in *The Spectator*.

Chapter 15

Some Devices of Effective Prose

READERS of good prose, admiring the beauty of its language and structure, seldom analyze the piece to learn how the effect has been secured; yet had they done so, they would have had an additional source of delight in the recognition of the skill of the artist. It would be impossible to detail all the devices by which authors have enhanced the effectiveness of their writing, but if we can discover a few of these and recognize the deliberation with which they have been made, we have a stimulation for personal endeavour to secure whatever effect we desire.

ON THE USE OF MODELS

Creative writing follows the mastery of technique, though there is no reason why the student should not make the occasional essay as he learns. For the learning process there is no more effective method than the study and imitation of good models. Professor Lounsbury says:

"The art of writing, like that of painting and sculpture, is an imitative art. Accordingly the culture and perception of beauty necessary to produce success in it are best and soonest acquired, not by the study of grammatical and rhetorical text-books, but by the imitation, conscious or unconscious, of some one, or some number of those whom the race regard as its great literary representatives. Different minds, or minds in different grades of development, will exhibit preferences for different authors. The choice is not a matter of moment, provided the one chosen is worthy and appeals to the chooser, not because the study of him is a duty, but because it is a delight. To become thoroughly conversant with the work of a great writer, to be influenced by his method of giving utterance to his ideas, to feel profoundly the power and beauty of his style, is worth more for the development of expression than the mastery of all the rhetorical rules that were ever invented. This has been the inspiration and salvation of numberless men, who have never seen the inside of an institute of learning. He who of his own accord has sat reverently at the feet of the great masters of English literature, need have no fear that their spirit will not inform, so far as in him lies, the spirit of their disciple. Connected with it, too, there is incidentally one further benefit. Constant familiarity with the language of authors of the first rank, imparts in time that almost intuitive sense of what is right or wrong in usage which distinguishes the cultivated man of letters from the sciolist who bases his judgment upon what he has found in grammars and manuals."

Similar evidence is given by Robert Louis Stevenson, one of the most finished stylists who has written in English.

Whenever I read a book or passage that particularly pleased me, in which a thing was said or an effect rendered with propriety, in which there was either some perspicuous force or some happy distinction in style, I must sit down at once and set myself to ape that quality. . . . That, like it or not, is the way to learn to write; whether I have profited or not, that is the way. It was so Keats learned, and there was never a finer temperament for literature than Keats'; it was so, if we could trace it, that all men have learned.

ON KILLING ORIGINALITY

Perhaps I hear some one cry out, But this is not the way to become original! It is not; nor is there any way but to be born so. Nor yet, if you are born original, is there anything in this training that shall clip the wings of your originality. There can be none more original than Montaigne, neither could any one be more unlike Cicero, yet no craftsman can fail to see how much the one must have tried in his time to imitate the other. Burns is the very type of a prime force in letters; he was of all men the most imitative. Shakespeare himself, the imperial, proceeds directly from a school. It is only from a school that we can expect to have good writers; it is almost invariably from a school that great writers, these lawless exceptions, issue. Nor is there anything here that should astonish the inconsiderate. Before he can tell what cadences he prefers, the student should have tried all that are possible; before he can choose and preserve a fitting key of words, he should long have practised the literary scales; and it is only after years of such gymnastics that he can sit down at last, legions of words swarming to his call, dozens of turns of phrase simultaneously bidding for his choice, and he himself knowing what he wants to do and (within the narrow limits of a man's ability) able to do it."—ROBERT LOUIS STEVENSON, *A College Magazine.*

By permission of the publishers, Charles Scribner's Sons.

From here to the end of our course we shall be studying the devices by which the artist and the artificer have worked their magic—which is often simpler than the uninitiated believe.

The two models and imitative exercises which follow will give you an idea how models may be imitated. It is not always necessary to follow so closely as the first of these, but it is sometimes good judgment to do so.

Model:

THE STRANGER

By Lafcadio Hearn

The Italian had kept us all spellbound for hours, while a great yellow moon was climbing higher and higher above the leaves of the bananas that nodded weirdly at the windows. Within the great hall a circle of attentive listeners, —composed of that motley mixture of the wanderers of all nations, such as can be found only in New Orleans, and perhaps Marseilles,—sat in silence about the lamplit table, riveted by the speaker's dark eyes and rich voice. There was a natural music in those tones; the stranger changed as he spoke like a wizard weaving a spell. And speaking to each one in the tongue of his own land, he told them of the Orient. For he had been a wanderer in many lands; and afar off, touching the farther horn of the moonlight crescent, lay awaiting him a long, graceful vessel with a Greek name, which would unfurl her white wings for flight with the first ruddiness of morning.

"I see that you are a smoker," observed the stranger to his host as he rose to go. "May I have the pleasure of presenting you with a Turkish pipe? I brought it from Constantinople."

It was moulded of blood-red clay after a fashion of Moresque art, and fretted about its edges with gilded work like the ornamentation girdling the minarets of a mosque. And a faint perfume, as of the gardens of Damascus, clung to its gaudy bowl, whereupon were deeply stamped mysterious words in the Arabian tongue.

The voice had long ceased to utter its musical syllables. The guests had departed; the lamps were extinguished within. A single ray of moonlight breaking through the shrubbery without fell upon a bouquet of flowers, breathing out their perfumed souls into the night. Only the host remained—dreaming of moons larger than ours, and fiercer summers; minarets white and keen, piercing a cloudless sky, and the many-fountained pleasure-places of the East. And the pipe exhaled its strange and mystical perfume, like the scented breath of a summer's night in the rose-gardens of a Sultan. Above in deeps of amethyst, glimmered the everlasting lamps of heaven; and from afar, the voice of muezzin seemed to cry, in tones liquidly sweet as the voice of the stranger—

"All ye who are about to sleep, commend your souls to Him who never sleeps."

By arrangement with the publishers, Houghton, Mifflin Company.

Imitation:

THE LECTURER

(*After* Lafcadio Hearn)

The lecturer had held our close attention for an hour or more, while the heavens grew dark above the towers of the steeple that crowned the church. In the hall, a circle of fascinated listeners, composed of hero-worshipping school girls in a group typical of a church club, sat in silence about their leader's chair, awed by the speaker's marvellous story and clear, deep voice. There was a witchery in those tones. The lecturer gazed at us as she spoke, like one hypnotized, and speaking to us in the common parlance of the day, she told us of the Arctic. And as she talked, the listeners discovered a strange new land with her. For the first time, they beheld the rough, wild beauty of a Northern springtime, and struggled under the ice-mailed fist of the tyrant winter. They sensed the overpowering vastness of earth and sea and sky, and felt the loneliness of the Barren Lands. For the lecturer had the distinction of being the first white woman to live in the R.C.M.P. post at Chesterfield Inlet; and already the tongueless, voiceless waste was calling her back to her Northern home.

"Now, I would like to leave your leader something from my collection of souvenirs," observed the lecturer, before she left. "May I give you this Eskimo lamp? I brought it from Chesterfield Inlet."

It was cut from rich black soapstone, in the fashion of all primitive races, and smooth about the lid, with an edge like the tapering blade of a knife. And a faint odour, as of some light oil, clung to its black bowl, whereon was attached a small, crude handle.

The voice had long ceased to utter its bell-toned syllables. The club members had departed, leaving the hall in quiet darkness. A quiet wind, wandering through the belfry, shook a few golden notes from the chimes, winging from their Gothic arches into the night. Only the leader remained, dreaming of a climate colder than ours, and of months-long nights; northern lights, cathedral-arched and rainbow-tinted, shifting through the sky; and the daring courage of the adventurous nomads who dwelt beneath them; the endless blinding snows—nothing but mounds of ice and age-old rock, and hills of rock, and age-old ice, and snow, and snow, and still more snow.

And the lamp exhaled its oily odour, like the warm breath of a fat-fed fire in an icy igloo. Above, through the branches, flickered the eternal candles at the altars of Heaven; and from afar the choir of the Arctic winds seemed to sing, deep as the voice of the lecturer:

"All ye who love to brave the danger of a great adventure, come, try your strength in the romantic North."—PUPIL.

Model:

THE WINE-SHOP

(*A Tale of Two Cities*, Chapter V)

This wine-shop keeper was a bull-necked, martial-looking man of thirty, and he should have been of a hot temperament, for, although it was a bitter day, he wore no coat, but carried one slung over his shoulder. His shirt-sleeves were rolled up, too, and his brown arms were bare to the elbows. Neither did he wear anything more on his head than his own crisply curling, short dark hair. He was a dark man altogether, with good eyes and a good bold breadth between them. Good-humoured-looking on the whole, but implacable-looking, too; evidently a man of a strong resolution and a set purpose; a man not desirable to be met rushing down a narrow pass with a gulf on either side, for nothing would turn the man.

Madame Defarge his wife, sat in the shop behind the counter as he came in. Madame Defarge was a stout woman of about his own age, with a watchful eye that seldom seemed to look at anything, a large hand, heavily ringed, a steady face, strong features, and great composure of manner. There was a character about Madame Defarge, from which one might have predicted that she did not often make mistakes against herself in any of the reckonings over which she presided. Madame Defarge, being sensitive to cold, was wrapped in fur, and had a quantity of bright shawl twined about her head, though not to the concealment of her large ear-rings. Her knitting was before her, but she had laid it down to pick her teeth with a tooth-pick. Thus engaged, with her right elbow supported by her left hand, Madame Defarge said nothing when her lord came in, but coughed just one grain of cough. This, in combination with the lifting of her darkly defined eyebrows over her tooth-pick by the breadth of a line, suggested to her husband that he would do well to look round the shop among the customers for any new customer who had dropped in while he stepped over the way.

The wine-shop keeper accordingly rolled his eyes about, until they rested upon an elderly gentleman and a young lady, who were seated in a corner. Other company was there; two playing cards, two playing dominoes, three standing by the counter lengthening out a short supply of wine. As he passed behind the counter, he took notice that the elderly gentleman said in a look to the young lady, "This is our man."

"What the devil do *you* do in that galley there!" said Monsieur Defarge to himself; "I don't know you."

But he feigned not to notice the two strangers, and fell into discourse with the triumvirate of customers who were drinking at the counter.

"How goes it, Jacques?" said one of the three to Monseiur Defarge. "Is all the spilt wine swallowed?"

"Every drop, Jacques," answered Monsieur Defarge.

When this interchange of Christian names was effected, Madame Defarge, picking her teeth with her toothpick, coughed another grain of cough, and raised her eyebrows by the breadth of another line.

"It is not often," said the second of the three, addressing Monsieur Defarge, "that many of these miserable beasts know the taste of wine, or of anything but black bread and death. Is it not so, Jacques?"

"It is so, Jacques," Monsieur Defarge returned.

At this second interchange of the Christian name, Madame Defarge, still using her toothpick with profound composure, coughed another grain of cough, and raised her eyebrows by the breadth of another line.

The last of the three now said his say, as he put down his empty drinking vessel and smacked his lips.

"Ah! So much the worse! A bitter taste it is that such poor cattle always have in their mouths, and hard lives they live, Jacques. Am I not right, Jacques?"

"You are right, Jacques," was the response of Monsieur Defarge.

This third interchange of the Christian names was completed at the moment when Madame Defarge put her toothpick by, kept her eyebrows up, and slightly rustled in her seat.

"Hold then! True!" muttered her husband. "Gentlemen—my wife!"

The three customers pulled off their hats to Madame Defarge with three flourishes. She acknowledged their homage by bending her head, and giving them a quick look. Then she glanced in a casual manner round the wine-shop took up her knitting with great apparent calmness and repose of spirit, and became absorbed in it.

"Gentlemen," said her husband, who had kept his bright eye observantly upon her, "good day. The chamber, furnished bachelor-fashion, that you wish to see, and were inquiring for when I stepped out, is on the fifth floor. The doorway of the staircase gives on the little courtyard close to the left here," pointing with his hand, "near to the window of my establishment. But, now that I remember, one of you has already been there, and can show the way. Gentlemen, adieu!"

They paid for their wine and left the place.

Imitation:

THE SIGNALS

The Chinese chop suey house stood alone, unlighted, and sinister-looking. Involuntarily the Englishman shuddered as he gave the rap—three long, two short. He was admitted by a Chinaman, who silently conducted him through a bare hall to a huge room where several people sat eating chop suey. This, the Englishman knew, was not the real business of the place, for behind the wall at the end was a gambling den, and it was the Englishman's duty to see that no one entered who was not to be trusted.

He ordered a drink and sat down at one of the tables. Presently three prosperous-looking business men came in, and strolling up to the bar addressed the man behind it.

"Very nice night," said one.

"Yes, velly nice night," came the response from behind the counter, as the bar-tender glanced up while he ran a damp cloth over the bar. But in the glance there was time enough to notice that round the Englishman there were floating placid rings of tobacco smoke.

"Too bad," spoke up the second of the businessmen, "that there are so few good chop suey houses in this city—really clean, fine places like this of yours," and he let his eyes wander over the comfortable appointments of the hall. Without any sense of wonder he noticed, as did the bar-tender, that the Englishman was still exhaling placid clouds of tobacco smoke round him.

"Likee oll place, ha?" the Chinaman was saying.

The third business man spoke up, "How about a quiet little table, and three juleps, China?"

More quickly, more casually than the most trained observer might have noticed, Chang looked up for his cue, at the Englishman. He was just finishing three luxurious smoke rings. Genially the Chinaman replied,

"Most cellanly, come wit me."

And he led the way to the end of the room. As they approached a curtained wall tapestried with exquisite dragons, the tapestries parted and admitted the men to the most luxurious gambling den in the western city.—Pupil.

It will be observed that whereas the student who imitated Lafcadio Hearn's little "fantastic" has imitated the rich rhythmic style with complete appropriateness, the second student, who has borrowed Dickens for a model has not tried to imitate the style of Dickens, but has borrowed the device of the signals for his plot.

PARALLELISM AND BALANCE

1. LICHENS AND MOSSES

Yet as in one sense the humblest, in another they are the most honoured of the earth-children. Unfading as motionless, the warm frets them not, and the autumn wastes not. Strong in lowliness, they neither blanch in heat nor pine in frost. To them, slow-fingered, constant-hearted, is entrusted the weaving of the dark eternal tapestries of the hills; to them, slow-pencilled, iris-dyed, the tender framing of their endless imagery. Sharing the stillness of the unimpassioned rock, they share also its endurance; and while the winds of departing spring scatter the white hawthorn blossom like drifted snow, and summer dims on the parched meadow the drooping of its cowslip-gold,—far above, among the mountains, the silver lichen-spots rest, star-like, on the stone; and the gathering orange-stain upon the edge of yonder western peak reflects the sunsets of a thousand years.—JOHN RUSKIN, *Modern Painters,* *Vol. V. Pt. vi. chap. 10.*

2. THE MASTER'S LOOK

She softly crept toward the door, but as she went the master lifted his gloomy chestnut-coloured eyes under their thatch of grizzled hair, and so transfixed her. She could not move with that brown fire upon her, engulfing her. So he always looked when he was deeply stirred. So he had looked down at his father's coffin years ago, at his mother's last year. So he had looked into the eyes of his favourite dog, dying in his arms. The look was the realization of the infinite within the finite, altering all values. Never once in all the fifteen years during which she had been calling here had he seemed to look at Margaret at all.—MARY WEBB, "Over the Hills and Far Away", from *Armour Wherein He Trusted.*

By arrangement with Jonathan Cape, Limited, Toronto.

Parallelism is one of the most effective of all devices; but it must be used sparingly. It is most effective at points of climax and in emotional passages. The passage from Mary Webb is perhaps the better model because it is more restrained, not so obvious. Notice that always the parallelism is given sufficient variation and change to avoid monotony.

PRACTICE 1. Parallelism

From your own reading, in magazines or books, bring to class five paragraphs where parallelism is effectively used.

PRACTICE 2. Parallelism

On one of the models above, or on one of those you have chosen, write a paragraph using parallelism effectively. Suggested topics:

1. Flowers of the prairie. 2. Stratified rock. 3. Beach combers. 4. Kittens playing. 5. A bear in a zoo (going round and round his cage). 6. A paragraph containing several 'when' clauses. 7. A paragraph containing three sentences beginning 'So' (or 'Thus' or 'Now' or 'Never').

REPETITION

1

Pines and pines and the shadows of pines as far as the eye can see.

—ROBERT SERVICE

2. THE DESERT

As long as you are journeying in the interior of the Desert you have no particular point to make for as your resting-place. The endless sands yield nothing but small stunted shrubs—even these fail after the first two or three days, and from that time you pass over broad plains—you pass over newly reared hills—you pass through valleys dug out by the last week's storm, and the hills, and the valleys are sand, sand, sand, still sand, and only sand, and sand, and sand again.—KINGLAKE, *Eothen*.

Before repetition can be effective it must be built up to, as you see in this second passage; and it must be varied again and again. You will find this device used by Dickens many, many times.

PRACTICE 3. Using Repetition

1. Imagine yourself in Captain Bligh's little boat when he was cast adrift. Describe the endless watching for land.

2. Elaborate Robert Service's line into a paragraph of description of the forests of the North seen from a mountain vantage point.

3. Describe one of the following: the Bad Lands of the West, the drought stricken prairies, burnt over forest region, northern Ontario, fruit valleys in bloom, the northern "wastes" in bloom during the short summer, the ice and snow fields of the Arctic or Antarctic, a fruitless search for a rooming house, the dreary grind of daily routine.

ALLITERATION

1. SUNRISE

What a sunrise it was on the morning! Yet I stood with my back to it, looking west; for there I saw, firstly, the foam on the reef—as crimson as blood—falling over the wine-stained waves: then it changed as the sun ascended, like clouds of golden powder, indescribably magnificent, shaken and scattered upon the silver snow-drifts of the coral reef, dazzling to behold, and continually changing.—CHARLES W. STODDARD, *South-Sea Idylls*.

By permission of Charles Scribner's Sons.

2. SPANISH FORCES AT GRANADA

Never had Christian war assumed a more splendid and imposing aspect. Far as the eye could reach, extended the glittering and gorgeous lines of that goodly power, bristling with sunlit spears and blazoned banners; while beside, murmured and glowed and danced the silver and laughing Xenil, careless what lord should possess, for his little day, the banks that bloomed by its everlasting course.—LORD LYTTON.

You will notice that alliteration is not confined to nouns and their modifiers, but is even more effectively used with verbs, and even adverbs. We must be warned with alliteration, as with repetition and parallel structure, not to make it too obvious nor to use it too often.

PRACTICE 4. Using Alliteration

Read the models given until the sound of the alliterative phrases becomes familiar and then try a passage of description choosing alliterative phrases wherever you can devise them. You will be struck with the readiness with which you can pick up this device. Suggested topics:

1. A sunset scene which you have particularly enjoyed. 2. The flowers of a valley. 3. The rolling of the tide. 4. A secluded spot in the woods. 5. Moonlight on the mountains. 6. A city street scene. 7. A section of the slums.

WORD SENTENCES

When a writer has become a master of clear and correct sentence structure, he is entitled to attempt effective impression, using verbal devices of any sort that may secure the effect he desires. These need not be grammatically complete so long as they are perfectly clear. Examine the following passage for unusual constructions.

1

POOH GREETS EEYORE

"Good morning, Eeyore," said Pooh.

"Good morning, Pooh Bear," said Eeyore gloomily. "If it *is* a good morning," he said. "Which I doubt," said he.

"Why, what's the matter?"

"Nothing, Pooh Bear, nothing. We can't all, and some of us don't. That's all there is to it."

"Can't all *what*?" said Pooh, rubbing his nose.

"Gaiety. Song-and-dance. Here we go round the mulberry bush."

"Oh!" said Pooh. He thought for a long time, and then asked, "What mulberry bush is that?"

"Bon-hommy," went on Eeyore gloomily. "French word meaning bon-hommy," he explained. "I'm not complaining, but There It Is."

Pooh sat down on a large stone, and tried to think this out. It sounded to him like a riddle, and he was never very much good at riddles, being a Bear of Very Little Brain."—A. A. MILNE, *Winnie-the-Pooh.*

By permission of the publishers, McClelland and Stewart, Limited, Toronto.

Do not try to make too much sense out of this delightful nonsense. About all it says is that Eeyore and Pooh are queer, muddleheaded little animals, and Eeyore is not very happy. But could it be better done!

2

Suddenly he put his foot in a rabbit hole, and fell down flat on his face. B A N G ! ! ! ? ? ? * * * ! ! !
Piglet lay there, wondering what had happened.—A. A. MILNE, *Winnie-the-Pooh.*

By permission of the publishers, McClelland and Stewart, Limited, Toronto.

3. HEYTHORP GROWS REMINISCENT

Lying in that steaming brown fragrant liquid, old Heythorp heaved a stentorous sigh. By losing his temper with that ill-conditioned cur he had cooked his goose. It was done to a turn! and he was a ruined man . . . His tree had come down with a crash! Eighty years—eighty good years! He regretted none of them, regretted nothing. . . . He smiled and stirred a little in the bath till the water reached the white hairs on his lower lip. It smelt nice! And he took a long sniff. He had had a good life, a good life! . . . He closed his eyes. They talked about an after-life—people like that holy woman. Gammon. You went to sleep—a long sleep; no dreams. A nap after dinner! Dinner! His tongue sought his palate! Yes, he could eat a good dinner! That dog hadn't put him off his stroke!—JOHN GALSWORTHY, *The Stoic.*

By permission of the publishers, William Heinemann, Ltd., London.

4. THE WILD DUCK

Twilight. Red in the West.
Dimness. A glow on the wood.
The teams plod home to rest.
The wild duck come to glean.
O souls not understood,
What a wild cry in the pool;
What things have the farm ducks seen
That they cry so—huddle and cry?
Only the soul that goes.
Eager, Eager. Flying.
Over the globe of the moon,
Over the wood that glows.
Wings linked. Necks astrain,
A rush and a wild crying.

. . . .
A cry of the long pain
In the reeds of a steel lagoon,
In a land that no man knows.
—JOHN MASEFIELD, *Ballads and Poems.*

By permission of the publishers, The Macmillan Company of Canada Limited, Toronto.

PRACTICE 5. Using Incomplete Sentences

Reputable writers rarely take liberties, but when the artist is skilful, the devices are extremely effective. Try a piece of descriptive writing similar to that of Masefield's.

1. A prairie sunset. 2. Moonlight over a lake. 3. Resting time for a threshing outfit. 4. The city lights over a river or a lake. 5. Shadows under a bridge. 6. A church spire silhouetted against the sky. 7. One of your own topics.

ADDRESSING THE INANIMATE AS IF ANIMATE

This device, like the apostrophe and the ode, gives opportunity for emotional expressions which otherwise would be impossible. It is reserved, obviously, for such personal experiences and reflections as that in the model.

TO MY OLD HIKING SHOES

It is a funeral pyre, not an ordinary rubbish heap, and I cannot give you to the flame without a backward glance at the days we spent together.

Do you remember the slopes of slippery pine needles that you trod so surely, the great fallen tree trunks and boulders over which you scrambled? All your scars are honourable. You never failed me on the roughest trails; on glistening deck and spray-glazed rocks you were as steady as on the level beach.

What adventures we have known! There was that perfect June day when we forded the noisy creek, and a great silver bass, mistaking you for a couple of his fellows, edged closer, until he was nuzzling your toes! And then you hung astride the rustic verandah railing of a certain small log cabin, glistening like Cinderella's slippers, until you were dried by the wind that made music in the nearby pines, and teased the water lapping on the rocks below.

Let's not forget the morning we hunted orange lilies. The wild cherry showered its snowy petals on our path, and the flowers we sought, glowing on the green slopes, tempted us on and up. We went home drenched with dew and that peace which fills the wilderness at sunrise.

But, best memory of all is the day when with one other we scaled Lookout Rock. How joyously we climed, laughing breathlessly as we overcame each obstacle. It was steep and rugged, but surely, without a slip, you brought me to the very peak. But, ah, you brought me down again, alone. Down from the height of Lookout, down from the highlands of the north, down into this southern valley of Reality, so far, so very far from all my dreams!

And you, travel-worn and weary, have come to rest on this bonfire at the foot of an orchard. The eager little flames leap towards you. I see you writhe at first, then settle down contentedly. Now little curls of blue smoke are rising from you. You'll go to make the sunsets that linger vividly behind the pines. At night you'll drift, a luminous veil, across the moon, and your shadow will touch the water of the little lake. Some day, I think, I'll join you there, and we'll wander on again together through the haunts we loved.—MARION ROWLAND, "The Home Forum," *The Globe.*

By arrangement with the publishers, The Globe, *Toronto.*

PRACTICE 6. Addressing the Inanimate as if Animate

Upon this model, write an address to some object of your own with which you have had interesting experiences. If this seems too personal, (though it need not) try your dramatic power by choosing some other object and, imagining yourself in the place of its supposed owner, and inventing their experiences together, write an address to it. Write sincerely, do not burlesque your topic.

1. To my fountain pen. 2. To my skating jacket. 3. To a pair of moccasins. 4. To an old glove. 5. To a cigarette lighter. 6. To a neck scarf. 7. To a party dress. 8. To a dress suit. 9. To a pair of dancing pumps. 10. To a favourite fireplace. 11. To a finger ring. 12. To some gift (book, crest, brooch, sweater, or any other.) 13. To a school pin.

AUTOBIOGRAPHY

A useful, but somewhat time-worn device for interesting people in objects which otherwise might escape notice is to represent them as telling their own story.

THE ADVENTURES OF A SHILLING

I was born on the side of a mountain, near a little village of Peru, and made a voyage to England in an ingot, under the convoy of Sir Francis Drake. I was, soon after my arrival, taken out of my Indian habit, refined, naturalized, and put into the British mode, with the face of Queen Elizabeth on one side and the arms of the country on the other. Being thus equipped, I found in me a marvellous inclination to ramble, and visit all parts of the new world into which I was brought. The people very much favoured my natural disposition, and shifted me so fast from hand to hand that before I was five years old I had travelled into almost every corner of the nation. But in my sixth year, to my unspeakable grief, I fell into the hands of a miserable old fellow, who clasped me into an iron chest, where I found five hundred more of my own quality who lay under the same confinement. The only relief we had was to be taken out and counted over in the fresh air every morning and evening. After an imprisonment of several years, we heard somebody knocking at our chest, and breaking it open with a hammer. This, we found, was the old man's heir, who, as his father lay dying, was so good as to come to our release: he separated us that very day. What was the fate of my companions I know not; as for myself, I was sent to the apothecary's shop for a pint of sack. The apothecary gave me to a herb-woman, the herb-woman to a butcher, the butcher to a brewer, and the brewer to his wife, who made a present of me to a non-conformist preacher. After this manner I made my way merrily through the world; for, as I told you before, we shillings loved nothing so much as travelling. I sometimes fetched in a shoulder of mutton, sometimes a play-book, and often had the satisfaction to treat a Templar at a twelve-penny ordinary, or carry him with three friends to Westminster Hall.

After many adventures, which it would be tedious to relate, I was sent to a young spendthrift, in company with the will of his deceased father. The young fellow, who I found was very extravagant, gave great demonstrations of joy at the receiving of the will: but opening it, he found himself disinherited and cut off from possession of a fair estate by virtue of my being made a present to him. This put him in such a passion, that after having taken me with his hand, and cursed me, he squirred[1] me away from him as far as he could fling me. I chanced to light in an unfrequented place under a dead wall, where I lay undiscovered and useless, during the usurpation of Oliver Cromwell.

About a year after the king's return, a poor cavalier that was walking there about dinner-time fortunately cast his eye upon me, to the great joy of us both, carried me to a cook's shop, where he dined on me, and drank the king's health. When I came again into the world, I found that I had been happier in my retirement than I thought, having probably, by that means, escaped wearing a monstrous pair of breeches.

I shall pass over many other accidents of less moment, and hasten to the fatal castastrophe, when I fell into the hands of an artist, who conveyed me underground, and with an unmerciful pair of shears, cut off my titles, clipped my brims, retrenched my shape, rubbed me to my inmost ring, and, in short, so spoiled and pillaged me that he did not leave me worth a groat. You may think what a confusion I was in, to see myself thus curtailed and disfigured. I should have been ashamed to show my head had not all my old acquaintances been reduced to the same shameful figure, except some few that were punched through the belly. In the midst of this general calamity, when everybody thought our misfortune irretrievable, and our case desperate, we were thrown into the furnace together, and (as it often happens with cities rising out of the fire) appeared with greater beauty and lustre than we could ever boast of before.

What has happened to me since this change of sex which you now see, I shall take some other opportunity to relate. In the meantime I shall only repeat two adventures, as being very extraordinary, and neither of them having happened to me above once in my life. The first was my being in a poet's pocket, who was so taken with the brightness and novelty of my appearance that it gave occasion to the finest burlesque poem in the British language, entitled, from me, "The Splendid Shilling". The second adventure, which I must not omit, happened to me in the year 1703, when I was given away in charity to a blind man, but indeed this was by mistake, the person who gave me having heedlessly thrown me into the hat among a pennyworth of farthings.—JOSEPH ADDISON (abridged)

PRACTICE 7. Autobiography

Write an imaginative autobiography based on one of the following topics. Notice the sidelights which further help Addison's story. What do you learn about English history, about church donations, about counterfeiting and debasement of coins, being "cut off with a shilling," the poverty of poets, and charity to the poor? These are, strictly

---

[1]*squirred—to throw away with a jerk.*

speaking, additional to his story, but they have helped the story to live for two hundred years. Use your own invention, take your time.

1. The story of a piece of coal. 2. The story of a violin. 3. A good luck piece. 4. A horse-shoe nail ("and all for the loss of a horse-shoe nail"). 5. A rosary. 6. A pocket-knife. 7. A library book. 8. A museum piece. 9. A mummy ("And thou hast walked about, How strange a story!"). 10. Nelson's Monument in Trafalgar Square. 11. Vimy Ridge. 12. The Four Horses in front of St. Mark's (consult Encyclopedia). 13. An adventurous engagement ring (!).

SUSPENSE

The principle of suspense is used in many ways. It consists in creating, by suggestion, a growing sense of climax. Things are reaching a head, but the outcome, however much anticipated, is still unsure. The two models immediately following illustrate this sense of apprehension. Notice the emphatic short paragraphs, the repetitions with change. Notice the pace, faster and faster; the false alarms. Study these models closely for words, for sentences, and for proportion. The third model is included as an example of this device used for the purpose of giving a humorous surprise ending.

1. LOST IN THE WILD WOOD

With great cheerfulness of spirit Mole pushed on toward the Wild Wood, which lay before him low and threatening, like a black reef in some still southern sea.

There was nothing to alarm him at first entry. Twigs crackled under his feet, logs tripped him, funguses on stumps resembled caricatures, and startled him for the moment by their likeness to something familiar and far away; but that was all fun, and exciting. It led him on, and he penetrated to where the light was less, and the trees crouched nearer and nearer, and holes made ugly mouths at him on either side.

Everything was very still now. The dusk advanced on him steadily, rapidly, gathering in behind and before; and the light seemed to be draining away like flood-water.

Then the faces began.

It was over his shoulder, and indistinctly, that he first thought he saw a face; a little, evil, wedge-shaped face, looking out at him from a hole. When he turned and confronted it, the thing had vanished.

He quickened his pace, telling himself cheerfully not to begin imagining things, or there would be simply no end to it. He passed another hole, and another, and another; and then—yes!—no!—yes! certainly a little narrow face, with hard eyes, had flashed up for an instant from a hole, and was gone. He hesitated—braced himself for an effort and strode on. Then suddenly, and as if it had been so all the time, every hole, far and near, and there were hundreds of them, seemed to possess its face, coming and going rapidly, all fixing on him glances of malice and hatred: all hard-eyed and evil and sharp.

If he could only get away from the holes in the banks, he thought, there would be no more faces. He swung off the path and plunged into the untrodden places of the wood.

Then the whistling began.

Very faint and shrill it was, and far behind him, when he first heard it; but somehow it made him hurry forward. Then, still very faint and shrill, it sounded far ahead of him, and made him hesitate and want to go back. As he halted in indecision it broke out on either side, and seemed to be caught up and passed on throughout the whole length of the wood to its farthest limit. They were up and alert and ready, evidently, whoever they were! And he—he was alone, and unarmed, and far from help; and the night was closing in.

Then the pattering began.

He thought it was only falling leaves at first, so light and delicate was the sound of it. Then as it grew it took a regular rhythm, and he knew it for nothing else but the pat-pat-pat of little feet still a very long way off. Was it in front or behind? It seemed to be first one, and then the other, then both. It grew and it multiplied, till from every quarter as he listened anxiously, leaning this way and that, it seemed to be closing in on him. As he stood still to hearken, a rabbit came running hard toward him through the trees. He waited, expecting it to slacken pace, or to swerve from him into a different course. Instead, the animal almost brushed him as it dashed past, his face set and hard, his eyes staring, "Get out of this you fool, get out!" the Mole heard him mutter as he swung round a stump and disappeared down a friendly burrow.

The pattering increased till it sounded like sudden hail on the dry leaf-carpet spread round him. The whole wood seemed running now, running hard, hunting, chasing, closing in round something or—somebody? In panic, he began to run too, aimlessly, he knew not whither. He ran up against things, he fell over things and into things, he darted under things and dodged round things. At last he took refuge in the deep dark hollow of an old beech tree which offered shelter, concealment—perhaps even safety, but who could tell. Anyhow, he was too tired to run any further, and could only snuggle down into the dry leaves which had drifted into the hollow and hope he was safe for a time. And as he lay there panting and trembling, and listened to the whistling and the pattering outside, he knew it at last, in all its fullness, that dread thing which other little dwellers in field and hedgerow had encountered here, and known as their darkest moment—that thing which the Rat had vainly tried to shield him from—the Terror of the Wild Wood!—KENNETH GRAHAME, *The Wind in the Willows.*

By permission of Charles Scribner's Sons, New York.

2. THE ESCAPE

The same shadows that are falling on the prison are falling, in the same hour of that early afternoon, on the Barrier with the crowd about it, when a coach going out of Paris drives up to be examined.

"Who goes here? Whom have we within? Papers!"

The papers are handed out and read.

"Alexandre Manette. Physician. French. Which is he?"

This is he; this helpless, inarticulately murmuring, wandering old man pointed out.

"Apparently the Citizen-Doctor is not in his right mind? The Revolution-fever will have been too much for him?"

Greatly too much for him.

"Hah! Many suffer with it. Lucie. His daughter. French. Which is she?"

This is she.

"Apparently it must be. Lucie, the wife of Evrémonde; is it not?"

It is.

"Hah! Evrémonde has an assignation elsewhere. Lucie, her child. English. This is she?"

She and no other.

"Kiss me, child of Evrémonde. Now, thou has kissed a good republican; something new in thy family; remember it! Sydney Carton. Advocate. English. Which is he?"

He lies here, in this corner of the carriage. He, too, is pointed out.

"Apparently the English advocate is in a swoon?"

It is hoped he will recover in the fresher air. It is represented that he is not in strong health, and has separated sadly from a friend who is under the displeasure of the Republic.

"Is that all? It is not a great deal, that! Many are under the displeasure of the Republic, and must look out at the little window. Jarvis Lorry. Banker. English. Which is he?"

"I am he. Necessarily, being the last."

It is Jarvis Lorry who has replied to all the previous questions. It is Jarvis Lorry who has alighted and stands with his hand on the coach door, replying to a group of officials. They leisurely walk round the carriage and leisurely mount the box, to look at what little luggage it carries on the roof; the country-people hanging about, press nearer to the coach doors and greedily stare in; a little child, carried by its mother, has its short arm held out for it, that it may touch the wife of an aristocrat who has gone to the guillotine.

"Behold your papers, Jarvis Lorry, countersigned."

"One can depart, citizen;"

"One can depart. Forward, my positilions! A good journey!"

"I salute you, citizens—and the first danger passed!"

These are again the words of Jarvis Lorry, as he clasps his hands, and looks upward. There is terror in the carriage, there is weeping, there is the heavy breathing of the insensible traveller.

"Are we not going too slowly? Can they not be induced to go faster?" asks Lucie, clinging to the old man.

"It would seem like flight, my darling. I must not urge them too much; it would raise suspicion."

"Look back, look back, and see if we are pursued!"

"The road is clear, my dearest. So far, we are not pursued."

Houses in twos and threes pass by us, solitary farms, ruinous buildings, dye-works, tanneries, and the like open country, avenues of leafless trees. The hard uneven pavement is under us, the soft deep mud is on either side. Sometimes we strike into the skirting mud, to avoid the stones that clatter us and shake us; sometimes we stick in ruts and sloughs there. The agony of our impatience is then so great, that in our wild alarm and hurry we are for getting out and running—hiding—doing anything but stopping.

Out in the open country, in again among ruinous buildings, solitary farms, dye-works, tanneries, and the like, cottages in twos and threes, avenues of leafless trees. Have these men deceived us, and taken us back by another road? Is not this the same place twice over? Thank Heaven, no. A village. Look back, look back, and see if we are pursued! Hush! the posting-house.

Leisurely, our four horses are taken out; leisurely, the coach stands in the little street, bereft of horses, and with no likelihood upon it of ever moving again; leisurely, the new horses come into visible existence, one by one; leisurely, the new postilions follow, sucking and plaiting the lashes of their whips; leisurely, the old postilions count their money, make wrong additions, and arrive at dissatisfied results. All the time, our overfraught hearts are beating at a rate that would far outstrip the fastest gallop of the fastest horses ever foaled.

At length the new postilions are in their saddles, and the old are left behind. We are through the village, up the hill, and down the hill, and on the low watery grounds. Suddenly, the postilions exchange speech with animated gesticulation, and the horses are pulled up, almost on their haunches. We are pursued!

"Ho! Within the carriage there. Speak, then!"

"What is it?" asks Mr. Lorry, looking out at window.

"How many did they say?"

"I do not understand you."

"—At the last post. How many to the guillotine to-day?"

"Fifty-two."

"I said so! A brave number! My fellow-citizen here would have it forty-two; ten more heads are worth having. The guillotine goes handsomely. I love it. Hi, forward! Whoop!"

The night comes on dark. He moves more; he is beginning to revive, and to speak intelligibly; he thinks they are still together; he asks him, by his name, what he has in his hand. Oh, pity us, kind Heaven, and help us! Look out, look out, and see if we are pursued.

The wind is rushing after us, and the clouds are flying after us, and the moon is plunging after us, and the whole wild night is in pursuit of us; but, so far, we are pursued by nothing else.—DICKENS, *A Tale of Two Cities.*

3

A hush came over the room. A dead silence fell upon the gay crowd. The dancing stopped, the laughing stopped, the shouts of gaiety stopped. Everyone was motionless, staring with wide open eyes at the dark brown object in the corner. What was to happen? Then, a low rumbling which grew louder and louder, a clang, a clash! a beating of drums and a wild savage cry, "Tarzan is on the air!"—PUPIL

PRACTICE 8. Creating Suspense

The devices given throughout this section are meant to stimulate your own invention and to draw your attention to the fact that effects may be produced—are produced—by conscious effort and invention. Use "The Terror of the Wild Wood" as a model and write a story using the short paragraph for emphasis, inventing a suitable cause for fear or apprehension.

Suggestions:

1. A small child wanders off into the woods. 2. You have to pass through an underground cave. 3. You are sleeping in a strange house in a strange city. 6. You walk through the narrow streets of Chinatown. 5. You sleep in the woods for the first time. 6. Two boys go exploring an abandoned castle. 7. Some experience you have had, suitably retold for its full effect.

PRACTICE 9. Creating Suspense

Write on one of the topics given below, managing the creation of suspense as in Dickens' story of the escape of Lucie Manette and her party, in *A Tale of Two Cities*. Do not omit the false alarm.

1. Mickey Mouse and Minnie move from the old barn. 2. Mrs. Duck takes Donald and starts to move from the mill pond. 3. Two girls lost in New York come at sundown to the negro section of Harlem. 4. Two boys have been kidnapped and manage to escape. 5. In John Buchan's story *Prester John* Davey escapes with the necklace and is pursued through the forest by the blacks. Retell the story after the Dickens' manner.

PRACTICE 10. Creating Suspense

Read in Dickens' *A Tale of Two Cities*, Book II, Chapter xiv, the story of Jerry Cruncher's Fishing Expedition. Young Jerry follows him, gets scared and is pursued home by the coffin. Notice that because Jerry said he was going fishing, Dickens maintains the language of fishing ("a saw, a crowbar, a rope and chain, and other fishing tackle of that nature" . . . "They fished with a spade first" . . . "The three fishermen" . . .). Make a story of your own where one person—not necessarily Father—gives another person a put-off answer, and does something else. Translate Dickens' terms to suit your own story.

1. Going fishing. 2. Late at the office. 3. Going to the dentist. 4. Off to see Bert. 5. Out for a walk. 6. To Martha's for a game of bridge. 7. Going to the hospital to see Aunt Bessie.

REPEATED SENTENCE AND PARAGRAPH

In the model on page 368, "The Escape," we noticed that the feeling of terror was created, or re-created, by the repetition of the sentence "Look back, look back, and see if we are pursued!"; and further by the repetition of the objects of scenery which gave the impression that the fugitives were going again over the same road. This repetition of a sentence, or even of a paragraph, may be very effective. Dickens has used it with fine effect in *Dombey and Son*.

In *A Tale of Two Cities*, Book III, chapter xiv, Madame Defarge sets out to trap Lucie Manette. Lucie has gone, fortunately, and only Miss Pross is in the house. When Dickens tells the story he says, "Thus accoutred, and walking with the confident tread of such a character, and with the supple freedom of a woman who had habitually walked in her girlhood, barefoot and barelegged, on the brown sea-sand, Madame Defarge took her way along the streets." Dickens' story then turns to Miss Pross and Jerry Cruncher who are planning to escape from Paris without attracting attention. The theme is pursued for a thousand words, when this paragraph is inserted "And still Madame Defarge, pursuing her way along the streets, came nearer and nearer." The story of Miss Pross continues, this time for one paragraph; then we find again, "Still Madame Defarge, pursuing her way along the streets, came nearer and nearer." Six lines more about Miss Pross and, "Madame Defarge was drawing very near indeed." Thereafter the two stories merge and the meeting of Miss Pross and Madame Defarge is given.

PRACTICE 11. Repetition

Read the story in *A Tale of Two Cities;* read the student exercise *The Artist* which follows, and then write a story of your own using the same device.

THE ARTIST
(Based on Dickens' *A Tale of Two Cities* Bk III. Ch. XIV)

It was dark—the darkest hour of the night, and the inky blackness lay like some dark spirit over the land. Not a single star shone in the heavens above, for a thick canopy of clouds covered the sky. It was a bitter night. The wind shrieked and moaned and, in its anger, blew down trees and destroyed barns. The stout little house that resisted its terrific strength seemed to incense it more as it thrashed at the building in an effort to raze it.

Inside that stout little house, which so bravely battled against the wind, there was also a storm—not a storm of the elements, but the storm of a human soul. In the awful darkness that filled the one room of the house, a man lay, sick unto death. Writhing with pain, the tortured man tried to calm himself for the coming ordeal; for off in the distance he saw death drawing towards him slowly and silently; and the gaunt figure was pointing a long white finger at him.

The man closed his eyes to shut out the awful vision; but as he listened to the wailing of the wind, it seemed only to be the echo of the tumult of his own soul. Then, as he listened more closely, a voice seemed to arise out of the wind, and whisper to him, "Get up! Get up! It is almost too late. He is coming. Get up!"

The sick man opened his eyes, and still he saw the tall, gaunt figure of death approaching him, and the long white finger seemed more accusing.

With a sob the man arose suddenly. Forgetting his pain and sorrow, he threw his one thin blanket around him, and in the darkness groped for a candle. Finding it, he lit it and looked about the room. Ah! there they were—his paints and easel in the corner. Praying that he would be given the strength to get them, the man stopped to get his breath. But as he stopped, the wind hissed at him, "Hurry! Hurry! It is almost too late. He is coming. Oh, hurry!" And again he saw the figure of death with its accusing finger, drawing very near indeed.

Frantically he grabbed for his brush and paints. Then seating himself, he tried to calm his spirit. He must complete his picture. He would paint the face of Jesus—Jesus whom he had forgotten in his wicked life. The numbness gone from his fingers, he took up his brush and painted. Gradually an outline appeared, then it grew more distinct; and soon, smiling, the painter put down his brush. He had finished his work, for before him was the face of the Christ, and around the picture a bright light shone.

Once more the artist shut his eyes and listened to the wind. But instead of the hissing, he heard soft music and sweet sounds, and when he opened his eyes he beheld in the place of the dark figure of death, a beautiful angel.

A party searching for him came to his lonely hut, and, as they opened the door, the picture caught their eye. Reverently they approached it, and found, lying beside it, the body of the dead artist. Solemnly they buried him, but the picture was shown to the world, which, seeing it, loved him and forgot his sins.—PUPIL

PERSONALITY TO ANIMALS

We omit, because of its length, the allegory proper which you may examine at its best in Bunyan's *Pilgrim's Progress* or any episode from it, such as 'Doubting Castle', and turn to such allegorical devices as have been so successful in *The Wind in the Willows* by Kenneth Grahame, and in A. A. Milne's *Pooh* books. Here the stories of animals are given in their own habitat but the actions are those of people, and their feelings and emotions are human. For example, *The Wind in the Willows* begins with this delightful paragraph:

The Mole had been working very hard all the morning, spring-cleaning his little home. First with brooms, then with dusters; then on ladders and steps and chairs, with a brush and a pail of whitewash; till he had dust in his throat and eyes, and splashes of whitewash all over his black fur, and an aching back and weary arms. Spring was moving in the air above and in the earth below and around him, penetrating even his dark and lowly little house with its spirit of divine discontent and longing. It was small wonder, then, that he suddenly flung down his brush on the floor and said, "Bother!" and "O blow!" and also "Hang springcleaning!" and bolted out of the house without even waiting to put on his coat. Something up above was calling him imperiously, and he made for the steep little tunnel which answered in his case to the gravelled carriage-drive owned by animals whose residences are nearer to the sun and air. So he scraped and scratched and scrabbled and scrooged, and then he scrooged again and scrabbled and scratched and scraped, working busily with his little paws and muttering to himself, "Up we go! Up we go!" till at last, pop! his snout came out into the sunlight, and he found himself rolling in the warm grass of a great meadow.—KENNETH GRAHAME, *The Wind in the Willows.*   *By permission of Charles Scribner's Sons.*

   In your stories of animals do not hesitate to introduce dialogue, as in any narrative.   Consider the effectiveness of Jerome K. Jeromes' account of Montmorency's experiences:

   Montmorency went for the cat at the rate of twenty miles an hour; but the cat did not hurry up—did not seem to have grasped the idea that his life was in danger.   It trotted quietly on until its would-be assassin was within a yard of it, and then it turned and sat down in the middle of the road, and looked at Montmorency with a gentle, inquiring expression, that said:
   "Yes, you want me?"
   Montmorency does not lack pluck; but there was something about the look of that cat that might have chilled the heart of the boldest dog.   He stopped abruptly and looked back at Tom.
   Neither spoke; but the conversation that one could imagine was clearly as follows:
   THE CAT: "Can I do anything for you?"
   MONTMORENCY: "No—no thanks."
   THE CAT: "Don't you mind speaking, if you really want anything, you know."
   MONTMORENCY (*backing down the High Street*): "Oh, no,—not at all—certainly—don't you trouble.   I—I am afraid I've made a mistake.   I thought I knew you.   Sorry I disturbed you."
   THE CAT: "Not at all—quite a pleasure.   Sure you don't want anything, now?"
   MONTMORENCY (*still backing*): "Not at all, thanks—not at all—very kind of you.   Good morning."
   THE CAT: "Good morning."

—JEROME K. JEROME, Three Men in a Boat.
By permission of the publishers, J. W. Arrowsmith (London) Ltd.

PRACTICE 12. Giving Personality to Animals

   Write an imaginative story on one of the following topics.   Give personality to each animal; give them human actions and re-actions, feelings, ambitions, emotions.   You will feel more in the way of it, if you read two or three chapters from *The House at Pooh Corner* by A. A. Milne, or Kenneth Grahame's *The Wind in the Willows.*

   1. That Monday Feeling. 2. Jenny Wren Puts on a Concert. 3. Ground-Hog Looks at the Weather. 4. Jimmy Skunk Attends the Animal Fair. 5. Mickey Serenades Minnie. 6. Toad Takes His Lady for a Drive. (Use as a sub-title Touchstone's sentence "We that are true lovers run into strange capers.") 7. Any other animal's adventures.

HUMOROUS EXAGGERATION

We all enjoy the "tall" story. There are Liars' Clubs where prizes are given for the most imaginative stretcher. These lies are not contravention of fact so much as exaggeration of it. It is the core of American humour, as under-statement and punning are at the base of much English humour. Both, of course, turn upon the unexpected.

1. MY FINANCIAL CAREER

When I go into a bank I get rattled. The clerks rattle me; the wickets rattle me; the sight of the money rattles me; everything rattles me. The moment I cross the threshold of a bank I am a hesitating jay. If I attempt to transact business there, I become an irresponsible idiot.

I knew this beforehand, but my salary had been raised to fifty dollars a month, and I felt that the bank was the only place for it. So I shambled in and looked timidly round at the clerks. I had an idea that a person about to open an account needed to consult the manager. I went up to a wicket marked "Accountant." The accountant was a tall, cool devil,—the very sight of him rattled me. My voice was sepulchral.

"May I see the manager?" I said, and added solemnly, "alone". I don't know why I said "alone".

"Certainly," said the accountant, and fetched him. The manager was a grave calm man. I held fifty-six dollars clutched in a crumpled ball in my pocket.

"Are you the manager?" I asked. Heaven knows I didn't doubt it.

"Yes," he said.

"May I see you?" I asked. "Alone?" I didn't want to say "alone" again, but without it my question seemed self-evident.

The manager looked at me in some alarm. He felt that I had a terrible secret to reveal.

"Come in here," he said, leading the way to a private room, and turning the key.

"We are safe from interruptions here," he said, "sit down."

We both sat down and looked at one another. I found no voice to speak.

"You are one of Pinkerton's men, I presume," he said.

He had gathered from my mysterious manner that I was a detective. I knew what he was thinking and felt all the worse.

"No, not from Pinkerton's," I said, seemingly to imply that I came from a rival agency. "To tell the truth," I went on, as if I *had* been prompted to lie about the matter, "I am not a detective at all. I have come to open an account. I intend to keep all my money in this bank."

The manager looked relieved, but still serious; he concluded now that I was a son of Baron Rothschild, or a young Gould.

"A very large amount, I suppose," he said.

"Fairly large," I whispered. "I propose to deposit fifty-six dollars now, and fifty dollars a month regularly."

The manager got up and opened the door. He called to the accountant.

"Mr. Montgomery," he said, unkindly loud, "this gentleman is opening an account; he will deposit fifty-six dollars. Good morning."

I rose. A big iron door stood open at the side of the room.

"Good morning," I said, and stepped into the safe.

"Come out," said the manager coldly, showing me the other way.

I went up to the accountant's wicket and poked the ball of money at him, with a quick, convulsive movement as if I were doing a trick. My face was ghastly pale.

"Here," I said, "deposit it." The tone of the words seemed to mean, "Let us do this business while the fit is on us."

He took the money and gave it to another clerk. He made me write the sum on a slip and sign my name in a book. I no longer knew what I was doing. The bank swam before my eyes.

"Is it deposited?" I asked, in a hollow, vibrating voice.

"It is," said the accountant.

"Then I want to draw a cheque."

My idea was to draw out six dollars for present use. Some one gave me a cheque-book through a wicket, and some one else began telling me how to write the cheque. The people in the bank had the impression that I was an invalid millionaire. I wrote something on the cheque and thrust it in at the clerk. He looked at it.

"What! Are you drawing it all out again?" he asked in surprise. Then I realized that I had written fifty-six instead of six. I was too far gone to reason now. I had a feeling that I could not explain my act. All the clerks had stopped writing to look at me.

Reckless with misery, I made a plunge.

"Yes, the whole thing."

"You withdraw your money from the bank!"

"Every cent of it."

"Are you not going to deposit any more!" said the clerk, astonished.

"Never!"

An idiot hope struck me that he might think some one had insulted me while I was writing the cheque and that I had changed my mind. I made a wretched attempt to look like a man with a fearfully quick temper.

The clerk prepared to pay the money.

"How will you have it?" he said.

"Oh." I caught his meaning and answered without even trying to think, "In fifties."

He gave me a fifty dollar bill.

"And the six?" he asked dryly.

"In sixes," I said.

He gave me the money and I rushed out. As the big doors swung behind me I caught the echo of a roar of laughter that went up to the ceiling of the bank. Since then I bank no more. I keep my money in cash in my trousers pocket, and my savings in silver dollars in a sock.—Stephen Leacock, *Literary Lapses.*
                                                                    By permission of the author.

2. PINEAPPLE FOR LUNCH

We are very fond of pineapple, all three of us. We looked at the picture on the tin; we thought of the juice. We smiled at one another and Harris got a spoon ready.

Then we looked for the knife to open the tin with. We turned out everything in the hamper. We turned out the bags. We pulled up the boards at the bottom of the boat. We took everything out on the bank and shook it. There was no tin-opener to be found.

Then Harris tried to open the tin with a pocket knife, and broke the knife and cut himself badly; and George tried a pair of scissors, and the scissors flew up, and nearly put his eye out. While they were dressing their wounds, I tried to make a hole in the thing with the spiky end of the hitcher, and the hitcher slipped and jerked me out between the boat and the bank into two feet of muddy water, and the tin rolled over, uninjured, and broke a teacup.

Then we all got mad. We took the tin out on the bank, and Harris went up into a field and got a big sharp stone and I went back into the boat and brought out the mast, and George held the tin and Harris held the sharp end of the stone against the top of it, and I took the mast and poised it high up in the air, and gathered up all my strength and brought it down.

It was George's straw hat that saved his life that day. He keeps that hat now (what is left of it), and, of a winter's evening, when the pipes are lit and the boys are telling stretchers about the dangers they have passed through, George brings it down and shows it round, and the stirring tale is told anew, with fresh exaggerations every time.

Harris got off with merely a flesh wound.

After that I took the tin myself, and hammered at it with the mast, till I was worn out and sick at heart. Whereupon Harris took it in hand.

We beat it out flat; we beat it back square; we battered it into every form known to geometry—but we could not make a hole in it. Then George went at it, and knocked it into a shape, so strange, so weird, so unearthly in its wild hideousness, that he got frightened and threw away the mast. Then we all three sat around it on the grass and looked at it.

There was one great dent across the top that had the appearance of a mocking grin, and it drove us furious, so that Harris rushed at the thing, and caught it up, and flung it far into the middle of the river.—JEROME K. JEROME, *Three Men in a Boat.*   *By permission of the publishers, J. W. Arrowsmith (London) Ltd.*

PRACTICE 13. Humorous Exaggeration

Write a humorous account of one of your own experiences, depending for its effect upon exaggeration and the unexpected. Copy the model as closely as you desire.

Suggestions:

1. A hike. 2. A weiner roast. 3. A picnic. 4. A motoring experience. 5. A fishing expedition. 6. A laboratory experiment. 7. A holiday episode. 8. An unusual incident in church. 9. At a wedding. 10. A rookie tries to harness (hitch, halter, bridle, or ride) a horse. 11. Any other amusing experience. 12. Writing a letter. 13. Learning to skate (remember Sam Weller). 14. Giving a toast at a banquet. 15. The first dance. 16. Invited to supper. 17. A formal presentation. 18. Explaining to mother. 19. A 'bit part' in a play. 20. Entertaining Mother's (sister's, brother's) friend till Mother (sister, brother) appears. 21. An impromtu entry!

Chapter 16

Preparing the Research Essay

The secret of handling any big job is to break it down into a number of smaller jobs which you can handle one at a time. Writing a research essay, though a "big" job, can be easily handled. This chapter will provide, step by step, a time- and effort-saving system of preparing a research essay.

"But I haven't anything to write about!" boys and girls often complain. "When I sit down at my desk with a blank sheet of paper in front of me, I can't think of a thing to say!" Well, what do other people use for material? Only a small part of the writing we find in books and magazines is entirely imaginative. By far the greater part is based on the author's own experiences, ideas, and investigations.

CHOOSING YOUR SUBJECT

Because you can write best about what you are interested in, the first step in preparing a good research essay is to choose the right subject.

HINTS ON CHOOSING A SUBJECT

1. Pick a subject that you would like to know more about. You might as well enjoy the work. What are you interested in? How do you spend your leisure time? Have you a hobby? What kind of clubs and other organizations have you joined? What subjects do you like to read about? What sort of television programs do you enjoy? What vocation do you wish to enter? What kind of work have you done after school and during vacations?
2. Pick a subject you can handle. You would not be able to explain what you can't yourself understand.

3. Pick a subject that permits library research. But, if you can, brighten your work with information secured from interviews, from pamphlets or booklets, or from your own observation and experience. For example, to supplement what you find in the library about teen-age drivers, you might interview the chief of police in your community or the judge of a traffic court.

4. Pick a subject narrow enough to be handled adequately in the space allotted.

Don't bite off more than you can chew. If you try to write on "Atomic Energy" in fifteen hundred words, you'll be doomed before you start. Cut your subject down to one phase or aspect which interests you particularly and which is small enough to be handled in the space of your research essay. This is the way to do it.

A SUBJECT FOR A WHOLE SERIES OF LEARNED WORKS!	A SUBJECT FOR A BOOK!	BETTER BUT—	JUST RIGHT!
Farming	Modern farming	Science and the modern farmer	Chemistry helps the farmer
Aviation	Commercial aviation	Advances in commercial aviation	Helicopter to the rescue

PRACTICE 1. Choosing a Subject for Your Research Essay

1. Bring to class a list of at least three subjects on which you would enjoy working. Be sure each of the subjects is narrow enough to be handled adequately in a 1500-word essay. The following subjects, most of them too broad, may suggest narrower ones.

Advertising
Artificial satellites
Auto design
Automation
Business machines
Cancer research
A career in government service
Conservation and reforestation
The documentary film
Educating the consumer
Educational television
Guided missiles
High school athletics
Historic places in Ontario

Modern design
Modern mining methods
Native ballet
New discoveries in medicine
The Olympic games
Opera
Photography
Plastics
Preventing labour disputes
Professional football
Scouting
Skin diving
South America
Square dancing

2. After discussing the lists in class, choose a subject for your essay. Be ready to tell why you think your subject is worth the research you will have to do on it.

STATING YOUR THESIS OR PURPOSE

After you have selected a subject, try to decide what you want to learn about it. For a start, list questions that occur to you. For example, if your subject is teen-age drivers, you may begin your research by considering questions like these: Why are insurance rates for young drivers so high? Do young women have a higher or lower accident rate than young men? What steps are being taken to train young people to drive cautiously and safely?

As you work, other questions may occur to you. The preliminary questions act as a self-starter.

Having considered these initial questions, set down on paper what you wish to accomplish. This sentence will become your thesis. Frequently the thesis sentence names the person or group to whom you are writing.

EXAMPLES OF THE THESIS SENTENCE

I wish to tell my classmates pertinent facts about progress made in rocketry, its present status and probable future, and to discuss the unsolved problems on which engineers are still working.

I shall try to recommend my favourite hobby, stamp collecting, to other students of the class—especially those who are not collectors already.

My purpose is to assess the role of television in high school education.

GATHERING YOUR MATERIAL AND LISTING YOUR SOURCES

Take to the library a fountain pen, 3 x 5 and 4 x 6 inch cards or slips of paper, paper clips, and a box, folder, or envelope in which to keep everything together. (Some students prefer to use the smaller size for source cards and the larger size for notes. The same size, of course, may be used for both.)

At the library you will probably begin your search with the *Encyclopaedia Britannica*, the *Encyclopedia Americana*, the *Encyclopedia Canadiana*, or another encyclopedia. If you don't find readily the information you want, look up your subject in the index. Follow up cross references in the articles. If they look helpful, copy the titles and authors of books listed in the bibliography at the end of an article.

Next, go to the card catalogue and try to locate the books suggested in the encyclopedia and other books on your subject. With the call numbers as guides, go to the shelves and examine as many books as possible. A quick glance through the table of contents of each book will help you to estimate its value to you. If it looks promising, use the index at the back of the volume to find material on your subject.

For accurate and up-to-the-minute information consult the *Readers' Guide* (an index to articles in many American magazines and journals), and the pamphlet and clipping file.

Don't overlook pamphlets and reports distributed by various governmental agencies, private corporations (like the Royal Bank of Canada) and charitable institutions. The following publications are invaluable to any study dealing with Canadian life: *The Canada Year Book*, *Vital Statistics* (a provincial government publication), and *The Canadian Who's Who*.

The Queen's Printer, Ottawa, issues a monthly catalogue of all federal government publications. A *Reference Paper* (issued by the Information Division of the Department of External Affairs, Ottawa) lists government and non-government sources of information about Canada.

PREPARING SOURCE CARDS

For each book, magazine article, or other source that you use, prepare a source card. Record in the upper right corner of each source card a number or the author's name. Then when you begin to take notes you can use the number or name—instead of the full title—to identify the source from which you took your information.

Follow the following forms for (1) a book, (2) a magazine article, (3) an encyclopedia article, and (4) a newspaper article.

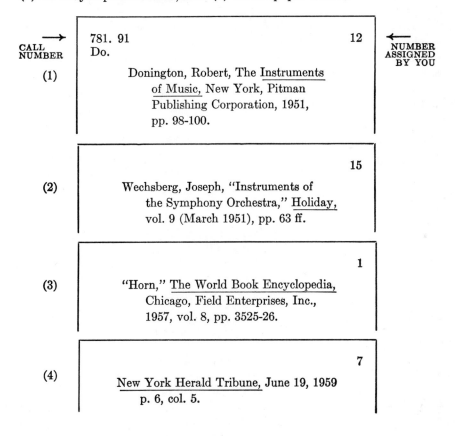

CALL NUMBER

(1)

781. 91
Do.

12

NUMBER ASSIGNED BY YOU

Donington, Robert, The Instruments of Music, New York, Pitman Publishing Corporation, 1951, pp. 98-100.

(2)

15

Wechsberg, Joseph, "Instruments of the Symphony Orchestra," Holiday, vol. 9 (March 1951), pp. 63 ff.

(3)

1

"Horn," The World Book Encyclopedia, Chicago, Field Enterprises, Inc., 1957, vol. 8, pp. 3525-26.

(4)

7

New York Herald Tribune, June 19, 1959 p. 6, col. 5.

PRACTICE 2. Preparing Source Cards

Find at least five reliable sources of information on your subject and list them on source cards in the form illustrated above. If you find that the library hasn't adequate material on your subject, or that most of the books are out, try another library—the main public library or a branch library. If it also lacks adequate material, choose another subject.

TAKING NOTES

If you read first, without taking notes, a general account of your subject in an encyclopedia, you will have some idea for a possible organization of your essay and some idea about what material you will find valuable and what useless.

When you do find valuable material—striking facts, statistics, quotations—take notes. Take plenty of them, but don't copy whole sections of articles.

Ordinarily take notes in your own words. If you copy something word for word, enclose the passage in prominent quotation marks, a reminder that the language is not your own. If you use a quotation in your paper, *give the exact source in a footnote*. If you paraphrase—that is, put another person's ideas in your own words—also credit the source in a footnote.

NOTE
CARD
(4" × 6")

	12
Phases in Development	pp. 98-100

1. Valveless natural horn—Bach & Handel's time
2. Hand horn—pitch changed by inserting hand into bell—Beethoven to Brahms
3. Valve horn—fully chromatic—popular after 1850—Wagner

HINTS FOR TAKING NOTES

1. Skim the selection. Reread the first paragraph. Notice headings and topic sentences. Don't take notes until you have discovered what you consider the important facts and ideas.
2. On each card write only one note, or related facts about only one topic.
3. Place the topic in the upper left corner. As you take notes and write down topics, a rough outline of your essay will begin to merge.
4. Write on one side only.

5. Use your own brand of shorthand, but be sure you can read your notes later. Make free use of contractions, the standard abbreviations, abbreviations of your invention, and mathematical signs such as &, $+$, $=$, $-$, $\therefore$, $\therefore$, $>$, and $<$. As a rule, omit articles, connectives, and the verb *to be*.

6. Ordinarily jot down only facts and ideas, not the author's words. Copy names, places, and figures accurately and clearly.

ORGANIZING YOUR NOTES

Read each note card and place it in one of two piles: (1) important facts, ideas, topics, and relevant figures, details, quotations, and illustrations; (2) irrelevant and unimportant information. Store pile 2 for possible future use. Arrange pile 1 in the order you want your report to read. Decide where each point may be most effectively presented. Don't be afraid to change your mind. All you have to do at this stage is to shift a note card to another place.

You are now ready to make an outline for your research essay. If you have arranged your note cards logically, the outline almost writes itself. The titles of important notes become main topics and subtopics in your outline.

For a report on nursing as a career these main topics might be selected:

I. Importance of nursing to society
II. Qualifications of a good nurse
III. Professional preparation
IV. Fields open to graduate nurses
V. The future of nursing

You are now ready to look over the remaining points, which are not of equal importance. Some will serve as subtopics under a main topic, some as subtopics under a subtopic, and a few will have to be dropped entirely.

ARRANGING DETAILS

The happenings in a story are ordinarily arranged in time order. The details of a picture are arranged in the order of observation, which is usually the space order. In explanation you will often place first the facts necessary for an understanding of later paragraphs. When in doubt, begin with a vital topic and lead up to a climax at the end. These patterns are (1) *time order*, (2) *space order*, (3) *necessary-facts-first order*, and (4) *emphasis order*.

Simple plans for the arrangement of material are: cause—effect; fact—explanation; easy—difficult; idea—action—consequences; disadvantages—advantages; physical—social—intellectual—moral; profit —duty; interesting happening—the big event; unnecessary—impractic-**a**ble—injurious.

When time order is possible, it is generally best.

HOW TO OUTLINE

Review the section on "How to Outline" in Chapter 4. In making your outline, watch for these further points:

1. *Avoid overlapping of topics.* See that no point disguised in different words is allowed to appear twice.
2. *Cover the subject completely.* Find subtopics that add up to the topic under which they fall.
3. *Avoid empty topics.* Fill your outline with information. Topics like "Value", "Purposes", "Results", "Economic results", and "Physical benefits" are empty unless subtopics give specific information.
4. *If you find any topics that are not on the subject cross them out.*

PRACTICE 3. Organizing Notes for Your Research Essay

Using the methods just described, take notes on your subject and arrange them in logical order. Then write the outline of your paper and hand it in with your note cards and source cards for checking.

SAMPLE OUTLINE FOR A RESEARCH ESSAY

YOUNG DRIVERS—A HIGHWAY MENACE

I. Young drivers in automobile accidents
   A. Number of young drivers in accidents.
   B. Number of young drivers in the country.
   C. Physical qualities of young drivers.

II. CAUSES OF AUTOMOBILE ACCIDENTS
   A. EXTERNAL FACTORS IN AUTOMOBILE ACCIDENTS
     1. Violation of traffic rules.
     2. Ignorant and reckless drivers.
   B. PSYCHOLOGICAL FACTORS IN AUTOMOBILE ACCIDENTS
     1. Per cent of accident-prone drivers.
     2. Characteristics of accident-prone drivers in general.
     3. Characteristics of accident-prone young drivers.

III. Need for Driver Education
   A. driver training in schools
      1. Program to date
      2. Effectiveness of school driving programs.
   B. driver training at home
      1. Parents' encouragement of proper driving by their children.
      2. Parents' supervision of the use of the family car.
      3. Parents' example—the strongest force of all.

IV. Young Drivers of the Future

SELF-CRITICISM CHART OF OUTLINE

1. *Is every main topic and subtopic on the subject?*
2. *Do my main topics cover the subject? Do the subtopics cover the main topics?*
3. *Have I avoided using too many main topics?*
4. *Does every subtopic belong under the main topic to which it is attached?*
5. *Are the main topics and the subtopics sensibly arranged?*
6. *Have I avoided duplications?*
7. *Is the grammatical construction for parallel topics the same—all sentences, for example, or all nouns with modifiers?*
8. *Is there a period after every topic number and letter, and after every sentence? Does every topic begin with a capital?*

WRITING YOUR FIRST DRAFT

With your note cards and your outline in front of you, you are ready to write the first draft. Use plenty of paper. For convenience in revising, write on one side of the sheet only and double space your writing. Write your first draft as rapidly as possible, without paying much attention to anything except getting your ideas down on paper.

Follow your outline, but make changes to improve your essay. As you use material for which you will give credit in footnotes, put the number of the source card and the page reference at the end of the sentence or paragraph you are writing. Don't worry about footnote form until you revise your essay.

When you wish to include a long quotation or a set of statistics from one of your authorities, don't laboriously copy your note card. Simply clip the note card to the rough draft and go on with your writing. Write as simply and clearly as you can. Compare, illustrate, explain, prove, give specific instances, develop.

PRACTICE 4. Writing Your First Draft

Write the first draft of the essay for which you have been preparing.

Give definite facts, examples, and illustrations. Indicate where foot notes will be required.

DEVICES FOR EFFECTIVE INTRODUCTION

1. A startling or relevant fact.
2. A pertinent narrative.
3. A series of questions which will be answered in the essay.
4. A simple statement of the purpose or theme of the essay.
5. A relevant comparison or contrast.

WRITING THE CONCLUSION

The last paragraph is usually a summary or enforcement of an important idea. It may be used to repeat the chief points, to strengthen conviction, or to emphasize an important idea. The last sentence should be so phrased that it will linger in the hearers' minds. A brief article or report needs no conclusion or just a sentence to enforce the main point. Don't feel that you must say something after you have said everything you have to say.

REVISING YOUR FIRST DRAFT

In writing your first draft you concentrated on getting all your facts down on paper and indicating where they belonged. Now you are ready to fill in the gaps and polish this rough copy. Read your essay critically several times. Pay particular attention to your introduction. Not only must it attract the reader's attention, but it must make clear to him the general theme of the essay. Be sure you have given credit for all borrowed material.

EXAMPLE OF REVISION

The French horn may be the problem child of the orchestra, but it's rich, beautiful, almost human tone makes it one of the most poetic of *musical* instruments. Although it is one of four members of the brass family, ~~only colloquially is the term "horn" applied to any brass instruments.~~ *In* orchestral circles the *term* "horn" ~~is~~ *refers to* always the French horn. It's great versatility makes it the bridge between the other brasses and the woodwinds. (7-40)

ADDING YOUR FOOTNOTES

You do not have to give credit for facts that are common knowledge or for accepted ideas. Anyone has the right to say that Florence Nightingale established nursing as a profession, or that a whale is an animal. Such facts are public property. When you include in your report, however, a discussion of an original theory, you should, by the use of such a phrase as "according to Adam Smith," "Mendel's opinion was," "Dr. Banting believed", acknowledge that the idea is borrowed.

Occasionally you will wish to quote directly a pertinent, vivid sentence or paragraph you have jotted down in your notes. Changing a few words doesn't make another writer's sentence or paragraph your property. Give credit for the following:

1. Material quoted verbatim.
2. Material only slightly reworded.
3. Ideas and opinions definitely borrowed.
4. Statements and figures which may be questioned.

Whenever there is anything in your paper which might cause a reader to ask "How do you know?" or "Who says so?" insert a footnote. Place a footnote number a little above the line at the end of the borrowed material and give the source in a footnote at the bottom of the page.

If you study several books or magazine articles that make use of footnotes, you may find the footnotes in different forms. Unless your teacher prefers another arrangement, you will find the following forms acceptable.

The first time you refer to a **book,** include the author's name, title of book, place of publication, publisher, date of publication, volume, and page numbers.
Hope Stoddard, From These Comes Music, New York, Thomas Y. Crowell Company, 1952, p. 91.

In a footnote for a **Magazine Article,** mention the author (first name or two initials), the title of the article, the magazine, the volume, the date, and the page number.
Ralph E. Rush, "The Brass Section—Strength of the Orchestra", Etude, vol. 73 (October 1955), p. 15.

In a footnote for a **Newspaper Article,** give the author's name (if known), the title of the article, the name of the newspaper (omitting the article), the date, the page number, and the column number. In special cases it might be advisable to indicate the edition. If such information is essential it should be placed before the date.
"The Symphony Orchestra", New York Herald Tribune, June 19, 1959, p. 6, col. 5.

In a footnote for an **Encyclopedia Article,** give the title of the reference, the name of the encyclopedia, the date of publication, the volume number, and the page number.

"Horn", Encyclopedia Britannica, 1957, vol. 11, p. 750.

For a later reference to the same source, use a shortened form. To refer to the author, work, and page numbers mentioned in the footnote immediately preceding, use ibid. (Latin ibidem, meaning in the same place). If the page number differs, place a comma after ibid. and give the page number.

Ibid., p. 19.

To refer to a book or an article quoted earlier but not in the immediately preceding footnote, give the name of the author if only one book or article by him is used.

Stoddard, p. 92.

If more than one book or article is used, give the name of the author and an abbreviated form of the title.

Rush, "Brass Section", p. 17.

There is a growing tendency today to insert specific page or line references directly in the accompanying text. Such statements as the following serve to identify the passages which they introduce and obviate the necessity of footnotes: "Somewhat more to the point are these lines from *Paradise Lost* (IX, 275-281)"; "The same thought is expressed more forcefully by Dante (*Inferno*, xxv, 1-3)." Equally explicit and space-saving is the practice of attaching to the last line of the quoted passage a notation (enclosed in either parentheses or square brackets) indicating the line, page, chapter, act, scene, etc. In such appended notations it is unnecessary to give the author's name or the title of the work if these have already been clearly indicated in the text; and it is proper to omit even the abbreviations if both page (or line) and volume, etc. are mentioned. Write (II, 36-40) instead of (VOL. II, pp. 36-40), and (IV, iii, 120-137) instead of (Act I, scene iii, ll. 120-137). [1]

[1]*Scholarly Reporting in the Humanities.* Humanities Research Council of Canada, Ottawa, 1951, pp. 10-11.

If the original work has been translated or edited, the name of the translator or editor, preceded by the abbreviation "trans." or "ed.", should be placed after the title.

Dante, *The Vision of Dante Alighieri*, trans. H. F. Cary, ed. Edmund G. Gardner, London and Toronto, Dent, 1915, p. 22.

Your footnotes should be numbered consecutively throughout your research essay. Some instructors prefer to have the footnotes assembled at the end of an essay; others prefer to have them appear on the page containing the material to which they refer.

If your footnotes are placed at the bottom of a page, draw a line to separate the footnotes from the text of your essay. Do not extend the line into the margins. See the model on page 133.

PREPARING YOUR BIBLIOGRAPHY

A research paper includes a bibliography—a list of books, encyclopedias, magazines, pamphlets, and newspapers consulted. A bibliography is valuable in supporting statements which may be questioned and in directing your reader to further information on the subject. A worth-while bibliography has complete and accurate information: author, title, publisher, date, volume, page.

Alphabetize the source cards for all the books, magazine articles, and other sources from which you got material for your research essay. On a separate sheet of paper copy the information from the cards, omitting the call numbers and your identifying numbers. Hand in the bibliography with the final version of your paper. Follow this form for a *lengthy bibliography:*

BIBLIOGRAPHY

ENCYCLOPEDIAS

"Horn", *Collier's Encyclopedia,* New York, P. F. Collier & Son, 1954, vol. 10, p. 159.

"Horn", *Encyclopaedia Britannica,* Chicago, Encyclopaedia Britannica, Inc., 1957, vol. 11, pp. 749-750.

"Horn", *The World Book Encyclopedia,* Chicago, Field Enterprises, Inc., 1957, vol. 8, pp. 3525-26.

BOOKS

Carse, Adam, *The Orchestra from Beethoven to Berlioz,* New York, Broude Brothers, 1949, pp. 38-39; 409-23.

Daubney, Ulric, *Orchestral Wind Instruments,* London, Wm. Reeves, 1920, pp. 14-17; 71-77.

Donington, Robert, *The Instruments of Music,* New York, Pitman Publishing Corp., 1951, pp. 98-100.

Johnstone, Arthur Edward, *Instruments of the Modern Symphony Orchestra and Band,* New York, Carl Fischer, 1928, p. 40.

Stoddard, Hope, *From These Comes Music,* New York, Thomas Y. Crowell Company, 1952, pp. 91-97.

MAGAZINES

Marek, George, "Instruments of the Orchestra", *Good Housekeeping*, vol. **129** (September 1949), pp. 4 ff.

Rush, Ralph E., "The Brass Section—Strength of the Orchestra", *Etude*, vol. 73 (October 1955), pp. 15 ff.

Wechsberg, Joseph, "Instruments of the Symphony Orchestra", *Holiday*, vol. **9** (March 1951), pp. 63 ff.

NEWSPAPERS

New York Herald Tribune, June 19, 1959, p. 6, col. **5**.

For a *short bibliography* an alphabetical order for all works consulted would be sufficient.

PREPARING THE FINAL COPY

1. Type your essay, double spaced, or write neatly and clearly in ink.
2. Write on only one side of the paper.
3. Leave a margin of at least an inch on the left side and about an inch on the right side.
4. As you write, don't forget to leave enough room for footnotes.
5. On the title page write the title of the essay, your name, and the date, as well as anything else your teacher requires. Centre this information.
6. On the first page write the title again, this time at least two inches from the top. Leave a space between it an the first line of the report. On pages after the first begin approximately an inch from the top.
7. Number the first page at the bottom (no period) and the rest at the top right-hand corner (one inch down and one inch in from the edge of the paper).
8. Include your outline, but number it separately.
9. Proof for errors and inconsistencies in form.
10. Assemble your pages in this order: title page, outline, essay, bibliography.

Your first page should look like the sample following:

SAMPLE FIRST PAGE OF A TERM PAPER
THE FRENCH HORN

> "The French Horn's sensitive; it's rumoured
> Its scale has notes which must be humoured.
> The players are a helpful team,
> So all comes out as smooth as cream."[1]

The French horn may be the problem child of the orchestra, but its rich, beautiful, almost human tone makes it one of the most poetic of musical instruments. Although it is one of four members of the brass family, in orchestral circles the term "horn" always refers to the French horn. Its great versatility makes it the bridge between the other brasses and the wood winds.[2]

In appearance the French horn is a coiled brass tube about seven feet, four inches long. At one end is a wide-mouthed bell from eleven to twelve inches in diameter; at the other, a long, funnel-shaped mouthpiece. Three valves controlling the length of the air passage in the tube give the French horn a chromatic range of three octaves.[3]

The French horn differs from the other brasses in that the diameter of its tubing is small compared to its length. It has a conical bore in contrast to the cylindrical bore of the trumpet. Whereas the other brasses have a flat, cup-shaped mouthpiece, the horn has a deep, funnel-shaped mouthpiece. Another important difference in the French horn is that the valves are managed with the left hand. The player inserts his right hand into the bell to control the pitch and tone quality of his instrument.[4]

---

[1] Hope Stoddard, From These Comes Music, New York, Thomas Y. Crowell Company, 1952, p. 91.

[2] Arthur Edward Johnstone, Instruments of the Modern Symphony Orchestra and Band, New York, Carl Fischer, 1928, p. 40.

[3] Ibid., p. 42.

[4] Stoddard, Music, p. 95.

SUBJECTS FOR A RESEARCH ESSAY IN LITERATURE

1. Forerunners of the modern mystery story (Edgar Allan Poe, Wilkie Collins, Arthur Conan Doyle).

2. The fathers of science fiction (Jules Verne, H. G. Wells, etc.).

3. Modern science fiction (Ray Bradbury's Fahrenheit 451, Karel Čapek's R. U. R. or War with the Newts, Robert Heinlein's The Puppet Masters).

4. Canada's dual culture—the conflict as it is expressed in the Canadian novel (MacLennan's Two Solitudes, Costain's High Towers, Gabrielle Roy's The Tin Flute).

5. The Utopian novel (Hilton's Lost Horizon, Bellamy's Looking Backward, More's Utopia, etc.).

6. George Orwell's debt to Arthur Koestler (Koestler's Darkness at Noon).

7. Steinbeck's social criticism.

8. Mark Twain's picture of the American West (Life on the Mississippi, Huckleberry Finn, The Celebrated Jumping Frog of Calaveras County, A Connecticut Yankee in King Arthur's Court, Roughing It, The Gilded Age—perhaps three of these).

9. Vance Packard's social criticism (The Hidden Persuaders, The Status Seekers, The Waste Makers).

10. Sinclair Lewis's picture of America (Dodsworth, Main Street, Babbitt).

11. The business man in fiction (Shaw's Major Barbara, Lewis's Dodsworth or Babbitt, Dreiser's Sister Carrie or The Financier, Sloan Wilson's The Man in the Gray Flannel Suit, Arthur Miller's The Death of a Salesman—perhaps three of these).

12. Man's inhumanity to man (Alan Paton's Cry, the Beloved Country, John Hersey's Hiroshima or The Wall, Arthur Miller's The Crucible, Jerome Weidman's The Enemy Camp, Charles Ferguson's Naked to Mine Enemies—perhaps three of these).

13. Man and nature—quest and conquest (Hemingway's *The Old Man and the Sea*, Heyerdahl's *Kon-Tiki* or *Aku-Aku*, Lindbergh's *The Spirit of St. Louis*, Costeau's *The Silent World*, Sir John Hunt's *The Conquest of Everest*—perhaps three of these).

14. A modern Canadian poet (E. J. Pratt, Earle Birney, A. M. Klein, etc.).

15. The poetry of Emily Dickinson (*or* some other poet).

16. George Bernard Shaw, the teacher. (Show that Shaw uses his plays as vehicles of instruction. State his main ideas and illustrate them by specific references to at least three plays—*Pygmalion, Man and Superman, Arms and the Man*, etc.)

17. The saintly life—an essay to illustrate St. Joan's qualities (simplicity, positiveness, eagerness, naivety, isolation, etc.).

18. Conway, Proctor, St. Joan, Babbitt, Winston Smith—as leaders.

19. The child in fiction—Little Eva, Little Lord Fauntleroy, Penrod, Tom Sawyer, Huckleberry Finn, Oliver Twist, etc. (Richard Hughes's *A High Wind in Jamaica*, William Golding's *Lord of the Flies* or J. D. Salinger's *The Catcher in the Rye*).

20. English spelling—an investigation into the ways words were spelled in previous ages and a consideration of Dewey's and Shaw's proposals for modernizations.

Chapter 17

Reports and Reviews

WRITING A REPORT

Reports and letters are the forms of writing you will use most. Through reports people communicate their observations, knowledge, and experiences. You may need to report on meetings, visits, interviews, job conditions, investigations, committee activities, and books you have read. In college, club, and church and in business, government, and the professions the ability to write accurate, clear, concise reports is always valuable and often essential.

PRACTICE 1. Evaluating a Report of a Visit

1. What makes the following report interesting?
2. What did you learn from the report?
3. What made you feel that the writer kept his eyes open during his visit?
4. Is the report clear, not too long? Does it leave unanswered questions?

OUR VISIT TO QUEBEC

Last summer I accompanied my uncle Ralph on an automobile trip to Quebec. The weather was perfect as we drove slowly through the countryside. Many of the villages we passed had impressive-looking buildings called "Hôtel Dieu" and "Hôtel de Ville". We learned later that these were not hotels, but hospitals and town halls. The farm communities seemed similar to American settlements. So too did the cities of St. Hyacinthe and Drummondville, with their supermarkets and parking meters. Odd-shaped houses, uniform church architecture, and French road signs were the chief reminders that we were in a province of French origin.

As we approached Quebec Bridge, however, we saw an astonishing sight. To the northeast, on a large hill overlooking the St. Lawrence River, was a huge mass of rock and fortifications. Towering above it like a medieval castle was the Château Frontenac, Quebec's biggest hotel.

Grande Allée, one of Quebec's three main thoroughfares, led us through an attractive residential section of luxurious homes, shade trees, spacious lawns, and neat flower gardens. On the right we passed the park leading uphill to the famous battlefield, the Plains of Abraham. The large gray building on our left was the Parliament Building, where the legislature of the province meets. The government libraries, too, are here. Parklike grounds and historical statues give added stateliness to the building.

Just beyond the Parliament Building a high stone wall crosses the city. At Grande Allée it arches to form the St. Louis Gate. The tower on one side gives the structure a medieval appearance. Past this gate is old Quebec—a quaint, compact little world. Narrow streets with queer-sounding names, steep hills, ancient houses, larger dwellings with French roofs and dormer windows, museums, monasteries, churches, government buildings—these are interspersed with modern stores and tall office buildings. The giant, red-brick Château Frontenac stands over this busy settlement.

A narrow road just beyond the Chateau dips downward and to the right to the Lower Town 350 feet below. Here, along a strip of water front crowded with old tenements, warehouses, and shops are Quebec's oldest buildings and landmarks. An "ascenseur", or elevator, crawls up the steep hill to the Château and the Upper Town.

The sight I enjoyed most was the Citadel, the thick-walled fortification which stands at the very top of the cape. This Gibraltar of America overlooks the battlefield on which Generals Wolfe and Montcalm were killed. Within the enclosure is the residence of Canada's governor general. During World War II, President Roosevelt and Prime Minister Churchill met at the Citadel to plan Allied strategy.

Our trip was an experience I shall never forget. Quebec's many interesting sights made me eager to go again.—HOWARD BOWMAN

From Tressler and Christ: English in Action, Course 3, 1960, 7th Edition, by permission D. C. Heath & Co., Boston.

PRACTICE 2. Reporting a Visit

Report to the class a visit to a place of interest—for example, an unusual house, a college, a model farm, a new shopping centre, an airplane factory, a harbour, an electronics laboratory, an art gallery. For help in using connectives to show clearly the relation between ideas.

REVIEWING BOOKS

Why do magazines and newspapers print pages of reviews of books, moving pictures, plays, operas, art exhibits, concerts, and recitals? Of what use are book reviews?

Book reviews are intended to help us choose, among the tens of thousands of books published each year, the books we may be interested in, and give us an appraisal of their worth. By helping us to decide what books we ought to read and giving us information about the books we have not time to read, reviewers make us more intelligent about books of the day. In the field of contemporary literature reviews are as useful as a history of literature is in the realm of older books: they guide and inform. And well-written book reviews are also entertaining.

FICTION

The job of the critic is to find out what the author was trying to do and whether or not he succeeded in doing it, and then to express what he thinks and feels about the book. The topics of a review vary with the type of book read. A fiction or drama report may be a discussion of a number of these topics: setting (time, place, atmosphere); plot; scenes that would be effective on the stage; characters; theme or central idea; suspense; beginning; ending; contrast; climaxes; clearness, force, and beauty of style; probability; methods of gaining a semblance of reality; movement of the story; humour; quotations; the best part of the story; reasons for liking or disliking the book; comparisons with other books by the same author or by other authors. That is a long list. Of course, no book review includes a discussion of all these topics. It is better by use of incidents, illustrations, and citations to prove three or four points than to mention and discuss a dozen vaguely. A pointed reason for liking or not liking the book makes an effective ending of a report.

POETRY

Many of the topics given under fiction and drama may be used in a report on poetry. Other topics often discussed are: themes treated, moods reflected, the sound (metre, rhyme, rhythm, onomatopœia, alliteration, assonance, most melodious lines); pictures; feelings expressed by the poet or aroused by the reader; lines worth remembering; word choice. Most good poetry has beauty of theme, imagination, emotion, sound, and diction.

BIOGRAPHY

A report on a biography should tell what the person discussed has done for the world, what he has added to the available hope, goodness, beauty, knowledge, or contentment. Useful topics are: the lasting work done by the subject of the biography; his early experiences as preparation for his life work; his traits; his ideals; his helps in achieving success; his handicaps or hardships; the author's style; the fairness and accuracy of the biographer; a comparison with other biographies; and reasons for liking or disliking the book.

ESSAYS

For a report on a volume of essays, letters, or orations good topics are: the author's purpose; traits of author shown; his style; his mood; humour; main thought of each essay, letter, or oration; ideas worth remembering; sentences worth memorizing; words added to reader's vocabulary; a comparison with other books; reasons for liking or disliking the book.

SEVENTEEN
BY BOOTH TARKINGTON

A lovelorn youth of seventeen, a beautiful young lady who talks baby talk, a few other youths, and a little sister who has a passion for sugared applesauce on bread—mix these ingredients and add Booth Tarkington. Place on a pedestal Miss Lola, and—oh, yes— Floppit! Underneath the pedestal, with an adoring expression in his eyes, place William Baxter, romantically aged seventeen, who discovers he can write poetry. The result is an extremely humorous and well-written book, for around those characters Booth Tarkington builds a delightful story. *Seventeen* could not be anything but utterly charming and entertaining, for Tarkington is at all times a master at portraying love-sick youth So to everyone, be he under seventeen, over seventeen, or just at that eventful age, I say, read this book—for it is an antidote for everything depressing—except, perhaps, seventeen-year-old lovesickness.— STUDENT

PRACTICE 3. Writing a Book Review

After reading the preceding review write a lively, pointed, entertaining one-paragraph report of a book you have recently read.

When you write a review, check it against the following check list for evaluating book or drama reviews.

CHECK LIST FOR A FICTION OR DRAMA REVIEW

1. General effect—gaiety, despair, courage, idealism, bitterness, etc.
2. How the effect is produced
   (a) Setting—place, time, atmosphere
   (b) Plot—probability, suspense, climaxes, movement of the story or play
   (c) Effective scenes

(d) Characters and dialogue—realistic? Are the characters likable, pathetic, understandable, different from people you know?

(e) Theme or central idea

(f) Beginning and ending

(g) Contrast—in mood, in characters, in pace

(h) Clearness, force, and beauty of style—word choice

(i) Humour

3. The best part of the story or play

4. Reasons for liking or disliking the book

5. Comparison with other books by the same or other authors.

CHECK LIST FOR A BIOGRAPHY REVIEW

1. The work achieved by the subject of the biography

2. His early experiences as a preparation for his lifework

3. The kind of person he is—physically, intellectually, emotionally

4. His ideals

5. His handicaps and hardships

6. The help he received in achieving success

7. The author's style

8. The fairness of the biographer

9. Sources of material. Did the subject or his family assist the biographer with letters, diaries, and other data?

10. A comparison with other biographies of the person

11. The reasons for liking or disliking the book

THE REVIEWER'S THREE BASIC QUESTIONS

(1) What was the author's purpose? (2) Was his purpose worth while? (3) Did he accomplish his purpose? If so, how? These are the three basic questions a reviewer usually considers. He answers them referring specifically to the story.

PRACTICE 4. Studying a Book Review

After you have read Lorraine Riesinger's review below, answer these questions:

1. What is Lorraine's general estimate of the book?
2. What specific information does she give about the theme or central idea, setting, main character, plot, effective scenes, author's style?
3. Which of these six topics does Lorraine discuss by using incidents and quotations from the book?   List the incidents and quotations.

THE OLD MAN AND THE SEA
BY ERNEST HEMINGWAY

This is an exciting book about an old man's struggle to keep his self-respect. Santiago, a wrinkled old man, lives alone in a one-room shack in a fishing village in Cuba.   He was once the best fisherman in the village.   Now for three months he has caught nothing.   Manolin, the young boy whom he taught to fish, has deserted him, for his parents have sent him to a luckier boat.

The proud old man will not admit defeat.   He tries fishing farther out in the Gulf.   A huge fish seizes his baited hook—the biggest marlin he has ever seen.   Without help he cannot pull the fish to his boat.   Putting the line around his body, he lashes himself to the vessel while the giant marlin drags the boat and its occupant farther out to sea.   Although cut and exhausted, the old man conquers through will power, skill, and intelligence.   His victory does not prove lasting, however.

The story is fast-moving.   Hemingway avoids unnecessary words, and his descriptions are clear and crisp.   For example, the fishing line was "as thick around as a big pencil."   The marlin's sword was "as long as a baseball bat and tapered like a rapier."   The most thrilling episode is the struggle with the marlin.   Other moments of great suspense occur when the fish is first hooked and when Santiago fights the mako shark.

Why in his old age did Santiago continue to go after big fish instead of concentrating on shrimp or tuna?   Hemingway suggests the answer: "Everything about him was old except his eyes and they were the same colour as the sea and were cheerful and undefeated."   Youthfulness of spirit also explains Santiago's unusual interest in baseball.   In the tensest moments of his sea experience he wondered how the big-league teams had fared or what Joe DiMaggio would think of him.

The theme of *The Old Man and the Sea* is man's persistent striving.   Although sea fiction ordinarily does not interest me, this short book was so gripping and its pictures of marine life so brilliant that I could not put it down.   I heartily recommend it therefore to both sea lovers and landlubbers.—LORRAINE RIESINGER.

Tressler and Christ: English in Action, Course 3, 1960, 7th Edition, by permission of D. C. Heath & Co., Boston.

PRACTICE 5. Analyzing a Book Review

From the *Saturday Review*, another magazine, or a newspaper, clip a good book review and paste it on a sheet of paper. Beside the review, indicate which of the check-list topics on page 396 the critic has discussed; for example, characters, effective scenes, etc.

Which topics has he discussed by using incidents or illustrations from the book?

Tell what you like about the review.

PRACTICE 6. Writing a Book Review

Write a clear, convincing, entertaining review of a book you have read recently. Base it on a number of the topics listed on page 396. Avoid trite phrases by explaining directly and pointedly why you like or dislike the book. A mere telling of the story or the life of the author is not a review. Reveal just enough of the plot to arouse the reader's interest. Build complete, varied sentences. Choose words which mean exactly what you wish to say.

REVIEWING A MOTION PICTURE

To review a motion picture requires somewhat the same skills as are required to review a drama, except that there are techniques peculiar to motion pictures, such as sound, colour, types of projection, which must be taken into account.

PRACTICE 7. Reviewing a Motion Picture

Using the following outline as a guide, write a review of a motion picture that you have lately seen.

OUTLINE FOR MOTION PICTURE REVIEW

General impression the motion picture made on you.
How the effect was achieved

STORY—good or bad, consistent or inconsistent, convincing or unlikely? Is the end appropriate?

DIRECTION—Who directed it? Did you enjoy his skill?

CAMERA WORK—kind of projection, good shots? was it artistically done?

SETTING—was it appropriate to the story?

ACTING AND CHARACTERIZATION—Who deserves special mention?

SOUND—was the sound pleasant? Does it make for good listening?

General Conclusion—Do you recommend it? with reservations?

PRACTICE 8.   Comparing Two Reviews of the Same Motion Picture

One of the great motion picture spectaculars of recent years was M-G-M's revival of Lew Wallace's *Ben-Hur*.   So great a spectacle was it that the viewer was apt to be carried away by the tremendous emotional impact of the film and lose his sense of perspective and proportion.   Different viewers reacted very differently to the film.

Compare the two following reviews of the motion picture *Ben-Hur*. Is each reviewer sincere in what he says about the film? Do the reviews complement each other? Is it likely that both reviews are correct? Why, then, are they so different?

BEN-HUR

Ben-Hur (M-G-M)."Did I set all this in motion?" gasped Major-General Lew Wallace.   In 1899, the hard-riding, hard-writing Civil War commander was already appalled by the smashing success of his first historical novel, *Ben-Hur*, which in 19 years had sold 400,000 copies.   And that, though the general did not live to see it, was only the beginning.   By 1920, a stage version of the general's work had been running 21 years, and had been seen by 20 million fans, had grossed $10 million.   In 1926, M-G-M turned it into the first of the cinemammoths, a $4,000,000, two-hour spectacle starring Ramon Novarro as Ben-Hur and Francis X. Bushman as Messala.   By 1936, the film had grossed almost $10 million, and the book had become the biggest bestseller (more than 2,000,000 copies) in U.S. history, not counting the Bible.

Last week, after five years of preparation, $6\frac{1}{2}$ months of shooting in Italy, nine months of editing in Hollywood, and a massive publicity campaign, M-G-M displayed a new version of *Ben-Hur* that is far and away the most expensive movie ever made—it cost $15 million to produce, $1,500,000 more than *The Ten Commandments*—and also one of the longest—3 hr. 37 min., not including a 15-minute intermission.   Only *Gone With the Wind* (3 hr. 42 min.) and *The Ten Commandments* (3 hr. 39 min.) ran longer.

Ben-Hur, 1959, by M-G-M's statistics, is adorned with more than 400 speaking parts, about 10,000 extras, 100,000 costumes, at least 300 sets   One of them, the circus built for the chariot race in Rome's Cinecitta, was the largest ever made for any movie.   It covered 18 acres, held 10,000 people and 40,000 tons of sand, took a year to complete, and cost $1,000,000.   The race itself, which runs only nine minutes on the screen, ran three months before the cameras and cost another million.   Three months before the shooting stopped.   Production Manager Henry Henigson had a serious heart attack, and two weeks later Producer Sam Zimbalist had a fatal one.   By the time the cameras had finally stopped rolling, M-G-M's London laboratories had processed at a cost of $1 a foot, some 1,250,000 feet of special, 65-mm. Eastman Color film.

Out of this sea of celluloid, a masterful director, William (*Wuthering Heights, The Best Years of Our Lives*) Wyler, has fished a whale of a picture, the biggest and the best of Hollywood's super-spectacles.   The story of *Ben-Hur* is reasonably faithful to the general's stirring "Tale of the Christ."   Prince

Judah Ben-Hur (Charlton Heston), a rich Jew born about the same time as Christ, falls out with his childhood friend Messala (Stephen Boyd), commander of the Roman garrison in Jerusalem, who demands that Ben-Hur inform against other Jewish patriots. When Ben-Hur refuses, Messala condemns him to certain death as a galley slave and shuts up his mother (Martha Scott) and sister (Cathy O'Donnell) in a pestilential dungeon. Ben-Hur is freed from the galley, taken to Rome and adopted by a Roman admiral (Jack Hawkins) whose life he has saved. As soon as possible, he goes back to Palestine, hears that his mother and sister are dead, enters against Messala in the chariot races and rides him into the ground. But Messala has his vengeance. With his dying breath he tells Ben-Hur that his mother and sister are alive, but are lepers. Heartbroken and crazed with hate, the hero sets out to raise a rebellion against Rome, but he is caught up in the procession to Calvary, and becomes a Christian. The picture ends with Christ's death and the hero's rebirth.

The film has its failures. The movie hero is pretty much an overgrown boy scout who never experiences the moral struggles that beset the hero of the book. Then, too, the story sometimes lags—not, oddly enough, because it is too long but because it is too short. For the final script, M-G-M eliminated an entire sub-plot that gives the middle of the story its shape and suspense. But the religious theme is handled with rare restraint and good taste. The face of Christ is never fully revealed. The Sermon on the Mount, The Trial, The Ascent of Calvary and The Crucifixion are pictured, without breathless reverence, in a matter-of-fact manner, as contemporary political events.

The script, written by Karl Tunberg, and touched up by S. N. Behrman, Gore Vidal and Christopher Fry, is well ordered, and its lines sometimes sing with good rhetoric and quiet poetry. The actors, for the most part, play in the grand manner, but with controlled firmness. Actor Boyd carries off the prize with a virile portrayal of Messala, and Hugh Griffith provides some skillful comic relief as a sheik who is crazy over horses. But what matters most and comes off best in the picture is the great scenes of spectacle, particularly the chariot race, a superbly handled crescendo of violence that ranks as one of the finest action sequences ever shot. All by itself it would be worth the price of admission.

Great credit goes to Producer Zimbalist, Scenarist Tunberg and Director Wyler, but the greatest belongs to Wyler. His wit, intelligence and formal instinct are almost everywhere in evidence, and he has set a standard of excellence by which coming generations of screen spectacles can expect to be measured. His virtues have been agreeably rewarded. Friends report that his percentage-of-profits deal with M-G-M will put him on easy street for the rest of his life. But it is probable that M-G-M, which was in a shaky financial spot when the project was launched, will not have any trouble keeping up the payments. *Ben-Hur* has run up the biggest advance sale (500,000) in film history, and the studio expects it to run at least two years at high-priced, ten-a-week showings in selected theaters, and to make more money than *The Ten Commandments*, which has already grossed more than $50 million.

Reprinted by permission of TIME *The Weekly Newsmagazine; Copyright Time Inc.* *1959.*

BEN-HUR 'MOST INSIDIOUS FILM OF 1960'
BY JOAN FOX

To mark the arrival of the new year, let us condemn rather than praise one of 1960's most successful films, *Ben-Hur*.

In Toronto alone more than a quarter of a million people have paid a handsome sum to witness this most latently insidious film to come from Hollywood in the past decade—notwithstanding all the lip-service its script pays to the humanitarian virtues of brotherhood and freedom.

Disturbing totalitarian tendencies, present like a slow sickness in current commercial films, are all there in primitive clarity in *Ben-Hur*. There is the master-slave world in which people are numbed, passive, and helpless to do anything; the submissive acceptance of violence as a means to an end; and an exposition of clinical horrors right out of an SS "medical" laboratory.

Far from "a tale of the Christ," William Wyler has unconsciously rendered a 20th-century parable of the unknown faceless Jew, "that young Rabbi from Nazareth," who is led off to be tortured and exterminated by the agents of the state, in the full knowledge of his fellow-citizens who stand mute and dry-eyed as He carries the cross to Calvary.

Ben-Hur offers Him water, but it is in the spirit of "tit for tat."

DOES NOT REALIZE

Wyler does not realize, even emotionally, that in turning Christ into just another victim figure he is subtly conditioning the world to accept anti-Semitism, genocide, and all the Nazi paraphernalia as facts of life.

Nor does the script offer a grain of what Christ had to offer the oppressed suffering world. The one character in the film suffused with good spirits and a happy soul is the pagan Arab horse-dealer.

He trains his horses with "love" and gentleness.   Ben-Hur races them in the famous chariot race and wins without ever touching them with a whip.

The character of Ben-Hur himself conforms to our contemporary cliche of the leader-hero of a colonial minority as innately right and good.   He has a strong will—as evidenced by his resistance to conversion.

His love-hate relationship with the Roman, Messala, is a reflection of the psychology of male military cults that rise when Fascist breezes stir the world.

For this reason, women are peripheral slaves in the story, as in "the warrior and the slave girl" complex that distinguishes second and third-rate spectaculars these days.   With Ben-Hur it is a case of "I could not love thee, dear, so much, Loved I not Israel more."

The Old Testament values of the film are high-lighted by the post-crucifixion fade-out on a gigantic Ben-Hur, the patriarchal father-god figure, embracing mother, wife, and sister all at once.

But the blasphemy, the enervated religiosity, and witless hypocrisy of *Ben-Hur* are surpassed by the depiction of the death of Messala, the most foul, stunning scene in recent films.

BEYOND WORDS

It is dangerous beyond words that present-day audiences can sit in passive comfort through this ghoulish butcher-shop scene and not utter a word of protest.

It is even more dangerous when the action on the screen enjoins the audience to watch the agonizing death of a skinned man strapped to a mortuary slab and enduring the amputation of his leg, and not feel any emotion or judgment on the matter.

For the audience identifies with the hero, Ben-Hur, who stands there expressionless. Compassion? Pity? Sorrow? Forgiveness? Charity? Horror? Revulsion? Hatred? or even satisfaction? Not a flicker of a recognizable human emotion!

The total effect of the scene is to consider how much pain a human body, of less consequence than a dog, can stand before death. Another statistic for Himmler.

Reprinted by permission of the Toronto Daily Star.

WRITING A SECRETARY'S REPORT

A secretary's report is a record of the business transacted, the motions passed, the committees appointed, and other important happenings. It should be concise, clear, and pointed.

In some English classes the pupils in turn act as secretary, write the minutes, and read them in class or write them on the blackboard. The Secretary's report of a meeting of an English class should, as a rule, include the date, the assignment for the next recitation, important announcements or business, a résumé of the work done, and a summary of what the class learned during the period. When you write a report of a meeting of your class, avoid stereotyped expressions. Omit matters of daily class routine which all the pupils understand—for example, "The class met in Room 208"; "The class came to order when the bell rang"; "The teacher then took the attendance"; "When the bell rang, the class was dismissed."

Keep in mind three purposes of the secretary's report: (1) to review at the beginning of a period the work of the preceding period; (2) to let the absent pupil know exactly what he missed and to guide him in the making up of his work; (3) to give the secretary valuable practice in summarizing and in reading aloud. Of course, you know that practice of any sort—summarizing, typing, or playing tennis or the piano, for instance—is of real value only when you take pains and do your best.

PRACTICE 9. Studying a Secretary's Report

Read the following report carefully.

1. What valuable discussion hints does the report include?
2. Are the sentences efficient and varied?   Give examples.

November 3, 19—

Miss Jergens began the work of the period by dictating the assignment for November 4. The class was instructed to read carefully pages 263-89 and

324-49 of *Microbe Hunters* in preparation for a test on the work of David Bruce and Walter Reed.

Miss Jergens then turned the class over to Fred Hamer, the class chairman. After a brief talk on "Modern Science", the topic of the day's panel discussion, Fred introduced Ethel Wolf, the first speaker. In her talk on "Science in the Home" Ethel pointed out that years ago people did not have in their homes such modern conveniences as washing machines, electric lights, vacuum cleaners, telephones, radios, and air-conditioning equipment.

Next Bert Schreiber spoke on "Methods of Microbe Hunters". After describing Koch's discovery of the anthrax bacillus, Bert discussed the four steps of microbe hunting: (1) isolate probable germ; (2) grow germ in artificial culture medium; (3) inoculate animal with suspected germs; (4) if animal dies, dissect it and look for germ. In conclusion Bert told how scientists stain germs to see them more easily under the microscope.

In his discussion of medical science today the third speaker, Alfred Deal, pointed out that it is only within the last fifty years that new scientific methods of prevention and cure of disease have been accepted. Because of them the life expectancy of a baby has, within thirty years, been raised fifteen years. To fight pneumonia, one of the chief causes of death, physicians have prepared serums. Although there are thirty-two different types of pneumonia, certain kinds are so rare that five serums cure 95 per cent of all the cases. Within recent years the sulfa drugs have also dramatically reduced pneumonia mortality. In penicillin, a drug obtained from mould, the medical profession has found a new cure for infections, and germ-caused diseases.

The last speaker, Charles Stein, sketched the future of aviation as experts envision it. Because of military experience in high altitude flying it is probable that in postwar years planes will cruise at heights well over 20,000 feet without unreasonable consumption of fuel. Bigger, more powerful engines—perhaps of the Diesel type—will be housed in the wings of tomorrow's planes. These planes may have four wheels, a front and a rear on each side of the fuselage. It is probable that the helicopter, a small aircraft which can fly forward, backward, and sideward, rise or descend vertically, and hover motionless in the air will be universally owned and operated as the automobile is today.

After the speakers had answered several questions, members of the class joined in the discussion. Next Miss Jergens was called on for a criticism. Ethel Wolf was criticized for talking to the floor rather than to the class and for telling the class what everyone knew. Bert Schreiber, on the other hand, had evidently investigated his subject thoroughly and spoke clearly and effectively. Alfred Deal was commended for interesting material. Occasionally, however, he mumbled instead of speaking clearly, and during his talk mispronounced *apparatus, benignant,* and *Becquerel.* Several times Charles Stein failed to make technical details clear to the class. He lacked vigour and animation and depended too much on his notes.

During the period the class learned many interesting facts about modern science and received valuable pointers about preparing and delivering a speech.

David Schwartz
Secretary

PRACTICE 10. Writing a Secretary's Report

Write, when your turn comes, a secretary's report of an English recitation. Summarize thoughtfully the work done during the period. Leave out unimportant details of the class routine.

DRESSING UP YOUR REPORT

SAMPLE LAY-OUT FOR REPORT TYPED IN BOOKLET FORMAT[1]

1

The Sno-Ball of 1958

Eleanor Forsey

June 6, 1958

2

Southside Collegiate Institute
June 6, 1958

To whom it may concern:

This report has been com-
piled for two purposes:
To present the organization,
the success, and the financial report of this year's
Sno-Ball; to help those
students who may be chair-
men of the Sno-Ball Com-
mittee of the future.

Yours sincerely,

Eleanor Forsey

3

Acknowledgements

My sincerest thanks go to
the committee members and
the many other people who
helped make this dance a
success. Thanks are
especially due to the
Collegiate Technicians
Club, the decorators, those
who cleared the cafeteria,
and the clean-up committee.

---

[1]*Reprinted from* Form and Content *by J. Bassett and D. Rutledge, with the kind permission of the publisher, McClelland and Stewart Limited, and of the authors.*

4

Table of Contents

(Sample Page of Body of Report)

5

I   THE COMMITTEE

The following were appointed members
of the Sno-Ball Committee for 1958:
Katherine Spring, Quentin Grant, Jean
Crups, John Braine, Lionel Fischer,
Ruth Cossini, Eric Dustinev.

II   DECISIONS ARRIVED AT

1. THE BAND

The Committee decided to hire Nels
Wismer and his twelve-piece band to
play from nine until one o'clock on
the evening of Friday, January 31.

2. MASTER OF CEREMONIES

It was decided that Charles Bloomfield,
President of the Student Senate, be
Master of Ceremonies.

3. GUESTS AND CHAPERONES

Invitations were posted in the
Teachers' Staff Rooms inviting the
Staff to attend the Sno-Ball.

Mr. and Mrs. B. C. Bell acted as
chaperones on behalf of the Staff.

The following were the guests:

```
                11                              13

VII  CONCLUSIONS                 IX   BIBLIOGRAPHY

     Because of the success           As references I used the
     of the dance and the             Sno-Ball reports of the
     obvious need for such a           last two years.
     formal·occasion, the
     Committee concludes
     that the Sno-Ball
     should be held annually.
```

```
                12


VIII RECOMMENDATIONS


     We recommend

     A. That there should
        be pencils at the
        door for the
        dancers to use for
        programs.

     B. That in future years
        a less expensive
        band be hired so
        that more money may
        be made for student
        activities.

     C. That a microphone
        be placed by the
        throne.

     D. That the Clean-Up
        Committee be en-
        larged and that it
        includes responsible
        students.
```

Chapter 18

The Familiar Essay

ALTHOUGH essays are commonly divided into the formal and informal or familiar, no sharp dividing line can be drawn between the two types. The formal essay is usually an orderly, logical, impersonal, instructive treatment of a subject. Carlyle's "Essay on Burns", Emerson's "Self-Reliance", Macaulay's "Life of Johnson", and Palmer's "Self-Cultivation in English" are four formal essays often studied in high school.

Of the familiar essay Mr. A. C. Benson says, "The true essay, then, is a tentative and personal treatment of a subject; it is a kind of improvisation on a delicate theme; a species of soliloquy, as if a man were to speak aloud the slender and whimsical thoughts that come into his mind when he is alone on a winter evening before a warm fire, and, closing his book, abandons himself to the luxury of genial reverie." He adds that the familiar essay is natural, clear, and rambling.

The personal note in the informal essay is one of its attractive features. The successful informal essayist writes as a man talks to his friend, and is so good-natured, fair, frank, reasonable, and entertaining that his readers come to know him. They learn of his whims, foibles, experiences, blunders, visions, likes, dislikes, and prejudices; feel his mood; and sense his personality.

THE IDEA

To write an informal essay one needs to have an interesting or unusual idea and to tell it skilfully. Of the subject matter Charles S.

Brooks says, "Pieces of this and that, an odd carrot, as it were, a left-over potato, a pithy bone, discarded trifles, are tossed in from time to time to feed the composition."

The idea must be the cornerstone on which rests the complete structure of the essay. No matter what digressions the writer may make later on, he must at length return to his original thought and make the reader feel that it permeates the entire work. Since the general idea or theme is so important, it should be introduced near the beginning of the essay.

STYLE

The style of the essay very often holds the chief interest of the reader. It should be adapted to the subject and mood, and may be gay and sprightly, or full of deep yet controlled feeling. One good test of the effectiveness of an essay's style is to read it aloud. If it has the cordial, intimate, sincere tone of good conversation, it is good essay style.

The essay is perhaps the literary form which needs the most polishing. To express skilfully an interesting or unusual idea takes time. Brooks says, "Essayists, as a rule, chew their pencils." Variety in sentence structure, in paragraph structure and length, and in vocabulary and phrase is the keynote. Use your dictionary freely, and consult Roget's *Thesaurus* and a good dictionary of synonyms when you find that you have fallen into worn-out words or hackneyed phrases.

Models of Familiar Essays:

1. THE EDUCATIONAL BENEFITS OF BOOK SALES[1]

It is a well-known fact that a person will spend his hard-earned money at a sale on something which he would not walk ten feet to purchase at its regular price. Thus does he acquire one of those hideous prints of "The Road to Jerusalem" done in chartreuse and violet, or similar *objets d'art* which are promptly relegated to the obscurity of the attic. But the most interesting— or alarming—results of bargain-hunting come from second-hand book sales, or from counters of books that have never left the store since their wholesale purchase some years ago and are consequently marked down.

The information accumulated in buying and reading these books is likely to be curious indeed. For example, I would never have spent $2.50 on a biography of William Jay Gaynor. This is not due to any prejudice against Mr. Gaynor (it would be impossible to conceive of such a prejudice, since I had never heard of him before I saw the book), nor is it due to any intense personal dislike of the biographer. It is because my earnings are about ten per cent higher than

---

[1] *A prize-winning essay in the annual Scholastic Awards competition. From* PRACTICAL ENGLISH *Magazine. Copyright 1956, by* Scholastic Magazines, Inc. *Reprinted by permission.*

those of Horatio Alger's bootblacks. But when the biography of Mr. Gaynor was offered for five cents, I threw financial caution to the winds and invested the required sum. This was one of those sales at which three or four cents is subtracted each day from the original price of the book, and I had the choice of buying it at an already much-reduced price or waiting until it came down to one cent.

And at this point I should add that there is an element of risk in waiting. When the prospective buyer decides to go back for the book, it may be gone. I almost had this experience with a copy of a book on the Revolutions of 1848. I regretfully spent $1.25 for it, when I might have waited for some days and bought it for 67¢. But it was the only copy, and I had visions of hungry historians descending *en masse* upon the bookstore after a three o'clock class and fighting for the book before I could even reach the store. Once a book I was about to get disappeared while I was *in* the store. It was a depressing and frustrating experience. If I had seen the purchaser, I would have wanted to knock him flat. But I am not a naturally aggressive person; in fact, I have a childlike gentleness, which some compare to that attributed to Abraham Lincoln. And I also have a reputation to preserve. So I contented myself by thinking that only a complete moron would buy such a book, forgetting— needless to say—that I myself had planned to buy it a moment before.

But I am wandering rather far afield from my original subject: the type of books a bargain hunter will buy and just what he is likely to read in them. With apologies to Mr. Gaynor and his biographer, I now hasten to say that I read the book and even rather enjoyed it. I counted myself somewhat richer culturally. And in doing so, I found a reason for buying the book—if one needs a reason when only a nickle is at stake.

Owing to book sales, I have read love poems of Abraham Cowley, about whom I know nothing. Having read them, I care less. I have read part of the Constitution of France with no excessive enjoyment, but rather with the grim zeal of the consecrated martyr who believes in self-education at the possible loss of friends, good spirits, and physical fitness. At the same time, I have tried to be duly consoled by the knowledge that the Austrian Socialist Party is becoming "ideologically closer" to the British Labour Party, though for the life of me I wouldn't know what to say to an Austrian Socialist if I met one on the street. Perhaps "Hello, there; I hear you fellows are becoming ideologically closer to the British Labour Party" would be a good icebreaker, although there is always the chance that an Austrian Socialist doesn't like to be compared to a British Labourite.

Owing to book sales, I have also learned of the existence of Adelaide of Savoy (1685-1712), who otherwise would have passed unnoticed and unsung by me. I have discovered a gentleman named William Henry Fry who seems to have written the first American opera; and upon scanning some of the musical excerpts from his work, reproduced in the biography concerning him, I have concluded that American music has suffered an irreparable loss by his demise, though not *too* irreparable. I have acquired the first volume of *The Manner of Holding Parliaments in England* by Henry Elsynge, who hastens to inform me on the subject of "Anno 25. E.3. Octab, purif. m. 25 for the abatement of fees for the Seale in the Kings Bench and Common pleas." I also have that nice fat volume on *The Course of Europe since Waterloo* which comes in handy as a seat for some of my piano students who are too small to reach the keyboard from the bench without some additional aid. And I fancy myself well qualified to deliver a discourse on Polish underground poets during World War II.

So, the educational advantages of buying books at sales cannot be over-emphasized. At least, that's the thought I leave with you. I don't want it. I prefer the remark of Sherlock Holmes, when informed for the first time by Watson of the Copernican theory: "Now that I *do* know, I shall do my best to forget it."—LARRY POSTON, University High School.

2. ON BIG WORDS

I was cutting down the nettles by the hedge with a bill-hook when a small man with spectacles, a straw hat, a white alpaca jacket, and a book under his arm came up, stopped, and looked on. I said "Good evening," and he said "Good evening." Then, pointing to my handiwork, he remarked:

"You find the nettles very difficult to eradicate?"

I said I found them hard to keep down.

"They disseminate themselves most luxuriantly," he said.

I replied that they spread like the dickens.

"But they have their utility in the economy of Nature," he said.

I replied that Nature was welcome to them as far as I was concerned.

He then remarked that it was most salubrious weather, and I agreed that it had been a fine day. But he was afraid, he said, that the aridity of the season was deleterious to the crops, and I replied that my potatoes were doing badly. After that, I think it occurred to him that we did not speak the same language, and with another "Good evening" he passed on and I returned to the attack on the nettles.

It is an excellent thing to have a good vocabulary, but one ought not to lard one's common speech or everyday letters with long words. It is like going out for a walk in the fields with a silk hat, a frock-coat, and patent leather boots. No reasonable person could enjoy the country in such a garb. He would feel like a blot on the landscape. He would be as much out of place as a guest in a smock-frock at a Buckingham Palace garden-party. And familiar conversation that dresses itself up in silk-hatted words is no less an offence against the good taste of things. We do not make a thing more impressive by clothing it in grand words any more than we crack a nut more neatly by using a sledge-hammer. We only distract attention from the thought to the clothes it wears. If we are wise, our wisdom will gain from the simplicity of our speech, and if we are foolish, our folly will only shout the louder through big words.

Take, for example, that remark of Dr. Johnson's about the swallows. "Swallows certainly sleep all the winter," he said. "A number of them con-globulate together, by flying round and round, and then all in a heap throw themsevles under water and lie in the bed of a river." It was a foolish belief, but it would be unfair to scoff at Johnson for not being better informed than his contemporaries. It is that bumptious word "conglobulate" that does for him. It looks so learned and knowing that it calls attention to the absurdity like a college cap on a donkey's ears.

A fine use of words does not necessarily mean the use of fine words. That was the mistake which Humpty-Dumpty made in *Alice in Wonderland*. He thought that "impenetrability" was such a magnificent word that it would leave Alice speechless and amazed. Many writers are like that. When the reporter says that So-and-So "manipulated the ivories" (meaning that he had played the billiard-balls into position), or that So-and-So "propelled the sphere" (meaning that he had kicked the football), he feels that he has got out of the rut of common speech when in fact he has exchanged good words for counterfeit coin. That is not the way of the masters of language. They do not vulgarize fine words. They glorify in simple words, as in Milton's description of the winged host:

> Far off their coming shone.

Quite ordinary words employed with a certain novelty and freshness can wear a distinction that gives them not only significance but a strange and haunting beauty. I once illustrated the point by showing the effects which the poets, and particularly Wordsworth and Keats, extract from the word "quiet." Shakespeare could perform equal miracles with the trivial word "sweet," which he uses with a subtle beauty that makes it sing like a violin in the hands of a master. Who can be abroad in the sunshine and singing of these spring days without that phrase, "the sweet o' the year," carolling like a bird in the mind? It is not a "jewel five words long." It is a dewdrop from the very mint of Nature. But Shakespeare could perform this magic with any old word. Take "flatter." A plain, home-spun word, you would say, useful for the drudgery of speech but nothing more. Then Shakespeare takes it in hand, and it shines bright as Sirius in the midnight sky:

> Full many a glorious morning have I seen
> Flatter the mountain tops with sovran eye.

I once wanted to use for purposes of quotation a familiar stanza of Burns, but one word, the vital word, escaped me. I give the stanza, with the word I lacked missing:

> To make a happy fireside clime
>   For weans and wife
> That's the true   and sublime
>   Of human life.

You, perhaps, know the missing word; but I could not recall it. I tried all the words that were serviceable, and each seemed banal and commonplace. I dare not, for shame, mention the words I tried to use as patches for Burns. When I turned up the poem and found that poignant word "pathos," I knew the measure of my failure to draw the poet's bow.

We carry big words in our head for the expression of our ideas, and short words in our heart for the expression of our emotions. Whenever we speak the language of true feeling, it is our mother tongue that comes to our lips. It is equal to any burden. Take the familiar last stanza of Wordsworth's: "Three years she grew in sun and shower":

> Thus Nature spake—the work was done—
> How soon my Lucy's race was run!
>   She died, and left to me
> This heath, this calm and quiet scene;
> The memory of what has been,
>   And never more will be.

It is so simple that a child might have said it, and so charged with emotion that a man might be forgiven if he could not say it. *A Shropshire Lad* is full of this surge of feeling dressed in homespun, as when he says:

> Into my heart an air that kills
>   From yon far country blows:
> What are those blue remembered hills,
>   What spires, what farms are those?
> That is the land of lost content,
>   I see it shining plain,
> The happy highways where I went
>   And cannot come again.

Even in pictorial description the most thrilling effects, as in the case I have quoted from Milton, are produced not by the pomp of words but by the passion of words. In two rapid, breathless lines:

> The sun's rim dips, the stars rush out,
>   With one stride comes the dark,

Coleridge flashes on the mind all the beauty and wonder of the tropic night. And though Shakespeare, like Milton and Wordsworth, could use the grand words when the purpose was rhetorical or decorative, he did not go to them for the expression of the great things of life. Then he speaks with what Raleigh calls the bare intolerable force of King Lear's:

> Do not laugh at me,
> For as I am a man, I think this lady
> To be my child Cordelia.

The higher the theme rises the more simple and austere becomes the speech, until the words seem like nerves bared and quivering to the agony of circumstance:

> *Lear.*   And my poor fool is hanged! No, no, no life!
> Why should a dog, a horse, a rat, have life,
> And thou no breath at all?   Thou'lt come no more,
> Never, never, never, never, never!
> Pray you, undo this button. Thank you, sir.—
> Do you see this?   Look on her, look, her lips,—
> Look there, look there!
> *Edgar.*   He faints! My lord, my lord!—
> *Kent.*   Break, heart; I prithee, break!
> *Edgar.*   Look up, my lord.
> *Kent.*   Vex not his ghost: O let him pass! he hates him
> That would upon the rack of this tough world
> Stretch him out longer.

The force of words can no farther go. And my friend in the white alpaca jacket will notice that they are all very little ones.—"Alpha of the Plough" (A. G. Gardiner), from *Many Furrows.*

By arrangement with the publishers, J. M. Dent & Sons, London and Toronto.

3. CANDILLI

James Elroy Flecker, author of the following delightful essay, was a young British poet, friend of Rupert Brooke. He served his nation for a few short years in the consular service in the Near East.

That there are landscapes whose beauty is intrinsically mournful, I admit; there are summer afternoons in England when the clouds lie low on the horizon, and the shadows of the hedges stretch out over the fields whose loveliness we recognize as sad. But in other lands than England reign endless sunshine and bright colour, and the scene that met my eyes all today should make the veriest dullard dance to behold its radiant joy. I have been staring for hours out of my window today, letting my thoughts and glances wander down the cobbled and precipitous street of Candilli, where dog and man lie sleeping, past the village minaret, out across the Bosphorus and all the myriad laughter of the tiny waves, to the further shore where rise the chivalrous old towers of Roumeli Hissar, which men called the Castle of Damalis five hundred years ago. If the world holds a fairer prospect, I, who have wandered a little, have not seen it; yet all its brightness and splendour does but fill my mind with sorrow and unrest. I have been watching for three hours the tracts of warm light on those giant-rounded keeps, and the thousand boats that ply the high-way of the salt sea-river, sad I know not why. I have waited till evening, idle in my chair, till the brown castle walls turned gold, and the blue sea white and wet, till the sun went down not amid the patches and pageantry of our Northern settings, but gently leaving a sky as softly coloured as the petals of a rose; and the lamps were swung high on to the masts of the great ships steaming out to Russia through the gloom. Sick at heart with so much loveliness was I, and then brief twilight came, netting the world in spectral blue, till I cried out for the darkness like a cave-beast blinded by the glare. And now darkness is here with her fixed and trailing stars, and the whole European shore is ablaze from Therapia to Stamboul; the Muezzin has cried from his little minaret, the Ottoman night has begun.

Is it unmanly or decadent of me to long for a slag-heap or a gaswork, or any strong, bold, ugly thing to break the spell of this terrible and malignant beauty that saps body and soul? Yet there are few who did not feel what they might call a "touch of sadness," in the sweet popular phrase, when first they saw the boundless sea, or mountains capped with snow. The misery I feel lies deep in the nature of man; such thoughts as I am thinking, millions have thought before. For here, it seems, is the very face of Beauty, here one may gaze into her eyes and watch them change. But who am I to enjoy this high gift of the gods? What can I do with it, how make it my own? Why is it there, part of my foolish daily life: can I treat it as a common thing? To deserve, to enjoy its magnificence, a man should have a high work, or at least a noble plan. A poet might sing of it, and find peace; or a painter paint it; glorious would it shine to a man returning from a long journey, if among those countless lights one light meant home. Even to me these scenes were joyful that day I rode over the Anatolian hills, and the weariness of the body banished all sickness from the mind, and my head was void of fancies, and I saw little as we cantered along the sandy tracks save spars of sunlight and flashes of sea. But now, though my limbs are aching to be up and doing, I am fascinated by deadly wonder; and he who sinks before this spell sits in his chair for hours and plays with his dreams. He dreams of a mistress as Thais gentle or as Helen fair, and of the palace one might raise upon the hill in marble symmetry and store with curious broideries of the East; and of all that life might be to a man who conquered it, and why Antony was wise. And he dreams vain private hopes of his own of which he is ashamed. And he ponders on the narrow lane of sea, and of all that Ancient histories have told him; of Sultans and Emperors; he remembers how the proud flags of Venice once flew splendid in the breeze, and how relentless Romans before them built walls and ways, and how once the little *Argo* rounded the point with blue-eyed Jason on her prow, and the merry, toiling crew, bound on the first adventure of the world. And a light fever distracts the dreamer's body, and his mind longs for some coercive chain, and he begins to understand why men of the East will sit by a fountain from noon to night, and let the world roll onward. —JAMES ELROY FLECKER, from *Collected Prose*.

By permission of Mrs. Flecker and the publishers, William Heineman Ltd., London.

PRACTICE 1. Thinking Up Topics for Informal Essays

After examining the titles in Practice 3, write five additional lively titles for informal essays on topics that you feel competent to handle. Some good titles begin with "The Art of . . ."—for example, "The Art of Getting into Trouble," "The Lost Art of Kiteflying," Some begin with "On . . ."—"On Boys," "On Pen Pals," "On Introductions." James Thurber has a number of essays beginning "The Night . . ." or "The Day . . ."—for example, "The Day the Dam Broke," "The Night the Ghost Got In."

PRACTICE 2. Making a Beginning

When you have decided upon a topic for your essay, consider how it can best be introduced, for it will depend usually upon the first sentence or the first paragraph whether the reader will go on to read your essay.

Study the first sentence of each of the essays in your book of essays to see how other writers have made their beginnings. Add other openings to the following possible list:

Open with a proverb or a familiar quotation.
Challenge a statement made by a speaker or writer.
Ask a question that will arrest the attention of the reader.
Begin with a personal experience or anecdote.

Add such other openings as you find illustrated in your book of essays.

PRACTICE 3. Writing an Informal Essay

On a topic you have just thought up, or on one of the following topics, write an informal essay. Write as if you were chatting with friends. Expand and illustrate your points. Enrich the essay with quotations and comparisons. Write clear, concise sentences. Revise and polish to make your essay interesting.

1. Cats	2. Snakes
3. Bells	4. The weaker sex
5. Do-it-yourself	6. Family chores
7. Sports cars	8. Family life on television
9. Hollywood's idea of the West	10. Going steady
11. Neighbours (or Relatives)	12. Gossip
13. On growing things	14. Keeping peace in the family
15. People I could do without	16. Alarm clocks
17. Christmas shopping	18. Crushes and hero worship
19. Practical jokers	20. Beach picnics

SELF-CRITICISM CHART—FAMILIAR ESSAYS

1. *Will my reader share the full flavour and significance of my ideas?*
2. *Have I particularized, expanded, illustrated sufficiently?*
3. *Is it easy to see how my ideas are related?*
4. *Have I chosen the most appropriate words?*
5. *Is my style easy and conversational?*
6. *Have I enriched the essay with quotations, allusions, experiences, comparisons, and figures of speech?*
7. *Are my sentences and paragraphs varied?*
8. *Have I revised and polished to make my ideas and expression clear and interesting?*

PRACTICE 4. The Familiar Essay

Write an informal essay on a topic of your own choice, but choose one that gives you a chance to write about your experience, observation, reading, or reflection. The topics listed below may suggest ideas and experience which are of interest to you and in which you can interest others. In your revision apply the eight standards above.

1. Dreams. 2. Family expectations. 3. Young experimenters. 4. Ho, for camp! 5. Eavesdropping. 6. On erasing boards. 7. A quiet afternoon with baby. 8. Table conversation. 9. Shoes. 10. Movies. 11. On hobbies. 12. Applying for a position. 13. Lightning. 14. Rubbish cans. 15. Stairs. 16. Back-seat driving. 17. On handshakes. 18. On sandwiches. 19. The radio. 20. On keeping a diary. 21. Radio advertising. 22. On wearing new clothes. 23. Overnight cabins. 24. Camping during a storm. 25. Mountain-climbing. 26. The uses of adversity. 27. In defense of rainy days.

Chapter 19

Literary Appreciation and Criticism

One of the commonest forms of the modern essay is that which seeks to appraise literary writing, poetry or prose. Usually if the emphasis is upon the merits of the piece we use the phrase literary appreciation; if upon its demerits we use the phrase literary criticism. The object of such writing is to recommend those works which have given the writer pleasure, and to evaluate others. This writing differs from book reviewing in not being, usually, professional, in not being confined to recent publications, and in not necessarily applying to whole books. It may treat a single poem or even portion of it.

Literary appreciation and criticism usually deal with (1) the author, (2) his personal style, (3) his place in literature, and (4) a review of the work under discussion, covering (*a*) the spirit of the piece, (*b*) its character, (*c*) particular merits, and (*d*) short excerpts, (*e*) comparison with other works of same author, or even by another author.

PRACTICE 1. Literary Appreciation

The following essay was written as an Introduction to *Gone to Earth* in a special edition of the works of Mary Webb.

1. Make a topical analysis of Buchan's essay on *Gone to Earth*. What subjects are treated?

2. For what purpose is each quoted excerpt chosen?

3. In a paragraph state what impression Buchan gives you of the book *Gone to Earth*. Does the essay give you a desire to read the book?

INTRODUCTION TO "GONE TO EARTH"

Gone to Earth was published in the dark days of 1917. It was the first of Mary Webb's novels to come into my hands. I read it at a time when everything that concerned the soil of England seemed precious, and one longed for the old things as a relief from a world too full of urgent novelties.

The scene is laid in the Welsh marches, a haunted country, like all borderlands. There are only a few human characters—a girl in her teens, the daughter of a gipsy and a crazy bee-keeper; a local squireen; a half-educated minister and his mother; a peasant or two. But there are multitudes of others, for winds and seasons, day and night, God's Little Mountains, the Callow, Hunter's Spinney, the house of Undern, are as much persons of the drama as the men and women. The animate and the inanimate combine to work out tragedy.

The book is partly allegory; that is to say, there is a story of mortal passion, and a second story behind it of an immortal conflict, in which human misdeeds have no place. Hazel Woodus suffers because she is involved in the clash of common lusts and petty jealousies, but she is predestined to suffer since she can never adjust herself to the straight orbit of human life. She is a creature of the wilds, with no heritage in the orderly populous world. In the end she is "gone to earth," as she has come from it. She is eternally a stranger.

The chief beauty of the book is the picture of Hazel, which is done with extraordinary tenderness and subtlety. She is at once the offspring of the mysterious landscape, and the interpretation of it. Wild and shy as a wood nymph, she has none of the natural world's callousness to pain. She is the protector of all wounded and persecuted things—a lame cat, a blind bird, bees frozen in winter, a fox-cub saved from the hounds. With the elemental things of hill and shaw she is at home, but when she travels beyond them she is a wild creature in a trap. Mary Webb is curiously insensitive to the cruelties of nature. To her *Natura* is only *benigna*. It is the world of men and their works in which alone dwells evil. "Oh, filthy, heavy-handed, blear-eyed world," she cries, "when will you wash and be clean?"

The progress of the tale is as simple and inevitable as a Greek tragedy. Hazel, in her innocence, becomes the prey of Jack Reddin, the yeoman-squire of Undern; craving for gentleness she finds it in Edward Marston, the minister, whom she marries; but Reddin drags her from her shelter. When she returns to it, broken and soiled, it is to find that the minister has become, through suffering, a man and a lover. But it is too late; destiny has set the game; in her efforts to save her fox-cub from the hounds she is driven over the rocks of the quarry—the victim of both man's cruelty and man's love.

The story marches to its close with a fierce impetus, but there are lovely interludes, like flutes among the trumpets. These are the quiet places which give relief, as when Hazel tries the charms which her mother had taught her, before returning to Reddin, or goes out to the stream side in the summer dawn, or wanders among the old, musty, haunted corridors of Undern. For grave irony I know few scenes in modern literature more effective than her interview with Reddin's discarded mistress. The character-drawing is on the same high level as the drama. Reddin is subtly conceived; his power over Hazel is due in part to the fact that he, too, is near the elemental world. The minister, Edward Marston, tends at first to be too much an embodiment of abstract virtues, but he awakes before the end into vivid life. His mother, the notable housekeeper, is a little masterpiece—the indoors, fireside dweller as a foil to the child of the woods. But apart from Hazel herself, the chief triumphs of portraiture are the gnarled figures of an elder England—the old father, harper and bee-keeper, coarse as a clod but gifted with a poet's fancy; Andrew Vessons, Reddin's servant, clipping his yews and philosophizing like one of Shakespeare's clowns.

The style, as in all Mary Webb's books, is impregnated with poetry, rising sometimes to the tenuous delicacy of music, but never sinking to "poetic prose". There are moments when it seems to me superheated, when her passion for metaphor makes the writing too high-pitched and strained. But no one of our day has a greater power of evoking natural magic. The landscape, the weather, the seasons, are made to crowd in upon us as we follow the doings of the protagonists, and we are perpetually aware of these things as a fateful background. That is right, for they are Hazel's world, and part of her character. Mary Webb need fear no comparison with any writer who has attempted to capture the soul of nature in words, and to "tease us out of thought" by glimpses into our ancient inheritance.

"The echoes are in us of great voices long gone hence; the unknown cries of huge beasts on the mountains; the sullen aims of creatures in the slime; the love-call of the bittern. We know, too, echoes of things outside our ken —the thought that shapes itself in the bee's brain and becomes a waxen box of sweets; the tyranny of youth stirring in the womb; the crazy terror of small slaughtered beasts; the upward push of folded grass, and how the leaf feels in all its veins the cold rain; the ceremonial that passes yearly in the emerald temples of bud and calyx—we have walked those temples; we are the sacrifice on those altars."

In her best moods the style clarifies to a rare beauty and simplicity. Take this of the old bee-keeper:

"Whenever an order for a coffin came, Hazel went to tell the bees who was dead. Her father thought this unnecessary. It was only for folks that died in the house, he said. But he had himself told the bees when his wife died. He had gone out on that vivid June morning to his hives, and had stood watching the lines of bees fetching water, their shadows going and coming on the clean white boards. Then he had stopped and said with a curious confidential indifference, "Maray's jead." He had put his ear to the hive and listed to the deep, solemn murmur within; but it was the murmur of the future, and not of the past, the preoccupation with life, not with death, that filled the pale galleries within."

And this of Hazel in the churchyard in the early morning:

"It was as if the dead had arisen in the stark hours between twelve and two, and were waiting unobtrusively, majestically, each by his own bed, to go down and break their long fast with the bee and the grass-snake in refectories too minute and too immortal to be known by the living. The tombstones seemed taller, seemed to have a presence behind them; the lush grass, lying grey and heavy with dew, seemed to have been swept by silent passing crowds."

If that is not the true magic, I do not know where to look for it.—JOHN BUCHAN, Introduction to *Gone to Earth*.

By permission of the publishers, Jonathan Cape Limited, Toronto.

EVALUATING PROSE STYLE

Akin to literary appreciation is an examination of the structure and development of selections of prose writing to ascertain its strengths and weaknesses.

Before attempting such an evaluation, refresh your memory of the principles of good prose writing.

A BRIEF REVIEW OF THE PRINCIPLES OF PARAGRAPH STRUCTURE, AND DEVELOPMENT

As a paragraph is the development of ONE thought, *Unity* or *Oneness* is its most important characteristic. *Unity of thought* is the adherence to one subject or to one aspect of a subject throughout a paragraph. The principal thought is given in the topic sentence and is developed in the supporting statements. Unity of thought may be achieved by the development of nothing but the topic sentence, by the elimination of all unrelated material, and by the introduction of a new paragraph when a new aspect of the subject, or, in direct narration, when a change of speaker is indicated.

A good paragraph has more than just unity of thought. It also *Impresses*, that is, affects, the reader in one dominant and predetermined way. A number of effects may be used as long as they combine to form ONE main impression. The impression left may be hatred, peacefulness, grandeur, beauty, and so on. A paragraph concerning mountains could leave an impression of height, cold, ruggedness, solitude, or vastness.

The use of one *Physical* and/or *Mental Point of View* is an aid to unity. In order that the reader may see the picture which is in the writer's mind, he must know the author's physical point of view; that is, he must know where the author was when he saw what he is describing. Good description indicates the physical point of view and indicates it early. The writer may change the physical point of view if it is logical to do so, but he must tell the reader of any change. A writer's mental point of view is the effect which the picture has upon his mind; it is thus the same as the impression or feeling that he wishes us to experience.

Coherence, literally, "hanging together", includes two things: (a) the *arrangement* of the ideas in their proper order and (b) the use of *word links* to bridge the gaps between sentences in order to show the exact relationship of one sentence to another. The connection of each sentence and each idea with the preceding context must be made clear and unmistakable. If the method of arrangement used by the writer is *chronological* (time, climactic, anti-climactic), then time links would be employed (*for example*, then, now, later, at the same time, meanwhile). If the method is *spacial* (place, topical), then place links would be employed (*for example*, on the right, in the distance, somewhat lower, just in front of, to the left, straight ahead). If the method is *logical* (familiar to unfamiliar, specific to general, etc.), then logical links would be employed (hence, thus, consequently, so, for this reason, therefore, as a result, it follows that). Miscellaneous linking words may be grouped under the following headings: addition (and, moreover, further, also, likewise, too); comparison (similarly, likewise); opposing, negating, limiting (but, nevertheless, on the contrary, however).

The following are the chief devices of *Emphasis:*

(a) **A forceful introduction or conclusion:** a question, a command, an exclamation, a sentence arousing suspense or bringing it to a climax, a sentence with universal appeal (human interest), a terse or unique expression, a positive statement, a negative statement.

(b) **Repetition.** The deliberate repetition of a key word or phrase strengthens a paragraph. Notice that repetition may take the form of synonyms or of sentence structure (parallelism). The use of appositives is also a kind of repetition.

(c) **Example and illustrations.** These help to express and to impress ideas.

(d) **Comparison and contrast.** The placing of similar or contrasting ideas side by side or in close proximity adds force to the ideas concerned. Consider black and white side by side: the black seems blacker; the white, whiter.

(e) **Climactic arrangement:** the arrangement of the details of the paragraph in an ascending scale of interest or importance.

(f) **Good proportion:** the concentration of the most important ideas or details in the larger part of the paragraph.

The following passage is a good example of effective arrangement in *description:*

From the top of Notre Dame, Montreal, is certainly to be had a prospect upon which, but for his fluttered nerves and trembling muscles and troubled perspiration, the traveller might well look back with delight, and, as it is, must behold with wonder. So far as the eye reaches, it dwells only upon what is magnificent. All the features of that landscape are grand. Below you spreads the city, which has less that is really mean in it than any other city of our continent, and which is ennobled by stately civic edifices, adorned by tasteful churches, and skirted by full-foliaged avenues of mansions and villas. Beyond it rises a beautiful mountain, green with woods and gardens to its crest, and flanked on the east by an endless fertile plain, and on the west by another expanse, through which the Ottawa rushes, turbid and dark, to its confluence with the St. Lawrence. Then these two mighty streams, commingled, flow past the city, lighting up the vast champaign country to the south, where, upon the utmost southern verge, as on the northern, rise the cloudy summits of far-off mountains.—WILLIAM DEAN HOWELLS, *Their Silver Wedding Journey.*

Reprinted by permission of the Heirs of William Dean Howells.

The following passage is a good example of effective arrangement in *exposition:*

We always speak of Canada as a new country. In one sense, of course, this is true. But there is another sense in which the Dominion of Canada, or at least part of it, is perhaps the oldest country in the world. According to the Nebular Theory, the whole of our planet was once a fiery, molten mass, gradually cooling and hardening itself into the globe we know. On its surface moved and swayed a liquid sea, glowing with such terrific heat that we can form no idea of its intensity.

As the mass cooled, vast layers of vapour, great beds of cloud, miles and miles in thickness, were formed and hung over the face of the globe, obscuring from its darkened surface the piercing beams of the sun. Slowly the earth cooled, until great masses of solid matter, rock as we call it, still penetrated with intense heat, rose to the surface of the boiling sea. Forces of inconceivable magnitude moved through the mass. The outer surface of the globe, as it cooled, ripped and shrivelled like a withering orange. Great ridges, the mountain-chains of today, were furrowed on its skin. Here in the darkness of the prehistoric night there arose, as the oldest part of the surface of the earth, the great rock bed that lies in a huge crescent round the shores of Hudson Bay, from Labrador to the unknown wilderness of the barren lands of the Coppermine Basin, touching the Arctic sea. The wanderer who stands today in the desolate country of James Bay or Ungava is among the oldest monuments of the world. The rugged rock which here and there breaks through the thin soil of the infertile north, has lain on the spot from the very dawn of time.—STEPHEN LEACOCK, "The Dawn of Canadian History" in *The Chronicles of Canada.*

PROSE APPRECIATION

An examination of the principles of good paragraph structure, sentence structure, and diction of this extract follows the selection.

THE CRUEL SEA

The scene from the bridge of the *Saltash* never lost an outline of senseless violence. By day it showed a square mile of tormented water, with huge waves flooding in like mountains sliding down the surface of the earth: with gulfs opening before the ship as if the whole ocean was avid to swallow her. Outlined against a livid sky, the mast plunged and rocked through a wild arc of space, flinging the aerials and the signal halyards about as if to whip the sea for its wickedness. Night added the terrible unknown; night was pitch-black, unpierceable to the eye, inhabited by fearful noises and sudden treacherous surprises: by waves that crashed down from nowhere, by stinging spray that tore into a man's face and eyes before he could duck for shelter. Isolated in the blackness, *Saltash* suffered every assault; she pitched, she rolled, she laboured: she met the shock of a breaking wave with a jar that shook her from end to end, she dived shuddering into a deep trough, shipping tons of water with a noise like a collapsing house, and then rose with infinite slowness, infinite pain, to shoulder the mass of water aside, and shake herself free, and prepare herself for the next blow.—NICHOLAS MONSARRAT, from *The Cruel Sea*.

By permission of the Author and Cassell & Co.

APPRECIATION

The writer of this passage has adhered to the principles of good paragraph structure. He has maintained unity of thought and of impression by the selection of suitable details to show the effect of a severe storm on the sea, on the ship, and on the crew: "tormented water", "pitching" ship, and "stinging spray that tore into a man's face and eyes". From the "tormented water" in the second sentence to the ship's efforts to "shake herself free" and prepare for the "next blow" in the last sentence, the writer has concentrated our attention on the "senseless violence" of the sea. The fixed point of view helps to achieve unity. The physical point of view is the bridge of the *Saltash;* the mental point of view, that of one of the ship's officers. The main impression—the fearful might of the storm is presented as a powerful enemy and that against which it is directed (the sea, the ship, and the crew) as helpless victims.

The arrangement of the details in a chronological order is an aid to coherence. The writer describes the terrors of the storm first by day and then by night. This method of arranging the details enables the author to conclude with an expanded description of the storm at night and thus to emphasize the features which he considers most significant. "Night added the terrible unknown." The passing of time is indicated by such word bridges as "by day," "night added", and "then". The details are also arranged in a place order with the description moving from the surface of the water up to the sky and the rigging, and then back again to the water. Since the time order is also a climactic order, the author's method of coherence enables him to build up to the ship's victory and her preparation to meet the next onslaught.

The senseless violence of the storm is emphasized in several ways—by climactic arrangement of details, purposeful sentence structure, well chosen diction and vivid imagery. Some of these devices have already been mentioned; others will be discussed later. The writer arouses our interest in the suspense of the opening sentence and holds it in the contrast between day and night—the visible horrors of daylight and the unseen terrors of night.

The sentence structure is purposeful. The short, simple topic sentence conveys the main impression of "senseless violence" right at the beginning of the paragraph. Most of the sentences, however, are long and loose. These heap up the descriptive details and thus help to create an overwhelming effect in keeping with the weather conditions. The long sentences at the end of the passage suggest the slow passage of time during the long night of the storm.

Numerous examples of balanced phrases and parallel structure convey the rhythm of the incessant pounding of the waves. One of the best examples of structural repetition is "she pitched, she rolled, she laboured," which conveys the supreme difficulty of the ship's struggle against the overwhelming forces of nature.

The passage is enlivened by good diction. To help his readers visualize the senseless violence of the waves, to hear their crash, and to feel their impact, the writer has used figurative language, specific adjectives, nouns and verbs, and onomatopoeic words. The vivid similes "huge waves flooding in like mountains sliding down the surface of the earth" and "shipping tons of water with a noise like a collapsing house" emphasize the tremendous force of the storm by suggesting its potential destructive power. To emphasize the size of the waves, the writer compares their troughs to "gulfs" and their crests to wild arcs of space. These are appropriate and original metaphors. The ship and the elements are personified in order to make the battle more realistic. Two of the best examples are "gulfs opening before the ship as if the whole ocean was avid to swallow her" and "the mast . . . flinging the aerials and the signal halyards about as if to whip the sea for its wickedness." Shouldering the mass of water aside and shaking herself free, the ship prepares for the next blow.

Almost every word in this passage is a sensory stimulus. Such vivid units of area and mass as "a square mile of tormented water", "shipping tons of water", and "mass of water" effectively suggest the vastness of the storm. Words of contour ("a wild arc of space" and "trough of waves"), colour ("livid sky" and "night was pitch-black"), and movement ("waves flooding in" and "mast plunged and rocked"), and vivid adjectives ("tormented water" and "treacherous surprises") help us to visualize the senseless quality of the storm's might. At the same time we feel the "stinging spray", the plunge and pitch and roll of the ship, and the jar of the breaking waves which shake the ship from end to end.

The writer makes good use of onomatopoeia and other sound effects. Cacophonous sounds in "crashed down," "stinging spray tore" and "dived shuddering into a deep trough" convey unpleasant sensations. Alliteration, especially the end-alliteration in "she pitched, she rolled, she laboured," emphasizes the tremendous exertion of the helpless vessel.

Thus, by means of unity of thought and impression, coherent and emphatic development, purposeful sentence structure, well chosen diction, and vivid imagery, the writer has successfully conveyed to his readers the fearful might of a storm at sea.

PRACTICE 2. Prose Appreciation

Write a prose appreciation of the following passage in which you discuss the principles of paragraphing, sentence structure, and diction.

The gorge bent. The walls fell suddenly away, and we came out on the edge of a bleak, boulder-strewn valley. And there it was.

Osborn saw it first. He had been leading the column, threading his way slowly among the huge rock masses of the gorge's mouth. Then he came to the first flat, bare place and stopped. He neither pointed nor cried out, but every man behind him knew instantly what it was. The long file sprang taut, like a jerked rope. As swiftly as we could, but in complete silence, we came out into the open ground where Osborn stood, and raised our eyes with his. In the records of the Indian Topographical Survey it says:

> Kalpurtha: a mountain in the Himalayas, altitude 28,000 ft. The highest peak in British India and fourth highest in the world. Also known as K3.   A tertiary formation of sedimentary limestone . . .

There were men among us who had spent months of their lives—in some cases, years—reading, thinking, planning about what now lay before us, but at that moment statistics and geology, knowledge, thought and plans were as remote and forgotten as the faraway western cities from which we had come. We were men bereft of everything but eyes, everything but the single, electric perception! There it was!

Before us the valley stretched away into miles of rocky desolation. To right and left it was bounded by low ridges which, as the eye followed them, slowly mounted and drew closer together until the valley was no longer a valley at all, but a narrowing, rising, corridor between the cliffs. What happened then I can describe only as a single stupendous crash of music. At the end of the corridor and above it—so far above it that it shut out half the sky—hung the blinding white mass of K3.

It was like the many pictures I had seen, and at the same time utterly unlike them. The shape was there, and the familiar distinguishing features—the sweeping skirt of glaciers; the monstrous vertical precipices of the face and the jagged ice line of the east ridge; finally the symmetrical summit pyramid that transfixed the sky. But whereas in the pictures the mountain had always seemed unreal—a dream image of cloud, snow, and crystal—it was now no longer an image at all. It was a mass, solid, imminent, appalling. We were still too far away to see the windy whipping of its snow plumes or to hear the cannonading of its avalanches, but in that sudden silent moment every man of us was for the first time aware of it, not as a picture in his mind but as a thing, an antagonist. For all its twenty-eight thousand feet of lofty grandeur, it seemed, somehow, less to tower than to crouch—a white-hooded giant, secret and remote, but living.—JAMES RAMSEY ULLMAN, from "Top Man".

Reprinted by permission of The Saturday Evening Post.

POETRY APPRECIATION AND COMPARISON

Read the following poems for pleasure.   Afterwards the exercises will be based on them.

TO AUTUMN

Season of mists and mellow fruitfulness!
   Close bosom-friend of the maturing sun;
Conspiring with him how to load and bless
   With fruit the vines that round the thatch-eaves run;
To bend with apples the moss'd cottage-trees,
   And fill all fruit with ripeness to the core;

To swell the gourd, and plump the hazel shells
  With a sweet kernel; to set budding more,
And still more, later flowers for the bees,
Until they think warm days will never cease,
  For Summer has o'er-brimm'd their clammy cells.

Who hath not seen thee oft amid thy store?
  Sometimes whoever seeks abroad may find
Thee sitting careless on a granary floor,
  Thy hair soft-lifted by the winnowing wind;
Or on a half-reap'd furrow sound asleep,
  Drowsed with the fume of poppies, while thy hook
    Spares the next swath and all its twined flowers;
And sometimes like a gleaner thou dost keep
  Steady thy laden head across a brook;
  Or by a cider-press, with patient look,
    Thou watchest the last oozings hours by hours.

Where are the songs of Spring? Aye, where are they?
  Think not of them, thou hast thy music too,—
While barred clouds bloom the soft-dying day,
  And touch the stubble-plains with rosy hue;
Then in a wailful choir the small gnats mourn
  Among the river sallows, borne aloft
    Or sinking as the light wind lives or dies;
And full grown lambs loud bleat from hilly bourn;
  Hedge-crickets sing; and now with treble soft
  The redbreast whistles from a garden-croft;
    And gathering swallows twitter in the skies.

                                    —JOHN KEATS

LONDON, SEPTEMBER 1802

O Friend! I know not which way I must look
For comfort, being, as I am, opprest,
To think that now our life is only drest
For show; mean handy-work of craftsman, cook,
Or groom!—We must run glittering like a brook
In the open sunshine, or we are unblest:
The wealthiest man among us is the best:
No grandeur now in nature or in book
Delights us. Rapine, avarice, expense,
This is idolatry; and these we adore:
Plain living and high thinking are no more:
The homely beauty of the good old cause
Is gone; our peace, our fearful innocence,
And pure religion breathing household laws.

                              —WILLIAM WORDSWORTH

THE SNAKE

A narrow fellow in the grass
Occasionally rides;
You may have met him,—did you not?
His notice sudden is.

The grass divides as with a comb,
A spotted shaft is seen;
And then it closes at your feet
And opens farther on.

He likes a boggy acre,
A floor too cool for corn.
Yet when a child, and barefoot,
I more than once, at morn,

Have passed, I thought, a whip-lash
Unbraiding in the sun,—
When, stooping to secure it,
It wrinkled, and was gone.

Several of nature's people
I know, and they know me;
I feel for them a transport
Of cordiality;

But never met this fellow,
Attended or alone,
Without a tighter breathing,
And zero at the bone.

—Emily Dickinson

SNAKE

A snake came to my water-trough
On a hot, hot day, and I in pyjamas for the heat,
To drink there.

In the deep, strange-scented shade of the great dark carob-tree
I came down the steps with my pitcher
And must wait, must stand and wait, for there he was at the trough before me.

He reached down from a fissure in the earth-wall in the gloom
And trailed his yellow-brown slackness soft-bellied down, over the edge of the
    stone trough
And rested his throat upon the stone bottom,
And where the water had dripped from the tap, in a small clearness,
He sipped with his straight mouth,
Softly drank through his straight gums, into his slack long body,
Silently.

Someone was before me at my water-trough,
And I, like a second comer, waiting.

He lifted his head from his drinking, as cattle do,
And looked at me vaguely, as drinking cattle do,
And flickered his two-forked tongue from his lips, and mused a moment,
And stooped and drank a little more,
Being earth-brown, earth-golden from the burning bowels of the earth
On the day of Sicilian July, with Etna smoking.

The voice of my education said to me
He must be killed,
For in Sicily the black, black snakes are innocent, the gold are venomous.

And voices in me said, If you were a man
You would take a stick and break him now, and finish him off.

But must I confess how I liked him,
How glad I was he had come like a guest in quiet, to drink at my water-trough
And depart peaceful, pacified, and thankless,
Into the burning bowels of this earth?

Was it cowardice, that I dared not kill him?
Was it perversity, that I longed to talk to him?
Was it humility, to feel so honoured?
I felt so honoured.

And yet those voices:
If you were not afraid, you would kill him!

And truly I was afraid, I was most afraid,
But even so, honoured still more
That he should seek my hospitality
From out the dark door of the secret earth.

He drank enough
And lifted his head, dreamily, as one who has drunken,
And flickered his tongue like a forked night on the air, so black,
Seeming to lick his lips,
And looked around like a god, unseeing, into the air,
And slowly turned his head,
And slowly, very slowly, as if thrice adream,
Proceeded to draw his slow length curving round
And climb again the broken bank of my wall-face.

And as he put his head into that dreadful hole,
And as he slowly drew up, snake-easing his shoulders, and entered farther,
A sort of horror, a sort of protest against his withdrawing into that horrid black
    hole,
Deliberately going into the blackness, and slowly drawing himself after,
Overcame me now his back was turned.

I looked round, I put down my pitcher,
I picked up a clumsy log
And threw it at the water-trough with a clatter.
I think it did not hit him,
But suddenly that part of him that was left behind convulsed in undignified haste,

Writhed like lightning, and was gone
Into the black hole, the earth-lipped fissure in the wall-front,
At which, in the intense still noon, I stared with fascination.

And immediately I regretted it.
I thought how paltry, how vulgar, what a mean act!
I despised myself and the voices of my accursed human education.

And I thought of the albatross,
And I wished he would come back, my snake.

For he seemed to me again like a king,
Like a king in exile, uncrowned in the underworld,
Now due to be crowned again.

And so, I missed my chance with one of the lords
Of life.
And I have something to expiate;
A pettiness.

—D. H. LAWRENCE

Reprinted by permission of Laurence Pollinger Ltd., and the Estate of the late Mrs. Frieda Lawrence, from The Collected Poems of D. H. Lawrence, Published by William Heinemann Ltd.

PÈRE LALEMANT

I lift the Lord on high,
Under the murmuring hemlock bough, and see
The small birds of the forest lingering by
And making melody.
These are mine acolytes and these my choir,
And this mine altar in the cool green shade,
Where the wild soft-eyed does draw nigh
Wondering, as in the byre
Of Bethlehem the oxen heard Thy cry
And saw Thee unafraid.

My boatmen sit apart,
Wolf-eyed, wolf-sinewed, stiller than the trees.
Help me, O Lord, for very slow of heart
And hard of faith are these.
Cruel are they, yet Thy children.   Foul are they.
Yet wert Thou born to save them utterly.
Then make me as I pray,
Just to their hates, kind to their sorrows, wise
After their speech, and strong before their free
Indomitable eyes.

Do the French lilies reign
Over Mont Royal and Stadacona still?
Up the St. Lawrence comes the spring again,
Crowning each southward hill
And blossoming pool with beauty, while I roam
Far from the perilous folds that are my home,

There where we built St. Ignace for our needs,
Shaped the rough roof-tree, turned the first sweet sod,
St. Ignace, and St. Louis, little beads
On the rosary of God.

Pines shall Thy pillars be,
Fairer than those Sidonian cedars brought
By Hiram out of Tyre, and each birch-tree
Shines like a holy thought.
But come no worshippers; shall I confess,
St. Francis-like, the birds of the wilderness?
O, with Thy love my lonely head uphold,
A wandering shepherd I, who hath no sheep;
A wandering soul, who hath no scrip, nor gold,
Nor anywhere to sleep.

My hour of rest is done;
On the smooth ripple lifts the long canoe;
The hemlocks murmur sadly as the sun
Slants his dim arrows through.
Whither I go I know not, nor the way,
Dark with strange passions, vexed with heathen charms,
Holding I know not what of life or death,
Only be Thou beside me day by day,
Thy rod my guide and comfort, underneath
Thy everlasting arms.

—Marjorie L. C. Pickthall

Reprinted by permission of McClelland & Stewart Ltd.

SEASCAPE

Over that morn hung heaviness, until,
Near sunless noon, we heard the ship's bell beating
A melancholy staccato on dead metal;
Saw the bare-footed watch come running aft;
Felt, far below, the sudden telegraph jangle
Its harsh metallic challenge, thrice repeated:
Stand to.   Half-speed ahead.   Slow.   Stop her!
They stopped.
The plunging pistons sank like a stopped heart:
She held, she swayed, a bulk, a hollow carcass
Of blistered iron that the gray-green, waveless,
Unruffled tropic waters slapped languidly.

And, in that pause, a sinister whisper ran;
Burial at Sea! a Portuguese official . . . .
Poor fever-broken devil from Mozambique:
Came on half tight: the doctor calls it heat-stroke.
Why do they travel steerage?   It's the exchange:
So many million *reis* to the pound!

What did he look like?   No one ever saw him:
Took to his bunk, and drank and drank and died.
They're ready! Silence!
                                        We clustered to the rail,
Curious and half-ashamed.   The well-deck spread
A comfortable gulf of segregation
Between ourselves and death.   *Burial at sea* ....
The master holds a black book at arm's length;
His droning voice comes for'ard: *This our brother* ....
We therefore commit his body to the deep
To be turned into corruption .... The bo's'n whispers
Hoarsely behind his hand: *Now, all together!*
The hatch-cover is tilted; a mummy of sailcloth
Well ballasted with iron shoots clear of the poop;
Falls, like a diving gannet.   The green sea closes
Its burnished skin; the snaky swell smoothes over ....
While he, the man of the steerage, goes down, down,
Feet foremost, sliding swiftly down the dim water,
Swift to escape
Those plunging shapes with pale, empurpled bellies
That swirl and veer about him.   He goes down
Unerringly, as though he knew the way
Through green, through gloom, to absolute watery darkness
Where no weed sways nor curious fin quivers:
To the sad, sunless deeps where, endlessly,
A downward drift of death spreads its wan mantle
In the wave-molded valleys that shall enfold him
Till the sea gives up its dead.

There shall he lie dispersed amid great riches:
Such gold, such arrogance, so many bold hearts!
All the sunken armadas pressed to powder
By weight of incredible seas!   That mingled wrack
No living sun shall visit till the crust
Of earth be riven, or this rolling planet
Reel on its axis; till the moon-chained tides,
Unloosed, deliver up that white Atlantis
Whose naked peaks shall beach above the slaked
Thirst of Sahara, fringed by weedy tangles
Of Atlas's drowned cedars, frowning eastward
To where the sands of India lie cold,
And heaped Himalaya's a rib of coral,
Slowly uplifted, grain on grain ....
                                        We dream
Too long! Another jangle of alarum
Stabs at the engines: *Slow.   Half-speed.   Full-speed!*
The great bearings rumble; the screw churns, frothing
Opaque water to downward-swelling plumes
Milky as wood-smoke.   A shoal of flying-fish
Spurts out like animate spray.   The warm breeze wakens;
And we pass on, forgetting,

Toward the solemn horizon of bronzed cumulus
That bounds our brooding sea, gathering gloom
That, when night falls, will dissipate in flaws
Of watery lightning, washing the hot sky,
Cleansing all hearts of heat and restlessness,
Until, with day, another blue be born.

—Francis Brett Young

Reprinted by permission of William Heinemann Ltd.

DOVER BEACH

The sea is calm to-night.
The tide is full, the moon lies fair
Upon the straits:—on the French coast the light
Gleams and is gone; the cliffs of England stand,
Glimmering and vast, out in the tranquil bay.
Come to the window, sweet is the night-air!
Only, from the long line of spray
Where the sea meets the moon-blanch'd land,

Listen! you hear the grating roar
Of pebbles which the waves draw back, and fling,
At their return, up the high strand,
Begin, and cease, and then again begin,
With tremulous cadence slow, and bring
The eternal note of sadness in.

Sophocles long ago
Heard it in the Aegaean, and it brought
Into his mind the turbid ebb and flow
Of human misery; we
Find also in the sound a thought,
Hearing it by this distant northern sea.

The Sea of Faith
Was once, too, at the full, and round earth's shore
Lay like the folds of a bright girdle furl'd.
But now I only hear
Its melancholy, long, withdrawing roar,
Retreating, to the breath
Of the night-wind, down the vast edges drear
And naked shingles of the world.

Ah, love, let us be true
To one another! for the world, which seems
To lie before us like a land of deams,
So various, so beautiful, so new,
Hath really neither joy, nor love, nor light,
Nor certitude, nor peace, nor help for pain;
And we are here as on a darkling plain
Swept with confused alarms of struggle and flight,
Where ignorant armies clash by night.

—Matthew Arnold

PROSPICE

Fear death?—to feel the fog in my throat,
    The mist in my face,
When the snows begin, and the blasts denote
    I am nearing the place,
The power of the night, the press of the storm,
    The post of the foe;
Where he stands, the Arch Fear in a visible form,
    Yet the strong man must go:
For the journey is done and the summit attained,
    And the barriers fall,
Though a battle's to fight ere the guerdon be gained,
    The reward of it all.
I was ever a fighter, so—one fight more,
    The best and the last!

I would hate that death bandaged my eyes and forbore
    And bade me creep past.
No! let me taste the whole of it, fare like my peers
    The heroes of old,
Bear the brunt, in a minute pay glad life's arrears
    Of pain, darkness and cold.
For sudden the worst turns the best to the brave,
    The black minute's at end,
And the elements' rage, the fiend-voices that rave,
    Shall dwindle, shall blend,
Shall change, shall become first a peace out of pain,
    Then a light, then thy breast,
O thou soul of my soul! I shall clasp thee again,
    And with God be the rest!

—ROBERT BROWNING

ON HIS BLINDNESS

When I consider how my light is spent
    Ere half my days, in this dark world and wide,
    And that one talent which is death to hide,
    Lodged with me useless, though my soul more bent
To serve therewith my Maker, and present
    My true account, lest He, returning, chide;
    'Doth God exact day-labour, light denied?'
    I fondly ask. But Patience, to prevent
That murmur, soon replies: 'God doth not need
    Either man's work or his own gifts. Who best
    Bear His mild yoke, they serve Him best. His state
Is kingly. Thousands, at His bidding, speed
    And post o'er land and ocean, without rest;
    They also serve who only stand and wait.'

—JOHN MILTON

THE HARE AND MANY FRIENDS

Friendship, like love, is but a name,
Unless to one you stint the flame.
The child, whom many fathers share,
Hath seldom known a father's care.
'Tis thus in friendships; who depend
On many, rarely find a friend.

    A Hare who in a civil way,
Complied with every thing, like Gay,
Was known by all the bestial train,
Who haunt the wood, or graze the plain.
Her care was never to offend,
And every creature was her friend

    As forth she went at early dawn
To taste the dew-besprinkled lawn,
Behind she hears the hunter's cries,
And from the deep-mouthed thunder flies.
She starts, she stops, she pants for breath;
She hears the near advance of death;
She doubles to mislead the hound,
And measures back her mazy round;
Till, fainting in the public way,
Half-dead with fear, she gasping lay.

    What transport in her bosom grew,
When first the Horse appeared in view!
"Let me," says she, "your back ascend,
And owe my safety to a friend.
You know my feet betray my flight;
To friendship every burden's light."
The Horse replied; "Poor honest Puss,
It grieves my heart to see thee thus;
Be comforted, relief is near;
For all your friends are in the rear."

    She next the stately Bull implored,
And thus replied the mighty Lord;
"Since every beast alive can tell
That I sincerely wish you well,
I may without offence pretend
To take the freedom of a friend.
Love calls me hence; a favourite cow
Expects me near yon barley-mow;
And when a lady's in the case,
You know, all other things give place.
To leave you thus might seem unkind,
But see, the Goat is just behind."

    The Goat remarked her pulse was high,
Her languid head, her heavy eye:
"My back," says he, " may do you harm;
The Sheep's at hand, and wool is warm."

The Sheep was feeble, and complained
His sides a load of wool sustained;
Said he was slow, confessed his fears;
For hounds eat Sheep as well as Hares!
      She now the trotting Calf addressed;
To save from death a friend distressed:
"Shall I," says he, "of tender age,
In this important care engage?
Older and abler passed you by;
How strong are those! how weak am I!
Should I presume to bear you hence,
Those friends of mine may take offence.
Excuse me, then.   You know my heart;
But dearest friends, alas! must part;
How shall we all lament!   Adieu,
For see the hounds are just in view."

—John Gay

MY LAST DUCHESS
Ferrara

That's my last Duchess painted on the wall,
Looking as if she were alive.   I call
That piece a wonder, now: Fra Pandolf's hands
Worked busily a day, and there she stands.
Will't please you sit and look at her?   I said
"Fra Pandolf" by design, for never read
Strangers like you that pictured countenance,
The depth and passion of its earnest glance,
But to myself they turned (since none puts by
The curtain I have drawn for you, but I),
And seemed as they would ask me, if they durst,
How such a glance came there; so, not the first
Are you to turn and ask thus.   Sir, t'was not
Her husband's presence only, called that spot
Of joy into the Duchess' cheek; perhaps
Fra Pandolf chanced to say, "Her mantle laps
Over my lady's wrist too much," or "Paint
Must never hope to reproduce the faint
Half-flush that dies along her throat": such stuff
Was courtesy, she thought, and cause enough
For calling up that spot of joy.   She had
A heart—how shall I say?—too soon made glad,
Too easily impressed; she liked whate'er
She looked on, and her looks went everywhere.
Sir, 'twas all one! My favour at her breast,
The dropping of the daylight in the West,
The bough of cherries some officious fool
Broke in the orchard for her, the white mule
She rode with round the terrace—all and each

Would draw from her alike the approving speech,
Or blush, at least.   She thanked men,—good, but thanked
Somehow—I know not how—as if she ranked
My gift of a nine-hundred-years-old name
With anybody's gift.   Who'd stoop to blame
This sort of trifling?   Even had you skill
In speech—(which I have not)—to make your will
Quite clear to such an one, and say, "Just this
Or that in you disgusts me; here you miss,
Or there exceed the mark"—and if she let
Herself be lessoned so, nor plainly set
Her wits to yours, forsooth, and made excuse,
—E'en then would be some stooping; and I choose
Never to stoop.   Oh sir, she smiled, no doubt
Whene'er I passed her; but who passed without
Much the same smile?   This grew; I gave commands;
Then all smiles stopped together.   There she stands
As if alive.   Will't please you rise?   We'll meet
The company below, then.   I repeat,
The Count your master's known munificence
Is ample warrant that no just pretence
Of mine for dowry will be disallowed;
Though his fair daughter's self, as I avowed
At starting, is my object.   Nay, we'll go
Together down, sir.   Notice Neptune, though,
Taming a sea-horse, thought a rarity,
Which Claus of Innsbruck cast in bronze for me!

—ROBERT BROWNING

A. POETRY APPRECIATION

A poetry appreciation is an assessment of the merits of a particular poem. Although a professional critic usually attempts a fairly comprehensive treatment of his subject, a student's appreciation would be considered satisfactory if it included a discussion of four or five of the following:

1. The quality or impressiveness or the importance of the *thought* expressed.
2. The effective use of *imagery* or *colour* or *sound patterns*.
3. The *emotional effects* of the passage.
4. The effects of particular *figures of speech*.
5. The kind of *diction* and the effect of its use.
6. The use of *literary devices* such as contrast, rhetorical questions, repetition, climax.
7. The merits of the *verse form* and *rhyme scheme* and the *rhythm* and *melody* of the language.

The merit under discussion should be named, illustrated from the text of the poem, and, if possible, commented on as to effectiveness or result.

JOHN KEATS' "TO AUTUMN"

There is, in this ode, a satisfying completeness which leaves the reader conscious that all has been said that could be fittingly said. Any attempt either to add or to subtract would spoil the picture. And what has been done is so good that one would not have a word or a phrase altered. The three stanzas give perfect pictures—the first of the generous beauty associated with autumn as it appears to the eye, the third of the sounds of the season as they strike the ear, and the second a portrait of Autumn himself which seems alive and carries conviction as such full-length personifications rarely do.

Keats' exact and careful observation is shown throughout his record of typical sights and sounds. There are the loaded vines running round the thatch-eaves, the heavy fruit bending the branches of the mossy trees, and the bees busying themselves about the late flowers as if it were still summer. All these express the bounty of the Autumn, scattering his gifts with a lavish hand so that all who will may gather. Equally significant are the bleating of the full-grown lamb, the whistling of the redbreast, and the twittering of the swallows—all rendering the pensive note that accompanies the fall of the leaf.

Then the figure of Autumn himself portrayed by the poet in the second stanza is perfectly natural and convincing. We see him amid the scenes that express him most effectively—in the granary with "hair soft-lifted by the winnowing wind"; in the half-reaped furrow amid the drowsy poppies; with the gleaners; or by the cider-press, watching "the last oozings hours by hours".

The flawless form of the ode is in keeping with these pictures. There are four lines rhyming alternately, followed by a septet in which the repetition of the third rhyme is suspended while the second is sounded yet once again, giving just that amount of surprise which most pleases the ear.

The use of alliteration is equally pleasing. There are plain and obvious effects, as in

> While *b*arred clouds *b*loom the soft-*d*ying *d*ay,

and the subtler touches in

> *S*eason of *m*ists and *m*ellow *f*ruit*f*ulness!
> Close bo*s*om-*f*riend o*f* the *m*aturing *s*un.

Here we first become conscious of the repetition of the sibilant. Chiming with this we hear the *m* and then the *f*, giving an interlacing of soft sounds that suggest the slumbrous music so appropriate to an autumn day.

There are wonderfully effective single lines. One has already been quoted in part—

> Thou watchest the last oozings hours by hours.

The repetition of the difficult *st* ending so delays the utterance of the line as to express exactly the "patient look" that cannot bear to miss a single drop as it falls from the press.

There is, too, the very delightful line

> Then in a wailful choir the small gnats mourn

which in itself gives a perfect autumn picture.

The quickness of the poet's apprehension is evident throughout the poem. Each sight and each sound, however delicate, registers its due impression and it is noteworthy that Keats is so concerned in the apt expression of what he has seen and heard that he forgets himself completely. Nowhere does he refer to himself, yet, such is the paradox of personality, no poet has ever more effectively secured self-expression than Keats has done in *To Autumn*.

(from *Exercises in Appreciation* by F. H. Pritchard, published by George G. Harrap & Co. Ltd.)

STUDENT'S APPRECIATION:

WORDSWORTH "LONDON, SEPTEMBER 1802"

The theme of Wordsworth's sonnet "London, September, 1802" is a sensitive man's anger and despair over the materialistic society which he sees around him.   Although his emotions are strong, he fits them neatly into the prepared mould of the sonnet form.   There are two closely related quatrains in the octave. The first expresses his sadness over life's present ostentation; the second, comparing life to a brook, is a sarcastic comment on the shallowness of life.   In the sestet Wordsworth fits two related ideas to each of the tercets.   First, high thinking is gone because of greed; second, the best qualities of human conduct have been abandoned.   The relationship between the octave and the sestet is clear.   In the octave the poet describes the present ideals of his country—materialism or ostentation—as the "mean handy-work of craftsman, cook, or groom."   In the sestet, however, he refers to the former ideals of England—the "pure religion breathing household laws" and the sober virtues of the "good old cause".   The contrast intensifies both sets of details and heightens the central theme.

The various moods of the sonnet are emphasized by the use of suggestive sounds and words.   In the first line, the short words containing long vowels tend to slow the rhythm of the line and express the poet's bewilderment.   To this is added the effect of the hard sounds in "opprest" and "drest", in "idolatry" and "adore".   Both the sound and the connotation of these words add to the mood of anger and disgust.   The sarcasm of the second quatrain, especially the line "The wealthiest man among us is the best," emphasizes the poet's disgust with the materialism of his countrymen.   His deep regret over the loss of something fine is reinforced in the last two lines by the use of euphonious words such as "peace", "fearful innocence" and "breathing."

The rhythm of certain lines is varied in a skilful manner.   In line four, for example, the word "mean" receives a heavy accent rather than the regular weak accent.   This helps to emphasize the central theme.   In line five, "glittering", with one strong and two weak accents, imitates the running of a brook. The lightness of the movement, however, suggests the superficial shallowness of the English life Wordsworth is criticizing.   In line eight, the strong, unusually heavy beats on the first syllable of each word—"rapine, avarice, expense"— suggest the poet's disgust.

The appeal of the imagery is strong.   The picture of the bewildered poet comes to our mind, and the image of "life . . . drest for show" is immediately apparent.   The visual appeal of the clear, shallow brook with its superficial beauty facilitates the detection of the poet's sarcasm.   The religious image of greed set up as an idol expresses the central theme vividly because we can see it clearly.   His countrymen are motivated by an inordinate desire to gain and worship wealth.

Thus, in a matter of fourteen lines, Wordsworth catches us up in a criticism which is as alive today as when he wrote the poem over 150 years ago.

PRACTICE 3. Writing a Poetry Appreciation

Write an appreciation, with illustrative reference to both content and poetic expression, of *one* of the poems studied in your literature course.

B. POETRY COMPARISON

In a poetry comparison a writer points out the similarities **or** differences between two poems.

Cautions:

1. Do *not* treat the poems separately, leaving your reader to make the comparison. For example, do not treat aspects (a), (b), and (c) for one poem followed by aspects (a), (b), and (c) for the second poem. Combine your comments on the two poems so that you establish the points of comparison.

2. Do *not* use vague general terms which might apply equally well to almost any poem. The following unsupported generalizations are almost worthless: "The theme of 'Composed upon Westminster Bridge' is the description of the emotional feelings of the poet caused by the perfect description of the scenery." "The theme of 'On First Looking into Chapman's Homer' is the revealing of emotional feelings and obsession of the poet caused by the recognition of the beauty of good poetry." Compare such vague generalizations with the following: "The theme of 'On First Looking into Chapman's Homer' is the poet's excitement and unbounded joy upon entering for the first time, through the medium of Chapman's translation of Homer, vast new realms of thought and imagination."

3. In stating the theme, do *not* paraphrase the poem. The theme is the underlying thought or emotion, the expression of the poet's attitude towards some universal truth. Since the theme is a reflection on some significant aspect of life, a mere paraphrase of the poem does not show that you have grasped the theme. A paraphrase may probably contain the theme, but not isolate it.

4. Do *not* attempt to give every example of a particular aspect of the poem. If, for example, the poet uses five similes, select the significant one or ones that most clearly express the central theme.

COMPARISON OF EMILY DICKINSON'S "THE SNAKE" AND D. H. LAWRENCE'S "SNAKE"

In both poems the snake is completely indifferent to man, but man is not indifferent to it. To show her distaste for the snake, Emily Dickinson avoids using its name, referring instead to "a narrow fellow" at the beginning and "this fellow" at the end of the poem. In the last two stanzas she contrasts the feeling of mutual good-will that exists between her and other objects of nature ("I feel for them a transport/ Of cordiality") and the intense dislike she instinctively but unaccountably has for the snake. Her strong distaste is emphasized by the description of the physical effects the snake has on her. In a vivid metaphor in the last line of the poem, she compares the cold dread which goes completely through her at the sight of the snake, even when she has a companion, with the freezing point of water.

> But never met this fellow,
> Attended or alone,
> Without a tighter breathing,
> And zero at the bone.

Reversing the ordinary hostile attitude of most human beings, D. H. Lawrence presents the strange fascination a snake has for him. Although the informality suggested by the phrase "in pyjamas" and by the repetition of the personal pronoun emphasize ownership, the poet becomes the "second-comer" who watches the perfect relaxation of the snake, the uninvited guest at his water-trough. The skilful repetition of the word "wait" in line 6 stresses the reversal of roles of guest and host. The voice of education, which urges the poet to kill the snake, comes into dramatic conflict with his instinctive admiration. He pictures the snake as a guest, a god, a king uncrowned in the underworld, and finally as one of the lords of creation. As the snake withdraws into the blackness of the "dreadful hole", the poet destroys by an act of thoughtlessness and violence the graceful control which he so greatly admired. There is a sort of pagan quality about Lawrence which leads him to repudiate his "accursed human education" and to identify himself with the grace and mystery of the snake.

Emily Dickinson's exact observation, simple diction, and familiar images paint a vivid picture of the appearance and movement of the snake. The verbs picture action accurately: "rides" captures the ease of its movement; "wrinkled", the swiftness of its disappearance. The simile "The grass divides as with a comb" and the metaphors "a narrow fellow", "a spotted shaft", and "a whip-lash" place the snake on a common scale. The description of the snake's house as a "boggy acre" and the reference to its habit of basking in the sun reinforce the impression of a known familiar environment.

Lawrence's description combines concrete with abstract details to suggest both the fear and the fascination he feels for the snake. The exact details of the third stanza paint a vivid picture:

> And trailed his yellow-brown slackness soft-bellied down, over
>   the edge of the stone trough
> And rested his throat upon the stone bottom . . . .
> He sipped with his straight mouth,
> Softly drank through his straight gums, into his slack long body,
> Silently.

The vivid similes "flickered his tongue like a forked night on the air, so black" and "writhed like lightning", and the coined phrase "snake-easing his shoulders" sustain the concreteness of the description. Contrasting these details are those suggesting exotic and mysterious qualities. Lawrence tells us that the snake comes from "the burning bowels of the earth" and returns to the "dreadful hole." (This is quite different from Emily Dickinson's known familiar environment.) By the skilful use of such similes as "he had come like a guest" and "looked around like a god, unseeing," the poet builds up a progressive admiration, culminating in the metaphor which compares the visitor to "one of the lords of life". This exotic atmosphere, which suits Lawrence's fascination for the snake, contrasts with Emily Dickinson's simple realism.

Each poet uses repetition effectively. The most noticeable example in Emily Dickinson's poem is the soft hiss of sounds in keeping, of course, with her attitude of distaste. The best examples are the end alliteration in "His notice" and "grass divides". The sounds in "notice" and "sudden" arrest pronunciation just as the snake's appearance arrests her attention. Lawrence's use of repetition serves many purposes. The hiss of sounds, especially in the third stanza, helps to create the initial feeling of horror. The repetition of long vowels slows up the reading in imitation of the snake's graceful movements:

> And looked around like a god, unseeing, into the air.
> And slowly turned his head.
> And slowly, very slowly, as if thrice adream,
> Proceeded to draw his slow length curving round
> And climb again the broken bank of my wall-face.

Another value of repetition, especially in such a long poem, is unity. The repetition of "wait" establishes the reversal of roles; that of "honoured" reveals the strange fascination; that of "blackness" indicates his horror; and that of the feeling of regret, his sense of wrongdoing.

Although the metric patterns are quite different, both poems capture in the rhythms of their lines the strange grace of the snake's movements. Dickinson's delicacy of pattern, with its alternating tetrameter and trimeter lines, iambic rhythms and run-on lines, creates the undulating effect of the snake's swift movement. Lawrence's pattern is of a different kind. His use of free verse, with its lines of varying length, is appropriate to the subject and to his emotional response. The long lines, for instance, convey great surges of emotion:

> And immediately I regretted it.
> I thought how paltry, how vulgar, what a mean act!
> I despised myself and the voices of my accursed human education.

The free verse permits this forceful, climactic arrangement, each succeeding line expressing more strongly the poet's remorse over what he had done.

In the use of diction and imagery, repetition and rhythmic pattern, and in the emotional response, the descriptions of the snake by Emily Dickinson and D. H. Lawrence form an admirable contrast.

EXAMINATION DIRECTIONS FOR POETRY COMPARISON

I

1. Compare the two poems in *one* of the following groups with regard to (i) the theme of each poem, (ii) the use in each poem of description to support the theme:

"Père Lalemant" (Pickthall) and "Seascape" (Young),

"Dover Beach" (Arnold) and **"Prospice"** (Browning).

The following student comparison is a satisfactory answer.

COMPARISON OF "DOVER BEACH" AND "PROSPICE"

1. (i) In "Dover Beach" the theme is a rather pessimistic view of life. Arnold emphasizes the beauty of the world, and then says that it is superficial, that beneath the calm of the night there is only confusion, destruction, and death. Personal love, he says, is the only thing man has to cling to.

Prospice, on the other hand, is full of energy and optimism. Browning welcomes the storm and darkness of death as a last trial. To Browning the real purpose of existence is to surmount life's pain; he sees death, not as the end of a meaningless life, but as an opportunity to complete life's struggle in a last glorious battle before entering Heaven where he will be reunited with his beloved wife.

1. (ii) Arnold employs a series of sustained and beautifully polished metaphors; all the description—the grating roar of pebbles, the ebbing sea, the nocturnal battle—supports his pessimism as he observes the beauty of the world and reflects on man's declining faith and his blind struggle.

Browning, however, uses a single sustained metaphor. He does not merely observe but actually participates. He feels the mist in his eyes, the fog in his throat, and the blasts of the wind as he faces the Arch Fear. The fight on the dark mountainside corresponds to Arnold's "darkling plain", but where Arnold's description ends in night, Browning's culminates in the light of Heaven.

HS4C, p. 9, 1956. By permission of the Department of Education, Ontario.

II

2. (a) Show how any *two* of "On His Blindness", "The Hare and Many Friends", "My Last Duchess", and "Dover Beach" differ in treating the subject of loyalty. (b) Compare the two poems chosen in (a) under the following headings:

(i) purpose, (ii) method of development, (iii) choice of words.

The following student comparison is a satisfactory answer.

COMPARISON OF "DOVER BEACH" AND "THE HARE AND MANY FRIENDS"

2. (a) In "The Hare and Many Friends", Gay satirizes the subject of loyalty, while in "Dover Beach", Arnold states that we "must be true to one another." The first poem deals with the fact that one cannot have many loyal friends. Rather, one may have one true friend or many casual ones, who will prove disloyal in times of stress. Arnold, on the other hand, speaks of times of stress and says that the means of overcoming the confusion and darkness is to be true to one another. Gay is metaphorical in that he takes an example of disloyalty in the animal kingdom, but Arnold treats the human race directly.

(b) (i) The purpose of "The Hare and Many Friends" is the presentation of a polished piece of poetry which expands the moral that one true friend is better than many false ones, and which cleverly satirizes the lack of fidelity among men when it is a question of helping a friend out of difficulty.

The purpose of "Dover Beach" is to present an intellectual appeal to people to be true to one another since the Sea of Faith is no longer at the full.

Although both poets treat loyalty, Gay treats disloyalty as a weakness of men (and animals) while Arnold treats loyalty as a means of overcoming the lack of faith among mankind.

(ii) Gay's poem is developed by means of elegant little rhymed closed couplets all in one stanza, while Arnold's poem makes use of an intricate rhyme scheme which interlocks between the several stanzas, which are of uneven length. The metre of "Dover Beach" is slow and irregular, with the result that the poem must be read slowly. "The Hare and Many Friends," on the other hand, moves quickly. Gay states his moral at the first of his poem and then develops it. Arnold deals with the theme of loyalty at the end, after opening with a description of the shore of England and the lights of France, and moving to a philosophical study later. Gay's poem has no beautiful description developing into a philosophy. Both poets develop their work by means of figurative language. Gay exemplifies human weakness by using the hare and the bull and the goat and the sheep. Arnold's use of figurative language to develop his subject is deeper, for he compares faith to a sea and says that it is no longer at high tide.

(iii) Gay's diction is prosaic; Arnold's is poetic. Examples are "bull" and "stint" in Gay's poem and "twinkle" and "fling" in Arnold's. Both poems use figurative language, but Gay's poem is figurative in idea, while Arnold's is figurative in language, for example, Sea of Faith.

HS4C p. 10, 1955. By permission of the Department of Education, Ontario.

PRACTICE 4. Writing a Poetry Comparison

Supporting your statements by specific references, compare the poems in any *one* of the following pairs with regard to (a) ideas and purpose of the poet, (b) methods of achieving effects, (c) choice of words.

1. E. J. Pratt's "The Dying Eagle" and Tennyson's "The Eagle".
2. Tennyson's "The Eagle" and Andrew Young's "The Eagle".
3. Siegfried Sassoon's "Morning Express" and W. H. Auden's "Night Mail".
4. Emily Dickinson's "Railway Train" and Stephen Spender's "The Express".
5. Charles G. D. Roberts' "The Skater" and Wordsworth's "Skating" (from *The Prelude*, Book I).
6. An ancient (traditional) ballad and a modern (literary) ballad.
7. Keats' "On First Looking into Chapman's Homer" and Wordsworth's "Composed upon Westminster Bridge".
8. Stephen Vincent Benét's "Autumn" and Robert Frost's "After Apple-Picking".
9. Keats' "To Autumn" and Nathaniel A. Benson's "Harvest".
10. E. J. Pratt's "The Shark" and Burns' "To a Mouse".
11. Earle Birney's "Atlantic Door" and Masefield's "Trade Winds".
12. Blake's "Tiger" and Gibson's "Tiger".
13. Arnold's "Dover Beach" and Young's "Seascape".

APPRECIATION OF POETRY

George Chapman (1559-1634) was an English dramatist who made a translation of the poems of Homer into English. John Keats (1796-1821), who was not himself a Greek scholar, was so impressed by the Homeric poems when he read them in Chapman's translation, that he wrote one of his most famous sonnets, "On First Looking into Chapman's Homer", in praise of Chapman's work.

PRACTICE 5. Writing an Appreciation

1. State in one sentence the substance of Keats' appraisal of Chapman's "Homer".

2. Since the appraisal of Chapman is too great a task, write an appreciation of Keats' sonnet "On First Looking into Chapman's Homer".

ON FIRST LOOKING INTO CHAPMAN'S HOMER

Much have I travell'd in the realms of gold,
 And many goodly states and kingdoms seen;
 Round many western islands have I been
Which bards in fealty to Apollo hold.
Oft of one wide expanse had I been told
 That deep-brow'd Homer ruled as his demesne;
 Yet did I never breathe its pure serene
Till I heard Chapman speak out loud and bold:
Then felt I like some watcher of the skies
 When a new planet swims into his ken;
Or like stout Cortez when with eagle eyes
 He star'd at the Pacific—and all his men
Look'd at each other with a wild surmise—
 Silent, upon a peak in Darien.

       —JOHN KEATS

Chapter 20

Further Exercises in Précis-Writing

Some Additional Suggestions

CAREFUL READING

The précis is one of the most useful means of developing careful reading and concise writing. On the one hand it demands analysis and comprehension; on the other, clear, accurate, and terse expression.

"Since careful reading comes first in importance as well as in order, you should *read the selection at least three times* before you attempt to write the précis. Each reading should have a definite purpose. The first should determine the theme or central idea. The second, especially in a passage of exposition, should trace the plan of development which gives the passage its coherence so that the reader may note the main sub-topics, logical thought divisions, and the use of more or less non-essential elements such as illustrative examples and repetition. When you read the passage a third time, you should be able to select the essential ideas intelligently. Then you may attempt to write your condensation directly from the original, dealing with several sentences at a time in logical units. Try to *re-state ideas* in your own words rather than translate individual words. Underlining of key phrases is a useful device, but it may encourage a patch-work effect. A point form outline as a preliminary to writing the précis is a safer practice, but it presents a problem on a timed test."—MARY K. CLEMENTS, *by permission.*

Unfamiliar Words.   You can sometimes guess intelligently at the meaning of an unfamiliar word by noticing the company it keeps. *Context* provides clues in the following sentences.

1. DEFINITION

   DIRECT: The *minuet,* a slow graceful dance, was popular in the eighteenth century.

   INDIRECT: Odysseus faced a real *dilemma,* for he had to choose between two possible courses of action—both bad.

2. EXAMPLE

   Like a tidal wave sweeping over a sandy beach, so the flood waters *inundated* the low-lying valley.

3. SENTENCE AS A WHOLE

   Predatory animals like the lion have a place in the scheme of nature by preventing the animal population from becoming too numerous for the available food supply.

   Removing the boulder that blocked the path was such a *formidable* job that we tried to find an alternate trail to the peak.

4. CONTRAST

   Though normally lazy and sluggish, Hap moved with *alacrity* when the dinner bell sounded.

5. COMPARISON

   Leaping from rock to rock, Greg looked as *agile* as a Rocky Mountain goat.

PRACTICE 1. Using Context Clues

Using context clues, give the meaning of each italicized word.

1. Madame Defarge's deep hatred for the Evrémondes made her a *vindictive,* unforgiving terrorist.
2. I am wholeheartedly in accord with your viewpoint, and I *concur* in your decision.
3. Though his remarks had seemed *impromptu,* actually they had been well rehearsed.
4. In the ascent of Mt. Everest a delay of a few days could have *jeopardized* the success of the expedition.
5. Though Nancy was apparently *contrite,* few of us believed she was really sorry for her thoughtlessness.
6. When angry, Emil is as *pugnacious* as an ill-tempered rattlesnake.
7. Though the family could afford few luxuries, they were by no means *indigent.*
8. Though the reporter persisted, Patterson refused to *divulge* the source of his information.

Reported Speech.   If the passage is one expressing a writer's opinion, it is advisable to begin your précis with a reference to the writer.   Since the following sentences may depend on the original verb of saying or thinking, there is no need to repeat the reference to the author or the introductory "that" after the first sentence.

> Divide your attentions equally between books and men. The strength of the student of books . . . .—SIR WILLIAM OSLER, *The Student Life.*
> Osler believes that the [medical] student should consider books and men equally. To study books successfully demands . . .

Imprecisions. The failure to read carefully may result in such imprecisions as the following.

ORIGINAL: Mary appeared to like washing, dusting, ironing, and cleaning.
IMPRECISE: Mary liked housework.
PRECISE: Mary *seemed* to like housework.

ORIGINAL: In the beginning of the eighth century before Christ
IMPRECISE: In 800 B.C. *or* In the eighth century before Christ
PRECISE: About 800 B.C. *or Early* in the eighth century before Christ

ORIGINAL: The Spartans were probably the finest soldiers that the world has ever seen.
IMPRECISE: The Spartans were the world's best soldiers.
PRECISE: The Spartans were probably the world's best soldiers.

ORIGINAL: Frenchmen, Germans, Italians, Spaniards and Belgians
IMPRECISE: Europeans
PRECISE: Some Europeans

Word Count. Keep strictly within the word limit, unless the word "about" appears in the directions. "About" generally means five words over or under the prescribed total. There is no advantage in using considerably fewer words than the number suggested. Write at the bottom of the passage the *exact* number of words that you have used. All articles and prepositions (*a, the, in*) must be included. Contractions such as *doesn't* (does not) and *haven't* (have not) count as two words. A hyphenated expression (*up-to-date*) is considered one word. Proper names and initials must be counted separately. For example, "Sir John A. Macdonald" is four words.

Extraneous Material. In précis-writing you must be careful *not* to introduce extraneous material by way of opinion, interpretation, or appreciation.

> ORIGINAL: Tom rose to his feet and said, "I cannot agree with your plan."
> EXTRANEOUS MATERIAL: Tom became angry and disagreeable again, as he usually does.

Summarizing Sentences. Summarizing sentences are important keys but do not necessarily preclude all that goes before.

The function of the statesman is not to decide upon what is theoretically the best in the world, but what is in practice the most feasible method of approaching an ideal goal. In other words, *statesmanship is compromise* in action. —*London Daily Telegraph*, October 15, 1901, page 9.

PRACTICE 2. Word Choice

Write after the number of each sentence that follows the single word which would accurately express the thought contained in the italicized words. Be careful as between synonyms. For example, the italicized words in the sentence, "He was *completely done out*," might be accurately expressed by *exhausted*, but not by *tired* or *weary*.

1. Fire-fighters, vigilantly patrolling the area, stamped out the embers before they gained headway and loss *of no consequence* was incurred.
2. Admitting *that he had committed the crime*, he was sentenced to six months' imprisonment.
3. The boys *got* the body *back again* and started their return journey to Aklavik.
4. Plants cannot grow in land without *those elements which plants feed on*.
5. He was dressed *in a very gorgeous manner*.
6. The orator was *not at all hesitant in his choice of words*.
7. His style is *that of a person who wrote long ago*.
8. A student must learn to *do as he is bid*.
9. The man is *continually without money, largely because of his own lack of industry*.
10. The old verb "pill", to rob or to plunder, from which our word "pillage" is derived, is now *entirely out of use* as a verb.
11. He is a *second year student* at the University.
12. Erasmus was a *man of great learning*.
13. The more I looked at him the more I was of the opinion that he was *the suspected person*.
14. There is a *difference* between *the facts of* the two stories.
15. Officials were unable to *come to an opinion about* the amount of money spent on the July road work.
16. British officials admit delays longer than they had *previously thought that they would be*.
17. The amount of our *goods sold outside Canada* has increased in the last two months.
18. We brought back a great many *tokens by which to remember the places we had visited*.
19. Charles Campbell, Canadian sculler, was *knocked out of all further championship chances* in the Olympic finals at Grunau.

Before attempting the following passages you should review the suggestions in Chapter 6.

PRACTICE 3.   Give the substance of the following passage, reducing it to about 100 words.   Your version should be connected in thought and expressed mainly in your own words.

LEARNED WORDS AND POPULAR WORDS

In every cultivated language there are two great classes of words which, taken together, comprise the whole vocabulary. First, there are those words with which we become acquainted in ordinary conversation, which we learn, that is to say, from the members of our own family and from our familiar associates, and which we should know and use even if we could not read or write. They concern the common things of life, and are the stock in trade of all who speak the language. Such words may be called "popular", since they belong to the people at large and are not the exclusive possession of a limited class.

On the other hand, our language includes a multitude of words which are comparatively seldom used in ordinary conversation. Their meanings are known to every educated person, but there is little occasion to employ them at home or in the market-place. Our first acquaintance with them comes not from our mother's lips or from the talk of our schoolmates, but from books that we read, lectures that we hear, or the more formal conversation of highly educated speakers who are discussing some particular topic in a style appropriately elevated above the habitual level of everyday life. Such words are called "learned", and the distinction between them and "popular" words is of great importance to a right understanding of linguistic process. (227 words)— J. B. GREENOUGH and G. L. KITTREDGE, *Words and Their Ways in English Speech. By permission of The Macmillan Company, New York.*

PRACTICE 4.   Write a précis of the following passage, reducing it to about 80 words.

A LIBERAL EDUCATION

That man, I think, has had a liberal education, who has been so trained in youth that his body is the ready servant of his will, and does with ease and pleasure all the work that, as a mechanism, it is capable of; whose intellect is a clear, cold, logic engine, with all it parts of equal strength, and in smooth working order; ready, like a steam engine, to be turned to any kind of work, and spin the gossamers as well as forge the anchors of the mind; whose mind is stored with a knowledge of the great and fundamental truths of Nature and of the laws of her operations; one who, no stunted ascetic, is full of life and fire, but whose passions are trained to come to heel by a vigorous will, the servant of a tender conscience; who has learned to love all beauty, whether of Nature or of art, to hate all vileness, and to respect others as himself.

Such a one, and no other, I conceive, has had a liberal education; for he is, as completely as a man can be, in harmony with Nature. He will make the best of her, and she of him.   They will get on together rarely: she as his ever beneficent mother; he as her mouthpiece, her conscious self, her minister and interpreter. (225 words)—THOMAS HUXLEY

PRACTICE 5.   Write a précis of the following passage, reducing it to about 100 words.

WILLIAM PITT, THE ELDER, SECRETARY OF STATE

While her great ally was reaping a full harvest of laurels, England, dragged into the Continental war because that apple of discord, Hanover, belonged to her King, found little but humiliation.   Minorca was wrested from her, and the Ministry had an innocent man shot to avert from themselves the popular indignation, while the same Ministry, scared by a phantom of invasion, brought over German troops to defend British soil.   But now an event took place pregnant with glorious consequence.   The reins of power fell in the hands of William Pitt.   He had already held them for a brief space, forced into office at the end of 1756 by popular clamour, in spite of the Whig leaders and against the wishes of the King.   But the place was untenable.   Newcastle's Parliament would not support him; the Duke of Cumberland opposed him; the King hated him; and in April, 1757, he was dismissed.   Then ensued eleven weeks of bickering and dispute, during which, in the midst of a great war, England was left without a government.   It became clear that none was possible without Pitt; and none with him could be permanent and strong unless joined with those influences which had thus far controlled the majorities of Parliament.   Therefore an extraordinary union was brought about; Lord Chesterfield acting as go-between to reconcile the ill-assorted pair.   One of them brought to the alliance the confidence and support of the people; the other, Court management, borough interest, and parliamentary connections.   Newcastle was made First Lord of the Treasury, and Pitt, the old enemy who had repeatedly browbeat and ridiculed him, became Secretary of State, with the lead of the House of Commons and full control of the war and foreign affairs.   (287 words) —FRANCIS PARKMAN

PRACTICE 6.   Write a précis of the following passage, reducing it to about 140 words.

THE COPERNICAN THEORY

The earth seems such a solid affair when we stand on it, and so big when we travel over it, that it is hardly surprising that men used to think of it as a vast immovable mass, forming the very centre of the universe.   Many of them pictured it as a sort of flat board, with the starry sky covering it—rather as a dish-cover covers a dish.   Of course they saw that the stars continually turned round the pole, and so they had to suppose that the dish-cover turned round over the dish; this was simpler than to suppose that the dish turned round under the dish-cover.   Yet there were some, especially among the Greeks, who held different opinions.   More than five centuries before Christ we find Pythagoras maintaining that the earth was of a globular shape: a ball floating in space, he said. Some centuries later, other Greeks and Aristarchus in particular, began to see that this ball must not only float in space but must also move through space—must in fact revolve around the sun. But the idea did not prove popular. Men did not like to think of their home as anything less than the centre of the universe; they found it simpler and more flattering to their self-esteem to think of the earth as standing at rest, while everything else revolved round it. And so they continued in their old beliefs for nearly two thousand years after Aristarchus had seen and proclaimed the truth.

Then, just about four hundred years ago, Copernicus, a Polish ecclesiastic, wrote a book of tremendous importance. He pointed out that the complicated motions of the sun and the planets across the sky could all be very simply explained by supposing that the sun stood still, while the earth and the planets revolved around it. While these ideas were still being discussed, Galileo, a professor in the University of Padua, made a small telescope with his own hands and convinced himself—and also showed to all the world—that things were as Copernicus said; the sun did not revolve round the earth, but the earth and also the planets revolved round the sun. In this way the earth had to abandon its proud claim to be the centre of the universe—to become an ordinary planet, a mere fragment of matter revolving round a much larger sun. (387 words)
—Sir James Jeans, *Our Home in Space.*
By permission of the Syndics of the University Press, Cambridge

PRACTICE 7. Give the substance of the following passage, reducing it to about 130 words. Your version should be neatly written and connected in thought, with all the essential points of the original.

THE MYSTERIOUS UNIVERSE

A few stars are known which are hardly bigger than the earth, but the majority are so large that hundreds of thousands of earths could be packed inside each and leave room to spare; here and there we come upon a giant star large enough to contain millions of millions of earths. And the total number of stars in the universe is probably something like the total number of grains of sand on all the sea shores of the world. Such is the littleness of our home in space when measured up against the total substance of the universe.

The vast multitude of stars are moving about in space. A few form groups which journey in company, but the majority are solitary travellers. And they travel through a universe so spacious that it is an event of almost unimaginable rarity for a star to come anywhere near another star. For the most part each voyages in splendid isolation, like a ship on an empty ocean. In a scale model in which the stars are ships, the average ship will be well over a million miles from its nearest neighbour, whence it is easy to understand why a ship seldom finds another within hailing distance.

We believe, nevertheless, that some two thousand million years ago this rare event took place, and that a second star, wandering blindly through space, happened to come within hailing distance of the sun. Just as the sun and moon raise tides on the earth, so this second star must have raised tides on the surface of the sun. But they would be very different from the puny tides which the small mass of the moon raises on our oceans; a huge tidal wave must have passed over the surface of the sun, ultimately forming a mountain of prodigious height, which would rise ever higher and higher as the cause of the disturbance came nearer and nearer.   And before the second star began to recede, its tidal pull had become so powerful that this mountain was torn to pieces and threw off small fragments of itself, much as the crest of a wave throws off spray.   These small fragments have been circulating around their parent sun ever since. They are the planets, great and small, of which our earth is one.

The sun and the other stars we see in the sky are all intensely hot—far too hot for life to be able to retain a footing on them.   So also no doubt were the ejected fragments of the sun when they were first thrown off.   Gradually they cooled, until now they have but little intrinsic heat left, their warmth being derived almost entirely from the radiation which the sun pours out upon them. (458 words)—SIR JAMES JEANS, *The Mysterious Universe.*

By permission of The Syndics of the University Press, Cambridge.

PRACTICE 8.   Reduce the following passage to not more than 130 words of connected prose.   (You may find it necessary to use an occasional word or phrase from the original passage where an adequate substitute cannot be found, but the final product should be mainly in your own words.)

LOAN-WORDS

Loan-words might be termed some of the milestones of general history, because they show us the course of civilization and the wanderings of inventions and institutions, and in many cases give us valuable information as to the inner life of nations when dry annals tell us nothing but the dates of the deaths of kings and bishops.   When in two languages we find no trace of the exchange of loan-words one way or the other, we are safe to infer that the two nations have had nothing to do with each other.   But if they have been in contact, the number of loan-words and still more the quality of the loan-words, if rightly interpreted, will inform us of their reciprocal relations; they will show us which of them has been the more fertile in ideas and on what domains of human activity each has been superior to the other.   If all other sources of information were closed to us except such loans-word in our modern North-European languages as *piano, soprano, opera, libretto, tempo, adagio,* etc., we should still have no hesitation in drawing the conclusion that Italian music has played a great role all over Europe.   Similar instances might easily be multiplied, and in many ways the study of language brings home to us the fact that when a nation produces something that its neighbours think worthy of imitation these will take over not only the thing but also the name.   This will be the general rule, though exceptions may occur, especially when a language possesses a native word that will lend itself without any special effort to the new thing imported from abroad. But if a native word is not ready to hand, it is easier to adopt the ready-made word used in the other country, nay this foreign word is very often imported even in cases where it would seem to offer no great difficulty to coin an adequate expression by means of native word material. (328 words)—OTTO JESPERSON, *Growth and Structure of the English Language.*

Fourth edition, copyright 1923, by D. Appleton and Co.   By permission of Appleton-Century-Crofts, Inc.

PRACTICE 9. Give the substance of the following passage, reducing it to about 120 words. Your version should be connected in thought and expressed mainly in your own words.

LANGUAGE REGENERATION

Most people who bother with the matter at all would admit that the English language is in a bad way, but it is generally assumed that we cannot by conscious action do anything about it. Our civilization is decadent, and our language—so the argument runs—must inevitably share in the general collapse. It follows that any struggle against the abuse of language is a sentimental archaism, like preferring candles to electric light or hansom cabs to aeroplanes. Underneath this lies the half-conscious belief that language is a natural growth and not an instrument which we shape for our own purposes.

Now, it is clear that the decline of a language must ultimately have political and economic causes: it is not due simply to the bad influence of this or that individual writer. But an effect can become a cause, reinforcing the original cause and producing the same effect in an intensified form, and so on indefinitely. A man may take to drink because he feels himself to be a failure, and then fail all the more completely because he drinks. It is rather the same thing that is happening to the English language. It becomes ugly and inaccurate because our thoughts are foolish, but the slovenliness of our language makes it easier for us to have foolish thoughts. The point is that the process is reversible. Modern English, especially written English, is full of bad habits which spread by imitation and which can be avoided if one is willing to take the necessary trouble. If one gets rid of these habits one can think more clearly, and to think clearly is a necessary first step towards political regeneration: so that the fight against bad English is not frivolous and is not the exclusive concern of professional writers. (298 words)—GEORGE ORWELL, *Politics and the English Language.*

By permission of Martin Secker & Warburg, Ltd., Publishers.

PRACTICE 10. Reduce the following passage to not more than 140 words of connected prose. (You may find it necessary to use an occasional word or phrase from the original passage where an adequate substitute cannot be found, but the final product should be mainly in your own words.)

TRADITIONS MAKE REBELS

Every man who possesses real vitality can be seen as the resultant of two forces. He is first the child of a particular age, society, convention; of what we may call in one word a tradition. He is secondly, in one degree or another, a rebel against that tradition. And the best traditions make the best rebels. Euripides is the child of a strong and splendid tradition and is, together with Plato, the fiercest of all rebels against it.

We are in reaction now against another great age, an age whose achievements in art are memorable, in literature massive and splendid, in science and invention absolutely unparalleled, but greatest of all perhaps in the raising of all standards of public duty, the humanizing of law and society, and the awakening of high ideals in social and international politics.   The Victorian age had, amid enormous differences, a certain similarity with the Periclean in its lack of self-examination, its rush and chivalry and optimism, its unconscious hypocrisy, its failure to think out its problems to the bitter end.   And in most of the current criticism on things Victorian, so far as it is not mere fashion or folly, one seems to feel the Victorian spirit itself speaking.   It arraigns Victorian things by a Victorian standard; blames them not because they have moved in a particular direction, but because they have not moved far enough; because so many of the things they attempted are still left undone, because the ideals they preached and the standards by which they claimed to be acting were so much harder of satis-faction than they knew.   Euripides, like ourselves, comes in an age of criticism following upon an age of movement and action.   And for the most part, like ourselves, he accepts the general standards on which the movement and action were based.   He accepts the Athenian ideals of free thought, free speech, democracy, "virtue" and patriotism.   He arraigns his country because she is false to them.   (329 words.)—GILBERT MURRAY, *Euripides and His Age.*

By permission of Oxford University Press, Publishers.

PRACTICE 11.   Reduce the following passage to about 120 words.

ST. PATRICK'S DAY

St. Patrick, if we are to believe a quarter of the stories, legends, and songs about him, was a true son of his own country, by arranging to be born out of it. We find him claimed by France, England, Scotland, and Wales, and, only half-heartedly, by Ireland itself.   As a matter of fact, as near as we can get at the truth, St. Patrick was born at Dumbarton, near Glasgow, in the year A.D. 372—some say 389—and when about sixteen was carried off by pirates under the order of King Niall of Ireland, and sold into slavery to a farmer of Sleamish in County Antrim, where he was employed as a swineherd.   In this lowly state he passed some years, and before he could escape, contrived to learn the Irish language, and made himself acquainted with the manners and customs of the people whom he also began to love.   But his captivity galled him, and when the long-sought opportunity arrived, after many adventures, he contrived to reach the coast, and, entering the service of the captain of a merchant ship, managed to get carried to France, and travelled as far south as Italy.

Here he entered upon the monastic life and was successively ordained deacon, priest, and bishop.   He then returned to Ireland "to preach the gospel to its then heathen inhabitants".

The most extraordinary thing about the majority of rhymsters of Ireland when dealing with the Saint, whether Roman Catholic or Protestant, is that they have penned the "poems"—with very few and rare exceptions—in a light-hearted and flippant manner.   For instance, one of the most universally popular songs in Ireland is Samuel Lover's "Birth of St. Patrick"—a momentous event, surely.

"On the eighth day of March it was, some people say,
That St. Patrick at midnight he first saw the day:
While others declared 'twas the ninth he was born,
And 'twas all a mistake between midnight and morn."

This "dividing" of the clans on the subject is supposed to have been the cause of the first faction fight in the country. (352 words)—S. J. ADAIR FITZ-GERALD, *The Graphic*

PRACTICE 12.   Give the substance of the following passage, reducing it to about 90 words.   Your version should be connected in thought and expressed mainly in your own words.

CHANGES IN THE ENGLISH LANGUAGE

Nearly all the changes in the English language, which now seem so clearly marked, took place very slowly and almost imperceptibly.   We can easily trace the gorge cut by Niagara, though we cannot at any particular moment mark the wearing of the rock.   As we review the history of the development of English speech, we can see, however, that these changes have come more rapidly at certain periods than at others; and that particularly in the fourteenth century, as Professor Lounsbury says, "the forces that gave stability and character to a language first began to operate upon the speech employed by the people." By this time the Norman conquerors had given up their efforts to make the English people learn to speak French and had realized that it was not only desirable but even necessary for them to speak English; Mohammed must come to the mountain.   Far more important, however, was the fact that in this century the dialect known as the East Midland came to hold a commercial, social, and literary preëminence over the numerous other dialects of the island. One of the reasons for this leadership lay in the nature of the dialect itself: it had not suffered the rapid changes which, due to the presence of a large number of Danes, had affected the Northern speech; on the other hand, it was far more progressive than the Southern dialect which hung tenaciously to many old forms and inflections.   Again, Midland England was the speech of London and of Oxford and Cambridge; consequently it was familiar to the merchant, the courtier, and the scholar.   Business, society, and education thus strengthened its claims to preëminence.   (276 words)

PRACTICE 13.   Write a précis of the following passage, reducing it to about 130 words.   Your finished work should be a connected passage and should be expressed mainly in your own words.

LINCOLN

To all appearance nobody could have been more than Abraham Lincoln a man of his own time and place.   Until 1858 his outer life ran much in the same groove as that of hundreds of other Western politicians and lawyers.   Beginning as a poor and ignorant boy, even less provided with props and stepping stones than were his associates, he had worked his way to a position of ordinary professional and political distinction.   He was not, like Douglas, a brilliant success.   He was not, like Grant, a hopeless failure.   He had achieved as much and as little as hundreds of others had achieved.   He was respected by his neighbours as an honest man and as a competent lawyer.   They credited him with ability, but not to any extraordinary extent.   No one would have pointed him out as a remarkable and distinguished man.   He had shown himself to be desirous of recognition and influence, but ambition had not been the compelling motive of his life.   In most respects his ideas, interests and standards were precisely the same as those of his associates.   He accepted with them the fabric of traditional American political thought and the ordinary standards of contemporary political morality.   He had none of the moral strenuousness of the reformer, none of the exclusiveness of a man whose purposes and ideas were consciously perched higher than those of his neighbours.   Probably the majority of his more successful associates classed him as a good and able man who was somewhat lacking in ambition and had too much of a disposition to loaf.   He was most at home, not in his own house, but in the corner grocery store, where he could sit with his feet on the stove swapping stories with his friends; and if an English traveller of 1850 had happened in on the group, he would most assuredly have discovered another instance of the distressing vulgarity to which the absence of an hereditary aristocracy and an established church condemned the American democracy.   Thus, no man could apparently have been more the average product of his day and generation.   Nevertheless, at bottom Abraham Lincoln differed as essentially from the ordinary Western American as St. Francis of Assisi differed from the ordinary Benedictine monk of the thirteenth century.   (377 words)—HERBERT CROLY, *The Promise of American Life.*

Copyright, 1909, by the Macmillan Company, New York.   By permission of The Macmillan Company

PRACTICE 14.   Reduce the following passage to about 140 words. The new version should be a connected passage containing the essentials of the original expressed mainly in your own words.

FROM MAGIC TO RELIGION

If an Age of Religion has thus everywhere, as I venture to surmise, been preceded by an Age of Magic, it is natural that we should enquire what causes had led mankind, or rather a portion of them to abandon magic as a principle of faith and practice and to betake themselves to religion instead.   When we reflect upon the multitude, the variety, and the complexity of the facts to be explained, and the scantiness of our information regarding them, we shall be ready to acknowledge that a full and satisfactory solution of so profound a problem is hardly to be hoped for, and that the most we can do in the present state of our knowledge is to hazard a more or less plausible conjecture.   With all due diffidence, then, I would suggest that a tardy recognition of the inherent falsehood and barrenness of magic set the more thoughtful part of mankind to cast about for a truer theory of nature and a more fruitful method of turning her resources to account.   The shrewder intelligences must in time have come to perceive that magical ceremonies and incantations did not really effect the results which they were designed to produce, and which the majority of their simpler fellows still believe that they did actually produce.   This great discovery of the inefficacy of magic must have wrought a radical though probably slow revolution in the minds of those who had the sagacity to make it.   The discovery amounted to this, that men for the first time recognized their inability to manipulate at pleasure certain natural forces which hitherto they had believed to be completely within their control.   (276 words)—Sɪʀ Jᴀᴍᴇs Fʀᴀᴢᴇʀ, *The Golden Bough* (Volume I, "The Magic Art and the Evolution of Kings")   *Reprinted by permission of Trinity College, Cambridge, and The Macmillan Company.*

PRACTICE 15.   Give the substance of the following passage, reducing it to about 95 words.   Your version should be connected in thought and expressed mainly in your own words.

SENSIBILITY

First of all we must recognize that the ability to think depends primarily upon the number and the quality of those impressions which are brought to the mind along the railways of the various senses.   Through the sensory nerves which have their receiving stations in the eye, ear, tongue, nose, and muscles of our bodies we gain our impressions of the manifold objects making up our world.   As these various senses are called into greater use, we come to recognize with keener and ever keener appreciation the nature of their messages, till those people who cultivate long and faithfully any one of these senses, as does for example the tea-taster, seem to their less-educated fellows to work marvels. The Indians so trained eye and ear to catch sounds and sights that the snapping of a twig or the gleam of a far distant fire, imperceptible to the less-acute senses of the white, seldom escaped them.   Such a man as John Ruskin owed his mental superiority to the majority of mankind, in part at least, to the fact that he deliberately and painstakingly schooled his senses, particularly his vision, to bear clear-cut, definite messages from the world about him, to supply him with an abundance of vivid images.   His mind was like a great well-equipped radio station which receives frequent and accurate news of what is doing in the world and thus possesses much valuable materials which may be turned to good use.   People differ markedly in their sensibility to these impressions; a few are as finely responsive as a delicate thermometer which registers a variation of a fraction of a degree in temperature; others, however, resemble those thermometers given away to advertise Dr. Quack's Cure-all, which are quite indifferent to a change of five or ten degrees.   (297 words)

PRACTICE 16.   Reduce the following passage to not more than 140 words of connected prose.   (You may find it necessary to use an occasional word or phrase from the original passage where an adequate substitute cannot be found, but the final product should be mainly in your own words.)

STATE VERSUS WORLD AUTHORITY

There is a good deal of apprehension over the control a world authority might have over the internal affairs of the individual state.   Natural and understandable though such concern may be, it has its source in confusion over a distinction that should be made between world *sovereignty* and state *jurisdiction*.   A common world sovereignty would mean that no state could act unilaterally in its foreign affairs.   It would mean that no state could have the instruments of power to aggress against other states.   It would mean that no state could withdraw from the central authority as a method of achieving its aims. But it would *not* mean that the individual state would lose its jurisdiction over its internal affairs. It would *not* mean the arbitrary establishment of a uniform ideology all over the world. It would *not* mean the forcible imposition of non-democratic systems on democratic states, any more than it would mean the forcible imposition of democratic systems on non-democratic states.

Though the idea of bestowing democracy on all other peoples throughout the world seems both magnanimous and attractive, the fact remains that democracy is not to be had just for the giving or the taking. It cannot be donated or imposed from without. It is an intricate and highly advanced mechanism capable of existing, like man himself, under certain conditions. It depends not only on the love of freedom, but on the ability to carry the responsibilities of freedom. It requires enduring respect for numberless principles, not all of them incorporated into formal law. It requires adherence to the principle of majority rule with preservation of minority rights. It is as much a way of living and a philosophy of life as it is a form of political organization. (391 words)—NORMAN COUSINS, *Modern Man is Obsolete.*

By permission of The Viking Press.

PRACTICE 17. Give the substance of the following passage, reducing it to about 160 words. Your version should be connected in thought and expressed mainly in your own words.

THE STUDENT OF BOOKS AND MEN

Divide your attentions equally between books and men. The strength of the student of books is to sit still—two or three hours at a stretch—eating the heart out of a subject with pencil and note-book in hand, determined to master the details and intricacies, focusing all your energies on its difficulties. Get accustomed to test all sorts of book problems and statements for yourself, and take as little as possible on trust. The question came up one day, when discussing the grooves left on the nails after fever, how long it took for the nails to grow out, from root to edge. A majority of the class had no further interest; a few looked it up in books; two men marked their nails at the root with nitrate of silver, and a few months later had positive knowledge on the subject. They showed the proper spirit. The little points that come up in your reading try to test for yourselves. With one fundamental difficulty many of you will have to contend from the outset—a lack of proper preparation for really hard study. No one can have watched successive groups of young men pass through the special schools without profoundly regretting the haphazard, fragmentary character of their preliminary education. It does seem too bad that we cannot have a student in his eighteenth year sufficiently grounded in the humanities and in the sciences preliminary to medicine—but this is an educational problem upon which only a Milton or a Locke could discourse with profit. With pertinacity you can overcome the preliminary defects, and, once thoroughly interested, the work in books becomes a pastime. A serious drawback in the student life is the self-consciousness bred of too close devotion to books. A man gets shy, "dysopic", as old Timothy Bright calls it, and shuns the looks of men, and blushes like a girl.

The strength of a student of men is to travel—to study men, their habits, character, mode of life, their behaviour under varied conditions, their vices, virtues and peculiarities.   Begin with a careful observation of your fellow-students and of your teachers; then, every patient you see is a lesson in much more than the malady from which he suffers.   Mix as much as you possibly can with the outside world, and learn its ways.   Cultivated systematically, the social circle will enable you to conquer the diffidence so apt to go with bookish-ness, and which may prove a very serious drawback in after life.   I cannot too strongly impress upon the earnest and attentive men among you the necessity of overcoming this unfortunate failing in your student days.   It is not easy for every one to reach a happy medium, and the distinction between a proper self-confidence and "cheek", particularly in junior students, is not always to be made.   The latter is met with chiefly among the student pilgrims who, in travelling down the Delectable Mountains, have gone astray and have passed to the left hand, where lieth the country of Conceit, the country in which, you remember, the brisk lad, Ignorance, met Christian.   (517 words)   SIR WILLIAM OSLER

By permission 'rom The Student Life *by Sir William Osler, Copyright, 1932, McGraw-Hill Book Company, Inc.*

Chapter 21

Clear Thinking

WHY LEARN TO THINK

IN an essay called "Citizenship", James Bryce says that the unwillingness or the inability of people to think is a real danger to democracy. If a person does not know the difference between sound and unsound reasoning, he can't distinguish between the truth and false propaganda and can't vote intelligently. Although thinking is the hardest kind of mental work and hence is heartily disliked by the mentally lazy, it is both an enjoyable and most profitable form of activity.

WHAT THINKING IS

Webster defines *to think* as *to reflect for the purpose of reaching a conclusion; to reason.* When, having a chance to elect either French or physics, you jot down the arguments in favour of each subject, compare them, weigh them, and then decide which would be more advantageous to you, you are thinking. When, having a chance to go to the movies, you compare the pleasure and profit of an evening at a photoplay and an evening of reading, you are thinking. If you

461

play baseball, you probably do some real thinking as you stand at bat. You see the ball leave the pitcher's hand, you watch it, you decide where it is going, and then you decide what you are going to do.

Examples:

1. HOW I DECIDED TO OWN A DOG

When last summer I visited Uncle Will on his big Alberta farm, I played with Punch, his bulldog puppy, and wished I had one just like him. A dog, I knew, is a faithful companion and enjoys playing with boys and girls. But a farm with a barn, sheds, and fields is quite different from a city home with a small yard and a garage. Isn't a dog in the city more bother than fun? When I put this question to two of my friends who have dogs, both said emphatically "No." Then I was ready to ask Father and Mother to buy me a bulldog puppy. They surprised me by saying without a moment's hestitation, "Yes, if you will take care of him." Father also told me what care a dog requires and how much bother he is. After weighing in my mind both the work and the fun, I said, "All right. How soon can we buy him?"—PUPIL.

2. FOREST SMELLS BETTER THAN THOSE OF THE SEA

And, surely, of all smells in the world the smell of many trees is the sweetest and most fortifying. The sea has a rude pistolling sort of odour, that takes you in the nostrils like snuff, and carries with it a fine sentiment of open water and tall ships; but the smell of a forest, which comes nearest to this in tonic quality, surpasses it by many degrees in the quality of softness. Again, the smell of the sea has little variety, but the smell of a forest is infinitely changeful; it varies with the hour of the day, not in strength merely, but in character; and the different sorts of trees, as you go from one zone of the wood to another, seem to live among different kinds of atmosphere. Usually the rosin of the fir predominates. But some woods are more coquettish in their habits; and the breath of the forest Mormal, as it came aboard upon us that showery afternoon, was perfumed with nothing less delicate than sweet-brier.—STEVENSON, *An Inland Voyage.*

By arrangement with the publisher, Charles Scribner's Sons.

3. BOTH RICH AND POOR NEED CULTURE

The poor require culture as much as the rich; and at present their education, even when they get it, gives them hardly anything of it. Yet hardly less of it, perhaps, than the education of the rich gives the rich. For when we say that culture is: To know the best that has been thought and said in the world, we imply that, for culture, a system directly tending to this end is necessary in our reading. Now, there is no such system yet present to guide the reading of the rich, any more than of the poor. Such a system is hardly even thought of; a man who wants it must make it for himself. And our reading being so without purpose as it is, nothing can be truer than what Butler says, that really, in general, no part of our time is more idly spent than the time spent in reading. —ARNOLD, *Essays.*

PRACTICE 1. Reaching a Decision

Explain clearly some thinking you have done before reaching a decision. Perhaps these topics will suggest some subject you have thought about.

1. Shall I buy a car? 2. Shall I play football? 3. Shall I smoke cigarettes? 4. Shall I leave school? 5. Shall I work after school? 6. Shall I work during the summer vacation? 7. What college shall I attend? 8. What course shall I take? 9. What subjects shall I elect? 10. Shall I copy my written homework or lend it to a friend to copy? 11. Shall I try out for the track team? 12. What book shall I select for supplementary reading? 13. Shall I buy this suit, dress, or hat, or that one? 14. Shall I subscribe for the school magazine? 15. Shall I go to the football game? 16. Shall I go to college? 17. Shall I cheat in an examination if I have a good chance?

FAULTY REASONING

There are many things which contribute to faulty thinking and reasoning, but commonest among them are these two:

1. *Reasoning without Facts*—It is one of the chief faults of children and immature adults to draw hasty conclusions without complete knowledge of the facts. Without sufficient evidence we accept political, social, and religious views as our own. Without sufficient evidence we condemn our leaders, our parents, our friends, our enemies. Reasoning based on wrong facts or too few facts has every chance of being wrong.

2. *Untrustworthy Authorities*—One of the first requisites of the student and the adult is to learn to distinguish between authorities. Always seek the authority in his own field. Sir James Jeans in astronomy Marconi in wireless, Sir Arthur Quiller-Couch in literature, are authorities in their fields; what they think in unrelated fields will depend entirely upon their studies in these other fields. When a distinguished actor talks about acting, he speaks with some authority on the subject; but when he speaks on science, religion, politics, health, beds, and cigarettes, he is no longer an authority, and his opinion is worth no more than that of any other man with equal intelligence and knowledge of the subject. Moreover, if he is receiving thousands of dollars for signing a recommendation of a brand of cigarettes, his statement is untrustworthy as evidence.

Because we like to think of ourselves as *reasonable* beings, we sometimes invent reasons for doing what we want to do. If we'd rather play tennis than clean the cellar, we say "I need relaxation. Playing tennis will give me the needed strength for that geometry test." This self-deception may, for the moment, lull our consciences into repose, but we generally feel uneasy about the rationalization just the same.

PRACTICE 2. Detecting Rationalization

Which of the following impresses you as an example of logical reasoning? Which sound suspiciously like rationalization? Can you add an example of rationalization of which you have been guilty?

1. Instead of doing my history homework, I'll go to see that historical movie at the Ritz. I'm sure to learn a lot of history by going.
2. I won't try out for the team after all. Probably the coach has already picked his squad and won't give a fair chance to newcomers.
3. Instead of shovelling the snow from the walks tonight I'll get my young brother Timmy to do it. Young, growing bodies need exercise to develop properly.
4. The ability to speak effectively is an asset, if not a requirement, for a successful lawyer. Because I expect to be a lawyer, I'm going to join the Debating Club.

LOGICAL FALLACIES

Errors in the reasoning process itself are called "fallacies".

HASTY GENERALIZATION. Civilization is based upon generalizations derived from the combined wisdom of many men. Generalizations about electromagnetic waves have led to television, radio, the telephone, and other scientific marvels. Generalizations based upon representative samplings are likely to be sound. For example, after observing many violet plants, in different places and during different years, you may rightly conclude that violets grow better in shade than in sun.

Generalizations based upon a few unrepresentative samplings are likely to be faulty. If you say, "Howard and Harold White are excellent students; therefore their three brothers will undoubtedly be excellent students," you are jumping to a conclusion. The generalization is based on only two examples. Besides, human beings are too complex to fit into simple categories. Often the members of a family vary widely as students.

Thus, hasty generalization consists in arguing that what is true of one or more special cases is true of *all* cases without exception.

MISTAKING THE CAUSE. During an eclipse primitive peoples may beat drums to frighten away the evil spirit gobbling up the sun. You may chuckle at this simple confusion of cause and effect, but are you guilty of the same kind of error? Even if your cold goes away after you've dosed yourself with lemon juice in water, you can't be certain the lemon was the cure. What of the fact that you spent a day resting in bed? How about the aspirin you took? Medicine may be the whole cause of a cure, the major cause, a minor cause, or no cause at all. In human affairs it's dangerous to ascribe any effect simply to the "cause" that comes to mind first. Take a minute to think of other possible causes, and then judge among them.

FALSE ANALOGY. To argue from analogy is to infer that two objects which are alike in some respects are alike in another particular. When we argue that because the squirrel buries nuts for the winter, we should prepare for old age; or that because Vancouver Technical Collegiate publishes a weekly newspaper, Weyburn Collegiate should have one, we are using analogies. The argument is valid only if (1) the points of similarity outweigh the points of difference and (2) if there is no essential difference. If, for example, Vancouver "Tech" has ten times as many students as Weyburn, this one essential difference destroys the value of the analogy.

IGNORING THE QUESTION. Ignoring the question is evading or missing the real point at issue. If on the question *"Resolved,* That pupils should receive credit for participation in atheltics" an affirmative speaker spends all his time proving that athletic sports are valuable to boys and girls, he is ignoring the question, for swimming during the summer, cutting the grass, making a dress, repairing the automobile, and many other activities are valuable but do not receive school credit.

Macaulay attacks this fallacy of arguing beside the point when he says, "The advocates of Charles, like the advocates of other malefactors against whom overwhelming evidence is produced, generally decline all controversy about the facts, and content themselves with calling testimony to character. He had so many private virtues! . . . A good father! A good husband! Ample apologies indeed for fifteen years of persecution, tyranny, and falsehood!" Cracking jokes instead of presenting proof and appealing to tradition and prejudice are common ways of ignoring the question.

BEGGING THE QUESTION. Begging the question is assuming the truth or falsity of what one is trying to prove. When a person argues that E. J. Pratt is not a great poet because there are no great living poets, he is assuming the truth of a larger statement which includes the one he started out to prove and hence is begging the question. When a debater states his question *"Resolved,* That the brutal game of football should be abolished," he is assuming that football is brutal instead of proving the game brutal, and therefore is begging the question.

ATTACKING THE PERSON, NOT THE ARGUMENT. " I don't care what Henderson says. He's a disagreeable, unreliable troublemaker." Such a statement attacks the person rather than the argument he presents. Name calling is not reasoning.

MISUSING STATISTICS. "Figures do not lie, but liars do figure" is an old saying. Careless, stupid, and dishonest people often use statistics to "prove" what the figures do not prove at all, because the units are not comparable or because the figures cover an abnormal period or do not cover a long enough period of time. If child labourers in one province include boys and girls who do housework and farm work and in another province exclude these classes, the totals are not comparable. In discussing wages, prices, street-car fares, and deposits in savings banks, one must remember that in the last thirty years the dollar has fluctuated widely in purchasing power.

There are many times when a single number is used to represent a group. When the group contains many members the *average* or arithmetical mean is often used. However, when the group is relatively small, or when a few members deviate widely from the others, the average is not a good number to use to describe the group. A better indication is provided by the *median*, which is the number that belongs to the middle member of the group. Then, half the group lies above the median, and half below it. For example, five boys graduated from high school ten years ago. To compare their financial success as a group with other groups, a single number is desired. The monthly wages of the five are $200, $250, $350, $800, $1400. The average of these, $600, is greatly influenced by the top figure. But the median, $350, would be the same whether the top earner received $900 or $2500 per month. The median has much more meaning in representing this group.

PRACTICE 3. False Statistics

1. Does the relative number of ships show the comparative strength of the navies of the world? Why?
2. Does the number of arrests for drunkenness show the comparative amount of drunkenness in various cities? Why?
3. Does the average wealth of the people of a community show whether there is need for charity? Why?

PRACTICE 4. Logical Fallacies

In most of the following the reasoning is faulty. In each case of unsound or unconvincing reasoning, name the fallacy or defect and show clearly that the argument is not convincing.

A. 1. Sweet peas don't grow well in Scarborough. I planted some in my garden and they didn't grow.

   2. Shelley, a great English poet, was a poor speller. Therefore spelling is not important.

   3. Going to college doesn't pay. Look at all the people who have been successful in business without education.

   4. The honour system will work in our high school, for it is successful in Central High School.

   5. Mrs. Brewer is an excellent housekeeper; therefore she would manage well the provincial housekeeping if elected premier.

   6. The B.M. Motor Sales is now a paying concern. Lindey A. Garrison, the company's accountant, made this assertion last night.

   7. The left-handed man lacks will power, for, if he did not, he would not be left-handed.

   8. I'm not superstitous, but I'll never again start anything on Friday the thirteenth of the month. We started to Cobourg on Friday the thirteenth and had two blowouts on the way.

   9. I won't pay $40 for that suit. I bought just as good a one five years ago for $30.

  10. Mr. Brown should never drive an automobile. Last week a runaway horse came down the street while Mr. Brown was driving; and Mr. Brown, being very nervous, drove his car into a telephone pole.

B. 1. Because our team won the championship this year, they will win it next year, too.

   2. Earl Christy, who is noted for his portraits of beautiful women, asked me to sit for a portrait; therefore I must be beautiful.

   3. I should have been given the job rather than Miss Hersey, for I have been working for the firm much longer than she.

   4. Since there is much dishonesty in politics, I shall not vote.

   5. In recent football games Hamilton defeated Queen's by a score of 50 to 0, and Sudbury defeated Queen's by a score of 30 to 0. Therefore Hamilton will defeat Sudbury.

   6. It is unnecessary for us to include meat among our provisions. Alfred McCann, a food expert, says that many vegetables cheaper than meat possess the same food value.

   7. Mrs. Knapp, the first woman elected to an important civic office, was sent to jail for misuse of city funds. Therefore women should not be elected to public office.

   8. This year we wish to cut down the expenses of our company. Because advertising is a big expense, we shall start by eliminating it.

   9. My father is a Conservative. Therefore I should regularly vote for Conservative candidates.

  10. There are almost a million people in Metropolitan Toronto. Why should I vote? One vote more or less won't make any difference.

C. 1. Hofmeister, the great inventor, sleeps only five hours a day. I require only five hours of sleep a day. Therefore I shall be a great inventor.

  2. Tobacco which has been toasted is kind to the throat.

  3. I have been troubled by rheumatism this year. Defective teeth often cause rheumatism. Therefore I shall have my teeth removed.

  4. Joan Evans was chosen to address the next parent-teacher meeting. Miss Collins always plays favourites.

  5. Jackson has six doctors, while Randolph has twelve. Evidently there is twice as much disease in Randolph as in Jackson.

  6. I've always enjoyed mysteries by A. Conan Doyle. Here's his *The Return of Sherlock Holmes*. I'll probably enjoy it too.

  7. Yesterday I found a horseshoe. Today I got 98 on a history test. The horseshoe must have brought me luck.

  8. Joel's plan for a self-service cafeteria is impractical. I just don't care for Joel anyway.

  9. You're buying yourself a new spring outfit. Don't neglect your kitchen. Give it a treat with Everglo paint.

  10. I pride myself on being unprejudiced, but I have found from experience that all people from the west end of town are sharp dealers and unreliable as workmen.

THREE JOBS FOR LANGUAGE

Language plays three roles. It communicates facts. It expresses our feelings or arouses the feelings of others. It gets people to act. When you tell your friend that you are going to camp, you communicate a fact. When you describe in glowing terms the good time you had camping last year, you express your feelings and perhaps arouse his. When you urge him to go along with you this year, you try to get him to act. In a few sentences you may perform all three functions. In a sense, you are a propagandist for your viewpoint.

PROPAGANDA

The propagandist usually tries to persuade you to think and act in the ways he desires.

"But," you say, "many people who I know have my interests at heart are trying to influence me to think in certain ways. My parents try to persuade me that cleanliness is next to godliness. My teachers want me to believe that I won't be able to get ahead in life unless I speak grammatically. Are these people propagandists?" Yes, in the good sense of the word your parents and your teachers are propagandists. Take a look at their motives. Your parents and teachers try to influence your thinking because they want what's best for you and for society.

Unscrupulous propagandists, on the other hand, are interested only in the good of the organizations they work for. They care little for the welfare of society, and they're willing to use every trick of their trade to influence you. They frequently stoop to distortion of the truth and to misstatement to make their points.

PROPAGANDA TRICKS

Twisting and Distortion. Fred Taylor said the Constitution of the United States is a weak document made by imperfect men.

Fred Taylor said, "I am proud of the Constitution of the United States. Though constructed by imperfect men, it has stood the test of time and has met the challenge of change. True, it has had its weaknesses here and there, but these have been met by amendment."

The first sentence, describing Fred Taylor's stand, completely distorts his point of view. Such distortions of the truth by dishonest propagandists are often difficult to see through.

Sometimes the distortion occurs by leaving something out.

Selective Omission. An incomplete truth can be more deadly than a falsehood. In an election campaign a candidate may emphasize that his opponent once voted against a popular measure. He will omit saying that the bill had an objectionable rider. By omitting important information the propagandists can give a wholly inaccurate picture.

Incomplete Quotation. "I don't enjoy reading when I'm completely tired out," said Jennie. Later, Charlotte quoted Jennie as saying, "I don't enjoy reading." By taking only part of the quotation, Charlotte gave a misleading picture.

PRACTICE 5. Studying Incomplete Quotations

Discuss how reporting only the words in parentheses would give an inaccurate picture of the speaker's original words and intentions.

1. (I can't stand my family) until I've had my morning coffee.
2. I don't agree that (Paula is unfriendly).
3. (Jim seemed unusually stubborn) before I came to know him better.
4. (At typing Neal is slow) but accurate.
5. (Skiing is a much overrated pastime) in the opinion of those who have never tried this thrilling sport.

Quoting out of Context. The women were teasing Ralph Erickson because he had not made his wife's breakfast on their wedding anniversary. "I guess I'll have to leave Ralph," said Mrs. Erickson with a laugh. Later, someone quoted Mrs. Erickson as having said she was about to leave her husband. In the context of good-humoured joking, her sentence was intended as a humorous retort. Taken out of context, it could easily cause misunderstanding. Quoting out of context may report the words and distort the message.

COMMON PROPAGANDA DEVICES

In addition to distortions and omissions, the dishonest propagandist makes much use of devices often harmless in themselves. The major objection to the following devices is that they encourage unthinking acceptance.

Testimonial. Though Ronald Ruddy, movie star, endorses a candidate for office, we should ask, "What qualifications make Ronald a political expert?" Don't believe everything you hear. Consider the reliability of the source. Is the speaker or writer habitually truthful? Has he had the opportunity to obtain reliable information about the subject? Is the speaker or writer biased? In whose employ is the speaker or writer? Don't be fooled by a sports hero's or actor's endorsement of a breakfast food, a soap, a cosmetic, or a razor. Always discount an endorsement that seems to have been paid for.

Band Wagon Appeal. "Everybody" may be voting for the Conservatives, reading the *Star*, or planting junipers in front of new houses. But if you think the Liberals, the *Telegram*, or azaleas are better, don't be swayed by the hop-on-the-band wagon appeal. Think and choose for yourself.

Plain Folks. "Hello, neighbours, it's mighty good to have a little heart-to-heart chat with all you kind folks." A propagandist may pretend to be just like us and use words of folksy connotation full of genial good fellowship. "A down-to-earth, friendly man just like us," say the gullible, and they give him their confidence—and their money.

Snob Appeal. This is the reverse of the plain-folks device. "These lovely exclusive creations by Mademoiselle Renée of Paris are individually designed for the discriminating woman." Words like *exclusive*, *discriminating*, and *individually designed* help to sell articles or ideas without respect to their merits.

Glittering Generalities. Big, abstract words of favourable connotation lead us to applaud a person or a cause without critically examining the proof. "Virtue words" like *public spirit*, *friend of the people*, *justice*, and *co-operation* are difficult to pin down. Nearly everyone agrees on what *oak tree* means. It is harder to agree on *ideal democracy* or *forward-looking reform*. Strip every idea of virtue words and judge it on its own merits.

Name Calling (EMOTIONAL WORDS). Sometimes speakers use loaded words—words having pleasant or unpleasant associations. Calling a person "a pillar of the community", "a friend of the people", or "a red-blooded Canadian" doesn't prove his qualifications and achievements. Merely labelling a man "a chiseler", "a City Hall crook", or "a Red" is not sufficient evidence against him. To avoid being misled by this device, ask yourself: (1) What does this name mean? (2) Is the speaker trying to secure an emotional rather than a reasonable reaction? (3) Has he proved that the name applies to the person?

PRACTICE 6. Studying Name Calling

1. List commonly applied words or expressions which currently have a bad connotation—*radical, reactionary, appeaser*, for example.
2. In news stories, editorials, feature articles, letters to the editor, or columns of newspapers or magazines, find examples of name calling. Copy in your notebook the expressions used and indicate the source.

Transfer. Even the speaker who has nothing but contempt for our country and its heritage will put a Union Jack on the speaking platform. Through the flag he hopes to induce the uncritical to transfer their patriotic feelings of loyalty and approval to the programs and principles he advocates. Symbols may encourage us to accept a program apparently endorsed by agencies we love and respect—church or nation, for example.

Scientific Slant. By giving their advertisements a scientific slant, many advertisers make use of another form of transfer. In most people science inspires awe and faith, which can easily be transferred to a product of science. Advertising a soap as containing *"Heliol,* the sunshine catalyst," wins purchasers who are awed by the impressive words.

PRACTICE 7.   Studying Propaganda Devices

In each of the following, which propaganda device is used? In some cases two or more devices are employed.

1. Give him the razor all men want: the precision-tooled razor with the double-honed blades.
2. Vote for a candidate who is as true as that glorious emblem you see on the platform. Vote for a man who embodies the finest principles of our democracy, who will lead us along the path to peace, prosperity, and security for all.
3. This woolly-headed, impractical dreamer would like to guide the destinies of this great and progressive city of ours. Why, this weak would-be leader cannot keep his own affairs in order.
4. Antikay, that great new toothpaste, contains *seriol,* the miracle ingredient. Give yourself the smile of charm and protect your teeth against decay: use Antikay—with seriol!
5. Through a fortunate purchase, we have just been able to acquire twenty handbags, individually designed and tooled by the master craftsmen of London. Wait until you see the graceful lines, the inimitable designs, the richly tanned leather! These bags are designed for the woman who doesn't have to count her pennies. They are expensive, but they are worth the money.
6. The advertisement shows a bearded old gentleman peering into a microscope. The advertisement reads, "Doctors everywhere are acclaiming Nopain, the new tablet for the relief of headaches."
7. Now, friends, we'll have a little chat with our good neighbour, Nat Gardiner, candidate for Board of Control. You all know Nat. He was born in that modest little gray house over on Main Street. Why, he worked as a delivery boy for old Mattson, the druggist.
8. Don't buy Willow Tea unless you are able to tell the difference between this and cheaper brands. Don't pay the extra money unless you are satisfied with only the best.
9. Nurses were among the first to discover how effective Smoothene is as a complexion aid. Smoothene contains medicated formula with Emollito. Listen to Hollywood star Sharon Farron, who says, "I always use Smoothene for complexion beauty."
10. Read the new, up-and-coming family magazine *Family Living.* In the past two years it has doubled its circulation.

Chapter 22

The Mass Media of Communication

Mass media is the sociologists' term for means of communication that reach huge audiences: magazines, television, newspapers, radio, paper-covered pocket books, the movies. We're so accustomed to these mass media that we seldom realize what a great influence they have in our lives.

CHOOSING A NEWSPAPER

Despite the inroads of other mass media, newspapers retain a powerful influence in Canadian life. Even adults who scarcely read anything else do look for their daily paper. But newspapers vary in quality. Choosing a good one is not always easy.

SUGGESTIONS FOR CHOOSING A NEWSPAPER

1. Look for these qualities: truthfulness, completeness, fairness, good taste. Comparing newspapers helps you judge these qualities.
2. Look for good balance and proportion in features and special departments: art, books, fashions, education, food, movies, music, radio, sports, television.
3. See whether the news is up to date.
4. Check the use of pictures. Good photographs enrich your reading of the news. Sensational photographs merely appeal to curiosity or morbid interest.
5. Change newspapers occasionally for a fresh viewpoint.

PRACTICE 1. Choosing a Newspaper

Of the newspapers available to you, which one seems best by the standards suggested above? Bring the newspaper to class and tell why you chose it.

SUGESTIONS FOR READING A NEWSPAPER

1. Read all the headlines on the front page. Skim through the rest.
2. Read important news stories as well as other stories that particularly appeal to you.
3. Sample special departments: theatre reviews, columnists, letters to the editor.
4. Try to read at least the first editorial.   Remember that this is an opinion, not a straightforward report of a fact.
5. Read those items that you enjoy most: a report of last night's baseball game, a new recipe, the fashion notes, or an account of the Davis Cup matches.

PRACTICE 2. Talking about a Newspaper Column

Choose your favourite newspaper column: political, sports, movie, or some other. Clip an example of one and bring it to class. Be ready to tell why you like it and why you would recommend it to others.

CHOOSING MAGAZINES

Among the thousands of magazines on the news stands are many you can read with interest and profit.

SUGGESTIONS FOR CHOOSING A MAGAZINE

1. Talk over magazines with friends. Which ones do they recommend?
2. Browse through the magazines in your school or local library. Sample the contents of magazines that might interest you.
3. In examining a magazine consider these: purpose, appeal, contents, appearance.
4. Learn the names of magazines that are tailored to your special interests and needs: hobbies, sports, travel, science, garden, teen-age problems, movies, television, news, mystery, science fiction.

PRACTICE 3. Reporting on a Magazine

Prepare to tell the class about your favourite magazine. Bring a copy to class and refer to it to illustrate your points. Give the name of the magazine and tell where and how frequently it is published. Consider the four elements mentioned above.

TELEVISION AND RADIO

Television and radio have extended the influence of the mass media to groups not reached by magazines and newspapers. Children of preschool age and persons who cannot or will not read are directly affected by television and radio even though the influence of other media may be slight.

CHOOSING TELEVISION AND RADIO PROGRAMS

1. Plan your listening. Look ahead. Budget your time. Don't watch something because "there's nothing else to do."
2. Decide on the programs you'd like to see during the week. Remember that you may have to compromise with members of your family who have different ideas.
3. If your week-end newspaper has a schedule of programs for the week, save it. Circle worth-while possibilities.
4. Don't "freeze" the dial to one channel or station.
5. Don't twirl the dial, getting meaningless fragments as you ceaselessly seek something that "sounds good".
6. Look for outstanding productions, like a great actor in a famous play. These productions are usually given adequate advance publicity.
7. Listen to parents, teachers, and friends whose judgment you respect. Their recommendations will help you.
8. Make a note of programs endorsed by newspapers and magazines.
9. If possible, find out what a program will be about. Some magazines, like *TV Guide*, include brief summaries of the programs.

PRACTICE 4. Reporting on Good Programs

List three excellent radio or television programs, and be ready to tell why you consider each worth watching or listening to.

PRACTICE 5. Comparing Television and Radio

Be ready to discuss these questions. Do you still listen to radio? What type of program do you seek principally on radio? What special needs does radio fill that cannot be met by television? What kind of program can be done immeasurably better on television?

CHOOSING MASS MEDIA

Newspapers, magazines, radio, and television all have special appeals, special interests and points of strength. Each is supreme in certain areas. For good music you might turn to radio; for great plays, to television; for detailed treatment of up-to-the-minute events, to newspapers; for leisure reading, to magazines. Don't expect from magazines what newspapers can do better. Choose the correct medium to meet a specific need.

PRACTICE 6. Comparing the Mass Media

Which of the mass media is well suited to reporting each of the following? If you choose more than one medium, tell the special advantages of each. Prepare to give reasons.

1. A band concert presented at the local park
2. A ventriloquist act
3. News of an earthquake
4. A new scientific discovery
5. An article on how to make a birdhouse

NEWS AND THE MASS MEDIA

Each medium reports the news, but each does it in a special way. Radio can present news bulletins as they are received. Some stations present news bulletins "on the hour," with roundups at longer intervals. Commentators on radio and television can analyze the news and present their own opinions. Television can show maps, graphs, photographs, filmed interviews, and newsreels. The newspaper presents a more complete picture of current events. Many newspapers print the full text of important speeches, for example, as well as detailed accounts of the event. Magazines present news summaries and try to give the background of news events. Thus it is possible to use all four media for a complete and up-to-date awareness of the news.

PRACTICE 7. Studying News on the Mass Media

For the next week follow an important news event through two or more of the mass media. One week from today be ready to report to the class, using these questions as a guide. Announce the news event before you begin.

1. How was the news treated by each of the media?
2. What special advantages did each news medium have in presenting the news?
3. Which presentation do you remember best? Why?
4. Was there a difference in interpretation? Explain.
5. Did one presentation seem biased? In what way?
6. If you had to choose only one medium for news, which would it be? Why?

BIAS IN NEWS REPORTS

By omitting information or by burying news in back pages of the newspaper, an editor can slant the news even though he writes nothing untrue. When you read your newspaper, notice whether it gives the same prominence to news of one political party as of another.

PRACTICE 8. Comparing Two Views of the Same Question

Find an article, editorial, or TV or radio analysis that gives one view of a political figure or political question. Then find another that gives a different view, and compare the two. Did both give facts to support their cases? Did the facts given differ? How much use did each make of emotional words?

Re-read Chapter 21 to refresh your memory, of the tricks of propaganda and bias.

EDITORIALS

An editorial or commentary on the news does not pretend to be a straight report. Rather it is someone's opinion about a current news item. Some readers and listeners, unfortunately, often accept opinion as fact.

Most newspapers take a definite political stand. A newspaper editorial writer can seldom give an unprejudiced view of a political question. Some magazines, especially news-commentary magazines, have definite political viewpoints. Now, there is nothing wrong with having opinions and reading opinions, but remember, opinions are not facts.

How do you spot bias in an editorial, an article, or a television (or radio) commentary?

The editorial columns of the great dailies are powerful instruments in the formation of public opinion, reinforced as they usually are by such selection and display of the news as will direct the attention of the reading public to the matters under consideration. And this is the function of the editorial: to mould public opinion. The news reporters glean the day's news and the editorial writers comment upon it. They may congratulate, criticize, commend, condemn, or crusade on political or social questions. They usually clarify the interpretation of news; they might be used for the opposite purpose, though this is beneath the ethical code of reputable editors.

"THIRD LEADERS"

The usual editorial "leaders" are not intended for preservation or expected to be of permanent interest. "Like the news of the day," says Professor Mackail, "the daily comment on it is transitory and soon forgotten. One thinks as little of rereading yesterday's leading articles as of re-reading yesterday's news . . . The news of the day and the daily comment made upon it give necessary information, and help (or are supposed to help) to interpret it to us. Between them, they rouse feeling and suggest action, as well as keep us in touch with the daily movement of the world; but they do not satisfy the intelligence, nor, except incidentally, do they enlarge the mind, or lead it toward the real realities. Those who read nothing but newspapers—how many!—are starving their minds; and the starvation is none the less real for those who gorge themselves with this food."

Metropolitan newspapers try to make up this editorial deficiency by including an editorial of a different, less occasional kind. This editorial, known as the "third leader", resembles the familiar essay, but is less personal and more topical. "They are meant," says Professor Mackail, "to turn the reader from affairs and interests of the moment to a consideration 'of man, of nature, and of human life' in their larger, more permanent aspects. They may still deal not indeed with events, but with fashions or tendencies, theories or experiences, of the immediate present. But even with these they deal in a more detached way, from a wider point of view. Oftener still they are concerned with things that have a more true permanence; with the elements of human nature, the springs of action, the problems of life and conduct; with the effective meaning of art or of science; with the recurrent and perpetual pageant of the visible world."

These headings are chosen from "third leaders": "On Friendship", "Ugliness", "On Being a Gentleman", "Childishness", "Amateur and Professional", "Castles in the Air", "Philosophy and Poetry", "Grumbling", "Strawberries", "Living in the Past".

MODELS (LEADING ARTICLES):

COURAGE OF CIVIL LIFE

Periodically the world hesitates in its every-day run of work and pleasure to contemplate some act of high courage. Such an incident seems to lift the average man or woman out of the mundane routine of life which they are at times tempted to term "meaningless."

In northern Canada the curtain has just been lowered on the final act in one of these great living dramas by the successful rescue of Flight Lieutenant Sheldon Coleman and Leading Aircraftsman Joseph Fortey by other members of the Royal Canadian Air Force.

For more than a month, the two lost airmen waited for help near a small lake, inadequately sheltered by timber and warmed by their ingenious camp-made stove. They had little to eat and the country afforded less provision than one would expect. There was the continuous pressure of the rapidly approaching Arctic Winter with its prospect of greater suffering and privation.

Thinking of these things, one wonders how many times their fitful sleep must have been broken by the lash of an imaginary propeller and how they stood for hours scanning the horizon hoping against hope for sign of a rescue ship. It is inactive waiting like that which breaks the nerve of most men.

Then there were the men who conducted the search. The leader of this party tended to minimize in his public statement the hazards his men undertook in their rescue work. Yet there will be few who read the story of airmen returning to their base with empty gasoline tanks or of the constant strain of flying in bad weather who do not feel that lift about the heart that comes from the contemplation of shining courage.

After witnessing a rescue like the one just completed, or many others that take place on the frontier or in the mines or on the sea, it seems almost senseless for certain kinds of ardent militarists to continue their arguments that war and slaughter are necessary to bring out the highest virtues of the human race.

SLAUGHTER STILL PREVAILS ON THE HIGHWAYS

Two judges of the High Court of Ontario have this week denounced the increase of motor accidents and the general practice of reckless driving on the highways. A few drivers have been sent to jail on charges of manslaughter when they were responsible for the deaths of others. Chief Justice Rose is quoted as saying: "I am not sure we are following the logical course in prosecuting only when there has been a serious accident or death." There must be punishment to suit the crime, but punishment will not be inflicted until public opinion is sufficiently aroused to demand it. The officers of the law should rigidly enforce existing regulations, and the courts should not hesitate to convict.

One of the causes of accidents on the highways is the persistence of the vast majority of drivers in neither dimming nor dipping their lights in the face of opposing traffic. We doubt if five per cent of the motor users of this part of the country ever think of lessening the glare from their own headlights in consideration for motorists who are travelling the other way. If a motorist driving south has to meet a succession of cars driving north, he is partially blinded so that he cannot discern what is on the road ahead of him. We have printed a series of editorials on the subject of glaring headlights. The Minister of Highways has appealed for courtesy on the road, but very few people appear to pay any attention to these appeals. It is probable that a few examples will have to be made of a few individuals before a very grave abuse is checked or even modified.

By Permission of The Globe and Mail, *Toronto.*

MODEL (THIRD LEADERS):

ON FRIENDSHIP

Friendship is above reason, for, though you find virtues in a friend, he was your friend before you found them. It is a gift that we offer because we must; to give it as the reward of virtues would be to set a price upon it, and those who do that have no friendship to give. If you choose your friends on the ground that you are virtuous and want virtuous company, you are no nearer to true friendship than if you choose them for commercial reasons. Besides, who are you that you should be setting a price upon your friendship? It is enough for any man that he has the divine power of making friends, and he must leave it to that power to determine who his friends shall be. For, though you may choose the virtuous to be your friends, they may not choose you; indeed, friendship cannot grow where there is any calculated choice. It comes, like sleep, when you are not thinking about it; and you should be grateful, without any misgiving, when it comes.

So no man who knows what friendship is ever gave up a friend because he turns out to be disreputable. His only reason for giving up a friend is that he has ceased to care for him; and, when that happens, he should reproach himself for this mortal poverty of affection, not the friend for having proved unworthy. For it is inhuman presumption to say of any man that he is unworthy of your friendship, just as it is to say of any woman, when you have fallen out of love with her, that she is unworthy of your love. In friendship and in love we are always humble, because we see that a free gift has been given to us; and to lose that humility because we have lost friendship or love is to take a pride in what should shame us.

We have our judgments and our penalties as part of the political mechanism that is forced upon us so that we may continue to live; but friendship is not friendship at all unless it teaches us that these are not part of our real life. They have to be; and we pay men, and clothe them in wigs and scarlet, to sit in judgment on other men. So we are tempted to play this game of judgment ourselves, even though no one has paid us to do it. It is only in the warmth of friendship that we see how cold a thing it is to judge and how stupid to take a pleasure in judging; for we recognize this warmth as a positive good, a richness in our natures, while the coldness that sets us judging is a poverty. Just as our criticism of a work of art begins only when we have ceased to experience it, so our criticism of our friends begins only when we have ceased to experience them, when our minds can no longer remain at the height of intimacy. But this criticism is harmless if we know it for what it is, merely the natural reaction, the cold fit that comes after the warm, and if we do not suppose that our coldness is wiser than our warmth.

There are men who cannot be friends except when they are under an illusion that their friends are perfect, and when the illusion passes there is an end of their friendship. But true friendship has no illusions, for it reaches to that part of a man's nature that is beyond his imperfections, and in doing so it takes all of them for granted. It does not even assume that he is better than other men, for there is egotism in assuming that. A man is your friend, not because of his superiorities, but because there is something open from your nature to his, a way that is closed between you and most men. You and he understand each other, as the phrase is; your relation with him is a rare success among a multitude of failures, and if you are proud of the success you should be ashamed of the failure.

There is nothing so fatal to friendship as this egotism of accounting for it by some superiority in the friend. If you do that you will become a member of a set, all, in their assertion of each other's merits, implying their own, and all uneasy lest they are giving more than they get. For if you insist upon the virtues of your friend, you expect him to insist upon your virtues, and there is a competition between you which makes friendship a burden rather than a rest. Criticism then becomes treachery, for it implies that you are beginning to doubt those superiorities upon which your friendship is supposed to be based. But when no superiorities are assumed, criticism is only the exercise of a natural curiosity. It is because a man is your friend, and you like him so much and know him so well, that you are curious about him. You are in fact an expert upon him, and like to show your expert knowledge. And you are an expert because in the warmth of friendship his disguises melt away from him, and he shows himself to you just as he is. Indeed, that is the test of friendship and the delight of it, that because we are no longer afraid of being thought worse than we are we do not try to seem better. We know that it is not our virtues that have won us friendship, and we do not fear to lose it through our vices. We have reached the blessed state of being nearer to heaven than anything else in this life, in which affection does not depend upon judgment; and we are like gods, who have no need even to forgive, because they know. It is a rare state, and never attained to in its perfection. We can approach it only if we know what friendship is and really desire it, and especially if we admire that man who is a friend without ever wondering at his choice of friends or blaming him for his faithfulness to them whatever evil they may do.—From *"Modern Essays from The Times"*.

By permission of the publishers, Edward Arnold & Co., London.

PRACTICE 9. Studying Editorials

Cut out and bring to school three editorials which you think are good ones and after pasting them in your exercise book write under each what you think its merits are.

PRACTICE 10. Writing an Editorial

Write an editorial (leading article) on some topic in this week's news.

PRACTICE 11. Writing a "Third Leader"

Write a "third leader" editorial for your school paper.

PRACTICE 12. Discussing the Impact of the Mass Media

1. What are some other ways (not mentioned in this chapter) in which we are influenced by the mass media? Be ready to tell how we are affected.

2. Is it true that the mass media are directed principally to minds at the thirteen-year-old level? What exceptions can be found? What can individual members of the public do to raise the level of their appeal?

3. Since advertising plays a crucial role in the mass media, should advertising be controlled in any way? How?

Chapter 23

Discussion, Argument, Debate

A. Discussion

Whenever a matter of the tactics used in a baseball game, an issue in school politics, or a question of club policy comes up, boys and girls gather in groups to talk over the subject, to consider the different angles of the situation, to exchange facts and opinions bearing on the matter. This is group discussion, in which each member of a group contributes facts and opinions that may help the group as a whole to arrive at a sensible conclusion or plan of action.

CHOOSING A DISCUSSION SUBJECT

Choose a subject of real interest to the group. Be sure it fits the time you have for discussion and the knowledge you bring to it. For example, you, as a high school student, would be better prepared to discuss student government than the theory of relativity.

Put the discussion subject in the form of a question. How can the legitimate theatre attract a wider audience? What kind of discipline is best for teen-agers? What subjects should high school students be required to take? How can labour unions be run so as to benefit both their own members and the community as a whole?

PREPARING FOR A DISCUSSION

Prepare to take an active and intelligent part in the discussion. Review your own knowledge of the subject. Observe the problem firsthand if possible. Consult the most factual, impartial sources that you can find, first for background material, later for details about the topic.

Next, organize your material in the form of a discussion outline. Ask yourself:

1. Just what is the scope of the question? What information are we seeking? What problem are we trying to solve?

2. What solutions have been proposed for this problem? What support exists for each solution?

3. Which solution seems to me best? (Keep this answer tentative; the discussion itself may give you a different slant on question 3.)

4. How may the preferred solution be put into effect?

TAKING PART IN A DISCUSSION

Come to the discussion prepared with facts, opinions, and a discussion outline. Be prepared to co-operate with the rest of the group, to pool your information, and to work with your classmates toward the best solution of the problem. Listen carefully. Make sure that each remark you offer relates to the point immediately under discussion. If someone disproves or rejects one of your pet ideas, accept the criticism in good spirit.

If the meeting is large and formally conducted, rise, address the chair, and wait for recognition before speaking. If it is small and informal, talk from your place. In either case, be brief and keep to the point. Speak courteously and impersonally. And don't forget—give the other fellow a chance to speak.

CHOOSING THE DISCUSSION LEADER

Choose as the leader of a discussion a pupil who (1) speaks clearly and pointedly; (2) listens understandingly; (3) is businesslike and efficient but also courteous, considerate, and fair. The chairman's duties are—

1. To state at the beginning the subject and the main points to be covered.

2. To keep the discussion on the subject. When a pupil wanders away from the subject, the chairman courteously reminds him of the topic under discussion.

3. To give all a chance to contribute. If a pupil talks too long or too often, the chairman reminds him that some pupils have not had a chance to speak.

4. To keep the discussion peaceful.

5. To keep the discussion moving forward until a plan of action is adopted or a resolution formed. The chairman may at any time sum up the points already made to keep them clearly in the minds of the group. He also occasionally asks a question or makes a statement to keep the discussion moving toward a goal. At the close of a discussion he may sum up the conclusions reached and mention points which have not been settled or may call on a member for such a summary.

Example of pupil's contribution to discussion:

ATTITUDE OF YOUNG PEOPLE TOWARD RELIGION

Mister Chairman, the present attitude of many boys and girls of high school and college age toward religion seems to be one of general laxity and indifference. Many declare that religion was all right for their parents to believe in, or for people of a few generations past, but that now things are different; people are more broad-minded—religion is for people with set standards and narrow points of view. As a result of these erroneous beliefs, many of the younger generation have discarded all so-called "old-fashioned" principles of religion, with the argument that we, of today, have a free right to express ourselves in word and action as we see fit, and not as others see fit.

In order to have any well-regulated and happy social order, it is, and always has been, necessary to conform to some higher authority—not only political authority, but religious authority as well. The very fact that crime, general lawlessness, and careless moral behaviour have increased these past few years seems to be fairly good evidence that lack of religious belief of some sort has hindered the world from achieving a better social order.

If we are to look for a more idealistic civilization in the future, we must hold on to less worldly ambitions and to more spiritual ambitions. Public laws will never be able to do away entirely with corruption; each individual must regulate his own moral behaviour so as to conform with laws that have been handed down throughout the ages by religions of all kinds—laws made by a higher power than man.

PRACTICE 1. Group Discussion

Choose a discussion leader and prepare to take an active part in the discussion of one of the following topics:

1. Is youth today irresponsible?
2. Is all education essentially self-education?
3. Is it desirable to have an international language?
4. Does how a young man spends his time after working hours concern his employer?
5. Being sick is a crime and being well the common duty of every good citizen.
6. The rigours of country life give young people initiative and ambition.
7. The further development of machines gives us more to fear than to hope.
8. The modern evaluation of success is generally with the money yardstick. Give your opinion of this with the purpose of establishing a true standard of success.
9. Emerson said, "There are 850,000 volumes in the Imperial Library at Paris. If a man were to read industriously from dawn to dark for sixty years, he would die in the first alcove." What books should a person read? How select?
10. Henry Ford says, "I believe America's educational system is all wrong. It turns out millions of high school graduates looking for any kind of job and not fitted for any one job in the world, unless it might be lecturing." Would this be true of the Canadian educational system? Why?
11. College. 12. Gambling. 13. Law enforcement. 14. Drinking. 15. The profitable use of leisure. 16. Honesty. 17. Courtesy in school. 18. The attitude of young people toward religion. 19. Modern advertising. 20. Books published this year.

PRACTICE 2. Discussing Motion Pictures

With the following criteria in mind, discuss motion pictures you have recently seen:

1. **Type of motion picture.** Comedy? Tragedy? Melodrama, arce? Travelogue? Musical drama?
2. **Setting.** Time? Place? Any outstandingly beautiful or unusual scenes? Harmony of setting with mood and theme of the picture?

3. **Main idea or theme running through the story.** Important?

4. **Story.** Is it by a well-known author? Sketch briefly the framework. Is the story original? True to life? What is the conflict inherent in it? What is the climax and in what part of the story is it reached? Is the ending logical? Name the two leading characters. What traits do you admire or dislike in each?

5. **Scene you liked best.** Why? What made it effective?

6. **Acting.** Lifelike interpretation of main character? Any outstanding performances of minor roles? Is the acting exaggerated? Which is more important—the story or the acting.?

7. **Direction.** Name the director. Any clever "shots"? Skilful introduction of characters? Of scenes? Use of photographic effects to produce a mood or suspense? Are useless scenes included or necessary ones left out?

8. **Photography.** Smooth transition from scene to scene? How? Fade-outs and close-ups used effectively? Lighting? Describe.

9. **Sound effects.** Subtle or prominent? Does speaking or action predominate? Does the dialogue seem real? Do the actors speak effectively? Are their voices pleasing and suited to the characters? Characteristic noises employed? Is the music suitable?

10. **Critics.** What do the critics say about the picture? Are their opinions sound? Prove your statements.

PRACTICE 3. Discussing Radio or Television Programs

With the following topics as guides, discuss the most interesting radio or television program you have listened to within a week:

1. **Name** of the program, time of broadcast, and broadcasting station. Was there a feature artist?

2. **Type** of program: concert, lecture, drama, news items, interview, forum discussion, sports broadcast.

3. **Highlights** of the program. Briefly sketch the main features.

4. **The plan** of the program. If a concert, was there any basis for the selection of compositions? Smooth transition between numbers? Good continuity? If a drama, how were the characters introduced? Scenes? How was the setting implied? Any sound effects?

5. **Speaking.** Good voice? Good articulation? Fluent?

6. **Advertising.** Inconspicuous? Boresome? Moderately entertaining because original? Did the advertiser give convincing reasons? Talk as if he believed what he said?

7. **Reason for liking** (or disliking) the program. Give definite, thoughtful reasons. Prove your points.

FORUM DISCUSSION

As a preliminary to a forum discussion two assigned speakers may present the *two major points of view*. When both speakers have been heard, the chairman leads the group in an informal discussion. The main purpose of a forum discussion is to present fairly both sides of a question, not to arrive at a plan of action or the adoption of a resolution. In a forum discussion on the subject "Is education by experience as important as education by books?" one speaker will defend the value of education by experience; the other, education by books. In the ensuing general discussion, the members of the group will present their opinions, but a final decision need not be reached.

PRACTICE 4.   Forum Discussion

Select one of the following topics and a speaker for each side. After each speaker has presented his argument, a student chairman will lead a discussion of the question.

1. Should the government own and operate radio and television stations?
2. Our present-day attitude toward criminals is too sentimental.
3. Debating should be eliminated from the high school English course.
4. The jury system should be abolished.
5. Canada should adopt compulsory military service.
6. Grades and marks should be abandoned in favour of semi-annual letters in which the teachers report to the parents the pupils' progress.

THE PANEL

The panel discussion is an *informal* group discussion before an audience. Panel members, whose number may vary, sit at a table on the platform or at the front of the room. The chairman, whose place is at the centre of the table, rises and introduces the topic and the speakers. He opens the discussion with an appropriate question or calls on one of the panel members to begin. There is no set order of speakers. The panel members talk over the topic informally in voices loud enough for the audience to hear easily. The chairman is familiar with the material each speaker wishes to present and sees to it that all points are covered in the discussion. After a certain fixed time he invites the audience to participate, either by asking questions or by contributing ideas and information.

PRACTICE 5. Holding Panel Discussion

Divide your class into committees of four or five "experts" and present a series of panel discussions based on such topics as: interspace travel, highway accidents, modern music, early marriages, adult education, labour unions, the farmer's problems, the movies, part-time jobs for high school students, hobbies, better housing for all, vocational training, value of a college education, educational television programs, the platforms of our two major political parties, marvels of modern science, compulsory voting.

THE SYMPOSIUM

The symposium is *more formal* than the panel discussion. Because it offers more information in a more unified form than does the panel, it is especially suited to large audiences. In the symposium prepared speakers, usually three to six in number, present different phases of a particular topic, usually not a controversial one. A chairman presides. Like the members of a panel discussion, the symposium chairman and speakers sit at a long table or in a semicircle on the platform or at the front of the room.

At a preliminary meeting the speakers analyze the topic and decide which phases of it they will cover. Each speaker chooses one aspect of the subject and by study and research prepares himself to speak as an authority on it. When all the material has been gathered and organized, the group present their information and ideas to the audience in a series of prepared speeches.

After the talks the chairman invites the audience to ask questions, contribute information, and join in the discussion.

EXAMPLE OF A SYMPOSIUM TOPIC:

SHOULD YOU GO TO COLLEGE?

FIRST SPEAKER	Analyzing your abilities and needs
SECOND SPEAKER	Reviewing college academic requirements
THIRD SPEAKER	Considering the economics of going to college
FOURTH SPEAKER	Surveying opportunities for college entrance

PRACTICE 6. Holding a Symposium

Divide your class into committees of four or five and present a series of symposia. With the other members of your class decide upon significant topics or choose from the following list. When you are a member of a symposium, speak clearly, use a pleasant voice, and pronounce every word correctly. When you are in the audience, follow the discussion carefully and jot down ideas and questions for the question and comment period.

1. The growth of suburbia.
2. Federal aid to education.
3. Science fiction.
4. Advertising in modern life.
5. Space travel.
6. Choosing a college.
7. Current job opportunities.
8. Television drama (or television commercials).
9. Problems of teen-agers.
10. The peacetime army.
11. The house of tomorrow.
12. Music fads and fancies.
13. Modern news reporting.
14. Outstanding English (or American) playwrights (or poets, or novelists).
15. Improving our national economy.
16. A free and responsible press.
17. Moral standards in politics and business.
18. Traffic problems.
19. Flood control.
20. Choosing a career.

B. Argument

VALUE

Concerning the value of argument the English syllabus of the state of California says, "The growing use of free speech in America and the dangers to our ideals and institutions which come from an inability to discriminate between sound and unsound reasoning make definite training in argument a necessity for every student." This is equally true of Canada.

PURPOSE

The purpose of argument is to change belief or secure desired action. Although the prime purpose of a school debate is to find the truth, an aim of the debaters is to convince the critic judge, the three judges, or the audience. In other arguments the purpose may be to sell tickets for a baseball game, to secure contributions for the Red Cross, to win votes for your candidate for the presidency of the student-body organization, or to sell a book or a pair of shoes. In these cases belief is not enough. In other words such an argument must be both *convincing* and *persuasive*.

PROOF AND ASSERTION

The most common fault in argument is assertion, mere "say-so", without proof. Don't say, "I think," "I believe," "It seems to me," "It is my opinion," "Statistics prove," and "Authorities on the subject say," for these expressions suggest easy-going assertion without proof. Really to argue at all, one must do more than state and restate the proposition and what he thinks about it; he must present facts, figures, quotations, maxims, theories, or comparisons to prove that his assertions are valid. Proof is giving (1) facts, (2) quotations from authorities, and (3) sound reasoning in support of a statement.

PRACTICE 7. Arguing

Speak convincingly on these topics. Assertion without proof is worthless.

1. Perhaps on a crowded street car you have seen a young man who neglected to offer his seat to a shabbily clad old woman suddenly become most polite when a stylishly dressed girl entered. To whom should a person give up his street car seat? Should a girl returning from a matinee expect a tired labourer to offer his seat? Give your opinion on this problem, and try to convince the class of its worth by being logical and definite.

2. "The ordinary vacation," says Walter B. Pitkin, "is a delusion and a snare, in so far as you use it as a rest period." What do you think? Why?

3. What should a high school do with its loafers, who waste their opportunity and the taxpayers' money? For example, would you favour debarring from the privileges of the school any pupil who through lack of work did not in two years complete the work of a year and a half? Prove that your answer is fair to the student and to the taxpayer.

4. Pope says, "A little learning is a dangerous thing." Is this true? Present proof.

5. James Harvey Robinson in *Mind in the Making* says, "Most of our so-called reasoning consists in finding arguments for going on believing as we do." Prove or disprove the statement.

C. Persuasion

To persuade is to move someone to action, to cause somebody to do what you would like to have him do. After deciding that you would like to go to camp, you must persuade Mother and Father to let you go and to pay the bills. To move a person to action you need to have good reasons, to be fair and sincere, to paint vivid pictures, and to look at the subject from the other person's point of view. To persuade your teacher, for example, you must try to look at the subject through his eyes.

Example of persuasion:

AN AMAZING SUMMERLAND

Now that summertime is here, don't you long for vacation time, and don't you wish to spend that vacation in British Columbia, where you can have a complete change and a continuous outdoor life? There nine nights out of ten you'll sleep under blankets and in the morning be wonderfully rested and refreshed for the thousand and one things to do by day. And just think of the summer sports, bathing in the ocean at the foot of mountain ranges, camping, fishing, hiking, riding horseback up wild mountain trails and over country that you've read about. Then a visit to the great national parks and forests, which are at their best in summer, and to the giant trees, tremendous waterfalls, and sky-blue lakes would be delightful. Don't you agree with me that it would be fascinating to spend a vacation in British Columbia?—STUDENT.

PRACTICE 8. Persuading

1. By effectively introducing a favourite book to the class, persuade some pupils to read it. You may tell a short, interesting incident, sketch an unusual character, read or reproduce a sparkling bit of conversation, or begin a sketch of the plot and stop at an exciting part.

2. You have twenty tickets for a Magic Evening to be given by the Science Club. In a short speech persuade the pupils in your class to buy them.

3. As campaign manager for a candidate for the secretaryship of your Student Council, make a short speech to persuade your classmates to vote for your candidate.

4. You are president of the Library Helpers' Club, the Book Club, the French Club, or another club. Make a speech to persuade your classmates to join your club.

5. Discuss places and ways to spend the summer. Try to persuade some in the class to spend a summer in a place you recommend or in a way you suggest.

6. With a partner dramatize a scene in which you try to persuade your father to let you go to camp, to teach you to drive the automobile, to permit you to take riding lessons, or to take up any other activity.

7. With a partner dramatize a scene in which you try to persuade a teacher to become a faculty adviser of a school club, to coach a club entertainment, to help you organize a club, or to help in any other school acitivity.

PRACTICE 9. Persuading

Suppose that the English Department of your school is revising the home reading list and has asked for the opinions of the pupils of the school about books. Discuss a book with the purpose of showing that it should be added to the list, should be removed from the list, or should be retained on the list.

Examples:

Why *A Son of the Middle Border* Should be Placed on the Home Reading List

In my judgment Garland's *A Son of the Middle Border* should most decidedly be placed on the home reading list. Considered from the standpoint of literary value, it is a masterpiece. Garland in this book makes one feel as if he were living in the West, playing with little Hamlin and Jessie, and sharing their troubles. From the standpoint of its interest to the reader, it is the best book of its kind that I have ever read, for it made me feel the despair and joy of these helpless farmers struggling to break down impassable barriers. It thrilled me and made me realize how many unknown heroes existed in those Middle Border days.—STUDENT.

Why *The Lost World* Should be Added to the Home Reading List

The Lost World by Conan Doyle is a story that should be added to our book list. It is a tale of adventures so vivid and exciting that, nearing the end, one lacks breath. The reader is led to a lost plateau in South America inhabited by prehistoric beasts and wild animals. Cut off from the outside world, four people explore this mysterious land, its wonders and hidden terrors. Tracked by enormous beasts, attacked by huge bird-creatures, half-killed by ape men, the little party finds danger at every step—but no way out. The book is rich in humour, suspense, thrills, chills—all that youth appreciates—then why not put this book on the list?—STUDENT.

D. Debate

Debate is formal discussion made into a game with definite rules.

THE QUESTION

For a debate choose an interesting two-sided question, and state it clearly, briefly, and definitely. The question should be a timely, vital one that is still unsettled. Avoid a broad or complicated question, a proposition which can never be proved or disproved, and a proposition which has *not* in it. State the question in a sentence having one subject and one predicate unless a modifying clause is needed.

PRACTICE 10. Questions for Debate

Criticize these questions for debate:

1. The trolley is more useful than the automobile.
2. Cigarette smoking is injurious to boys.

3. The pen is mightier than the sword.

4. Foch was a greater general than Napoleon.

5. Moral requirements for high school graduation should be as high as scholastic requirements.

6. Canada should not belong to the United Nations.

7. Law is a better profession than medicine.

FINDING MATERIAL FOR A DEBATE

Webster said, "I first examine my own mind searchingly to find out what I know about the subject, and then I read to learn what I don't know about it." The *Readers' Guide*, a debater's best friend, is an index of magazine articles. The card catalogue is a guide to the books in the library. The clipping file is convenient for up-to-the-minute information. In your reading watch for a bibliography or references to other books or magazines. On a local question ask the people who know the facts; on a school question interview the principal, superintendent, teachers, pupils, and parents.

Other publications which contain information valuable in debate are:

> *Encyclopedia Britannica*
> *New International Encyclopedia*
> *New International Year Book*
> *Statesman's Year Book*
> *The Canada Year Book*
> *World Almanac*
> Schlichter's *Modern Economic Society*
> *Encyclopedia of Social Science*
> *Hansard*
> *The Canadian Almanac and Directory*
> The publications of the Canadian Institute of International Affairs.
> The publications of the Foreign Policy Association

DECIDING ON MAIN ISSUES

The main issues map out the work that a debater must do to win. They are the divisions of the proposition, the points which must be proved to prove the case, the points on which there is a clash of opinion. Each is narrower in scope than the main question, but together they cover the whole question. In classroom debate the two sides frequently agree on the issues.

On the question "Examinations in high schools should be abolished," the affirmative will maintain that—

1. Examinations are not fair to the students.

2. Examinations injure the health of pupils.

3. Examinations cause loafing during the term and cramming at the end.
4. Examinations do not prepare for life.
5. Examinations encourage dishonesty.

The negative will maintain that—

1. Examinations aid in the accurate measurement of progress.
2. Examinations motivate study.
3. Examinations prepare for college and later life.
4. The abuses in examinations can be corrected without abolishing the whole system.

Opinions clash on the value of examinations in (1) measuring progress, (2) inducing pupils to study their work thoroughly and intelligently, and (3) preparing for life. The main issues therefore are—

1. Do examinations aid in the accurate measurement of progress?
2. Do examinations motivate study?
3. Do examinations prepare for college and later life?

The health and honesty arguments will be used by the affirmative as proof of the third issue.

Don't select too many issues. Usually two, three, or four are better than six or eight. Combine minor issues. Be sure, however, that the main issues cover the ground, prove the case. In a debate on examinations one team used these issues:

1. Are examinations injurious to the health of pupils?
2. Do examinations help teachers to mark accurately?
3. Do examinations cause cramming?

These issues do not cover the ground, because one of the most important points, the value of examinations as a preparation for later life is omitted.

Avoid also overlapping issues. One debater decided on these issues:

1. Do examinations result in the students' acquiring greater knowledge of the subjects they are studying?
2. Do examinations affect the health of students?
3. Is anything gained by examinations?

These are overlapping issues, because the first is just one part or phase of the third.

INTRODUCTION, BODY OF ARGUMENT, AND CONCLUSION

Every debate includes an introduction, body, and conclusion. The introduction clears the way for the argument; the body of the argument is the proof of the issues; and the conclusion is a summary of the proof.

INTRODUCTION

The history of the question is usually given in the introduction but may be omitted if the audience know the origin of the question, its importance, and its relation to them. If any word or expression is not clear to the audience or might be interpreted in two ways, define it. Supplement the dictionary definition by a common-sense analysis of the expression, an appeal to authorities who have defined it, or a study of the history of the question. Exclude irrelevant matter. If points are by agreement omitted from the discussion, state these. Finally, state the main issues.

The introduction should also win the sympathy of the audience. Hence it should be simple, straightforward, modest, and fair. Explain. Do not argue, overstate, or make assertions that need proof.

When in the introduction of the debate you reach the issues, it isn't enough to state them—unless, of course, the two sides have agreed on the issues. Your opponent may in a few minutes show that your issues aren't the main issues. The most important part of the introduction therefore is such an analysis of the question as will make clear to the audience that you have selected the real issues and that if you prove these issues the decision must be in your favour.

PRACTICE 11. Introducing a Debate

Criticize these statements in introductions:

1. Examinations have always been a Waterloo for most students.
2. The question of examinations increasing the mental ability of a student is irrelevant, because there isn't anything gained in this way which could not be gained without examinations.
3. Pupils study so hard for an examination that they get nervous in the examination and forget what they know.
4. Moving pictures have degenerated so rapidly that they are now a menace to public morality.
5. The moving picture is admittedly the chief cause of juvenile delinquency.

BODY OF ARGUMENT

The body of an argument should be a logical and emphatic grouping of *facts, authoritative opinion,* and *reasoning* to prove the main issues. Don't advance weak arguments. Hit hard. One good reason is more convincing than several poor ones. An old couplet runs,

> When one's proofs are aptly chosen,
> Four are as valid as a dozen.

PREPARING A BRIEF

A brief, as the word indicates, is an argument boiled down. This special kind of sentence outline written by a debater as he organizes his material has three parts: introduction, brief proper (which is the brief of the body of the argument), and conclusion. When completed, it is a storehouse of information so arranged or pigeonholed that the debater can easily find what he needs in his argument on the subject.

Introduction. Include in your introduction (1) the history of the question (origin, immediate cause for discussion, and importance), (2) the definition of terms (if definition is necessary), and (3) points at issue expressed in declarative or interrogative sentences. If there are admitted facts—points on which the two sides have agreed— state them. If your opponents are likely to introduce a point which is off the subject, set it down as irrelevant matter. As every statement requiring proof is excluded, the introduction is the same for the affirmative and the negative. Don't connect the topics of the introduction by *for.*

The Brief Proper. In the brief proper each subtopic is proof of the main topic and is connected with it by *for.* Use a comma before *for* and no punctuation after.

Begin the brief proper with a statement of the question for debate. In a negative brief insert *not* in the question.

In the brief proper the points at issue are the main topics. In the introduction the points at issue are numbered *A, B, C;* in the brief proper, I, II, III.

Use complete sentences. In the brief proper avoid the compound sentence.

Number and indent the points or topics as in an outline.

CONCLUSION

Make the conclusion a one-sentence summary of the points proved.

Use the words *introduction, brief proper, conclusion,* and *refutation,* but don't number them.

FOR BRIEFS WITH PROOF OF ALL ASSERTIONS

In the brief proper distinguish facts or proof from assertion by starring definite, convincing proof.

BRIEF FOR THE NEGATIVE WITHOUT FULL PROOF
OF ASSERTIONS

Resolved, That examinations in high schools should be abolished.

Introduction

I. Because examinations have played an important part in our secondary educational system ever since its inception, and because the abolition of examinations would probably work a radical change in our entire school life, this question concerns everyone interested in secondary education.

II. The question of the abolition of examinations has always been a source of contention.

   A. Students in medieval universities (where examinations originated) questioned the value of examinations.

   B. Many progressive schools have abolished examinations.

   C. In recent years, Johnson, Starch, Elliot, Kelly, Dearborn, and other educators have investigated the accuracy of examinations as measuring instruments and have found wide variations in the marks which different teachers give to the same answer paper.

III. By *examinations* is meant the tests given by the Department of Education and full-period tests at the end of a quarter, third, half term, or term. Short quizzes are excluded.

IV. The points at issue are:

   A. Do examinations aid in the accurate measurement of progress?

   B. Do examinations motivate study?

   C. Do examinations prepare for college and later life?

Brief Proper

Examinations in high school should not be abolished, for

I. Examinations aid in the accurate measurement of progress, for

   A. Examinations gauge for the instructor and student the increase in knowledge made since previous examinations.

   B. Examinations indicate the student's increased ability to apply and adapt to new situations information learned.

   C. Examinations put the entire student body on an equal footing, for,

      1. All students are given the same questions.

      2. All students are given the same length of time.

      3. Shy pupils do not need to talk to the class.

D. Although teachers vary somewhat in the marking of an essay answer, there is no such variation in the marking of a short-answer test.

II. Examinations motivate study, for

    A. They furnish a goal toward which every student must strive in order to pass his work.

    B. They stimulate a spirit of competition.

    C. A pupil will study harder and more thoroughly when he knows that a day of reckoning is approaching.

III. Examinations prepare for college and later life, for

    A. Many colleges require entrants to pass the examinations of the College Entrance Examination Board.

    B. To succeed in college a student must be able to pass examinations.

    C. Ability to pass examinations helps young people to enter professions, secure positions, and win promotions, for

        1. To engage in such a profession as medicine, law, or nursing, one must pass a lengthy, difficult examination.

        2. Corporations, as a rule, examine job-seekers.

        3. To enter the civil service one must pass a competitive examination.

        4. In many communities a teacher must pass a competitive examination to secure a position.

        5. In civil service, teaching, banking, and other vocations promotion is often dependent on the passing of competitive examinations.

    D. Every day a worker passes or fails an examination when he is called on to think quickly in an emergency and to use intelligently his knowledge and skill.

    E. Passing examinations gives the student confidence in facing a difficult job.

Conclusion

Since examinations in high school aid in the accurate measurement of progress, since examinations motivate study, and since examinations prepare for college and later life, high school examinations should not be abolished.

BIBLIOGRAPHY

Alilunas, J. L. "What Do Essay Examinations Show?" *Social Education.* Vol. 7, pp. 313-14. November, 1943.

Albjerg, V. L. "Students Insist Upon Examinations." *School and Society.* Vol. 77, pp. 325. May, 1953.

Brereton, J. D. *The Case for Examinations: an Account of their Place in Education, with Some Proposals for their Reform.* Cambridge University Press, 1944.

Gasking, D. A. T. *Examinations and the Aims of Education.* 2nd Edition Melbourne University Press, 1948.

Greene, H. A. and others. *Measurement and Evaluation in the Secondary School.* 2nd Edition. Longmans, 1954.

Mann, M. J. "Creativity and Productivity in Evaluation and Measurement." *Educational and Psychological Measurement.* Vol. 19, no. 44, pp. 505-13. Winter, 1959.

Nunnally, J. C., jr. *Tests and Measurements.* McGraw-Hill, 1959.

Remmers, H. H. and others. *Practical Introduction to Measurement and Evaluation.* Harper, 1960.

Strieker, L. D. "Examinitis." *Educational Forum.* Vol. 19, pp. 41-4. November, 1954.

Notice that the four main topics in the introduction of the preceding brief are the importance of the question, the history of the question, the definition of terms, and the points at issue, and that the three main headings (I, II, III) of the brief proper are the points at issue.

PRACTICE 12. Proof

Show that in the preceding brief proper each subtopic is proof of the main topic under which it stands.

PRACTICE 13. Writing a Brief

Write a brief on either side of one of the school questions at the end of the chapter.

DEBATING

CLEARNESS

The English of debate should be clear as crystal. The audience have no opportunity to return to a statement to search out its meaning. Debaters are prone to forget that matters simple to them after weeks of study on a question may seem complicated or abstruse to the audience, who have never given the question a serious thought.

ACCURACY

The debater must say exactly what he means. Exaggeration and inaccuracy destroy the confidence of the audience. One foolish statement is usually enough to lose a debate.

UNITY

A debate must be rigidly unified. Sometimes it will be hard for you to eliminate. You may like an argument or an illustration because it is picturesque or because it sounds learned, and yet know that the argument isn't part of your case. Be a hero. Omit everything that doesn't bear directly on a main issue you are proving.

COHERENCE

Coherence in debate includes (1) logical order, (2) announcement of that order, and (3) attention to transitions. The logical arrangement of a speech or an entire debate is sometimes hard to determine. Often two or more arrangements of the material are possible. A debater should imitate the English dramatist who said he first told the audience what the character was going to do, then showed him doing the act, then told that he had done it. The second speaker, for example, at the beginning of his speech should state briefly what the first speaker proved and what is the task set for the second speaker. When he has proved one point, he should make clear to the audience that he is passing on to another point. He should, however, avoid such hackneyed transitional phrases as "now"; "my next point is"; "I have just proved to you—. I shall now prove to you"; "let us now consider"; "let us now take up." The logical structure of the debate must at all times be kept before the eyes of the audience.

EMPHASIS

Emphasis includes (1) placing important ideas at the beginning and the end, (2) giving extra time to the chief arguments, and (3) making the entire speech concrete and vigorous. To grip the audience, place at the beginning a strong point vividly phrased and aptly illustrated; to secure a climax put the most convincing argument at the end. The beginning must catch the attention and win the sympathy of the audience, the body of the speech must present convincing proof, and the end must clinch the point. If you and your two colleagues decide on three main issues, don't assume that each debater should prove one issue. Perhaps one issue needs more proof than the other two combined. The concrete, the specific, and the imaginatively picturesque make an argument more forceful. Don't rely on bare statistics. They may be both dull and meaningless. Statistics take hold when comparisons give them significance. For example, the statement that the United States spent during World War I forty-four billion dollars means little to most people. The explanation that this sum exceeded by a half the total government expenditure in the preceding one hundred and twenty-eight years of the republic gives it significance.

DEBATE CUSTOM

Address the presiding officer as "Mister Chairman" or "Madam Chairman." Do not separately address the judges or other groups in the audience. Do not refer to opponents or colleagues by name. Say "the first speaker on the affirmative," "my colleague," "the preceding speaker," or "the second speaker on the negative." In direct proof, the order of speakers is, first affirmative, first negative, second affirmative, etc. In rebuttal the negative usually speaks first. This plan gives the affirmative the advantage of the last speech—a fair arrangement because the burden of proof rests upon the affirmative. In other words, if neither side advances definite proof or if the negative speakers overthrow the arguments of the affirmative without presenting any of their own, the affirmative have lost the debate, because they have failed to prove the proposition. A warning signal one or two minutes before a speaker's time is up helps him to close before the final gavel instead of leaving his speech hanging in the air. If he is speaking when the final gavel falls, he should conclude the sentence quickly and take his seat.

In refutation use notes freely, but in your direct proof limit your use of notes to sets of statistics and long quotations.

FIRST SPEAKER AFFIRMATIVE

The first speaker affirmative clears the way for the argument by presenting the introduction and then proceeds to the proof of his issue or issues. Because a case well explained is half won, the first speaker ordinarily spends about half his time on introductory matter and the rest on proving an issue or beginning the proof of the issue.

FIRST SPEAKER NEGATIVE

The first speaker on the negative side must be prepared to supply any important introductory material omitted by the first speaker affirmative but should not repeat facts already presented. He may either accept the definition of terms and issues or substitute his own and prove to the audience that the affirmative definition is not fair and that the issues they have presented are not the main points to be proved. After this introductory work he proceeds to the proof of his issue.

If the first speaker affirmative explains clearly and argues convincingly and persuasively, he commonly wins the sympathy of the audience of his side. The first speaker negative should by his knowledge of his subject, clearness, earnestness, fairness, sense of humour, and enthusiasm endeavour to win the audience over to the negative side.

OTHER MAIN SPEECHES

A good debate, unlike a series of orations or declamations, is a closely connected series of speeches on a subject. Each debater should listen attentively to what his opponents say, and, by referring to their arguments, changing his speech, if necessary, to meet their case, or refuting thoroughly a point, adapt or adjust his argument to his opponents'.

The last speaker on each side should conclude his speech with a clear, brief, forceful restatement of the main issues and proofs. A good conclusion is neither a bare summary nor a spread-eagle peroration.

ASKING QUESTIONS

If you insist that your opponents answer a fair question, you may enforce your point and drive them upon the horns of a dilemma. A dozen questions, however, will make the audience think that your arguments are interrogation points rather than facts.

REBUTTAL METHOD AND MATTER

To be ready for refutation prepare rebuttal cards with facts, statistics, statements of authorities or experts, illustrations, analogies, or reasoning for the attack of every important argument your opponents are likely to advance. During the debate take a few notes. Many a debater makes the mistake of spending his entire time in taking notes instead of using most of it for listening, finding the prepared rebuttal cards, and thinking what arguments are worth answering and how he will meet them.

In preparing to refute an argument, ask these two questions: "How do you know?" and "What of it?" Perhaps you can deny your opponent's facts or statistics or present other facts and figures that put the matter in a different light. Perhaps you can point out that his authorities and experts are prejudiced or unreliable, his reasoning faulty, or his statements inconsistent. An analogy or humorous absurdity may enforce your point. Possibly you can refute his authority with a better authority or produce from one of his authorities a quotation which indicates that the authority's attitude was not fairly presented. Or you may admit what he has said and show that his proofs are inadequate, are beside the point, or really strengthen your case. The last type of refutation is called turning the tables.

FALLACIES

A part of the job of refutation is exposing fallacies, which are errors in the reasoning process.

The main logical fallacies were discussed in Chapter 21, Clear Thinking.

REBUTTAL MISTAKES

A few common rebuttal mistakes should be guarded against.

1. Don't misrepresent your opponent's argument. If possible, use his exact words in stating the argument to be refuted.

2. Don't begin the refutation of each point with some unvarying formula like "My opponent says—."

3. Don't advance constructive arguments in the rebuttal.

4. Avoid "scrappy rebuttal" by striking at your opponents' main issues. When you chop down a tree, the branches go with it; when the main arguments fall, the little ones go with them. Don't spend your refutation time clipping off the branches; chop away at the trunk.

5. When your opponent makes a good point, or gives a sound reason or a fact, either admit it or pass it by without comment. Don't attempt to refute arguments which you know you can't overthrow.

6. Refute only the arguments your opponents advance. Memorized refutation answering the arguments the debater thinks his opponents will use is called 'canned" rebuttal.

7. Don't be smart or discourteous.

CLOSING REBUTTAL SPEECHES

In addition to refuting arguments, the speaker who closes the refutation on each side should, by summarizing briefly the arguments of his side which are still standing and pointing out the important arguments of his opponents that have been overthrown, give a bird's-eye view of the debate as it stands at the time. He should, in other words, review quickly and compare the arguments of the two sides.

PRACTICE 14. Refutation

1. Refute a point in the brief in this chapter.

2. Assume that some proof has been advanced by the negative on each of these seven points. Refute number one and two others.

1. Motion pictures do not incite to criminality, for Charles Evans Hughes, Lloyd George, and other famous men read detective stories without emulating the criminals.
2. Masterpieces would be rejected by the censors.
3. The federal censors would be grafters.
4. As the stage, books, magazines, and newspapers are unregulated, the censorship of the moving picture is an unjust discrimination.
5. No board can satisfactorily censor all pictures.
6. Provincial censors have erred in their judgment of pictures.
7. The people themselves are the best censors.

DECISION

In intercollegiate debates the no-decision contest, which emphasizes the fact that the purpose of debate is to find the truth, not to win a victory, is growing in favour. Years ago three judges, who either met and discussed the arguments at the close of the debate or voted without such discussion, regularly decided the debate. This system is still used. Sometimes, however, a critic judge, a person who understands argument, takes the place of the three judges; and in some debates the audience vote.

PRACTICE 15. Classroom Debate

Prepare for a series of classroom debates on questions selected from the following list or on other questions. Present proof; don't merely assert.

SCHOOL QUESTIONS FOR DEBATES

1. Our high school should adopt the honour system.
2. Week-end homework should be abolished.
3. Our student government should be given authority to —— (Insert the particular power you think it should have.)
4. The age limit for compulsory attendance at school should be raised.
5. High school students should wear uniforms.
6. Formal term examinations should be abolished (or reduced) in our school.
7. Pupils should be permitted to read newspapers and magazines in the study room.

8. Every high school boy should have a course in the elements of carpentry, plumbing, and electric wiring.
9. Every high school girl should be required to take cooking and sewing.
10. Pupils should receive school credit for music taken outside of school.
11. Pupils should receive school credit for gardening, sweeping, washing dishes, tending the furnace, delivering papers, clerking after school, and other work done outside of school hours.
12. The Board of Trustees should furnish (or discontinue furnishing) textbooks for high school pupils.
13. An hour should be added to the school day.
14. Ability to swim twenty-five yards should be a requirement for high school graduation.
15. No girl should be required to study algebra.
16. High school pupils should be charged a tuition fee of five dollars a year.
17. No pupil who is failing in a subject should be permitted to take part in school athletics.
18. Every pupil should be required to take a course in typewriting.
19. There should be a summer session of our high school to provide an opportunity for pupils to make up failures and to take advanced courses.
20. Every high school student should be required to study Latin for at least one year.

See also the topics under Forum Discussion on page 490.

CITY, PROVINCIAL, AND DOMINION QUESTIONS

1. Canada should adopt the principle of economic nationalism.
2. Canada should adopt compulsory military service for boys eighteen to twenty years of age.
3. The majority vote of a jury should be substituted for the unanimous vote.
4. The sale of intoxicating liquor should be prohibited (or permitted) in our city.
5. Suffrage in Canada should be restricted by an educational test.
6. A citizen of Canada who neglects to vote should be fined or imprisoned.
7. A Prime Minister should serve but one five-year term.
8. The Canadian Prime Minister should be elected by direct vote of the people.
9. The federal government should make a system of complete medical care available to all its citizens at public expense.
10. In this province capital punishment should be abolished (or re-established).
11. Billboard advertising should be prohibited.
12. The country boy or girl has a better chance to succeed than the city boy or girl.
13. The province should institute more rigid tests for candidates for the license to drive an automobile.

14. War should be declared only by popular vote.
15. Gambling on the races should be prohibited.
16. Sweepstakes should be legalized in Canada.

IN A LIGHTER VEIN

1. The comic strip as at present constituted should be barred from the public press.
2. Unmarried men over the age of thirty should be subjected to a bachelor tax.
3. Dagwood Bumstead is a greater benefactor of the human race than Einstein.
4. The emancipation of women is a mistake.
5. The modern girl is superior to her great-great-grandmother.
6. The barbarian is happier than the civilized man.

Chapter 24

The Short Story

TELLING EXPERIENCES

Example:

A BEAR STORY

Several years ago I was camping out in Maine one March, in a lumberman's shack. A few days before I came, two boys in a village near by decided to go into the woods hunting, with a muzzle-loading shotgun and a long stick between them. One boy was ten years old, while the other was a patriarch of twelve. On a hillside under a great bush they noticed a small hole which seemed to have melted through the snow, and which had a gamy savour that made them suspect a coon. The boy with the stick poked it in as far as possible until he felt something soft.

"I think there's something here," he remarked, poking with all his might.

He was quite right. The next moment the whole bank of frozen snow suddenly caved out, and there stood a cross and hungry bear, prodded out of his winter sleep by that stick. The boys were up against a bad proposition. The snow was too deep for running, and when it came to climbing—that was Mr. Bear's pet specialty. So they did the only thing left for them to do: they waited. The little one with the stick got behind the big one with the gun, which weapon wavered unsteadily.

"Now, don't you miss," he said, "'cause this stick ain't very sharp."

Sometimes an attacking bear will run at a man like a biting dog. More often it rises on its haunches and depends on the smashing blows of its mighty arms and steel-shod paws. So it happened in this case. Just before the bear reached the boys, he lifted his head and started to rise. The first boy, not six feet away, aimed at the white spot which most black bears have under their chins, and pulled the trigger. At that close range the heavy charge of number six shot crashed through the animal's throat, making a single round hole like a big bullet, cutting the jugular vein, and piercing the neck vertebrae beyond.

The great beast fell forward with hardly a struggle, so close to the boys that its blood splashed on their rubber boots. They got ten dollars for the skin and ten dollars for the bounty, and about one million dollars' worth of glory.

From Samuel Scoville's *Everyday Adventures* by permission of the Atlantic Monthly Press, Boston.

How to Narrate

What can we learn about storytelling by studying Scoville's "A Bear Story"?

The author at the start answers the questions "Who?" "When?" "Where?" and "What?" by telling us that in Maine one March several years ago a boy of ten and a boy of twelve went hunting with a stick and a shotgun between them.

2. He plunges right into the story. He doesn't tell us how it happened that these two boys went hunting alone, whose shotgun it was, what school the boys attended, or what they ate for breakfast.

3. By introducing the conflict between the boys and the bear, he arouses our curiosity and makes us eager to know whether the boys escaped from the bear.

4. He keeps the climax or the point of the story back till near the end. He doesn't give the story away in the first paragraph by telling us that the older boy shot the bear.

5. The author plunges out of the story. He doesn't take time to tell us what the story teaches us, how large the bear was, how they got him home, or what their parents said.

6. He adds life to the story by having the boy with the stick talk. Notice the separate paragraph for each speech, the quotation marks, and the commas. All boys and girls prefer stories which have a good deal of dialogue or conversation.

7. He pictures the boys and the bear. We can see the cross and hungry black bear rising on his hind legs, the boy of twelve, not six feet from the bear, with his gun pointed unsteadily at the white spot under the bear's chin, and behind him the little boy with the pointed stick.

8. He uses words accurately.

9. By omitting unnecessary words and details he makes the story move swiftly.

10. He tells the events in the order in which they happened.

PRACTICE 1. Studying Narratives

Read carefully the three following true stories:

1. What is the best part of number 1? Why?

2. The author of number 3 wrote first a plan and placed this at the top of his paper. Of what use is such an outline?

3. Which is the best story? Why?

1. MY FIRST VISIT TO THE THEATRE

Of all the things that have happened to me, I think that my first visit to the theatre was the most exciting. Though I was only five years old at the time, I can remember very clearly everything that happened.

As I sat waiting for the curtain to go up, I wondered if the play would be just like the story of the same name, "Jack and the Beanstalk." It was! Most assuredly it was! All the thrilling situations and hairbreadth escapes of the story were in the play. My nerves grew more and more taut. My blood raced; my hands tingled. Finally I could stand it no longer. Just as the brutal giant raised his axe to chop off the head of the pretty little princess, I shrieked. My bored father awoke in annoyance from a sound sleep. My mother looked at me with murder in her eye. If, however, the giant had threatened me with his axe, I could not possibly have restrained myself, for indeed if I were actually beheaded, the sensation could be no worse than the one which my imagination produced.—PUPIL

2. MY BURGLAR

"Crackle, crackle, crackle" in the middle of the night!

"Huh?" I asked myself sleepily.

"Crackle, crackle." I sat up in bed quickly, and as I was lying at one side, I narrowly escaped falling out. Then, making no noise, I listened. More crackles.

"It can't be the fish," I reasoned, "because they can't make any noise. I wonder what it is." Noiselessly getting out of bed, I grabbed my flashlight and crept down to the living-room. The crackles certainly weren't coming from there. I went on, and so did the noise. Next on my route was the dining room. I looked under the table, under the chairs, even in the chandelier, but nowhere could I find the source of those mysterious crackles.

"Maybe it's a burglar!" I thought, and rushed to wake my parents. In doing this I passed through the kitchen and beheld the source of the crackles. It was Pinky, my white mouse, sitting calmly in his cage and philosophically chewing the paper lining.

"You go to sleep," I told him and then, being very tired, I obeyed these instructions myself.—PUPIL

3. AN EXPERIENCE I'LL NEVER FORGET

SITUATION
    1. Uncle Herb's interest in trials
    2. His size and peculiar habit

EVENTS IN
   TIME ORDER

3. Our going to hear a robbery trial
4. Examination of the defendant
5. My uncle's habitual motion

CLIMAX

6. My uncle accused of making signs

ENDING

7. Results of the experience

If there's anything Uncle Herb used to love, it was a good stiff trial in the Criminal Court. Whenever he had spare time, he hastened to the building, and always got a seat in the front row.

Whenever my uncle became excited, he had the curious habit of sliding his finger around his mouth in a circular motion. As he is about six feet five inches in height, you can just imagine how conspicuous he is.

One day, with no work before him, he decided to take me to the trial of a dangerous criminal charged with robbery. Uncle Herb made me put on long pants and a felt hat, and I got in safely to one of his "ring-side" seats.

We both enjoyed the tricky questions fired at the defendant by the attorney for the prosecution. After a while the prosecutor asked, "Did you pawn this watch on the morning of October 16?"

The room was tense. So excited was my uncle that he at once resorted to his peculiar habit. "No," said the defendant timidly.

The defense attorney breathed a sigh of relief. "Just one moment!" almost shouted the prosecutor. "That man," pointing an accusing finger at Uncle Herb, "was making signs to the defendant. I demand that he be held!"

You can well imagine what a scare my poor Uncle Herb got. Of course, when everything was over and the criminal put where he belonged, my uncle was let go with many apologies. From that time on, he did his best to conquer his habit and, what was more important, stayed away from courts except when when he had a summons.—PUPIL

PRACTICE 2. Telling an Experience

Using one of the following titles, write entertainingly about an experience of yours. Plan, write, revise thoroughly, copy neatly. Apply what you have learned about narrating. Lead up to a climax or surprise. Tell the truth.

1. A childhood adventure. 2. Our burglar. 3. Lost. 4. A snowball fight. 5. At night alone on a country road. 6. An unexpected bath in January. 7. A narrow escape. 8. An experience with a horse, a mule, or an automobile. 9. A long evening at home alone—noises. 10. My first attempt at learning to swim, skate, fish, snowshoe, or ride a bicycle. 11. An exploration. 12. No gas. 13. Locked out. 14. Caught in a storm in the country. 15. A hasty retreat. 16. The cost of carelessness. 17. Our circus. 18. My part in the game. 19. Just scared. 20. My first airplane ride. 12. A fishing experience.

PRACTICE 3. Studying a Narrative

In Numbers 1 and 2 following, Virginia and Ted have told the same story.

1. Which telling do you prefer? Give three good reasons for your choice.

2. What words or sentences in Virginia's story make you see pictures?

1. WE DIDN'T GO IN

"Yes," said my mother one morning while we were at Seaside Park, "you may walk down to the beach, but remember you can't go in swimming now."

"Well," said Cousin Ted, as though he had lost his last friend, "we can at least look at the ocean even if we can't go in." And down to the beach we went.

"I can't see why we have to wait for the rest," I remarked gloomily.

"Just look at that water all going to waste while we sit around and wait for some worthless friends to come from the city," Jack said.

"Say," I howled, slapping Ted on the back so that he nearly fell off the jetty where we were sitting, "why couldn't we take off our shoes and socks now and have some fun wading around until they come?" In a second our shoes and socks were off and we were in.

"This isn't as good as swimming, but it's pretty good at that," observed Cousin Ted.

In a short time we had forgotten all about Mother, friends, clothes, and everything else that we should have remembered. Splashing around in the waves, having a wonderful time, we grew careless about getting out of the way of large breakers.

Before long the inevitable happened. My cousin was facing shore. "Look out!" I screamed at him, but he didn't hear me. A huge wave was breaking over him. I can see yet his white blouse and blue tie disappearing beneath the green comber.

Of course, I fell down trying to help him up. Out of the water we came, our light summer clothes soaking wet, and a more unpleasant feeling I cannot describe. Add to that the pricking of a guilty conscience and you see that we were pretty miserable.

My mother met us at the door. "Go in the back way," she said with the air of one who was ready for anything. "You know, I thought you'd do something like that if I didn't watch you."

We weren't scolded. I guess it was because we looked so funny. When the company came we all went for a swim, and my mother mercifully spared us by not telling of our morning's escapade.

2. WE DIDN'T GO IN

Aunt Ellen told Cousin Virginia, Jack, and me not to go in swimming in the morning but to wait and go in after dinner with our friends from the city. We didn't go in but took off our shoes and stockings and waded in the water. After a while a big wave knocked me down, and Virginia fell down trying to help me up. Aunt Ellen didn't scold us and let us go swimming that afternoon.

WRITING CONVERSATION

To write good conversation isn't easy. No, it isn't hard to learn to use a separate paragraph for each speech and the introducing words, to place a comma between the speech and the introducing words, and to set off the whole speech or its parts with quotation marks. But to make the conversation natural, lifelike, and appropriate is work. As we have to learn to see with our eyes, so we have to get into the habit of hearing with our ears—that is, of noticing how people talk. Three suggestions may help you to improve the conversation in your stories:

1. Study the conversation you hear, and practise imitating the talk of a variety of people.

2. Write contracted forms as they are spoken—*who's, they'll, where's, wasn't,* etc.

3. Avoid repetition of *said*. Either use a word that tells how the person spoke—*cried, exclaimed, whispered, growled,* or *argued,* for example—or, if the introducing words are not needed to make clear who the speaker is, omit them.

Some substitutes for *said* are—

added	cried	murmured	roared
admitted	declared	muttered	screamed
announced	exclaimed	pleaded	shouted
answered	explained	remarked	sighed
argued	growled	repeated	whined
begged	inquired	replied	whispered
bellowed	mumbled	returned	yelled

PRACTICE 4. Writing Contractions

Learn to spell the following contractions which are frequently used in conversation. Notice that the apostrophe always takes the place of the omitted letter. *Did + not = didn't; does + not = doesn't; you + have = you've* (two letters omitted).

aren't	hasn't	mustn't	we've
can't	haven't	she's	won't
couldn't	I'll	shouldn't	wouldn't
didn't	I'm	that's	you'd
doesn't	isn't	there's	you'll
don't	it's	wasn't	you're
hadn't	I've	weren't	you've

Ain't, hain't, 'tain't are incorrect forms used by some careless and uneducated people.

REPRODUCING A CONVERSATION

The preparation for writing natural, lifelike conversation includes reproducing conversations overheard, and studying the dialogue in good stories.

Example:

IN AFRICAN FOREST AND JUNGLE

While I was walking along the park towards the library the other day, a voice hailed me with, "Hey there! Got any good books?"

Turning around, I saw my friend Bernard walking toward me. "A few," I answered.

We sat down on a park bench for a little chat. "Is this one any good?" he asked, picking up *In African Forest and Jungle.*

"The best of the four. I've finished it. Would you like to read it?"

"What's it about?"

"It's about an explorer and his adventures in Africa."

"Is there a lot of description in the book?"

"Some—when he describes the dress and customs of the natives."

"They're pretty superstitious, aren't they? I mean the natives."

"Somewhat. One incident is about a native who locks himself in a hut for a week to avoid the 'curse of the new moon'."

"Is that all it tells about?"

"Oh, no, there's plenty of adventure, romance, and even pathos."

"Pathos?"

"Yes, in the jungle Du Chaillu's dog has a fight with some animal and dies of loss of blood after killing it, and his pet monkey dies soon after being bitten by a centipede."

"Well, I guess the book must be pretty good."

"It certainly is—I advise you to read it."—PUPIL

PRACTICE 5. Writing Conversation

1. How is conversation paragraphed?

2. What punctuation marks enclose a direct quotation?

3. What punctuation regularly separates a direct quotation from the rest of the sentence?

4. How has the pupil avoided repeating *said*?

5. Why is this reproduction entertaining?

PRACTICE 6. Reproducing a Conversation

Reproduce a conversation you have overheard or in which you have taken part. Without evesdropping, keep your ears open for talk that is unusual, characteristic, bright, or laughable.

1. At the ticket window. 2. In the theatre. 3. At the movie. 4. At the baseball game. 5. At the bargain counter. 6. At the dinner table. 7. Waiting for the train. 8. In the street car. 9. At the concert. 10. After the school entertainment. 11. On the street corner. 12. In the barber shop. 13. In the grocery store. 14. In the meat market. 15. In class. 16. At the football or the basketball game. 17. A quarrel. 18. An automobile accident. 19. A newsboy and a customer. 20. In the restaurant. 21. An interview with father. 22. On the railroad train. 23. Asking the way. 24. Pupil just home from school and his mother. 25. Generous woman and tramp. 26. About homework. 27. Over the radio. 28. About a book. 29. About a movie. 30. On the way to school.

WRITING AN AUTOBIOGRAPHY

Chapter I

How much do you know about your ancestors? Would you like to know more? When you ask your father, mother, grandparents, or other relatives about their lives or the lives of their parents or grandparents, don't be discouraged if they say they have nothing to tell. Be a good interviewer; ask such definite questions as: What hardships did you have when you were young? What fun did you have? What thrilling and exciting experiences? How did you select your vocation and get started in it? How did your food, clothing, school, or work as a boy or girl differ from mine? What do you know about our ancestors who had the pluck to leave their homes in Europe for a new world? How did they get their start in Canada? What war stories of our family do you know?

PRACTICE 7. Studying a Story

As you study the story "Lost" get ready to answer these questions:

1. Does the writer at the start answer the questions "Who?" "When?" "Where?" and "What?"
2. Does she plunge right into the story or bore us with unnecessary explanation?
3. Does she arouse our curiosity and keep us in suspense? If so, how?
4. Does she hold our interest to the end? If so, how?
5. Is the ending abrupt or leisurely?
6. What use is made of conversation?
7. What word pictures are there in the story?
8. Does she tell how she felt and how her mother felt? Where?
9. In what order are the events told?

LOST

On a hot day in summer when I was a child about seven years old, Florence, the girl who took care of me while my mother was away, took me to the woods near home.

"Come, Anna," said Florence. "Let's see who can pick the bigger bunch of flowers."

"All right," I replied and immediately started to work. It seemed that the farther I went the more beautiful the flowers grew. Slowly but surely I moved away from Florence until she was entirely lost to my view. I was unconscious of all this until I heard Florence call to me in a frightened voice, "Anna, Anna, where are you?"

Thinking she was fooling, I hid behind a bush. She continued to call until her voice seemed to be far away. I got up laughing to myself. In fact I was rather proud of myself to think that I had fooled Florence, but no Florence could be seen. I called and called, but my calling was of no avail. Only my echo came back to me to increase my fear. Crouching down behind the bush, I feared every moment the bogeyman would take me, or lions, bears, or tigers would spring on me and gobble me up, as in the stories I had heard from my mother and father.

My heart was in my mouth. I hardly dared to breathe. Every move of the branches startled me. How I wished for my mother, for her comforting words and caresses! The trees were darkly lined against the blue sky, and seemed like great giants ready to fall on top of me.

After a while I felt as if something or somebody was scratching on the back of my neck. I didn't dare to look. All sorts of imaginary giants, dragons, evil spirits came to my mind. I wondered what it was. At last a little courage came to my assistance and made me speak.

"Let me go," I cried in terror. "Let me go. I will give you my dolly. I'll promise not to fight with Pauline any more. I'll do whatever Florence tells me to do if you will only let me go." With that I turned around, expecting to see some awful beast. And guess what it was. Why, a sticker that was lying against my dress and partly against my neck, and every time I moved it would scratch my neck.

If I hadn't been in such a sad plight, I would have laughed, but anyway I felt much relieved and began to have a little more courage to look around. Seeing a path, I got up and followed it. Every step I took, I thought some wild animal or a bandit would jump at me.

At last I came to the end of the path and found I was a few blocks from home. My heart leaped with joy. But it suddenly misgave me when I thought of what my father and mother would do to me. This thought quite vanished when, turning a corner, I met my friend Pauline, looking rather excited. Staring at me as if she had seen a ghost, she exclaimed in astonishment, "Anna is it really you? Nearly everybody you know is looking for you. Where have you been?"

Just as I began to explain, Florence came running up to me in tears. She picked me up bodily, and held me so tightly I could hardly breathe, as if her life depended on me.

When we reached home, there were about a dozen children and some grown-ups on the porch talking excitedly. As soon as they saw me, a shout arose that would have made a deaf man hear. I was borne in triumph to my mother like some grand princess arriving from a foreign land.

The next moment I was locked in my mother's arms with my head against her breast. How happy I felt to be safe and sound in my mother's arms! I think I shall never again be so happy as I was at that moment.

Seeing my mother's eyes full of tears, I said, "What's the matter, Mother? Are you angry at me?"

"No," she replied. "I cry because I am happy." At that time I didn't understand her, but now I realize what she meant. Those were tears of joy and not of sorrow.

When my mother told my father, he didn't spank me, as I had expected. Instead, he laughed till the tears rolled down his cheeks. I felt rather insulted that he should laugh instead of feeling sorry for me, and immediately after supper I took my doll and went to bed. There I told her my adventure but she looked at me so foolishly that I spanked her and turned her face to the wall.—PUPIL

PRACTICE 8. Writing an Autobiography

Write another chapter of your autobiography. Picture people and places. Tell how you felt. Select your own subject. One class wrote an entertaining book on the following topics:

1. An adventure. 2. My trip to Italy. 3. The country school I attended. 4. My trip to Germany. 5. A storm at sea. 6. My best vacation. 7. Lost. 8. At the circus. 9. My trip to Europe. 10. Two weeks in the Catskill Mountains. 11. My trip to Algonquin Park. 12. Points of interest in Toronto. 13. A visit. 14. My trip to Waskesiu. 15. In Glacier National Park. 16. My first week in camp. 17. An adventure I had last summer. 18. My first visit to the zoo. 19. A thrilling game. 20. Vacation experiences in France and England. 21. My first acquaintance with a policeman. 22. My first dance.

PRACTICE 9. Telling a Story

On one of the following topics write entertainingly about one of your experiences. Use words that will make your readers see pictures.

1. The greatest surprise of my life. 2. An incident that taught me a lesson. 3. Something funny in school. 4. The joke was on me. 5. A punishment I deserved. 6. An experience of a bargain hunter. 7. How I earned my first dollar. 8. I was cook. 9. In the nick of time. 10. The trick that failed. 11. A camping experience. 12. The meanest thing I ever did. 13. It never rains but it pours. 14. An experience I shall not forget. 15. A spoiled adventure. 16. The hornets' nest. 17. Why I didn't go swimming. 18. My first visit to the dentist. 19. When Mother was away this summer. 20. The best Christmas I ever had. 21. My bicycle stolen. 22. My birthday party. 23. An embarrassing experience. 24. A dog in school. 25. When I lost my money. 26. My first experience riding along on a train. 27. What happened when the rising tide turned the streets into canals.

THE SHORT STORY

WHAT IS A SHORT STORY?

We all long for interesting experiences. If we could have them first-hand, we would choose to do so, but since it is obviously impossible, because we are bound to time and space, to experience first-hand more than a fraction of the things we should like, we learn to substitute vicarious experiences for the real ones. Fiction, drama, poetry, and the short story furnish us with the nearest approaches to actual experiences. Of these possible sources, the most easily available is the short story. This fact helps to account for its great popularity.

The short story has this advantage over factual biography and tales of travel, that it may be more real in the sense of being less circumscribed, more compressed, more immediate to the life of the protagonist. In a word, it is more artistic.

Dr. Blanche Colton Williams says, "The short story is a narrative artistically presenting characters in a struggle or complication which has a definite outcome." J. Berg Esenwein points out other characteristics: (1) a single predominant incident; (2) a single pre-eminent character; (3) imagination; (4) plot; (5) compression; (6) organization; and (7) unity of impression.

WHY WRITE SHORT STORIES

If we are going to read short stories in and out of school, it is well to learn how to judge and evaluate them. It is with short stories as it is with sports, those persons enjoy and appreciate the most who have participated in them, who know the skills and the techniques involved, and who have some competence themselves. Those who have written short stories select more discriminatingly the stories they read and appreciate most fully their artistry and truth.

The following story, "A Student of Languages", will repay careful examination and study to learn some of the techniques and skills that have helped Elsie Singmaster to create a good short story.

A STUDENT OF LANGUAGES

Mrs. Wagonseller, waking early, heard Victoria above her head. The tapping of her heels was regular, unremitting, masterful. Victoria was a masterful young woman.

Having blinked her eyes open, Mrs. Wagonseller turned them upon her sleeping husband. His name was James but before her marriage she had been too shy to address him familiarly and afterward she called him "Mister," and then when he had a right to the title, "Pop." His round head was an almost perfect sphere against the white pillow and his hands folded and laid under his cheek gave him the look of a cherub. His wife would have made no such comparison, however; to her he was a man of personal distinction, profound wisdom, and wide learning.

He yawned and threw his short arms above his head. At this instant the clock struck five.

"It is early," he said. "Something must a waked me."

"It is Victoria," explained Mrs. Wagonseller, pronouncing the *V* carefully. "She is already at it. Just listen once!"

"Like a steam hammer," he remarked, grinning. "What has got into her at this hour?"

Mrs. Wagonseller sat up. At the same instant there was a snapping sound which came apparently from outside the window.

"She is shaking her sheets in the air," said Mrs. Wagonseller. "That means she will make her bed right away. Now she's pounding her pillow." Mrs. Wagonseller stepped from bed. "Something is up, Pop."

"She knows her lessons all right," said Wagonseller.

But he too sat up, glancing humorously at his pleasant wife. He knew what worried her; she was always anticipating the day when Victoria would marry and leave them, and lately her fear had been sharpened by the elopement of a young neighbour. It was true that so far as they knew Victoria was unsought and she was only seventeen, but no one had dreamed that Alice Aughinbaugh had a lover and she was only sixteen. It was not because Victoria was unattractive that she lacked attention; it was because she held herself too high.

Wagonseller rose and began to dress. In his heart he, too, feared for Victoria. He had wished to be a preacher but he had not been able to afford an education and he dreamed of Victoria becoming a distinguished scholar. Thanks to his increasing urging and assistance and to Victoria's own ambition and ability she had never stood elsewhere than at the head of her class.

"*Ach*, it isn't anything serious," he assured his wife. "She is now quiet; it is just a little extra work. Perhaps she forgot something. Mom, have no fear."

At six-thirty Victoria came down to the kitchen. The sun's rays fell upon a half-bushel basket of freshly gathered tomatoes on the table. Breakfast was ready, substantial ham and eggs and molasses cake for Mr. and Mrs. Wagonseller, toast and coffee for Victoria. Mrs. Wagonseller mourned every day because Victoria ate so little but Victoria's red cheeks and her hundred and forty pounds distributed over five feet four inches of height made starvation seem remote.

"Well," said Victoria cheerfully, looking at the tomatoes, "what's up?"

"I will today make catsup," explained Mrs. Wagonseller. "It is a long work." She spoke not in the least complainingly but with pleasure in the prospect. Nor did she imply a desire for Victoria's help.

Victoria set the coffee pot on the table, transferred the fried potatoes from the pan to a hot dish and filled the glasses; then she walked to the door and called toward the garden, "Pop. Breakfast." When Wagonseller entered she sat at the table eating her toast with delicate precision. All the Wagonsellers had good manners but Victoria's were of a later generation than her father's and mother's.

"Pop," announced Victoria briskly, "you must hear me a little Latin yet before I go." At school Victoria spoke correct, sometimes painfully correct English, but at home she dropped into the vernacular.

"But you knew it good last night!"

"This is tomorrow's lesson. I studied it this morning."

Mrs. Wagonseller's frightened eyes sought her husband's. Victoria never had engagements which made advance preparation necessary. Wagonseller's eyes twinkled back—did she suppose that if Victoria meant to elope she would continue to study Latin? He finished his breakfast and took up Victoria's Caesar—this was happiness! Sometimes while he waited for customers at the stocking counter in the store where he worked, he wrote down the following words: *English, Pennsylvania German, German, Latin, French;* and in moments like that, and like this, his proud heart swelled almost to bursting.

In Victoria's Caesar he found written two lists of words, one Latin, one English, and he began to pronounce them distinctly.

"*Ducit.*"

"Third person singular, present tense, verb *duco*, to lead," rattled off Victoria. "*Duco, ducere, duxi, ductum.*"

"*Dare.*"

"To give," translated Victoria. "Present infinite of *do. Do, dare, dedi, datum.*"

Having finished the Latin words, he pronounced the English and Victoria gave their Latin equivalents. He did not correct her; whether he was able to or not, she seemed to need no correcting. She took her book and read two sections first in Latin, then twice in English, once in a literal and then in a free translation. There was no scamping for Victoria.

"Now who were the Sequani?" asked Mr. Wagonseller proudly. "And who was Dumnorix? And how many were in a legion?"

"It is one thing I hope," said Mrs. Wagonseller from her place at the sink, "and this is it, that Victoria will not have to read any more stories like last year, about boiling fathers in hot oil and poisoning people and tearing them up."

"Pelias, you mean?" said Wagonseller, smiling condescendingly. "Those are different times from ours, Mom, and it was one of those sort of goddesses that done it."

"I haven't any use for those goddesses, either," said Mrs. Wagonseller. "And the words were so hard."

"Do you mean Symplegades and Eumenides and Agamemnon and Clytemnestra?" asked Wagonseller. His pronunciation was perfect and the airiness with which he said the words indescribable. "Anything else, Victoria?"

"I have yet a few French verbs, such irregular ones."

"Victoria handed her father a third list and took out pencil and pad. Wagonseller had often heard that French was easier than Latin and that, to one who knew Latin, French offered no difficulties, but he had not found this to be the case. These words he spelled.

"*B-o-u-i-l-l-e-r*," said he.

Victoria wrote rapidly.

"*V-o-i-r*," said Wagonseller.

Victoria dashed off the part of "*voir*." There were ten verbs in all. When she had finished she compared her writing with the grammar.

"More yet?" asked Wagonseller.

"No," said Victoria. "I have everything else."

She fetched her hat from the hall and took her books under her arm.

"It is surely a nice day," she said happily. Then, unconscious of their curiosity, she ended their suspense. "There is a lecture this evening on the Value of Science to Mankind. That is why I learned my lesson this morning."

"We will not have so much dinner today as sometimes, "announced Mrs. Wagonseller. "But this evening I will cook *schnitz und knep*. I will feel by that time for something hearty."

Wagonseller went to the store and Mrs. Wagonseller began to scald and peel tomatoes. She was very happy—who would not be with a good husband and a bright daughter and sufficient income and plenty to do?

But such bliss is almost sure to be a precursor of trouble and at dinner Mrs. Wagonseller's castle crashed to earth. As she sat at table her cheeks were flushed, her eyes shone, and there was a smile on her cheerful face—until Victoria spoke. Victoria had finished her dinner and was folding her napkin.

"Mom," said she, "we will have company for supper."

"Who, who?" asked Mrs. Wagonseller astonished.

"A teacher from the high school," said Victoria.

"Then I will not bottle my catsup till tomorrow," said Mrs. Wagonseller, not in the least disturbed but on the contrary very much pleased. "I will make a good supper."

"No," said Victoria, blushing a little. "That isn't the idea. You have what you said. This teacher has never eaten *schnitz und knep;* that is the reason I fixed it for this evening. We will have *schnitz und knep* and good pie and preserves and cake and coffee. If you have too much besides you cannot enjoy *schnitz und knep*."

"*Ach*, Victoria!" This time Mrs. Wagonseller's *v* was a *w*.

"The teacher is coming especially for *schnitz und knep*. Mom," answered Victoria firmly. "Afterwards I go along to the lecture." Rising and putting on her hat, she continued to talk: "Remember, Mom! To those who have never eaten *schnitz und knep* it is a wonderful thing. And I will be home to set the table and fix flowers."

"All right," said Mrs. Wagonseller, somewhat ruefully. "But sometime we have this teacher for a right meal."

Her father saw Victoria blush. He was brighter than his wife and his brow had clouded as hers had cleared.

And what is this teacher's name?" he asked.

"Mather," said Victoria as she went through the door. "*M-a-t-h-e-r*."

"*Ach*" said Mrs. Wagonseller when he was out of hearing. "This is no way. I have a mind to fry chicken."

Wagonseller went toward a table in the corner of the room and taking up yesterday's newspaper turned to an inner page and pointed to a brief personal. His wife read it over his shoulder.

Mr. Charles Mather, teacher of mathematics in the high school, has returned from a visit to his home.

"Not a man!" gasped Mrs. Wagonseller "Is this teacher then a man?"

"We will see how much of a man he is," said Wagonseller grimly. "I was afraid something was up when I heard her this morning." His wife was too unhappy to remind him that it was she who had scented trouble in advance; besides she was not that kind of person.

According to his custom Wagonseller tried to meet the situation with humour.

"Have I then all my great learning for nothing?"   But his voice shook.

"Victoria was always so quick," said Mrs. Wagonseller.   "It is no telling what she might do.   It cannot be that she would bring him here married! That is what Alice did to her Mom and Pop."

"Now don't be foolish," answered Mr. Wagonseller.   But he did not speak with any heartiness.

"A teacher!" said Mrs. Wagonseller.

"You wouldn't expect Victoria to take anyone lower than that," said Wagonseller.

Wagonseller entered the kitchen at a quarter past five o'clock.   In four hours he had had ample time to see his home despoiled of its pride.   No more would he sit watching Victoria add to her learning by the dining-room lamp, no more would he leave his companions at the barber shop with the excuse that he must hear his daughter's lessons, adding casually and invariably that Victoria always stood first.   She might even go elsewhere to live, or her husband (especially one named Mather) might consider her parents beneath him. Wagonseller had had a very unhappy afternoon.

The kitchen was in perfect order except for the few utensils needed in preparing supper.   Beyond, in the dining room, the table had been set with a stiff outstanding starched cloth, the best china, and a bowl of asters.   The house was deliciously scented with cloves and allspice which had gone into the catsup.

Wagonseller looked round uneasily; then he called "Mom!" and his wife appeared from the dining room.   She wore a blue and white striped gingham dress and large stiff white apron.

"Were you then listening to them?" asked Wagonseller, trying to be gay.

Mrs. Wagonseller turned tearful eyes upon him.

"He is a big good-looking young man," she said.   "Victoria said I must come in.   I think he looks already down on me.   But they are sitting on chairs yet and not on the sofa."

"I should hope so!" protested Wagonseller.   He tiptoed up the back stairs to change his suit.

"You don't know how far this has gone," Mrs. Wagonseller called after him in a mournful whisper.

Having completed his change of raiment and brushed his brown hair with a wet brush, Wagonseller descended the steps.   He felt the same embarrassment as his wife but he was too proud to show it.   Mrs. Wagonseller had not ceased to cry and her nose was growing red.

"You must brace up," said Wagonseller sternly.

"But he is such a learned one!"

"Well, the preacher is learned and you are not afraid of him, are you?"

"I'm afraid of my manners," wept Mrs. Wagonseller.   "I never thought I would have to have such a one in the family.   If I could only stay in the kitchen."

"That you can't do," said Wagonseller firmly.   "You won't need to talk; let Victoria do the talking.   She brought him here.   And I will help along too." For the first time in Victoria's life her father thought of her with irritation. "I'm now going in."

Passing through the narrow hall toward the parlour. Wagonseller heard no sound and remembered with a sinking heart the rapturous silences of his courtship. It might be that already they had reached the point where speech was unnecessary.

Victoria rose when her father entered, not from the young man's side but from a chair across the room. Her cheeks were a little brighter than usual and her motions a little jerky.

"This is Mr. Mather," she said. "Mr. Mather, this is my father." Yesterday Victoria would have said, "Meet my father"; but last evening in an advertisement of a book of etiquette on the back of a magazine she had read that this was an abominable form of introduction. Victoria needed but one hint.

It seemed at first as though the young man did not intend to rise. When finally he made up his mind, he did not quite get to his feet before Wagonseller was directly in front of him holding out his hand.

"I'm pleased to meet you." Wagonseller began in a loud cordial tone but his voice dropped toward the end of the sentence. This was, as Mrs. Wagonseller had said, a very big and good-looking young man and he did seem to look down.

"It is a very nice day," Wagonseller continued pleasantly.

"I thought it hot," said Mr. Mather.

A short response like this was not according to Wagonseller's rule for polite conversation and he backed away.

"I will help Mom a little," he said as he went through the door. "It will soon be everything ready".

In the hall Wagonseller slipped his finger inside his tight collar as though to move it away from his neck. His face was red with shame; he knew that he had not made a good impression.

Then Mrs. Wagonseller announced supper. She had bathed her eyes in cold water and she stood in the doorway and said, "Supper, Victoria," in a fairly steady voice; then she went to her place at the table. The preacher always pulled out her chair for her and she was uncomfortable throughout the meal—would this young man shove her halfway under or leave her too far away?

The young man did neither; he walked to the place indicated to him and sat down and opened his napkin and fixed his eyes upon the covered dish before Mr. Wagonseller.

"I hear this is a wonderful concoction," said he in a deep voice.

Mr. Wagonseller smiled and then unaware of the astonishment of his guest he bowed his head and prayed. At the head of his table with so much good food before him to dispense he lost his uneasiness. *Schnitz und knep* was, as Mr. Mather said, a wonderful concoction. Made of dumplings boiled with pork and dried sweet apples and cooked in Mrs. Wagonseller's fashion, it was a delicious and substantial viand. Wagonseller helped the guest and then Victoria and then his wife, and as the aroma reached him it sent a reviving impulse through his brain.

"It has often wondered me what those old Romans ate," he remarked pleasantly.

The menu of the old Romans was apparently of less interest to the guest than the menu of the modern Wagonsellers. Mrs. Wagonseller had not finished pouring the coffee, Victoria obedient to the laws of good behaviour was still sitting with her hands clasped lightly in her lap as though the food before her were nonexistent, Wagonseller was just beginning to help himself— not too generously the first time, he remembered: but the young man had already begun to eat. He was really a very fine-looking young man but his good looks seemed eclipsed as he bent over his plate.

"Those old Sequani, for instance," continued Mr. Wagonseller after a pause. "And old Caesar and old Dumnorix—what did they eat now? For every day and for a feast?"

The young man made no answer.

"They had grain and meat like we have," said Victoria, making no motion toward beginning her supper. With despair her mother saw her bright colour and remembered her own lack of appetite when Wagonseller had taken his first meal at her father's house. "They made bread and cakes and we hear about their roasting meats and, of course, they had wine." She looked intently at Mr. Mather but his eyes were on his plate.

"Now Mrs., she don't like to hear of those old times," said Wagonseller pleasantly. "She don't like to hear about how Pelias was boiled and killed or how the other chap had the same treatment and come out a young man."

"I never heard of them," said Mather.

Victoria was astonished.

"What Latin did you study?"

"Never studied Latin," said Mr. Mather with his mouth full of dumpling. "Math's my specialty. Went to technical school where they had no use for that stuff."

"Well, well," said Wagonseller. "I thought you all had to study Latin." He refilled Mr. Mather's plate for the second time. What could one talk about? "You studied history, of course, and you know about old Caesar?"

"I know about old George Washington and his cherry tree," answered the young man, laughing at his own wit. "That was enough history for me." He began to talk in his deep voice and continued until he had finished his *schnitz und knep* and until Victoria had removed the main dish and brought on three kinds of pie, a cherry pie, and apple pie, and a delectable raisin pie. At sight of them the young man's eyes glittered, but before they were offered to him he had said a good deal. He had a really beautiful voice and his pronunciation was excellent. It was his voice and his broad *a's* and his elided *r's* which had captivated Victoria.

"We had a gump of a history teacher, an old maid with false hair. She was a perfect fool for history and we wouldn't learn to spite her. She used to say to me, 'Now, Charlie,' in a tone like that. Once she cried. No use anybody teaching unless they can slam the kids around. She had to stop. Now math I liked, and I had a teacher I could respect—he used to swear at us like the dickens. The rest I didn't care for, taught a lot of rot. In the Latin room— ye gods!" Suddenly the young man looked at the cloth beside his plate. "I have a fork here for this pie but no knife."

It is astonishing how large a little room may suddenly become when the silence of a great amazement spreads over it. Wagonseller flushed a little and Mrs. Wagonseller bent her head. To eat pie with a fork was, according to Victoria, the conspicuous and essential hallmark of good manners. Their hearts ached for Victoria. Then her father almost groaned. Victoria did not mind! She rose with the pleasantest face in the world and went to the sideboard drawer. Moreover, Victoria told a lie!

"It's my fault," said she gaily. "I set the table. I forgot your knife."

Then Victoria began to talk. She had eaten almost no *schnitz und knep* and now she did not touch her pie. She talked about everything and nothing, about the weather, about the tricks played in school, speaking rapidly as her father and mother had never heard her speak. She urged more pie on Mr. Mather and he consented to have a second piece of each variety. When he finished he took his watch from his pocket and looked at it and rose.

"Come on, Victoria," said he. "We got to beat it." Then he glanced around. "Got any toothpicks?" he asked.

For this too Victoria fell—thus Wagonseller phrased it in the slang which he heard daily. His colour was now as red as Victoria's. The phrase was exact—it was a fall for Victoria. A toothpick belonged, according to her creed, with a toothbrush and a nail file and a washcloth, in one's bedroom or bathroom. But Victoria opened the sideboard drawer. Back in a corner was a forgotten and long outlived receptacle and this Victoria brought forth and offered. She opened the door into the hall and the young man preceded her through it. He said, "Good-bye," for both him and Victoria.

Still at his place at the table, Mr. Wagonseller sat motionless. The door was shut tight and the voices came faintly to his ears. Victoria was speaking in her positive tones; her voice sounded gay. Wagonseller put his elbows on the table and cradled his head in his hands. He heard a door close with a slam and then there was silence. Mrs. Wagonseller came and stood beside him and put her hand on his shoulder.

"*Ach*, don't take it so hard, Pop! Perhaps he isn't such a bad fellow."

Wagonseller shook his head. He heard Victoria's voice, which had been music to his ears; he saw her capable and strong body, which had been the delight of his eyes. He seemed to hear her quick step on the stairs and so real was his delusion that he lifted his head. To his astonishment the door opened and there stood Victoria, not dressed for the street but with a book under her arm.

"Aren't you going then?" gasped Mrs. Wagonseller.

"No," said Victoria with flaming cheeks. "I certainly am not going with him anywhere. It is all right to give such a person a meal but there it stops."

"Did you have to hurt his feelings?" asked Mrs. Wagonseller.

"No," said Victoria. "He hasn't any. But I told him I had work to do; I made up my mind that I, at least, would show I had manners."

"Have you work to do?" asked Mrs. Wagonseller. Now that Victoria had begun, was she going to keep on lying?

"Yes, I have. Father, listen once."

Wagonseller lifted his head. Above his clasped hands, which hid his mouth, his eyes glittered.

"Well?" he said.

"I have a plan," said Victoria. "There is a Greek class starting in the high school and I'm going to get into it. I can easily do that along with my other studies. They say it is more interesting than Latin."

"And what am I to do?" asked Wagonseller, trying to look grave.

"Well, I thought if you could just learn the letters you could help me. Here is the alphabet."

Wagonseller bent his head over the page. At sight of the strange characters he was both terrified and inexpressibly proud.

Then I could get into college with an examination," continued Victoria. "You can do it, Pop."

Wagonseller's head bent still lower. There was a college in the town—it would mean years more of Victoria. He lifted his head and blinked at her, his face sober, almost blank. It was the way he looked when he was about to say a good thing.

"All right," he said, pretending a weary patience. "I have already five languages, but I never thought I'd have to learn Greek yet."

He saw a long list: *English, Pennsylvania German, German, Latin, French, Greek.*

Were there, Mr. Wagonseller wondered with ambitious hunger, any more?

—ELSIE SINGMASTER

Reprinted by permission of the author.

RAW MATERIALS

"A Student of Languages" deals with material within the experience of high school boys or girls—the friendly, understanding relationship between a girl and her parents; her methodical performance of daily household duties; her interest in her school lessons, especially Latin and French; and her corresponding interest in the finer points of living as evidenced by good manners.

First we should study ourselves. Arnold Bennett says that all the greatest novels are autobiographical. If a person thoroughly understands the working of his own mind, he knows much about other people. Next we should observe. Every professional writer knows that setting down in a notebook what he sees opens his eyes so that he sees more to jot down. Only by developing a seeing eye can one really know the people, scenes, and characters he wishes to write about. We should also read. The newspaper, histories, biographies, travel books, and magazine articles present characters and incidents that may be used as starting-places for stories.

ELEMENTS OF A SHORT STORY

The four elements of a short story are plot, character, atmosphere, and theme. In a character story the emphasis is on the presentation of a character; in a plot story, on complicated, novel, or surprising plot; in an atmosphere story, upon the setting and subjective colouring. A story of theme illustrates strikingly an idea or a truth of human life. The short story writer may begin with a theme; begin with a plot and fit characters to it; start with a character and fit the action and setting to it; or start by creating an atmosphere to which he fits people and actions. One of the four must dominate.

"A Student of Languages" is primarily a study of character, with the action based on the contrast between the sincere, sensitive, considerate, and courteous Wagonsellers and the self-centred, inconsiderate, crude Mr. Mather.

PLOT

A story is more than a mere sequence of events. It is a sequence which has a logical development through cause and effect, leading from a state or condition which is accepted by the reader as an agreed starting point, through complication and conflict, which is imposed upon or discovered in this *status quo*, and leads to a climax and re-arrangement where a new and final condition is accepted. A plot must make provision for these stages of development, and furnishes the vehicle by which they are created and resolved.

The author may be arrested by some striking incident, and ask himself how it came about, and how it will end, for he knows that every event has had a past and will have a future. As soon as his imagination begins to fashion this casual sequence into a coherent story he has begun to plot, and when he has so arranged it, he has created a plot and arranged his observations as a logical part of a piece of fiction.

A common germ-idea or starting-point of a short story is an incident, a situation, or an anecdote. The incident may be an experience of the writer or of one of his friends, a happening recorded in a history, biography, or newspaper, or an imagined happening.

Goethe says that there are only thirty-six tragic situations. Some of these that are useful to the story writer are the pursued, revolt, fatal imprudence, rivalry of kinsmen or friends, unequal rivalry, obstacles to love, an enemy loved, ambition, mistaken identity, the saviour, self-sacrifice for an ideal, self-sacrifice for kindred or friends, discovery of the dishonour of a loved one, and recovery of a lost one.

EXAMPLES OF INCIDENTS OR SITUATIONS THAT HAVE STORY VALUE

1. A man crossing the street is knocked down by an automobile. He crawls to his feet and calls a traffic officer. Much to his amazement, he discovers his wife to be the driver of the machine.
2. A man has just moved into a neighbourhood where the houses are all alike. Coming home late at night, he finds he has no key, climbs through an open window, and discovers he has entered the wrong house.
3. A poor woman loses the diamond necklace she borrowed from a wealthy friend.
4. A man steals to pay for his son's college education.
5. Two young people whose families are enemies secretly become friends.
6. At a masquerade party a young man falls in love with a beautiful and fascinating oriental princess, who proves to be a boy.

PRACTICE 10. Finding Story Material

1. Find in the newspaper, a history, or a biography an incident or a situation that might be used as a story-germ—for example, the headline *Dog Saves Master Who Broke His Leg on Ice.*

2. What experience of your own or of a friend's might be the starting-point of a short story?

3. Find an anecdote that might be expanded into a short story.

4. Find or invent three other incidents, situations, or anecdotes that might be used as starting-points for stories. Do not include hackneyed material such as the weird experiences that prove to be a dream or the athletic hero who wins the game and thus wins the hand of the beautiful girl he loves.

BUILDING A PLOT

A simple plot may be diagrammed in this **way:**

A is the cause or initial impulse, the incident or force which starts the story. In "A Student of Languages" it is Mrs. Wagonseller's announcement that she will have *schnitz und knep* for supper. Without this decision there would have been no story that day. The line AB represents the complication, entanglement, mix-up, or rising action; B is the effect or the climax. In "A Student of Languages" the entanglement includes Victoria's announcement that she has invited a teacher to supper, the discovery that the teacher is a young man, the careful preparations for the meal and the Wagonsellers' concern about the impression they will produce on the guest, the increasing evidence of his bad manners, and Mather's saying good-bye for Victoria and himself.

In this story the climax comes with Victoria's almost immediate return, "not dressed for the street but with a book under her arm." Barrett defines climax as "the apex of interest and emotion, the point of the story." The untangling, consisting of Victoria's explanation of her decision to remain home that evening, is brief. The conclusion, the picture of Victoria continuing her studies with her father, follows swiftly. A good rule for story-writing is to make the untangling and conclusion as brief as possible.

MOTIVATION

An essential difference between the incidents of a plot and the incidents of a fishing trip is that the happenings of a fishing trip are like a string of beads or a train of cars, whereas the incidents of a short story are related by cause and effect or are motivated. In "A Student of Languages", Mrs. Wagonseller's desire to make catsup causes her to plan a supper of *schnitz und knep;* this leads Victoria to invite her teacher to supper; his conduct at the table reveals to the parents and Victoria how ill-bred he is; and scorn of him causes Victoria to decide to remain at home and study Greek with her father that evening, so easing the minds of her parents, who feared she was in love with Mr. Mather.

COMPLICATION

The essential difference between an incident and the plot of a short story is complication. When Victoria Wagonseller, a high school girl, wishing to go to a lecture at night and yet be well prepared the next day, gets up at five o'clock to prepare her next day's lessons in advance, her overcoming an obstacle to her going out at night is an incident. When her parents, however, fear it may be the first sign of a secret love affair, the complication gives the incident story value.

"The Gift of the Magi" illustrates a favourite method of O. Henry —complicating by having the characters work at cross-purposes. Della and Jim need money to buy Christmas gifts. Della's love for Jim prompts her to sell her hair to buy him a platinum fob chain for his watch; Jim sells his watch to buy Della pure tortoise shell combs, side and back, with jewelled rims.

STRUGGLE

Conflict is the essence of the short story. Everyone is interested in a race between two men for the quarter-mile championship, the control of a corporation or political party, or the hand of a girl in marriage, or the conflict between the man who wants his son to carry on the family hardware business and the son who is determined to be an actor. The struggle in a man's mind when he has a chance to "get even" with a rival is no less dramatic. All are interested, too, in the mysterious—the strange noise, the secret door, the letter written in code, the haunted house. Everybody also enjoys action, especially unusual or striking action in which the performers arouse our sympathy —marching soldiers, a hero aviator riding up Main Street, a man rescuing a horse from a burning barn, the freshman substitute fullback winning the game.

The struggle is an important element of plot construction. The struggle may be physical or mental and may be between man and nature, man and animal, man and man, man and supernatural forces, or man and himself. When, for example, Jim Vaughn hesitates between rescuing an enemy and letting him die, the mental struggle has story value. Stevenson's "Markheim" and De Maupassant's "The Coward" are other illustrations of the struggle between a man and himself.

Suspense

Complication and struggle lead to suspense, an important element in a plot. When the action is complicated and the struggle between man and man, man and himself, or man and a supernatural power seems equal, the reader does not like to lay down the magazine or book until he knows how the story ends. If the reader knows early in the story that the substitute will win the game, that the girl will marry her guardian, that Margy will prevent the robbery, that the ghost is a mischievous boy, that the girl has lost all respect for the crude young man, he is not likely to finish the story. Conceal something from the reader; let him have something to look forward to.

In "A Student of Languages" there is suspense at the very beginning. Why does Victoria get up so early? The answer does not come until after breakfast. Likewise, the author leaves us in doubt as to whether or not Victoria will go to the lecture with Mr. Mather, placing this information at the end. The paragraph near the climax which begins "Still at his place at the table Mr. Wagonseller sat motionless" is a good example of suspense.

DEVELOPMENT

In developing the plot, and (as we shall see later) in developing character, the unit of progress is the incident or episode. It is to the management of episode that the student should direct his greatest care, for the story is no more than the logical and natural sequence of episodes, each of which has one, and sometimes more, specific purposes.

Our story "A Student of Languages" has eleven episodes:

1. Victoria is heard bustling about at five in the morning.
2. They have breakfast.
3. Mr. Wagonseller hears Victoria's lessons for the following day.
4. They all go about the day's labours.
5. Victoria announces a visitor for supper.
6. Mr. and Mrs. Wagonseller talk it over.
7. Preparing for supper.
8. Mr. Wagonseller meets Mr. Mather.

9. They have supper.
10. Victoria announces her decision not to go out.
11. They plan to begin the Greek class.

In this sequence of events the emphasis is upon character and most of the episodes are for character portrayal. Strictly speaking, the plot is contained in the announcement of Mrs. Wagonseller that there will be *schnitz und knep*, in the invitation, in the display of rudeness, and in Victoria's decision.

Episode 1 gives a picture of the three Wagonsellers and distinguishes them clearly one from the other. We learn also the family character, devotion, and apprehension. Suspense is roused and we are fully prepared for the action which follows.

Episode 2—Time sequence is maintained; reason is provided for the *schnitz und knep* supper; Victoria is further characterized.

Episode 3—Character development of Victoria and Mr. Wagonseller and the fine family spirit is established, which is to rouse our favourable concern and prepare for the possibility of trouble—making disaster not unreasonable.

Episode 4—Plot development. Time goes forward, and the important announcement is made.

Episode 5—Plot development. Announcement of visitor.

Episode 6—Rouses apprehension. Visitor is a man. Anything may happen.

Episode 7—Character development. Fears are increased by reason of Mather's appearance.

Episode 8—Character episode. Mr. Mather makes his first mistake.

Episode 9—The plot grows to a head. Mr. Mather is revealed in all his selfish, uncultured person.

Episode 10—The climax is reached. Victoria justifies her parents' (and our) fine opinion of her.

Episode 11—The story is resolved into a new and final settlement to our evident satisfaction.

PRACTICE 11. Recognizing Episodes

Select any favourite short story or one-act play and analyze it into episodes and say what purpose each episode serves in the story or the drama.

CREATING CHARACTERS

The recent trend has been toward placing the stress on the characters, rather than on plot, setting, or theme. Commonly in a story there are not more than six persons, one of whom occupies the centre of the stage. "A Student of Languages," which has four characters, Mrs. Wagonseller, Mr. Wagonseller, Victoria, and Mr. Mather, is the record of an important decision which Victoria made.

As a rule, the prominent character is an unusual, striking, or fascinating person who has a dominant, individual trait, characteristic, desire, weakness, power, ambition, or ideal upon which the plot is built—kindness, shrewdness, ability to reason, faithfulness to duty, devotion to a master, desire for revenge, interest in crimes, determination. In "A Student of Languages" the outstanding trait of Victoria is a determination to be a cultured woman.

Sometimes a minor or humorous weakness or striking contradiction is associated with a desirable dominant trait. For example, a benevolent gentleman loves everybody and everything but hates cats; a prosperous, generous man never throws away a string; or a hero in battle is afraid to face an audience.

LEARN TO OBSERVE

To put real people into stories one must first know thoroughly some interesting people. Hence students of life and of story-writing should form the habit of studying and understanding the boys, girls, men, and women they see or meet in the home, the church, the theatre, the classroom, and the streetcar, discovering the distinguishing mark or trait of each, and using in their stories these people, not army officers, industrial leaders, racketeers, farmers, or the "four hundred", unless they really know these people.

Examples:
1. A young man who instead of taking responsibility relies on his widowed mother, a saleswoman, to get him to school on time, to see that he does his homework, to pay his college bills, to find a job for him, and to get him to work on time.
2. A woman who, like a child, builds air castles and then tells her friends again and again about trips abroad, country estates, servants, and expensive cars which she expects soon to enjoy but which never become realities.
3. A mechanical genius who enjoys taking a car apart more than riding in it and thinks out ways to improve his automobile, radio, and other machines. Sometimes the "improved" machines don't work.
4. A girl who is never sincere, who always wears a mask to hide her real self.
5. A boy who attends a private school and spends much of his time telling how popular he is and how much he does for the school, when in reality he plays but a very small part in the school's life.

PRACTICE 12. Character Study

In the manner indicated, describe briefly four people who belong in a book. Start with people you know, have studied on the street or at a meeting, have heard about, or have read about, but change them if you wish.

CHARACTER TRAITS

Traits of character are best portrayed by acts and by speech, but may be suggested in a description of the person or explained in an analysis of his character. In "A Student of Languages", Elsie Singmaster does not tell us Mr. Mather was rude and inconsiderate; she tells us what Mr. Mather said and did, and how he did it and said it, so that we may get acquainted with him as we do with a person we meet. Mr. Mather's failure to rise promptly when his host entered the room, his brief "I thought it hot," his haste to begin eating, his request for a knife and a toothpick, the glitter in his eyes at the sight of the three kinds of pie, his taking "a second piece of each variety," and his "good-bye" unaccompanied by any word of thanks, present dramatically his rudeness and selfishness.

PRACTICE 13. Studying Character Traits

1. What is the outstanding trait of Mrs. Wagonseller? Mr. Wagonseller? Mr. Mather?
2. How does Elsie Singmaster make her people real to us? What significant incidents, habits, or actions are shown?
3. Using the preceding analysis of Mr. Mather as a model, discuss the author's portrayal of the character of Mr. Wagonseller, Mrs. Wagonseller, or Victoria.

PRACTICE 14. Writing a Biographical Sketch

Write the biography of a person you intend to put into your story. Start with someone you know but change the character as you see fit and use your imagination for details. Include in your biography birth, parentage, childhood, later life, achievement, character, dominant trait, temperament, and appearance.

INDIVIDUALIZING

In character drawing there are two important and distinguishable processes. The first of these is individualization, giving to each character a name and individual traits or differences which will set him off in the mind as a person. Literature is filled with these individuals who would never be mistaken, even in appearance, for any one else: Sir John Falstaff, Long John Silver, Uriah Heep, Captain Cuttle, Mr. Micawber, Prester John. The distinguishing marks differ very much, for we would grow very tired if they were always the same. Sir John has his "tun of flesh"; Silver his wooden leg; Heep his lashless eyes, his writhing, moist, fishy hands; Micawber his pomposity, his love of big words, his pet phrases ("in short", "turn up"); Captain Cuttle, like Silver, his sea language for land purposes; Prester John his superb physique, and his colour. Jerry Cruncher (from *A Tale of Two Cities*) cannot pronounce a *v*,—he calls his wife an "aggerawaiter", he desires to "circumwent ewents"; his hair is like spikes; he has rust always on his fingers.

PRACTICE 15. Individualizing

Either from life or from imagination choose a character well distinguished from others by appearance and so vividly describe him (or her) as to make him stand out unmistakably to the mental eye of the reader as never to be mistaken for anyone else.

Suggestions:

1. A very stout person. 2. A very thin person. 3. A man with misshapen features, prominent nose, ears, lips; a hare-lip, cast in the eye, protruding or receding chin, etc. 4. A dour face. 5. A face wreathed in smiles. 6. One-armed man. 7. A club-footed man. 8. A very tall man. 9. A man with a square jaw. 10. A hunchback.

(*Warning:* Characters that are misshapen or deformed are usually reserved for stories of crime and mystery, or unnatural stories; yet some of the best stories have shown how absurd this natural feeling toward deformity is. It is not necessary to choose such unusual persons for stories, but they are less likely to be confusing at the start.)

PRACTICE 16. Individualizing by Speech

Choose either the same or another character, and invent an episode including conversation in which the character is individualized by his speech.

Suggestions:

1. Oddities of pronunciation, such as: pronouncing 'v' for 'w', or 'w' for 'v' as Germans sometimes do (as Mrs. Wagonseller did under excitement); or pronouncing 'j' like 'y' as Scandinavian peoples often do in learning English; or 't' for 'th'; or 'l' for 'r' such as we attribute to Orientals. 2. Some one who stutters. 3. A man who whistles in his speech. 4. A girl who has some pet word or phrase which is used habitually, *lovely, grand, wow, keen, gosh!, and everything, you know, don't you think*. 5. One who hesitates and repeats without making progress.

PRACTICE 17. Individualizing by Actions

Invent other episodes for the same or other characters who are distinguishable from others by habitual actions.

Suggestions:

1. Walks or handles his legs and arms oddly.   2. Has a peculiar eye affliction which makes him wink frequently (sometimes at embarrassing times).   3. A nervous, fidgety person.   4. A hacking, habitual cough.   5. A writhing, wriggling person like Uriah Heep.   6. One who habitually uses his hands in talking. 7. One who smacks his lips as he talks.   8. A giggling person.

CHARACTERIZATION

Individualization is already a good step toward revelation of character and often the two things go forward together, but yet two persons may have much the same individual traits and be very different in character. Characterization must reveal the personality, the sincerity, frivolousness, honesty, cupidity, selfishness, thoughtfulness, pride, modesty of the person. These may be shown by description as Chaucer has so well done; by action or speech, or by both, as has been done by nearly all writers.

In this important part of the short story technique, the episode is again the chief instrument. Many story episodes, incidents, and situations are for character drawing almost entirely.

Consider individually the episodes in "A Student of Languages" and in the story analyzed in Practice 2 for what each reveals of character.

PRACTICE 18. Characterizing

Write an episode which will reveal by his speech one of the following characters:

1. A man given to very great exaggeration for personal advertising.   2. A man who likes to tell 'tall' stories, stretchers, merely for the sake of their artistic effect, but with no malice.   3. A girl who is very snobbish.   4. A student who is fond of self-display.   5. An incident in the life of Casper Milquetoast, or one in the life of Major Hoople.   6. A southerner, fond of saying "Down South", makes unfavourable comparisons between your district and his beloved South. 7. A newly-rich man betrays his lack of culture among cultured folk.   8. A girl of sound good sense keeps up her end in a verbal battle with some haughty rival.

PRACTICE 19. Characterizing by Action

Write an episode which will reveal by action, without saying it in so many words, one of the following characters:

1. A dishonest rogue.   2. A furtive, sneaking individual.   3. A thoughtful, considerate boy.   4. A motherly woman.   5. A selfish boy.   6. A brave, courageous person.   7. An untrained, unmannerly boy.   8. A girl who would sacrifice another girl in an attempt to save herself.   9. A girl who would take undeserved blame to shield a timid, fearful classmate.   10. A bullying boy, man.   11. A self-sacrificing boy, man, teacher.   12. A student with high ideals.   13. An avaricious person.   14. A dreamy, slow, indolent man.

NAMES

The names chosen for your characters should be in keeping with their personality, background, and surroundings.   An Italian immigrant would hardly be called "Ruby Kaufman".   "Knute Axelbrod" suggests a sturdy pioneering farmer; "Hetty", a practical, reliable person; "Wagonseller", a Pennsylvania "Dutch" family.   "Willie" is a soft little boy; "Bill", a sturdy one whom "Percival" thinks rather rough; "William," a dignified, serious young man.

PRACTICE 20. Studying Names in Fiction

1. Choose five names from short stories, novels, or plays you have read. Does each name fit the character? Why do you think so?

2. List five names of people that you think have good story value. Suggestions may be found in the telephone book, "Who's Who," or a catalogue.

THEME

Sometimes the story writer starts with an idea or theme; most novels and short stories illustrate an idea or present in concrete form a truth of human life.   James Lane Allen's *The Kentucky Cardinal* instills a love of birds; *Silas Marner* shows the influence of a little child upon a man; Tarkington's *Alice Adams* shows the effects of posing; his *Seventeen* interprets the youth of high school age; Sinclair Lewis's *Main Street* pictures the self-satisfied dullness of small-town life; his *Babbitt* shows the foibles of successful and self-sufficient city people; Dickens' *Nicholas Nickleby* attacks the abuses of charity schools and brutal schoolmasters; his *Oliver Twist* exposes the wretched condition of the poor in the English workhouses.   The text of Hawthorne's *House of Seven Gables* is, "The fathers have eaten sour grapes, and the children's teeth are set on edge."

EXAMPLES OF THEMES FOR SHORT STORIES

1. Jealousy leads to folly and injustice.
2. A mother's sacrifice, while seeming to benefit her child, in reality causes the girl to lose the most precious thing in life.

3, Judge a person by what he does, not by what he says.

4. Sudden wealth is dangerous.

5. A friend to everybody is a friend to nobody.

6. All is not gold that glitters.

PRACTICE 21. Studying Story Themes

1. What is the theme of "A Student of Languages"?

2. Find or invent three themes which might be used as starting-points for stories.

SETTING

Occasionally an author starts with a setting. Stevenson says, "Some places speak distinctly. Certain dank gardens cry aloud for a murder; certain old houses demand to be haunted; certain coasts are set apart for shipwreck." High school students, however, as a rule write more easily and entertainingly when they begin with an incident, a situation, an anecdote, a character, or a theme than when they use setting as the starting-point for an atmosphere or local-colour story.

Setting includes time, place, occupations, and conditions. When the curtain rises, one sees the setting of a scene of a play. Although important features of the background or setting are pictured near the beginning of the story, details are often presented as the story progresses. Long paragraphs of description slow up the story and confuse the reader; brief vivid descriptions help the reader to visualize the action.

LOCAL COLOUR AND ATMOSPHERE

Local colour suggests the London streets of Dickens' stories; the Wessex country-side of Thomas Hardy; the Mississippi river life of *Tom Sawyer;* the Yukon of the *Trail of 98,* the French regime in old Quebec of *Seats of the Mighty.* Each of these presents in details the manners, customs, dress, dialect, and scenery of a particular district. In "A Student of Languages" the references to the pronunciation of *v* and to *schnitz und knep,* Mr. Wagonseller's including Pennsylvania German among his languages, and such constructions as "I will today make catsup" and "Pop, you must hear me a little Latin yet before I go" are illustrations of local colour.

The *Winston Simplified Dictionary* defines atmosphere as "the influence effected by a work of art or literature upon the spirit or emotion." Edgar Allen Poe says that there should be no word in a short story which does not help to produce a preconceived effect. His stories illustrate his theory and influence us by their atmosphere of gloom, mystery, weirdness, and horror. An effective ghost story has an atmosphere of uncanniness, spookiness, or creepiness. The snapping of Victoria's sheets, the sunshine in the kitchen, the substantial breakfast, the good manners of the family, the house "deliciously scented with cloves and allspice" from the catsup suggest a busy, wholesome, refined atmosphere.

PRACTICE 22. The Story's Setting

Picture the setting of your story. Does it have a definite atmosphere? What? How will you make your reader feel it?

POINT OF VIEW

Before writing the first word of a story, one should decide whose story it is or who should tell the story. The common narrators are a major, a minor, or a silent character who tells the story in the first person; the author who tells the story objectively; and the author who looks over the shoulder of the main character and tells the story from that person's point of view. Stockton's "The Lady or the Tiger?" Ellis Parker Butler's "Fleas Is Fleas", Mary Wilkins Freeman's "The Revolt of 'Mother' ", and Elsie Singmaster's "A Student of Languages" are examples of stories told objectively in the third person. Poe's "The Cask of Amontillado", "The Pit and the Pendulum", "The Manuscript Found in a Bottle", and "The Gold Bug" are told in the first person.

Barrett Wendell says, "Most people have a strong impulse to preface something in particular by at least a paragraph of nothing in particular, bearing to the real matter in hand a relation not more inherently intimate than that of the tuning of a violin to a symphony." A good beginning catches the reader's interest.

OPENING

The student can find out how to begin his story by studying the openings of successful stories. "A Student of Languages" begins with incident and characterization.

Freeman's "The Revolt of 'Mother' " begins with dialogue:
"Father!"
"What is it?"
"What are them men diggin' over there in the field for?"

Stockton's "The Lady or the Tiger?" begins with characterization:
In the very olden time, there lived a semibarbaric king, whose ideas, though somewhat polished and sharpened by the progressiveness of distant Latin neighbours, were still large, florid, and untrammelled, as became the half of him which was barbaric.

In "The Gold Bug", Poe starts with setting, characterization, and needed explanation:

Many years ago I contracted an intimacy with a Mr. William Légrand. He was of an ancient Huguenot family, and had once been wealthy; but a series of misfortunes had reduced him to want. To avoid the mortifications consequent upon his disasters, he left New Orleans, the city of his forefathers, and took up his residence at Sullivan's Island, near Charleston, South Carolina.

Brand Whitlock's "The Gold Brick" begins with incident and characterization:

Ten thousand dollars a year! Neil Kittrell left the office of the *Morning Telegraph* in a daze.

The rule is to begin a character story with character delineation, an atmosphere story with setting, and a plot story with incident or dialogue. When in doubt, begin with action and tuck in a bit at a time the antecedent explanation, characterization, and setting.

Often, as in Poe's "The Cask of Amontillado", the first part of the story is omitted. Poe does not include the incidents which made Montresor desire revenge. This story is represented by the numbers 7, 8, 9, 10, 11, 12; incidents 1, 2, 3, 4, 5, and 6 are omitted. A safe rule for the opening is to start as near to the climax as possible.

The order of the detective story is 12, 11, 10, 9, 8, 7, 6, 5, 4, 3, 2, 1. The author begins with the commission of a crime and gradually unwinds the tangled incidents until he reaches the first one and hence completes the solution of the problem.

PRACTICE 23. The Opening of the Story

1. Study the openings of a dozen stories. How many open with incident? With dialogue? With setting? With characterization? With necessary antecedent explanation? With a general proposition, or theme, which the story will illustrate? With a combination of these?

2. Decide whether in your story you will stress plot, character, theme, or setting. Then write the opening of your short story. Arouse the reader's interest.

DIALOGUE

Although uncritical readers like a story with "lots of conversation in it", a story by a beginner usually contains little dialogue. Conversation is hard to write, and no conversation is preferable to stilted, unnatural talk that does not fit the characters. Likewise conversation which does not serve a purpose—characterize or advance the plot, for example—should be rigidly excluded from the story.

To learn to write dialogue one must get out among people, know them, and also observe carefully the details of their speech—coherence, point, accuracy, length of sentences, type of sentences, fluency, vocabulary, grammar, pronunciation, tone, mannerisms.

Instead of a string of *he saids* and *he replieds*, a story writer can use for variety *grunted, roared, snarled, sneered, maintained, contradicted, explained with icy precision, cried angrily, shouted, corrected, asked, drawled, whispered, volunteered, yelled, mumbled, rejoined, retorted, ventured, muttered, stammered, snickered, boasted, chuckled, dashed in, exclaimed, gasped, growled,* or *hinted darkly.*

The introductory *he said, he mumbled,* or *he shouted* may be placed at the beginning of the speech, in the middle, or at the end. When there is no possibility of confusion, the introductory expression is omitted.

Other ways of making dialogue natural, interesting, and sprightly are by having the speeches short, using freely for most characters contradictions and colloquialisms, having one speaker break in on another before a speech is completed, letting a character ask another question instead of answering the question asked, having a person anticipate a question and answer it before it is asked, and breaking the dialogue with brief passages of description and comment.

PRACTICE 24. Conversation

1. Study the conversation of "A Student of Languages". Show how it is made natural, interesting, and lively. Is there any talk out of character, any wooden or dull talk?

2. Jot down in your notebook words and turns of speech you hear used by special classes of people: a fisherman, a small boy, a gardener, a typist, a ribbon salesgirl, a farmer, a German, an Italian, a Norwegian, an Irishman.

3. Write a conversation that will form a part of the story for which you have already written the opening.

SELF-CRITICISM CHART—CONVERSATION

1. *What variations of* he said *and* he replied *have I used?* *Is it always clear who the speaker is?*
2. *Is the talk in character?*
3. *Is tone of voice suggested?* *Manner?* *Pronunciation?*
4. *If I have used dialect, is it accurate?* *Easily understood by the reader?*
5. *Are speeches long or short?* *Broken by questions, description, narration?*

PICTURES AND CONTRAST

One way to make the story seem real is by picturing vividly but tersely the characters and the setting. The writer who does not observe or see in imagination the sparse hair, wrinkled face, faded coat, square jaw, and keen, kindly eyes of the heroic figure in his story will write about phantoms, not about real people.

Another device for making clear and forceful what one has to say is contrast. Elsie Singmaster contrasts the courtesy of the Wagonsellers with the bad manners of Mr. Mather, and the calmness of Victoria with her parents' agitation.

PRACTICE 25. Pictures and Contrasts

1. In "A Student of Languages" find another example of contrast expressed or implied.

2. In "A Student of Languages" what are two illustrations of the fact that Elsie Singmanster is an accurate observer?

3. Find two vivid pictures in "A Student of Languages".

PLAUSIBILITY

Because "truth is stranger than fiction", to say of an incident in a short story that it really happened is not proof that it is plausible. To be plausible an incident must seem true. In other words, in a story every effect has a cause; every act grows out of the character delineated and the preceding action. Although no one probably ever lived on a desert island in the manner depicted in *Robinson Crusoe*, yet because of the minuteness of detail and absolute naturalness, the story has the air of truth, and is really more plausible than are many happenings recorded in the newspapers.

STYLE

In "How *Flint and Fire* Started and Grew", Dorothy Canfield tells how she wrote one of her stories. After "the materials were ready, the characters fully alive" in her mind "and entirely visualized, even to the smoothly braided hair of Ev'leen Ann," she scribbled the story as rapidly as her pencil could go. "After this came a period of steady desk work, of rewriting, compression, more compression," rewriting of "clumsy, ungraceful phrases", and revision for correctness, suggestiveness, accuracy, movement, proportion, and sound.

In answer to the question "How can I acquire style?" Robert W. Neal says, "Don't try to . . . directly. Strive rather to report accurately what you observe and think and feel." Although struggling for a literary style is likely to lead to affectation and emptiness, by taking pains one can acquire the knack of building varied, lively, forceful, and natural sentences. Writing "A Student of Languages" in one's own words without referring to the story and then comparing one's sentences with Elsie Singmaster's simple, lucid, accurate, crisp, terse language is a good exercise.

TITLE

The title is rarely decided when one starts to write. Often it is suggested by an event in the course of the story; it may not come until after the story is complete. In a letter to Tom Taylor, Lewis Carroll describes the evolution of the title for *Alice in Wonderland*.

I first thought of "Alice's Adventures under Ground"—but that was pronounced too much like a lesson book about mines. Then I took "Alice's Golden House", but that I gave up. Here are the names I thought of: "Alice among the Elves", "Alice among the Goblins", "Alice's Hour in Elf Land", "Alice's Doings in Wonderland", "Alice's Adventures in Wonderland".

A good title should be brief, specific, colourful, and original, should be suitable for the story, and should excite curiosity. Comparatively few titles of short stories are more than five words long. The title, like the opening, should allure readers, as clover attracts bees.

PRACTICE 26. Studying Titles

1. Which of these are good titles: "The Moon Coin", "The Commutation Chophouse", "A Thrifty Man", "The Only Child", "The Restaurant", "A Convert to Christmas", "Clothes", "A Bus Ride," "Footfalls", "Beyond the Horizon", "In the Distance", "Old Judge Priest", "One against the World", "The Striker", "All or Nothing", "A Decision", "Percival Galahad Barnose", "The Hired Baby", "Rikki-Tikki-Tavi", "Wee Willie Winkie"? Why?

2. From magazines or a book of short stories select five excellent titles.

3. Decide upon a title for your story.

SELF-CRITICISM CHART—SHORT STORY

1. *Is plot, character, theme, or atmosphere conspicuously emphasized?*
2. *Show that the story has (or has not) a single predominating incident.*
3. *Has it a single pre-eminent character? Prove.*
4. *Does the story give a unified impression. What is it?*
5. *How much time does the story cover? Does the length of time destroy the unity of the story?*

6. *What is the setting?   Does the entire action happen in one place?   If not, do unnecessary changes of scene destroy the unity?*

7. *In the plot what is the cause or inciting impulse, what are the incidents, and what is the effect or climax?*

8. *Show that the plot is (or is not) compressed.*

9. *What is the outstanding trait of each character?*

10. *Do the characters show their traits by their speech and acts?   Does the author describe, analyze, and explain the characters?*

11. *Is each character colourful?   Individual?   Interesting?   Do you know him intimately?*

12. *Is each character's name suitable?   Suggestive?*

13. *Are there any touches of local colour?   What?*

14. *Is there a struggle or conflict?   What is it?*

15. *Is the plot complicated?   If so, how?*

16. *If the story has suspense, show how it is secured.*

17. *Is there any variation from the chronological order, 1, 2, 3, 4, 5, 6, 7, 8, 9, 10, 11, 12?*

18. *Has the story a theme?   If so, what is it?*

19. *Who is the narrator?*

20. *How does the story open?*

21. *What proportion of the story is dialogue?*

22. *Show that the dialogue is (or is not) natural, interesting, and sprightly.   What substitutes for* said *and* replied *are used?*

23. *What pictures are there?*

24. *What use is made of contrast?*

25. *Is the story plausible?*

26. *Use five adjectives to characterize the style.*

27. *Is the title brief?   Vivid?   Attractive?   Suitable?   Suggestive?   Does it arouse curiosity?*

PRACTICE 27. Writing a Short Story.

1. Complete the story you have been working on. Test it by the above standards; then revise thoroughly.

2. Go to life for another plot. Start with a cause, an incident, an effect or a climax, a character, or a theme. Invent needed details. Then write the short story.

Chapter 25

The One-Act Play

The one-act play is a short story in dramatic form. Instead of being read silently from a book it is intended to be presented by actors before an audience, solely by means of dialogue and action, aided by costumes, scenery, and lighting. Like the short story, the one-act play must aim for a single unified impression. "It is," says a playwright, "a story of ones—one simple setting, one continuous, unbroken scene, one main character, one main incident, and one climax. A good one-act play leaves one clean-cut impression."

WHAT MAKES A SITUATION DRAMATIC?

Any situation is dramatic which can arouse the emotions of the audience. A conflict, physical or mental, between two or more characters or within the mind of one character, usually arouses an emotional reaction in an onlooker. In the one-act play a conflict is revealed mainly through the actions of the characters, and partly through dialogue. The elements of conflict are identical in the play and short story.

THEME

Often, as explained in the section on the short story, an idea comes in the form of a theme—general truth which may be used as the subject of the play: Fortune is fickle; A stitch in time saves nine; Dishonesty doesn't pay. But the theme should be merely implied by the action, not drummed into the minds of the audience through constant repetition in the speeches of the characters.

The one-act play may be tragic—a character fails in what he sets out to do, or in doing it, unhappiness, ruin, or even death results. It may be comic—the hero, successful in what he sets out to do, achieves happiness. Or it may be melodramatic—an exaggerated picture of right conquering wrong.

PLOT

Theme alone is not sufficient. There must be a story or plot, presented dramatically, with beginning, middle, and end. Pantomime plays an important part. It has been said that a writer should not start to write speeches for his characters until the play is perfectly understandable to an audience in pantomime alone.

The beginning is occupied with introducing characters and explaining previous action through the speeches of characters. These preliminaries pave the way for the main action.

"The middle," as one playwright puts it, "depends for its interest on the ability of the author to swing the balance of power from one character to another." In the middle or main action the conflict takes place. The main action should reach a climax or turning point, followed swiftly but naturally by the end or result of the main action. But throughout, says George P. Baker in *Dramatic Technique*, the audience must feel "a compelling desire to know what will happen next."

THE MASTER IN THE HOUSE[1]

SCENE: *The kitchen of* KATE BURKE'S *typical middle-class home. It is early evening, and the kitchen is flooded with warm light. The blinds are down, shutting out the windy dusk. There is a door U C,[2] elevated above the level of the floor and reached by two steps, which leads upstairs to the bedrooms. In the L wall, about centre, is a door leading outside, with a curtained window above and below it. L C is a kitchen table with kitchen chairs above and right of it. In the R wall, down stage, is a door leading to another part of the house. Above the door is the kitchen stove. U R C is the kitchen sink. Below the door D R is an old armchair. There is a clock on the wall above the sink U R C, a cupboard U L C, and a large rocking chair R C. There may, also, be innumerable objects about suggesting the atmosphere of a kitchen.*

AT RISE OF CURTAIN: KATE *is working between the stove and sink, evidently preparing dinner. She is a large, comfortable-looking woman of middle age, with dark hair and blue eyes. She is dressed neatly in a gingham house dress and has a large apron tied around her waist. As she moves around the spotless kitchen, she sings softly to herself. Her voice is filled with an undercurrent of—not exactly grief—perhaps resignation.*

[1]Copyright, 1934, by Scholastic Corporation. Copyright, 1934, by Betty Fitzgerald. Copies of the play may be obtained for 35 cents each from the Dramatic Publishing Company, 59 East Van Buren Street, Chicago, Illinois.
[2]Up stage (U) means away from the footlights; down stage (D), towards the footlights. Right (R) and left (L) are used in regard to the actor as he faces the audience. (C) means centre.

KATE: But come ye back, when summer's in the meadow,
        Or when the valley's hushed and white with snow,
        It's I'll be here—

[*There is a knock on the door* L. KATE *breaks off with an exclamation of annoyance and then, wiping her hands on her apron, crosses to the door* L.]

KATE. Now I wonder who could that be, at this hour? [*She opens the door* L.] How do you do? [*Then she recognizes the figure.*] Denny! Oh, Mother of God, it's my boy come back! Denny, darling, come in!

[DENNY *enters* L *and stands just inside the doorway, a suitcase in his hand. He is a tall young Celt of about twenty-five, with a worn, nice grin. His suit is old and not too well pressed, and he carries a dark hat. He is followed by* ANNE. *She is a pretty, young girl of about twenty-three, with a worried look and manner. She wears a shabby suit and hat, which were originally of good cut and material, but are now plainly well worn.* ANNE *stands self-consciously in the doorway, unnoticed, while* DENNY *drops the suitcase above the door, sweeps* KATE *into his arms, and kisses her.*]

DENNY. Two years is a long time, isn't it, Mother?

KATE [*hugging* DENNY *roundly*]. With never a word nor a letter from you, you young scamp!

DENNY [*releasing* KATE, *holding her off, and grinning*]. But I'm back for a visit now—if you'll have me.

KATE [*indignantly*]. Have you? Don't talk so foolish, Denny!

DENNY. And, Mother—[*He turns to* ANNE.] this is Anne—[*There is pride in his voice.*] my wife.

ANNE [*putting out her hand timidly to* KATE *and stepping into the kitchen*]. How do you do, Mrs. Burke?

KATE [*startled at first, but now completely herself again, crossing warmly to* ANNE]. Come here 'til I look at you. And don't you be calling me "Mrs. Burke." Denny's wife is like one of my own. [*She kisses* ANNE *warmly and then stands back, her voice very gentle.*] You chose yourself a pretty wife, Denny, and I know I'll love her. [*Then, matter-of-factly*]. You must be tired out, the two of you, and it's that cold the wind would be to your bones. [*She puts her arm around* ANNE *and leads her to* C.]

[ANNE *and* DENNY *take off their wraps.* KATE *takes their wraps and goes out* D R, *returning immediately without them.* ANNE *sits gingerly right of the table* L C. *After a moment's hesitation,* DENNY *sits down in the rocking chair* R C. *He sighs as he relaxes, and his face is white and drawn.*]

ANNE. It's so beautifully warm here.

KATE [*crossing from* D R *to* C.]. It is that, with the fire going all day for the washing. Well, Denny, I don't know what I'm doing, I'm that excited. [*She stands* C, *gazing proudly at* DENNY.]

DENNY. I am, myself, Mother. It's been a long time.

KATE. It seems longer, Denny, when you're old.

DENNY. Listen to her, Anne! Old, with those eyes, and her hair still black as coal!

KATE [*with a pleasant shrug*]. It's all blarney. [*She crosses to the chair above the table* L C *and sits.*] Well now, I want to hear every little thing you've been doing. It's a queer feeling to be two weary years and not knowing what your own son's doing at all!

DENNY [*gently*]. I know, Mother. You see, I wouldn't write at first, and after a while, when I tried, I couldn't.

KATE. I understand.

DENNY. Mother, I'm sorry that I had to hurt you.

KATE [*lightly*]. Well now, if you hadn't, you wouldn't have met Anne, and I'm thinking I'd look a long way before I found a daughter-in-law I'd like better. [*She lays her hand gently on* ANNE'S *shoulder.*]

ANNE [*her face glowing*]. Oh, thank you!

KATE [*rises and crosses to* DENNY *and gently strokes his hair*]. Come, tell me about yourself. And don't tell me you're well. I've eyes on me, and you look peaked, Denny.

DENNY [*throwing his head back, smiling up at* KATE]. I'm all right. Just a little tired. Do you want me to begin at the very first?

KATE. Yes, Denny, I've wondered.

[KATE *remains standing behind* DENNY, *her one arm lovingly placed about his shoulders.* DENNY *looks straight ahead as he tells his story.*]

DENNY. Well, after—that night, I went to Boston as I'd intended to. The job was still open, and I took it. I liked it—every bit as much as I had known I would. I found a little boarding house where they had fairly good meals and comfortable beds, and settled down. I was a little lonely at first, of course, and then one day I met Anne.

[DENNY'S *eyes meet* ANNE'S *and the two young people smile bravely.*]

DENNY [*continuing*]. We saved up a little money and got married, and that's the best thing that happened to me while I was gone, for after that everything was fine. We got a little apartment and some secondhand furniture, and got along splendidly. Anne's a grand cook. And then—[*His face darkens and his voice drops low.*] that's all, I guess. [*He stares down at his feet.*]

[*There is a short pause.* ANNE *looks away.* KATE *looks at* DENNY *with shrewd, pitying eyes. Then, brightly, she breaks the silence.*]

KATE [*crossing C.*] Well, now, isn't that fine? A good job and a wife at your age. . . . .

By BETTY FITZGERALD

PRACTICE 1. Studying a Play

1. Read the selection from *The Master in the House*, a student-written one-act play.
2. How much of the story does this selection tell you? What part of your information did you receive from the speeches of Kate? Of Anne? Of Denny? From action?
3. Are the characters skilfully introduced? Prove your points.

CHARACTERS

As in the short story, the one-act play should have one principal character and a few minor ones, all true to life and individualized. Unlike the short-story writer, the playwright must make his characters reveal themselves entirely by what they say, what others say to them or about them, and how they act. Kate's kindliness to Anne, her gentleness and tact, her quick perception of Denny's true situation stamp her as a motherly, understanding woman.

DIALOGUE

Next to action, dialogue is the most important thing in the play. The speeches of the actors explain what has gone before, prepare for what is to follow, and reveal character. Make the sentences short, even clipped, like those of people in real life. Avoid cramming too much information into a speech; the audience will miss half you have to give, and your characters will seem stiff and unnatural. A fundamental rule many dramatists follow is, "One idea to the speech."

Although speeches in a one-act play cannot reproduce every word or phrase of daily life, they may be short, yet convincing, if you use specific and telling words and include only the necessary details. To avoid jerkiness, questions and comments by other characters serve as connecting links. Above all, every word that is uttered should seem so typical of the person who is speaking that no one else in the play could possibly have said it.

Beware of using dialect unless you are both thoroughly familiar with it and are also able to reproduce it so skilfully on paper that the actor will be able to interpret it convincingly. In *The Master in the House* the dialect, readily understandable, accurate, and consistently used, is a real asset.

DEVELOPMENT

As in the short story, development both of plot and character is by episode. Our selection from *The Master in the House* is the first two episodes. The first episode reveals to the audience the setting, and briefly, the character of Kate. Episode 2 is the arrival of Denny and Anne. We have a fine development of the character of Kate; we learn from the dialogue the story which has preceded the lifting of the curtain; and we have formed surmises of the future plot, rousing our interest and creating suspense.

SCENARIO

A scenario is a synopsis or outline of the play, the purpose of which is to clarify the whole play in the writer's own mind and to make the writer's wishes absolutely clear to the producer. First comes the cast of characters, each carefully described, then the time and place, the setting for the stage, the list of stage properties necessary, and finally a detailed explanation of the action by episodes, with a new episode every time a character enters or leaves. Unlike the play, the scenario may include description, narration, and characterization. A detailed plan of the action (entrances, exits, stage business) is also helpful. The completed scenario should be brief, clear, and well-proportioned, with stress on the important points of the story.

STAGE DIRECTIONS

Stage directions, as evidenced by *The Master in the House*, should be brief and concise, concerned chiefly with suggestions for the arrangement of the stage properties, the lighting, and the more important action. Properties should be simple, suggestive of time and place, and in keeping with the mood. Costumes should harmonize in style and be appropriate to the character. For the actor, the stage directions should be explicit and practical, concerned only with what cannot possibly be conveyed in the dialogue: with pantomime, tone of voice, expression, gestures.

MANUSCRIPT

In writing the final draft of your play, refer to *The Master in the House* as a guide for form. Notice that in the dialogue the names of the characters are written out, not abbreviated with initials. People are always referred to in the same way: Mrs. Burke as *Kate*, not *Mrs. Burke* at one time and *Kate* at another. Stage directions precede the speeches, are enclosed in parentheses, and are underlined to indicate italics in print.

PRACTICE 2. Dramatizing a Story

Select from your own reading some short story which has dramatic quality and dramatize it. Be careful in your selection to choose a plot which can be presented in one place—for your scene should not shift; and at one time, for there should be only one curtain. Before starting, write a scenario. Necessary previous actions can be covered by conversation.

PRACTICE 3. Writing a One-Act Play

1. Around an interesting incident based on personal experience, school life, a newspaper clipping, or a story you have heard, build a story suitable for a one-act play. What is the theme? Is it tragedy? Comedy? Melodrama?

What is the main incident? Who is the main character? What is the conflict behind the action?

Write a synopsis or scenario to clarify your ideas. Do you depend too much on dialogue? Are there long, awkward pauses while necessary action is going on?

Do your characters enter naturally? Be sure that your exposition of previous action is neither long nor involved. Is there an element of suspense in the development of the action? Does the end quickly follow the climax?

Make your characters real people. It is better to choose types you know (high school boys and girls, mothers, fathers, storekeepers, people of your community) than bizarre and fantastic personalities.

Take great pains with dialogue. Study the speech of people about you as a model for the speech of your characters.

Supply brief, pointed stage directions.

2. Write out the final draft of your play with careful attention to form.

Chapter 26

Public Speaking

I learned to speak as men learn to skate or cycle—by doggedly making a fool of myself until I got used to it.—George Bernard Shaw

Speaking, like writing, is largely a matter of habit. You can break the bad habit of fidgeting when you speak by (1) determining to break this habit, (2) practising standing still when you converse, answer questions in class, and make a speech, and (3) never allowing an exception, never making purposeless movements when speaking to one person or a group. Think how you learned a dance step or a stroke in tennis or swimming, and learn to speak by the same methods.

To make progress in speech you must practise at every opportunity. A person might make three or four speeches each year for forty years without noticeably improving. To acquire proficiency you need to speak at least two or three times each week. A few weeks of concentrated, purposeful speech work will accomplish more than years of scattered attempts.

PREPARING A SPEECH

Just as the passengers on a ship see only the one ninth of an iceberg which is above water, so the audience is aware of only a small part of the energy expended in preparing and delivering a speech. No matter how talented the speaker, a talk without adequate preparation is usually a failure.

WHAT IS YOUR PURPOSE?

Many speakers are like the man in the old song: "I don't know where I'm going but I'm on my way." To be a successful speaker, however, you must know why you are speaking and what you wish to accomplish by your speech. The five common purposes of speech are to entertain, to inform, to impress, to convince, and to move to action.

Do you, like a radio humourist or an after-dinner speaker, wish to entertain? Or, like a teacher, a manager, or a foreman, to make your ideas clear to beginners? Or, like a patriotic orator, to impress upon your hearers their duties in wartime? Or, like a debater, to convince the judges or the audience? Or, like a speaker selling war bonds or raising funds for the Red Cross or the Community Chest, to collect cash or secure subscriptions?

To speak without preparing is to shoot without taking aim. Decide what your aim is; then state it in a complete topic sentence; as, "My purpose is to convince the class that it should vote for the adoption of the honour system in the Long Branch High School." Make sure that your subject is definite and not too broad.

GATHERING MATERIAL

"Blessed is the man," says George Eliot, "who, having nothing to say, abstains from giving us wordy evidence of the fact." If one talks much and says little, he is set down as a bore. But where can you find material? Your school and city libraries, first of all, will furnish you with newspapers, magazines, and reference books. Never base a speech on just one newspaper, magazine, or book. Investigate several sources, select the best, combine the information, and make it your own. Search for facts rather than for opinions; learn to use the facts to draw your own conclusions.

Don't thoughtlessly seize every idea you happen upon. Think whether the idea is sound and, if so, whether it belongs in your speech. Notes on your reading are only raw materials for a speech; to them must be added your own experience, your imagination, your thinking. If you fail to digest and organize your material and deliver it in your own language, your speech will be a serving of "library hash".

Your materials should include not only notes on your reading but also thoughts and scraps of information gathered from other sources. A good speaker keeps his eyes and ears open and with them gathers a variety of firsthand material. Wherever he goes—to the movies, the theatre, on a shopping trip—he is prepared to shape his experience so that it will be useful. He recalls past experiences of his own and of his acquaintances. The result is a speech which can be definitely identified with the speaker himself.

OUTLINING

Outlining is nothing more than the association of ideas, showing the relationship of one part to the other parts and to the whole. Good outlining means good thinking; good thinking means good outlining. If you cannot outline a topic, you need more information on the subject and a better understanding of it. By learning the outline form and subjecting every speech you make to this rigid discipline, you will improve your thinking and make better speeches.

A first step is to find the main props supporting your contention or the big divison of the subject and to jot them down in logical order. This statement of main points may be very simple; as,

REASONS FOR VOTING FOR JAMES WILSON FOR PRESIDENT OF THE ATHLETIC ASSOCIATION

I. His scholarship
II. His executive ability
III. His athletic record

The next job is to arrange appropriate facts and examples under the main points. See pages 148-50 for an example of an outline.

DEVELOPING THE OUTLINE

An outline is only a skeleton. Undeveloped, it is to a speech as a skeleton is to an animal. Somehow you must get some meat on the bones. Do you know how to go about it? Do you know how to transform a topical outline into a fully developed speech? The following methods of development may solve your problem.

1. *Statements of authorities.* The leading men in any field are authorities on their subject. Use statements from them. Always give full credit.

2. *Statistics.* To make your speech more convincing, use statistics, facts, and figures. Choose your statistics carefully, check their accuracy, and they will stand like a stone wall.

3. *Examples.* Well-chosen examples are vital, interesting, and forceful. You can hardly cite too many, but be careful to select those that are strictly appropriate and have punch.

4. *Quotations.* Quotations include not only direct statements from authorities in a specialized field, but also gems of thought and emotion. Literature is rich in truth crystallized in a line or two. A great speaker invariably possesses wide literary knowledge on which he draws as from a treasure house. The Bible, Shakespeare, other poets, philosophers, and essayists can help you. "A dwarf," says Coleridge, "can see farther than a giant—if he stands on the giant's shoulders." Hoyt's *New Cyclopedia of Practical Quotations* and H. L. Mencken's *A New Dictionary of Quotations* are arranged alphabetically by subject.

5. *Analogies.* An analogy is an inference that two objects which are alike in some respects are alike in another particular. For example, to show the absurdity of electing magistrates from the Athenian Senate by lot, Socrates asked, "Would it be wise for sailors about to set out on a long and dangerous journey to cast lots among themselves to see who should be pilot?" The first paragraph on "Developing the Outline" includes an analogy. Analogies are useful in arousing interest and clarifying a subject. Use them sparingly, if at all, as proof of a point. False analogy is evidence of loose or dishonest thinking.

6. *Personal experiences.* You can speak with conviction because it has happened to you.

PRACTICE 1. Outlining and Delivering a Speech

Select a subject in which you are especially interested—for example, "A Hero of World War II" or "A Person Who Succeeded in Spite of a Handicap". List haphazardly all the points relating to it that pop into your head. Now organize these items in outline form. Be sure that your main headings are really main headings and include the points you place under them. Using at least three of the methods suggested, develop the outline into a good speech. In the margin of your outline, opposite the proper place, write the method of development used. When you deliver the speech, enunciate distinctly and pronounce every word correctly.

BEGINNING AND ENDING

Introduction. Before an audience the first ten seconds are important. A striking, sparkling beginning grips the audience; a pointless, weak beginning induces yawns. Notice the directness with which Franklin D. Roosevelt began one of his wartime broadcasts.

My friends: Yesterday, on June 4, 1944, Rome fell to American and Allied troops. The first of the Axis capitals is now in our hands. One up and two to go.

Besides suggesting the purpose of the speech your introduction may contain a brief history of the subject, a pointed anecdote, a striking illustration, a quotation, or a general statement to be illustrated.

Conclusion. A famous chef once remarked that, no matter how he had to economize on a banquet, he always tried to serve delicious coffee, for that is the taste diners go away with. Similarly your clincher or conclusion is the idea your audience go away with. Sum up forcefully, yet briefly, what you have tried to prove. If your purpose has been to persuade your listeners to act, repeat your appeal in a well-worded sentence. Then sit down.

USING NOTES

After completing the outline, think how the main topics are linked in thought and fix them in your mind so thoroughly that during your speech you will always know what point comes next. When delivering a prepared talk, have no notes unless you wish to use a long quotation, a number of quotations, or a set of statistics.

To memorize or not to memorize is an important question. Because the ordinary memorizer sounds like a reciter, not a speaker, it is better to talk a speech—that is, to speak extemporaneously with the exception perhaps of memorized opening and closing sentences. In later life the ability to speak extemporaneously is much more valuable than skill in reciting memorized speeches. An extemporaneous speech is prepared but the wording is not memorized. Impromptu speaking is offhand, unprepared.

PRACTISING YOUR SPEECH

After preparing the outline, deliver the speech several times to real or imaginary listeners. Parents, brothers, and sisters are a good audience for one or two deliveries and are usually frank and helpful critics. Talk to the cat or canary rather than just into the air. Don't try to fix the exact words. Each time you speak you make a path through your subject and thus become better acquainted with it. Adjust the length to the time assigned you. Listen to your voice, and watch for errors in enunciation and pronunciation grammar, sentence structure, and word choice.

Profit by the criticism of anyone who will listen to you. Watch your hearer to see whether he is actually interested in what you are saying. If he isn't, find the reason and try again.

PRACTICE 2. Speaking about Books

Prepare to speak on one of the following topics. For the book named, substitute a book you have recently read. If you like the book, make it so attractive that your classmates will read it. Use examples to prove your points. Hand in your outline. Speak distinctly and pronounce every word correctly.

1. An unusual setting in a book I read recently. 2. A book (or play) I'd like to write. 3. A novel that would make a good motion picture. 4. Comparison of a novel and the motion picture based on it. 5. What I like in John Buchan's *Prester John*. 6. What I disliked in George Eliot's *Silas Marner*. 7. What I liked about Peter Freuchen's *Adventures in the Arctic*. 8. Why Ernie Pyle's *Brave Men* is worth reading. 9. A review or criticism of J. F. Hayes' *Treason at York*. 10. Contrast in Charles Rann Kennedy's *The Servant in the House*. 11. The plot of James Hilton's *Lost Horizon*. 12. Why read biography? 13. A book I have recently enjoyed. 14. My favourite book. Why? 15. My favourite character in fiction. Why? 16. The value of novel reading. 17. Why study the drama? 18. A character sketch. 19. The best book of the year. 20. Books I have outgrown.

IMPROVING YOUR POSTURE

Stand easily with chest up, weight well forward, shoulders square, head erect, and chin at right angle to the throat. Relax your arms and hands. Avoid swaying from side to side, twitching the fingers, and other purposeless movements. Usually a speaker stands with the weight on the ball of one foot and with the other foot at a comfortable distance diagonally in front. In this position the weight foot may point straight to the front or be slanted out; the free foot is turned out. Don't jam your hands into your pockets or lean on a desk or a chair. Although it is permissible to put a hand in a pocket or let it rest lightly on a desk at the speaker's side, such a position should be the exception, not the habit. Don't stand regularly with your arms behind your back as if impersonating an armless statue.

Change position occasionally at the beginning of a paragraph. Stand still until you are ready to paragraph in this way. Make the change as you begin to speak the paragraph.

If you find that your hands don't "feel right" when you are talking to the class, or if you think they "look funny" hanging at your sides, stand in front of a large mirror at home and watch the effect of every position you assume and every movement you make while you rehearse a speech. Watch not only your hands but your whole body, including your hands, eyes, and facial expression. There are no short cuts to becoming a good speaker, but if you will take this exercise for half an hour two or three times each week, you will soon find yourself freed of the feeling of awkwardness and lack of ease. Look yourself over. That is the quickest, surest road to self-improvement.

COMMUNICATING YOUR IDEAS

To maintain good audience contact, face the audience squarely and look right into the eyes of your listeners, not at the ceiling, the floor, or the windows.

Talk to your hearers, not at them. Use the tone of conversation but speak slowly and especially distinctly if the audience is large. Adopt the style of speech you would use in an earnest and serious dialogue with someone at the other end of the table. Think every idea as you express it. If you think about it, your audience will also. Don't parrotlike recite a memorized speech.

Talk to various parts of the audience. Speak in turn to different individuals—one in the last seat at the right, another in the centre, and a third in the last seat at the left. From the expressions on the faces of these three discover whether they (1) hear you easily and (2) are interested.

SUGGESTIONS FOR OVERCOMING NERVOUSNESS

1. *Remember that nervousness before an audience is normal for beginners and is a good sign. It shows that you have a wholesome respect for your audience.*
2. *The cure for stage fright is repeated practice in speaking.*
3. *Choose a subject in which you are deeply interested.*
4. *Prepare your talk thoroughly. Knowing that you have something worth saying will give you confidence.*
5. *Practise your speech several times before your family and friends.*
6. *Take several deep breaths just as you go to face the audience.*
7. *Think of each member of the audience as a single person and a friend; don't be concerned about the group.*
8. *Speak slowly at first. Take deep breaths. Make sure that everybody hears your opening words but don't begin in a high-pitched voice.*
9. *Avoid such mannerisms as tensing your fingers in awkward positions, rubbing your hands together, playing with a bracelet, a lead pencil, or the buttons on your coat, and clearing your throat, for they advertise your nervousness and distract the attention of your listeners from what you are saying.*
10. *Concentrate on communicating your ideas to your audience. When you think about what you are saying and forget about yourself, you are not nervous.*
11. *Don't exaggerate the importance of the speech or the solemnity of the occasion. In a month's time you and your hearers will have forgotten all about it.*

12. *If your topic and the occasion permit, make your audience laugh at the beginning of your talk. When they laugh, you will relax. You don't have to be screamingly funny; most hearers respond gratifyingly even to mild humour or a witticism.*

USING A CONVERSATIONAL TONE

A good speaker makes each member of the audience feel that he is being talked to as in a private conversation. A conversational tone has the ring of truth and sincerity, and is worth working for. Here are two suggestions:

1. When speaking to a group, keep your mind on the thought you are expressing, rather than on the words.

2. Prepare to speak extemporaneously; don't memorize. **The conversational tone and the memorized speech are deadly enemies.**

ENUNCIATING DISTINCTLY

Good enunciation is a matter of using the tongue and the lips properly. Lazy lips and tongue produce slovenly sounds. Do you admire the speaker whose words leap from his mouth, each one sharp and clean-cut? It is hard work for us to improve our enunciation, but the will to succeed, with plenty of serious practice, will show results.

THE LANGUAGE OF SPEECH

If you do not grasp the ideas in an essay, you can re-read and study it until you understand it. A listener, on the other hand, can't go back.

The language of an effective speech, therefore, is simpler than that of an essay. Short, clipped sentences are easy to listen to and to absorb. More examples and illustrations are necessary. Comparisons and contrasts help to make the speech vivid. Pointed, appropriate, original figures of speech enliven it.

CONCISENESS

To talk much and say little is commonplace. To talk little and say much is genius. At Gettysburg, Edward Everett, the orator of the day, spoke for hours. His speech was soon forgotten. Lincoln spoke only a few minutes, but his *Gettysburg Address* is a masterpiece.

Boil down. Eliminate unnecessary words and repetitions. Avoid long sentences and complicated sentence structure. Gain sentence variety by the use of an occasional question, exclamation, or command.

Omit every unnecessary *well, why, and, but,* or *so.* Don't fill pauses with *ur's.* By pausing before conjunctions and prepositions, not after them, avoid *and-ur, but-ur, that-ur, to-ur.* The *ur* has been described as a whisker on the word and as a grunt. Professor Winans says, "Grunting is no part of thinking." Oliver Wendell Holmes says,

> And when you stick on conversation's burs,
> Don't strew your pathway with those dreadful *ur's.*

USING TRANSITIONAL EXPRESSIONS

Just as the bones of the body are joined by ligaments, so the sentences of a speech are held together by connective words and phrases. To avoid overworking a few connectives, study the list on pages 122-23. Use some of these words and phrases deliberately in your next speech as you prepare it. Don't substitute *well-ur, why, and,* and *so* for genuine transitional expressions. When you pause between ideas, shut off your voice.

PRACTICE 3. Making a Five-Minute Speech

Have you ever thought seriously about your own school, its problems, its good points and its weak spots, its courses of study, its activities? Perhaps there is something you have always wanted to praise or to defend; perhaps there is something you have always wanted to help to improve. Select a phase of your school for consideration in a speech of not more than five minutes. Be specific. Don't deal in generalities. Select an attractive and appropriate title. In a single sentence tell exactly what, in your five minutes, you propose to accomplish. Stick to this thesis throughout the speech. Apply the suggestions for organization and delivery learned so far. You might base your limited subject upon one of these broad topics:

1. Our library
2. Our music department
3. Cliques
4. The honour society
5. Sports
6. Dramatics
7. Recreation facilities
8. Conduct
9. Grades, tests, homework
10. The value of the work done in the classes
11. The school as preparation for earning a living
12. The school as preparation for college
13. The school as preparation for citizenship
14. Our student government
15. Tardiness and absence
16. Habitual failures
17. School parties
18. The cafeteria

HOLDING ATTENTION

A practical problem of the speaker is holding the attention of the audience. Because in every audience there are numerous distractions the speaker's task is not an easy one. For one the room is too hot; for another it is too cold; one girl's shoes hurt her; another drops her compact or handkerchief; somebody coughs; and a latecomer enters. The wise speaker foresees these distractions and plans to overcome them.

Illustrations and comparisons. Be concrete. Avoid glittering generalities and meaningless abstractions. Keep your hearers wide awake by a free use of *for instance, to illustrate,* and *for example.* Repeat and illustrate your idea until it sinks in but not until your hearers are bored.

If you use statistics, dramatize them. Put them into human terms. In talking about the future of aviation, for example, don't point out

Interest, Like Inattention, is Contagious

that Bombay is only 7875 air-line miles from Toronto. Instead, show that a Torontonian with only a week's vacation will be able to fly to India, visit the Taj Mahal, buy an Indian rug, and return home in time for work the following Monday.

Visual aids. Blackboard talks are popular because they help the audience see as well as hear the main points of the speech. Don't neglect the blackboard or other visual aids when giving an informational talk. Demonstrate if possible.

Variety. "No one," says William James, "can possibly attend continuously to an object that does not change." Because monotony puts an audience to sleep, have a variety of subject matter and vary your rate of speaking and the pitch and volume of your voice.

Enthusiasm. Interest, like inattention, is contagious. If you are enthusiastic about your subject, your classmates are likely to attend to what you say.

ON THE PLATFORM

1. When introduced, walk straight to a position well forward on the platform and pause momentarily to get your bearings.

2. When you rise or when you reach the front of the platform, recognize the chairman with "Mr. Chairman", a bow, or both.

3. Walk on the platform as you walk along the street. Avoid both the stride and the tiny step. When you are walking toward the audience, look at them, not at the floor as if searching for a stray dime.

4. Don't begin to speak at the very edge of the platform. If you do, it will be difficult to change position, and the audience will wonder whether you are likely to step off the edge.

5. Avoid haste in beginning to speak. Take a breath before speaking the first sentence.

6. If you use a salutation, say merely "Fellow Students", "Members of the Speech Club", or something similarly brief.

7. Speak slowly and distinctly enough for everyone to hear easily your opening words. Don't begin in a high-pitched, loud voice.

8. If you forget a point, keep looking at the audience and go on without it; don't break the link of sympathy and response established by eye contact.

9. Don't walk the platform as if impersonating a caged lion at feeding time.

10. Take time to impress your last sentence on the minds of your hearers. Don't say, "I thank you."

11. When you finish your talk, pause momentarily and then turn and walk back to your chair.

12. If other speakers follow you on the program, listen courteously. Don't imply by an inattentive manner that no one else will say anything worth hearing.

13. Practise correct posture and platform behaviour until the correct becomes habitual. Then, when you address an audience, you may forget these details, forget yourself, and centre attention on what

you have to say to the audience and their reception of the message. But you can't forget until you have first learned.

MAKING A SPEECH TO INFORM

Have you ever poured water out of a big jug with a small neck? Have you ever sympathized with or laughed at a person who blubbered like such a jug when he tried to tell you something? Many persons— most of us, in fact—are like a big jug with a small neck. Daily our minds are taking in information through all the senses. But what good is all this knowledge if we can't get it out? There is no one of us who does not daily need to give somebody information about something. Every one of us knows more about one thing than does the average person. It is important, therefore, for us to seize every opportunity to bring our ability to speak abreast of what we have to say.

Remember that your speech to inform will be judged, not by how much you tell your classmates, but by how many important facts or ideas they remember. Cold encyclopaedic facts without examples or illustrations arouse little interest and are quickly forgotten.

CHECK SHEETS FOR TALKS

1. Energy and enthusiasm
2. Posture and platform behaviour
3. Communicativeness or audience contact
4. Conversational tones, not recitation of a memorized speech
5. Adequate volume of voice without strain
6. Enunciation and pronunciation
7. Clear, correct, concise sentences
8. Effective timing
9. Variety of rate and force
10. Emphasis of important ideas
11. Beginning
12. Organization
13. Ending
14. Fluency
15. Avoidance of *ur*
16. Avoidance of useless *well, why, and, but,* and *so*
17. Examples and facts
18. Audience reaction—attention and interest

PRACTICE 4. Making a Speech to Inform

From among the things you know best, select one on which to talk to your class for two or three minutes. It may be something personal —a hobby, or a job you have held. Perhaps in school you have carried on an investigation that no other pupil has undertaken. Perhaps you have read an interesting, informative book. Perhaps you have a pet subject you always like to talk on. Choose something you know about, are interested in, and want others to know about. Remember that your single purpose is to inform. Turn in your outline for your teacher's criticism. Speak in sentences. Enunciate distinctly and pronounce every word correctly.

Group programs may be based on subjects studied in school. On a physics program, for example, pupils may speak on topics like these:

1. Link trainers
2. What frequency modulation means to radio
3. How a thermostat works
4. History of television
5. How lenses correct nearsightedness
6. Gasoline and Diesel engines
7. Uses of compressed air
8. How a boat sails into the wind
9. Why an airplane flies
10. Centigrade and Fahrenheit thermometers
11. The lie detector
12. Unusual effects of modern photography
13. Electricity on the farm
14. A laboratory experiment
15. The work of a great scientist
16. The use of blood tests of dairy animals
17. Science, the timesaver
18. The contribution to progress made by the electromagnet
19. Noise and musical sounds
20. Making aviation safer
21. How a camera takes a picture
22. Radar, its operation and use
23. Rockets or space travel
24. How sounds are made and carried

MAKING A SPEECH TO ENTERTAIN

Do you know what made Will Rogers the most loved comedian for many years? It was his ability to speak and write entertainingly. Certain of his secrets we know—that he was always himself, was never merely silly, drew constantly on his store of personal experience, never said anything mean, and flavoured all he said with his own personality. The ability to make an entertaining speech is like any other highly prized personal skill. If we acquire the ability, one of the roads to success in school and out is paved for us. The entertaining speech is always informal, subject to few rules. Organization is least important here, and what is said is perhaps less important than how it is said. Wit, originality, exaggeration, variety, and wholesome fun are at a premium. An entertaining speech does not, of course, have to be funny; it may be made on a serious subject, but it should be colourful and lively.

PRACTICE 5. Making a Speech to Entertain

Elect a master of ceremonies for the occasion, and let each one in the class be responsible for an informal talk of not over three minutes. The only purpose is to entertain. The one rule to follow is: Don't be merely silly! In a class discussion, talk over possible subjects.

One of the best subjects is "The Funniest Thing I Ever Saw." After a little discussion of this topic you will probably recall an incident that you will be bursting to tell. Rehearse your speech enough to tell it smoothly. The idea is to have a good time yourself and to give others a good time. Make your story funny by telling it seriously.

PERSUADING

Logical reasoning and substantial proof are ordinarily sufficient to convince your audience. Often, however, you may find it necessary to carry your audience one step farther, so that they will take action. Persuasion, by appealing to the emotions (loyalty, pride, fear, admiration, pity), transforms conviction into action.

The *United Appeal* each Christmas asks for contributions for the neediest cases in Toronto. Instead of giving statistics and generalities about the needy, it prints on successive days word pictures of these poor homes.

PRACTICE 6. Persuading other Students

Persuade your class to act on one of these matters. Enunciate distinctly, pronounce every word correctly, and use your best voice.

1. Your class has been asked to contribute to the Red Cross. The teacher has appointed you to take charge of the collection. Talk to the class.
2. Money is being collected to provide a party for wounded veterans at a near-by hospital. Urge pupils to contribute.
3. Around school you have seen some examples of bad manners. Urge pupils to be courteous and considerate of the rights of others.
4. Persuade your classmates to subscribe for the school publications. Convince them that the school newspaper and magazine are worth what they cost.
5. Prepare a "pep talk" to persuade every classmate to become a member of at least one club or team.
6. Your school has been asked to contribute to the nation-wide collection of books to be sent to Europe. Persuade your classmates to canvass their homes and neighbourhood. Make clear how, when, and where the collection will be made.
7. Your class has decided to study during the term one magazine and before voting will devote a period to discussion. Which magazine do you think best for class study? Why? Be specific and persuasive.

ANNOUNCEMENT

A good announcement is clear, complete, and persuasive. In

announcing a game include the place, the opposing team, the day, the hour, and the price of tickets, and, if the game is being played away from home, directions for reaching the field. In an appeal for a large attendance make the game or entertainment so attractive that pupils will not want to miss it; don't overwork the appeal to school spirit.

PRACTICE 7. Making an Announcement

Announce to your class one of the following. Include an appeal for a large attendance or for a large number of entrants.

a game	an exhibit	an entertainment
a debate	a play	a new club
an open meeting of a club	a concert	a field day
a contest	an excursion	another school event

NOMINATING SPEECH

A speech of nomination commonly includes these points:

1. The kind of boy or girl needed to fill the office.

2. The name of the candidate.

3. His record, qualities of character, and abilities—to speak and manage, for example.

4. His platform or the improvements he can be expected to make.

Although the name is often held till the end of the speech, it is better to mention it earlier unless everybody knows who is being nominated.

PRACTICE 8. Nominating, Presenting, or Accepting

1. Nominate a candidate for a school, a class, a club, a town, or a city office.

2. Present or accept a gift, a medal, a trophy, or a banner—for example, a baseball championship trophy, a birthday gift, or a gift to the retiring president of a society.

RADIO SPEECH

A radio or television address differs from other talks in that the audience, invisible to the speaker, consists mostly of family groups seated comfortably in their own homes. The speaker therefore has to compete with many possible distractions—the evening paper, family conversation, a visitor. The moment the speaker becomes uninteresting, the relentless hand of Mother or Jimmy will reach out and twirl the dial. Also, because his time is allotted to the fraction of a second, the average radio speaker must write out his talk and read it before the microphone.

To secure the immediate interest of the audience, radio or television speakers often begin with a question, story, or problem common to many people. Quiet humour helps to hold the attention of the invisible audience; but flippancy, overfamiliarity, and cheap wisecracks bore or annoy the average listener. Short, crisp sentences, vividly worded, are preferable to long, involved ones that lead the hearer into a mental labyrinth. "The essential rules for radio speaking," says Frank Dunham, "are: (1) have something to say and say it in a few words; (2) speak so as to be understood; (3) create a feeling of being *en rapport* or at ease with your audience." The same rules apply to television.

Think of your audience not as a mass of thousands of people but as a small family group. Then you will achieve the vivid conversational quality so necessary to holding attention. Don't imitate some famous radio personality. Tricks are unnecessary. Simply work hard at achieving good voice quality.

Pitch should be low but natural; don't try to make over your voice for radio. *Volume* should be fairly uniform; it is unnecessary to shout for emphasis. Keep a conversational tone, but be sure to sustain normal volume even on the very last word of every sentence. *Pause, stress,* and *inflection* are your best methods of obtaining variety, emphasis, and interest, of reflecting your mood and personality. Many famous news commentators mark on their manuscripts every pause, every emphasized word, every rise and fall of the voice which they find effective in rehearsal. Naturally, distinct *enunciation* is important. Don't, however, make your speech overprecise just for air delivery. Speak distinctly but naturally. And of course check the pronunciation of difficult words before you go on the air. One mispronounced word often brings two hundred letters of protest to the broadcasting company.

Although the radio audience can't see you, good posture is important for poise and relaxed breathing. Stand or sit erect about a foot and a half in front of the microphone. Hold your script slightly above eye level and a little to one side of the microphone. That will keep your chin up and direct your voice outward, not down. As you finish reading from each sheet of paper, slip it behind the others. Never rattle papers in front of the microphone. If necessary, mount each sheet on a piece of cardboard.

TELEVISION APPEARANCE

Many devices are used to make it convenient to speak into the television microphone, for the speaker is within sight, as he is in platform speaking. The producer of the program may hang a small microphone round the speaker's neck; he may seat the speaker where his manuscript, if he is using one, may be partially concealed by some object of furniture, or by lying flat on the speaker's knee, or whatever is most easily arranged. Try to accommodate yourself to the desires and advice of the producer.

PRACTICE 9. Rehearsing a Radio or Television Speech

Imagine that you have been asked to broadcast on one of the following topics. Rehearse your speech in class. Enunciate distinctly, pronounce every word correctly, and use your best voice.

1. Scholarship and the part-time job. 2. The radio (or motion picture) in education. 3. The student court. 4. Why I like the agricultural (or another) course. 5. High school education for rural districts. 6. Project work in vocational agriculture. 7. Health education in the high schools. 8. The importance of vocabulary enrichment. 9. Educational hobbies. 10. Educational vacations. 11. Getting the most out of high school. 12. Why complete the high school course? 13. Working in the vocational agricultural shop. 14. Place of social life in high school. 15. Student government. 16. Why study history (or another subject)?

PRACTICE 10. Comparing Radio or Television Speakers

Compare two speakers you have recently heard over the radio. Which is the better speaker? In what respects is he more effective?

Mastering Effective English

HANDBOOK

When in doubt consult your Handbook

A. Grammar and Usage

B. Punctuation

C. Mechanics

D. Spelling

E. Poetry

F. The Library

G. Parliamentary Practice

Grammar and Usage

A. Parts of the Sentence

Can you always recognize the subject, predicate, and other parts of the sentence? The diagnostic test will help you to answer this question.

TEST 1A (*Diagnostic*). PARTS OF THE SIMPLE SENTENCE

Copy the italicized words in a column and number them 1 to 26. Then, using the abbreviations given below, indicate the use in the sentence of each word. Write the abbreviations in a column to the right of the words.

s.s.—simple subject	*o.p.*—object of preposition
v.—verb	*i.o.*—indirect object
p.a.—predicate adjective	*ap.*—appositive
p.n.—predicate nominative	*n.a.*—nominative of address
d.o.—direct object	*a.o.*—adverbial objective
o.p.a.—objective predicate adjective	*o.p.n.*—objective predicate noun

1. Samuel de Champlain, *founder* of Quebec, was a *native* of France.
2. That *afternoon* the Village of the Turtle and the Shark lay very still and *clean* in the hot sun.
3. The blue *eyes* of the okapi in the zoo were mild and *content*.
4. The wife of Mr. McNamara, the cab *driver*, gave *me* a piece of griddle bread with currants in *it*.
5. In the morning the gypsies strung *beads* around the *neck* of the donkey and *tied* her tail with a bright red ribbon a *yard* long.
6. *Beatrice*, what *kind* of fruit do *you like* best?
7. The next *morning* the *servants* brought *Henry* a *breakfast* of goat's milk and black *bread*.
8. Viscount Alexander of Tunis, a famous soldier, was *made Governor-General* of Canada.
9. The lightning struck him dead.
10. They made him chairman.

SUBJECT, PREDICATE, AND MODIFIER

1. A sentence is a group of words expressing a complete thought.

The Jersey cow is rated high by dairymen.

2. The predicate verb makes a statement, asks a question, or gives a command.

STATEMENT A primitive type of wheat *was grown* in the Stone Age by the "Lake Dwellers" of Switzerland.

QUESTION What *is* the normal temperature of the healthy human body?

COMMAND *Bring* me *These Men Shall Never Die* from the library.

3. The simple subject names the person, place, or thing spoken of. The simple subject answers the question "Who?" or "What?" before the verb.

Where does your *community* get its water supply? (*Community* answers the question "Who does get?")

From the top of the blockhouse came a single *shot*. (*Shot* answers the question "What came?")

4. The complete subject is the simple subject with its modifiers.

A small black turtle clung lovingly to the lobe of Sam's left ear.

5. A modifier is a word or an expression which changes the meaning of the word to which it is attached.

Lois arranges dahlias *skilfully*. (*Arranges skilfully* means something different from *arranges; skilfully* modifies *arranges.*)

He *who hesitates* is lost. (This sentence means something different from "He is lost." *Who hestitates* modifies *he.*)

6. The complete predicate is the predicate verb with its modifiers and the words that complete its meaning. Words which complete the meaning of a verb are "completers" or "complements."

A ribbon | is worn on the service uniform in place of a medal. (The vertical line separates the complete subject from the complete predicate. The simple subject is underscored once and the predicate verb, twice.)

Captain Robert S. Johnson, the famous World War II ace, | made his first solo flight at the age of fourteen.

7. When the complete predicate or part of it is before the subject, the order is inverted.

INVERTED ORDER From the direction of the main highway came the sound of footsteps on crisp sycamore leaves.

NATURAL ORDER The sound of footsteps on crisp sycamore leaves | came from the direction of the main highway.

When *there* introduces an inverted sentence, it is called an "expletive" or "introductory adverb". It is never the subject.

There are lakes of asphalt in the West Indies. (The simple subject is *lakes*. It answers the question "What are?")
Lakes of asphalt | are in the West Indies.

8. A simple sentence has one subject and one predicate, either or both of which may be compound.

COMPOUND SUBJECT   The quality and quantity of a harvested crop | depend to a large extent upon the proper timing of the harvest.

COMPOUND PREDICATE   A searchlight beam | dipped from the sky and swept across the bay.

COMPOUND SUBJECT AND COMPOUND PREDICATE   Big three-place torpedo planes and tiny, stubby fighters | roared away from the field in groups and headed for the carrier.

PRACTICE 1. Underlining Subjects and Verbs

Copy the following sentences, arranging inverted sentences in the natural order. Then draw one line under the simple subject and two lines under the predicate verb. With a vertical line separate the complete subject from the complete predicate.

Examples:

a. Articulate every word distinctly. (The subject *you* is understood.)
(You) | Articulate every word distinctly.

b. In the days of the pioneer most industries were carried on in the home.
Most industries | were carried on in the home in the days of the pioneer.

A. 1. Josiah Wedgwood was the son of an English potter.
   2. At fourteen the boy was molding clay in his brother's workshop.
   3. In 1759 he formed a partnership with Thomas Wheildon.
   4. Before long the young man produced a beautiful cream-coloured earthenware.
   5. Never before had Queen Charlotte of England seen such exquisite china.

B. 1. The fame of the young British potter spread throughout Europe.
   2. From the Empress of Russia came an offer of fifteen thousand dollars for a service of the new china.
   3. In later years Wedgwood produced matchless vases, tablets, and cameos of jasper.
   4. Have you seen in museums specimens of his art?
   5. Look for examples of Wedgwood china in the homes of your friends.

THE PARTS OF SPEECH

9. A noun is a name.   Nouns name:

a. Persons, animals, places, things—*Ernie Pyle, lion, Toronto, tractor.*

b. Collections or groups of persons or things—*army, Parliament, team, club, audience, crowd, platoon, fleet.*

c. Qualities, conditions, actions, and ideas—*ambition, perseverance, happiness, beauty, wealth, mercy, time, length.*

10. A pronoun is a word used instead of a noun.

That is the girl about *whom I* wrote *you.*

11. A substantive is a noun or pronoun, or another part of speech or a word group used as a noun.   The word group may be any kind of phrase or clause used in place of a noun.

Only the *brave* deserve the *fair.*
Seeing is *believing.*
As a girl Amelia Earhart liked *to play baseball.*
Captain Taylor told us *that soldiers like to receive automatic pencils, wrist watches, pocket-size books, pocket flashlights, and small toilet kits.*

12. Words which make statements about persons, places, or things, ask questions, or give commands are verbs.   Three forms of the verb—the infinitive, the participle, and the verbal noun (gerund)— do not make statements, ask questions, or give commands.

STATEMENT   The captain *told* my brother about his promotion.
QUESTION   Who *told* you that ridiculous story?
COMMAND   *Tell* Gwen to come to the block party tonight.

An auxiliary helps a verb to make a statement, ask a question, or give a command.

For some time the *Hispaniola* had been sailing easily before the wind along the coast of Treasure Island. (*Had* and *been* are auxiliaries.)

The auxiliaries are: *is, be, am, are, was, were, been, has, have, had, do, does, did, may, can, might, could, must, shall, will, should,* and *would.*

13. An adjective is a word that modifies or describes a noun or pronoun. An adjective usually answers one of these questions: "Which?" "What kind of?" "How many?"

> *The narrow little* streets shone with *the copper* light from *a hundred petrol* torches.

14. An adverb is a word that modifies a verb, an adjective, or an adverb. Adverbs commonly answer the questions "When?" "Where?" "How?" and "How much?"

> Speedy, carrier-based fighter planes zoomed almost continually overhead. The adverbs *continually* and *overhead* modify *zoomed;* the adverb *almost* modifies the adverb *continually.*

15. A preposition is a word used to show the relation of a substantive to another word.

> The wealthy planters *along* the banks *of* the river lived almost *like* feudal lords. (*Along* shows the relation between *banks* and *planters; of,* between *river* and *banks; like,* between *lords* and *lived.*)

a. The substantive following a preposition is its object.

> On the *fields* of *Ecuador* in the high *mountains* the harvest season comes in *May.*

b. A preposition and its object, with or without modifiers, is called a prepositional phrase.

> The first Distinguished Service Cross (of World War II) was awarded posthumously (to Captain Colin P. Kelly) (for action) (in the Philippines). (Each prepositional phrase is enclosed in parentheses.)

PRACTICE 2. Recognizing Parts of Speech

Copy the following sentences, leaving a blank line after each line you write. Underscore the simple subject once and the predicate verb twice. Write *adj.* over every adjective and *adv.* over every adverb. Enclose prepositional phrases in parentheses.

A. 1. The tiny, blue-eyed kitten mewed pitifully.
2. The draftees were quickly assigned to barracks.
3. The entire bow of the huge carrier was enveloped in flames.
4. The age of sheep is estimated by the appearance of their teeth.
5. For the twentieth time Lieut. Bulkeley looked anxiously at his watch.

B. 1. Planes are sometimes launched from the decks of carriers by catapults.
   2. The purchase of an ice-cream machine is recorded in an expense ledger of George Washington's. (*Ice-cream* is one modifier.)
   3. Rocket guns are of comparatively recent origin.
   4. Helmeted soldiers careened along the beach in speedy jeeps.
   5. Amid the brilliance of the field floodlights a big Douglas transport was settling down gently on the paved runway.

16. A conjunction connects words or groups of words.

After I wash *and* dry the dishes, I'll knit an inch *or* two more on my sweater. *When* a succession of different crops is grown upon the same soil, it is said *that* crop rotation is being practised.

Conjunctions used in pairs are called correlatives: *both, and*; *either, or*; *neither, nor*; *not only, but also*.

Neither Dr. Watson *nor* Mrs. Hudson suspected Sherlock Holmes's ruse.

17. An interjection is a word or form of speech that expresses strong or sudden feeling.

Hurrah! We've found the cave!
Oh, what a delightful spot this is!

18. To find the part of speech of a word, always ask yourself the question, "What does the word do in the sentence?" Some words may be used as a number of different parts of speech.

ADJECTIVE   *That* package is not for you. (*That* modifies the noun *package*.)
PRONOUN   *That* won't make any difference to Sybil. (*That* is used in place of a noun.)
CONJUNCTION   Didn't Edward notice *that* Mother looked tired? (*That* connects *Mother looked tired* with *did notice*.)
ADVERB   *Out* flew the packages in the back of the sled. (*Out* modifies the verb *flew*.)
PREPOSITION   Without a word Oku Hung waddled solemnly *out* the door. (*Out* joins its object *door* to the verb *waddled*.)

PRACTICE 3. Using a Word as Different Parts of Speech

Write sentences in which you use each of the following words as the different parts of speech named after it.

A. 1. *what*—pronoun, adjective, interjection
   2. *near*—verb, preposition, adverb
   3. *wrong*—noun, verb, adjective
   4. *off*—adverb, preposition

     5. *since*—preposition, conjunction, adverb

     6. *free*—adjective, verb, noun

B. 1. *until*—preposition, conjunction

     2. *patrol*—noun, verb, adjective

     3. *slow*—adjective, adverb, verb

     4. *after*—preposition, conjunction, adverb

     5. *like*—verb, noun, preposition

     6. *while*—noun, verb, conjunction

PRACTICE 4. Parts of Speech

Copy the following sentences, leaving a blank line after each line you write. Then, using the following abbreviations, show what part of speech each word is. Write the abbreviation above the word.

n.—noun	*adv.*—adverb	*prep.*—preposition
pron.—pronoun	*v.*—verb	*conj.*—conjunction
adj.—adjective		

A. 1. In population, Mexico, a land of warm colour and charm, ranks second among the Latin American countries.

     2. At the time of the Spanish conquest in the sixteenth century the Indians of Mexico had a unique civilization.

     3. They devised several kinds of calendars, studied the stars, the sun, and the moon, and produced art and architecture of high quality.

     4. On the peninsula of Yucatan a great pyramid, where religious ceremonies were performed, still stands.

     5. Near by is the Sacred Well, in which beautiful maidens were sacrificed to the angry gods.

B. 1. Under Spanish rule Mexico was exploited until Father Hidalgo, a noble priest, led the people in a revolution.

     2. Although the Spaniards captured Father Hidalgo and shot him, his followers carried on the fight and won the independence of their country. (*Their* may be called an adjective or a pronoun.)

     3. After years of bitter internal strife Benito Juarez became president and worked unceasingly for education and the equitable distribution of land.

     4. Although most of the people are still quite poor, within recent years social and economic conditions have improved.

     5. Mexicans are artistic, courteous, and intelligent, with sensitive dignity and a great love for their land.

OTHER IMPORTANT PARTS OF THE SIMPLE SENTENCE

Every sentence has a subject word and a predicate verb, as a backbone to which modifiers are attached. A sentence may have also as part of this backbone a complement or completer of the verb. Four kinds of completers are **the predicate adjective, the predicate nominative, the direct object,** and **the indirect object.**

19. A predicate adjective completes the predicate and describes the subject.

> The meadows were *gay* with buttercups and bluebells.
> The constable was desperately *weary* from lack of sleep.

20. A predicate nominative is a substantive that completes the predicate and explains or renames the subject. The predicate nominative, except with a negative, denotes the same person, place, or thing as the subject.

> The most common trophy of the Pacific War is the Japanese personal battle *flag*. (trophy = flag)
> The lemming is a roly-poly little *mouse* with a furry stump of a tail. (lemming = mouse)

21. A direct object is a substantive that completes the predicate and names the receiver or the product of the action. If the subject acts, the noun or pronoun which answers the question "What?" or "Whom?" after the verb is the direct object of the verb.

> On the rocks just above the line of full tide Edward found the baby *seal*. (*Seal* answers the question "Found what?")
> Red Cross dogs found the wounded *men* for the stretcher-bearers. (*Men* answers the question "Found whom?")

a. A verb that has a direct object is transitive active.

> At 0700 on Tuesday the lookout *sighted* land.

b. If the subject is acted upon, the verb is transitive passive.

> At 0700 on Tuesday land *was sighted* by the lookout.

c. All other verbs are intransitive. Many verbs may be used both transitively and intransitively.

> All Tuesday night our ship *plowed* uneventfully through the waves of the Atlantic. (*Plowed* is intransitive.)
> Our ship *plowed* a path through the waves. (*Plowed* is transitive.)

22. An indirect object is a noun or pronoun that tells to or for whom something is done. An indirect object is regularly followed by a direct object.

> Bolton gave the little *seal* a breakfast of warm milk and bread crumbs. (*Seal* answers the question "Gave to whom?")
> From Montreal an old friend of my father sent my *sister* and *me* a set of brushes and a box of paints. (*Sister* and *me* answers question "Sent to whom?")

23. An adverbial objective is a noun used like an adverb.

The Indians of Peru generally work six *days* of the week and shop on
Sunday. (*Days* answers the question "How much?")

That *night* little Daniel rolled up in a bearskin and slept by the fireplace.
(*Night* answers the question "When?")

In the desert a plane on the ground is invisible thirty or forty *feet* away.

Charles Dickens often walked ten or fifteen miles at a time. (*Miles*, the
adverbial objective, is a noun used like an adverb to modify the verb
walked.)

**24. An appositive is added to a noun or pronoun to explain it and
denotes the same person or thing.**

**Mr. Fields, a chef at the Hotel Commodore, won the tennis
championship.**

Jon, the cabin *boy*, was well liked by the officers, crew, and passengers of
the freighter. (Jon = boy)

An appositive and a predicate nominative are similar. The difference is that a verb connects the subject and the predicate nominative,
while an appositive follows a word directly and is generally set off by
commas.

25. A nominative of address is the name of the person spoken to.

Ring for more speed, Lieutenant Barston.

**26. A nominative absolute with a participle expressed or under-
stood has the force of an adverb modifier, but has no grammatical
connection with the rest of the sentence.**

Its *head* held up like a little periscope, a water snake slipped across the creek.

The candles were scattered about the room, two tall white *ones* standing on the chimney piece.

PRACTICE 5. Recognizing the Parts of the Simple Sentence

Find the subject words, verbs, predicate adjectives, predicate nominatives, direct objects, indirect objects, adverbial objectives, appositives, and nominatives of address.

A. 1. Officer Brady, give me your report.
  2. The freshman girls on the winning team were Kathleen and I.
  3. Hydrogen is the lightest of all substances.
  4. For vitamins the soldiers in the desert drink quantities of lime juice.
  5. Frank Buck, the big game hunter, is a friend of birds.
  6. Carlsbad Caverns are one thousand feet deep.

B. 1. By mistake my brother sent my cousin and me two miles out of the way.
  2. During the Middle Ages barley was the most important bread grain of Central Europe.
  3. The Quartermaster Corps has trained thousands of carefully selected dogs for various jobs in the Army.
  4. In World War I, Major General Ernest Swinton, a retired British officer, invented the tank.
  5. Read me the last line of that paragraph about the use of camouflage, Alfred.
  6. In airplane vernacular the ceiling is the distance between the ground and the base of a cloud layer.

PRACTICE 6. Recognizing the Parts of the Sentence

Copy the subject and the verb of each sentence. Copy also the italicized words, leaving a blank line after each line you write, and write above each word *p.a.* (predicate adjective), *p.n.* (predicate nominative), *d.o.* (direct object), *o.p.* (object of preposition), *i.o.* (indirect object), *ap.* (appositive), or *a.o.* (adverbial objective).

A. 1. Selma Lagerlöf, the famous *author*, was the *daughter* of a Swedish *soldier*.
  2. During her *childhood* she became seriously *ill* and could not walk for many *years*.
  3. For consolation the little girl, an eager *student*, turned to books of poetry and *prose*.
  4. Sometimes she wrote *plays* for her own *amusement*.

5. One *day* Selma made a great *decision*.

6. She would be a *teacher*.

7. With *difficulty* Lieutenant Lagerlöf and his wife scraped together the *money* for her *education*.

8. Ten *years* later Selma was a capable young *teacher* in an elementary *school*.

9. She was *happy* in her work and for a long while had written *nothing*.

B. 1. Then one day she saw the *announcement* of a contest for *writers*.

2. In her childhood Lieutenant Lagerlöf had told *Selma* weird *tales* of the deeds of Gosta Berling, a Scandinavian *hero*.

3. Now Selma wrote down the stories from *memory* and entered *them* in the *contest*.

4. To her great *amazement* the judges gave *her* the *prize*.

5. Soon Brandes, a famous Danish *scholar*, was singing the *praises* of Gosta Berling.

6. The book, in his *opinion*, was a *masterpiece*.

7. Overnight Selma Lagerlöf became *famous*.

8. People journeyed many *miles* for a glimpse of the young *author*.

9. In 1909 the Nobel prize for literature, a *gift* of $40,000, was presented to *her*.

TEST 1B (*Mastery*). PARTS OF THE SIMPLE SENTENCE

Median 16.8

Copy the italicized words in a column and number them 1 to 26. Then, using these abbreviations, indicate the use in the sentence of each word. Write the abbreviations in a column to the right of the words.

s.s.—simple subject	*o.p.*—object of preposition
v.—verb	*i.o.*—indirect object
p.a.—predicate adjective	*ap.*—appositive
p.n.—predicate nominative	*n.a.*—nominative of address
d.o.—direct object	*a.o.*—adverbial objective
o.p.n.—objective predicate noun	*o.p.a.*—objective predicate adjective

1. The next *day* Sally, a little black and tan *puppy*, became a *member* of Aunt Ida's *household*.

2. Is that old *man* a *relative* of *yours*, *Bob?*

3. A few *hours* later Elizabeth Ann was *feeling* small and *lonely* and just a little *homesick*.

4. For Christmas, Grandmother gave *Helen* a little silk *bag* with four shiny new *quarters*.

5. The Indians adopted the *captive* as a member of their tribe and *taught him* all their customs.

6. Dash, the seasoned *actor*, took his *cue* with a friendly yip.

7. The chief *source* of radium is *pitchblende*, a shiny black *rock*.
8. Were the *children* of colonial parents *helpful* around the home?
9. Mary was elected *president*.

PARTICIPLE, VERBAL NOUN, AND INFINITIVE

   27. Verbals are forms of the verb that do not make statements, ask questions, or give commands. Verbals are used as adjectives, adverbs, and nouns. Like verbs that say, ask, and command, verbals take objects and predicate nominatives and are modified by adverbs. The three classes of verbals are **participles, verbal nouns** (or **gerunds**), and **infinitives.**

   28. A participle is a form of the verb that is used as an adjective. It is *part* adjective and *part* verb. Many participles end in *ing* and *ed.*

> *Perched* upon a high boulder at the edge of a *melting* snowbank, Oreos, the mountain goat, lazily chewed his cud. (*Melting* immediately precedes the noun modified and may be called a participle or an adjective.)
>
> *Shifting* grenades from one pocket to another, the men twisted and turned in the *crowded* barges. (As an adjective the participle *shifting* modifies *men;* as a verb it has a direct object, *grenades. Crowded* is an adjective.)

PRACTICE 7. Telling the Use of Participles

   Copy every participle and explain its use in the sentence.

A. 1. Standing in the rear cockpit, Sandy adjusted his goggles.
   2. The speedboats circled the island, towing the amateur water skiers.
   3. The first subway, invented by Alfred Beach, was opened in New York City in 1870.
   4. Stroking at a lively pace, the college crew pulled ahead.

B. 1. Led by the guide, the boys soon found their camp.
   2. Along the crowded beach were lying the soldiers in grotesque positions.
   3. The porcupine goes placidly through life, sometimes dawdling for a whole day in a tree with delicious-tasting bark.
   4. Reluctantly leaving their banquet hall, the porcupines waddled off up the beach.

   29. A verbal noun (gerund) is an *ing* **form of the verb that is used as a noun.**

OBJECT OF PREPOSITION   After *sipping* fragrant tea from little bowls, we went into a large courtyard.

SUBJECT   *Hunting* for butterfly and moth eggs is a fascinating pastime in spring and summer.

DIRECT OBJECT   Patricia enjoys *keeping* house.

PREDICATE NOMINATIVE An important industry of Australia is *raising* sheep.

APPOSITIVE My favourite exercise, *walking* through the woods, is particularly enjoyable in the autumn.

> *Grazing* with livestock is a cheap and effective way of *harvesting* pasture and forage crops.
>
> The verbal noun *grazing* is the subject of the verb *is*. As a noun the verbal noun *harvesting* is used as the object of the preposition *of;* as a verb it has a direct object, *crops.*

PRACTICE 8. Explaining the Use of Verbal Nouns

Copy every verbal noun and explain its use in the sentence.

A. 1. Clyde enjoys playing golf.
   2. Fishing by torchlight was once a popular sport in Hawaii.
   3. The minimum cost of training a bomber crew is forty thousand dollars. (*Forty thousand* is one modifier.)
   4. His new hobby, building model planes, is one shared by many high school boys. (*High school* is one modifier.)

B. 1. Men in the Air Force often wear fur-lined jackets or electrically heated suits for flying at high altitudes.
   2. Part of the fun of photography is developing your own negatives.
   3. Much of the success in growing crops depends upon preparing the seed bed and planting the seed.
   4. Aerial navigation is the science of piloting a plane from one point to another and establishing its position at any time.

30. An infinite is a verb form ordinarily introduced by *to* and used as a noun, an adjective, or an adverb.

ADJECTIVE The radioman, with headphones clapped to his ears, sat listening for orders *to proceed.* (*To proceed* modifies *orders.*)

ADVERB Hamlin Garland once set out *to look* for gold in Alaska. (*To look* modifies *set.*)

NOUN *To help* a ship in distress is the first rule of the sea. (Subject of verb.)

NOUN Winnie-the-Pooh sat down at the foot of the tree, put his head between his paws, and began *to think.* (Direct object of verb.)

NOUN Part of Hamlin Garland's job was *to keep* the water jug cool and well filled. (Predicate nominative.)

1. Crop rotation helps to control weeds and plant diseases.
   The infinitive phrase, *to control weeds and plant diseases,* is the direct object of the verb *helps.*
2. Planes from a near-by airfield occasionally swooped down to practise a dive against a ship.
   The infinitive phrase, *to practise a dive against a ship,* is used as an adverb **to** modify the verb *swooped.*

To, the sign of the infinitive, is commonly omitted after *bid, dare, need, see, make, let, hear, please, feel, help,* and sometimes after a few other verbs.

After a while Serge saw an old woman *stop* in front of his window.

PRACTICE 9. Explaining the Use of Infinitives

Copy every infinitive and explain its use in the sentence.

A. 1. To graduate with distinction was the main ambition of my sister.
   2. A determination to graduate *magna cum laude* was my sister's chief ambition.
   3. Her plan was to enter the University of Toronto.
   4. From the time she was sixteen she began to prepare herself.

B. 1. Edison tried to send a message by train whistle.
   2. Using a parachute to screen the fire on the side toward the sea, the aviators flashed signals in Morse code.
   3. The only way to save the puppies was to put them in the canoe.
   4. Before we left camp several of the boys were equipped with extra rations to use in bringing back the prisoners.

31. After verbs of *making, telling, letting, wishing, expecting, thinking, knowing, commanding, believing,* **and the like, the infinitive has a subject.**

We know *him* to be the culprit.

PRACTICE 10. Recognizing Verbals

Copy every participle, verbal noun, and infinitive in the following sentences. Draw one line under a <u>participle</u>, two lines under a <u>verbal noun</u>, and a dotted line under an <u>infinitive</u>. Copy the whole participle or verbal noun, whether it is one, two, or three words. Include the sign *to* of the infinitive if it is expressed.

A. 1. Pulling out of the dive, the pilot spotted the landing strip. (*Out of* is a preposition.)
   2. The breakers took infinite delight in tossing us against the black rocks along the coast.
   3. The half-back, having intercepted the pass, was set upon by the left line-backer.
   4. The cheer section, filled with enthusiasm, made a fruitless attempt to save the day.
   5. The ship was travelling at full speed, making every possible attempt to evade the attacking plane.

6. A profitable trade carried on in colonial days by travelling workers **was** making candles.

B. 1. Entertaining children by telling them stories was a favourite pastime of Lewis Carroll.

2. Horses tied at hitching posts along the street reared wildly to get free.

3. The teacher in charge came out, trying his best to rally the flagging team.

4. Picking huckleberries was a good excuse for wearing worn-out clothes.

5. In hand-to-hand fighting the U.S. Marines shoved back the Japanese soldiers through jungles infested with snakes and cannibals.

6. The Western cowboys show great skill in handling the lasso for roping cattle.

32. A phrase is a group of related words which does not contain a subject and a predicate. Phrases may be used as noun, adjectives, or adverbs.

At an early age (adverb) an Indian boy learned *to follow the trails* (noun) *of men and beasts* (adjective).

a. A participial phrase consists of a participle and the words which modify it or complete its meaning.

The children watched the seals *swimming happily about.*

b. An infinitive phrase consists of an infinitive and the words which modify it or complete its meaning.

Roger was sent by the principal *to help Arnold.*

COMPOUND AND COMPLEX SENTENCES

TEST 2A (*Diagnostic*). KINDS OF SENTENCES

Classify the following sentences by writing *S* (simple), *Cd* (compound), or *Cx* (complex) on your paper after the number of each sentence.

1. When the passengers went on deck after dinner, they noticed that the wind had increased and that snow was falling.
2. The children sat on top of the scraggly old fence like bright-coloured snowbirds, waiting for the king to pass by.
3. Colonial churches were very cold in winter, and only by the aid of foot warmers and wood stoves could the congregation keep from freezing.
4. Jimmy lowered his voice as the big farm hand came around the corner with an armful of cornstalks.
5. The puma picked up the tawny ball of fur by the tough skin on the back of its neck and carried it to the foot of the cliff.
6. Never trouble another for what you can do yourself.
7. Thomas Edison possessed the invaluable gift of getting from a book just what he wanted and nothing else.
8. The revolving beacon on the airplane field threw its beams into the snow-filled darkness to guide the pilot bringing the holiday mail from Montreal.
9. The glow of the sun from above, its thousandfold reflection from the waves, the sea water that fell and dried upon me, caking my very lips with salt, combined to make my throat burn and my brain ache.
10. A bowl of warm barley porridge was brought to us, and with a big wooden spoon I fed my little charge his frugal supper.

33. A compound sentence is made up of two or more independent statements, questions, or commands.

Suddenly a window above the two boys opened, and a tramp looked out.

The two independent statements joined are:

1. Suddenly a window above the two boys opened.
2. A tramp looked out.

34. The independent statements, questions, or commands joined to form a compound sentence are called principal clauses.

35. A clause is a part of a sentence that has a subject and a predicate.

When the newspapers speak of the ABC countries of South America, | they are referring to Argentina, Brazil, and Chile. (The two clauses of this sentence are separated by a vertical line.)

36. Co-ordinate conjunctions connect words, phrases, and clauses of equal rank. Principal clauses are of equal rank. Co-ordinate conjunctions used to connect the clauses of a compound sentence are *and, but, or, nor, for, so, yet,* and *while* (meaning *but*).

Not all deserts are made up entirely of sand, *nor* are they uninhabited by living creatures.

37. A subordinate clause is used as a noun, an adjective, or an adverb. Two tests of a subordinate clause are: (1) as a rule, it does not make complete sense when standing alone; (2) usually a subordinate conjunction or a relative pronoun is either expressed or can be supplied without spoiling the sense.

NOUN   Dr. Iago Gladston states *that half of all disabling diseases begin with a cold in the head.* (*That* introduces the clause.)

ADJECTIVE   The sheep were forced to walk through a tank containing a disinfectant solution *which freed them from insect pests.* (*Which* introduces the clause.)

ADVERB   A little later in the afternoon, *when the rose of sunset lay on the snowy hills,* a stranger knocked at the door of Navelle's home. (*When* introduces the clause.)

38. A sentence with a principal clause and one or more subordinate clauses is called a complex sentence.

Although the other villagers lived in one-room huts of mud thatched with straw, Heera Singh had a two-storied house with a tile roof and a central courtyard.

30. A noun clause is used as a noun. It may be:

SUBJECT OF VERB   *What makes the Grand Canyon a scenic feature of the first order* is its marvellously variegated volcanic colouring.

OBJECT OF VERB   From the heights above the city the enemy could see *that every one of their shells hit.*

OBJECT OF PREPOSITION   During the Renaissance, Francis Bacon laid the foundation of *what may be called the modern laboratory method of research in natural science.*

PREDICATE NOMINATIVE   One of Sir Ronald Ross's greatest disappointments was *that the world did not make better use of his scientific instruction on tropical sanitation.*

APPOSITIVE   Dr. Howard made the statement *that the medicinal properties of Hot Springs were known to the Indians long before the Spanish invasion.*

APPOSITIVE   The discovery *that no two fingerprints in the world are exactly alike* has been of great importance in criminal investigation.

PRACTICE 11. Recognizing Noun Clauses

For each sentence write the noun clause, underline the subject once and the verb twice, and explain how the noun clause is used.

A. 1. Paul Eipper believes that snakes do not hypnotize their prey.
   2. What I want is to become a navigator in a D.C.4.
   3. An interesting feature of the Carlsbad Caverns is that another region to explore lies beyond each cave.
   4. Thomas Edison once said that the American people eat too much.
   5. It is an old saying that the workman is known by his tools.
   6. Do you know what blind flying is?

B. 1. Everyone thought that Curly would make a good pilot because of his initiative and coolness.
   2. That my brother was immediately commissioned a second lieutenant was due to his C.O.T.C. training. (*Due* is a predicate adjective.)
   3. Do you know who was elected president of the Engineering Club?
   4. The little cottage nestled among the old elms was what we wanted.
   5. Give this package to whoever comes to the door.
   6. Major Alexander de Seversky made the statement that victory can come through air power.

40. An adjective clause modifies a noun or a pronoun.

During the next week Dad insisted on running off the reels for everybody *who came into the house.* (*Who came into the house* modifies the pronoun *everybody.*)

a. An adjective clause may be attached to the word it modifies by:

(1) A relative pronoun (*who, which,* and *that*)

The battle cry of Carlson's Raiders was "Gung Ho!" *which* is Chinese for *work—harmony.*

(2) A subordinate conjunction

Fearing Indian raids, Miles Standish, the captain of the Pilgrim militia, trained his men for the time *when* battle should come.

b. The connecting word may be omitted.

The three skippers were there to give the survivors of the *Judith* a warm welcome and to marvel at the yarn (which) they spun.

PRACTICE 12. Recognizing Adjectives Clauses

For each sentence write the adjective clause, underline the subject once and the verb twice, and explain how the clause is used.

A. 1. All that glitters is not gold.

2. Birds which destroy harmful insects should be protected.

3. The helicopter is a plane that is held up by horizontal propellers.

4. We recalled a tiny café where we had had a delicious fish concoction.

5. The Victoria Cross, which is the highest-ranking decoration, was established in 1856. (*Victoria Cross* is the name of the medal.)

6. Our circling barges churned up the water in great swells, which splashed over us.

B. 1. A tall, red-haired young man, who was frying bacon over a stove, gazed at us in mild surprise.

2. Lemmings are particularly common in the mountainous regions where the juniper tree grows.

3. The colonists purchased their sugar in huge loaves which weighed nine or ten pounds.

4. The two white-robed figures silently disappeared in the direction from which they had come.

5. The conditions under which people dwell have an important influence upon their health and character.

6. By the beach lay the skin canoes in which the Indians had come up the river.

41. An adverb clause modifies a verb, an adjective, or an adverb.

Cautiously Renny and his sister crept forward *until they could distinguish dim shapes in the fog.* (The clause *until they could distinguish dim shapes in the fog* modifies the verb *crept.*)

In most parts of Holland waterways are cheaper to construct and keep in operation *than railroads.* (The clause *than railroads* [*are*] modifies the adjective *cheaper.*)

George Washington's hands were so big *he had to have his gloves made to order.* (The clause *he had to have his gloves made to order* modifies the adverb *so.*)

PRACTICE 13. Recognizing Adverb Clauses

For each sentence write the adverb clause, underline the subject once and the verb twice, and explain how each clause is used.

A. 1. When the thermometer drops to —40° the wind usually falls too.

2. When the snow falls in the city, it usually disrupts traffic.

3. A young eel is so transparent that print can be read through its body.

4. When water is heated to 212°, it comes to a boil.

5. Canada produces more asbestos than any other country.

6. If the wing of a single-engine plane is located at the bottom of the fuselage, the ship is called a low-wing monoplane.

B. 1. No man ever had a harder struggle for success than Frank Woolworth.

    2. Small flights of mallards could be seen as far as we could penetrate through the fog.

    3. Our Cubs held out as long as their food and water lasted.

    4. The deck of the transport was so crowded with barges and gear that only small groups of men could exercise at a time.

    5. As the plane plunged to the bottom of the ocean, a deflated rubber boat and a cushion came to the surface.

    6. When the horseless or steam carriage was first used, drivers frequently stopped to get up more steam.

42. A subordinate conjunction connects a subordinate clause with the clause to which it is attached. Frequently used subordinate conjunctions are:

after	before	in order that	that	whenever
although	but that	lest	though	where
as	even if	provided that	till	whereas
as if	for	since	unless	whether
as though	how	so that	until	while
because	if	than	when	why

43. A compound-complex sentence has two or more principal clauses and one or more subordinate clauses.

Now and then a blue cart filled with peasants drew aside *as the tourists approached,* or a shepherd in a vividly embroidered cloak guided his flock into a huddle at the roadside and stood watching, pipe in mouth, *as they passed.* (The two subordinate clauses are in italics.)

44. A complex sentence in which a subordinate clause is itself complex is called complex-complex.

I remembered what Silver had said about the current that drifts northward along the whole west coast of Treasure Island. (*What Silver had said about the current* is a noun clause used as direct object of the verb *remembered; that drifts northward along the whole west coast of Treasure Island* is an adjective clause modifying *current.*)

PRACTICE 14. Recognizing Clauses

For each sentence write the subordinate clause, underline the subject once and the verb twice, identify the clause as a noun, an adverb, or an adjective clause, and tell how it is used in the sentence.

A. 1. The leaders of the United Nations now know that justice must be tempered with patience.

    2. Alexander Hamilton re-entered the city to the deafening shouts of a multitude that escorted him to his doorway.

3. Juanita tickled her baby brother under the chin so that he would laugh at her.

4. Antarctic explorers say that penguins are totally unafraid of man.

5. Moist paper is more clearly printed from engraved plates than dry paper.

6. In 1772 the first umbrella was shipped from India to Baltimore, where it was regarded as an item of feminine apparel.

B. 1. A high wind rattled the windows of the deserted old house until it creaked like a ship in a heavy sea.

2. What had happened to the little mascot of the ball team was a deep mystery.

3. The stranger told the girls fascinating tales of the wandering gypsies who pitched their tents on the high steppes of eastern Hungary.

4. The second mate made the discovery that the ship had grounded on the mud flats of Smith Bay.

5. To the colonists starvation and disease were worse enemies than the Indians.

6. The Louvre, in which the kings of France once lived, now contains the largest picture gallery in the world.

7. That we had no place to land soon became evident.

PRACTICE 15. Recognizing Subordinate Clauses

Write the subordinate clauses in the following sentences, underline a simple subject once and a predicate verb twice, label a clause *n.*, *adj.*, or *adv.*, and indicate what word or words an adjective or an adverb clause modifies and how a noun clause is used.

Examples:

a. Benjamin Franklin gained fame among the scientists of the world by a kite-flying experiment through which he proved that lightning and electricity are one.

through which he proved—adj., *experiment*

that lightning and electricity are one—n., direct object of *proved*

b. There are trees in the New England forests that are still called the King's trees, because in colonial days an officer in the British navy walked through the forest with a branding axe and marked every tree that would be suitable for a mast on one of His Majesty's vessels.

that are still called the King's trees—adj., *trees*

because in colonial days an officer in the British navy walked through the

  forest with a branding axe and marked every tree—adv., *are called*

that would be suitable for a mast on one of His Majesty's vessels—adj., *tree*

A. 1. That Louis Agassiz was one of the great naturalists of all time is the opinion of authorities.

    2. At the age of fourteen he wrote his parents that he would like to become an author on scientific subjects.

    3. Mr. Agassiz's answer was that the boy might study the natural sciences at the College of Lausanne and at the universities of Zurich, Heidelberg, and Munich.

    4. Whatever Agassiz undertook at college was well done.

    5. In his room several lively monkeys and a tub full of fish bore evidence to the fact that Agassiz had not lost his early interest in nature.

    6. About this time he wrote to his father, "I wish it may be said of Louis Agassiz that he was the first naturalist of his time, a good citizen, and a good son."

B. 1. When a well-known naturalist who had been commissioned by the king of Bavaria to edit a book on Brazilian fishes died in 1829, Agassiz took up the task and published a comprehensive volume.

    2. When his work led him to study fossil fishes preserved in rocks, Agassiz became interested in geology, in which he soon made himself an expert.

    3. Agassiz proved that most of Europe was once covered by glaciers, which had played an important role in the formation of the earth.

    4. In 1846 Agassiz, who was deeply in debt, sailed for Boston, where he had been invited to deliver a course of lectures at the Lowell Institute.

    5. Because Agassiz showed in his addresses that he was a master in his field, Harvard University offered him a position on its staff.

    6. Although many European countries extended tempting offers, Agassiz refused to leave the United States, where he worked happily until his death in 1873.

PRACTICE 16. Building Complex and Complex-complex Sentences

Using the ideas in each of the following groups of sentences, build one forceful complex or complex-complex sentence.

Example:

SIMPLE SENTENCES Captain Cook and his companions landed on the shores of a bay. A naturalist in the party found many different kinds of plants there. So he named the bay Botany Bay.

COMPLEX-COMPLEX SENTENCE Captain Cook and his companions landed on the shores of a bay which a naturalist in the party named Botany Bay because he found there many different kinds of plants.

A. 1. On the next block a hooting mob of boys and girls pursued a sprinkling truck. The truck washed the street with a strong sideward current of water.

2. Emily and Henry knew that the salvation of their home depended on their efforts. They worked till midnight in the cornfield.

3. Young Ronald arrived in England for the first time. Then he was taken to the Isle of Wight. Here he lived with an elderly uncle and aunt.

4. In the seventeenth century the castle was purchased by a dashing French pirate. His pointed beard was a peculiar dark bluish colour. Therefore he was nicknamed Edouard de la Barbe Bleue.

5. A squirrel was leaping from tree to tree. It fell and broke its paw. Saint Florentin placed the broken paw in splints.

6. We arrived by train two days later. Rita and Horace were waiting for us at the tiny railroad station. The station is in sight of the long, white-walled house.

7. Major André boarded the *Vulture*. His youthful head carried the details of the scheme. By it he hoped to win the war practically single-handed.

8. Mary Elizabeth waved good-bye to Nancy and the other passengers. Then she secured her portfolio from Nancy's cabin and carried it to the middle of the ship. Here a consignment of grain was stored.

B. 1. I strolled through the peaceful streets of Santa Maria del Carmine one November afternoon. A small boy told me a bloodcurdling tale. I was sharing some tangerines with him.

2. The picnic lunch was all packed. Then Sarah went out and rang the ship's bell. This hung near the kitchen door.

3. Spider monkeys often wrap their tails about themselves. They are very sensitive to cold. Their tails keep them warm.

4. Washington made Clinton think he intended to attack New York. Then he slipped away southward.

5. His leg obviously hurt him sharply when he moved. Yet it was at a good, rattling rate that he managed to trail himself across the quarter-deck.

6. The captain and the spy were in the adjoining room. They were speaking very low. Not a sound was heard. Yet Major Williams guessed the subject of the conversation.

7. Marion Tyler thought little of the manuscript of her first story. She consigned it to the wastebasket. Her mother rescued it.

8. I remember the appearance of his coat. This he himself patched upstairs in his room. After a while it was nothing but patches.

TEST 2B (*Mystery*). KINDS OF SENTENCES
Median—6.7

Classify the following sentences by writing *S* (simple), *Cd* (compound), or *Cx* (complex) on your paper after the number of each sentence.

1. Timothy slid down from a load of hay and came in to see if dinner was ready.

2. Crouched in a corner of the dungeon, the cat howled loudly for someone to come down and get him.

3. After deciding where you are going and making reservations, you must next consider your wardrobe.

4. The dirigible fought every yard of the way, and throughout the night an anxious world waited for a message from the airship.

5. John Ryan clattered into the city at eight o'clock on the morning of January 30 and placed the message in the hands of the governor.

6. The captain of the nearest ship shouted through his brass trumpet, but the skipper of the *Cecile* had no voice to answer back.

7. As the last rays of twilight dwindled and disappeared, absolute blackness settled down on Treasure Island.

8. Marine zoology students at the University of Miami attend class in diving helmets and take notes under water on zinc tablets with yellow wax crayons.

9. Marta and Emil were almost sorry when they saw the white gateposts before their little house, glistening with snow and moonbeams.

10. Benjamin Franklin once said, "I never sought an office, never refused one and never resigned."

Enter your mark on your achievement graph.

B. Grammatical Usage

Recently a radio quiz program presented a contestant with ten dollars for knowing the answer to a grammatical puzzler. A knowledge of grammatical usage will bring you a cash bonus, too, for the better jobs go to those who express themselves correctly and forcefully.

CORRECT PRONOUNS

TEST 3A (*Diagnostic*). PRONOUNS

In each of the following which pronoun is correct or preferred? On your paper write the answer after the number of the sentences. (Right — Wrong = Score)

1. Ferrari offered the hand of his daughter to —— made the best violin (whoever, whomever)

2. The church officials issued a solemn warning to Galileo, ——, they said, was printing statements contradictory to the Holy Writ. (who, whom)

3. Everyone at the minstrel show enjoyed —— immensely. (himself, themselves)

4. The ballad is passed down from generation to generation; —— usually based on a heroic deed or a terrible tragedy. (it is, they are)

5. The success of Class Night depends on —— doing his part. (everyone, everyone's)

6. To his horror Dr. Beebe found himself in the presence of a giant cobra, —— fortunately failed to notice the naturalist. (that, which, who)

7. Frantically the men on board the ship pulled in the diver, —— they feared was seriously injured. (who, whom)

8. Burton was surprised at —— offering to help him build the birdhouse. (me, my)

9. The next morning Carlton and —— set out at five o'clock for Loon Lake. (I, myself)

10. The Ancient Mariner told his terrible story to those —— he thought would profit by the tale. (who, whom)

11. The average buyer is a question asker, and a salesman must be able to answer —— questions. (his, their)

12. Joan Deary, —— I think is a senior in Alma College, has offered to tutor me in Latin this summer. (who, whom)

13. If you see a pupil throwing papers on the floor, remind —— that wastebaskets are more than mere decorations for the classroom. (him, them)

14. The persecuted and poverty-stricken —— the governor welcomed to the colony helped to build a great commonwealth. (who, whom)

15. The king promised a royal reward to —— made the most beautiful lace for the little princess Maria. (whoever, whomever)

16. In India lives the mongoose, the only animal —— can catch and kill the deadly cobra. (that, what, who)

17. No one can study effectively when there is noise around ——. (him, them)

18. Whenever the monk found a wounded bird or a suffering animal, he did his best to nurse —— back to health and strength. (it, them)

19. Neither Harold nor Albert finished —— homework. (his, their)

20. If you neglected some of your work during the first third, you may hand —— in now but will receive reduced credit. (it, them)

CASE OF PRONOUNS

45. The subject of a verb (except of an infinitive) is in the nominative case.   The case of a pronoun depends upon its use in its own clause.

He and Bob manage a small chicken farm after school.
Celia's brother Gerald is six inches taller than *she*. (*She* is the subject of the verb *is* understood).
Those are the girls I met at the skating rink. (Not "them.")

a. An expression like *he says, I think,* **or** *I suppose* **between** *who* **and its verb does not change the case of the pronoun.**   The case-form of the relative pronouns *who* and *whoever* is determined by the use of the pronoun in its own clause.

Who did she say sang the lead in *Naughty Marietta?* (*Who* is the subject of *sang.*)

The governor praised the work of the "bondadiers," *who* he said had sold or taken pledges for $250,000,000 worth of bonds. (*Who* is the subject of *had sold* and *taken; he said* is parenthetic.)

For the task of building a pontoon bridge across the swift stream, the lieutenant picked men *who* he knew were expert swimmers. (The three clauses are *for the task of building a pontoon bridge across the swift stream the lieutenant picked men; he knew;* and *who were expert swimmers. Who* is the subject of *were.*)

b. Do not let *who* or *whoever*, when the subject of a verb, be attracted into the objective case by a preceding verb or preposition.

Give the message to *whoever* answers the telephone. (*Whoever* is the subject of *answers*, not the object of *to*. The object of *to* is the noun clause *whoever answers the telephone.*)

46. The verb *to be* and other linking verbs take the same case after them as before them. *To be* never takes an object. A linking verb joins a predicate adjective or a predicate nominative to the subject.

Was it *he* who joined the Air Raid Patrol? (*He* is a predicate nominative.)
The villagers often wondered *who* Mr. Stafford's mysterious visitor really was. (*Who* is the predicate nominative after the verb *was.*)
I believed my masked visitor to be *her*. (*Visitor*, the subject of the infinitive *to be*, is in the objective case.)

47. Direct objects of verbs, indirect objects, and objects of prepositions are in the objective case.

DIRECT OBJECT   The scout *whom* Colonel Cochran *had sent* ahead to locate the enemy returned with an accurate report.

INDIRECT OBJECT   Who gave Fred and *him* that set of tools?

OBJECT OF PREPOSITION   That morning in front of the entire regiment Colonel Ryan presented the Distinguished Service Cross to Corporal Faust and *me*.

To determine the correct case of a pronoun in an inverted sentence, arrange the sentence in the grammatical or natural order: (1) subject and modifiers; (2) verb; (3) object, predicate adjective, or predicate nominative.

1. (Who, Whom) do you think will win the scavenger hunt?

NATURAL ORDER   You do think (who, whom) will win the scavenger hunt? (*Who* is the subject of the verb *will win*. The noun clause *who will win the scavenger hunt* is the direct object of *do think.*)

2. (Who, Whom) do you think I met on Connor Avenue yesterday?

NATURAL ORDER   You do think I met (who, whom) on Connor Avenue yesterday? (*Whom* is the direct object of the verb *met.*)

NOTE   "Who is that package for?" "Who does the book belong to?" **"Select for your captain whoever you want," and similar expressions** are correct colloquial or informal English. The formal English sentences are: "For whom is that package?" "To whom does the book belong?" "Select for your captain whomever you want."

48. An appositive agrees in case with the word to which it refers.

This term our school is sending two students, Francis Lake and *me*, to the convention of the Columbia Scholastic Press Association. (*Students* is the direct object of *is sending*. The objective *me* is correct because it is in apposition with *students*.)

49. The subject of an infinitive is in the objective case. After verbs of *making, telling, letting, wishing, expecting, thinking, knowing, commanding, believing,* **and the like, the infinitive has a subject.**

I told *him* to meet me at the main entrance to the Maple Leaf Gardens. (*Him* is the subject of the infinitive *to meet*.)

50. A pronoun modifying a verbal noun is in the possessive case.

I was surprised to hear of *his* joining the Navy on his seventeenth birthday.

KINDS AND FORMS OF PRONOUNS

1. Personal Pronouns

First Person

	SINGULAR	PLURAL
Nominative	I	we
Possessive	my, mine	our, ours
Objective	me	us

Second Person

SINGULAR AND PLURAL

Nominative	you
Possessive	your, yours
Objective	you

Third Person

		SINGULAR		PLURAL
	Masculine	*Feminine*	*Neuter*	
Nominative	he	she	it	they
Possessive	his	her, hers	its	their, theirs
Objective	him	her	it	them

2. Relative Pronouns

SINGULAR AND PLURAL

Nominative	who	which	what	that	whoever
Possessive	whose	whose			whose-ever
Objective	whom	which	what	that	whomever

3. Demonstrative Pronouns

SINGULAR	PLURAL
this	these
that	those

4. Compound Personal Pronouns

	SINGULAR	PLURAL
First person	myself	ourselves
Second person	yourself	yourselves
Third person	himself, herself, itself	themselves

PRACTICE 17. Using Correct Pronouns

Supply the correct or preferred pronoun and explain its use in the sentence.

A. 1. Charlotte Bronte, ——, some critics think, was one of the most important English novelists, had a hard and lonely life. (who, whom)

2. For many years she and her sisters, Emily and Anne Bronte, were completely under the domination of their father, —— has been described as a man of cold and harsh nature. (who, whom)

3. Branwell, the only brother of the Bronte sisters, —— Emily in particular loved dearly, was an idler and a drunkard. (who, whom)

4. Always, however, his fond sisters cherished hopes of —— writing a wonderful poem or story. (him, his)

5. During the dreary years on the Yorkshire moor the three girls, ——, we know from their books, were often lonely and unhappy, turned to writing as an emotional outlet. (who, whom)

6. In 1847 Charlotte published her novel about Jane Eyre, ——, the author tells us, was created to prove that heroines may be small and plain. (who, whom)

B. 1. Charlotte did not at first admit that the author of *Jane Eyre* was ——. (her, she)

2. For some time the question, "—— do you suppose wrote *Jane Eyre?*" aroused lively discussion in English literary circles. (Who, Whom)

3. Authors and critics heaped praise on the head of —— had written the forceful, original novel. (whoever, whomever)

4. That same year Emily Bronte, —— most modern readers think was an even greater writer than Charlotte, published *Wuthering Heights.* (who, whom)

5. Both —— and Charlotte are considered eminent British novelists. (her, she)

PRACTICE 18. Using Correct Pronouns

Eleven of the following sentences are wrong. Correct them, giving a reason for each change you make.

Example:

> The puppy curled up between he and I.
> The puppy curled up between him and me. (*Him* and *me* are objects of the preposition *between*.)

1. I looked around and selected a boy whom I thought would carry out my orders intelligently.
2. Didn't you suspect that it was her?
3. Into her knitting Madame Defarge, whom everyone feared, worked the names of people whom she considered enemies of the republic.
4. Sydney Carton, whom I think is the hero of the book, is first seen at the trial of Charles Darnay.
5. No one in the family had heard of his sailing for Spain.
6. Distribute the rest of the posters among friends whom you know will vote for our ticket.
7. I knew it to be he by the way he walked.
8. The men who Squire Trelawney thought were honest sailors turned out to be bloodthirsty buccaneers.
9. Whom do you suppose dressed the kitten in baby's bonnet and sweater?
10. The time has come for we students to give our active support to the Junior Red Cross.
11. I shall vote for whomever I think is best qualified to hold office.
12. Miss Marlowe was delighted at his offering to build a stage for the puppets.
13. Dr. Watson was surprised to see Sherlock Holmes, whom he thought was dangerously ill with a rare tropical disease.
14. The pilot whom President Roosevelt praised in his radio address was Captain Hewitt T. Wheless.
15. Lieutenant Pearson believes the approaching battalion to be they.
16. I recommend *Dragon Seed* to whoever wishes to read a novel about modern China.
17. My dog enjoys me taking him for a run.

AGREEMENT OF PRONOUN AND ANTECEDENT

51. A pronoun agrees with its antecedent in number, person, and gender. Find the antecedent of the pronoun. Then decide whether the antecedent is singular or plural.

The past record of an applicant is investigated before *he* is hired.

Every pupil had a Union Jack in *his* right hand.

a. A collective noun takes a singular pronoun when the group is thought of and a plural pronoun when the individuals are thought of.

The crew had *its* gear in readiness for a quick take-off.

The crew discussed *their* parts in the forthcoming manoeuvres.

b. Two or more singular antecedents joined by and require a plural pronoun.

Correspondent Sherrod and a marine companion spent *their* first night at Tarawa in a foxhole on the beach.

c. Two or more singular antecedents joined by *or* or *nor* require singular pronouns.

Either Gary or Ray will bring *his* tennis racket to school.

d. As a rule, *each, every, either, neither, one, many a, a person,* and compounds with *body* and *one* take singular pronouns. Antecedents like *each, anyone,* and *everybody* are especially troublesome.

Each of the pilots reported that *his* mission had been successfully completed.

Every soldier and sailor in the crowd of bystanders raised *his* hand in a snappy salute as the flag passed. (Although the subject *soldier and sailor* is compound, the word *every* changes the meaning to "every one of the soldiers and sailors", treating each individually.)

e. Every pronoun should agree with its antecedent in person.

My mother makes *me* eat spinach, because it puts iron in ~~your~~ *my* system.

f. *His* is generally preferable to the clumsy *his or her*.

Every pupil in Room 112 brought as *his* contribution to the scrap drive five pounds of waste paper.

g. Masculine pronouns are used in referring to most animals: neuter pronouns, in speaking of insects or small animals.

When Mrs. Kennicott entered the room, the *puppy* stood up on *his* hind legs and whined softly.

Creeping quietly up behind the *fly*, the cook demolished *it* with a vicious blow.

The *mouse* made *its* home in the granary.

h. *His* may be used to refer to *one*. Some authorities, however, consider *one's* better usage.

Accurate, vivid words will help one to express *his* (or *one's*) reasons for considering a particular event the biggest news of the week.

PRACTICE 19. Using Correct Pronouns

Select the correct or preferred words. What is the antecedent of each pronoun chosen?

A. 1. Taking a picture of a person when —— not looking is often lots of fun. (he is, they are)
  2. If candidates for these scholarships are required to take an examination, when and where will —— be held? (it, they)
  3. Many a reader skips the words with which —— familiar. (he isn't, they aren't)
  4. At the first crash of thunder everyone had started for —— tent. (his, their)
  5. At the end of the summer neither of the Bennet boys had passed —— swimming test. (his, their)
  6. If Louis Pasteur or Thomas Edison had been easily discouraged, —— could never have made such great contributions to science. (he, they)
  7. It is neither polite nor fair to ridicule a loser, for —— bad enough about the defeat. (he feels, they feel)
  8. I recommend *My Friend Flicka* to anyone who wants a good book to read during —— leisure time. (his, their)

B. 1. In the Middle Ages, if one did not know Latin, —— considered uneducated. (he was, they were)
  2. When Japanese troops invaded Manchuria in 1931, the League of Nations tried to stop the aggression, but —— had no way of forcing the Japs to withdraw. (it, they)
  3. If everybody does —— share, we shall have enough gasoline, rubber, and food for the armed forces and the civilians. (his, their)
  4. Any pupil can learn to spell common words correctly if —— systematically. (he studies, they study)
  5. Everyone will do —— best to make the visitors feel at home. (his, their)
  6. A person naturally tries to secure as good clothing as possible for —— money. (his, their)
  7. If one drinks too much coffee, it speeds up —— heart, makes —— nervous, and keeps —— awake. (his, their) (him, them) (him, them)

COMPOUND PERSONAL PRONOUN AND RELATIVE PRONOUN

52. A compound personal pronoun ordinarily refers to the subject or emphasizes the noun or pronoun to which it is attached.

REFLEXIVE   Did Helen cut *herself* with the can opener?
EMPHATIC   Joe *himself* sent to get the tickets.

53. Most careful speakers and writers do not substitute the compound personal pronoun for the simple personal pronoun, especially in the nominative case. "Hisself" and "theirselves" are incorrect forms.

> *You   your*
> ~~Yourself~~ and ∧ friends are cordially invited to attend the lecture on Saturday evening.

> *I*
> Tomorrow Julius and ~~myself~~ are going to the aquarium to see the electric eels.

54. *Who* refers chiefly to persons: *which*, to animals or things: *that*, to persons, animals, or things. The relative pronoun *that* is often used in essential subordinate clauses—that is, in a clause the omission of which would change or destroy the meaning of the principal clause—but is not used in non-essential clauses.

> The Distinguished Flying Cross is awarded to any person *who* has distinguished himself by heroism or extraordinary achievement in an aerial flight.
> With telling precision the formation of torpedo planes launched their tin fish, *which* converged on the enemy carrier from all directions.
> That morning Buzz Wagner with a single P-40 had done a job *that* ordinarily would be assigned to an entire squadron. (The omission of the essential clause *that ordinarily would be assigned to an entire squadron* would change the meaning of the principal clause.)

a. *What* never has an antecedent. The relative pronoun *what* is equivalent to *that which.*

b. *As* is used as a relative pronoun after *such* and *same.*

My translation of the sixth sentence is the same *as* yours.

PRACTICE 20. Choosing Correct Pronouns

Select the correct or preferred words. Give the reason for each selection. Sometimes two words are correct, but one sounds slightly better than the other.

A. 1. Such promises —— my opponent makes in his campaign speeches are difficult to fulfill. (as, that)

    2. My sister —— was married last Christmas lives in New Westminster. (which, who)

    3. In my class are sixteen boys, only five of —— were accepted by the R.C.A.F. (which, whom)

4. This afternoon Madge, Dorothy, and —— will decorate the girls' gymnasium for the Hallowe'en dance. (I, myself)

5. Everything —— lives in the desert must learn to get along with little water. (that, which, who)

6. Mother, Dad, and —— expect to spend the Christmas vacation in Regina. (I, myself)

B. 1. France, —— happened at that time to be stronger than Spain, decided to strip the Spanish kingdom of its riches. (what, which, who)

2. How far away is the beach —— we are going? (that, to which)

3. The War Relief Committee's work is closely associated with that of the Red Cross, —— we have belonged to for a number of years. (which who, whom)

4. The largest percentage of criminals is found among those —— have least education. (what, which, who)

5. Tomorrow George and —— are going for a bicycle ride along the Belt Parkway. (I, myself)

6. Jane has a dog —— she calls Punch. (which, whom)

TEST 3B (*Mastery*). PRONOUNS

Median—14.2

In each of the following which pronoun is correct or preferred? On your paper write each answer after the number of the sentence. (Right − Wrong = Score)

1. Mother and Father were delighted to hear of —— winning the scholarship to Queen's. (him, his)

2. The natives, —— Emperor Jones thought were too much afraid to rebel, eventually rose against him and overthrew him. (who, whom)

3. —— do you think it was? (Who, Whom)

4. The hermit offered food and shelter to —— passed by on the lonely forest path to Eislich. (whoever, whomever)

5. Lucie Manette, —— both Charles Darnay and Sydney Carton loved, is the heroine of *A Tale of Two Cities*. (who, whom)

6. For a short time Lady Mary Carlisle was extremely gracious to Monsieur Beaucaire, —— she thought was a wealthy nobleman. (who, whom)

7. Miss Marshall was greatly surprised at —— failing the Latin test. (him, his)

8. That evening the tall man —— Sherlock Holmes thought had been the purchaser of the white goose called at the detective's lodgings in Baker Street. (who, whom)

9. Give this medal to —— wins the hundred-yard dash. (whoever, whomever)

10. If I took home a cat, a dog, or a parrot, my mother would give —— away. (it, them)

11. Labour has the right to bargain collectively with employers and choose —— own representatives for this purpose. (its, their)

12. Last Sunday my father, mother, and —— visited my brother at Camp Davis. (I, myself)

13. Dr. Stefansson set to work to collect his dogs, some of —— had gone squirrel hunting on Cooper Island. (which, whom)

14. Playing on the beach were several happy youngsters, two of —— I recognized as the children of my host. (which, whom)

15, 16. It is sometimes difficult for a boy or girl to select a vocation unless —— the advice of an older person to guide ——. (he has, they have) him, them)

17. The title would never induce one to read this book for —— supplementary report. (his, their)

18. Neither Hilda nor Mildred has done —— share of the camp work. (her, their)

19. When in a trolley you see an old person standing, get up and give —— your seat. (him, them)

20. If lectures and programs on the subject of education were given over the radio, —— would inspire the students to strive for higher marks in school. (it, they)

Enter your mark on your achievement graph.

CORRECT VERBS

Because about half the grammatical errors made by pupils are mistakes in the use of the verb, this section has many exercises to help you understand verbs and habitually use correct verbs.

TEST 4A (*Diagnostic*). VERB EXCEPT AGREEMENT OF VERB AND SUBJECT.

Select the correct or preferred verb to complete each sentence. On your paper write each answer after the number of the sentence. (Right − Wrong = Score)

1. As the detective advanced into the room, he gazed curiously at the rose petals —— on the floor. (laying, lying)

2. After Alice had —— the little cake, she grew to a height of nine feet. (ate, eaten)

3. If Frank —— a tactful boy, he would not have criticized Beatrice's new hat. (was, were)

4. Marshall and I intended —— dinner at Murray's. (to eat, to have eaten)

5. If Nancy —— really interested in the Dramatic Club, she would attend the meetings. (was, were)

6. A large chart was —— on the table in the captain's cabin. (laying, lying)

7. If Mathilde —— known the borrowed necklace as only paste, she would not have been frantic at its loss. (had, would have)

8. When the children —— back from lunch, they found a gaily decorated Christmas tree set up in one corner of the schoolroom. (came, come)

9. This afternoon we —— probably finish our class paper. (shall, will)

10. When Mr. Holder was collecting his tools for an afternoon of gardening, he discovered that someone —— the handle of his favourite hoe. (broke, had broken)

11. No sooner had we assembled in Kathleen's room and —— our preparations for the feast than there came a stern rap at the door. (began, begun)

12. Later Paragot sent Asticot to school, where he —— educated. (is, was)

13. All this time the Great Seal of England had —— in the armpiece of the Milanese armour on the wall. (laid, lain)

14. Father strode to the foot of the stairs and —— in an outraged bellow the instant return of his white fur rug. (demanded, demands)

15. Patricia and her sister —— to leave so much work for Helen. (hadn't ought, ought not)

16. If Sam —— off the radio, he would be able to concentrate on his spelling lesson. (turned, would turn)

17. An hour later a messenger —— Major O'Neill a letter from Captain Stimson. (brought, brung)

18. After we had —— under the hickory tree for an hour, a fierce-looking bull drove us away. (laid, lain)

19. All night the prisoner —— by the barred window, staring with terrified eyes over the dark and lonely moor. (sat, set)

20. Four Maltese kittens —— on the soft padding in the basket. (laid, lay)

PRINCIPAL PARTS OF VERBS

PRACTICE 21. Supplying Verb Forms

Insert in each sentence the verb form named. Supply the active voice of a transitive verb unless the passive is asked for. When in doubt, consult a dictionary for the principal parts. The passive voice always includes a form of the verb *to be*.

A. 1. When the mischievous little boy stuck a pen in Arthur's balloon, **it** (past of *burst*) with a loud pop.

2. While touring the Middle East army camps, Nelson Eddy (past of *sing*) many times on request "Oh, What a Beautiful Morning!"

3. John (past of *do*) his homework in such a hurry that I can't read his handwriting.

4. For my birthday Aunt Gertrude (past of *give*) me a war bond.

5. The thieves killed the three priests of Klesh, who (past perfect of *come*) to find the ruby stolen from the forehead of the idol.

6. After the soldiers (past perfect of *eat*) their K rations, they stretched out on the ground to get a little sleep.

7. My brother (present perfect of *drive*) a jeep ever since he (past of *become*) attached to Message Centre.

8. Amid much excitement Gaspard (past passive of *hang*) over the fountain in the town square.

9 When the alarm bell (past of *ring*), the townspeople (past of *come*) running in frightened groups to the town hall.

10. The enemy (past of *know*) that our scouts (past perfect of *see*) the column advancing up the hill.

B. 1. On the morning of the thirteenth day the exhausted survivors of the torpedoing (past of *see*) a ship on the horizon.

2. The precious Ming vase (past perfect of *fall*) from the table and (past perfect of *break*) into a hundred fragments.

3. This morning Craig (present perfect of *swim*) the length of the pool three times.

4. The letter which (past perfect passive of *write*) by Captain Anthony so many years ago (past passive of *tear*) into several pieces.

5. The Russian guerrillas waited until the river (past passive of *freeze*) solid before carrying out their raid.

6. Every pupil in my class (present perfect of *give*) twenty-five cents to the Junior Red Cross.

7. When Dr. Jekyll (past perfect of *drink*) the drug, he changed into Mr. Hyde, an inhuman brute.

8. "A" Company's softball team (present perfect of *beat*) "E" Company's team in both games by a margin of two runs.

9. To our surprise nothing (past perfect passive of *take*) except the little sandalwood box from Ceylon.

10. If I (past subjunctive of *be*) you, I would try again.

PRACTICE 22. Supplying Verb Forms

Insert in each numbered sentence the verb form or forms named. Supply the active voice of a transitive verb unless the passive is asked for.

1. As the white rabbit scurried past Alice, he (past of *take*) a watch from the pocket of his waistcoat and looked at it anxiously.

2. Recovering from her amazement, Alice (past of *spring*) to her feet and (past of *run*) across the field after the rabbit.

3. He (past of *dive*) into a large hole under the hedge.

4. When Alice (past of *come*) to the rabbit hole. she, too, popped into it.

5. Down, down she (past of *sink*), until she (past of *begin*) to think she would never reach the bottom.

6. After she (past perfect of *fall*) for some time, she landed with a thump on a heap of leaves and sticks.

7. First Alice made sure that she (past perfect of *break*) no bones; then she set out to explore.

8. On a crystal table she (past of *see*) a tiny gold key and a little bottle, on the label of which (past passive of *write*), "Drink me."

9. After Alice (past perfect of *drink*) the contents of the bottle, she (past of *shrink*) until she was only ten inches tall.

10. But now, alas, she was too small to reach the top of the table, where (past of *lie*) the golden key.

11. On the floor, however, Alice spied a little cake; when she (past perfect of *eat*) it, she (past of *grow*) to be nine feet tall and could easily reach the key, but now she was too big to go through the low gate.

12. In a moment she (past perfect of *burst*) out crying and before long had a deep pool of tears around her.

13. Suddenly Mr. Rabbit, elegantly dressed, (past of *become*) visible in the distance, and Alice determined to ask his help.

14. As soon as she (past perfect of *speak*), however, the rabbit hurriedly retreated, dropping his fan and white kid gloves.

15. Feeling a little warm, Alice picked up the fan and waved it gently back and forth.

16. Soon she (past of *see*) that she was shrinking again, and quickly dropped the rabbit's fan.

SIT, SET; LIE, LAY; RISE, RAISE

The principal parts of six troublesome verbs are:

	PRESENT TENSE	PRESENT PARTICIPLE	PAST TENSE	PAST PARTICIPLE
Sit (*occupy a seat*)	sitting	sat	sat
set (*place*)	setting	set	set
lie (*recline*)	lying	lay	lain
lay (*put down* or *place*)	laying	laid	laid

| rise (*ascend*) | rising | rose | risen |
| raise (*elevate*) | raising | raised | raised |

55. *Set, lay,* and *raise* are, as a rule, transitive verbs; in the active voice they require objects. *Set* is intransitive in "The sun is setting" and "He set out on a long journey." To *set* usually means *to cause to sit*; *to lay* means *to cause to lie*; *to raise* means *to cause to rise.*

56. *Sit, lie,* and *rise* are intransitive; they never take objects; they lack voice.

> Mr. Meredith *laid* the new linoleum in the kitchen and then *lay* down in the hammock to read the paper.
>
> Ray *set* the baby in her high chair, and while she *sat* there gurgling happily, Burke snapped a picture of her.
>
> As the sun *rose* over the horizon, the German troops *raised* the white flag of surrender.

PRACTICE 23. Using Sit, Set; Lie, Lay; Rise, Raise

Select the correct word to complete each sentence. Give the **reason** for each choice.

1. After eating his lunch David —— down on the grass and went to sleep. (laid, lay)

2. At the request of a soldier in the fourth row Joyce —— down and played Beethoven's "Moonlight Sonata". (sat, set)

3. Under the force of Denis' blow the masked knight fell from his horse and —— motionless on the dusty plain. (laid, lay)

4. After Robin Hood had —— for some time in dreamless slumber, he awoke, hung his broadsword at his side, and started out to seek adventure. (laid, lain)

5. As Kenneth travelled through the desert, he came upon a wounded Saracen —— on the burning sands. (laying, lying)

6. "—— down, Rover; —— down," ordered Elmer. (Lay, Lie) (lay, lie)

7. In the dirty flat Lillian Wald found a sick woman —— on the bed. (laying, lying)

8. The black-and-white pig —— in the mud puddle for several hours. (laid, lay)

9. While Professor Malzius was —— in his cell, his guard unlocked the door and told him to come out. (laying, lying)

10. All morning Audubon —— dreaming in the thick grass. (laid, lay)

11. —— on the floor was Jane's party dress. (Laying, Lying)

12. The song of the birds in Sherwood Forest awakened Robin Hood, who had —— all night under a tree. (laid, lain)

13. We made the mistake of —— the patient up in a chair instead of —— him flat on the floor. (setting, sitting) (laying, lying)

14. After marching for two hours the scouts —— down to rest. (sat, set)

15. Please —— the clock back ten minutes. (set, sit)

16. —— down and tell me the whole story. (Set, Sit)

17. With unerring instinct Jerry chose the most comfortable chair in the room and —— down with a sigh of relief. (sat, set)

18. Since you forgot to put in the baking powder, you really shouldn't expect the cake to ——. (raise, rise)

19. Just then the submarine —— to the surface to recharge its batteries. (raised, rose)

20. Why doesn't this bread ——? (raise, rise)

SUBJUNCTIVE MOOD

57. The subjunctive mood is preferred for a wish or request and for a condition (an *if* clause) that is contrary to fact (untrue).

Right now I wish I *were* an Eskimo. (Wish.)
Heaven *help* him!
If I *were* twenty-one (but I'm not), I should join the Women's Reserve Marine Corps. (Condition contrary to fact.)
If this *were* gold, our fortune would be made.

TENSE

58. Do not carelessly shift from the past tense to the present or from the present to the past.

Waving her tail furiously the cat stalked into the room and
went
~~goes~~ straight to Grandma's chair.

59. The past tense represents action completed in the past. The present perfect tense is used if the action began in the past and con-- tinues in the present.

> I *lost* my umbrella. (The umbrella may since have been found.)
> I *have lost* my umbrella. (Here the consequences extend to the present. The umbrella has not been found.)
> The rosebush *bloomed* every summer for ten years. (It doesn't bloom now.)
> The rosebush *has bloomed* every summer for ten years. (It still blooms.)

60. The past perfect tense is used if the action was completed before some past time.

> When the army entered Cassino, they discovered that the city *had been* almost completely *demolished* by the fierce bombing assaults. (The discovery took place in past time, and the demolishing was completed before the discovery.)
> The next day the foreman received the news that the shafts *had been sunk* thirty feet. (*Had been sunk* is correct, because the sinking took place before the past act of receiving.)

61. To express action earlier than that expressed by the main verb, use the perfect tense of the participle or the infinitive; otherwise use the present tense.

> I intended to *see* Violet before she left Pineville. (*To see* is correct, because the seeing did not occur before the intending.)
> I am happy *to have been* of assistance in this matter. (The being of assistance preceded the being happy.)
> *Having received* his Eagle Scout award, Russell became assistant scoutmaster of our troop. (The receiving preceded the becoming.)

62. The present tense may be used for the past in vivid narration.

> The house lights *dim,* a soft bluish light *floods* the stage, and the audience *grows* silent.

63. *Might, could, would,* **and** *should,* **not** *may, can, will* **and** *shall,* are used after a past tense.

> The outlaws then *told* Gurth that he *might go* free.

Note these correct forms:

> *had*
> If we ~~would have~~ heard about the rodeo in Cheyenne on August 21, we would have planned to be there that day.

> *had*
> I wish I ~~would have~~ known the real reason for Shirley's queer behaviour.

told
If I ~~would tell~~ you what really happened, you wouldn't believe me.

had
I wish I ~~would have~~ studied art.

not
Bernice ~~hadn't~~ ought ∧ to spend so much time in the house.
(*Had* is never used with *ought*.)

PRACTICE 24. Using Correct Tense

Nineteen of the following are wrong. Correct them and give a
reason for each change in sentences 1-25.

Example:

Ninety-seven enemy planes have been brought down yesterday.
Ninety-seven enemy planes were brought down yesterday. (The past
tense is used for action completed in the past.)

1. I have entered Queen Elizabeth High School last September.
2. In assembly today two girls who are in this country only four months
   told us why they came to Canada.
3. Last summer and the preceding summer I have worked on a dairy farm.
4. The meteorologist pointed out that Greenland in time might have great
   strategic importance.
5. When I reached home, I discovered that I forgot my suitcase.
6. If Brutus had taken Cassius' advice, he would not have given Antony
   permission to speak.
7. Although these cases were shipped a month ago, the purchaser did not
   receive the goods yet.
8. The president closed his address with the hope that what has been done
   during his administration may benefit the people.
9. I intended to write the letter on Saturday.
10. If Squire Cass's sons loved him, they would have considered his feelings.
11. Since Shakespeare's time the stage settings became more elaborate.
12. Circe told Odysseus that he should fill the ears of his men with wax, so
    that they may not hear the song of the Sirens.
13. Modern history is the record of events that happened recently.
14. Enclose you will find a check for seventy-five dollars.
15. The colonists were the descendants of the English and had the English
    conception of liberty.
16. Sir Walter Scott wished to have repaid the total indebtedness of his
    publishers.

17. I intended to have gone to the museum last week.
18. You hadn't ought to go in swimming right after dinner.
19. A dividend of ten cents a share of common stock, amounting to $1,265,000, was paid on February 1.
20. During my visit to Roosevelt Field I hoped to have seen an autogyro.
21. Ernest said that he may be absent from the rehearsal.
22. Carl came into the meeting late and begins to talk to another boy.
23. The public health nurse told Mrs. Bianchi that she hadn't ought to feed the baby bacon.
24. If I had sneezed, the broadcast would have been ruined.
25. I wish I would have taken a course in typing while I was in high school.

SHALL, WILL; SHOULD, WOULD

64. To express simple futurity (mere expectation), use *shall* **in the first person and** *will* **in the second and the third.**

> I *shall* probably *plant* the marigolds and cosmos along the fence.
> I *shall be delighted* to have lunch with you next Friday.
> The journalism class *will publish* next week's edition of the *Brookdale Record.*

NOTE. "I will probably enter the University of Manitoba in September," although not the best usage, is accepted colloquial English. The rule, however, indicates the practice of most writers.

65. To express the will of the speaker, use *will* **in the first person and** *shall* **in the second and the third.**

PROMISE   You *shall* not *be annoyed* by these rowdies any longer.

WILLINGNESS   We *will* gladly *mind* the baby this evening, Mrs. Hunt.

THREAT OR DETERMINATION   I *will see* that your father hears of this.

COMMAND   You *shall* not *use* the car again this week.

66. In first person questions use *shall*.

Whom *shall* we *invite* to the puppet show?
How *shall* I *return* the book to you?

67. *Should* is, as a rule, used like *shall*, and *would* like *will*.

After graduation I *should like* to play on a professional basketball team.

EXCEPTIONS.   *Would* is used for habitual action.

All summer I *would rush* home from business every evening to work in my garden.

Should is used (1) to express duty and (2) to express an opinion modestly.

DUTY   She *should help* her mother get dinner for all those people.
MODEST EXPRESSION OF OPINION   I *should think* so.

PRACTICE 25.

Insert the correct or preferred word. Give the reason for each choice.

A. 1. I —— like to listen carefully to both recordings before deciding which one to buy. (should, would)
2. How —— we celebrate Mother's birthday? (shall, will)
3. The work —— be completed by January 15. (A promise.) (shall, will)
4. I —— be glad to play on the baseball team you are organizing. (should, would)
5. Most of the material for my report on television I —— obtain from the *Britannica Book of the Year*. (shall, will)
6. I —— like to visit the planetarium. (should, would)
7. I —— be there on time. (Determination.) (shall, will)

B. 1. When the final examinations are over, I —— be ready for my summer job in a garage. (shall, will)
2. What belt —— I wear with this gray dress? (shall, will)
3. I —— like very much to see your collection of tropical fish. (should, would)
4. I hope I —— be able to write short stories like these some day. (shall, will)

5. I —— never give my consent to such a ridiculous request. (Determination.) (shall, will)

6. I —— be glad to teach you to knit. (shall, will)

7. I —— probably spend my vacation making a Youth Hostel bicycle trip. (shall, will)

TEST 4B (*Mastery*). VERB EXCEPT AGREEMENT OF VERB AND SUBJECT

Median—14.1

Select the correct or preferred verb to complete each sentence. On your paper write each answer after the number of the sentence. (Right — Wrong = Score).

1. In an instant Edwin discovered that he had —— down on a freshly painted bench. (sat, set)

2. If Harold —— begun earlier to prepare his report, everybody would have enjoyed it more. (had, would have)

3. You —— to put that fragile goblet into boiling water. (hadn't ought, ought not)

4. For a half hour I —— on the living room floor while Jane practised for her artificial respiration test. (laid, lay)

5. Suddenly over the roar of the motors —— the dismal wail of a foghorn. (came, come)

6. After Sherlock Holmes had —— the advertisement, Dr. Watson took it to the office of the *Evening News*. (written, wrote)

7. Some of the most skilful bowmen in Lincoln and Nottinghamshire were gathered in the forest, and Little John —— tallest of the group. (is, was)

8. When I reached home, I discovered that I —— my history book in school. (had left, left)

9. What programs —— we listen to this evening? (shall, will)

10. The letter brought the good news that on the previous Friday I —— elected a member of Senior Arista. (had been, was)

11. After Helen and I had bought our yarn and —— to take lessons, we discovered that knitting a sweater is more difficult than we had supposed. (began, begun)

12. Halfway to Chicago we ran into a storm which worried Father John because he never —— in a plane before. (had been, was)

13. If Marcus —— in his own home, he wouldn't throw paper on the floor. (was, were)

14. Last night I wanted —— *The Courage and the Glory* before going to bed. (to finish, to have finished)

15. If the weather —— warmer, we could canoe up Lake George to Fort Ticonderoga. (was, were)

16. Rogers circled over the canyon to study the white markers —— spread out on its floor. (laying, lying)

17. Tom Canty dragged himself to his wretched bed and —— down to dream of palaces, princes, and kings. (laid, lay)

18. With one mighty effort Tim and I lifted the heavy chest and —— it on the rude table in the cabin. (sat, set)

19. For two days before his rescue Carter had —— helpless on the ice pack. (laid, lain)

20. When we reached Harrisburg after a two hours' drive over icy roads, I was almost ——. (froze, frozen)

Enter your mark on your achievement graph.

AGREEMENT OF VERB AND SUBJECT

TEST 5A (*Diagnostic*). AGREEMENT OF VERB AND SUBJECT

In each of the following sentences which word or expression is correct? On your paper write each answer after the number of the sentence. (Right − Wrong = Score)

1. I think three dollars —— too much for a book on amateur photography. (are, is)

2. A hundred years ago there —— Indians all over this neighbourhood. (was, were)

3. Examinations to test scholarship —— given in medieval universities. (was, were)

4. The description of the tiny islands —— so vivid that you can almost see them as you read. (are, is)

5. *Young Americans* by Cornelia Meigs —— stories of real boys and girls. (contain, contains)

6. The churches of this community —— a great opportunity for service. (has, have)

7. Two thirds of Martha's free time —— spent in experimenting with new and unusual recipes. (are, is)

8. You, like every other candidate for graduation, —— to serve on one of the class committees. (want, wants)

9. Gradually, as your skill and courage ——, you become more and more confident of your superiority over this throbbing giant of steel and iron. (increase, increases)

10. The animals that particularly attracted my attention —— the bears. (was, were)

11. At first everyone, including Bernice and her parents, —— convinced of Kenneth's guilt. (are, is)

12. Leon is one of the boys who —— constructing a tennis court behind the high school. (are, is)

13. In the small envelope which Mr. Openshaw received in the mail —— five dried orange seeds and a mysterious message signed X.Y.Z. (was, were)

14. The number of deaths caused by traffic accidents —— decreasing. (are, is)

15. In our last municipal election all the Labour candidates but one —— elected. (was, were)

16. Many of the contributors to *Popular Science* —— how to make useful articles out of junk. (explain, explains)

17. Buckwheat cakes and maple syrup —— one of my favourite breakfast dishes. (are, is)

18. A will left by J. M. Glenarm, bequeathing his nephew a large estate under unusual conditions, —— wild adventures for Jack and his two sisters. (start, starts)

19. Where —— your committee decided to hold its final meeting? (has, have)

20. The mayor, together with the president of the Canadian Legion, and two veterans, —— dedicated the town honour roll. (as, have)

68. A verb agrees with its subject in number and person. First find the subject; then determine its number. If the subject is a pronoun, notice also the person.

They agree   They don't agree

In recent years there *have been* many changes in methods of teaching.

Allen *doesn't* know how to drive a tractor.
Why *weren't* you at the meeting of the Science Club yesterday?
(The subject *you* always takes a plural verb.)

Millicent, not her twin sisters, *has offered* to bake a pie for our picnic. (The verb agrees with the positive subject, not the negative.)
The Count of Monte Cristo is one of those rare books that *appeal* to almost every boy and girl. (*Books*, not *one*, is the antecedent of *that*. The relative pronoun is therefore plural.)

69. Do not be deceived by a modifier after the subject. Search out the subject and make the verb agree with it. *With, together with, as well as,* and *including* after subjects are troublemakers.

In general the procedure of our assemblies *varies* little.

Parts of *A Son of the Middle Border are* as entertaining as an
adventure story.

Bob Frederickson, together with Sam Davis and Ed Morse,

is building a model airplane.

One of Jane's finest characteristics *is* her composure.

**70. As a rule, compound subjects connected by *and* take plural
verbs.** "Lillian and Mary were absent" means that two girls were
absent.

EXCEPTION. A compound subject that names one person, thing,
or idea takes a singular verb.

> The secretary and treasurer of the Senior Class *writes* the minutes of the
> meetings, *carries* on the class correspondence, and *collects* dues. (One
> person is both secretary and treasurer.)
> At first bread and milk *was* the baby seal's favourite breakfast dish. (Bread
> and milk is one breakfast dish.)

**71. A verb having a compound subject connected by *or* or *nor*
agrees with the nearer subject.**

> Either Scotty or Towser *has eaten* the chops. (Because one dog has eaten
> the chops, the verb is singular.)
> Either Ted or the girls *have eaten* the chocolates. (The verb agrees with the
> nearer subject word, *girls*.)

RIGHT   Either you or I *am* responsible for the error.

BETTER   Either you are responsible for the error, or I am.

**72. A word that is plural in form but names a single object or idea
takes a singular verb.**

> Do you think five dollars *is* too much for this hat? (Five dollars is one sum
> of money.)
> *Younger Poets is* an anthology of the work of high school students.
> Two thirds of a pie *is* far too much for a little boy to eat.
> Mathematics *is* important to the aviator.

**73. As a rule, *each, every, neither, one, many a, a person,* and com-
pounds with *body* and *one* take singular verbs.**

> One of the boys *has caught* five big trout.
> Every tree and every shrub *is covered* with snow.
> Neither of us *was* able to finish the experiment in one period.

74. A collective noun takes a singular verb when the group is thought of and a plural verb when the individuals are thought of.

My physiography class *has decided* to visit the Hayden Planetarium.
My physiography class *are* now *discussing* plans for the visit.

75. A verb agrees with its subject, not with its predicate nominative.

To me the most fascinating collection *is* the jewels.
A gunner and a navigator *were* his crew.

PRACTICE 26. Choosing Correct Verbs

Twenty-one of the following sentences are incorrect. Correct them and give a reason for each change you make.

1. Under the fake forecastle there was two cannons.
2. I admit that civics never were my favourite subject.
3. Many a would-be nurse has been inspired by the story of Florence Nightingale.
4. Winnie, not the committee members, were responsible for the success of Senior Day.
5. The committee are discussing plans for a masquerade party.
6. Charles, as well as his young sisters, were frightened by the piteous groans.
7. Mother is anxious to know whether Marion or June are also interested in the Cadet Nurse Corps.
8. During the next quarter the Queen's team weren't able to cross the Varsity goal line.
9. My favourite among summer sports is swimming.
10. There has been a number of robberies in my neighbourhood recently, and not one of the thieves have been caught.
11. There was several requests at the library yesterday for books about radar.
12. He don't know how to study a spelling lesson.
13. Neither of these jobs offers much scope for creative talent like yours.
14. Every stick and stone have been cleared from the west field.
15. Strangely enough, not one of the five boys has the slightest idea who batted the baseball through Mrs. Bascom's window.
16. Is it the black puppy or the white one which have just made a meal of Father's new hat?
17. Tom Eadie was one of the expert divers who was summoned by the Navy to help in the salvage of the S-4.
18. The next day Barbara and I was summoned to the principal's office.
19. Each of the stories in *Short Stories for Study and Enjoyment* are different from the others and leave a vivid impression on the reader's mind.
20. In our class fourteen dollars has been collected for the Red Cross.

21. Twenty-five years ago there was not so many large and beautiful schools as there is to-day.
22. The expression "free textbooks" means books lent to the pupils by the Board of Education.
23. Neither of us like ripe olives.
24. An alligator don't make an ideal pet.
25. Every bud and blossom are opening wide.
26. Not one of the seven passengers in the plane was injured.
27. Is it Juliet or Mary who stand first in the class?
28. It is one of the numerous books that is published by the Harvard University Press.
29. By nine o'clock James and I was ready to go home.
30. Every one of the boys is to blame for the disorder.

PRACTICE 27. Agreement of Verb and Subject

This rapid drill is to help you form the habit of using correct verbs. First use each of the subjects listed below with *is* or *are*, then with *wasn't* or *weren't*, then with *doesn't* or *don't*. Choose quickly.

1. you	2. everyone in the class
3. a person	4. he and his twin sister
5. a set of encyclopedias	6. every pen and pencil
7. ten dollars	8. van Loon's *Ships*
9. three of the crew	10. his choice of words
11. many an engineer	12. he
13. either the pilot or the co-pilot	14. stamps and envelopes
15. a bunch of radishes	16. one of my assignments
17. a box of cookies	18. either Marie or Betty
19. students at Shaw High School	20. three quarters of the period
21. a number of boys	22. the number of accidents
23. it	24. this kind of apples

TEST 5B (*Mastery*). AGREEMENT OF VERB AND SUBJECT
Median—14.9

In each of the following which word or expression is correct? On your paper write each answer after the number of the sentence. (Right − Wrong = Score)

1. As far as I could see, there —— only two ways to escape. (was, were)
2. Ten minutes after the end of the performance the audience —— still calling for their favourite actors. (was, were)
3. Either Bryce Canyon or Zion Canyon —— worth a trip across the continent. (are, is)

4. Captain Bligh, who has been sent to sea in a little boat with several mid-shipmen, —— in court to accuse the mutineers. (was, were)

5. Plenty of rest, as well as exercise and nourishing food, —— essential to the normal growth of a young puppy. (are, is)

6. The gate was open but in the yard —— two fierce-looking bulldogs. (was, were)

7. The setting of these two poems —— a farm in New England. (are, is)

8. The changes made by the new coach —— based upon his wide experience with high school baseball teams. (was, were)

9. A number of my friends —— members of the Engineering Club. (are, is)

10. In front of the parish church —— fifty or more boys and men. (was, were)

11. Apple pie and cheese —— Uncle Henry's favourite dessert. (are, is)

12. *Heroes of Progress* —— of the achievements of great scientists, inventors, naturalists, and artists. (tell, tells)

13. Two dollars —— seem an exorbitant price for that air-mail stationery. (doesn't, don't)

14. Why —— two thirds of the work always left to Margaret? (are, is)

15. Not one of us fifteen boys —— been late this term. (has, have)

16. The lines "Ten thousand saw I at a glance, tossing their heads in sprightly dance" —— a thrilling scene. (picture, pictures)

17. Sherlock Holmes and Dr. Watson discover the criminals' plans and —— their scheme for robbing the bank. (upset, upsets)

18. In Pittsburgh —— located some of the largest steel mills in the world. (are, is)

19. Clyde R. Hunt, president of the Canadian Legion, together with Thomas P. Ohlert, president of the Woodhaven Lions, —— been busily working out the final details of the dedication. (has, have)

20. During recess the children at the nursery play games which —— them fairness and co-operation. (teach, teaches)

Enter your mark on your achievement graph.

CORRECT ADJECTIVES, ADVERBS, NOUNS, PREPOSITIONS, AND CONJUNCTIONS

TEST 6A (*Diagnostic*). GRAMMAR EXCEPT PRONOUN AND VERB

In each of the following select the correct or preferred word or expression. On your paper write each answer after the number of the sentence. (Right − Wrong = Score)

1. I hope that when I return a year from now —— will be ready for college. (that you, you)

2. We could not see the lake very ——, as it was foggy. (good, well)

3. After finishing her homework Betty practised her piano lesson for a half ——. (an hour, hour)

4. I enjoy swimming more than —— sport. (any, any other)

5. When Charlie and I awoke the next morning, we were so stiff we ——
hardly move a muscle. (could, couldn't)

6. Masefield's poetry is different —— Robinson's. (from, than)

7. Sherlock Holmes refused to listen to the stranger's story —— Dr. Watson
was permitted to remain in the room. (unless, without)

8. Just then the puma gave an angry snarl and jumped —— the ledge.
(off, off of)

9. After an early morning fishing trip broiled trout tastes ——. (delicious,
deliciously)

10. —— will be many opportunities for this generation to practise the Good
Neighbour policy. (Their, There)

11. In a short detective story you don't have to read three hundred pages to
discover who the murderer is, —— you have to do in a full-length mystery
novel. (as, like)

12. For a long time the divers couldn't find —— way to enter the sunken
submarine. (any, no)

13. Why don't you like —— kind of dress? (that, those)

14. On Christmas Eve the baby was —— excited to eat her supper. (to, too)

15. For a long time law appealed to Clifford more strongly than —— profession. (any, any other)

16. Although the commander gave the order to surface, the submarine did
not rise as it should ——. (have, have risen)

17. No extensive training is needed to pilot —— kind of helicopter. (that,
those)

18. Do you know the difference between a politician and ——? (a statesman,
statesman)

19. Aunt Miranda's opinion of the new dress was quite different —— Rebecca's.
(from, than)

20. The letters RHHS are engraved on the ring in a —— way. (most unique,
unique)

CORRECT ADJECTIVES AND ADVERBS

76. Use the comparative when comparing two.

Vivian is the *taller* and *prettier* of the two sisters.

**77. When the comparative is used for more than two, exclude
from the group the object compared.**

                                                              other
New York has more electoral votes than any ‸ state in the
Union. (The wrong sentence says that New York has more
electoral votes than itself, for New York is one of the states
in the group *any state in the Union.*)

78. Avoid double comparison.   Double comparison ("more wiser",) "most beautifulest") was correct when Shakespeare wrote but has gone out of style.

> Of the two magazines, *Good Housekeeping* has a ~~more~~ wider selection of recipes and homemaking articles.

79. *This* and *that* are singular and modify singular nouns; *these* and *those* are plural.

that

I can't understand why you enjoy ~~those~~ kind of books.

Say *this boy*, not "this here boy"; *that boy*, not "that there boy".

80. Repeat the article before a second noun in a series for contrast, clearness, or emphasis.

> In those days life was kind to neither the old nor *the* young.
> The captain and *the* manager of the football team have agreed to address the cheering squad.

81. Say *a half hour* or *half an hour*, **not "a half an hour".**

> By working energetically for a half ~~an~~ hour, Father and I made the car shine like new.

82. Omit the article after *sort* and *kind.*

RIGHT   The other pupils in Schuyler Academy considered Fred Laughton a likeable *kind of* boy.
COLLOQUIAL   The other pupils in Schuyler Academy considered Fred Laughton a likeable kind of a boy.

83. Use *a* **before a consonant sound and** *an* **before a vowel sound.** Don't make the mistake of thinking of letters instead of sounds.   "An hour" is right, because the *h* is silent.

PRACTICE 28. Correct Adjectives and Adverbs

Select the correct or preferred word or expression in each sentence and give a reason for the choice.

A. 1. English is spoken by more people than —— language in the world. (any, any other)
   2. —— mile farther on, the platoon came to the rifle range. (A half, A half a)
   3. Which is the —— educational of these two magazines? (more, most)
   4. Diamonds are the —— substance known to man. (hardest, most hardest)

5. Clarence Day's *Life with Father*, which I finished last night, is different from —— book I have ever read. (any, any other)

6. Ontario produces more winter wheat than —— province. (any, **any other**)

7. Go south on Park Avenue for about a half ——. (a block, block)

8. No one would order —— kind of oranges. (that, those)

B. 1. Home nursing is —— for me than first aid. (easier, more easier)

2. It is —— honour to present Major Charles P. Coates as our next speaker. (a, an)

3. Which have the —— opportunities for advancement, chemical **or** electrical engineers? (best, better)

4. —— kind of song has never appealed to me. (That, Those)

5. Patsy is a peculiar sort of ——. (a dog, dog)

6. A half —— away I met Dr. Foster, who had been calling on Mr. Reisman. (a block, block)

7. The birds of Brazil are more beautiful than —— in South America. (any, any others)

8. The Navy's eyesight tests are —— than the Army's. (more stricter, stricter)

84. Avoid the double negative. Most negatives begin with *n*— *not, no never, nothing, none, nobody.* The negative is not used with the half-negatives *hardly, scarcely, only,* and *but* when it means *only.*

> When Jane returned from training camp, I couldn̶'̶t̶ hardly wait to see her.
>
> *anything*
> I had to admit I didn't know ~~nothing~~ about ventriloquism.
> There is̶n̶'̶t̶ but one high school for the children of the three towns.

PRACTICE 29. Avoiding Double Negatives

Seven of the following sentences are wrong. Correct them.

1. My grandfather hadn't never seen a technicolour movie.
2. The pilot searched for a landing strip, but there wasn't none.
3. Industrial engineers haven't hardly begun to find uses for plastics.
4. There was but one taxi waiting at the station.
5. In August we haven't had scarcely one rainy day.
6. By the end of the week Mr. Rogers hadn't no more gym shoes for sale.
7. Donors may give blood for plasma only five times a year.
8. The captain wouldn't take but one volunteer with him.

9. Jim Connors has said hardly a word this evening.
10. Isn't there no one here who saw the rocket flares last **night?**

CORRECT NOUNS

Use these correct forms:

The high school is two miles from my home. (NOT "mile".)
Yesterday we sold ten bushels of apples. (NOT "bushel".)
My music teacher is only five feet tall. (NOT "foot".)
Last winter I lost two pairs of gloves. (NOT "pair".)

WRONG PARTS OF SPEECH

85. Do not interchange conjunctions and prepositions. *As, than,* **and** *unless* **are commonly conjunctions. Avoid the use of** *like* **or** *without* **as a conjunction.** *Different from* **is always correct.**

The slums of a great city are far *different from* the homes of the rich.
Florence interpreted the third question *as* I did.

86. Use an adverb to modify a verb, an adjective, or an adverb.

RIGHT   I *surely* was frightened when I heard that noise.
SLANG   I sure was frightened when I heard that noise.

Slow, loud, quick, fast, smooth, cheap, right, wrong, clear, ill, well, hard, high, long, deep, and *close* are used as adjectives or as adverbs.

Drive *slow*.   Come *quick*.   Speak *louder*.   (Of course, "Drive slowly" and "Come quickly" are also correct.)

87. After *be, become, grow, seem, appear, look, feel, taste, smell,* **and** *sound,* **use a predicate adjective to describe the subject.**

Everyone thought that Louise looked beautifully.

88. Do not carelessly use *to* **and** *their* **as adverbs.**

There are *too* many adjectives in your sentences.

PRACTICE 30. Nouns and Parts of Speech

Eleven of the following sentences are wrong. Correct them and give a reason for each change you make.

1. How many bushel of potatoes did your father raise last year?
2. Rolly Marvin looks like he could play a great game at tackle.
3. The salutation of a friendly letter is usually different from that of a business letter.
4. Nancy wanted to talk and act as the wealthy people of Glen Shore did.
5. The first Eddystone lighthouse, which resembled a Chinese pagoda, was very different in appearance than the lighthouses of today.
6. No other knight in the king's court could entertain the young prince like Richard could.
7. My hobby, fashion designing, I take very serious, for I expect to make it my vocation after I graduate from high school.
8. Mother is feeling somewhat better today.
9. In some states, however, the candidates are chosen different.
10. Alice found that the mixture in the bottle tasted rather sweetly.
11. The voice in the next room sounded harshly.
12. Write your essay legibly on one side of the paper.
13. Constance is always to busy to have any fun.
14. Walter and George were to frightened to move from the spot.
15. There was no doubt that the letter had been read by the naval **censor.**
16. Other fountain pens are filled different.

SYNTACTICAL REDUNDANCE

89. A pronoun and its antecedent are not used as subject of the same verb.

The aviator who made the rescue he declined to consider it an unusual **feat.**

90. Omit every unnecessary preposition or other word.

In Rome we saw the house in which Keats died ~~in~~.
A strong gust of wind nearly blew us off ~~of~~ the observation tower.

PRACTICE 31. Getting Rid of Unnecessary Words

Twelve of the following sentences are incorrect. Correct them and give reasons.

1. Shelley ends up "Ode to the West Wind" on the optimistic note, "If Winter comes, can Spring be far behind?"
2. The newsreel man noticed that on both trial runs when the driver brought the car to a stop, that the car swerved to the right.
3. One day a high summer flood washed the mongoose out of the burrow where he lived with his father and mother, and carried him, kicking and clucking, down a roadside ditch.
4. In this chapter we meet Charles Darnay, of whom we hear a great deal of later in the book.
5. This poem tells of a person who, although she never saw a moor or the sea, can imagine the appearance of the heather and the waves.
6. Will this extra work take the unprepared mark off of my record?
7. When Godfrey decided to claim his daughter, Silas he left the decision to Eppie.
8. It was a fresh, crystal-clear morning, with icicles hanging like dazzling pendants from the trees and a glaze of pale blue on the surface of the snow.
9. Constance is a girl of about seventeen years old, with short curly hair, dark blue eyes, and a turned-up nose.
10. When Emma Jane went home, she told her brothers of what she had done.
11. The reason for my absence yesterday was on account of illness.
12. "In Flanders Fields" by John McCrae is another poem of which I never tire of reading.
13. The first and most important step is to decide on what the biggest news of the week is.
14. Entering an arched doorway, the two found themselves in a beautiful little vaulted chapel about eighteen feet long.
15. This news dispatch tells about a young aviator who, though he had a chance to bail out, he gave his parachute to a passenger who had none.

INCORRECT OMISSION

91. Do not omit a repeated verb if it differs in form from the verb expressed.

RIGHT The Western team hoped to defeat Queen's as decisively as they *had* already *defeated* McGill.

COLLOQUIAL   The Western team hoped to defeat Queen's as decisively as they had already McGill. (*Had defeat* is not grammatical.)

92. Do not make a single form of the verb *be* serve as both a principal and an auxiliary verb.

WRONG   Public speaking is (principal verb) valuable training and preparing (present participle) me for the employment interview.

RIGHT   Public speaking *is* (principal verb) valuable training and *is* (auxiliary) *preparing* (present participle) me for the employment interview.

93. Include every word needed to complete a comparison.

that of

The salary of a travelling companion is in many cases larger than ∧ a private secretary or a stenographer.

94. Do not omit a needed preposition.

RIGHT   Franklin D. Roosevelt *graduated from* Harvard University. (Both *graduated from* and *was graduated from* are correct.)

WRONG   Franklin D. Roosevelt graduated Harvard University. (*Graduate* in this sense does not take an object.)

PRACTICE 32. Adding Needed Words

Ten of the following sentences are wrong. Correct them and give reasons.

1. My sympathy has always been with the poor people and have decided that the only way I can really help them is by becoming a doctor.
2. Quinidine is a rare drug and being distributed only to the armed forces.
3. Webster told his hearers they were on the same ground their fathers stood fifty years before.
4. The ideal vocation for a person is the one for which he is best fitted and which he most enjoys.
5. Received your letter in this morning's mail and hasten to assure you that I shall be on hand on May 18.
6. Scientists say that synthetic quinine is as good, if not better than natural quinine.
7. I am hoping in your next letter to hear a great improvement in your work.
8. Richard studied Diesel engineering just as many others have and are doing.
9. More than ten thousand schools have used or are using our service.
10. Is the salary of an engineer larger than a teacher or an accountant?
11. Topography is an interesting subject and helping to prepare me for a job as surveyor.
12. Fred Waring graduated Flushing High School last June.

TEST 6B (*Mystery*). GRAMMAR EXCEPT PRONOUN AND VERB
Median—16.5

In each of the following select the correct or preferred word or expression. On your paper write each answer after the number of the sentence. (Right — Wrong = Score)

1. Take-offs and landings of a bus-plane would make fares —— high. (to, too)
2. Bill's courtesy, efficiency, and willingness —— have made a good impression on Mr. Burroughs. (sure, surely)
3. Thomas Edison patented more inventions than —— person who has ever lived. (any, any other)
4. Within a few months I —— hardly see the scar on my arm. (could, couldn't)
5. In our school cafeteria we never get —— kind of unbalanced meals. (that, those)
6. The secretary and —— of the Writers' Club were absent from yesterday's meeting. (the treasurer, treasurer)
7. Is an autogyro different —— a helicopter? (from, than)
8. Each year Americans consume more pounds of sugar than the people of —— nation in the world. (any, any other)
9. Your delicious hot dinner will taste —— it had been cooked aboard the plane, not at the airport hours before. (as if, like)
10. At graduation Anita Cromwell won more awards than —— member of her class. (any, any other)
11. When I visited the aquarium last week, I saw the —— fish imaginable. (most oddest, oddest)
12. —— is never any justification for discourtesy. (Their, There)
13. I don't think Miss Jordan will —— that excuse for tardiness. (accept accept of)
14. Miss Shuyler never has forgotten and never —— that one of her distant relatives was a signer of the Declaration of Independence. (will, will forget)
15. Which of the dresses do you like better, the blue or —— one? (green, the green)
16. What is the rate for a half —— program over a major radio network? (an hour, hour)
17. You cannot understand a difficult topic —— you give the subject your undivided attention. (unless, without)
18. This afternoon I played tennis with a boy with whom I had never —— before. (played, played with)
19. Your method of learning a poem is different —— mine. (from, than)
20. After taking one bite out of a Northern Spy, Harold said, "I like —— kind of apple." (these, this)

Enter your mark on your achievement graph.

GRAMMAR POSTERS

By drawing a grammar poster you will impress a correct form **on** your own mind and on the minds of other pupils who see your **poster** on the bulletin board.

STANDARDS FOR POSTERS

1. *Is the error real, common, and serious?*
2. *Is the correct form conspicuous and the incorrect preceded by* not, *crossed* **out,** *printed smaller, or otherwise subordinated?*
3. *Is the lettering easily read from all parts of the classroom?*
4. *Is the workmanship careful?*
5. *Is the picture appropriate?*
6. *Is there a touch of humour?*

Pupil Cartoon

PRACTICE 33. Making Grammar Posters

After studying the cartoons in this book, especially the student cartoon on this page, draw a grammar poster to help eradicate **a** common error.

HANDBOOK: B

Punctuation

PUNCTUATION marks help the writer to make his ideas clear and help the reader to understand what is meant. Because punctuation marks are conventional signals, a writer needs to know what marks are ordinarily used to indicate the relationship he desires to express. Because of the tendency toward less pointing it is wise to omit punctuation marks which do not help the reader.

MASTERY TEST "A"—PUNCTUATION

Copy the following sentences, punctuate them, and insert needed apostrophes. Overpunctuation is just as bad as underpunctuation. Therefore if you either omit a needed mark or insert a mark that is not needed, the sentence is wrong. Do not divide one good sentence into two sentences.

1. Ships are warned off these sunken reefs by lighthouses buoys and fog-horns
2. The task of framing the constitution was performed by fifty-five of the best men that the provinces could send to the convention
3. Cuba which was thought to be a part of Asia was discovered by Columbus
4. Have you read about Marie Fish the young biologist who hatched the eels eggs
5. The terrific storm of hot air which sweeps the Arabian desert is called a simoom which in Arabian means poison
6. Next year however we shall make another attempt said Fred
7. If you and Janet can come to see us this summer for we are always delighted to have you
8. He was respectful not servile to superiors and affable not improperly familiar with equals
9. These are his exact words I rise Mr. President to ask for information
10. An adverb is a word used to modify a verb an adjective or another adverb as *rapidly often completely* and *altogether*
11. War means murder and destruction peace life and plenty
12. The food supply had to be organized and back of the various centres of organization stood the whole city glad to do whatever it was asked to do
13. Health ability education and opportunities in various fields should be considered in the choice of a vocation

14. We find the heart of the address in this sentence Our purpose is to build in this nation a human society not an economic system

15. By the way Tom did you ever get that dictionary you were saving your money for I asked

16. Many an Indian dazzled by glittering ornaments and gaudy blankets eagerly offered valuable furs in exchange a profitable transaction for the wily traders

17. Strange to say I found good air pilots hard to get

18. I was very glad to hear that you are coming to visit me soon

19. Hundreds of thousands of miles of rail must yet be laid millions of miles of hard-surface roads will yet be needed

20. In that moment sir continued Walker that crocodile had become a demon of fury lashing with its tail slashing at its tormentor with its huge jaws

PERIOD

1. The period is used after imperative and declarative sentences.

Stunt flying requires altitude and speed.
Open the window.

2. The period is used after abbreviations: P.M., *Mass.* **Do not** use a period after *per cent* or Roman numerals in a sentence.

At 9:15 P.M. seventy-five per cent of the votes had been counted.

COMMA

3. To set off an expression requires two commas unless the words to be set off come first or last in the sentence.

4. The comma is used to set off the name of the person addressed.

Why don't you speak for yourself, John?

5. As a rule, appositives are set off by commas.

Cheerfulness is health; the opposite, melancholy, is disease.

a. Appositives preceded by *or,* and titles and degrees after a name, are set off.

The ounce, or snow leopard, has a tail three feet long.
Thomas Kite Brown, M.A., Ph.D., is one of the editors of the dictionary.

b. The comma is not used to set off restrictive appositives:

The poet Browning. The orator Burke. The year 1930. My friend Kirby. The word *one.*

6. Most parenthetical expressions are set off by commas—for example, *however, on the other hand, for instance, by the way, to tell the truth, to say the least, I think, I believe, I repeat.*

Lewis and Clark could not, however, have crossed the United States without the help of the Indian squaw.

The lion, like everything great, has his share of critics and detractors.

a. The comma, as a rule, is not used to set off *also, perhaps, indeed, therefore, at least, nevertheless, likewise,* and other parenthetical expressions that do not require a pause in reading aloud.

b. Well, why, or *now* at the beginning of a conversational sentence is commonly set off; *etc.* is always set off.

Why, I hadn't thought of that.
2, 4, 6, 8, etc., are even numbers.

7. The comma is used to separate expressions in a series. When a conjunction is used between the last two items only, it is correct to place a comma before the conjunction or to omit the comma.

There is no substitute for thorough-going, ardent, and sincere earnestness.
Verdun, Jutland Reef, the Somme, and the Marne were four important battles of World War I.
If I cannot correspond with you, if I cannot learn your mind, if I cannot co-operate with you, I cannot be your friend.

a. When all the conjunctions are used, no comma is required unless it makes the sentence clearer.

He is brave and courteous and generous.
We found very few huckleberries that were ripe, and finally decided to pick blackberries instead.

b. In the word group *two little hens,* no comma is used, because the adjectives are not co-ordinate in thought. *Little* modifies *hens,* but *two* modifies *little hens.* Likewise in *solid gold watch, gold* modifies *watch,* but *solid* modifies *gold watch.* Likewise in *puny right hand, right* modifies *hand,* and *puny* modifies *right hand.*

c. Expressions like *an honest, ambitious man* and a *ferocious, straggling mustache* require the comma. If inserting *and* between the adjectives does not change the sense, the comma is needed: *an honest and ambitious man; a ferocious and straggling mustache.*

8. In an address or date each item after the first is set off by commas.

On Congress Street, Portland, Maine, stands the home of Henry Wadsworth Longfellow.
On November 11, 1918, an armistice dictated by General Foch was signed.

9. The comma is used to set off a contrasting expression introduced by *not.*

Francis Scott Key is famous, not as a lawyer, but as the author of "The Star-Spangled Banner".

10. Use a comma after *yes* or *no* at the beginning of a sentence.

Yes, you're right.

11. The comma is used after the salutation of a friendly letter and the complimentary close of any letter.

Dear Isabel,
Yours truly,

12. Occasionally, when no other rule justifies the use of a punctuation mark, a comma is necessary to prevent misreading.

Ever since, Carter House has been deserted.
The night before, we bought a tent to take with us.
To the wise, youth is a time for training.

13. As a rule, the comma is used between the principal parts of a compound sentence if they are joined by a conjunction—*and, but, or, nor, so, yet, while* (meaning *but*).   In a short sentence the comma may be omitted.

Man was made to be active, and he is never so happy as when he is doing something.
Experience keeps a dear school, but fools will learn in no other.
His country called and he went.

Note.   Either the comma or the semicolon may be used when *so, yet* or *then* connects the principal clauses.

14. The comma occasionally takes the place of an omitted verb.

General Haig was the commander of the British; General Petain, of the French; and General Pershing, of the Americans.
We respect deeds; they, words.

15. The comma is used to set off a short direct quotation.

"Why, Silver," said the captain, "if you had pleased to be an honest man, you might have been sitting in your own galley."

16. Use a comma after an introductory adverb clause.

When a man is wrong and won't admit it, he always gets angry.
If you want to live and keep well, you must eat proper food.

a. The comma may be omitted after a restrictive introductory clause, especially a short one.

Right   When he reached home he found the telegram.
Right   When he reached home, he found the telegram.

17. Use the comma to set off non-restrictive phrases and clauses. If the omission of the subordinate clause would change the meaning of the principal clause or destroy its sense, the clause is restrictive, and no comma is required.

A restrictive adjective clause answers the question "Which one?" or the question "Which ones?"

A nonrestrictive adjective clause does not answer the question "Which one?" or the question "Which ones?" It gives additional information.

1. Peter is a boy *who watches goats.* [Answers the question "Which *boy?*"]
2. The highwayman wore boots *that reached to his knees.* [Answers the question "Which *boots?*"]
3. I was sent back to a butcher shop *which was two miles from camp* to get another pound of bacon. (Answers the question "Which *butcher shop?*")
4. The man *who does everything for gain* does nothing for good. [Answers the question "Which *man?*"]

Nonrestrictive Clauses

1. I called to my brother Ralph, *who ran quickly for Mother.* [Does not answer the question "Which *brother Ralph?*"]
2. My father and I planned to climb Mount Washington, *which is about sixty-four hundred feet high.* [Does not answer the question "Which *Mount Washington?*"]
3. Soon we crossed Bright Angel Creek, *which comes from Bright Angel Canyon.* [Does not answer the question "Which *Bright Angel Creek?*"]
4. Tom Sawyer, *who felt like playing,* tried to get out of whitewashing the fence. [Does not answer the question "Which *Tom Sawyer?*"]
5. We flew over Brooklyn, *which from an altitude of two thousand feet appeared to be a miniature playground.* [Does not answer the question. "Which *Brooklyn?*"]

a. As a rule, a participial phrase at the beginning of a sentence is nonrestrictive and is therefore set off from the rest of the sentence by a comma.

Deprived of the possibilities of importing foodstuffs, Great Britain could **not** sustain herself for more than six weeks without the most severe rationing.

b. Always use a comma before *as, for,* and *since* when the clause gives a reason.

I have elected advanced algebra, for I need it to enter a college of engineering.

PRACTICE 1. Classifying Clauses

Classify the phrases and subordinate clauses as restrictive and nonrestrictive, give a reason in each case, and punctuate the sentences:

1. Mrs. Akeley was received with friendliness by the Pygmies for her gifts of salt and tobacco delighted them.
2. Any boy who is intelligent can learn to punctuate correctly.
3. Mary Rafton who is in the eleventh-year English class seldom makes a mistake in punctuation.
4. Paris which is the most beautiful city in France is the world's fashion centre.
5. The Paris which is located in Kentucky is a country seat.
6. Charles Thomas running to catch a car stumbled and fell.
7. A fat man running to catch a car may injure his heart.
8. A permanent home for raccoons has been established near the southern end of the bear dens where its inmates will be near their relatives.
9. Union painters never work on a job where a spraying machine is used.
10. Be sure to visit Healthland where you will find plenty of fresh air sparkling drinking water and pure milk.
11. I lay down on the grass where for nine hours I slept soundly.
12. The next day we reached Nelson which is a divisional point on the C.P.R. Kettle Valley—Crowsnest route.

MASTERY TEST "A"—THE COMMA

Copy the following sentences and punctuate them correctly. Overpunctuation is just as bad as underpunctuation. Therefore if you either omit a needed punctuation mark or insert a mark that is not needed, the sentence is wrong. Three of the sentences are correctly punctuated.

1. On the right the runway was blocked by two Canadian Air Line planes on which some men were loading mail and express packages.
2. The telegram said that my mother's only brother who has been travelling for years was coming the next day to visit us.
3. The woman who maketh a good pudding in silence is better than she who maketh a tart reply.

4. As there were Indian horse thieves in the neighbourhood a guard was put on duty at the corral.

5. The flaw in King Lear was that he liked to be flattered.

6. *Kim* written by Rudyard Kipling tells the life and experiences of a young boy in northern India.

7. "At present" said our guide "there are but two herds of wild bison in existence."

8. It is the guilt not the scaffold which constitutes the shame.

9. A book that is filled with good stories is what I like.

10. For two days the boys trailed the big cats through the tangled forest but in the end they failed to track them down.

11. There is however a limit at which forbearance ceases to be a virtue.

12. "About three o'clock" Big Tim recounted "we had to stop for the cattle were blind with thirst."

13. Virtue is usually though not necessarily connected with intelligence; vice with ignorance.

14. On August 30 1935 I came home from my vacation brown and strong for I had spent most of the month in climbing mountains canoeing swimming playing golf and sleeping.

15. Margaret Deland has immortalized her birthplace Manchester a suburb of Allegheny Pennsylvania in *Old Chester Tales*.

16. Yes Harry I wish I had taken chemistry.

17. The night before we had stayed at the Chateau Frontenac in Quebec.

18. The girl who was called on to recite said "Uriah's hair which was red was cropped close to his head."

19. Disraeli who is responsible for all the action of the play is an old man very clever and witty.

20. Realizing that the son was not responsible for what his father had done Jim led the party and rescued the lad.

MASTERY TEST "B"—THE COMMA

Copy the following sentences and punctuate them correctly. Overpunctuation is just as bad as underpunctuation. Therefore if you either omit a needed punctuation mark or insert a mark that is not needed, the sentence is wrong. Three of the sentences are correctly punctuated.

1. Lincoln rewrote five times the famous speech which he delivered at Gettysburg.

2. Paul carried the blankets; Kit the folded tent; and I a frying pan a coffee pot and two tin cups.

3. Terrified by the smoke and flames the horses beautiful Kentucky thoroughbreds reared and plunged in their stalls.

4. Eppie quickly cut the linen strip which bound her to the loom and in a moment she had run out into the sunshine.

5. Shylock made the loan to Antonio not to make a large profit but to secure revenge.

6. While inspecting his racing stables however King George got a chill which later caused his death.

7. The knot which is most commonly used for tying two ropes together is the reef knot.

8. Toads bats and nonpoisonous snakes deserve man's protection since they are valuable in destroying harmful insects.

9. Mike's big locomotive which weighed over one hundred tons came roaring down the grade at fifty miles an hour.

10. If green plants are kept in the aquarium the fish and other animals need not be fed for long periods of time.

11. Dr. Gorgas who has already freed Havana and Cuba of yellow fever was asked to continue his work in Panama.

12. This temple which was the largest in Ceylon was the home of an ugly two-headed idol.

13. In colonial times it was impossible to foretell the length of a sea voyage for everything depended on wind and weather.

14. On September 1 1905 Saskatchewan and Alberta the two prairie provinces were admitted to the Dominion.

15. Ever since Meg has rushed to the cellar at the first sign of a storm.

16. "Well sir" demanded the colonel in a freezing tone "where have you been these past two days?"

17. Returning to England in 1801 Alexander Mackenzie published *Voyages from Montreal to the Frazer and Pacific Ocean.*

18. "Yes my lad" murmured the captain "a twelve-mile row in such a gale was hard on even the huskiest men."

19. Mr. Pickwick who has not been on the ice for thirty years slid gravely across the pond with his feet a yard and a quarter apart.

20. Our chief trouble was that we could not persuade the natives to guide us up the cliffs.

SEMICOLON

The semicolon is regularly a strong comma or a weak period.

18. (Weak period) As a rule, the semicolon is used between the clauses of a compound sentence if they are not joined by a conjunction. When the connecting word is *moreover, consequently, thus, hence, therefore, besides, also, nevertheless, still, otherwise, likewise,* or another independent adverb, the semicolon is used.

Caesar was dead; hence Rome was in confusion
The big ape beat his mighty chest with rage; his enormous hands rattled the iron bars of the cage.
Property can be paid for; the lives of peaceful and innocent people cannot be.

Exception. If three or more short clauses are similar in form and are closely connected in thought, the comma is used to separate them.

I came, I saw, I conquered.

19. (Strong comma)   The semicolon is used frequently to separate co-ordinate parts of a sentence when they have commas within themselves.

For further information about my character, ability, and training you may write or telephone to Reverend H. B. Jackson, Viscount, Saskatchewan; Professor J. W. Inglis, 207 Thirty-second Street, Saskatoon; and Mr. J. W. Pichon, 131 Elm Avenue, Saskatoon.

The grazing zebra presents a picture of grace and gentleness; but if his anger is aroused, not even a lion is safe from his flying hoofs.   [Either a comma or a semicolon after *gentleness* is correct.]

20. *Namely, for instance, for example, that is,* **and** *as,* **when introducing explanations, are preceded by the semicolon or the dash and followed by the comma.**

A pronoun is a word used in place of a noun; as, *he, we, who.*

A restrictive modifier limits the word modified; that is, it makes a general word more specific in its application.

COLON

21. Use the colon after the salutation of a business letter.

Dear Mr. Webster:

22. The colon is used to introduce a list of items or a long or formal quotation or statement. If such introducing word or expression as *this, thus, as follows, the following,* or *these words* is used, the colon follows it.

Christopher Morley's delightful essay, *What Men Live By,* begins as follows:

"What a delicate and rare and gracious art is the art of conversation."

Each first aid kit must contain the following articles: bandage, adhesive plaster, gauze, mercurochrome, tube soap, and burn lotion.

INTERROGATION POINT

23. The interrogation point is used after a direct question, but not after an indirect question.

Why is it difficult to raise seals in captivity?

Mr. Carr asked why it is difficult to raise seals in captivity.

a. A period is used after a request courteously worded in interrogative form.

Will you please hand in the report before nine o'clock tomorrow morning.

Will you please send me your latest catalogue.

EXCLAMATION POINT

24. The exclamation point is used to mark an expression of strong or sudden emotion.

> Three cheers for the Premier!
> Whew! That's over!
> Oh, what a wreck!

Notice the comma after the interjection *oh*. An interjection which **is a** real exclamation is followed by an exclamation point.

a. O is used with a noun in direct address and is never followed by **an** exclamation point.

> O John, why did you tease your little brother?

DASH

25. The dash is used to indicate an abrupt change in the thought or grammatical construction of a sentence.

> And, as for money—don't you remember the old saying, "Enough is as good as a feast"?
> I mean—you know what I mean.

26. Dashes may be made to make parenthetical, appositive, or explanatory matter stand out clearly. Dashes are less formal and more common than parentheses.

> There were diamonds—some of them exceedingly large and fine—a hundred and ten in all.—Poe
> Peters was thunderstruck—absolutely astounded—at this piece of good fortune.

27. The dash is used before a word that sums up preceding particulars.

> The rolling green hills, the rocky seacoast, the prim white cottages—all were typical of New England.
> Fishing, camping, touring—all kinds of outdoor activities now demand attention.

The dash is seldom used with any punctuation mark except the period.

QUOTATION MARKS

28. Quotation marks are used to enclose a direct quotation, but not to enclose an indirect quotation.

1. "Come on!" yelled Ed.
2. "Have you ever heard of Count von Luckner?" my father asked me.

3. "I found him in his cabin about twenty miles northwest of here," said Sergeant Perth.

In Sentence 1 an exclamation point follows the quoted exclamation; in Sentence 2 a question mark follows the quoted question; in Sentence 3 a comma is placed after the quoted statement.

4. Harold said, "Now you're joking."

Here the quotation follows the introducing words. Notice the comma after *said* and the capital letter in *Now*.

5. "Well," said Ruth, "here we are."
6. "Throw these papers out of the window," said the Southerner to his servant, "and pay the boy for them."

When a quotation is broken by an expression like *said Ruth*, two pairs of quotation marks are needed. Notice that *here* in 5 and *and* in 6 begin with small letters. Note also that the quotation marks follow the commas and the periods.

Use a comma to set off a short direct quotation.

7. "No, I don't believe in luck," replied Dick. "There's really nothing to it."

What Dick said was two sentences:

No, I don't believe in luck.
There's really nothing to it.

When you enclose the two sentences in quotation marks you still have two sentences.

Put a period after introducing words placed between two sentences.

29. Single marks surround a quotation within a quotation.

Benjamin Franklin said, "It requires a good, strong man to say, 'I was mistaken, and am sorry.'"

30. A quotation mark following a period or comma always comes after it. Other punctuation marks should be placed inside the quotation marks only if part of the quotation.

The captain demanded, "Can you reef a jib sail?"
Will you say to him, "Come at once"?

31. When two or more paragraphs are quoted, place quotation marks at the beginning of each paragraph and at the end of the last paragraph.

32. Quote the titles of chapters, articles, essays, lectures, and short poems.

Have you read Keats' ode "To Autumn"?
The subject of the lectures was "The Future of Russia".

33. In print the name of books, plays newspapers, and magazines are usually italicized.   In a composition or letter they may be enclosed in quotation marks or underscored.

I have been studying *Macbeth* this term.

PARENTHESES

34. Parentheses are used to enclose a side remark that does **not** affect the structure of the sentence.

I told him (and who would not?) just what I thought.

BRACKETS

35. Brackets surround words inserted in an article or speech **by** a reporter or editor.

Mr. Fess.   The Chair rather gets me on that question.   [Laughter] I did not rise—[Cries of "Vote!" "Vote!"]

APOSTROPHE

36. The apostrophe is used (1) to denote possession, (2) to **take** the place of an omitted letter, and (3) to form the plural of letters, figures, and signs.

John's brother makes neat *b*'s, *l*'s, ¼'s and *6*'s
He knows you're right and he doesn't care.

The Possessive

37. The possessive case of a noun always has an apostrophe; the possessive case of a personal pronoun never has an apostrophe; *his, its, hers, theirs.*

a. To form the possessive singular of a noun, add *'s* to the nominative.   The possessive sign is always at the end of the name.[1]

fox's, James's, enemy's, lady's, policeman's, son-in-law's

b. To form the possessive plural of nouns, first write the plural. Then add *'s* to the plurals that do not end in *s* and an apostrophe to the plurals that end in *s*.

---

[1]Nouns ending in *s* may take the apostrophe only: *Moses', James', Dickens', Burns', Jones'*. The easy way is always to add *'s* at the end of the word. Stabbing the name by putting the apostrophe before the *s* (*Dicken's*) is a serious blunder.

SINGULAR	POSSESSIVE SINGULAR	PLURAL	POSSESSIVE PLURAL
policeman	policeman's	policemen	policemen's
Jones	Jones's	Joneses	Joneses'
mouse	mouse's	mice	mice's
enemy	enemy's	enemies	enemies'
lady	lady's	ladies	ladies'
child	child's	children	children's

For joint possession only one apostrophe is needed: *Allyn and Bacon's New York office.* If the possession is individual, the possessive is added to the name of each owner.

Isabel's, Mildred's and Josephine's shares were as 1, 2, and 3.

PRACTICE 2. Possessives

Write in four columns the singular, the possessive singular, the plural, and the possessive plural of each word:

alley	donkey	Murphy	teacher
ally	fly	Norman	trout
boy	fox	officer	week
Burns	it	one	who
child	Keats	potato	whoever
day	lady	sheep	woman
deer	man	sister	year
Dickens	manservant	spoonful	you

MISCELLANEOUS EXAMPLES

38. Notice the punctuation of the following:

1. MS.
2. 5,647,982
3. August 3, 1914—November 11, 1918
4. Meet me at 8:15 P.M.
5. That's good advice, isn't it?
6. I have read many autobiographies, such as *Autobiography of a Super-Tramp* and *Roads of Adventure.*
7. *Resolved,* That every automobile driver should be required to carry liability insurance.
8. Maitland barely made the goal, the ball teetering on the rim of the basket but finally dropping inside.   [The comma sets off the absolute phrase.]

PRACTICE 3. Review of Punctuation

Give the rule for every punctuation mark except a period at the end of a sentence:

1. *The Last of the Mohicans,* which relates the heroism of Hawkeye and Uncas, is the second of Cooper's Leatherstocking series.

2. The girth hitch, or larkshead knot, is used only for fastening a saddle to a horse.

3. Don't be satisfied with one; buy as many as you can.

4. Open your purse and your mouth cautiously; and your stock of wealth and wisdom shall, at least in repute, be great.

5. When you see a crime committed or observe a person acting very suspiciously, it is your duty to notify the police.

6. The soul of a man is a garden where, as he sows, so shall he reap. If ye would gather roses, do not sow rotten seeds.

7. True eloquence consists in saying all that should be, not all that could be said.

8. Two old men, dragging a heavy bundle of household goods between them, abandoned it in the street and fled screaming.

9. Her soul was noble—in her own opinion.

10. The word *that* may be used as follows: first, as a relative pronoun; second, as an adjective, third, as a subordinate conjunction.

11. War is the law of violence; peace, the law of love.

12. Fascinated by romantic tales of adventure, Shorty joined the Klondike gold rush.

13. Success, fame, wealth—are these all you demand of life?

14. *Julius Caesar* opens with this sentence: "Hence! home, you idle creatures, get you home."

15. "Will not someone arise," asks Mr. E. V. Lucas, "to remind young people of the fun, to say the least of it, of choosing the right word?"

PRACTICE 4. Punctuating Correctly

Punctuate the following sentences and give a rule for each mark used. Insert needed apostrophes. Some sentences require no further punctuation.

1. On the first day one of the horses went lame on the second they lost the trail and wandered around for hours on the third a buffalo stampede destroyed the chuck wagon nevertheless they pushed on.

2. If a man has a job to which a large salary is attached he is said to be holding a lucrative position.

3. The chameleon which has naturally a bright green skin can change colour to suit its surroundings.

4. The trout which we caught in the pool were already broiling over the coals when the boys returned from their hike.

5. The ungrateful King Charles however made no attempt to rescue Joan of Arc from her captors the English.

6. He uses very few words which the average educated person doesn't understand.

7. He noted the men who tried hard but were naturally slow and awkward.

8. What is becoming is honourable and what is honourable is becoming.

9. Our château lies in the valley between two hills so to obtain a clear view of the horizon I hurried to the roof with a pair of field glasses.

10. Just as we had seated ourselves comfortably in the auditorium Mr. Reynolds began a selection on the organ but soon the speaker appeared and gave us glimpses of Cairo and the Nile.

11. Hope is the mainspring of efficiency complacency is its rust.

12. Draw down the blind Jim whispered my mother they might come and watch outside. And now said she when I had done so we have to get the key off that and whos to touch it I should like to know and she gave a kind of sob as she said the words.

13. When buying goods if you are satisfied with the price and quality make sure that you get full weight or measure.

14. As charity covers a multitude of sins before God so does politeness before men.

15. Men are born with two eyes but with one tongue in order that they should see twice as much as they say.

16. A needle made of fish bone and thread made of deer sinew were the only sewing tools the Indian squaws possessed.

17. There are more than a thousand different forms of ice crystals nevertheless each one always has either six points or six sides.

18. Dr. Frederick Grant Banting discovered insulin which is claimed to be a cure for diabetes.

19. He who works will be rewarded.

20. For information concerning my school record you may write or telephone to Mr. J. R. MacKay principal of Bedford Road Collegiate Institute Saskatoon.

21. When water power sets dynamos and turbines in action we get power to drive trains to run factory machines and to generate light and heat.

22. The boy who won the peace medal lives in Philadelphia which is often called the City of Brotherly Love.

23. The University of British Columbia which is situated on Point Grey has one of the finest sites in Canada.

24. A New York newspaper quotes John J. Pershing as follows I pray fervently that there will be no more war.   With all my soul I hate it.

25. The question was thus stated Should our national defenses be increased?

26. For the old boatman the Mississippi still was something human it raged at him wept for him laughed at him and smiled for him.

27. He asked whether our national defenses should be increased.

28. A sudden and violent wind blew their tent so far away that they never found it again then torrents of rain beat down on the unprotected group.

29. The membership of the Board of Trustees was made up as follows labourers 2 lawyers 2 business men 3 doctors 2.

MASTERY TEST "B" PUNCTUATION

Copy the following sentences, punctuate them, and insert needed apostrophes. Overpunctuation is just as bad as underpunctuation. Therefore if you either omit a needed mark or insert a mark that is not needed, the sentence is wrong. Do not divide one good sentence into two sentences.

1. The sunbonnet which every African baby wears to protect it from sunstroke is made of a hollow gourd.
2. This is a trick he learned from William A. Muldoon who used to be able to run as fast backward as the average man can run forward
3. Man is a strange mixture of good and evil even the worst criminal has admirable qualities
4. All his life he had known activity people something going on here there was nothing to do but to eat drink and loaf
5. If the air about us did not move man beast and vegetation would die for the motion of the air keeps it pure and sweet
6. The Eskimo woman who allows her seal oil lamps to smoke is considered to say the least a poor housekeeper
7. The first settlers in Pennsylvania finding only snow-covered forests lived in holes in the river bank during the winter a miserable existence indeed
8. The human body it has been estimated gives off about as much heat as is produced by a candle flame
9. The next morning the sky was dark with threatening rain clouds but we determined to push on down the river until noon at least
10. Sealskin fur comes from sea bears which are not really seals at all
11. An old manuscript lists the seven wonders of the world as follows the pyramids the hanging gardens of Babylon the statue of Zeus at Olympia the temple of Diana at Ephesus the mausoleum of Halicarnassus the Colossus of Rhodes the Pharos lighthouse at Alexandria
12. The murex a shellfish like the mussel was prized by the ancients not for food but for a purple dye which it yields
13. My way of joking says George Bernard Shaw is to tell the truth
14. Since the earliest times shells have been used for all sorts of curious things for instance for money ornaments buttons dinner horns
15. Be not simply good be good for something
16. Admiral Peary was adored by Ootah and Seeglo who accompanied him on his expedition to the North Pole
17. Caroline asked Why should a lifesaver always approach the drowning person from the rear
18. Placing a knife between his teeth Chambers dived over the side of the boat into the very centre of the group of black shark fins
19. Lad never killed a sheep in his life Stan said Seward and you know it
20. Some are satisfied with their work during the past term most of us however are not

HANDBOOK: C

Mechanics

Be original in what you have to say, but be conventional in putting it down. Weird abbreviations and fancy systems for writing numbers are out of place in letters and themes. You want your reader to pay attention to the content of your message. Use conventional form to put your content across.

CAPITALIZATION

TEST 7A (*Diagnostic*). CAPITALIZATION

Copy correctly the words that should be capitalized according to literary practice. If you omit a needed capital or insert a capital that is not needed, the sentence is wrong. (Number of correct sentences = Score)

1. Linda attended a junior high school in vancouver, british columbia, before entering wildwood high school.
2. The prime minister and senator potter addressed a first of july rally in ottawa.
3. Uncle frank said, "while flying to winnipeg on a trans-canada airlines plane, i read part of *around the world in eighty days* by jules verne."
4. At a newsstand on king street i bought copies of the *london free press*, the *toronto daily star*, and the *globe and mail*.
5. As we drove down to key west, the southernmost city in the united states, we saw the beautiful blue waters of the gulf of mexico on our right.
6. After lester had attended a meeting of the junior red cross committee, he went to the office of senator charles e. potter.
7. A committee of the house of commons compared the work of the united nations with that of the league of nations.
8. The social credit party won its first chance to form a government in the province of Alberta.
9. While searching for a northwest passage around north america, henry hudson discovered hudson bay and hudson straight and explored the hudson river as far as albany.
10. The morning after the news of pearl harbour reached washington, president roosevelt appeared personally before the united states congress, saying "i now ask the congress for a declaration of war against japan."

1. **FIRST WORDS** Capitalize the first word of (1) a complete sentence, (2) a quoted sentence, and (3) a line of poetry or verse.

> There was only one catch to the bright idea: Who would bell the cat?
> Oliver Goldsmith said, "People seldom improve when they have no other model but themselves to copy."
> Full many a flower is born to blush unseen,
> And waste its sweetness on the desert air.—THOMAS GRAY

Do not capitalize the first word of (1) a quoted phrase or (2) the second part of a one-sentence broken quotation.

> Plato called thinking "the talking of the soul with itself".
> "Quarrels would not last long," declared Rochefoucauld, "if the fault was only on one side."

2. **PROPER NOUNS, PROPER ADJECTIVES** Capitalize proper nouns, proper adjectives, and their abbreviations.

A proper noun names a particular person, place, or thing.

> Robert Frost, North America, New Year's Day, Victor Herbert

A common noun refers to any one of a class of persons, places, or things.

> poet, continent, holiday, composer

Proper adjectives are derived from proper nouns.

> France—French pastry   Shakespeare—Shakespearean sonnet

Some words derived from proper names are not capitalized.

> fez, ohm, ampere, bohemian, braille, odyssey, shanghai, quixotic, pasteurize, macadam

The names of school subjects except languages and specific numbered courses are common nouns.

> trigonometry, home economics, civics, physics, bookkeeping

BUT   English, French, Latin, History 9, Chemistry 1B

RULES FOR CAPITALIZING PROPER NOUNS AND PROPER ADJECTIVES

a. Capitalize names of particular persons.

PROPER	COMMON
Helen Hayes	an actress
Mr. John Lee	a man

b. Capitalize the titles of organizations and institutions.

ASSOCIATIONS Veterans of Foreign Wars, Salvation Army, Boy Scouts of
    Canada
CLUBS   Kiwanis Club, Rotary Club, Oxford and Cambridge Club
FIRMS   Chrysler Corporation, Beacon Musical Instrument Company
INSTITUTIONS   High School of Performing Arts, University of Manitoba

c. Capitalize the names of definitely defined groups of persons.

POLITICAL PARTIES   Liberal, Progressive Conservative, Canadian Common-
    wealth Federation
RELIGIONS AND SECTS   Baptist, Catholic, Jew, United Church, Moslem
NATIONALITIES AND PEOPLES   Danes, Japanese, Arab, Mexican, Indian

d. Capitalize geographical names and the names of buildings.

Rio Grande, St. Lawrence River, Lake Charles, Gulf of Mexico, Rocky
Mountain National Park, North Fifth Avenue, Royal York Hotel, Grand
Central Station, Cleveland Museum of Art, First Congregational Church

Do not capitalize words like *province* and *city* when not used as
individual names or parts of such names: *republic of Liberia, city of
Boise, state of Oregon.* In *the Bay of Funday, Bay* is capitalized because
it is part of the name. *Fundy* is not the name. In *the city of Knoxville*
the name is *Knoxville.*

e. Capitalize the names of government bodies and agencies.

COURTS   Supreme Court of Canada, Muncipal Court
LEGISLATURES   Senate, House of Commons, Parliament, Chamber of Deputies
AGENCIES AND DEPARTMENTS   Federal Bureau of Investigation, National
    Labour Relations Board, Toronto Fire Department

Do not capitalize inexact or incomplete names.

the association, the division, the corporation, the appeals court

f. Capitalize the names of publications.

Do not capitalize *the* as the first word of the name of a newspaper
or magazine.

NEWSPAPERS   the *Globe and Mail,* the *Vancouver Province*
MAGAZINES   the *Chatelaine, Maclean's Magazine*

In titles of books, articles, reports, and poems capitalize the first
and the last word and all others except articles (*a, an, the*), prepositions,
and conjunctions.

BOOKS   *The House of the Seven Gables, North with the Spring*

ARTICLES   "History Comes to the Plains," "The Discovery of the Electron"
POEMS   "My Heart's in the Highlands," "The Tuft of Flowers"

g. Capitalize the names of ships, trains, planes.

the T*itanic*, the C*onfederation*, the C*hief*, the C*annonball*

h. Capitalize the days of the week, months of the year, and holidays (but not seasons).

Wednesday, Friday, October, January, Hallowe'en, Washington's Birthday
BUT   winter, spring, summer, autumn, fall

i. Capitalize *North, South, East, West, Southeast,* etc., when they refer to particular regions. When they refer to directions, they are not capitalized. *Westerner, Southerner,* and the like are capitalized when they refer to inhabitants of parts of the country.

REGION   Americans of the East, the South, the Midwest, and the Far West have regional differences in their speech.
DIRECTION   If you sail through the Panama Canal from the Atlantic to the Pacific, you will actually be going from north to south, not east to west.

j. Capitalize titles before proper names, titles of the highest governmental officers used without proper names, and abbreviations of academic degrees.

TITLES BEFORE NAMES   Governor Harold W. Handley, General Lauris Norstad
TITLE STANDING ALONE   the Prime Minister, the Secretary of the Treasury
ACADEMIC DEGREES   Ph.D., M.D., B.S., D.Lit., B.A.

Capitalize *uncle, aunt, cousin,* and *grandmother* before proper names.

Aunt Sylvia and Uncle Jerry are flying to Bermuda this Easter.

Mother, Father, Dad, Grandfather, and similar titles without names are preferably capitalized.

PREFERRED   I hope that Mother and Dad will some day be able to visit the little English town where Mother was born.
LESS COMMON   I hope that mother and dad will some day be able to visit the little English town where mother was born.

When a possessive precedes *mother, father, dad,* or *grandfather,* no capital is used.

My mother and father hope to visit England some day.

k. Capitalize historical events, periods, and documents.

Age of **R**eptiles, the **B**oston **T**ea **P**arty, the **A**rticles of **C**onfederation, the **M**onroe **D**octrine, the **B**attle of **S**even **O**aks.

l. Capitalize the specific part of the trade name of a product.

Camay soap, **C**hevrolet station wagon, **G**leem toothpaste

3. COMPOUND WORDS   In capitalizing a compound word do not capitalize the second part, unless the second part is a noun or a proper adjective.

Forty-second **S**treet, **E**ighty-seventh **C**ongress, *Best-loved Dog Stories*
BUT   *The Ox-Bow Incident, Twentieth-Century Authors, An Index to One-Act Plays, Pan-American plane*
NOTE   pro-**F**rench, un-**A**merican

4. DEITY, BIBLE   Capitalize names of the Deity and names for the Bible, divisions of the Bible, and other sacred writings.

Is this the dream **H**e dreamed who shaped the suns
And marked their ways upon the ancient deep?—EDWIN MARKHAM
Genesis, **H**oly **W**rit, the **K**oran, the **O**ld **T**estament

5. LETTER   In the salutation of a friendly letter capitalize the first word and all nouns; in the complimentary close capitalize the first word only.

Dear old **S**tan,   **Y**our old friend,
My dear **M**r. **C**arter: **S**incerely yours,

6. OUTLINE   Capitalize the first word of each division of a topical outline.

7. PART OF BOOK   Capitalize a word indicating an important division of a book or of a series of books.

Act II, **V**ol. IV, **P**art V, **N**o. 8, **C**hapter IX
If the division is a minor one, do not use the capital.
scene 3, article 7, page 98, line 18, section 2, paragraph 4

8. PERSONIFICATION   Capitalize nouns clearly personified.

O **M**emory! thou fond deceiver.—OLIVER GOLDSMITH

9. I, O   Capitalize the pronoun *I* and the interjection *O.* Do not capitalize *oh* unless it begins a sentence.

PRACTICE 1. Capitalizing Correctly

Capitalize the following according to preferred literary practice.

Which need not be capitalized? Be prepared to give a reason for each capital inserted.

1. eiffel tower
2. fifty-third street
3. carter's ink eradicator
4. *the wonderful world of mathematics*
5. thanksgiving day
6. a trip to the southwest
7. act iii, scene 1, line 17
8. ten eyck hotel
9. spring and summer
10. barrie's *the little minister*
11. denver museum of natural history
12. city of winnipeg
13. federal communications commission
14. smugglers' notch inn
15. chapter vii, page 118, line 14
16. the university of toronto
17. admiral arthur w. radford
18. algebra, home economics, and spanish
19. hindu
20. the president and the secretary of defense
21. the columbia river
22. very truly yours,
23. dear old bill, (salutation)
24. the senate
25. *the edge of the sea*
26. my mother and my father
27. mother and dad
28. canadian red cross
29. the imperial oil company
30. john evans, ph.d.
31. peter the great
32. french
33. the declaration of independence
34. liberals and conservatives
35. un-american
36. twenty-third congressional district
37. aunt nora and my cousin
38. clara barton high school
39. battle of saratoga
40. palisades park

PRACTICE 2. Capitalizing Correctly

Capitalize the following. Prepare to give a reason for each capital you insert. Do not write in this book.

Last spring you probably doubted that bob, larry, and i would ever get to california in our aging ford. Yes, we made it across the plains and the rocky mountains and here we are. Since july 20 we've been camping out in sequoia national park.

We've seen plenty of sequoias, including the general sherman tree, which is almost four thousand years old. Why, that tree was about a thousand years old when the greeks were building the parthenon.

Yesterday we visited tharp cabin, a shelter made by blocking off the ends of a fallen sequoia already hollowed out by fire. The discoverer of the giant trees, hale tharp, once lived here, and the naturalist john muir used it for a while in 1875. Although the place looks comfortable, it would never be featured in *house beautiful* as an example of ideal american architecture.

Just so we wouldn't become too unused to people, we went to several campfire programs. Last tuesday a ranger gave a talk with coloured slides on "wild flowers of the sierras"; one of the guests played gershwin's *rhapsody in blue:* and the whole group sang "home on the range" and "shine on, harvest moon." We finished with "the sequoia song," which begins "we've been to crescent meadow and we've seen the sherman tree."

When I get back to Toronto, w. c. porter high school won't know the new mcginty. In botany this fall i'll have all sorts of firsthand knowledge to spring on mr. naylor.

No kidding, i'm going to write to the department of agriculture for information about the forest service. It's a more adventurous life than selling arrow shirts. I'm sure dad and mother will encourage any honest ambition in their shiftless son.

I've been trying to persuade bob and larry to yield to the spell of the west and become foresters too, but they seem to prefer the glitter of montreal or toronto. From september till june i'll concentrate on persuading you to join me.

Your rambling pal,

Art

TEST 10B (*Mastery*). CAPITALIZATION

Median-8

Copy correctly the words that should be capitalized according to literary practice. If you omit a needed capital or insert a capital that is not needed, the sentence is wrong. (Number of correct sentences = Score)

After your test is scored, enter your mark on your achievement graph.

1. Lieutenant collins said, "you two follow the river north while the rest of us circle snowy mountain."
2. Francis parkman's travels in the northwest were preparation for writing his fascinating history, *the oregon trail.*
3. The parliament of england, consisting of the house of commons and the house of lords, was established over six hundred years ago.
4. The board of education of the city of new york maintains numerous vocational high schools, which train pupils for various trades.
5. Mount desert island off the coast of maine was discovered in the fall of 1604 by champlain, the french explorer.
6. In 1957 one of the most discussed questions in ottawa was: how can the united nations prevent war in israel?
7. The statue of liberty, the gift of france to america, stands on liberty island in new york harbour.
8. Dr. henry marshall tory was the founder and first president of carleton college (now carleton university).
9. Many pupils from jamaica high school visited queen's university and heard talks on college life by student leaders.
10. In september 1787 a messenger on horseback took a copy of the constitution of the united states of america from philadelphia to the continental congress in new york.

ABBREVIATIONS

Abbreviations are handy short cuts in note-taking. Be cautious in using them elsewhere.

10. AVOIDING ABBREVIATIONS In a letter, theme, or report, write out all words except for tabulated matter and a handful of common abbreviations that are correct in all writing. Among the correct abbreviations are these: A.D.; B.C.; *Y.M.C.A.; C.O.D.; a.m.; p.m.; Co.* in the name of some firms; and *No.* with numbers expressed in figures. The names of some organizations and agencies are commonly abbreviated, frequently without periods: FBI, AFL-CIO, TWA, CBS, CBC, CCF.

WRONG My cousin lives on Fifth Ave. bet. 86 St. and 87 St. in N.Y.C.

RIGHT My cousin lives on Fifth Avenue between 86 Street and 87 Street in New York City.

11. END OF SENTENCE Use only one period for an abbreviation at the end of a sentence.

Our plane is scheduled to take off at 8:37 a.m.

12. ETC. Do not use the abbreviation *etc.* unless it helps avoid needless repetition. The use of *etc.* is usually an admission of ignorance.

WRONG The New England states are Maine, Vermont, etc.

RIGHT The New England states are Maine, Vermont, New Hampshire, Massachusetts, Connecticut, and Rhode Island.

RIGHT The numbers 2, 4, 8, 16, 32, etc., form a geometric progression. (Notice the comma after *etc.*)

13. TITLES Do not abbreviate a civil, professional, military, or political title—except *Mr., Mrs., Messrs., Dr.,* and *St.* (as in St. John's Hospital), which are always abbreviated. *Rev.* and *Hon.* may be spelled out or abbreviated. Abbreviate *Jr., Sr., Esq., Ph.D., D.D.* after a name.

Mr. Jonathan Carlson, Jr.   Professor Edward Chickering
Dr. Mark Loring   Captain William Kelly
Rev. (*or* Reverend) William Bedell   William Bedell, D.D.

14. NOT ALONE Many abbreviations which are proper when combined with other expressions are improper when standing alone.

WRONG The dr. arrived at our house early in the a.m.

RIGHT Dr. Thomas arrived at our house early in the morning.

RIGHT ALSO Dr. Thomas arrived at our house at 7:00 a.m.

15. LITERARY ABBREVIATIONS Certain special abbreviations are used in reports, especially in footnotes, to save space and needless

repetition. These include *i.e.* ("that is"), *e.g.* ("for example"), *et al.* ("and others"), *viz.* ("namely"), *ibid.* ("in the same place"), *pp.* ("pages"). In most writing, the unabbreviated form is more appropriate.

16. **&** The symbol *&* is used only in note-taking and in the names of some firms. In replying to a letter, follow the form which the firm uses in its letterhead—*& Co., & Company,* or *and Company.*

      and   company's
Mother ~~&~~ Dad took us to the ~~co.'s~~ plant at Oakville for a guided tour.

PRACTICE 3. Eliminating Abbreviations

Rewrite the following letter substituting complete words for improper abbreviations and contractions.

Dear Aunt Alice and Uncle Ted,

    I arrived home in the middle of the a.m. on Tues. & discovered that Mother didn't expect me till the p.m. of Sept. 3rd. The letter I sent at the end of Aug. arrived after I did. The trip home through the Eastern townships was pleasant & fairly cool, but my heart was back in Bruce Co.

    Thank you both for inviting me. The two wks I spent with you on the bay will give me many pleasant memories for the long winter mos. ahead. I gained six lbs. on the creamy milk furnished by the local dairy co. Mother says the wt. I gained should keep the dr. away for at least a yr.

    I've already planned to write an acct. of my vacation for the h.s. mag. That adventure with the skunks should make good reading! The p.o. will close in twenty min. I want to get this letter off.

    Love from us all.

Your niece,
Carol

WRITING NUMBERS

17. FIGURES Use figures for dates, street numbers, room numbers. telephone numbers, page numbers, and numbers of divisions (parts, chapters, paragraphs, sections, rules) of a book, and for statistics.

    On January 4, 1960, we moved to 119 East 75 Street.
    Review pages 92-123 for a test on the rise of nationalism.

18. AGE, TIME Ordinarily spell out ages and hours of the day.

    Mr. Curtis, our principal, always begins commencement exercises promptly at eight o'clock.
    Mozart gave a concert performance before he was six.

Use figures with the abbreviations *a.m.* and *p.m.*

Leona and I will take the train at 4:27 p.m. and arrive at Bay Shore at 5:30 p.m.

19. ONE OR TWO WORDS   Ordinarily spell out numbers that can be expressed in one or two words: *fifty-eight, four hundred, six thousand, eighteen hundred.*   Use figures for numbers that require three or more words: 180; 2539; 5,736,000.

   The greatest known depth of the Atlantic Ocean is about thirty thousand feet, near Puerto Rico.
   The greatest known depth of the Pacific Ocean is 34,440 feet, near Mindanao in the Philippines.

20. STREET   Spell out the name of a numbered street if it is one word without a hyphen: 127 East Ninth Street.   The name of a numbered street with a hyphen may be spelled out or given in numbers.

   2417 Twenty-eight Street   2417 28 Street   2417 28th Street

21. SEVERAL NUMBERS   Ordinarily use figures when several fairly long numbers follow each other closely.

   Records for rainfall throughout the world include 46 inches in a single day at Baguio in the Philippines; 150 inches in 5 consecutive days at Cherrapunji in India; and 366 inches in a month, also at Cherrapunji.

   BUT   At the picnic Tommy ate two hamburgers, three hot dogs, five slices of watermelon, two peaches, two pieces of pie, a piece of cake, and a bar of chocolate.

22. MONEY   When representing money, use figures (1) for a sum in dollars and cents and (2) for a sum in dollars if the number requires three or more words.

   Jeff paid two hundred dollars for the car.
   Sale dresses are priced at $3.95, $4.95, and $5.95.
   We sold the tickets at thirty-five cents each, or three for a dollar.

23. BEGINNING   Spell out a number at the beginning of a sentence or rewrite the sentence.

   One hundred two
   ~~102~~ seniors are planning to go to Ottawa this Easter.
   BUT   This Easter 102 seniors are planning to go to Ottawa.

24. PER CENT   Use figures for percentages but write out the words *per cent.*   Do not put a period after *per cent* unless it comes at the end of a sentence.

   This Easter 70 per cent of our seniors are planning to go to Ottawa.

PRACTICE 4. Writing Numbers

Prepare to write the following sentences from dictation.

1. Ty Cobb, lifetime batting leader of the major leagues, made 4,191 hits in 11,429 times at bat and scored a total of 2,244 runs.

2. In 1926 A. L. Monteverde walked from New York to San Francisco, a distance of 3,415 miles, in 79 days 10 hours 10 minutes.

3. On our property we have six dogwoods, two elms, four oaks, four maples, and a beautiful flowering cherry.

4. On television tonight *Peter Pan* is scheduled to begin at 8:30 p.m. and run until 10:00 p.m.

5. Entered in the race were two Fords, three Chevrolets, two Plymouths, and four Nash Ramblers.

6. The 3300-pound capstone of the Washington National Monument is crowned by a small pyramid of pure aluminum 5.6 inches square at its base and 8.9 inches in height.

7. The Golden Gate Bridge is 4200 feet long, it towers are 746 feet high, and its centre span is 220 feet above the water.

8. Glacier National Park has more than two hundred glacier-fed lakes, sixty small glaciers, and precipices thousands of feet high.

9. The club spent $25.30 on the Halloween Dance—$4.90 for cider, $3.60 for doughnuts, $8.60 for records, $3.20 for crepe paper and balloons, and $5.00 for prizes—leaving $4.27 in the treasury.

10. You can find an interesting explanation of the term *St. Vitus's dance* in Volume 3, page 4035, column 2, paragraph 3, of *The New Century Cyclopedia of Names.*

ITALICS

In typewritten or longhand work underline whatever is to be italicized in print.

LONGHAND

For my birthday I received copies of <u>The Columbia-Viking Desk Encyclopedia</u>, <u>Webster's Dictionary of Synonyms</u>, and <u>The Reader's Encyclopedia</u>.

TYPEWRITTEN For my birthday I received copies of <u>The</u> <u>Columbia—Viking</u> <u>Desk</u> <u>Encyclopedia</u>, <u>Webster's</u> <u>Dictionary</u> <u>of</u> <u>Synonyms</u>, and <u>The</u> <u>Reader's</u> <u>Encyclopedia</u>.

PRINTED For my birthday I received copies of *The Columbia-Viking Desk Encyclopedia, Webster's Dictionary of Synonyms,* and *The Reader's Encyclopedia.*

25. TITLES Italicize titles of newspapers, magazines, pamphlets, books, plays, motion pictures, symphonies, and operas. When *a, an,* or *the* is the first word in the title of a book, it is capitalized and italicized. When *the* is the first word of the title of a newspaper, do not capitalize or italicize it.

Lou Wexler wrote an excellent review of *The Return of the Native* in the *Star,* our school magazine.
Did Mozart write his opera *The Magic Flute* after he had written his *Jupiter Symphony?*

Short poems, essays, and parts of a book are enclosed in quotation marks: "Ode on a Grecian Urn", "On Doors", "Mr. Micawber's Transactions".

26. SHIPS, AIRCRAFT Italicize the names of vessels and aircraft.

The first round-the-world solo flight was made by Wiley Post in a Lockheed-Vega, *Winnie Mae,* in July, 1933.
Did the *United States* beat the speed record of the *Queen Mary?*

27. FOREIGN WORDS Italicize foreign words and expressions which have not been naturalized.

Sinclair Lewis liked to poke fun at the troubles of the *nouveaux riches,* the newly rich who don't know what to do with their money
BUT It is usually more expensive to order food à la carte.

28. LETTER, WORD, PHRASE Ordinarily italicize a letter spoken of as a letter, a word as a word, or a phrase as a phrase.

How many *m's* are there in *committee?*
The word *muscle* originally meant "a little mouse".
The expression *to be in the same boat* means "to share risks equally, to have similar obligations".

29. EMPHASIS Use italics sparingly for emphasis.

SCHOOLGIRLISH The basketball game was simply *thrilling.* Jack seemed to be scoring *every* time I looked around. Our team was simply *wonderful* in winning the game by more than *ten* points.
EFFECTIVE No, I will *not* accept that plan.

PRACTICE 5. Using Italics Correctly

As you copy the following sentences, underline the words that should be italicized.

1. My dad subscribes to Time, Life, Natural History, the Saturday Evening Post, and the Reader's Digest.
2. In Information Please Almanac find out which of these newspapers had the largest circulation last year: the London Free Press, Winnipeg Free Press, or the Detroit Free Press.
3. Does the plural of leaf end in fs or ves?
4. Mr. Harkness says he'll be happy when all of us spell too, its, their, separate, and until correctly.
5. Of all the books about Mt. Everest I prefer Tiger of the Snows and Conquest of Everest.
6. As you pronounce rough, though, hiccough, plough, cough, and through, notice the different sounds of ough.
7. We are flying to the Netherlands on the Flying Dutchman but shall return on the Queen Mary from Southampton, England.
8. Did you know that au revoir and auf Wiedersehen have the same meaning?
9. Does the opera Faust closely resemble Marlowe's play The Tragical History of Dr. Faustus?
10. In Charles Earle Funk's book Heavens to Betsy! I learned the origin of expressions like weasel words and fly-by-night.

Improving Your Spelling

The poor speller finds himself severely handicapped every time he picks up a pencil or pen. Fortunately no matter how poor a speller you are you can learn to spell. You can learn a few useful rules and apply them. You can learn to take clear mental pictures of troublesome words. And you can learn to look up in the dictionary words you're not sure of.

WORDS FREQUENTLY MISSPELLED

1. TEN HARDEST WORDS Spell these words correctly every time you write them.

believe	its	pleasant	receive	their
committee	occurred	principal	separate	too

2. TWENTY HARD WORDS Master these words too. The hard spots are underlined.

acquaintance	cafeteria	disappoint	necessary	privilege
all right	definite	immediately	noticing	pronunciation
benefit	dependent	independent	occasionally	recommend
business	describe	meant	opinion	writing

3. SINGLE O forty   lose (lo͞oz)   move   prove   whose

4. CEED, SEDE, CED Three words end in *ceed.*

exceed   proceed   succeed

One word ends in *sede: supersede.*
Other words have *ced.*

concede   precede   preceding   procedure

PRACTICE 1. Using Words Frequently Misspelled

Write lively sentences using *all right, its, it's, principal, principle, their, there, to, too,* and *separate* correctly. You may include several of the words in one sentence.

EXAMPLE If the *principal* says *it's all right, there* will be a *separate* cheering section for seniors.

EI AND IE

5. EI, IE

> Put *i* before *e*
> Except after *c*
> Or when sounded like *a*,
> As in *neighbour* and *weigh*

i BEFORE *e*		EXCEPT AFTER *c*	SOUNDED LIKE *a*
achieve	handkerchief	ceiling	freight
besiege	mischievous	conceive	neighbour
cashier	piece	deceit	reign
chief	relieve	receipt	vein
grief	siege	receive	weigh

EXCEPTIONS

Isn't it *weird* that at the *height* of his success the *financier* could *neither seize* a bit of *leisure* nor afford a *foreign* trip? Four other exceptions are *counterfeit, forfeit, heifer,* and *sleight.*

Where *c* is pronounced *sh, ie* follows the *c: ancient, conscience, efficient, proficient, sufficient.*

PRACTICE 2. Spelling Words with *ei* and *ie*

Write these words with *ei* or *ie*. Prepare to give a reason for each *ei* or *ie*.

anc—nt	dec—ve	h—fer	p—ce	s—ve
bel—f	f—rce	hyg—ne	rec—ve	th—f
c—ling	for—gn	l—sure	rel—f	th—very
conc—t	forf—t	misch—vous	s—ze	w—gh
consc—nce	front—r	n—ce	shr—k	w—rd
counterf—t	gr—vous	perc—ve	s—ge	y—ld

COMPOUNDS

HYPHENATED COMPOUNDS

6. COMPOUND NUMBERS Use the hyphen in compound numbers from twenty-one to ninety-nine: *forty-four, ninety-five.*

Hyphenate a fraction used as a modifier, but do not hyphenate fractions used as nouns.

　　a two-thirds majority　　BUT　　two thirds of the class

7. COMPOUND ADJECTIVES Hyphenate an adjective made up of two or more words if it precedes the noun modified: *first-class cabin, ocean-going liner, well-manned ship.* Do not put a hyphen between an adverb ending in *ly* and the adjective or participle it modifies: *tastefully decorated stateroom.*

When a modifier is after the noun, the hyphen is ordinarily omitted.

BEFORE NOUN	AFTER NOUN
He's a well-known author.	That author is well known.
That's a worth-while book.	His latest book is worth while.
It includes up-to-date statistics.	Its statistics are up to date.

Some compound adjectives are hyphenated when used before or after the noun modified: *blue-eyed, flat-footed, full-blooded, good-natured, gray-haired, long-legged, middle-aged, old-fashioned, two-faced.* In these compounds the *ed* word is formed from a noun, not a verb.

8. IN-LAW, GREAT Usually hyphenate compounds of *father, mother, brother, sister, daughter, son,* and *great: daughter-in-law, father-in-law, great-grandparents, great-uncle.*

EXCEPTIONS

godfather, grandfather, stepmother, stepson, half brother, half sister

Write these words with a hyphen:

bird's-eye	know-it-all	make-believe	U-boat
good-by *or* good-bye	know-nothing	make-up	X-ray

SOLID COMPOUNDS

9. POINTS OF THE COMPASS Write solid—that is, without a hyphen or a space—these points of the compass: *northeast, southeast, northwest, southwest.*

10. PREFIXES, SUFFIXES Prefixes joined to root words do not, as a rule, require the hyphen: *coeducation, extracurricular, infrared, misstep, nonrestrictive, semiofficial.*

EXCEPTIONS

1. Between a prefix and a proper noun or proper adjective: *Anglo-American, mid-Victorian, pro-British, un-Christian.*

2. After the prefix *self: self-defense, self-interest, self-reliant, self-respect.*

3. After the prefix *ex,* when *ex* means "former" or "formerly": *ex-convict, ex-fighter, ex-salesman.*

4. *Bell-like* (to avoid three *l*'s); *re-elect, re-enter, re-examination* (to avoid two *e*'s); *re-cover* (to cover again, *not* to get back).

11. Compound Pronouns Write solid the following compound pronouns: *oneself, himself, themselves, ourselves, myself, herself, itself, yourself.*

12. Body, Thing, Where Write solid pronouns and adverbs ending with *body, thing,* and *where: anybody, everybody, nobody, somebody, anything, anywhere.*

Write these words solid:

altogether	forehead	nevertheless	serviceman
anyone	foresee	notebook	snowstorm
baggageman	framework	nowadays	someone
basketball	grapefruit	outdoors	sometime
bathroom	handwriting	overcharge	stockholder
bookkeeper	heretofore	pillowcase	taxpayer
businessman	homework	postmaster	teamwork
classroom	horsepower	roommate	throughout
downstairs	inasmuch	safekeeping	typewritten
everyone	indoors	scrapbook	wastebasket
farmhouse	livestock	secondhand	watermelon
fireproof	mailbox	semicolon	woodwork

EXCEPTIONS

Some time ago I ordered Pan Amercan's *New Horizons.* (*Time* is a noun.)
Every one of these overcoats has been marked down. (*One* is emphasized.)

SEPARATE WORDS

all right	grape juice	living room	parcel post
dining room	in spite of	no one	post office

The trend is toward writing compounds solid. When in doubt, consult the dictionary.

HARD SPOTS

The hard spots are underlined.

abundant	descend	intimate	relative
acquainted	determined	lieutenant	renowned
agriculture	difference	medal	response
analysis	difficulties	muscles	restaurant
annual	discipline	museum	sacrifice
apartment	disgusted	necessity	sandwich
apologize	duplicate	nickel	semester
apology	embarrass	offense	sergeant
attitude	endeavour	opponent	similar

authority
bicycle
capacity
chosen
clothes
column
comfortable
control
courteous
curiosity
defense

expense
extension
fascinate
genius
gentlemen
grateful
ignorance
imagine
imitate
imitation
interfere

opportunity
original
pastime
permanent
pneumonia
possess
possession
prejudice
pursue
quantity
quartet

spontaneous
stretch
successful
surprise
sympathy
temporary
thorough
tragedy
valuable
wretched
written

FINAL Y

13. Y After Consonant *Y* preceded by a consonant becomes *i* before a suffix: *pity, pities, pitied; icy, iciest; ready, readily.*

EXCEPTIONS

1. Before *ing* and *ish* to avoid double *i*: *studying, trying, babyish*
2. In proper names: *Jerrys, Healys*
3. In some derivatives of some adjectives of one syllable: *dryness, shyness* (Notice *drier, driest.*)

14. Y After Vowel When a word ends in *y* preceded by a vowel, the *y* remains unchanged before all suffixes: *delay, delayed; destroy, destroyed; journey, journeys; pray, prayed.*

EXCEPTIONS *lay, laid; pay, paid; say, said,* and most of their compounds.

PRACTICE 3. Final *y*

1. Change each adjective to a noun by adding *ness: busy, friendly, happy, kindly, lonely, lovely, uneasy.*

2. Write the third person singular of the present tense and of the past tense of these verbs (*reply, replies, replied*): *apply, carry, cry, deny, hurry, marry, occupy, play, repay, satisfy, study, supply, try.*

3. Study these words. For each word explain why *y* is or is not changed to *i*.

accompanied
annoyance
appliance
burglaries
duties
families

hastily
heartily
hurrying
industrious
likelihood
necessarily

opportunities
ordinarily
prepaid
prophecies
readily
replying

satisfactorily
satisfying
specified
stayed
studying
worrying

FINAL E

15. FINAL E Final silent *e* is usually dropped before a suffix beginning with a vowel and kept before a suffix beginning with a consonant. (This rule applies to more than two thousand words.)

VOWEL—*e* DROPPED

hop*e* + ing = hoping
us*e* + age = usage
din*e* + ing = dining

CONSONANT—*e* KEPT

hope + ful = hopeful
use + less = useless
nine + teen = nineteen

16. FINAL IE Words ending in *ie* drop the *e* and change the *i* to *y* before *ing* to avoid two successive *i*'s: *die, dying; lie, lying; tie, tying.* Note *dye, dyeing* to distinguish from *die, dying*.

PRACTICE 4. Adding *ing*

Add *ing* to each of the following words:

acknowledge	change	enclose	owe	shine
advertise	choose	encourage	produce	suppose
advise	come	interfere	pursue	taste
argue	complete	lie	receive	type
arrange	continue	lose	rule	use
bore	define	oblige	separate	write

17. FINAL CE, GE Keep the *e* when adding *able* and *ous* to words ending in *ce* or *ge*: *advantageous, changeable, courageous, serviceable.* If the *e* were dropped, the *c* and *g* would be pronounced as in *car* and *gate*.

PRACTICE 5. Adding *able* or *ous*

Form adjectives by adding *able* or *ous* to these words. Write the words and prepare to explain in each case why you drop or keep the *e*.

admire	charge	imagine	notice	recognize
advise	conceive	monotone	outrage	use
believe	desire	note	peace	value

PRACTICE 6. Adding Suffixes

1. Form adjectives by adding *ful* to the following nouns: *care, force, grace, peace, revenge, shame, spite, use*. No adjective ends in *full*.

2. Add *ly* to each of these words: *absolute, affectionate, approximate, bare, complete, entire, extreme, fortunate, immediate, immense, late, like, lone, love, mere, rare, scarce, severe, sincere, sure*.

3. Add *ment* to each of these words: *achieve, advertise, announce, arrange, commence, encourage, excite, replace, require*.

4. Add *ty* to *nine, safe, sure*.

EXCEPTIONS Twelve exceptions to the rules about final *e* are: [1]

acknowledgment	canoeing	judgment	shoeing
argument	duly	mileage	truly
awful	hoeing	ninth	wholly

[1] The spellings *acknowledgement* and *judgement* are permissible but rare.

PRACTICE 7. Using Words Frequently Misspelled

Write sentences for these words frequently misspelled by graduates of senior high schools. You may put two or more of the words in one sentence. Know why the final *e* in each word is kept or dropped.

coming	writing	immediately	severely	valuable
losing	useful	likely	truly	achievement
pursuing	completely	lonely	ninety	amusement
studying	entirely	merely	safety	argument
using	extremely	scarcely	desirable	arrangement

DOUBLING FINAL CONSONANTS

18. FINAL CONSONANTS Double the final consonant before a suffix beginning with a vowel if (1) the word has one syllable or is accented on the last syllable and if (2) the word ends in one consonant preceded by one vowel: *stop, stopped, stopping; beGIN,*

beginning. (This rule applies to more than three thousand words.)

1. stop, stopping. *Stop* has one syllable. The final consonant *p* is preceded by the single vowel *o*. The rule applies.

2. shine, shining. *Shine* has only one syllable, but the final letter is a vowel. The rule does not apply.

3. reMIT, remitted, remittance. *Remit* is accented on the last syllable. The final consonant *t* is preceded by the single vowel *i*. The rule applies.

4. DIFfer, differing, differed. *Differ* is accented on the first syllable. The rule does not apply.

EXCEPTIONS Words, like *PREFerence* from *preFER* and *REFerence* from *reFER*, in which the accent is shifted to the first syllable. *EXcellent* from *exCEL*, however, has two *l*'s.

PRACTICE 8. Adding Suffixes Beginning with Vowels

Add the suffix to the word or words that follow it. Be ready to explain in each case why the rule for doubling final consonants does or does not apply.

ed	benefit	*ed*	drop	*ed*	omit	*ed*	transfer
	commit		equip		prefer	*ence*	occur
	compel		occur		refer		refer
	control		offer		stop	*ee*	commit
est	big	*ing*	commit	*ing*	omit	*ing*	stop
able	prefer	*ing*	dig	*ing*	put	*ing*	swim
ance	remit		interfere		refer	*er*	propel
ing	begin		occur		run	*ion*	rebel

TROUBLE SPOTS

Can you spell these words? The hard spots are underlined. Look up a word if you don't know what it means.

absurd	consequently	expedition	patience
accustomed	considerably	exquisite	patients (*in*
acknowledge	council	extraordinary	*hospital*)
affectionate	(*assembly*)	guardian	possibility
alcohol	counsel (*advice*	handsome	prairie
analyze	*adviser*)	inconvenience	professor
anniversary	cylinder	invalid	recollect

appendicitis	decidedly	irrigation	recommendation
ascertain	desert (*waste*	kindergarten	registration
bachelor	*place*)	lavender	representative
campaign	desperate	license	scenery
complexion	dessert (*food*)	liquor	solemn
condemned	destination	millinery	specimen
conscience	distinguish	mutual	surgeon
(*moral sense*)	enormous	originate	sympathize
conscientious	enthusiastic	pamphlet	testimony
conscious	exhausted		
(*aware*)	exhibition		

ADDING PREFIXES AND SUFFIXES

Have you learned to attach a prefix or a suffix to a word without losing or adding a letter? As a rule, words can be divided into syllables between the prefix and the root and between the root and the suffix. Note that *recommend* is an exception to this rule.

usual + ly = usually   study + ing = studying
especial + ly = especially   drunken + ness = drunkenness
hurry + ing = hurrying   formal + ly = formally (*ceremoniously*)
marry + ing = marrying   former + ly = formerly (*at a former time*)
fore + see = foresee   re + commend = recommend
govern + ment = government   un + necessary = unnecessary
mis + spell = misspell   un + doubted + ly = undoubtedly

19. MIS, DIS As a rule, the *s* in the prefixes *mis* and *dis* is not dropped or doubled in combinations. *Dis* means "apart", "from", or "not". *Mis* means "wrong" or "bad".

dis + appoint = disappoint   mis + lead = mislead
dis + satisfied = dissatisfied   mis + step = misstep

dis			*mis*	
disapproval	disposal	dissimilar	misarrange	misspell
disgust	dissect	dissolve	misquote	misspend
dismissed	disservice	distrust	misspeak	misstate

20. AD The consonant of the prefix *ad*, meaning "to" or "toward", is often changed.

ad + breviate = abbreviate   ad + sociation = association
ad + parent = apparent   ad + commodate = accommodate

accelerate	accuracy	appearance	approximate
acceptance	acquaintance	appendix	assault
accessible	acquire	applause	assemble

accommodation	acquit	appointment	assent
accomplish	aggrandize	appreciate	assistance
accordance	aggravate	appropriate	attempt
accumulate	alluded	approve	attract

Before *sp*, *sc*, and *st* the *d* of *ad* is lost.

ad + scribe = ascribe   ad + spect = aspect

21. In The consonant of the prefix *in*, meaning "in", "into", or "not", is often changed.

For example, *in* becomes *il* in *illiterate*, *im* in *immoral*, and *ir* in *irresponsible*. These changes make the words easier to pronounce.

PRACTICE 9. Adding Prefixes and Suffixes

1. Add the suffix *ly* to these words:

accidental	cordial	grateful	original	respectful
actual	economical	immediate	partial	special
annual	equal	incidental	personal	successful
apparent	eventual	mutual	practical	total
artificial	final	natural	real	useful
careful	general	occasional	regular	usual

2. Prefix *un* to these words: *certainty, conscious, natural, necessarily, neighbourly, noticed, numbered.* What does *un* mean?

3. Prefix the correct form of *in* to these words:

legal	measurable	mortal	penetrable	prudent
legible	memorial	movable	perfect	rational
legitimate	migrate	numerable	personal	regular
literate	mobile	partial	possible	relevant
logical	modest	passable	practical	resistible
mature	moral	patient	probable	responsible

4. Add the suffix *ous* to these words: *humour, marvel, peril, poison, rigour, scandal, vigour.* What does *ous* mean?

GROUPS OF WORDS

OU	IE	OR		IA
course	audience	author	artificial	official
courtesy	convenient	compulsory	brilliant	parliament
fourteen	experience	governor	comedian	partial
fourth (4th)	fiery	senator	familiar	peculiar
mourning	ingredient	successor	financial	physician
source	society	tailor	marriage	politician

CAN YOU SPELL ALL OF THESE?

Know the meaning of every word.

adequate	delinquent	itinerary	philosopher
adieu	development	jewelry	picturesque
amateur	dimensions	legitimate	propaganda
architecture	emphasis	loyalty	psychiatrist
audacious	emphasize	masquerade	psychoanalysis
auxiliary	equivalent	miscellaneous	psychology
bouquet	erroneous	monotonous	Pullman
career	fascinated	morale	qualifications
characteristic	hypocrisy	municipal	reservoir
commemorate	immaculate	nuisance	sincerity
community	immense	optimism	site
controversy	inaccurate	orchestra	vacuum
copyright	intellectual	perseverance	volunteer

Chances are you could spell most of these words in your elementary-geography days. Can you spell them now?

Connecticut	Massachusetts	Morocco	Puerto Rico
Cyprus	Mediterranean	Pakistan	Saudi Arabia
Israel	Mississippi	Pittsburgh	Tennessee
			Trois Rivières

PRACTICE 10. Dictation

Study the spelling, capitalization, and punctuation of these sentences in preparation for writing them at your teacher's dictation.

A. 1. The inexperienced author views his characters as mere specimens pinned on a board for analysis and dissection.

2. Four card players—an intellectual from Connecticut, an immaculately dressed senator from Tennessee, and a successful financier and his accompanying physician—met quite accidentally in a Pullman car and proceeded to play a brilliant game of bridge.

3. The audience, thoroughly delighted by the performance, burst into applause, which the smallest monkey acknowledged with an irresistible grin and an extraordinary exhibition of leaps and back flips.

4. The committee for good government in our community recommends that all local clubs and societies, civic improvement groups especially, send representatives to the February meeting.

5. Professor Wilkins' appointment as leading psychiatrist at Municipal Hospital immediately touched off an unfortunate controversy about his qualifications.

B. 1. Because of its natural loveliness and excellent business opportunities, Massachusetts is an unusually attractive state.

2. Mother and Dad have requested Pullman reservations to Sudbury; after a week's stay with my aunt they will proceed with their itinerary, which includes most of Muskoka, for they want to visit a number of well-known sites in the North.

3. The lieutenant was grateful to the sergeant for assisting him in maintaining morale and good discipline in spite of the difficulties of forced marches in the desert.

4. Illiterate people sometimes fall prey to propaganda and to the promises of irresponsible politicians.

5. When my bachelor uncle's car finally stopped running, he found an opportunity to sell it and then bought as its successor a serviceable two-year-old Ford.

WORDS FREQUENTLY USED IN BUSINESS LETTERS

If some of these words are new to you, or if you have only a hazy idea of their meaning, look them up in the dictionary. Then make sure you know how to spell them. Attack ten words at a time.

accountant	approval	awaiting	circumstances
activities	architect	bankruptcy	clerical
adaptable	arrears	beneficiary	commercial
additional	arrival	bookkeeper	commodity
affidavit	article	bulletin	communication
allotment	assessment	calendar	competent

aluminum
amount
apparatus
apparel
contractor
corporation
correspondence
corrugated
currency
customary
debtor
demonstration
depreciation
desirability

directory
disastrous
discrimination
dividend
economy
effective
electrician
emergency
endorsement
engineers

essential
executive
expenditure
experience
facilitates
facilities
fashions
further

assigned
auditor
authentic
available
galvanized
grievance

guarantee
guidance
handicapped
hospitalization
implement
incorporated
indebtedness
indefinite
inflammable
influence

initiative
inspector
installation
institution
instrument
inventory
laboratory
liabilities
linoleum
locomotive

maintenance
manufacturers
material
maximum
mechanical
memorandum
mercantile

cancellation
carburetor
cashier
certificate
merchandise
mere
minimum

mortgage
negotiations
notary
personnel
petroleum
porcelain
practical
premises
previously
professional

proprietor
publicity
questionnaire
receipt
reconcile
reimburse
requisition
resignation
resources
responsibility

reversible
salaries
satisfactory
schedule
scientific

competitor
complimentary
concession
conference
secretary
shipper
solicit
specifically
specification

stationery
    (*paper*)
statistics
stenographer
substantial
superintendent
supervisor
system

tariff
technical
telephone

television
temporarily
transcript
typewriter
typographical
underwear
unfortunate
unique
universal
utilities

vacancy
wholesale

SPELLING TESTS

Number your paper from 1 to 20. Find the misspelled word in each group and write it correctly on your paper. Write C for each of the three groups in which all the words are spelled correctly.

1. apparatus, dimensions, losing, outrageous, remitance

2. appliance, greatfully, likelihood, notebook, receipt
3. alright, dining room, essential, minimum, reversible
4. bouquet, calendar, lavender, license, professor
5. bankruptcy, bookeeper, bulletin, perseverance, responsibility
6. adieu, appendix, desireability, illegible, personnel
7. canoeing, mileage, occassionally, occurred, succeed
8. especially, formally, secretary, truly, wholly
9. bicycle, controversy, Mississippi, Murphys, replys
10. accompanying, notable, owing, reconize, renowned
11. difference, familar, maintenance, seize, thief
12. embarassed, guarantee, morale, pamphlet, recommend
13. copyright, inflammable, practical, sincerely, stopped
14. courteous, experence, marriage, peculiar, useful
15. beginning, benefited, disatisfied, omitted, referred
16. ancient, business, committee, immediatly, mischievous
17. acquaintance, definite, cashier, conscience, weird
18. independent, labratory, resources, superintendent, writing
19. Israel, jewlery, linoleum, Mediterranean, Puerto Rico
20. assistance, auxiliary, changable, correspondence, necessarily

PRACTICE 11. Time Out for Review

Copy the following anecdote, correcting all errors in spelling, punctuation, and usage. Be prepared to give a reason for every change you make.

MOVE OVER, PLEASE

The subway stoped with an ear splitting shreik, as the waiting passengers were just about to surge aboard they noticed a blind man and his Seeing Eye dog. Carefully leading his master the dog pushed onto the train and led the man to the only available space on the seat runing the length of the car. It was to small to accomodate even a child but the dog nudged the passengers on either side with his nose and every one squeezed closer to their neighbor. When their was room enough for two people the dog signaled his master a fairly slight man to be seated. Naturaly every body is watching these procedings with great interest.

The dogs final act brung apreciative chuckles from the audiance. After the man had seated hisself the dog clumb into the remaining space beside his master and laid down with his head on the mans lap.

Poetry

THE MUSIC OF POETRY

RHYTHM is found everywhere about us in nature and in life: the beat of the heart, the tick of the clock, the rain pattering on the roof, the *left*-right of marching soldiers, the *one*-two or *one*-two-three of music and dancing, the ta-*rum*, ta-*rum*, ta-*rum-tum-tum* of the drum, the tolling of a church bell, the clang of a fire bell, the moaning of the wind in the trees, the alternation of the seasons and of day and night, the rise and fall of waves, the ebb and flow of the tide. Because of the rhythm children enjoy hearing poetry even when they don't understand it. Rhythm in speech and writing is a pleasing or tuneful arrangement of the accented and unaccented syllables.

Metre is a regular recurrence of accented and unaccented syllables.

FEET

A line of peotry is called a **verse**. The verse is made up of **feet**, groups of regularly recurring accented and unaccented syllables. The commonly used feet are:

NAME	ADJECTIVE FORM	ACCENT	EXAMPLE
iambus	iambic	‿ ′ (ta tum)	for**give**
anapest	anapestic	‿ ‿ ′ (ta ta tum)	una**fraid**
trochee	trochaic	′ ‿ (tum ta)	**kind**ly
dactyl	dactylic	′ ‿ ‿ (tum ta ta)	**but**tercup

Dactyl is from a Greek word meaning *finger*. A finger has three bones, one longer than either of the others.

PRACTICE 1. Metrical Measure

List ten iambic words, ten trochaic words, five anapestic words, and ten dactylic words.

Feet used less frequently are:

NAME	ACCENT	EXAMPLE
pyrrhic	‿ ‿ (ta ta)	of the
spondee	′ ′ (tum tum)	**white dawn**
amphibrach	‿ ′ ‿ (ta tum ta)	un**cer**tain

A verse is made up of one or more feet, and is named according to the type and number of feet.   A verse having five iambic feet is called **iambic pentameter.**

$$\breve{~}~'~|~\breve{~}~'~|~\breve{~}~'~|~\breve{~}~'~|~\breve{~}~'$$
They al | so serve | who on | ly stand | and wait.

NAME	NUMBER OF FEET IN LINE	NAME	NUMBER OF FEET IN LINE
monometer	1	tetrameter	4
dimeter	2	pentameter	5
trimeter	3	hexameter	6

The most popular metres are tetrameter and pentameter, with trimeter and hexameter next in favour.

THE EFFECT OF EACH FOOT

Each foot has a different rhythmic effect.   The iambus has been called the walking foot; the trochee, running; the anapest, galloping; and the dactyl, waltzing.   The iambus is bold, masculine; the trochee is gentle, sweet, and feminine.

Coleridge describes poetically the use or effect of each foot:

> Trochee trips from long to short;
> From long to long in solemn sort.
> Slow Spondee stalks, strong foot, yet ill able
> Ever to come up with Dactyl trisyllable.
> Iambics march from short to long;
> With a leap and a bound the swift Anapests throng.

Notice the "leap and bound" of "swift Anapest" in Robert Browning's "How They Brought the Good News from Ghent to Aix."

> I sprang to the stirrup, and Joris, and he;
> I galloped, Dirck galloped, we galloped all three.

Robert Browning in "Boot and Saddle" makes use of quick "Dactyl trisyllable".

> Rescue my castle before the hot day
> Brightens to blue from its silvery grey.

Notice the "tripping" of Trochee.

> Then the little Hiawatha
> Learned of every bird its language.
> —LONGFELLOW

PRACTICE 2. Metrical Measure

Discuss the metre of Browning's "My Star", Noyes's "The Barrel-Organ" or "The Highwayman", Longfellow's "Hiawatha" or "Evangeline", Byron's "The Destruction of Sennacherib", Hood's "The Bridge of Sighs", Stevenson's "Requiem", Markham's "Lincoln, the Man of the People", Moore's "A Visit from St. Nicholas", Milton's "L'Allegro", Tennyson's "Passing of Arthur" or "The Bugle Song", Gray's "Elegy", Wordsworth's "Daffodils" or "Reverie of Poor Susan", Masefield's "Cargoes" or "Sea Fever", De la Mare's "The Listeners", Thornburg's "The Cavalier's Escape", Buchanan's "The Green Gnome", or any other poem. What is the metre? Does it help to express the thought or feeling? How?

VARIATIONS

A verse lacking the last syllable is called **catalectic.**

$$\text{´} \quad \text{˘} \mid \text{´} \quad \text{˘} \mid \text{´}$$
Hate, and | pride, and | fear.

A verse with an added syllable is called **hypermetrical.**   If the extra syllable is at the end of the line, the verse is **hypercatalectic.**   The added syllable is a **weak** or **feminine** ending.

$$\text{˘} \quad \text{´} \mid \text{˘} \quad \text{´} \mid \text{˘} \quad \text{´} \mid \text{˘} \quad \text{´} \mid \text{˘}$$
The down | y clouds | go soft | ly steal | ing.

These and similar variations in the metrical scheme prevent monotony, make the verse more musical, and help the poet to express his thought and feeling.

The occasional adding or omitting of an unaccented syllable does not interfere with the rhythm but may give a leap or a bound to the line. Hence feet with the accent on the first syllable or on the last syllable are interchanged freely.

SCANSION

To scan is to divide a verse into its feet. To scan a line mark first the accents of words of two or more syllables. Then mark monosyllables that are clearly emphatic. Usually these accents will give you a clue to the verse pattern or the prevailing foot.

Example:

$$\text{´} \qquad \text{´} \qquad \text{´} \qquad \text{´}$$
But mercy is above this scepter'd sway.

Mer, bove, and *scep* are the accented syllables of the words of two syllables; *sway* is an important noun. The metre of the line is iambic pentameter.

RHYME

"You hunt the rhyme," says Gamaliel Bradford, "and the ideas come trooping after like quaint satyrs and nymphs after the pipe of Pan."

Rhyme is a similarity of sound, usually at the ends of lines. **Words** which rhyme perfectly have—

1. Accent on the rhyming syllables
2. The same vowel sounds in the accented syllables
3. The same sounds after this vowel sound
4. Different consonant sounds before this vowel sound

Rhyme is a matter of pronunciation or sound, not of **spelling.** *Laid, shade; hate, weight; kite, tight; pealing, reeling; nation, exclamation; gleaming, seeming; laugh, giraffe; after, laughter,* rhyme; *dough, cough; divine, routine; prey, key; map, hat; pain, flame,* do not. Occasionally we find such imperfect rhymes as *given, heaven; shadow, meadow; earth, hearth; bare, are; move, rove; love, move; never, river.*

Single (or masculine) rhyme consists of one rhyming syllable— *sound, found;* **double** (or feminine) rhyme, of two—*shaken, waken;* **triple** rhyme—of three—*tenderly, slenderly.* In double or triple rhyme the rhyming syllables may be in two or three words—*brink of it, think of it.*

Blank verse is verse without rhyme. Shakespeare wrote usually **in** unrhymed iambic pentameter, a dignified, noble verse form, suitable for the expression of the loftiest ideas.

Alliteration is the repetition of the same initial sound in words closely following each other.

> Then star nor sun shall waken,
>   Nor any change of light;
> Nor sound of water shaken
>   Nor any sound or sight.
>   —SWINBURNE

Here Swinburne uses the *s*-sound effectively to suggest the hushed silence of the long sleep of death.

PRACTICE 3. Alliteration

Read these lines aloud. Is alliteration skilfully used in each? Give **a reason** for your answer.

1. The fair breeze blew, the white foam flew,
   The furrow followed free.—Coleridge
2. Bareheaded, breathless, and besprent with mire.—Longfellow
3. Too English to bargain, bully, and browbeat; to wheedle, whine, or weep.
   —Trader Horn
4. The ploughman homeward plods his weary way.—Gray
5. A man to match the mountains and the sea.—Markham

ONOMATOPOEIA

Onomatopoeia is the fitting of sound to meaning. Examples are *buzz, roar, howl, splash, cackle, whistle, whizz, rumble, clatter, clash, hiss, murmur, clang, plunge, bubble, tap, grate, drowsy, bang, gurgle.*

Some time ago in England a vote was taken on the most expressive, the most romantic, the most beautiful, the most poetic, and the most completely onomatopoetic word. The winner was *murmuring.*

Keats told how the sound of the word *forlorn* affected him:

> Forlorn! the very word is like a bell
> To toll me back from thee to my sole self.

PRACTICE 4. Onomatopoetic Language

Is onomatopoeia used skilfully in each of the following? Prove your answer.

1. Oilily bubbled up the mere.—Tennyson
2. When Ajax strives some rock's vast weight to throw,
   The line too labours, and the words move slow.—Pope
3. The sails did sigh like sedge.—Coleridge
4. Moan of doves in immemorial elms
   And murmuring of innumerable bees.—Tennyson
5. No more! Alas, that magical sad sound
   Transferring all!—Poe
6. Bang-whang-whang goes the drum, tootle-te-tootle the fife.—Browning
7. The ice was here, the ice was there,
   The ice was all around;
   It cracked and growled, and roared and howled,
   Like noises in a swound!—Coleridge
8. Hear the loud alarum bells—
   Brazen bells!
   What a tale of terror, now, their turbulency tells!
   In the startled ear of night
   How they scream out their affright!
   Too much horrified to speak,
   They can only shriek, shriek.—Poe

STANZAS

A stanza is a regular combination of two or more verses.   **A couplet is a** stanza containing two rhyming lines.

> What wonder if Sir Launfall now
> Remembered the keeping of his vow?
>
> —LOWELL

Pope used the iambic pentameter couplet, called the **heroic couplet,** to express pointedly and tersely his ideas. Do you see why this is sometimes called the rocking-horse measure? Does the first line of each couplet seem to climb higher and higher and the second slide down?

> In words, as fashions, the same rule will hold,
> Alike fantastic, if too new or old;
> Be not the first by whom the new are tried,
> Nor yet the last to lay the old aside.
>
> —POPE

The **triplet,** a stanza of three lines rhyming together, is used by only a few poets.

> The wrinkled sea beneath him crawls;
> He watches from his mountain walls,
> And like a thunderbolt he falls.
>
> —TENNYSON

A quatrain is a stanza of four verses.

> About, | about, | in reel | and rout
> The death- | fires danced | at *night;*
> The wa | ter, like | a witch | 's oils,
> Burnt green | and blue | and *white.*

This quatrain, made up of iambic tetrameter alternating with iambic trimeter, is the typical **ballad stanza.** The second and fourth lines rhyme.

PRACTICE 5. Ballad Writing

Write a ballad about a school subject, a person, or a school happening, or tell a biblical, Robin Hood, or other story in ballad form. Write, for example, the ballad of the lunchroom, the football game, the excursion, commencement, the study hall, the athletic assembly, the election, examinations, the annual play, the concert, the speaking contest, the debate, the school paper, the library, camp, a ride, a hike, or an adventure. Base your ballad, if you wish, on a newspaper article, a story, or a paragraph or chapter of a history, a novel, or a biography.

Four other quatrain rhyme schemes are favourites. Lines marked *a* or *b* or *c* rhyme. The *abab* after number 1 shows that the first line rhymes with the third, and the second with the fourth. A line which has no rhyme is called *x*.

1

Full many a gem of purest ray *serene,*	*a*
The dark unfathomed caves of ocean bear;	*b*
Full many a flower is born to blush un*seen*	*a*
And waste its sweetness on the desert air.	*b*

2

(Called the *In Memoriam* stanza because used by Tennyson in *In Memoriam*. Also called the Tennysonian stanza.)

I sometimes hold it half a *sin*	*a*
To put in words the grief I feel;	*b*
For words, like Nature, half reveal	*b*
And half conceal the Soul with*in*.	*a*

—TENNYSON

3

Speed slackens now, I *float*	*a*
Awhile in my airy *boat*	*a*
Till, when the wheels scarce crawl,	*b*
My feet to the treadles fall.	*b*

4

(Called **Omaric stanza** because used in Fitzgerald's translation of *The Rubáiyát* of Omar Khayyám. Also called the **Rubáiyát stanza.**)

Yet Ah, that Spring should vanish with the *Rose!*	*a*
That Youth's sweet-scented manuscript should *close!*	*a*
The Nightingale that in the branches sang,	*x*
Ah whence, and whither flown again, who *knows!*	*a*

—FITZGERALD

The five quatrain rhyme schemes illustrated are: (1) *abab;* (2) *abba;* (3) *aabb;* (4) *aaxa;* and (5) (ballad stanza) *xaxa*. The last line must figure in the rhyming. By varying the rhyme scheme and the metrical pattern poets construct a great variety of quatrains.

PRACTICE 6.   Stanza Forms

Using any metrical pattern (iambic trimeter, iambic pentameter, trochaic tetrameter, etc.) and one of the rhyme schemes just illustrated (*abab*, *abba*, *aabb*, *aaxa*), write a stanza on a topic of your own choice.

Stanzas of five, six, seven, eight, and nine lines are common. The **Spenserian stanza** consists of nine lines; the first eight are iambic pentameters, and the ninth is an iambic hexameter. The rhyme scheme is *ababbcbcc*. Spencer's *Faerie Queene* and Byron's *Childe Harold* are written in this stanza.

There is a pleasure in the pathless woods,	*a*
There is a rapture on the lonely shore,	*b*
There is society, where none intrudes,	*a*
By the deep sea, and music in its roar;	*b*
I love not man the less, but nature more,	*b*
From these our interviews, in which I steal	*c*
From all I may be, or have been before,	*b*
To mingle with the universe, and feel	*c*
What I can ne'er express, yet cannot all conceal.	*c*

—Lord Byron's *Childe Harold*

FIXED FORMS

The **limerick**, an absurd five-line poem with an unexpected snap or twist in the fifth line, is easy to write. Lines 1, 2, and 5 are anapestic trimeter and rhyme; lines 3 and 4, anapestic dimeters, also rhyme. The pattern is—

Anywhere in the pattern an iambus ($\smile$ ') may be substituted for an anapest ($\smile \smile$ ').

1

There was a young lady of Niger
Who smiled as she rode on a Tiger;
   They came back from the ride
   With the lady inside,
And the smile on the face of the Tiger.

2

There was an Old Man with a beard,
Who said, "It is just as I feared!—
   Two Owls and a Hen,
   Four Larks and a Wren,
Have all built their nests in my beard!"

—Edward Lear

PRACTICE 7. Writing Limericks

Edward Lear, the author of example 2, wrote more than two hundred limericks. If you have never written a limerick, you have missed some good fun. Write, not two hundred, but two limericks about people you know, have seen, have heard of, or have read about.

A **cinquain** is a poem of five unrhymed lines, with one foot in the first line, two in the second, three in the third, four in the fourth, and one in the fifth.

Student Cinquains;

DREAMS

Lost on
A pleasant sea,
Afloat in a magic boat
Which takes him to a fairy land
Of dreams.—CATHERINE PETRILLO

TWILIGHT

At dusk
The day and night
Embrace for one light kiss;
A purple mist enfolds the two. . . .
Then dark.—DORIS M. GORDON

The **sonnet** is a poem of fourteen iambic pentameter lines. The Italian sonnet is made up of an octave rhyming *abba abba* and a sestet commonly rhyming *cdecde* or *cdcdcd*. The octave usually presents an idea, story, picture, doubt, problem, query; the sestet, a reflection, conclusion, answer, or solution. The Shakespearean sonnet is rhymed *abab cdcd efef gg.*

SONNET WRITTEN BY A LITTLE INDIAN GIRL

I own 'twas so. She said I dreamed in class—
Who would not dream? 'Twas some chance word she said;
I have forgotten what; the colour red
Perhaps, or just a prism through the glass.
Enough to free my soul and let it pass
From those four walls. Stripped of the dead,
Dull commonplace, singing through space it sped
Above cold seas of azure and topaz,
To lands whose ships lay gleaming in the sun
Laden to sail for ports of mystery;
Past gardens fair, where Dido waits for one
Who does not come, and Pan laughs secretly.
Poor, cheated class that heard but chemistry,
And missed the evening bells of Arcady.

Other examples of student verse;

THE SEA

I am in love with the purple twilight
From a dim plain,
With her star-sweet raiment blown and drifted
By the grey rain.

I am in love with silver laughter
Of a bright sea-maid,
As she binds her emerald hair with a slender ribbon
Of amber shade.

I am in love with the starlight falling
On a blue rock,
And the moon-canoe and Indian Summer in it
Drifting to dock.

I am in love with the lift and fall of the silver
Of sea-gull's wings,
Flashing above the blue wave's restless brightness
Where the sunlight swings.

I am in love with the wistful water creeping
Over the lea,
With the mystery of death and the wonder of life within it,
I am in love with the sea.

—KATHLEEN DAVIDSON.
By permission of the author.

AUTUMN DUSK

Here, where the star-locked gateway of the blue sky opens
Into the infinite bosom of the purple hills
We have drunk sunlight from flasks of the golden hours
That summer fills.

Now in a tender west the fires of Autumn
Burn—a supernal rose round a core of gold—
And stray winds whisper among dead leaves and grasses
A secret old.

Up from the old gray river that winds through the silence,
Like a tarnished strand from the silver skein of the moon
Stretches the stubble-field dark in the deepening shadows
That gather so soon.

An old witch-willow sifts through her trembling fingers
Fairy-gold bright from the moon-handled cup of night,
And whispers an ancient charm o'er her stolen treasures
That fade with the light.

Soon will the old world draw her white shawl about her,
Tenderly wrap her children under the sod,
Then, her work ended, will spend the last night keeping
A tryst with God.

—KATHLEEN DAVIDSON
By permission of the author.

WHEN I AM DEAD

When I am dead and have no longer need
Of earth-born things that once were life to me,
Take up my noblest thoughts and dreams, O Wind,
And bear them with thee to the mournful sea;
And let her tint them with her varying hues,
And fill them with her power, her depth, her strength,
And wash them with her ceaseless shadowed waves
Until, some quiet, moonlit night, at length
Some lonely, restless heart cries out, and craves
The comfort and the peace of quiet hours.
And then, O Wind, catch from the seething foam
Of some far sea my scattered salt-washed flowers
Of thought, and bear them back with thee to him
Who caused thy journey, and then softly say,
As in his groping hands thou layest them,
"Take these, the thoughts and dreams of yesterday;
Make of them what thou canst. Use but the best,
And from them gather peace and hope, and build
Upon them better, greater things." And if
He does, my greatest dream shall be fulfilled.

—M. RUTH FARNAM.
By permission of the author.

The Library

PLAN OF THE LIBRARY

MANY high school pupils approach the library with timidity and awe. Too often they regard the catalogue, the files, and the arrangement of the books as unsolvable mysteries. The truth of the matter is that using the library is an enjoyable game if one knows the rules. Go to your public or school library, explore for a half hour, and test your powers of observation. Locate the card catalogue, the magazine rack, the clipping file, novels, biographies, reference books. Then wander around among the book shelves and see what you can find out for yourself about the arrangement. Notice the numbers printed on the backs of the books. Most libraries are arranged according to the Dewey Decimal Classification, which divides all books into ten groups according to subject.

DEWEY DECIMAL CLASSIFICATION

010-099 General works
010 Bibliographies
030 Encyclopedias

101-199 Philosophy
170 Conduct

200-299 Religion
220 Bible
290 Myths

300-399 Sociology
330 Economics
350 Government
394 Holidays
398 Folklore, fairy tales, legends

400-499 Language
420 English language

500-599 Natural science
500 General science
510 Mathematics
520 Astronomy
530 Physics
537 Electricity

591 Animals
595 Insects
598 Birds

600-699 Useful arts
607 Vocational guidance
608 Inventions
613 Hygiene
620 Engineering
630 Agriculture, gardening
640 Home economics
680 Manual training, handicrafts

700-799 Fine Arts
740 Drawing
770 Photography
780 Music
790 Amusements, sports
792 Theatre, movies

800-899 Literature
810 American literature
811 Poetry, American
812 Drama, American
814 Essays, American

540	Chemistry	820	English literature
570	Biology	821	Poetry, English
580	Nature study	822	Drama, English
824	Essays, English	920	Biography, collective
		930	Ancient history
900-990	**History**	940	European history
910	Travel, geography	973	United States history

PRACTICE 1. Dewey Decimal Classification

To which of the ten groups does each of the following books belong?

1. *Creative Chemistry*
2. *Oxford Book of Canadian Verse*
3. *Appreciation of Music*
4. *Essays of Elia*
5. *Trades and Professions*

6. *Behind the Scenes at the Opera*
7. *Book of the Ancient World*
8. *As You Like It*
9. *Travels in Alaska*
10. *Story Lives of the Master Writers*

In the literature group the second figure shows the country; and the third, the kind of writing.

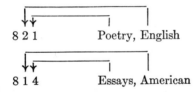

8 2 1   Poetry, English

8 1 4   Essays, American

Some libraries use 820 for both English and American literature.

If you find the 100 group and then walk around the library, you will see that the numbers are in order—200, 300, 400 etc.

Books of fiction have no call numbers but are arranged alphabetically on a separate set of shelves according to the author's name. Books by the same author are arranged alphabetically by title.   On the shelf four books by Kipling will be in this order: *Kim, The Light That Failed, Plain Tales from the Hills, Under the Deodars.*

Books of individual biography, numbered *B* or *921*, are usually grouped together on a separate set of shelves and are arranged alphabetically according to the name of the person written about.   Thus a biography of George Washington precedes one of Walt Whitman.

CARD CATALOGUE

The card catalogue, which indexes the library by author, by title, and by subject, will help you to find quickly any book in the library.

An author card has at the top the name of an author; a title card, the name of the book; and a subject card, a topic treated. In most libraries the heading of the subject card is in red. All these cards are filed alphabetically in a cabinet of small drawers or trays. Cards are filed according to the first word or words on the first line, other than an article.

The card catalogue answers the three questions which users of a library frequently ask:

"Has the library a book with this title?"

"Are there any books in the library by this author?"

"What books on this subject are there in the library?"

Suppose you want to find a book about Theodore Roosevelt by Henry Pringle. First look under the author's last name and find—

Author Card

> B   Pringle, Henry Fowles
> R781Pr   Theodore Roosevelt; a biography. 627p. por.
>   New York. Harcourt, c1931.

In the upper left corner is the call number: *B* for individual biography, *R* for *Roosevelt*, and *Pr* for the author, *Pringle*. The title of the book is *Theodore Roosevelt. 627p. por.* means that the book has 627 pages and contains a portrait of Roosevelt. *New York* is the place of publication; *Harcourt* stands for Harcourt, Brace and Company, the publishers; and *c1931* gives the copyright date.

The copyright date is important in selecting material for a talk or class paper. A book on motion-picture photography published in 1920 would be of very little value in a discussion of present-day trends. If, however, you wish to trace the development of the modern motion-picture industry, you will find books copyrighted in 1900, at the birth of the industry, both interesting and valuable.

If you know the title of the book but not the author, look in the catalogue for the—

Title Card

> B   Theodore Roosevelt; a biography
> R781Pr Pringle, Henry Fowles
>   Theodore Roosevelt; a biography. 627p. por.
>   New York. Harcourt, c1931.

Under the subject *Roosevelt, Theodore,* you will probably find a—

Subject Card Referring to Whole Book

> B   ROOSEVELT, Theodore   1858-1919
> R781B   Burroughs, John
>   Camping and tramping with Roosevelt. 110p.
>   Boston. Houghton, c 1907.

Among the subject cards you may also find this one:

Subject Card Referring to Part of Book

> 920   ROOSEVELT, Theodore
> W12R   See pp. 1-65 in
>   Wade, *Mrs*. Mary Hazelton (Blanchard)
>   Real Americans, Boston, Little, Brown, 1929

PRACTICE 2. Using the Card Catalogue

Answer the following questions by using only the card catalogue:

1. List the books or parts of books in your library which contain information about short-story writing, Greek myths, the American Revolution, cartoons, world peace.

2. Find one book of collected plays by James M. Barrie, W. S. Gilbert, John Galsworthy, or Lord Dunsany. What plays are included in the volume?

3. What books by the following authors does your library contain: Wilfred T. Grenfell, Washington Irving, Eugene O'Neill, Richard Halliburton, Christopher Morley?

4. Which of the following books are in your library? Copy the name of the author of each book that has a title card in the catalogue.

Edge of the Jungle	*Adventures in Contentment*
The Winged Horse	*Self-Cultivation in English*
North of Boston	*The Life of the Spider*
Innocents Abroad	*Only Yesterday*
Lyrics of Lowly Life	*Literary Lapses*

5. Where can you find "The Luck of Roaring Camp", a short story by Bret Harte?

6. Find the call number, author, title, and date of the most recent book in the library on one of these topics: aviation, moving pictures, history of Canada, travel in Europe.

PAMPHLET AND CLIPPING FILE

Important pamphlets and clippings from newspapers, booklets, and magazines are kept in folders or large envelopes arranged alphabetically by subject in a filing cabinet. In classifying clippings librarians use such topics as—

Airplanes	Authors	Boy Scouts	College
Athletics	Birds	Camping	Cooking

A clipping file has up-to-the-minute information about prominent people and important events. If you are permitted to use it, remember that the librarian trusts you to return every clipping to its proper folder.

READERS' GUIDE

Like the index, which is a guide to a book, and the card catalogue, which is a guide to a library, the *Readers' Guide,* an index of magazine articles since 1900, is a guide to more than a hundred magazines. To search through all the magazines for recent articles on aviation or football would take hours. In the *Readers' Guide* you can find the answer to your question in a few minutes.

The Guide is published every month. Occasionally during the year a larger number covering two or more months is published. In the summer the paper-bound numbers of a year are combined into a bound volume. Every three or five years these annual numbers are combined into larger volumes.

In the alphabetical list in the Guide an article is entered under the subject and the author's last name; a story, under the author and the title; and a poem, under the author and alphabetically according to the title under *Poems.*

Here is a typical excerpt from the *Readers' Guide:*

MORLEY, Christopher Darlington

> Effendi. Sat R Lit 10:471 F 10 '34

Notice the order of the items:

1. Author's full name
2. Title
3. Abbreviations for the name of the magazine. *Sat R Lit = Saturday Review of Literature.* (See the key to abbreviations at the front of the Guide.)
4. Volume number, before the colon.
5. Page number, after the colon.
6. Date of the magazine (February 10, 1934). If the magazine is published weekly, the day is given; if monthly, only the month.

Il, por, diag, or *bibliog* after the title shows that the article has illustrations, a portrait, a diagram, or a bibliography.

Like the encyclopedia and the card catalogue, the *Readers' Guide* uses cross references:

RADIO plays.   See Radio Broadcasting—Drama

PRACTICE 3. Using the Readers' Guide

Using the *Readers' Guide*, answer the following questions. In your answers to questions 1, 2, 3, 4, 5, and 6, give for each article (1) the author, (2) the title, (3) the magazine, (4) the volume, (5) the pages, and (6) the date.

1. In preparation for a class discussion of leisure find references to three magazine articles.
2. To prepare for a debate on the question *"Resolved,* That high school examinations should be abolished," find references to three magazine articles.
3. Find a reference to a magazine article in which Heywood Broun discusses cowardice.
4. Find a reference to an article on white ants published in recent years. Under what heading did you find the article?
5. Find references to two recent articles on school journalism. Under what heading did you find the articles?
6. Many of Stephen Leacock's humorous articles have been published in magazines. Find references to two of them.
7. Give the titles of two of Arthur Guiterman's poems which have appeared in magazines.
8. In 1933 Mrs. Helen Wills Moody wrote a series of articles on her tennis career. In what magazine were they published?
9. In 1933 the *Saturday Evening Post* published two articles about Charles A. Lindbergh. Give the titles and authors.
10. What current magazines are in your school or town library? What bound magazines are on the shelves? How are they arranged?

Parliamentary Practice

To accomplish anything, a meeting, like a business office, must have order and system. Parliamentary law is a set of rules which provide a method of transacting business smoothly, swiftly, fairly, and, above all, courteously. A good sportsman learns the rules of the game and abides by them.

The following pages are a short handbook on parliamentary practice for a school club.

FIRST MEETING

1. A temporary chairman and a temporary secretary are elected (see page 690).

2. Someone may state the object of the meeting or move that a permanent organization be formed.

3. A motion is made to appoint a committee on constitution and by-laws. The motion may state the number to be appointed. The chairman appoints the committee at the time or at a later time. Or the motion may name the members of the committee.

SECOND MEETING

1. The meeting is called to order. The minutes are read. The chairman says, "You have heard the minutes. Are there any corrections?" After a pause he says, "If there are no corrections, the minutes stand approved as read."

2. The Committee on Constitution and By-Laws reports its work complete and hands a copy to the secretary.

3. A member moves that the constitution and by-laws be adopted.

4. The chairman asks the secretary to read the constitution and by-laws one article at a time. After each article is read, he asks whether there are any amendments. If an amendment is offered, it is discussed and voted on. After the reading he says, "The entire constitution has been read and is open to amendment."

5. The president calls for a vote on the adoption of the constitution and by-laws as amended.

6. If the constitution and by-laws are adopted, permanent officers are elected.

7. The meeting is open for the transaction of business.

CHOICE OF OFFICERS

NOMINATIONS

1. Nominations may be made from the floor or by a nominating committee. By the second method other nominations are in order after the nominating committee has reported.

2. A member says, "I nominate Clifford Watts." The chair says, "Clifford Watts has been nominated," and writes his name on the blackboard.

3. The chairman may use his judgment about accepting a declination or he may call for a vote of the assembly on it.

4. A nomination does not need seconding.

5. If the motion to close nominations is seconded and carried, further nominations are shut off.

6. Without a motion, if there are no further nominations, the chairman may declare the nominations closed and say, "You may prepare your ballots."

7. One who makes or seconds a nomination may at the time speak of the fitness of the candidate.

ELECTION

1. To save time, a standing or a show-of-hands vote is sometimes permissible. The candidates by these methods are voted on in the order of nomination.

2. Commonly election by secret ballot is required by the constitution.

3. Unless the constitution or a standing rule provides otherwise, a majority is necessary to elect.

4. If no candidate receives a majority on the first ballot, the members ballot again.

5. By motion the one receiving the fewest votes may be eliminated after each ballot.

6. If there is but one candidate, a member may rise and say, "I move that the secretary cast one ballot for Marie Wilson for treasurer." If the motion is carried, the secretary writes the ballot, rises, and says, "Mr. Chairman, Marie Wilson receives one vote for the office of

treasurer, and there is no vote for any other candidate." The chairman then declares Marie Wilson elected.

CONSTITUTION AND BY-LAWS

The constitution contains the most important and permanent rules of the society. The by-laws are rules somewhat less important and permanent than those included in the constitution.

The constitution commonly includes:

1. The name and purpose of the organization
2. Qualifications for membership and method of admission to the club
3. Time and manner of electing officers, and duties of each officer
4. Appointment and duties of standing committees
5. Time and place of meetings
6. Method of amending the constitution

The by-laws may include:

1. Attendance necessary for a quorum
2. The book on parliamentary practice accepted as authority
3. Fees and dues
4. Order of business
5. Method of amending the by-laws

The by-laws may contain also details about membership, officers, meetings, fines, and standing committees. There is no sharp line between the constitution matter and by-law matter.

The order of business should be somewhat like this:

1. Roll call
2. Reading and adoption of minutes
3. Reports of standing committees
4. Reports of special committees
5. Unfinished business
6. New business
7. Program or speaker
8. Adjournment

In an English club, discussion of the program or a criticism by the teacher or a pupil usually follows the program.

CHAIRMAN OR PRESIDENT

1. The chairman calls the meeting to order at the appointed time,

announces the business to be transacted, announces the result of a vote, decides points of order, and preserves order in the meeting.

2. When a motion is made and seconded, the chairman says, "It has been moved and seconded that this club challenge the Wilson Club to a joint debate. Are there any remarks on the motion?" or "Is there any discussion?" He should be careful to use the exact words of the maker of the motion and may ask the secretary to read the motion. The chairman may require the maker of a motion to hand it in writing to the secretary. When, after some discussion, no member rises to debate, the chairman says, "Are there any further remarks? If not, are you ready for the question?" If there is no reply or if members call out "Question!" he says, "It has been moved and seconded that this club challenge the Wilson Club to a joint debate. Those in favour say 'Aye.' Those opposed say 'No.' The ayes have it; the motion is carried." If the chairman is in doubt, he says, "Those in favour of the motion will rise." After the count he says, "You may be seated. Those opposed will rise." After a voice vote any member may call for a standing vote or show-of-hands by saying, "Mr. Chairman, I call for a division."

3. The president sits except when stating a motion, putting a question to vote, announcing the result of a vote, and speaking upon a question of order.

4. To obtain the floor a member rises and says, "Mister Chairman" (or "Madam Chairman"). The chairman says "William." When a number wish to obtain the floor at the same time, the chairman recognizes first:

(1) The maker of the motion if he has not spoken
(2) A member of the opposite side from the one who has just spoken
(3) One who hasn't spoken on the question
(4) One who seldom rises to speak

In other cases he gives the floor to the one who first addresses the chair. If a member stands while another is speaking to make sure of obtaining the floor, raises his hand instead of addressing the chair, or otherwise makes himself objectionable, the chairman should not recognize him.

5. The chairman should always call for a second to a motion by saying, "Is the motion seconded?" or "Is there a second to the motion?" and declare the motion lost for want of a second if there is no response. A second, however, is in order even after this announcement. The seconder of a motion does not need to rise or obtain the floor.

6. The chairman should warn a member who is not speaking on the question, and if he does not then keep to the point, deprive him of the floor.

7. If the chairman wishes to debate a question, he should call to the chair the vice-president, the secretary, or another member, take a seat in the assembly, and speak only when recognized by the chair. He should likewise call a member to the chair to put a motion which refers to the chairman.

8. The chairman may vote when the voting is by ballot and in other cases when his vote would defeat the motion by making a tie or carry it by breaking a tie. For example, if the vote on a motion is 8 to 7, the chairman may vote "No," thus making a tie and defeating the motion.

9. By unanimous consent, the chairman may take any action that does not violate the constitution or by-laws. He says, "If there are no objections, the next meeting will be held at 3:15 instead of 3:30." After a pause he says, "It is so ordered." If objection is raised, a motion is necessary.

10. The chairman should be prompt and decisive in his rulings, should not himself waste time, and should not permit members to delay the business to be transacted.

11. The chairman refers to himself as "the chair".

VICE-PRESIDENT

The vice-president should render valuable aid to the president and be ready to take the president's place at any time.

SECRETARY

1. The secretary should keep an accurate record of everything that is done in a meeting. The minutes should include the kind of meeting, name of body, time of meeting, name of chairman, motions lost as well as motions passed, names of members appointed to committees, important remarks, and the like.

2. He notifies members of appointment on committees and of regular or special meetings.

3. He assists the president by counting in a division, by reading the exact wording of a motion, or by giving information about unfinished business or action already taken by the meeting.

4. He is custodian of the constitution, by-laws, minutes, and correspondence.

He carries on correspondence and reports to the society, calls the roll and keeps a record of the attendance, and in the absence of the president and vice-president calls the meeting to order.

TREASURER

1. The treasurer should keep in ink a detailed record of all sums received and expended and be ready at any meeting to make a complete report. The treasurer's book should be clear to any member who may be called upon to audit it.

2. He should give receipts for dues and assessments and secure a receipt when money is paid out.

3. The by-laws or constitution should specify how bills are to be paid. In many organizations the rule is that money is to be paid out only after it has been voted by the society.

COMMITTEES

1. The constitution or by-laws may provide for the appointment of an executive committee, a program committee, a membership committee, a publicity committee, a refreshment committee, and the like. These are standing committees with a fixed term of office. A special committee is appointed for a particular task. For example, the club may authorize the appointment of a committee to devise a plan for raising funds for the purchase of medals to be presented. Such a committee ceases to exist when it has done its work and reported to the society. The society either takes no action on a committee report or votes to adopt it. If the committee recommends a public mock trial to raise money, a vote to adopt the report means that the mock trial is to be held.

2. Committees are commonly appointed by the presiding officer. The first member named is the temporary chairman unless another is specified. If no chairman is named, the committee may select its own chairman.

3. A committee meets at the call of the chairman. A majority of a committee constitute a quorum.

RULES OF DEBATE

1. Do not refer to a member by name. Say "the preceding speaker", "the chair", "the secretary".

2. Don't rise to speak a second time unless everybody has had an opportunity to speak.

3. Address your remarks to the chairman and stick to the question.

4. A member may rise to debate up to the time that the negative vote is called for.

5. After a member has obtained the floor, he may hold it except for the question of consideration, a point of order, a call for the order of the day, a question of privilege, or a call to enter on the minutes a motion to reconsider.

PRECEDENCE OF MOTIONS

To fix time of next meeting **A, D?, R** (Symbols are explained on page 695-96.)
To adjourn (if next meeting time has been fixed) **r**
Question of privilege **D, A, T, P, C, R,—F?** (The first six symbols apply to a privileged motion, not to a request.)
Point of order **F—, —S**
To appeal from the decision of the chair **T, D?, R**
To suspend the rules ⅔
To withdraw (or renew) a motion **R**
Objection to consideration of question⅔, **—F, —S, R**
To lay on the table **r, R?**
Previous question (closes debate) ⅔, **r, R?**
To postpone to a certain time, **r, D?, A?, R**
To refer **D + , A, r, R**
To amend an amendment **D, R**
To amend **D, A, T, R.**   To postpone indefinitely **D + , R**
Main question **D, A, P, C, T, R**

1. To amend and to postpone indefinitely are of the same rank. Neither yields to the other.

2. The question mark after a symbol indicates that there are exceptions to the general statement. These exceptions are given in the discussion of the motions on pages 696-700.

3. The motions in the preceding list are arranged according to their rank, the highest first and the lowest last. Any motion takes precedence over any motion below it. For example, if a motion is before the house, an amendment is made and seconded, and a motion to adjourn is made and seconded, the motion to adjourn is acted on first. If it is lost, the amendment is discussed and voted on. If the amendment is carried, the motion as amended is discussed and voted on.

KEY TO SYMBOLS

A—Amendable.
C—May be referred to a committee.
D—Debatable.   Previous question applicable.
D+—Opens whole question for debate.   Previous question applicable.

—F—In order when another has the floor.
P—May be postponed definitely or indefinitely.
R—May be reconsidered.
r—Renewable after other business.
—S—Second not required.
T—May be laid on the table.
$\frac{2}{3}$—Two-thirds vote necessary.

Common Motions Classified According To Use

To *postpone* action, move (1) to lay on the table or (2) to postpone to a certain time.

To *defeat* the question, move (1) to postpone indefinitely or (2) to lay on the table.

To *stop debate*, move the previous question.

To *change the motion*, move to amend.

Main Motion

MEMBER [*rising*]. Madam President [*pausing for recognition*], I move that we hold a declamation contest.

1. A main motion is not in order if any other motion is pending.

2. If the motion is defeated, it cannot be introduced again at the same meeting.

Postpone Indefinitely

MEMBER [*rising*]. Mr. Chairman [*pausing for recognition*], I move that we postpone consideration of this motion indefinitely.

1. When a motion is postponed indefinitely, it is really defeated, because it may not be considered again during the meeting.

2. Sometimes leaders use this motion to find out how many are opposed to the original motion.

Amend

MEMBER. I move to amend the motion by striking out *declamation* and inserting the word *speaking*.

1. To amend means to change. The wording of the motion is changed by an amendment.

2. A change in the motion may be made by adding, subtracting, substituting, or dividing.

3. By unanimous consent a maker may change his motion without moving to amend.

4. An amendment must keep to the question but may be hostile to it. An amendment to add *not* or eliminate *not* or a silly amendment should be ruled out of order.

5. When an amendment is laid on the table, it takes with it the original question.

AMEND AN AMENDMENT

MEMBER. I move to amend the amendment by inserting the word *extemporaneous* before *speaking*.

The amendment to the amendment is acted on before the amendment or original motion. To illustrate, after discussion a vote is taken on inserting *extemporaneous*. If the meeting votes to change the amendment, the amendment is amended, that the words *extemporaneous speaking* be substituted for the word *declamation*, is discussed and voted on. If the amendment as amended is lost, the original motion, that the club hold a declamation contest, is discussed and voted on.

REFER

MEMBER. I move that we refer this question to a committee of three.

MEMBER. I move to refer the question to the Executive Committee.

1. The motion is useful when further investigation is desirable.

2. Amendments may change the size or selection of the committee or instruct the committee.

3. The motion should state the size of the committee and may include a method of selection.

POSTPONE TO A CERTAIN TIME

MEMBER. I move that we postpone consideration of this question till the next meeting.

1. The motion gives time for consideration.

2. At the time set the matter comes up under old business.

3. Debate must concern the wisdom of the postponement.

4. A change in the time at which the matter is to be considered is the only amendment in order.

PREVIOUS QUESTION (CLOSE DEBATE)

MEMBER. I move the previous question.

After a second to the motion the chairman says, "The previous question has been called for. Shall debate now be closed?"

1. The motion stops debate and requires a vote on the original question.

2. If a main motion and an amendment are before the house, the previous question unlimited requires a vote on both the amendment and the main motion without further debate. To limit the closing of debate to the amendment, the motion should be, "I move the previous question on the amendment."

3. The motion to limit debate, like the previous question, requires a two-thirds vote.

LAY ON THE TABLE

MEMBER. I move that we lay the main motion on the table.

A motion laid on the table is really lost unless a majority vote to take it from the table. Hence the motion is used both to delay action and to defeat a motion.

OBJECTION TO CONSIDERATION OF QUESTION

MEMBER. I object to the consideration of this question.

1. This motion is used to dispose of improper motions without debate.

2. The objection is in order only before the question has been debated.

WITHDRAWAL OF A MOTION

MEMBER. I move that George Howard be allowed to withdraw his motion.

Before a motion has been stated by the chairman, the maker has the privilege of withdrawing it. After it has been stated by the chair, he may withdraw it only by unanimous consent or on motion to withdraw.

QUESTION OF ORDER

MEMBER. I rise to a point of order.

CHAIRMAN. State your point of order.

MEMBER. My point of order is that parliamentary rules are being violated because a majority is necessary for election.

CHAIRMAN. Your point of order is well taken. Prepare your ballots again.

1. A point of order may properly be raised if the chairman permits a violation of the constitution, by-laws, or parliamentary law.

2. If a member is disorderly or discourteous in debate, the chairman names him, gives him an opportunity to explain his actions, and then requires him to withdraw from the room. The assembly then decides to overlook the offence or to punish the member by a reprimand, fine, or expulsion.

APPEAL FROM THE DECISION OF THE CHAIR

MEMBER. I appeal from the decision of the chair.

CHAIRMAN. The decision of the chair has been appealed from. Shall the decision stand?

1. The chairman may state the reasons for his decision without leaving the chair.

2. A member may speak but once.

3. If the chair is overruled, he takes the action approved by the assembly.

QUESTION OF PRIVILEGE

MEMBER. I rise to a question of privilege.

CHAIRMAN. State your question of privilege.

MEMBER. I move that a member be appointed to stop the noise outside.

1. Privileged questions relate to the rights of the meeting and of individual members. Examples are disorder, poor ventilation, and lack of chairs, heat, or light.

2. The chairman decides (subject to appeal) whether the question is really a question of privilege.

3. If immediate action is required, the maker may interrupt a member speaking.

ADJOURN

MEMBER. I move we adjourn.

1. A quorum is not necessary for a vote on adjournment.

2. If the motion to adjourn also fixes the time of the next meeting ("I move we adjourn to meet on Thursday at three o'clock"), the rules for a main motion apply.

3. The motion is not in order while a member is speaking or while a vote is being taken.

Fix Time or Place for Next Meeting

MEMBER. I move that the next meeting be held on December 22 at 3 P.M.

1. This motion is of highest rank, because, if the constitution and by-laws do not specify the regular meeting place and time of the body, there must be every opportunity during a meeting to set the time of the next one.

2. It is debatable if no other question is before the meeting.

Reconsider

The details about the motions to reconsider are complicated. Only the main facts about the unprivileged form, which is in common use, are given.

1. If the motion is carried, the original question is again before the assembly for consideration.

2. The motion must be made by one who voted with the majority.

3. The motion must be made at the meeting on which the original vote was taken or at the following meeting.

Use and Abuse of Parliamentary Motions

In a meeting motions should never be introduced to confuse the chairman or delay business. The purpose of parliamentary law is to secure a speedy expression of the will of the majority. School practice in presiding and making motions prepares a person to take part intelligently in the transaction of business in any meeting.

PRACTICE 1. Parliamentary Practice

1. On Parliamentary Practice Day in your English Club let A move that the class adopt a uniform for all members, B amend the motion by specifying the kind of uniform, and C amend the amendment with a change in the uniform.

2. Let D move that the class organize a literary club, E amend the motion by substituting *book* for *literary*, F move the previous question on the amendment, and G move to lay on the table.

3. Let H move that the class hold a party or a picnic, I amend by specifying the time, J move to postpone the question to the next recitation, K move to refer the matter to a committee, L rise to a question of privilege.

4. Let others make main motions and a variety of motions which take precedence over the main questions.

MANUALS

"M.P."—Canadian Young Men's Parliamentary Guide.

ROBERT—Rules of Order.

GREGG—Parliamentary Law.

GAMES—The New Cushing's Manual.

PALMER—Manual.

REED—Rules.

PARSONS, MRS.—Manual for Women's Meetings.

INDEX